THE ROCK YEARBOOK 1984

THE ROCK YEARBOOK 1984.

Copyright © 1983 by Virgin Books Ltd.

ISBN 0-312-68786-9

For information, address: St. Martin's Press, 175 Fifth Avenue,
New York, NY 10010.

Printed in Great Britain.

Design by David Fudger.

First U.S. Edition

10 9 8 7 6 5 4 3 2 1

THE
ROCK
YEARBOOK
1984

EDITED
BY
AL CLARK

CONTENTS

FEATURING THE BILLBOARD AND MUSIC WEEK CHARTS

CONTRIBUTORS

EDITOR

AL CLARK has edited *The Rock Yearbook* for longer than he cares to remember. The author of *Raymond Chandler in Hollywood* and editor of *The Film Yearbook*, he has now become a powerful and unpleasant film tycoon.

US CORRESPONDENT

DREW MOSELEY is being held in New York City against her will. Her ambition is to get married, raise children and write novels in her spare time. Meanwhile, she works for a public television news programme by day and for rock publications on weekends.

LLOYD BRADLEY is a former chef and associate of George Clinton, and now writes for the *New Musical Express* and *Look-In* and does deejay work. His spare time activities include making cakes and making a great deal of noise.

IAN CRANNA was a contributor to *New Musical Express* before leading *Smash Hits* to new heights during two years as editor. These days he looks after his ten children (four in Orange Juice and six in The Virgin Prunes) and becomes increasingly sure that there must be easier ways to become rich and famous.

KARL DALLAS had his first piece published in Melody Maker in 1957. He still writes regularly on music, though he now concentrates on videos and microcomputers. He has recently launched *Showtape*, a video magazine, and has just completed a "definitive study" of Pink Floyd.

ROBIN DENSELOW is a film director and presenter for BBC television and writes on pop music for the *Guardian*.

SIMON FRITH writes for the *Sunday Times* and *New York Rocker*, and teaches sociology at Warwick University.

JOHN GILL, after five years as *Sounds*' pet egghead, is now joint music editor of *Time Out*. He claims he still doesn't know who The Residents really are.

JIM GREEN has written for all manner of rock publications, especially *Trouser Press*.

MARY HARRON is a Canadian freelance writer who covers rock and television for the *New Statesman* and the *Guardian*. She is also interested in parts of the animal kingdom and wild flowers.

JOHN HAYWARD has been editor and publisher of *Circuit*, live music editor of *Music Week*, publisher of the short-lived monthly *Road Crew*, news editor of *Record Business* and is now editor of *Video Business*, as well as a national newspaper freelance on music business topics.

DAVID HEPWORTH is managing editor of *Smash Hits*, co-presents BBC TV's *Whistle Test* and makes odd contributions to various BBC radio programmes.

COLIN IRWIN is an avid cat-lover whose prime ambition was to cover the Moscow Olympics as a sports reporter. Instead he became features editor of *Melody Maker*. He also broadcasts regularly on folk music and once appeared drunk on television.

ALLAN JONES is the tirelessly productive assistant editor of the cheerful pop weekly, *Melody Maker*. He is also the author of *Great Belgians*, a slim volume of sociological profiles: curiously, it remains unpublished. He has never appeared on Channel 4.

MAX JONES is a freelance writer and co-author of the book *Louis* (with John Chilton). He retired in 1982 after nearly 38 years as chief jazz reporter on *Melody Maker*. He has written and broadcast on blues and jazz since 1942.

BARRY LAZELL, a former *Record Business* staffer, is a co-director of MRIB (the Media Research and Information Bureau) and the regular trivia man at *Sounds*.

DAVE MARSH was a founding editor of *Creem*, a music critic at *Newsday* and an editor at the *Real Paper* in Boston before joining *Rolling Stone* as an associate editor in 1975. His books include *Elvis*, *Born to Run: The Bruce Springsteen Story*, *The Book of Rock Lists* and *The Rolling Stone Record Guide*.

CHARLES SHAAR MURRAY is co-editor of *David Bowie: An Illustrated Record* and contributing editor of *New Musical Express*, for which he has written since 1972. He is currently playing guitar with Dance Hall Style, working on a book about Jimi Hendrix, and collecting the most gruesome Hawaiian shirts he can find.

IRA ROBBINS was educated as an electrical engineer, but wound up as a publisher and editorial director of *Trouser Press* and publisher of *Trouser Press Collector's Magazine*. As a freelancer, he has written for *Creem*, *Circus*, *New Musical Express*, *Crawdaddy* and numerous others.

TONY RUSSELL writes a column in *Jazz Journal* and edits/publishes *Old Time Music*.

JON SAVAGE has left Manchester and Granada Television for London and TVAM. He continues to write regularly for *The Face* and is an occasional contributor to *Time Out* and the *Sunday Times*. He is at present flat hunting.

STEVE TAYLOR is a former freelance magazine writer and was Assistant Editor of *The Face* magazine until February 1983, when he left to produce and present *Loose Talk*, an irreverent chat show on Channel 4. He now only writes for the music press when offered outrageous financial inducements.

JOHN TOBLER has written several rock books. Among the most recently published are *The Rock Lists Album*, *The Record Producers*, *Guitar Greats*, *25 Years of Cliff Richard* and *Elvis Presley — The Legend and the Music*. He broadcasts as often as he can on BBC Radio One.

RICHARD WOOTTON is a freelance writer who has contributed to *Melody Maker*, *Time Out* and *Country Music People*. His books include *Honky Tonkin'*, *The Illustrated Country Almanac* and children's books on Elvis Presley and John Lennon.

ACKNOWLEDGEMENTS

It took forever, as it always seems to, but it got done. This is largely because of:

The contributors and the design team, listed above and elsewhere.

Cat Ledger, who subbed ferociously, and John Brown, who looked over my shoulder with a weary paternalism.

The numerous — too numerous to enumerate here — record companies, book publishers and film distributors who supplied material promptly and efficiently.

Simon Fowler, Terry Lott, Anton Corbijn, Jean Bernard Sohiez, Steve Rapport, Bob Gruen, Chris Barclay, Colm Henry, Ian A. Anderson, Adrian Boot, Roxana Knight, BBC Photographs, ZEFA Picture Library, Popperphoto, Gorden Means, Irmgard Pozorski, who did likewise.

The editors of *New Musical Express*, *Melody Maker*, *Sounds*, *Record Mirror*, *Creem* and *Boston Rock*, who gave permission for bits of their reviews to be used.

Ian Cranna, who once again provided emergency assistance at a moment's notice.

Alex Sparks of the Virgin Megastore, who allowed us to wheel several trolleys around his shop in search of LP covers one morning.

Mary Volk, who was heroically good-tempered, tirelessly industrious.

To all of them, a deep bow, a raising of the trilby, a house by the sea.

This has been for Herbie and Lupe.

A.C.

1982 AUG.

1. *The Israelis seize Beirut Airport after a 15-hour bombardment.*

1. The recession hits clubland: the Zigzag Club closes, followed by the Fair Deal in Brixton.

4. *Prince William Arthur Philip Louis, son of the Prince and Princess of Wales, is christened in the Music Room of Buckingham Palace.*

7. 'Come on Eileen' takes Dexy's Midnight Runners to the top of the UK singles chart, where they remain all month, while *The Kids From Fame* starts an eight-week run as Britain's best-selling album. In America,

FLEETWOOD MAC

Mirage by Fleetwood Mac displaces Asia's debut to become the number one album.

9. *Health workers intensify their campaign in support of a 12% pay rise with a week of industrial action.*

12. Soul star Joe Tex, who came to prominence in 1965 with 'Hold What You Got', dies of a heart attack, aged 49.

12. *Actor Henry Fonda dies, aged 77.*

13. As the American record industry plunges to "the worst shape in its history", CBS, Capitol, Elektra Asylum, Atlantic and Warner Bros all make draconian staff cut-backs.

18. The city of Liverpool pays tribute to its favourite sons, The Beatles, by officially naming four local streets in their honour: John Lennon Drive, Paul McCartney Way, George Harrison Close, Ringo Starr Drive.

24. *Unemployment in Britain rises to 3,292,702 — one in seven of the work-force.*

27. Budgie, Iron Maiden and The Michael Schenker Group headline at the annual Reading Festival.

30. *As the last of the vanquished PLO fighting force evacuates Beirut, their leader, Yassir Arafat, also leaves.*

31. *In cities across Poland, demonstrations mark the second anniversary of the foundation of Solidarity.*

A month of many personnel shuffles. Terry Williams replaces Pick Withers in Dire Straits; Don Baldwin replaces Aynsley Dunbar in Jefferson Starship; John Sykes replaces Snowy White in Thin Lizzy; Eddie Martinez replaces Frank Infante in Blondie; Gary Barden replaces Graham Bonnet in The Michael Schenker Group. Guitarist Billy Bremner and bassist Tony Butler temporarily bring The Pretenders back to full strength, while the two birds in Tight Fit are replaced by two new birds. Phil Collen joins Def Leppard; Vince Ely quits the Psychedelic Furs; Pete Way quits UFO; and Phil Lewis quits Girl. Miles Over Matter and The Professionals pack it in.

THE PROFESSIONALS

1982 SEP.

1. Blondie cancel their British tour after poor advance ticket sales. Rumours of their subsequent dissolution are confirmed in October. Meanwhile, Frank Zappa says he no longer considers Europe viable touring territory: "It's too expensive and too violent."

2. Redlands, the 500-year-old Sussex residence of Rolling Stone Keith Richards, catches fire for the second time in nine years; a considerable portion of the house is destroyed. Richards was out of the country at the time.

4. After seven weeks as America's best-selling single, 'Eye of the Tiger' by Survivor makes number one in Britain

YAZOO

too. Yazoo top the independent single and album charts with 'Don't Go' and *Upstairs at Eric's.*

5. *Second World War fighter pilot hero Sir Douglas Bader dies, aged 72.*

8. *Daley Thompson regains the world decathlon record and wins the gold medal at the European Games in Athens.*

11. *American Fool* by John Cougar becomes America's number one album as Chicago's

'Hard to Say I'm Sorry' reaches the top of the singles chart. New Order and The Damned headline the fourth annual Futurama Festival.

13. *Princess Grace of Monaco dies in a road accident, aged 52.*

18. *Hundreds of defenceless civilians are massacred in two Palestinian refugee camps in West Beirut. The occupying Israeli Army blames Christian Phalangist militia.*

22. *The TUC call a day of action in support of the Health Service workers.*

22. The Institute of Environmental Health warn of the potential dangers of stereo headphones: "Their high sensitivity raises their potential for hearing damage above that of all other sources."

23. Charles Levison, Managing Director of WEA Records, threatens to withdraw all advertising from "any newspaper which supports or encourages home taping."

25. 'Abracadabra' returns Steve Miller to the top of the US singles chart.

27. *Michael Foot wins a gigantic vote of confidence at the Labour Party conference for his plan to drum leaders of the Trotskyist Militant Tendency from the party.*

29. *The Home Secretary announces plans to extend police powers of stop and search.*

During the month, Mark Fox leaves Haircut 100; Trudi Baptiste leaves King Trigger; and Geoff Deane leaves Modern Romance. Former Skid Richard Jobson joins Paines Plough Theatre Company; Stephen Lironi replaces both Titch and Jim McKinven in Altered Images; Troy Tate and Al Derby replace Dee Harris in Fashion. The Radio Stars and The Vibrators re-form and two punk pioneers unveil new bands: ex-Buzzcock Steve Diggle fronts Flag of Convenience and former Sex Pistol Glen Matlock returns in The Hot Club. Linx and Theatre of Hate call it a day.

1982 OCT.

1. America suffers John Cougar fever: 'Jack and Diane' and *American Fool* top the singles and album chart all month.

2. For the first time since 1975, Peter Gabriel reunites with Genesis for a WOMAD benefit at Milton Keynes Bowl.

2. Musical Youth head the UK singles list with 'Pass the Dutchie', while Dire Straits enter the album chart at number one with *Love Over Gold*.

2. *In America, the police hunt for a killer intensifies after Tylenol painkillers, contaminated with cyanide, claim a seventh victim.*

5. On the 20th anniversary of its original release, EMI reissues 'Love Me Do', the first Beatles single.

7. Jimmy Page is given a 12-month conditional discharge and fined £100 costs after being found guilty of possessing 198 milligrammes of cocaine.

8. Joan Jett arrives to start a UK tour but encounters the attendance slump which has gripped British venues. Iggy Pop and Grace Jones also visit Britain.

8. *US employment surges to its highest level since the Great Depression; over 10% of the work-force are now jobless.*

9. *577 men of the Falklands task force are honoured with medals.*

10. The British Phonographic Industry reveals that album sales in the third quarter of 1982 were down by 21% over the previous year. "Home taping is the main reason for the industry's problems" says a spokesman.

11. *Henry VIII's warship the Mary Rose is raised from the sea-bed and towed into Portsmouth.*

12. *The Hunt Committee recommends the unrestricted introduction of multi-channel cable television in Britain.*

16. UB 40's *UB 44* is the best-selling independent album in Britain.

19. *The De Lorean car firm in Belfast is closed by the official*

receiver. The following day, its owner, John De Lorean, is arrested on drugs charges in Los Angeles.

20. *In elections for the Northern Ireland Assembly, Sinn Fein candidates win five seats — but subsequently declare their intention not to attend.*

23. Culture Club have the number one single in Britain: 'Do You Really Want to Hurt Me'. Meanwhile, as 'I Ran' makes the Top Ten, A Flock of Seagulls become the first British technopop band to be conspicuously more successful in America.

25. *The New York Stock Exchange suffers its biggest one-day fall since 1929.*

27. Marillion embark on their first major "progressive (?!) rock" revival.

29. One concert-goer is stabbed to death, another killed by a gunshot, and a third seriously wounded in a knifing in three apparently unrelated incidents at a Peter Frampton gig in Hermann Park, Houston.

30. Robert Wyatt's 'Shipbuilding', co-written by Elvis Costello, is UK's top-selling indie single.

31. *For the first time, all ten gates of the Thames flood barrier are raised to test the mechanism.*

31. *The Kids From Fame returns to the top of the UK album chart.*

Kim Wilde and Yazoo play their first-ever live dates; Martin Atkins rejoins Public Image Ltd; Jane Munro leaves The Au Pairs; and Anti Pasti sack vocalist Martin Roper. The Doobie Brothers, Black Sabbath, Mood Six and TV Personalities all fold.

ROBERT WYATT

1982 NOV.

1. Top-selling UK independent single is 'How Does It Feel to Be Mother of a Thousand Dead?' by Crass.

2. Elton John starts a 42-date UK tour — his first British dates since 1979. The core of his backing group are the original early seventies' Elton John Band.

5. First broadcast of 'The Tube', Channel 4's live rock show.

5. *French film director/actor Jacques Tati dies, aged 75.*

JOE COCKER   **JENNIFER WARNES**

6. 'Up Where We Belong' sees Joe Cocker and Jennifer Warnes at number one in the US singles chart. Depeche Mode's album *A Broken Frame* is UK's best-selling indie.

10. *President Brezhnev of the Soviet Union dies of a heart attack at 75. Yuri Andropov, former head of the KGB secret police, is subsequently sworn in as his successor.*

10. *Geoffrey Prime is sentenced to 35 years in prison after admitting spying for the Soviet Union.*

13. Eddy Grant's 'I Don't Wanna Dance' is number one single in UK.

14. *Lech Walesa, leader of the outlawed Solidarity union, rejoins his family in Gdansk following his release by the Polish military government.*

16. *Comedian Arthur Askey dies, aged 82.*

20. Australia's Men at Work reach number one in America with their *Business As Usual* album.

27. Abba's *Singles* album removes *The Kids From Fame* from the top of the UK album chart.

30. *The previously unknown Animal Rights Militia claims responsibility for incendiary devices posted to various politicians including Margaret Thatcher.*

A month of resignation: Squeeze, The Teardrop Explodes, Gillan, Monsoon, The Modettes and Japan all throw in the towel.

EDDY GRANT

1982 DEC.

2. David Blue, 41, a Greenwich Village contemporary of Dylan's during the early sixties' folk boom, dies of a heart attack whilst jogging in New York.

3. *Comedian Marty Feldman dies while filming in Mexico City, aged 49.*

4. The Jam's 'Beat Surrender' enters the UK singles chart at number one. *The John Lennon Collection* is Britain's best-selling album all month.

6. *Seventeen are killed and 65 injured by an Irish National Liberation Army bomb detonated at a disco in a Ballykelly pub. The murders raise the total Ulster-connected civilian/troop killings to 2,264 since 1970.*

8. Country & Western star Marty Robbins dies of a heart attack, aged 57.

8. *The Home Secretary signs exclusion orders preventing Sinn Fein leaders from accepting Ken Livingstone's invitation to visit London for discussions on the problems in Northern Ireland.*

10. *Plans are revealed for the US Government to build new European war headquarters near High Wycombe in Buckinghamshire.*

THE JAM

11. The Jam, most successful of the 1976 New Wave bands, play their final gig at Brighton. Paul Weller subsequently signs a solo deal with Polydor.

12. *Tens of thousands of women converge on Greenham Common RAF base in Berkshire to protest against the siting of 96 American Cruise missiles.*

15. *The TUC Health Services Committee end eight months of disruption and resume talks on new pay proposals.*

17. The Who complete their 39-date "final tour" at Toronto's Maple Leaf Gardens. Since they kicked off on 22 September, they have grossed some $23 million to make it the top money-making tour of the year.

21. *Soviet leader Andropov offers to reduce nuclear missile strength to match that of Britain and France if USA abandons plans to deploy Cruise and Pershing 11 missiles in Western Europe. The proposals are met with scepticism in Britain and rejection in America and France.*

25. Seasonal UK hits include 'Blue Christmas' by Shakin' Stevens and 'Peace on Earth' by David Bowie & Bing Crosby.

30. *Martial law is suspended in Poland.*

During the month, Ian Dury returns to the stage for the first time in over a year and The Specials release their first single since 'Ghost Town'. Simon Gallup leaves The Cure and Pete Way joins Ozzy Osbourne's band. Wasted Youth, The Blues Band, Ten Pole Tudor, The Jam and The Who all play their last gigs.

IAN DURY

1983 JAN.

1. *Two women are trampled to death and 140 people severely injured as crowds disperse after New Year celebrations in Trafalgar Square.*

HALL AND OATES

1. Best-selling single in America is 'Maneater' by Daryl Hall and John Oates.

2. *Comedian Dick Emery dies, aged 63.*

7. *Australia regain The Ashes in the final test at Sydney.*

12. *Former Traffic percussionist Reebop Kwaku Baah dies of a brain haemorrhage in Stockholm.*

13. *Margaret Thatcher returns from a five-day visit to the Falklands.*

14. *Police seeking escaped criminal David Martin shoot and critically wound Stephen Waldorf by mistake. Martin is subsequently recaptured two weeks later in a tunnel at Belsize Park underground station.*

15. 'You Can't Hurry Love' by Phil Collins dislodges Renee & Renato from the top of the UK singles chart. As 'Down Under' rises to number one, Men at Work top both single and album charts in America.

18. *The Franks Report on the Falklands concludes that the Argentinian invasion could not have been foreseen or prevented.*

19. London rock club Dingwalls opens a chain of five provincial venues in Hull, Bristol, Newcastle, Liverpool and Sheffield.

23. *29,000 water and sewage workers start an all-out strike in support of a pay claim, having rejected a 7.3% rise.*

24. *Bjorn Borg confirms his retirement from first-class tennis at 26.*

24. *Sixty-three Red Brigade terrorists are sentenced to terms of imprisonment in Rome on some 200 charges, including 17 murders.*

25. Lamar Williams, 36, bassist with the Allman Brothers Band and Sea Level, dies of cancer in Los Angeles.

29. Fifties' pop idol Billy Fury dies of a heart attack, aged 41. After eleven Top Ten hits, recurrent illness had forced semi-retirement in the mid sixties, but he had recently returned to the charts with 'Devil or Angel'.

29. Men at Work's 'Down Under' becomes Britain's best-selling single; their *Business as Usual* the best-selling album. They still hold similar positions in America and in so doing become the first act to top all four charts since Rod Stewart in 1971.

31. Number one indie single in UK is 'Heartache Avenue' by The Maisonettes.

31. *The wearing of front-seat belts becomes compulsory for motorists in Britain.*

During the month Nidge leaves Blitz; Stu P. Didiot leaves Charge; and Nick Heyward leaves Haircut 100. Nicko McBain replaces Clive Burr in Iron Maiden. Angela Jaeger joins Pigbag. Trimmer & Jenkins and UK Decay break up.

1983 FEB.

1. Newly released statistics reveal the extent of the recession in the US record industry during 1982. The number of certified gold (sales of 500,000) and platinum (sales of one million) albums dropped by 15%. The year's two top-selling albums, John Cougar's *American Fool* and Asia's début, each sold some three million copies — less than half as many as REO Speedwagon's *Hi Infidelity* sold the previous year.

3. *Unemployment figures in Britain reach a new record — 3,224,714 or one in seven of the working population.*

THE CARPENTERS

4. Karen Carpenter dies of a heart attack in Los Angeles, aged 32. As The Carpenters, she and her brother Richard were one of the seventies' most successful duos.

5. 'Africa' gives Toto the number one single in America.

10. *The General Synod of the Church of England rejects unilateral nuclear disarmament and supports the continuation of a British nuclear deterrent — conditional on a commitment not to be the first to use it.*

10. A former civil servant, Dennis Nilson, 37, is charged with murder following the discovery of dismembered human bodies in a drain in Muswell Hill, North London. Up to 16 victims are thought to be connected to the murder investigation.

12. Ragtime composer and pianist Eubie Blake dies in Brooklyn, New York, five days after his 100th birthday.

16. *Bush fires fanned by 50 m.p.h. winds in Southern Australia, dry after the worst drought of the century, kill over 70 people, injure several hundred, and destroy much property, livestock and wildlife.*

16. *Newbury magistrates jail 36 women for breaches of the peace at Greenham Common Air Base. Following further incidents, another 34 women are arrested.*

19. KajaGooGoo's début 'Too Shy' becomes Britain's best-selling single.

25. *American playwright Tennessee Williams dies, aged 71.*

26. Men at Work are deposed after heading the US album chart for 14 weeks — the longest-running chart-topping début, breaking the record set by The Monkees in 1967. *Thriller* by Michael Jackson is the new number one.

26. *GLC leader Ken Livingstone incenses politicians by flying to Belfast for a two-day meeting with Provisional Sinn Fein leaders.*

28. Fifties' pop star Winifred Atwell, famed for her jangling piano, dies aged 69.

In a month of many changes, Ian Gillan joins the resuscitated Black Sabbath and former Uriah Heep mainstay Ken Hensley joins Blackfoot. Beki Bondage leaves Vice Squad, Troy Tate leaves Fashion, Pete Wells and Dallas Royal leave Rose Tattoo, and sax player Clare Hirst leaves The Belle Stars. Rick Wright's departure from Pink Floyd is confirmed. Former Jam leader Paul Weller unveils his

STYLE COUNCIL

new group, The Style Council. Stiff Little Fingers play their farewell gigs, while The Fun Boy Three play their first live dates. Terry Chimes, their original drummer who rejoined to help them out of a predicament in May 1982, leaves The Clash again "to get back to my own plans".

1983 MAR.

1. The second British Invasion gains ground as Culture Club, Duran Duran, The Pretenders, Dexy's Midnight Runners, The Thompson Twins, A Flock of Seagulls, Musical Youth, ABC

THOMAS DOLBY

and Thomas Dolby all move up the American charts.

2. Three major companies, Sony, Philips and Polygram, launch a new digital audio system. A five-inch Compact Disc contains up to an hour of music, reproduced as sound by a laser beam. Playing equipment, currently expensive, is expected to drop in price as its popularity spreads.

3. A Cleveland based Hell's Angel tells a Senate Judiciary Panel that the California Chapter has had a contract out on Mick Jagger since The Stones' Altamont concert in 1969, when a biker was jailed for stabbing a spectator to death. During the 14-year period, two abortive attempts had been made on the singer's life, he said. An unconcerned Jagger shrugs off the threats and continues to work on his autobiography.

3. *California is ravaged by storms in which at least 20 die and 15,000 are made homeless.*

5. 'Billie Jean' by Michael Jackson becomes the best-selling single in both Britain and America, joining his album, also number one on both sides of the Atlantic.

12. The U2 album *War* enters the UK chart at number one as 'Total Eclipse of the Heart' by

BONNIE TYLER

Bonnie Tyler becomes the best-selling single.

15. *Britain's Charlie Magri wins the Flyweight Championship of the World, defeating defender Eleoncio Mercedes when the fight is stopped in the second round.*

18. *Following dismal audience ratings during its first 50 days, TV-AM undergoes severe personnel shake-up. Chairman Peter Jay resigns.*

18. *The Prince and Princess of Wales leave for a six-week tour of Australia and New Zealand.*

21. *Following serious long-lasting drought in Ethiopia, over a million are in urgent need of famine relief.*

23. *President Reagan, speaking on television, claims to have evidence of a "relentless Soviet military build-up" and urges more research on a laser beam space defence programme.*

26. 'Is There Something I Should Know' by Duran Duran enters the UK singles chart at number one. Tears for Fears head the album chart with their début *The Hurting*. New Order have the best-selling indie single, 'Blue Monday'.

28. *After management proposals to axe a three-minute washing-up period at the end of each shift, 5,000 car workers at British Leyland's Cowley plant start a strike which halts production of the new Maestro for almost a month.*

29. *The Labour Party publishes its campaign document, advocating unilateral nuclear disarmament, withdrawal from the Common Market, and a public spending programme designed to reduce unemployment drastically.*

During the month, The Teardrop Explodes and Southern Death Cult confirm their dissolution. Punk pioneers Chelsea and The UK Subs throw in the towel but revised groups soon reappear under identical names.

1983 APR.

1. 100,000 CND protestors join hands to form a 14-mile human chain stretching from Greenham Common to Burghfield Ordnance factory. Easter demonstrations take place in cities across Europe.

2. The Final Cut by Pink Floyd becomes Britain's best-selling album within a week of release.

4. Challenger, America's second space shuttle, is launched from Cape Canaveral for a five-day mission. Two of the astronauts subsequently spend over three hours outside the craft — the first American ''space walk'' for almost a decade.

4. Film star Gloria Swanson dies, aged 84.

5. Danny Rapp, leader of Danny & The Juniors, still playing the oldies circuit on the strength of their late fifties' hits, dies of self-inflicted gunshot wounds, aged 42.

9. 'Let's Dance' returns David Bowie to the top of the UK singles chart — and the album chart two weeks later.

11. General Galtieri, former Argentine leader who instigated the Falklands invasion, is sentenced to 60 days imprisonment for criticising the conduct of the war.

11. Gandhi, the British film directed by Sir Richard Attenborough, wins eight Hollywood Oscars — including those for Best Film and Best Actor.

13. Eleven people are murdered in Sicily during violent conflict between Mafia factions.

16. Bonnie Tyler's Faster Than the Speed of Night is new top UK album.

16. EMI, initially reluctant to commit themselves, announce their intention to join the Compact Disc market.

16. Bass-player Pete Farndon, 30, who left The Pretenders last June, is found dead in the bath of his London home.

18. Felix Pappalardi, producer of Cream and bassist with Mountain, is shot dead in his New York apartment. Police charge his wife with second degree murder.

18. Sterling rises to $1.56, its highest level against the dollar for three months.

22. 77-year-old jazz piano great Earl ''Fatha'' Hines dies of heart failure in Oakland, California.

22. The German magazine Stern announces the discovery of Adolf Hitler's diaries, dating from 1932 to 1945. Scientific tests later find them to be forgeries.

23. Some ten months after its domestic success, 'Come on Eileen' by Dexy's Midnight Runners dislodges Michael Jackson from the top of the US singles chart — but only for one week, when 'Beat It' takes over.

27. President Reagan asks Congress to approve a further $110 million in military aid for El Salvador. He denies any suggestion of sending American combat troops to Central America to create another Vietnam.

28. New Civil Defence regulations prevent local authorities from declaring themselves ''nuclear free zones'' and defying Government instructions which include the building of bomb-proof bunkers.

29. The Argentine Junta officially declares that the many thousands of missing persons reported since the 1970s must be considered dead.

30. Spandau Ballet have the top UK single, 'True'.

30. Muddy Waters, the R&B giant whose music influenced three generations, dies in his sleep in hospital at Downers Grove, Illinois, aged 68. He had been intermittently ill and away from the touring circuit for more than a year.

Manfred Mann, The Yardbirds, Man and Caravan are among bands to regroup for the 25th anniversary of the Marquee Club celebrations. The original Animals, meanwhile, decide to re-form on a more permanent basis, planning an album and a world tour. During the month, Marc Riley leaves The Fall after five years and Billy Currie leaves Visage. Thin Lizzy and UFO both play their last gigs before disbanding. Joni Mitchell plays her first British dates since 1974. Among new bands to rise from the ashes are Babaluma (ex-King Trigger), The Truth (ex-Nine Below Zero), Cry (ex-The Cure), Fast Way (ex-Motorhead and Humble Pie) and The Tudors (ex-Tenpole Tudor).

1983 MAY

2. The town of Coalinga in central California is devastated by an earthquake measuring 6.5 on the Richter scale.

6. Jazz trombonist Kai Winding dies of complications resulting from a brain tumour, in Yonkers, New York, aged 60.

13. The stream of lava from Mount Etna, erupting for over six weeks, is diverted by explosives to avert danger to threatened villages.

SPANDAU BALLET

14. Spandau Ballet's True heads both UK single and album charts.

16. Following an out-of-court settlement with former manager Billy Gaff, Rod Stewart secures publishing, recording, television and video rights, together with ''a seven figure sum''.

21. 'Let's Dance' takes Bowie to US number one. Thriller returns Michael Jackson to the top of the UK album chart after a break of nine weeks.

24. In Paris, student demonstrations against university reforms escalate into rioting and street fighting.

26. In the FA Cup Final replay, Manchester United beat Brighton 4-0.

NEW EDITION

28. 'Candy Girl' by New Edition is number one UK single.

28. A Rembrandt portrait valued at £3 million is stolen from Dulwich College art gallery for the fourth time in 16 years.

31. During a four-day sit down protest and blockade at the US Air Force base at Upper Heyford, Oxfordshire, 752 demonstrators are arrested.

31. Jack Dempsey, world heavyweight boxing champion from 1919-26, dies aged 87.

During the month, Pete Jones, their bassist for seven months, leaves Public Image Ltd; Dee O'Malley replaces bassist Tracey Lamb in Rock Goddess; drummer David Palmer quits ABC; Andy Ward, ex-Camel, replaces Mick Pointer as drummer in Marillion. The Business and The Birthday Party announce their intention to disband, as do Yazoo — currently at the peak of their success. Richard Jobson, former Skid leader, unveils his new group The Armoury Show, featuring ex-Banshee John McGeoch and ex-Skid Russell Webb, and seventies' megagroup Yes get back together to record and tour.

MICHAEL JACKSON

1983 JUN.

1. *Lester Piggott wins his ninth Derby on Teenoso.*

4. The Police storm back to head the UK singles list with 'Every Breath You Take'. Meanwhile, 'Shipbuilding' by Robert Wyatt tops the Indie chart.

5. *The People's March for Jobs, which started from Glasgow on April 23rd, ends with a rally in Hyde Park.*

9. *The Conservative government win a landslide victory to return for a second term of office.*

12. *Michael Foot announces that he will stand down as leader of the Labour Party.*

14. *After 9,000 miles in ten months, storms force Peter Bird to abandon his attempt to become the first man to row the Pacific alone — only 33 miles from his target.*

16. *The Pope returns to his native Poland, denouncing the constrictions of martial law and meeting former Solidarity leader Lech Walesa for secret talks.*

17. *The inflation rate falls to 3.7% — the lowest since March 1968.*

FUN BOY THREE

17. Curtis Mayfield, King Sunny Adé, The Beat and The Fun Boy Three headline a three-day CND festival at Glastonbury.

18. 'Pills and Soap', recorded by Elvis Costello under the pseudonym of The Imposter, is best-selling independent UK single.

24. *The US space shuttle Challenger returns after a successful six-day mission. Among the crew of five is Sally Ride, America's first spacewoman.*

25. *India's cricket team beats West Indies by 43 runs in the final of the Prudential World Cup at Lords.*

25. *Synchronicity, the new Police album, enters the UK chart at number one, while in America, the Flashdance*

IRENE CARA

soundtrack dislodges Michael Jackson's *Thriller* after 17 weeks at the top. For the first time ever, America's Hot Hundred includes more records by foreigners than native Americans. The ratio is highest in the Top 40 where outsiders hold 24 against the US tally of 16.

30. *The first batch of jobless school-leavers swells unemployment figures by 63,000.*

Perennial heroes Rod Stewart and David Bowie return to the

British stage for sold-out tours. Rick Buckler, former Jam drummer, discloses details of his new group, Time UK. Drummers Hugo Burnham, Phil Rudd and Bob Rondinelli leave Gang of Four, AC/DC and Rainbow respectively. Keith Levine leaves PIL, reducing the group to two: singer John Lydon and drummer Martin Atkins. Pigbag disband. Haysi Fantayzee play their first live dates. Former Magazine frontman Howard Devoto comes out of the cupboard after two years.

1983 JUL.

2. Rod Stewart returns to the top of the UK singles chart with 'Baby Jane'.

2. *Defending champion John McEnroe defeats unseeded New Zealander Chris Lewis in the men's singles final at Wimbledon. In the ladies, the holder Martina Navratilova retains her title against Andrea Jaeger.*

5. The fourth annual New Music Seminar is held in New York City.

6. The British Phonographic Industry launches a new crackdown following the proliferation of pirate cassettes. Despite having taken 20 people to court, the BPI seems unable to locate the major sources or stem the supply. Meanwhile, in Los Angeles, William Minor is given an eight and a half year prison sentence plus a $90,000 fine for heading an Elvis Presley bootleg album operation.

9. *Fantastic*, the début by Wham, enters the UK album chart at number one. Michael Jackson's *Thriller*, by far the biggest selling album of the year, returns to the top of the US chart once more. 'Every Breath You Take' by The Police heads the singles chart — the fastest rising US number one since The Beatles' heyday.

9. The British Invasion continues to dominate the US charts — with The Police, Eddy Grant, KajaGooGoo, Culture Club, Madness, Elton John, Duran Duran, Rod Stewart, The Eurythmics, A Flock of Seagulls, The Human League, David Bowie, Naked Eyes, Def Leppard and Billy Idol all in the Top 40, alongside The Kinks and The Hollies — heroes of the 1964/5 invasion!

11. *Sir James Goldsmith wins £85,010 in libel damages and costs against* Private Eye *— the biggest settlement the magazine has ever had to pay.*

12. Chris Wood, former sax player with Traffic, dies of liver failure, aged 39.

13. *The House of Commons votes against the restoration of the death penalty by an unexpectedly large majority of 145.*

16. Tom Robinson's comeback single 'War Baby' tops the UK independent chart.

16. *A British Airways helicopter en route from Penzance to the Scilly Isles plunges into the sea with the loss of 20 lives.*

18. *In a return to the political arena, former US Secretary of State Dr Henry Kissinger is appointed by President Reagan to head the National Commission on Future Policies Towards Central America.*

18. EMI open their Abbey Road studios to the public. Tourists flock to inspect where The Beatles recorded 188 of their 210 tracks.

19. Scotland Yard's Obscene Publications Squad removes stocks of *Live in Yugoslavia* by The Anti-Nowhere League from a distributor's warehouse. In June, 8,000 copies of their single, 'So What', had been destroyed under the direction of Croydon County Court.

21. *Sir Harold Wilson, Gerry Fitt and Jo Grimond are among 17 new Life Peers.*

23. *Synchronicity* by The Police is best-selling US album; *You and Me Both*, the final offering from Yazoo, is best-selling UK album. 'Wherever I Lay My Hat' takes Paul Young to the top of the British singles chart.

26. *President Reagan goes on television to dispel public anxiety over the build-up of US forces in Central America.*

30. *In Britain, temperatures rise to the highest figures recorded for 300 years.*

31. *Tragedy strikes at the British 500cc Grand Prix at Silverstone when competitors Norman Brown and Peter Huber are killed in a collision on the track.*

Steve Winwood starts his first tour since the break-up of Traffic at the end of 1974. The Undertones play their final gigs before splitting. Bad Company, inactive for some time, confirm their dissolution. The Beat and The Fun Boy Three both throw in the towel.

STEVE WINWOOD

ROCK

In the immortal words of Elvis Costello, I just don't know where to begin. Attempting to impose some sort of shape on a music which got out of hand a long time ago gets that little bit more ludicrous with each passing year. I remember... what? Meat Loaf filing for bankruptcy, Blondie breaking up, Muddy Waters dying, Elvis Costello giving interviews, Neil Young taking up electronics, *everyone* doing cover versions, Malcolm McLaren scooting round the Third World with a tape recorder, Elton John making up with Bernie Taupin, and Michael Jackson introducing a hapless interviewer to Muscles, his pet python. Significant events indeed, but signifying what?

On the one hand we had U2 announcing the return of Progressive Rock; on the other were Duran Duran seemingly sewing up the Western World with the sort of emotionally neutral music that any advertising agency would be proud to put its name to. Only KajaGooGoo seemed to be able to produce some kind of accord. Needless to say, it was a consensus against. Just about everyone could be relied upon to administer a swift kick in their direction. It was the only thing they agreed on. The *Face*-reading art student with the wedge haircut and Banshees album could be cajoled into abusing KajaGooGoo without any trouble; likewise the rock-loving Springsteen fan, who would tell you what an affront they were to the music's integrity; even Duran Duran fans could draw themselves up to their full height in order to look down on them.

This much was not especially surprising. It was only when I came across a middle-aged BBC executive waxing near-apoplectic on the subject that I fully realised the extent to which they'd polarised opinion. KajaGooGoo, the case for the prosecution alleged, were a grotesque figment of EMI's imagination, cast as Monkees

KAJAGOOGOO

to Duran Duran's Beatles, cynically gift-wrapped like a pre-adolescent's cotton candy day-dream. Then the argument moved up a gear. KajaGooGoo were the last throw of a dying industry, a betrayal of all that is good and fine and precious. Dammit, they spluttered, this time they've gone too far!

At this point we should pause to remember that we're talking here about a pop group and not a killer virus. Just a pop group. Five youngish blokes with nice teeth, perfect manners and unfortunate haircuts, who

made an inoffensive noise and had a few hits. It's my belief that what aroused the ire of every self-appointed guardian of rock's eternal flame was KajaGooGoo's refusal to explain their existence, their refusal to explain *what they were trying to do*. In certain musical circles it was important that you were trying to do something. Indeed, to some people it was probably a good deal more important than what you actually did. Your aims and schemes could be broadcast in interviews, telegraphed in your

sleeve artwork, semaphored via your wardrobe; so much easier than wrestling with troublesome things like tunes.

And if, as their critics suggested, EMI had actually manufactured KajaGooGoo like so much software, who could blame them? The music industry is in deep trouble and nowhere more so than in the UK. A vast proportion of the potential consumers of pop records are out of work. Young teenage boys are turning to computer games in increasing numbers. Their sisters are

13

probably quite happy to listen to the radio and buy the odd magazine. The older, more affluent audience who were responsible for the albums boom of the early seventies can only be lured into the shops for a new Dire Straits record, a commodity that isn't exactly flooding the market.

In slack times it only takes 25,000 sales to penetrate the British singles chart. The audience is smaller and gets bored more quickly; its attention has to be constantly excited by new fads, snazzy videos, changes of costume. As a record market, the UK is very nearly a write-off and only retains importance as a proving ground for new acts, a panic-stricken laboratory where elements are desperately combined in search of that elusive compound with export potential.

The curious thing is that it appears to be working. Cropping up with increasing regularity among the Dan Fogelbergs and Pat Benatars of the US charts are names like Dexys, Yazoo, Adam Ant, Musical Youth, Duran Duran and Culture Club, groups that could only have been formed in a country where idiosyncrasy is all. Similarly, Australasia is proving itself a source of ingenious but derivative pop groups, with Men at Work's compulsive 'Down Under' leading the way.

In this new storming of the US citadel, video has played a vital part. With the rise of MTV and the world-wide advent of cable, satellite and "narrowcasting", the video has completely replaced touring as the route to fame and acceptance. For a sum in the region of £25,000 a record company can buy complete control over the way an act is packaged and disseminated. Compared to the old method of tour subsidy over a period of time this is laughably cheap. However, these new economics have implications which the music business is finding less palatable. Britain has more TV pop shows than any other country and it also has the highest proportion of VCRs per head of population. The promotional video is no longer simply a useful selling tool. In cases like David Bowie's 'China Girl', Michael Jackson's 'Billie Jean' or almost any Madness single you care to name, it is indivisible from the record that prompted it. It was intriguing

DAVID BOWIE

this year to watch Britain's fledgling breakfast television companies using a sprinkling of pop videos to lure teenagers into turning on the family set at this unaccustomed hour of the day.

It appears that the record companies have unwittingly evolved a new form of audio-visual entertainment, a form of entertainment which is hugely popular but nearly impossible to actually *sell*, partly because of the intractable economics of video manufacture but also because promotion dictates

that the desired object is being effectively given away for free, piped into the home and gratefully swallowed by the waiting VCR. More than one executive must have taken a look at the balance sheet and yearned fondly for the days when Peter Grant made Led Zeppelin a major attraction by refusing to let them release singles, give interviews or appear on TV.

Technology has made a nonsense of the music business. The laser disc, which could have offered new

horizons, has instead been trimmed down to a half-hearted gesture in the direction of better reproduction for twice the money. This from the same people who've been happy to press pop records from recycled vinyl, saving the virgin material for classical releases. It's little more than we've grown to expect from an industry hamstrung by the conventions of Tin Pan Alley.

Popular music is currently going through the stage that professional sport passed through ten years ago: the incursion of TV is hitting attendance figures at the grassroots while a small clique of superstars, secure in their pulling power, demand increasingly unrealistic sums of money just to cross their front doorstep. Not surprisingly, sponsors are starting to make tentative moves into the arena. Budweiser bankrolled The Who's final US tour, Levis shelled out a substantial sum for a piece of David Bowie's homecoming, while Eddy Grant, in the scam of the year, ensured massive coverage in the British press by getting the local airline to fly out a succession of journalists to his Barbados home, in return for their logo on his album sleeve.

But only the big earners can expect to attract this kind of support and they're proving a somewhat exclusive club. Of the hordes of acts who've achieved fame and fortune in the last five years, only The Police have really managed to haul themselves into the august company of sixties' and seventies' luminaries like Bowie, McCartney, Dylan and The Rolling Stones.

Bowie's return to the stage emphasised once again the huge gap that yawns between genuine stars and the legions of the merely well-known. Like most grand stadium shows it was musically mediocre, the incisive funk of the *Let's Dance* LP turned blunt and boorish. But in this super league the priorities are no longer musical. Millions of dollars spent on promotion, staging and hokum, but a paltry squabble over a few hundred dollars is responsible for the absence of Stevie Ray Vaughan, the young guitarist who did so much to give the album its distinction. The fact that he was replaced by the ghastly Earl Slick ensured that he was missed even more.

These kind of shows have a

MICHAEL JACKSON

WHAM

PAUL WELLER

corrosive momentum of their own. Bruce Springsteen thankfully took steps to get back to basics with *Nebraska* a bleak, erratically telling look at hope and despair in Middle America. As a comment on the contemporary malaise it was more successful than most, though neither as entertaining as 'The Message' by Grandmaster Flash nor as resonant as 'Shipbuilding', the Falklands War song that Elvis Costello gave to Robert Wyatt.

But all three worked in varying degrees because the relevant idioms had been mastered. Would that the same could be said of the various fumbled attempts at significance made by those alumni of the new pop academy who lay claim to heavyweight status. With sinking hearts we watched as carts were repeatedly and proudly placed before horses.

One such, Paul Weller, broke up The Jam and announced a project (we were not short of

"projects" this year) called The Style Council. Their second single, 'Money-go-round', illuminated a lot of things wrong with British pop. Weller is an honourable man fallen among theorists, one who has consequently become so obsessed with meaning and significance that he no longer has any grip on what sounds good and what doesn't. 'Money-go-round' was an orgy of ideological correctness — anti-capitalist rap over funk

backing, black backing singer — and it was truly awful; wooden, mannered and dreary. The sleeve exhortation to "keep on burning" only increased one's frustration with a record that was so barren of the spirit it claimed to embody.

Read Britain's music papers regularly — and most of us are hooked — and you quickly become familiar with terms like "radical dance music" (about as meaningful as "radical ice hockey") and "subversive

SPANDAU BALLET

DEXY'S MIDNIGHT RUNNERS

pop". Music is lauded for being "disconcerting" as if that were an end in itself. Such idle chat is the staple diet of musical discourse and its effect is generally pernicious. A good rule of thumb seems to be that those who talk most about "spirit" or "conviction" are those whose records are least likely to deliver said qualities.

Dexy's succeeded because they recorded 'Come On Eileen', a catchy tune, and when they couldn't follow it with another equally catchy tune, all Kevin Rowland's talk about passion and commitment could not seduce people into handing over their hard-earned. Similarly, Spandau Ballet have a picture of themselves as boulevard soul boys, selflessly dedicated to something-or-other, but when you hold 'True', their biggest hit, up to the light, it actually sounds like sub-standard Toto. And the truth is that sub-standard Toto is actually *better*, hard though it may be to accept.

This disparity between the claims made for the music and the music itself was one of the banes of the year and reached some kind of pinnacle of pretension with a two-man electro pop enterprise called Tears for Fears who had one track on their album labouring under the extraordinary title 'Ideas as Opiates'. Anyone who can find it in them to contrive a title like that is suffering from incorrectable wrong-headedness. I would at this point catalogue the atrocities committed in the fair name of jazz during 1983 but I haven't the heart. Suffice it to say that noises were produced on newly-purchased brass instruments that simply beggared description.

KING SUNNY ADÉ

THE POLICE

Not that the chic interest in traditional black music was entirely fruitless. The splendid King Sunny Ade visited the UK long enough for would-be High Lifers to see a master at work. Whether any rock group can come close to mastering this most slippery of forms is doubtful. Most likely African music will remain a minority taste until it produces a recognisable rock star figure like Bob Marley. Meanwhile we can look forward to white groups replacing their obligatory reggae number with an obligatory Nigerian one. There's a prospect to gladden the heart.

As the Atlantic continues to shrink, the musical two-way traffic gets heavier. New York's "hip-hop" school of mad scientists seized upon the Kraftwerk electronic manual and put it to the service of a whole string of wickedly playful records from people like The Jonzun Crew, Afrika Bambaata and, most surprisingly, Divine.

Wham! took up the challenge and produced that most unlikely of creatures, the good British rap record. They also set a different precedent as just about the only British act who could actually dance. In the year that *Fame* and *Flashdance* were major attractions, choreography was a strong card to play. Hoofers of the year were Jeffrey Daniels of Shalamar, who secured the nomination with a show-stopping demonstration of body popping on *Top of the Pops*, and previous winner Michael Jackson, executing one spin on the video for 'Beat It' which this writer would swap for 90% of the records of the day. For sheer polish and *élan*, his 'Thriller' cut just about every other offering in the vicinity to shreds and sometimes sounded as if it had been designed for that very purpose.

CULTURE CLUB

The least likely candidate for Most Popular Newcomer used to spend his days sitting in the doorway of a clothes shop around the corner from my office, got up like a dread version of the Bette Davis character in *Whatever Happened to Baby Jane?* The very idea that he would lead a group who in 1983 would find favour all over the world via a string of subtle, alluring pop-soul singles seemed obscure to say the least. But Boy George and Culture Club did it, emphasising in the process that androgyny and vulnerability seem to be the qualities that adolescent girls find the most attractive. But although it was the pancake and the dreadlocks and the gauche smiles that made him a talking point, it was the music itself that put Culture Club there in the first place and that music was simple stuff that belied the exotic image. Its aims were relatively modest but its grasp was refreshingly sure.

The same could be said of others who distinguished themselves; The Pretenders' brilliant 'Back on the Chain Gang' (recorded after the death of James Honeyman-Scott and the departure of Pete Farndon, who was himself to die within months); Donald Fagen's *The Nightfly*, a better album than Steely Dan ever made and the only pop "concept" worthy of the name; Richard Thompson's healing *Hand of Kindness*; Van Morrison's touchingly fuzzy 'Rave on John Donne'; Elton John's deft 'I Guess That's Why They Call It the Blues'; Eddy Grant's joyous 'Electric Avenue'. Nothing of the order of a great stylistic departure but each of them assured and affecting.

When you get right down to it, it's musical noise that we're dealing with here and all the propaganda and hype and flim-flam in the world won't save you if you've got those three chords in the wrong order. Great records are always built on little triggers; the downbeat that opens 'Every Breath You Take' by The Police, Nile Rodgers' descending rhythm break on Bowie's 'Cat People', the snippets of conversation woven into Malcolm McLaren's 'Buffalo Gals', the great gasp of relief when the rhythm section put the boot into Prince's '1999'. All the rest is idle chatter.
DAVID HEPWORTH

ELECTRONIC

For the second year running, America scores tops; solely for the first ever European tour by the mysterious San Francisco band, The Residents, following on a series of autumn dates on the West Coast.

Invited — maybe lured would be a more accurate description — onto their European tour, I came away none the wiser. Well, I now know that they're *not* The Beatles. Nor, the most recent allegation, The Police. And they're all too young to number Thomas Pynchon in their line-up, a personal suspicion for some years now.

I contrived to happen upon their 18-strong entourage in Vienna, in the vain hope of eliciting some comment on their obvious affection for Anton Karas' soundtrack to *The Third Man* (it's all over their *Fingerprince* LP). Certainly, a number of the masked and boiler-suited people on the tour admitted to having seen the film, but not even at the top of the gigantic Reisenrad ferris wheel — where, I'd daydreamed, they might care to stage a rerun of the confrontation between Orson Welles and Joseph Cotten — would anyone, whoever they were, deign to comment on the link.

As a French promoter had cannily pointed out on his posters, "The Residents Mole Show" — taken from the first and second acts of their culture-clash trilogy, *Mark of the Mole* — is more an "Opera" than a rock show; not in the pretentious, aspiring manner of most rock theatre, but simply in the nature of its conception and presentation. Not only is the trilogy still unfinished, but both they and their representatives refuse to explain the action so far. The oppressed, primitive Moles have left their underground workplace, and are marching on the fat and rich Chubs, but the grinning endomorphs may only accept the bug-like critters in order to enslave them...

The show, accompanied by a

THE RESIDENTS

narrator/fire-eater/juggler, dancers, Mole and Chub cut-outs, 30-odd towering Pore No Graphic backdrops and numerous other pyrotechnics, was dogged through Europe by street riots, illness, rip-offs, car crashes, disappearing and

exploding equipment, but someone who may or may not have glimpsed the inner sanctum claimed they've now got a taste for touring. Not before time — ten years is a long time for anyone to expect their audience to content

themselves with an airmail version of Courtly Love...

Nothing else this year came close to the wit, lunacy and bizarre invention of The Residents. Once again, Kraftwerk remained cloistered at Kling Klang Studios in

Dusseldorf — rumour had it because of head injuries sustained by Ralf Hutter in a bicycle accident, although visitors to Dusseldorf reported him, and them, in fine health. For a week or so in the spring (perhaps tellingly, around the time of Cherry Red's re-release of 'Moonshake' as an EP), rumours circulated London that Can were rehearsing together again somewhere in France. Guitarist Micky Karoli, visiting from his home near Nice, laughed at the idea.

The sensible ears lent themselves to *You Gotta Say Yes to Another Excess*, the third album from Zurich's Residents-nurtured trio, Yello. After the fizzy pop conceits on their first two albums, the ferocious dancefloor blow-outs of *Excess* established them as the most extraordinary electronic dance crew around, at times making even the likes of Grandmaster Flash's 'Scorpio' sound tame. They played a rather chaotic PA at the Camden Palace nightclub in London early in the summer, inviting four weirdos in top hats, tails and giant eyeballs onstage to shimmy around for a number. Quite correctly, the audience didn't notice, care or respond to this intrusion. Alas, this collective *faux pas* inspired Some Bizzare (sic) supremo Stevo (who always reminds me of John Lydon's line on *Flowers of Romance* about that "butterball turkey") to get onstage and bawl them out. Ho hum. Still, for once, big business agrees with your sybil; Yello transferred from Ralph to Stiff and were subsequently snapped up, at some expense it's said, for the relaunch of Elektra in the US.

After last year's four-hour version of Laurie Anderson's open-ended work in progress, *United States*, this year's eight-hour version stretched my attention span to unconscionable lengths. The earlier performances, a haunting, alarming and very funny series of stand-up comedy routines, future-shock newsflashes, Gregory Peck impersonations, metallic-tasting love songs and storm warnings for paranoids, were here stretched to twice the length, and while still entertaining and effective, convinced this observer that he was sitting through one of the longest tautologies in the world.

Anderson's triumphant

arrival of last year was almost repeated by New York composer Glenn Branca, also finding his first British audience at London's adventurous Riverside Studios arts complex. Once of that city's noted punk guerrilla act The Theoretical Girls, in recent years Branca has been lining up with the dubiously-titled New York Minimalist scene, recording solo, collaborating, like Anderson, with poet-performer John Giorno and writing Symphonies. His shock of hair, knuckle-length cuffs and increasingly violent "conducting" of his group gave him the look of a punky, maybe even preppy, Mozart as he threw himself around the stage, veins protruding and face reddening as he hefted tons of (invisible) chordal sound slabs up into the air, his band performing a deafening aural approximation of same. Powerful if very bombastic, and I can understand, if not agree with, Cage's accusation that his music is "fascistic".

Anyone who read last year's *Yearbook* will probably be aware that I am not beyond a nominal magnanimity. After last year's apology to The Tangs, this year I must say sorry to Philip Glass. That his record company flew me to New York to interview him may not be entirely divorced from this, but Glass deserves more than being tagged as the Mike Oldfield of the post-Cage scene.

Following CBS's release of *Glassworks*, Glass brought his Ensemble to London for a sold-out show at Sadler's Wells. Although studio multi-tracking gave way to "gaps" in the sound — musicians literally dropping out for a bar to catch their breath — pieces like 'Spaceship', the climax of his mammoth opera *Einstein on the Beach*, had this listener whirling towards satori.

Glass also released a follow-up to *Glassworks*, the (for him) miniature opera *The Photographer*, which contains some of the most powerful work he's committed to record since *Einstein* or *Music in Similar Motion*. He's also set this summer to release the soundtrack to *Koyanisqaatsi* (pron. 'Ko-yan-iss-kot-see') a spectacular, if somewhat hippyish, widescreen eco-warning film exploring, uh, macro- and micro-structures in nature and mankind.

The emergence of a new

YELLO

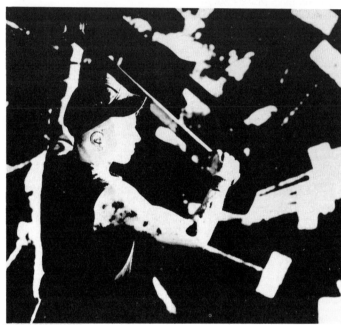

TEST DEPARTMENT

"school" of systems music mentioned last year *has* begun (did you ring your bookie?), and if it has yet to burgeon technically it still promises vindication for this widely influential but much-ignored music. The robust, cheery repetitions of Michael Nyman became known to thousands through his soundtrack to Peter Greenaway's *The Draughtsman's Contract*, a Sterne-into-Borges seventeenth century murder mystery intended, as is Greenaway's post-structuralist design, never to be solved. (If you can/want to, check out earlier Nyman/Greenaway collaborations like 'The Falls', 'A Walk Through H' and 'Vertical Features Remake'.)

The vari-sized orchestra Lost Jockey started out as a group of friends playing Glass and Reich in small galleries and arts centres, but is now a fully-fledged touring unit able, like Glass, to pull an audience in either the rock or the classical zone. With two albums (one a mini-LP) and a double-album-sized cassette available, they're probably the most successful of the new systems bands. The recent addition of a swinging rhythm section, to me jarring with the precise keyboards and reeds/woodwind/brass, has nudged them towards jazz-rock à la Neil Ardley, but at their best they can stand alongside their mentors with pride. Also worth hunting out here are Regular Music, who are assured of a powerful and inventive rock pulse by the presence of excellent This Heat drummer Charles Hayward, and Belgium's Soft Verdict, who record for Crepuscule.

You've heard this music refined through anything from the Kraftwerk/Cluster school to modern European and American disco productions. Why not try the real thing?

At what I can only unfortunately term the grassroots, the most, indeed only, exhilarating arrival this year was that of Test Department, a young quartet from the run-down South London area of New Cross. Having warm memories of Faust, been in the thick of a riot at a Throbbing Gristle gig, found Berlin's Einsturzende Neubauten rather harmless, and baulked at the repulsive antics of deranged West Coast kinetic sculptor Mark Pauline, I can vouch that Test Dept are the most extreme, dangerous act around. A bunch of six-years-too-late poseurs based around the West Coast rag *Re/Search* claim Pauline's exploding-machine installations are revolutionary — this, I can only presume, in ignorance of the fact that Switzer Jean Tinguely did it much better two decades ago before an invited audience of New York trendies in the yard of the Museum of Modern Art. So far, neither Pauline's nor Tinguely's audience have risked death at one of their performances. Test Dept's have.

The first TD gig I caught took place in a bricked-in space under a railway arch. Eschewing "real" instruments, they hoard metal water tanks, oil drums, sheet metal, large iron springs, corrugated iron, all of which was arrayed on a scaffolding stage. To a roaring electronic tape accompaniment, while arcane logos and Nazi and Fascisti propaganda films were projected onto walls and glistening torsos, they beat out hellish, hypnotic polyrhythms with hammers and lumps of metal, sometimes veering into improvisations, finally destroying the set with sledgehammers, but not before turning on their oil drums — as everyone could smell, still containing, and leaking, their contents — with an industrial saw, producing fountains of sparks. Which is when we started making *serious* attempts to locate the one tiny exit.

"It's a risk you take," one of them said archly, safely outside. Possibly it was a wind-up, but the end result was the same; a number of performances in the past have left me speechless, but none of them so scared. The immediate reaction to their performance might seem to lay them open to the same sort of accusations of "fascism" levelled at early Throbbing Gristle, but — perhaps as the name implies — their exploration of the processes of persuasion is a million miles away from Music From the Death Factory and Violence Chic...

From the soggy texture these pages are taking on, soaking up the steam issuing from the ears of people still waiting for the *real* scam — has Phil Oakey really slept with Joanne? What foundation cream does David Sylvian prefer? Are the Thompsons really Twins? — I see I can no longer put off addressing that interface between atelier and high street, Electropop. After (again) last year's comment that you can now buy electronic music in Woolworths, the situation has deteriorated. This year, mums and dads and aunts and uncles are rolling back the front room carpet and dancing to it themselves.

Having achieved world-wide success, The Human League have lain low, barring the release of 'Mirror Man', which merely offered further proof that the most successful electropop is that which play-acts at 1960s Motown soul production. After throwing a wobbly with the cloying 'Waves', Blancmange continued on with their bold, adventurous and substantial dance music (to this listener's ears, among the very best of the genre). Although now in a state of some disarray, Soft Cell finally won me over with Dave Ball's gorgeous, blowsy and again soul-influenced tearjerkers on *The Art of Falling Apart*.

Marc Almond's chosen role of Judy Garland portraying Edith Piaf in something scripted by Jean Genet still smells very funny, and no better odours attended the live outings by his Marc & The Mambas, which merely added Ida Lupino to his gallery of roles and reached a nadir of bad camp with a troupe of dancing poodles appearing on stage. Thomas Dolby finally, and deservedly, won acclaim on both sides of the Atlantic with his clever, knowing egghead pop, and so did The Thompson Twins, but seeing the downhill race they've embarked on since their early, large line-up improvisational days, the less said about that the better. Ultravox are still dining out on the style that won them a second lease of life with 'Vienna'.

Salvation is at hand, though. With *Power, Corruption & Lies*, New Order bettered all previous releases, and finally convinced this observer that their sometimes dubious marketing/imagery and the glimpses of ambiguous misanthropy are a small price to pay for the overwhelming, bursting emotion of their work. The Passage once more presented a positive, engaged alternative to NO's power with the swingeing hard funk 'Enflame', apart from The Poisongirls' *Where's the Pleasure?*, the only politically commendable album of the year. Ex-Wire operators Graham Lewis and B.C. Gilbert proved, with their *Will You Speak This Word* on the Scandinavian indie label Uniton (more of which elsewhere), that they're still at the vanguard of rock-originated electronics, priming and planting semantic land-mines (in a manner suggesting a hybrid of Beckett and Burroughs) in shifting, looming and stuttering drones and pulses that sounded like the noise from an unseen sound sculpture.

While their one-time collaborators Chris'n'Cosey continue to mine a vein of admirably combative electropop, I'm not at all sure what to make of the earliest manifestations of Genesis P. Orridge and Peter "Sleazy" Christopherson's Psychic TV Ltd — the most talked about almost-event of the year. With their WEA début, *Force the Hand of Chance*, the no-pussyfooting sonic combat of the past was replaced by a musical equivalent of luring children into cars with bags of sweets — the sweets represented by gentle ballads, polite pop tunes and other uncharacteristic diversions included among the electronics, drones and Tibetan thigh-bone trumpets. From an edited playback, the follow-up — employing the 3-D "surround-sound" Zucarelli Holophonic Sound system — is even stranger. Gen and Sleazy say that the aims are still the same, but that this time they're working from within the system, and that the "romantic existentialism" of their Temple ov Psychic Youth is a means of combating the horrors TG exposed. Others have called them hippies, but I tend to agree with them, at least theoretically. You'll have to make up your own mind.

TG camp-followers 23 Skidoo and Cabaret Voltaire followed a similar line, but while applauding the experiments of the former (especially on *The Culling Is Coming*) and sympathising with the messy noise of the latter, I've never been able to bring myself to trust them completely.

Others lent themselves to no theme or school: John Hassell's continuing work with dreamy electronics drones and pulses mixed with ethnic music reappeared with *Aka-Dabari-Java*; Deutsche-Amerikanische Freundschaft's sweatily erotic/heroic farewell LP *Fur Immer* and Gabi Delgado-Lopez's shocking solo album singing the praises of sexual power games, *Mistress*; Portsmouth's bizarre Residential Renaldo & The Loaf settled into a more sombre mood with *Arabic Yodelling*; Danielle Dax pushed her work with Lemon Kittens even further with the startling *Popeyes*; Bunnyperson Will Sargeant surprised us all with his highly effective ambient/process album *Themes for 'Grind'*; and Jah Wobble won my undying affection with the dazzling, majestic global dance music of The Invaders of the Heart. He won't earn enough to buy his own football club, but over the next year idiot-savant Wobble and band (a British Can if you need one) should achieve such a stature that the sky will go dark.

The most cherishable moment of the whole year came, however — and at, of all places, a small recital room at the 9th Bracknell Jazz Festival — when world-class saxophonist John Surman played a duo set with the fine Norwegian singer Karin Krog. Surman's untreated playing is a revelation in itself, but when cast into a discreetly-introduced echo unit, accompanied by understated pre-set synthesiser and fronted by Krog's deft, imaginative and alluring voice, it was heaven. They have their second album, *Such Winters of Memory*, due out on ECM this summer. It'll tell you more about what electronics should really sing of than 90% of the acts you just read about.

JOHN GILL

19

REGGAE

On an international level, reggae music has perhaps enjoyed its most successful 12 months ever, as many of the trends of the previous year were swiftly and surprisingly reversed. The breezy exuberance of five Birmingham schoolkids, the simplistic melodies of a Guyanese expatriate who emigrated from North London to Barbados, and the soulful voice and lilting rhythms of a group built around an androgynous trend-setter conquered charts (and hearts) the whole world over.

Musical Youth, Eddy Grant and Culture Club had, each in their own style, transformed reggae into a marketable and acceptable pop commodity. It was a three-pronged attack that saw 'Pass the Dutchie', 'I Don't Wanna Dance' and 'Do You Really Want to Hurt Me' all in the same Top 20 during October and November. A genius of strategy could not have planned it better, yet it was nothing more than a series of coincidences.

Musical Youth ended two years of waiting under the watchful eye of Freddy Waite — father of two of them and an accomplished Jamaican sessioneer — for the right song (and for their hands to grow) by taking everybody, including their newly acquired record company, by surprise. Both their adaptation of the Mighty Diamonds' song — substituting 'dutchie' (a cooking pot) for 'kutchie' (a receptacle for illegal substances) — and its accompanying video of five young people landing in court for playing music then getting the judge and jury to dance, were so utterly disarming that they proved reggae need not be a threat.

Record buyers across the spectrum jumped to Youth's lively skank, it shot to number one and the ground was cleared for Boy George. The image was perfect for a teen scene looking for a new prince of glamour, who may well have rocked to Youth's rhythms but

MUSICAL YOUTH

CULTURE CLUB

found the packaging none too fashionable. Culture Club irritated many reggae specialists with an attitude that ensured their place in the world

of pop. They removed all the stigmas — racial, social, cultural — from the music they played with their bizarre appearance and odd public

statements, yet they performed their reggae with such expertise and accomplishment that a strong affinity was suggested.

These two groups had scored with very different sections of the purchasing public and established reggae as the flavour of that month. With impeccable timing Eddy Grant, who a year back had quit England for a sunnier clime and a custom-built studio in Barbados, sent over a sample of easy-action Caribbean pop that was completely his own work, and the trinity was complete — three national number ones in a row that owed their entire being to reggae.

This situation should have delighted the music's many unknown exponents who were biding their time waiting for "a break", yet for the purist the frustrations continued. It was a year of problems best illustrated by the fact that its finest album was made by a man who had been dead for twice that length of time. Bob Marley's *Confrontation* set stood proud above the best Jamaica had to offer like a statue, both a fitting monument and an immovable, ominous reminder casting a shadow across all those who had ignored his teachings.

In its country of origin, reggae music had perhaps become more polarised than ever. DJs such as Sister Nancy, Yellowman, Fathead and Michegan and Smiley sensed the ears of the world were cocked in their direction, and issued a string of boast toasts that drew on gimmick rather than substance, thus lasting only as long as their novelty value.

Roots performers, on the other hand, seemed to shy away from the chances they had complained about not getting, and, instead of moving up through opening doors, chose to dig deeper. Few of their talk-overs, quasi-hymns and dubs had much meaning or any more impression outside the island or its tightest offshore communities.

This state of affairs was highlighted in the USA, where efforts by empathetic governments to expand American tourism in Jamaica involved package deals to the country's larger music festivals. Reggae had begun to make its mark in the black community through the efforts

EDDY GRANT

of many soul artists, and, more recently, the above-mentioned British chart heroes had scored heavily in the mainstream. This proved that a nation-wide acquiescence to the actual music existed, provided that the backgrounds and stances of the performers appeared to hold no serious social undertones. However, without a diplomat such as Marley with his gift for the cultural *and* the commercial in perfect harmony, black America's flirtation with roots reggae's heavier politics and rhythms tailed off. As the output from Jamaica became more and more impenetrable, sources of support dried up. On the mass market side, what in many cases were thought of as light commercial ditties were still too raw and uncompromising in their production to suit popular US tastes, leaving any capitalisation on British reggae's success waiting in the wings and now maybe too late to make an entrance.

Apart from the college and expatriate Jamaican followings of two years since — among whom, incidentally, English rockers Steel Pulse now earn a good living — reggae's only significant legacy in the past year has been the dub

techniques borrowed and adapted by East coast funk producers, and on the whole used to better effect than by their originators.

At the moment the UK is the reggae capital of the world. The superstars produced in this country, though, are only the tip of a huge mound of potential that has suddenly bubbled up from rehearsal rooms to recording studios, and is laced with a few veterans who felt the time was right to reappear.

The Beat fall into the second category. After toying with pop/rock for a while, they returned to doing what they do best and hit exciting and entertaining form as toast master Ranking Roger led the band to a string of acclaimed live dates and a couple of hit albums. The demand for Dennis Bovell's production talents stretched as far as Bananarama, and he gave them a crisp, spacey sound on perhaps the best song of their career, 'Tell Tale Signs'. Between his studio work, Bovell took to the road with his Dub Band, the cream of London's reggae session men, and put on an excellent and innovative show that drew from roots'n'culture and *The Beano* in equal amounts.

Clint Eastwood and General Saint still lurked purposefully on the verge of greatness, having weathered a critical storm that broke when they decided to use their English-based touring band in the studio instead of importing rhythms from Jamaica. They continued to sell records in respectable amounts, yet never quite reached the national chart placings and related exposure they deserved. This has not

CLINT EASTWOOD AND GENERAL SAINT

affected their first love, touring, and as the duo perfect their stage show and their following grows, so does their influence.

Eastwood and Saint are proving that it is possible to have a sense of fun and the ridiculous, and still play reggae — this lack of a sense of entertainment has long been cited as the chief obstacle in the development of the music. Chief usurpers to their position are the South London pair Laurel and Hardy, also known as The Pop Up Toasters or The Cockney Rappers. As their name suggests, the pair are taking a none too serious view and promise simply to

entertain. Yet in spite of a media fanfare at the close of 1982, and the backing of CBS records, Laurel and Hardy have still to come up to expectations. Under the guidance of ex-Nightdoctor man, Martin Poole, the pair seem to be dithering at the crossroads too long between their sound-system beginnings and pop chart aspirations. It results in product that, although excellently produced, is nothing more than amusing words, often in unintelligible dialect, toasted over a bass'n'drums backing — too silly to be taken seriously yet too heavy to be accepted lightly.

LAUREL AND HARDY

DENNIS BROWN

ASWAD

cultish, but any or all of those three names have the talent to take on much larger audiences, and one hopes it is only a matter of time.

In the world of British roots, artists came and went with little or no progression from the lovers' rock or JA styles of this time last year. The wall was still up. Aswad provided a welcome relief as they decided they had had their fill of uptown dealings and left CBS for the sanctuary of Ladbroke Grove and the Simbal label, where they added what they learned in the West End to their already wide knowledge and put out two blistering singles. The first, 'Promised Land', has Dennis Brown on vocals, and he proves that his last few years of so-so releases have in no way affected one of the best voices in reggae music.

As we come to the end of "The Year of the Youth" — for surely it must be dedicated to those five boys from Brum — we have a very different picture of British reggae than at this time 12 months ago. Instead of looking lost, it can now boldly go where . . . wherever it likes, with confidence. Sadly, that is much more than can be said for Jamaica.

The prevailing attitude there can be summed up by looking at the incident in which Gregory Isaacs refused, quite

GREGORY ISAACS

With just a little more care, Laurel and Hardy could go far, but as it is, even with the minor hit of their début single 'Clunk Click', they split with CBS after just one release.

Amazulu, the multiracial former all-girl group (but now sporting a male drummer) have come forward in the past year to become one of the future's brightest hopes. Their freewheeling, many-influenced style, that has mercifully kept away from the reggae-based musical clutter favoured by newcomers such as Farenji Warriors and Echo Base, has won the band support all over the country. Their appearance, though, might prove a little too unconventional. Completely uncontrived, it serves to

promote their personal approach to what they do, but it might be proving a bit too much for those with a fixed idea of what a female reggae group should look like.

On the roots scene, by far the most interesting development has been the rise of the dub poets. Whether they came about, like Eastwood and Saint did, as a reaction to the stagnant toasting that was dominant, or whether it was a continuation of the work of Linton Kwesi Johnson, Gil Scott-Heron and the like, is open to speculation; but the rhythmically spoken word that concentrated on lyrical content and not music has become commonplace.

Among the first to reach the

public eye were Michael Smith and Mutaburuka from Jamaica. Smith became the subject of much media attention during a visit to Britain, and Mutaburuka secured space in the sharper music papers. Yet due to the unavailability of the latter's material and Smith's somewhat vitriolic, often rather irrational viewpoints, the two were quickly overtaken by a UK posse led by the maniacal Benjamin Zephaniah, Valerie Bloom and Pepsi Poet.

A cynical vein of humour running through their work gives it an extra cutting edge and, perversely enough, means their comment is taken more seriously as it is listened to more readily. At present they remain in that watershed of the

unpleasantly, to appear in or even assist with a BBC film of Musical Youth in Jamaica. Golden opportunities are not always recognised. Perhaps the presence of three English acts headlining at this year's Sunsplash Festival (it's been increasing by one every year since 1981) will open a few eyes.

LLOYD BRADLEY

FOLK

It was, as I recall, the summer of 1965. Bob Dylan abrasively informed us that the times were a-changing and was arm-wrestling up the charts with the likes of The Beatles and The Beach Boys to prove it; Lyndon Johnson was getting edgy and Vietnam became a dirty word; and Joan Baez was marching for peace, publicity and a whole bunch of causes too obscure to recall here.

For a moment there we really thought we *would* overcome. Folk clubs were throwing open their doors up and down the country with lavish abandon, festivals were being launched like Fireworks Night rockets amid a fog of incense and slightly dodgier substances, and the Establishment winced and wagged its little finger with hilarious ineptitude. The folk movement was considered a *threat*...and the glory of that alone swept it along in a flood of euphoria.

All, seemingly, except my friend John. He always was a perverse bugger, that John. He was the one who never stopped complaining that Dylan was ripping off Phil Ochs and he sulked for months when he heard that Young Tradition were splitting up.

So John just sniffed in that contrary way of his, glanced cynically at all the euphoria, and shook his head. "That's it then," he said coldly. "The end of the folk revival. After a peak you have a decline. Once you scale the heights you don't climb any more. Once you get success your values alter, you settle for less. From here the folk scene starts to die." He was right, of course.

Since that revered age when folk music was central to a social struggle and helped to speak for a generation, it has shrivelled progressively to a point where it meets widespread ridicule. That it is still there at all is a tribute to the strength and durability of the circuit that emerged in the sixties, and the tradition of artistry and integrity among

ANDREW CRONSHAW

the musicians it produced.

Today, resilient if not always successful, the folk scene stoically battles on from a ferociously committed nucleus. The folkies wait in the shadows like King Arthur's knights, ready for the call to rescue England in its hour of need. Strangely enough, in a year that a right-wing Tory government has been given the mandate for another five years and CND is on the move again with as much determination as it had first time round, there's a widespread belief that the call may be imminent.

Certainly in the last year or so the hardcore folk circuit has eased its attitude of hard-bitten independence. Unlike other parallel minorities like country music and jazz, it has never — even in its heyday — been completely bought by the industry. Yet this admirable trait has had the dual effect of maintaining not only its basic honesty, but its self-imposed isolation too.

The recession has finally *forced* a crack in this isolation. There are fewer professional folk musicians in operation than at any time since the pioneering days of the folk revival and those still going seek additional outlets to keep their heads above water. No bad thing, as it's turned out.

Until they hook on to the anger of the radical youth of Britain and rediscover a genuine bite and direction, the folk clubs themselves will lack the excitement to attract a younger audience (that and the hoary old problem of an appalling public image). Because of the various reactionary conditions prevalent in Britain right now, the time is ripe for such a development; but, as Martin Carthy has pointed out, folk clubs are too anxious to fulfil the Trades Descriptions Act. They are currently dominated by English folk music, with too little American and other types of music to give the breadth

and variety needed to make them work. Like Bob Davenport before him, Carthy even suggested it was racist in its preoccupation with the music of the British Isles. There's much in what he says, though it's a simplification to forever blame the clubs — the perennial scapegoats — for their lack of foresight and unimaginative booking policies. The artists themselves need to be looking ahead, discarding their blinkers, and taking risks again. If there's been one firm positive development for folk in the last year, it has been the signs that this very thing has been happening — and not just from that guru of experimental folk music, Andrew Cronshaw.

As much folk now is being heard outside the folk clubs as inside them. Bands are now emerging beyond the guidance — and therefore the constrictions — of the orthodox folk revival. It's happening in pub sessions, in village dances, local organisation functions,

23

informal concerts, and it has resulted in some refreshingly uninhibited, unconsciously irreverent and even *exciting* approaches to folk music, particularly on the dance side. *Southern Rag* magazine has dubbed it "Rogue Folk" and it is beginning to shatter barriers at every turn, as well as causing some confusion.

The electric band Jumpleads, for example, disarmingly unconcerned about the more refined qualities of the tradition, have created extreme responses virtually every time they've set foot on stage and raised more than eyebrows with their explosive single — the traditional classic *False Knight on the Road* set to a rugged reggae arrangement. And Sussex pub band The Amazing Catsfield Steamers became involved in an almighty row with Rod Stradling, who claimed they'd nicked much of their repertoire from The Old Swan Band, the band Stradling used to front. The Catsfields, unaware or unimpressed by folk niceties, and used to picking up tunes in pub sessions without enquiring about their ancestry, disclaimed knowledge of their origins.

The politics of folk notwithstanding, the music is no longer in the vacuum it has occupied for so long. The result has been an encouraging cross-fertilisation that may, in turn, whip the clubs out of their torpor. And, for that matter, some of the less enlightened festivals. Even Cambridge — Britain's biggest and most prestigious, but hardly the most progressive — looked shamefully backwards in the summer of 1982, featuring several front-line acts irrevocably associated with the past — Joan Baez, Pentangle and Lindisfarne all dredged up for the occasion. Very depressing it turned out to be too.

For if folk ever had the chance to look positively forward instead of longingly back, then this was the time. Moving Hearts spent the year living up to their name in gloriously strident fashion, charging into the eighties with folk, jazz and rock aboard as comfortable co-passengers. "This band won't last," muttered an Irish friend, moved almost to tears by the sheer *passion* as Hearts blazed away on stage, "they're just too damn *good*. Too good to last."

Within a couple of weeks, Christy Moore, their legendary singer, had quit just like he'd twice left Planxty as the consequence of musical success became a more complicated lifestyle offstage. Hearts quickly replaced the irreplaceable with a solo singer of unimpeachable pedigree — Mick Hanly, whose vocal style and political beliefs corresponded remarkably with the departed Moore. Yet no sooner had Hanly been installed than Declan Sinnott, lead guitarist and important songwriting ingredient, had also gone. A decidedly dodgy second album, *Dark End of the Street*, and the incomprehensible disinterest of British record companies, piled pressures on them and threatened the various financial and business problems that have destroyed several similarly gifted Irish bands before them. If Moving Hearts don't make it, then it's a tragedy both for the thrilling enterprise of the people involved in the band, and for folk music itself.

There was even a modicum of cross-fertilisation from the other side, too, which briefly raised a few temperatures. Various extravagant claims have been made about the folk influences on rock bands like XTC, The Skids and Squeeze, but the most obvious example of a rock band actively *using* folk music in a tangible way occurred when Kevin Rowland's new-look Dexy's Midnight Runners came out with their *Too-Ry-Aye* album, complete with a glut of fiddles and accordions. When the Irish flavoured 'Come on Eileen' topped the chart in Britain and later went high in America, anticipation was rampant that a folk boom really was on the way. Perhaps wisely, Rowland vigorously disassociated himself from folk music, and his little indulgence was left well alone by other rock bands, though the example may still prove to have had an undercurrent effect on the attitudes of young musicians.

Nobody was really taken in, on the other hand, by the news that Malcolm McLaren was travelling the world recording ethnic folk musics for his first album as an artist in his own right. The eventual album, *Duck Rock* — brilliant though it was — merely used the ethnic element to give the album some kind of token basic credence, though the very mention of folk in such exalted company as

MOVING HEARTS

Malcolm McLaren did wonders for the morale of the much-derided folkies. The McLaren project will probably still prove to wield a rather more profound long-term effect than the massive chart success suddenly enjoyed by Clannad at the end of 1982.

For other reasons, though, it was a tragic year for folk music. Two of the scene's prime legends, A.L. Lloyd and Seamus Ennis, died within a few weeks of one another, a dual loss that not only deprived us of a couple of hugely colourful and crucially influential characters, but emphasised the irretrievable chasm between the current slightly directionless circuit of clubs and the trail-blazing movement a decade and a half ago. Both were elderly men, both had suffered severe ill health on and off in recent years, yet both were still doggedly pursuing their art almost to their graves, with their reputations untarnished by the ravages of age.

SEAMUS ENNIS

Only a few months before his death, Ennis had been helped on stage at the Irish Lisdoonvarna Festival looking frail and pale, but he still played the uillean pipes like the genius he was, still told stories with a uniquely vivid turn of phrase. An eccentric man, to be sure, but there's not a piper in Ireland who doesn't owe him a massive debt.

Bert Lloyd travelled the world researching and recording ethnic music — I wonder if Malcolm McLaren has ever heard of him — and was the indisputable authority in his field. His *Folk Songs of England* was/is the definitive textbook in the field, though his skill as a lecturer and raconteur often unfairly overshadowed his prowess as a singer. Fairport Convention once asked him to join them as lead singer in succession to Sandy Denny; his wealth of sea songs was extraordinary (he spent much of his early life as a merchant sailor), and his classic version of the epic magic ballad 'Tam Lin' remains a standard bearer for revival singers. Only Ewan MacColl now remains from the giants of those pioneering years.

The grandmother of Irish traditional singing, Sarah Makem, also died early in 1983. The mother of Tommy Makem and an enormous source of material, Sarah's death left a sad void in Ulster folklore. Another fine traditional singer, Bob Roberts, the Singing Bargeman, collapsed and died while out riding his bike at home in the Isle of Wight, and the general bleakness was underlined by the awful accident suffered by Noel Murphy. Attending a golfing function in the Isle of Man, Murphy sipped a pint of beer and felt his throat being ripped apart by a stray piece of glass in the drink. He was critically ill for a couple of days, but happily pulled through only to embark on an arduous (finally successful) attempt to get his vocal chords working again, and a long legal battle for compensation.

The most tragic news of all, however, came from Canada in May. A DC9 bound from Dallas to Toronto caught fire in mid-air. It landed in flames at Cincinnati, but 23 people were already dead in the first class area. One of them was Stan Rogers, Canada's top folk singer and a man respected all over the world both for his deep, relaxed singing and his classy songwriting. One of his songs in particular, 'Jeannie C.' — like much of his material, a sea song — is fast becoming a standard around the British clubs and plans were well in hand for a British tour at the time of the disaster.

On the brighter side, Nic Jones' miraculous recovery after his terrible road crash early in 1982 continues. It will still be some time before he can contemplate performing again, but now he's walking and singing again at home, and there's an entire folk scene willing him on. The sense of unity and identity with its own still, it seems, prevails and has perhaps been reinforced by the struggles it's had to endure these past few years.

An odd year at the more public end of folk music. In the writers' poll for *Rolling Stone* magazine, Richard and Linda Thompson's excellent *Shoot*

Out the Lights was voted top album of the year jointly with Bruce Springsteen's *Nebraska* and Linda won the female vocalist section on her own. Ironically, the duo had just separated when the results were announced, but prestige like that won't do Linda any harm as she nervously embarks on a solo career, while Richard's solo album in 1983, *Hand of Kindness*, is spectacularly powerful — his best work for a decade. It's dangerous to be too analytical about the split, but musically it does seem to have completely rejuvenated Richard, and he's fully justifying the American accolades being bestowed on him.

Maybe the chilling political winds blowing through Britain right now *are* making an impact on the folkies. While hard-bitten politico-folkies like Leon Rosselson, Frankie Armstrong and Steve Ashley now move more outside folk circles than in them (CND and the women's movement have been particularly receptive to their strident messages), other less likely characters have been taking up the sword. Ralph McTell, for example, emerged with his most passionate, convincing and political album in years, *Water of Dreams*. Is it a coincidence that it also sees McTell for the first time completely independent and free of the restraining influence of a major record company?

Elsewhere the most encouraging music came from bands with a fresh outlook and

a new angle on which to approach dance music. The Martin Carthy-John Kirkpatrick collaboration, Brass Monkey, at last looked like emerging as a determined regular force rather than simply as an occasional pick-up band, and with the use of brass perhaps fulfilling the role earmarked for the criminally underemployed Home Service.

De Danann, meanwhile — the most consistently inventive band of recent years — survived all manner of trauma to come up yet again with the goods. The departure of their exceptional singer Maura O'Connell to make a country album in Nashville was a major blow, and when it was followed by the departure of their virtuoso accordion player Jackie Daly and multi-instrumentalist Charlie Piggott their demise looked imminent, especially when fiddler supreme Frankie Gavin was nearly blinded in a shooting accident. But resilient to the last, Gavin recovered, Mary Black and Martin O'Connor — both highly-rated in their own right — were hauled in as replacements for O'Connell and Daly, and the band came out of the tunnel as rewardingly innovative as they had been when they'd gone into it.

Even Planxty re-emerged with a startling new line-up following the exodus of Christy Moore and Donal Lunny to Moving Hearts and the release of their marginally disappointing (for them) *Words & Music* album. Like De Danann they got in some impressive replacements for the dearly departed — Artie McGlynn on guitar, James Kelly on fiddle, and Dolores Keane on vocals — the result of which were the concerts of the year.

The Albion Band, complete with Cathy LeSurf and Simon Nicol, pursued a slightly uncomfortable pop-folk path, fulfilling a certain glee function, but producing a patchy album, *Light Shining*, and failing badly in comparison with the exhilarating boldness of Albion Bands of the past. In keeping with the general trend of the day they were at their strongest with dance material, though even here the fast-improving Oyster Band outstripped them. The Oysters' *Lie Back and Think of England* must rank as one of the most satisfying LPs of the year, surpassing even their own

highly recommended *English Rock'n'Roll: The Early Years 1800-1850*, though the title is less inspired.

There were other causes for celebration in the romping uninhibited development of Blowzabella with their bagpipes, hurdy gurdys and bizarre range of British-Eastern European material (resulting in a lively album, *In Colour*); the equally forthright progress of the multi-faceted Pyewackett (an impressive album called *The Man in the Moon Drinks Claret*); the increasing maturity of Jenny Beeching (who came of age with her *No More Sad Goodbyes* album); and the ingenuity of Alistair Anderson, whose *Steel Skies* concept grew from a straightforward album into a full-blown stage production.

VIN GARBUTT

Further honours to the Battlefield Band, Silly Wizard, Roaring Jelly, Proper Little Madams, Maxi & Mitch, Cosmotheka and Vin Garbutt for their persisting magnificence in front of an audience, though Garbutt, curiously, also became the villain of the year in a lot of eyes. The release of his album *Little Innocents* finally exploded a bombshell that's been simmering for some time: the title track is a ten-minute diatribe about the horrors of abortion, bringing in the Nazi massacre of Jews, the crucifixion of Christ, and Christians being thrown to the lions to illustrate his much-laboured point. Hysteria breeds hysteria and Garbutt was abused on stage, had gigs cancelled, and was reviled by women's movements over that one desperately emotive song.

While the folk scene can still inspire *that* sort of passion, it's still got a few kicks left in it . . .
COLIN IRWIN

STAN ROGERS

BLUES

A bits-and-pieces sort of year it's been, with no fresh developments, no clear trends emerging. As usual, blues activity has been divided between resurrecting past reputations and trying to promote new ones — with perhaps rather more apparent success for the resurrectionists. At any rate, reissues, from the twenties through to the sixties, kept rolling out as if there was no today.

But for those with their sights fixed upon the present there was encouragement in the gathering momentum of Johnny Copeland. Building on the previous year's breakout album *Copeland Special* he spread his name as a more than impressive club performer and kept the temperature up with a decent, if by comparison unspectacular, follow-up LP, *Make My Home Where I Hang My Hat*. In the 1982 W.C. Handy Blues Awards he was voted Contemporary Male Artist of the Year, and in the summer of 1983 he displayed his powers for the first time in Europe, playing prestigious continental festivals like the Northsea in Holland and Montauban in France, and squeezing in a London one-nighter that must have been the most eagerly awaited blues gig in years.

Copeland's south-western guitar style — he learned the ropes in Houston — associates him with artists like Albert Collins and the still largely unrecognised Phillip Walker, but his soul-singing past (he evinces a great respect for Sam Cooke) and his ability to work well, as on *Copeland Special*, with quite uncompromisingly modern jazzmen like saxophonist George Adams, powerfully underwrite what looks like being a great future.

Responding to Copeland's hot deep-Texas blast, Chicago singer-guitarist Magic Slim started a hurricane of his own in the Windy City. Rescued from the doldrums of an ill-handled recording career, he

MUDDY WATERS

cut a session for the British-American co-operative venture Rooster Blues, issued as *Grand Slam*, which cleverly conjured up a dirty, clubby PA sound in the studio and genuinely redeployed the city's musical roots. Radical Chicago, as you might say.

Otherwise the year's news from Chicago contained few surprises. Several of the city's ambassadors visited Europe to generally warm response, though Buddy Guy and Junior Wells, featured in May's London Blues Festival, once again snoozed on their laurels.

Their companions on the bill, John Lee Hooker and Albert King, were somewhat more positive, but what is clearly called for at events like this is a moratorium on old pros with good agents and a spirit of temperate experiment. It's time we saw Albert Collins again, Magic Slim for the first time, or Larry Davis (whose LP *Funny Stuff*, lauded in this column last year, went on to top its poll in the Handy awards), Gatemouth Brown, Lowell Fulson . . .

The most unwelcome story filed from Chicago during the

year was the report of the death, in April, of Muddy Waters, corner-stone of the city's blues Establishment for some 35 years. Other serious losses to the music were Big Joe Williams, an itinerant rogue who endeared himself to blues-lovers all over the world and (what was sometimes forgotten, even by Williams himself) a creative musician of the first rank; and another country guitarist and singer from Mississippi, Sam Chatmon, one-time Mississippi Sheik, whose ingratiating old-time style and long white beard had ensured him a measure of fame in his old age.

The torchbeam of international interest, which for some years has been tending to swing away from Chicago, passed once more over New Orleans, where the influence in particular of Professor Longhair was posthumously celebrated on both records — *The Last Mardi Gras* and *Mardi Gras in New Orleans* — and film. The most moving sequence of Stevenson Palfi's documentary *Piano Players Rarely Ever Play Together* (shown in Britain on Channel 4 TV) was shot at Fess's funeral. Earl King *(Let the Good Times Roll)*, Snooks Eaglin *(New Orleans 1960-62)* and singer-pianist Archibald *(The New Orleans Sessions 1950-52)* were also awarded reruns of their past R&B successes.

Drifting further south-west the beam then lighted upon Houston, Texas, city of the Astrodome, the expressway and, as was now revealed, the urban honk. Time was, the place rocked to a sax-combo boogie half native, half learned from the textbook forties' recordings of T-Bone Walker. Krazy Kat did a concise Baedeker job with their anthology *Houston Jump*, then lingered awhile, for the length of an LP *(Dowling Street Hop)*, on the singer-guitarist Lester Williams.

That other forties' forefather, alongside T-Bone Walker, of

the jumpin' blues — Louis Jordan — continues to haunt the environs of R&B, and the year saw more of his vintage stuff decanted, notably onto *Choo Choo Ch'Boogie* and *Reet Petite & Gone* — the former a virtual "greatest hits" collection, the other a distillation of rare movie soundtracks.

Among the other forties' and fifties' concoctions cooked up by specialist labels were Elmore James' *King of the Slide Guitar* — not a lot of slide, but regal stuff all right — and the lovely, atmospheric L.A. sounds of Pee Wee Crayton, *Rocking Down on Central Avenue*. Knockabout Memphis piano-player and throat-cold singer Rosco Gordon was further archived on both *The Memphis Masters* and *No More Doggin'*, while his surprise 1982 visit to England was enshrined, a trifle indulgently perhaps, on *Rosco Rocks Again*, which also spotlit some monstrously accomplished guitar work by famed session-man Wayne Bennett.

From Charly came a pair of sets series-titled *Chicago Bluesmasters*, derived from the fifties' catalogue of Vee Jay and associated labels. *Combination Boogie* combined J.B. Hutto, Snooky Pryor and Willie Nix, while *Ain't Times Hard* lined up Lazy Bill Lucas

(another recent loss), Homesick James and, pick of the bunch, topical blues composer and sensitive singer Floyd Jones.

Easily the most deeply-laid reissue project of recent times, however, is the one that started in late 1982 on a British label little heard from since the seventies, Matchbox. This series, which also waves a "Bluesmaster" banner, plans to cut a broad swathe through the acreage of pre-war country blues — as many as a hundred albums are being contemplated. Much of the material will, of course, be known from earlier reissues, but the big deal offered by Matchbox is that these are not anthologies predicated on the philosophy of "It's all great music, man" but, for the most part, tidy single-artist collections with the tracks in chronological order. So far the series has yielded some important items — the complete works of Skip James, for one, or the almost Edwardian charm of the Dallas String Band — along with rather more that are useful but not exactly stunning. Still, there is plenty of ground to be covered yet, and certainly some more treasures to be excavated or newly exhibited.

Helping Matchbox to make light work of a strikingly ambitious project are two

JOHN LEE HOOKER

Austrian sister-labels, Wolf and Earl. Both are concentrating on "all of", "best of" or "the rest of" sets by artists of the twenties and thirties, from the legendary (Charley Patton, Blind Willie McTell) to the obscure-but-interesting, like the rough-grained Mississippi rustic Robert Petway, or the young Josh White before he had become artistically neutralised by the cabaret folk circuit.

Speaking of circuits, Eddie "Cleanhead" Vinson was travelling on the British jazz-club route this past spring, still delighting audiences with his bellow-and-squeak vocalistics and hearty sax-playing. The LP issued closest to his tour, *Back in Town*, was a 1957 session with pleasant jazz settings (featuring, among others, the lately deceased tenorist Paul Quinichette) and, by and large, still an accurate enough account of Vinson's capabilities.

But not all the good work in restoring lost classics is being conducted within Britain. In Scandinavia the Route 66 bandwagon rolls on, cutting paths to the doors of yet more neglected forties' and fifties' R&B figures, such as Sanders King, Arbee Stidham, saxophonist Preston Love and Percy Mayfield. The high standard of presentation which has distinguished this set-up from the start is being maintained, and many of the sleeves contain what amount to

hefty monographs on their subjects.

LARRY DAVIS

Meanwhile, in Germany, Crosscut did a service to all blues enthusiasts when it re-released Otis Spann's 1960 Candid session on two LPs, *Otis Spann Is the Blues* and *Otis Spann . . . and His Piano*. This was the pianist's first work away from the Muddy Waters band, and the date — shared with guitarist/singer Robert Junior Lockwood — gave Spann plenty of room to move. There are boogies, fine accompaniments and good Chicago-style numbers, but what gives the records their enduring quality is Spann's memories of farm life in the Mississippi of his boyhood, encapsulated in songs like 'The Hard Way' and 'Beat-Up Team'. These are that rare thing, the blues as straight-forward, unvarnished auto-biography, and their artless beauty tells you most of what you would ever want to know about the point of the blues.
TONY RUSSELL

MAGIC SLIM

27

SOUL/DISCO

It has been, if not a vintage year in terms of music, at least an interesting one in terms of trends and events, in the world of soul, disco, and black music in general.

In the superstar bracket, Michael Jackson reigned supreme, with everything he touched turning to platinum. Marvin Gaye re-emerged from the blue with a world-conquering single, only to let his momentum fade again. Lionel Richie emerged from the ranks of The Commodores (who felt his loss *savagely*) a fully-fledged black superstar, and his momentum has just kept growing.

Artists on the ascendant during the year have included several with long apprenticeships: Evelyn King, Melba Moore, Prince, Maze featuring Frankie Beverly (who managed to sell out Hammersmith Odeon on their UK visit), and George Clinton. Clinton, of course, is a soul music veteran as leader of outfits like Parliament and Funkadelic, but his signing to Capitol as a soloist has shot him into the top echelon.

Amongst the soul and funk groups, the year has provided varying fortunes. Shalamar, who have been around since the late seventies with a fair rate of success, all of a sudden became America's hottest black group export to Britain, via a string of Top Ten pop hits and a massive-selling album in *Friends*. The trio's leader Jeffrey Daniels suddenly found himself with a fashionable face and image in the UK which has made him familiar to the public to an unprecedented degree for a member of a black American group. Perhaps the oddest point about Shalamar's bonanza year, though, has been that their success was by no means repeated in the US, where they sold records healthily enough but remained firmly in the minor chart league, particularly in pop crossover terms.

Kool & The Gang, who really

MARVIN GAYE

do seem to have found a funk-dance-pop formula which can't go wrong, continued to rack up transatlantic Top 30 hits with spot-on regularity. Earth, Wind and Fire, in contrast, struggled to maintain past consistency, with a comparatively lukewarm reception for their *Power-Light* LP and the singles taken from it.

The Dazz Band took America's R&B Grammy for their 'Let It Whip' single, and found some follow-up action in the US, although their success failed to cross into Britain at

all. The Gap Band, The Time, Zapp and Vanity 6 also scored consistently on home territory and less well outside it. Again in complete contrast, New York's Kid Creole & The Coconuts established themselves firmly in Britain with several big pop hits, and another fashionable face and voice emerged by way of the "Kid" himself, August Darnell.

Perhaps the most exciting influx of successful new groups coincided with the arrival of a clutch of New York-based independent record labels, notably Streetwise, run by producer Arthur Baker, and Tom Silverman's Tommy Boy outfit. Between them, these provided major new chart talent in the shape of Rockers Revenge, Afrika Bambaata & Soul Sonic Force, Nairobi, The Jonzun Crew, Planet Patrol, and The New Edition. These labels and their products struggle for mainstream airplay and appropriate nation-wide pop sales in the US, yet in urban areas with large young black populations they can sell hundreds of thousands of 12-inch records, effectively taking soul/disco music marketing back to its original stance in the 1950s.

Britain, without formularised radio, has actually given these new wellsprings of talent their biggest chart successes, with a Top Five pop hit for Rockers Revenge, and a number one placing for New Edition's 'Candy Girl', which also turned the clock back somewhat by reconjuring the 1970-era Jackson Five sound on what was only half a lawsuit away from being a remake of the J5's 'ABC'.

On the purely British side of things, developments have again been more interesting than spectacular. Linx broke up feeling that they had run their creative course as a team. David Grant has moved on to a promising start as a solo act, but in the summer of 1983 developments were still awaited from his former

EVELYN KING

DAVID GRANT

partner Sketch.

Last year's big British arrivals Imagination had a quieter period largely because they spent much of the 12 months riding on the depleted momentum of material from their *In the Heat of the Night* album, but a new album and hit single recently proved that nothing had been lost. The same, unfortunately, could not be said for Junior, who after being named by *Billboard* as "Top Black Newcomer of the Year" at the end of 1982, has struggled for success with ostensibly strong recordings like 'Communication Breakdown'. No such problems, though, for Eddy Grant, who wrapped his ever-familiar reggae/soul dance style around 'I Don't Wanna Dance' and 'Electric Avenue', and reaped two gigantic British hits, the former one of the biggest UK sellers of the year, and the latter poised to take the top slot on the American pop chart as the period under review closed.

There was noticeably less activity amongst the British independent disco/soul labels than in earlier years, with some of them obviously finding the economic climate impossible to work in. Nonetheless, new acts and hits did emerge from independent launching pads in a fairly steady stream through the year, turning up acts like First Light, Steve Harvey, and The Funk Masters, who seem assured of continued success through major labels. TMT and Streetwave are among the indie specialist labels who

succeeded in maintaining a solid profile with their releases throughout the year.

A close chronological look at the year helps tie down specific records, names and achievements as they came and went. August 1982 saw Zapp's 'Dance Floor' as America's top-selling soul single, closely pursued by Jeffrey Osborne's 'I Really Don't Need No Light', Jennifer Holliday with 'And I'm Telling You I'm Not Going' (from the Broadway musical 'Dreamgirls'), 'Love Is in Control' by Donna Summer, and Afrika Bambaata with 'Planet Rock', which was destined to sell over half a million copies with hardly a pop radio station in the USA programming it. Britain's big sellers of the month were Rockers Revenge with 'Walking on Sunshine', 'Big Fun' from Kool & The Gang, Evelyn King's 'Love Come Down', 'Stool Pigeon' by Kid Creole & The Coconuts, and 'The Message' by Grandmaster Flash and The Furious Five. This latter record almost singlehandedly recreated British interest in the tough New York Rap sound, originally popularised by the Grandmaster's label-mates The Sugarhill Gang, with their 'Rapper's Delight'. The success of 'The Message' in the pop market as a whole in Britain almost certainly paved the way for the otherwise unprecedented success at the end of 1982 of the UK's own white soul boy rappin' duo Wham!, who were to become one of the major pop successes of 1983 with three massive Top Ten hits in a row.

ARETHA FRANKLIN

Aretha Franklin made a triumphant return in September, when her Luther Vandross-produced 'Jump to It' was the biggest soul seller in America, closely attended by Evelyn King, Grandmaster Flash, Donna Summer, and two new biggies, 'You Dropped a Bomb on Me' from the Gap

Band, and Jermaine Jackson with 'Let Me Tickle Your Fancy'. In Britain, Evelyn King, Grandmaster Flash and Rockers Revenge still held sway, but the notable new big sellers were Shalamar's 'There It Is', and Howard Johnson's double-sided success 'So Fine'/ 'Keepin' Love New'. Also a surprise big seller was the Boys Town Gang's 'Can't Take My Eyes Off You', the only record to have crossed over in a really big way to pop and soul consciousness from the active but generally self-contained gay dance market in Britain. The only other gay escapee to approach it in popularity was 'Do You Wanna Funk', featuring the voice of Sylvester and the electronic keyboards of Patrick Cowley (who, sadly, died of cancer within months of this success).

Evelyn King's 'Love Come Down' had become America's best seller by October. Evelyn and The Gap Band were joined at the top by The Time with '777-9311' (probably the biggest-selling phone number since Wilson Pickett's '634-5789'), Luther Vandross and his medley of 'Bad Boy' with Sam Cooke's oldie 'Having a Party', and another single on which the extremely active Vandross duetted with Cheryl Lynn — 'If This World Were Mine', a revival of a Marvin Gaye song. In the UK, out of the blue came one of the soul ballads of the year in the form of 'Zoom' by Fat Larry's band, a disco chart topper which held off multiple strong challenges from Shalamar's 'There It Is', Sharon Redd's 'Never Gonna Give You Up', 'Love's Comin' at Ya' from Melba Moore, Raw Silk's 'Do It to the Music', and 'Annie, I'm Not Your Daddy' from Kid Creole. All of these records were chart successes in the overall pop market as well as being disco top-fivers, and it is notable that the soul and dance hits from the upper end of Britain's disco charts do achieve a much higher overall penetration of the pop chart than is the case in the USA, where the separationist effect of format radio makes the crossover far more difficult unless the artist concerned is a recognised star.

November saw the triumphant return of Marvin Gaye, newly signed to CBS after a long post-Motown silence, and effortlessly soaring to take the number one soul

chart position on both sides of the Atlantic with the exquisite 'Sexual Healing'. The single heralded the album *Midnight Love*, which also became a platinum seller in fairly short order, though oddly failed to deliver follow-up singles with quite the commercial potency of 'Healing'. This fact, combined with a subsequent long wait for more new material, has cooled the excitement which surrounded Marvin's return.

The other November successes were, in America, Lionel Richie with 'Truly' (the first of three major hit singles from his first solo album *Lionel Richie*, which was itself Motown's biggest-selling album of the year), 'Muscles' from Diana Ross, 'Love's Comin' at Ya' from Melba Moore, and Prince with '1999'. In Britain, Marvin Gaye was chased by Eddy Grant with 'I Don't Wanna Dance' (a pop chart-topper), Kool & The Gang's 'Ooh La La (Let's Go Dancing)', the return of Dionne Warwick on 'Heartbreaker', and 'E.T. Boogie' from the Extra Ts.

The last of these is worthy of some comment, as it was by far the biggest-selling disco 12-incher imported from America into Britain where it was not released domestically. Never a huge US hit, the disc ran into copyright problems with MCA/Universal, owners of the E.T. trademark, who forced its withdrawal from manufacture. The American Sunnyview label complied, but it took a remarkably long time for the flood of imports, which were coming in to meet UK demand, to dry up — and well into 1983 copies were still arriving which had been pressed in European countries with uncertain copyright laws.

November's hits maintained their supremacy in the USA until the end of the year, but Gaye, Richie and Prince were joined by Michael Jackson, duetting with Paul McCartney on 'The Girl Is Mine', and giving the first hint of a batch of super-successful material which was to make Jackson a virtual resident of the American charts for much of the next six months. Britain's year-end hits were mostly the same, except that Prince failed to find a foothold, and the American outfit Montana Sextet, fronted by Vincent Montana Jr, scored massively instead with their brand of jazz-funk on 'Heavy Vibes'. After missing initially with their 'Wham Rap', the British duo Wham! got into their chart-cracking stride with 'Young Guns (Go for It)', and Shalamar finished the year with yet another biggie in 'Friends'.

Soul and dance albums during these latter months of 1982 were dominated by the huge-selling Marvin Gaye and Lionel Richie sets already mentioned, but the other major LPs included Luther Vandross's *Forever, for Always, for Love,* Evelyn King's *Get Loose,* Aretha Franklin's *Jump to It,* and in Britain, Shalamar's *Friends.*

1983 got underway with what was to be the most consistently successful album in any style on both sides of the Atlantic during the first half of the new year — Michael Jackson's *Thriller.* Already featuring one proven hit single, it had plenty more platinum still to be extracted.

January's major singles successes were the long-lasting Jackson/McCartney, Gaye and Richie in America, though joined by Michael's younger sister Janet Jackson with 'Young Love', and by Sonny Charles and Tyrone Davis, two rediscovered veterans of soul music, who charted 'Put It in a Magazine' and 'Are You Serious' respectively, both on the same label, Highrise Records — another freshly launched independent putting its money where black music is. Britain's surprising big disco seller of the month was 'Last Night a DJ Saved My Life', from the New York team Indeep, a straightforward dance and rap disc which nevertheless found immediate pop acceptance.

February brought Michael Jackson's second *Thriller* single 'Billie Jean', a rapid number one seller on both sides of the Atlantic and obviously the top soul seller in each country too, assisted by an excellent and widely-programmed video. Custom-made videos have never played any significant role in the marketing of disco music until now, but a genre in which rhythm and movement are vital ingredients obviously stands to benefit from the possibilities of visual interpretation offered by video. The 'Billie Jean' clip and the one which was to follow for 'Beat It' were dynamic demonstrations of what could be achieved in this area, though

the high cost factor involved — even when offset against promotional value — could mean that for the time being video may remain the prerogative of wealthy major labels.

Other major February sellers were Patti Austin's duet with James Ingram on 'Baby Come to Me' — an across-the-board smash on both sides of the Atlantic in traditional soul duet style — plus the Gap Band's 'Outstanding'. Britain got an 'E.T.'-related disco hit after all, in the form of Johnny Chingas' largely instrumental 'Phone Home', a record which was not only highly commercial, but sufficiently ambiguous this time not to fall foul of Universal's eagle-eyed copyright department.

The big American sellers during March were Lionel Richie's follow-up 'You Are', in which he raised the tempo but hardly lowered the sales, plus 'Atomic Dog' from George

GEORGE CLINTON

Clinton, and new Motown family group DeBarge with 'I Like It'. Britain had a flood of disco/soul sellers which almost immediately became pop hits as well — Forrest's revival of 'Rock the Boat', the Icelandic jazz-funk of Mezzoforte on 'Garden Party', Sunfire's 'Young Free and Single' (which also inspired a successful reggae-flavoured domestic cover by Lorita Grahame), and a gigantic home-grown hit from David Joseph, one-time lead singer of Hi-Tension, in 'You Can't Hide (Your Love From Me)'. This one was sufficiently strong to immediately attract American ears (and feet) as well, and it benefited from a transatlantic re-mix before going on to become one of the biggest US club favourites of the first half of 1983.

George Clinton's 'Atomic Dog' was America's top soul single of April, sandwiched between Michael Jackson's 'Billie Jean' and 'Beat It'. Champaign, who had originally scored in 1981 with 'How 'bout Us', returned with 'Try Again', while chart veterans The Whispers returned to big sales with 'Tonight', and producer Kashif donned his performer's togs for the highly successful 'I Just Gotta Have You'. In Britain, I-Level had a biggie with 'Minefield', while Man Parrish far exceeded their American sales on 'Hip Hop Be Bop (Don't Stop)'. Even a 20-year-old dance craze, the Twist, got a brief revival through 'Twist (Round'n' Round)' by Chil Fac-Torr. This was one of the year's hottest American imports prior to its UK release, and again did significantly better in the UK than at home.

Several soul veterans returned with their first major hits of the year during May, as Gladys Knight's 'Save the Overtime for Me', The Isley Brothers' 'Between the Sheets', and the Chi-Lites' 'Bottoms Up' (on yet another energetic soul indie label, Larc Records, distributed by MCA) all crowded 'Beat It' for top sales. The one which did make the chart top, though, was 'Candy Girl', by the teenage newcomers from Boston, New Edition, referred to earlier. Two weeks after topping the American soul chart, the disc was top of the British pop chart, making it easily the most successful black music début of the year. Mtume's insistent dance groove 'Juicy Fruit', complete with slightly *risqué* lyrics, also hit simultaneously on both sides of the Atlantic.

Several more domestic names scored significantly in Britain during this month, notably Galaxy featuring Phil Fearon, whose 'Dancing Tight' was a national Top Five hit as well as a disco chart topper, against all expectations. London duo First Light also broke big with 'Explain the Reasons', as did Aberdonian funker Steve Harvey with 'Something Special', and The Funk Masters, featuring the uncredited but outstanding guest lead vocal of Londoner Julie Roberts on 'It's Over'.

Finally, as mid 1983 approached, the disco pace was being made once again by a mix of established and new artists. Britain's biggest

dancefloor record of the month was a single in a solidly traditional soul dance style from Booker Newberry III, titled 'Love Town'. Bob Marley had a big hit in a commercial crossover style with the posthumous 'Buffalo Soldier', and local lads Wham! scored with their third solid rap mover 'Bad Boys'. America and Britain extracted different singles from the long-awaited new album from George Benson, 'In Your Eyes', going for 'Inside Love' and 'Lady Love Me (One More Time)' respectively. Benson scored effortless hits with both — and the album.

June closed with Mtume's 'Juicy Fruit' as the month's biggest soul seller in the US, closely pursued by Debarge (yet to register in Britain) with 'All This Love', and 'Love Is the Key' from Maze featuring Frankie Beverly. In Britain, we witnessed the return of Imagination to top commercial form with 'Looking at Midnight', and the chart return — with one of the strongest dance productions of the year in 'I.O.U.' — of North London funkers Freeez. Interestingly, this group, which had been part of the spearhead of the British indie specialist label push into disco/soul music-selling in 1980/1 with their 'Southern Freeez' hit, turned to New York's hot indie entrepreneur Arthur Baker to produce the new disc. 'I.O.U.' was publicised as "The sound of New York from the streets of North London"; a phrase coined, no doubt, tongue-in-cheek, but indicative of a formula which could well herald exciting new directions for disco/soul music over the coming year if its philosophy is explored further.

It may not appear a vintage year when the black music historians of the future look back — 'Sexual Healing', 'Billie Jean' and 'Beat It' will probably get the most plays as the representative golden oldies of the period, and they, of course, would have been big in *any* year, along with their artists. But there was plenty of activity, there were lots of newcomers — even new labels and producers with a commitment to the genre — and the established stars generally moved with the times and were justly rewarded for it. There was plenty to listen to — and dance to.

BARRY LAZELL

30

COUNTRY

The recession finally caught up with country music in 1983, somewhat later than other areas of the entertainment business. After five years of rapid growth, particularly in the middle-of-the-road pop market, the year saw a fall back and widespread belt-tightening as Nashville-based publishing houses and record companies cut down on their staff and trimmed their rosters.

Record sales were down, promoters struggled to fill concert halls and many small venues went out of business. It was a bad year for acts in the middle range — the stars of yesterday who play the small club circuit — but even harder for the aspiring new writers and performers. After three years when a lot of new acts had broken through, there were suddenly few openings.

Yet, despite the increasingly hard times, business at the top end of the country music market-place was as good as ever. An indication of the money to be made as a country superstar came with the revelation that six of the top money-earners in Las Vegas are country entertainers. *The American Almanac of Jobs and Salaries* disclosed that weekly earnings in Vegas for Dolly Parton are $350,000; Kenny Rogers $250,000; Willie Nelson, Tom Jones (the Welsh

DOLLY PARTON

singer is generally recognised as an American country star these days) and Glen Campbell $200,000; and Tammy Wynette $150,000.

Dolly, incidentally, is top, ahead of Diana Ross and Frank Sinatra. She is now one of America's top cinema box-office stars too — *The Best Little Whorehouse in Texas* grossed over $65 million — and she has ambitious plans for the future, including a lavish Tennessee theme park called "Dollywood" and a Broadway musical called "Wildflower". "It's a story I've written about mountain folk," she told a London press conference. "It's my story but exaggerated a little!"

Despite the fall in record sales and concert revenue, country music's popularity in North America still seems to be growing. The 1983 Radio Survey by the Country Music Association revealed a 7%

increase in stations programming country all day — a total of 2,266 outlets in the US and Canada — which seems to indicate that a lack of money rather than interest has caused the slump.

Many observers see cable television providing country music with a new boost in the coming year. The success of the rock-oriented MTV has led to the launching of the Nashville Network, a cable channel run by WSM (who also own the long-running country music institution, The Grand Ole Opry) and available to cable subscribers throughout the USA — seven million at launch date but growing rapidly.

The Nashville Network screens a six-hour block of programmes, repeated three times daily, including *I-40 Paradise*, a sitcom set in a truck-stop on a busy road that leads to Nashville; *Fandango*, a quiz show introduced by Bill Anderson; *Tumbleweed Theatre*, which features clips from old western movies and songs from the contemporary group Riders in the Sky; and *Bobby Bare and Friends*, an original talk show from a Nashville recording studio in which the likeable Bobby Bare chats and sings with some of Music City's best singer-performers.

Recently launched is CMTV (Country Music Television), which is closer in format to MTV and structured like a contemporary country radio station with vision, screening continuous video clips.

These two cable stations have precipitated a rush of country acts making promotional videos, as there had previously been little demand and few outlets — MTV being particularly reluctant to screen country-orientated videos, even from acts like Alabama and Rosanne Cash who have made the pop charts.

Alabama, the four-piece band with a close harmony sound deeply rooted in country but

ALABAMA

flavoured with a strong rock beat, have been the undisputed country success story of the year. Their sound and energetic stage performance attracts an across-the-board audience of teenagers; 30-year-old former fans of country-rock bands like Creedence Clearwater Revival and The Eagles; and older country enthusiasts.

They dominated the *Billboard* country charts all year, hogging the top spot of the LP listings for eleven months, first with *Mountain Music* and then *The Closer You Get*, which defied prevailing trends by achieving platinum status. They succeeded with the long-established country music traditions of hard work, humility and awe in the face of success, and by putting the interests of their fans first.

Few people in the entertainment business work as hard as Randy Owen, Jeff Cook, Teddy Gentry and Mark Herndon, the four members of Alabama, except perhaps the 60-strong entourage who manoeuvre their stage show around the USA. Their 1983 tour began in Asheville, North Carolina, on February 18th and was due to close in Oakland, California, on December 4th. There were days off for award ceremonies — they were easy winners of Vocal Group of the Year and Entertainers of the Year titles at both the Country Music Association and Academy of Country Music shows; but most of the year was spent on the road.

Alabama's "Wild Stallion" operation accompanies the band on their travels, selling T-shirts and souvenirs and employing 22 people, but they've been boycotting venues which try and impose a hefty levy on sales — "It's unfair to the fans," an angry Teddy Gentry told *Billboard*, "because they're the ones who would have to end up absorbing the extra costs."

Before Alabama's mammoth tours, Willie Nelson was the country act who seemed to be on the road most frequently, but he's been taking things more easily, though he has had another very prolific year in the recording studio and hardly a month has gone by without the release of a new LP, including several duet packages with friends like Waylon Jennings, and a concept album about reincarnation entitled *Tougher Than Leather*.

This year Nelson begins filming the title role of *The Red Headed Stranger*, the movie based on the 1975 album which brought him to the top of the country music business. With George Jones, Merle Haggard and Conway Twitty, Willie is one of a rapidly diminishing group of country veterans who still sell records in large quantities.

Younger performers, many of whom only scored their first big hits in the last few years, now dominate the charts, including such rising stars as Reba McEntire from Oklahoma; Lee Greenwood, a natural successor to Kenny Rogers; the duo of David Frizzell and Shelly West, the daughter and younger brother of two of country music's best loved performers, Dottie West and the late Lefty Frizzell; the pop-orientated Sylvia, whose 'Nobody' was one of the few country singles to achieve gold record status; and Janie Fricke,

RICKY SKAGGS

backing singer on hundreds of country hits by other people but now the most recent CMA Female Vocalist of the Year.

JOHN ANDERSON

The most welcome new trend has been the increasing popularity of performers with roots deep in bluegrass and traditional country music, a trend that can be traced to Emmylou Harris's classic pure country album from 1980, *Roses in the Snow*, which showcased the talents of a brilliant young instrumentalist named Ricky Skaggs.

The performance encouraged Epic to sign Skaggs to a solo deal and he's had remarkable chart success with hits like 'Highway 40 Blues' and 'Heartbroke', won the coveted Best Male Vocalist award from the CMA, and the highest praise from fellow artists, like Merle Haggard who described him as "the brightest thing that's happened to country music."

Skaggs' popularity has encouraged other companies to sign similar contemporary bluegrass performers, including the family group The Whites (which features Ricky's wife Sharon, and whose excellent album *Old Familiar Feeling* was produced by him); and Delia Bell, who's made numerous fine LPs for specialist labels but is now signed to a major. She had

JANIE FRICKE

Emmylou Harris making her début as producer for *Delia Bell*.

Other performers having their best ever year include John Anderson, still in his twenties but performing in an authentic honky-tonk style which merits comparisons with the great George Jones; and three of America's best pure-country vocalists, Gene Watson, John Conlee and Vern Gosdin.

Anderson scored one of the biggest and most surprising crossover pop hits of the year with the gimmicky 'Swingin''; Gene Watson racked up a string of number one hits; and John Conlee's 'Common Man' was the best of many singles that reflected the troubled economic times of ordinary American working people.

The memory of the great Marty Robbins, who died after a heart attack in December 1982, remained strong throughout the year and he was honoured with three of the most important awards at the

MARTY ROBBINS

Music City News ceremony in Nashville, the only awards that are voted for by country fans. His last hit, ironically, had been 'Some Memories Just Won't Die' and just before his death he'd been elected to the Country Music Hall of Fame. Though his record sales were well below some of the other big country stars, Marty Robbins was one of the most popular artists with the hardcore fans and will be sorely missed.

Finally, the year managed to throw up the usual collection of extraordinary song titles, and the best included 'The Night Dolly Parton Was Almost Mine', 'I'm Gonna Hire a Wino to Decorate Our Home' and Loretta Lynn's definitive, 'Lyin', Cheatin', Woman Chasin', Honky Tonkin', Whiskey Drinkin' You'.
RICHARD WOOTTON

JAZZ

How is jazz now, and how's it been doing this past 12 months or so? Hard to find a straight answer. Jazz never quite flourishes in this country, being forever a minority taste. If it makes a bit of ground here — in the clubs or pubs for example — it sheds a little there. If concert tours proliferate, the number of patrons at each venue tends to decrease. A foothold gained is often not held.

Jazz always has been a dodgy occupation in Britain, for player and promoter alike. Though more jazz actually gets played here as the years roll by, it is a bonus for the audience (especially the committed listener) rather than the performer, home-grown that is. "There's no money in jazz," they say. "They" always did say that.

In the USA — with its vast land mass and population producing a regular and healthy crop of jazz musicians and an audience for the music — things can be better ordered. The jazz end of the business looks brighter than it does in Europe, despite a deep depression in the record industry and the fact that the average age of what we think of as the ordinary fans-in-the-street has advanced to the stage where it is beyond the top of most market charts.

In America, and not only in New York and Chicago, jazz venues thrive; the brilliant newcomers keep coming and the old-timers keep on working, often to a great age. Sam Wooding's name cropped up the other month; he's now 88, and a pioneer jazz leader who first brought his band to Europe in 1925. As for pianist Eubie Blake, the "Wizard of Ragtime" and a prolific composer, he was still performing until just before his 100th birthday (on February 7, 1983) which was suitably celebrated. He died at his Brooklyn home five days later. Another active veteran, Benny Goodman, 74, who was

WYNTON MARSALIS

reunited with Lionel Hampton and Teddy Wilson (no kids either) at the 1982 Kool Jazz Festival, is still powering along when he feels good. Incredibly, he won first place — an old spot for him — in *Down Beat*'s latest Readers' Poll. Young Wynton Marsalis scored three wins in the same poll.

It is encouraging to note that in July 1983 *Down Beat* began its 50th year of publication. The magazine does not place jazz in a ghetto, so its July issue welcomes Andy Summers of The Police, as well as Pat Metheny's multi-keyboardist, Lyle Mays, ace bassist Ron Carter and that perennial visionary, Miles Davis. A disc review praises trumpeter Terence Blanchard, 20, replacement for Marsalis in Art Blakey's Messengers and a youngster to watch. Everywhere the young lions test their strength. The outlook for them is OK. For the youthful British jazz *arriviste*

the situation is bleak.

The recession bites deeper, and a glance at the face of government does nothing to dispel alarm and suspicion. Musically, jazz is alive and fairly well. Players mix it with other idioms, particularly African and Afro-Latin just now, and many young rock musicians continue to flirt with jazz, from forties' swing and jump music to avantist free improvisation. Probably this cross-fertilisation bodes well for the future of innovative jazz and free music in the later eighties, should we reach same, but at this moment some of it sounds unlike simple rock and not enough like good jazz.

Straight-ahead jazz which swings hard, keeps a beat going for more than a minute or two without altering time or tempo, and has the sound of hot jazz as opposed to legit music, that sort of prime jazz is becoming almost a rarity. Musicians are inclined to knock

it as old hat, and the élitist critics like to have avant-garde names to "discover" or promote. This is understandable. New directions are interesting to follow (and publicise for profit), and it is a quirk of human nature to tire of something familiar and pass on to fresh faces.

Not much immediate harm is done by these games of what is *passé* and what fashionable, what's new and what's next, except that as a general rule it is liable to widen the gap between artist and audience and, for that matter, the critics' mafia and the crowd. And, of course, it is the crowd, no matter how we regard its taste in art, that pays the bills.

Look around you at the current scene and you'll notice the music-trade *aficionados*, the opinion-setters and a few musicians (players seldom go out to hear other players) dashing off to catch a contemporary free spirit in a club where he draws a couple of hundred customers. Meanwhile, the same evening, a mass of punters with a liking for jazz, and perhaps a desire to know more about it, flock to a theatre to enjoy Pat Metheny or Weather Report, or perhaps Al Jarreau or George Benson. Pundits do not care for popularisers. But pundits don't buy tickets.

Miles Davis, as we noted a year ago, crossed the line dividing jazz from rock and funk and attracted much attention. His return to the UK, in 1983, was successful and there were many who felt he played "more" horn than in April of 1982. But he created no furore this time and the theatre didn't quite sell out twice. Among trumpet players, 1983 was Wynton Marsalis' year. He got written up all over the place and drew long queues to Frith Street for his season at Ronnie Scott's. The reborn MJQ failed to fill The Dominion twice. So times are a-changin'.

The big concert tour and the commercially organised series of festival concerts are not what they were. Norman Granz, famed US impresario and record producer, introduced a note of splendour recalling the halcyon days when he brought Ella Fitzgerald, Oscar Peterson, Joe Pass and the Count Basie Orchestra to the Royal Festival Hall for a week (not all shows well-attended). Granz has the clout and the saleable names to do this; few in the private-money sector here could attempt to stage such a string of concerts by world-famous jazz artists.

What's needed more than ever today is subsidy, and a heap of it. Most of our festivals are supported, either by industry of the Arts Council, the GLC and various councils, regional arts and local radio, or by organisations like the ICA, the National Jazz Centre and the MU.

Capital Radio earned the gratitude of buffs by sponsoring George Wein's Capital Jazz Festival for four years despite sundry fires and fears. Now luck has run right out for Wein and the buffs, and for summer 1983 Capital staged a five-week music festival in which the jazz slots fought for space among clutches of pop, folk, rock, Afro-Caribbean, dance, brass band and classical music plus

theatre, fireworks and what-have-you. This is not the grand open-air jazz experience, after the style of Nice's annual bash in the Cimiez Gardens, which Wein promised at the 1979 inception of the Capital extravaganza.

So 1983 is the year England lost its jazz superfest. The reasons may be complex but they are not unconnected with the fact that Capital's franchise is shortly up for renewal — or rejection. Their diffuse Music Festival 1983 is a good thing to be seen to be doing for the communities involved. Otherwise, our festivals roll on as usual, changing very little and seemingly not greatly affected by the economic climate. Sheffield, Edinburgh, Cardiff, Chichester, Kendal, Bradford, Camden... the list is lengthy, and we must not forget the modest but forward-looking Bracknell Festival at South Hill Park at the start of July. It's a genuine alfresco affair, with marquee and indoor back-up sessions, in pleasant surroundings.

London, though, is still the shiny tip of the iceberg, and it is said you still need to gravitate there in order to make a marketable reputation, but a great deal of the important jazz playing and promoting is done elsewhere.

The Arts Council's Contemporary Music Network assist exponents and composers of newer jazz forms, and many a tour of uncommercial improvised music has taken place which could not have happened without the CMN bounty. The Jazz Centre Society (and allied National Jazz Centre), Platform organisation, London Musicians Collective and a number of regional Arts Associations all help at grassroots level (sorry about that phrase) and the worry now must be about what effect the coming government cash cuts are going to have.

What chance, for instance, would Birmingham, Manchester, Leicester, etc., have had of seeing *Piano Forty*, by four improvising pianists, without the Arts Council's initiative? These players — Jaki Byard (USA), Alex Von Schlippenback (West Germany), Irene Schweizer (Switzerland) and Howard Riley (UK) — made up an international quartet. Often the Network's grants go to British musicians (the majority do),

and some of our players feel aggrieved at the sight of precious subsidy reaching foreign hands. Our jazz players have lately complained, in print and to their union, about the large number of regular bookings given to Americans.

There is justification for the moans when hard-working local talent finds many of its gigs filled by foreign competition. However, jazz-making should be an international activity; EEC rules benefit our musicians abroad as much as their visitors to Britain; and I have always believed that the local jazz scene draws nourishment and ultimately financial support from the stimulation provided by "glamorous" American figures. To think of returning to the infamous embargo on foreign jazz players, however the move was disguised, would be a most reactionary step. But perhaps working visits could be restricted to two a year per person or band.

Of course it's unfair that Brits with the ability of Stan Tracey, Tony Coe or Michael Garrick (to name but three of scores of fine musicians) should lack the drawing-power to win them star billing on the international circuit. But when has artistic or business life been fair? Those who run high-overheads clubs, festivals and the like, all tell me that they could not survive without the excitement generated by major US names.

In Nice, a few years back, I asked George Wein why he didn't devote one festival evening to British jazz alone. "Because nobody would come to it," he replied. If true it is a harsh truth.

A glance at the bill of fare for the more important fests — from the Kool in New York to those in New Orleans, Monterey, Montreal, Ottawa, Saratoga, Nice, Montreux, The Hague and heaven-knows-where-else — is sufficient to convince a doubter that America is still the home of jazz. The music has spread around the world and taken firm root in many countries whose indigenous styles and outstanding stylists in turn wield an influence upon US jazz. In America, however, the music still derives advantage from being, as you might say, a natural language. Today it appears to be enjoying yet another revival — in clubs, bars, hotel lounges,

restaurants, concert halls, colleges, theatres, on radio and TV, and even in the street I'm told.

The number of new festivals being launched is astonishing. The first American Jazz Festival in Lexington, Kentucky...the first Mary Lou Williams Jazz Festival at Duke University...the Kool Jazz Festival in Cleveland...the first jazz major-fest in Las Vegas for 20 years...these are a few of the new events. Think of a town that's not quite Hicksville, and if it doesn't have its own jazz bash the chances are it soon will. The grants, the scholarships, endowments, sponsorship, television and radio support, all are forthcoming on a generous scale unknown to the impoverished Brit.

There are good tidings, though, and one is that TV has looked up and recognised jazz. And in London, at any rate, clubs and pubs and jazz bars and cafés (new and old) rolled along smoothly enough in spite of periodic scares and rumours of impending bankruptcy. Prices grew a bit hairy at the upper-market spots and impoverished jazz buffs claimed that inflation was squeezing them out. Ronnie Scott's, however, introduced a Mon-through-Thurs free admission for members which made club-going feasible for dedicated cats.

Too much stuff passed through the Frith Street portals for me to itemise, but it was a well-mixed assemblage, reflecting a broadening of club policy. Other West End jazz places — The Canteen, The Dean Street Pizza Express, The 100 Club — showed similar catholicity. Losses included The Roundhouse, which housed Gil Evans in March; the irreplaceable Earl Hines; trumpeter-leader Harry James, Al Haig, Wingy Manone, Sonny Stitt, Kai Winding, Ernie Royal, Bobby Plater, Pat Smythe. There were others.

To end, though, on an international note: Bill Ashton and NYJO toured the USSR not long ago and hit on an enthusiastic jazz following there. Now the Arts Council says it will be importing Soviet jazz over here in 1984 in the form of the Ganelin Trio. Jazz marches on.
MAX JONES

THE YEAR'S ALBUMS

A

ABBA
The Singles — The First Ten Years (Epic)
Its documentation of the group who altered the course of pop more than anyone else — *anyone* — is flawless.
NEW MUSICAL EXPRESS

ABRASIVE WHEELS
When The Punks Go Marching In (Riot City)
A W specialise in the usual breakneck brutality and lyrical banality spiced up with mob chants extracted from many a dodgy soccer match.
SOUNDS

Heartily encouraging signs of musical agility.
MELODY MAKER

BRYAN ADAMS
Cuts Like A Knife (A&M)
Exquisitely asinine drivel...second-rate Saccharine rock.
MELODY MAKER

If I were Bryan Adams, I think I would see Nick Gilder haunting my dreams, and a million other scrumptious boys with photogenic faces and fixations on jukebox pop.
CREEM

THE ADICTS
Sound Of Music (Razor)
Stinks of as much premeditation and cold blooded pecuniary forethought as anything perpetrated by the likes of Shitti Scritti.
NEW MUSICAL EXPRESS

Consummating the ideal marriage of fizzy, fizzical pop music and rampant, unrelenting and uncompromising punk rock...Wacky, wizard, wheezy.
MELODY MAKER

Thank Christ for the Adicts. In this often grey and depressing world, they entertain us, uplift us and unify us.
SOUNDS

ALLEZ ALLEZ

AEROSMITH
Rock In A Hard Place (Columbia)
As soon as the stylus hit the wax, it melted and my speaker covers blew across the living room floor.
SOUNDS

AIR
80 Below 82 (Antilles)
The best album I've heard this year...this music will wring you out. It is not difficult or tuneless, but it demands the full gamut of your responses, and will tax your spirit.
MELODY MAKER

ARTHUR ALEXANDER
A Shot Of Rhythm And Soul (Ace)
A welcome and important collection... great, great music.
NEW MUSICAL EXPRESS

ALLEZ ALLEZ
Promises (Virgin)
Promises remain unfulfilled.
NEW MUSICAL EXPRESS

Sounds unfinished.
MELODY MAKER

Hardly one piece of music indicates any sense of sure-footedness.
SOUNDS

ALTERED IMAGES
Bite (Epic)
More acceptable, more in vogue, more nauseatingly calculated than anything they've ever had the wit to produce up until now.
MELODY MAKER

Musical anorexia...it reminds me of one of those Mr Kipling fudge cakes that looks delicious on the package but when you look inside you see a bun half the size you expected.
SOUNDS

Miss Grogan is probably the most obvious star to come down from Scotland since Ramsay MacDonald.
NEW MUSICAL EXPRESS

ANGELIC UPSTARTS
Reason Why? (Anagram)
An articulate street-socialist alternative to punk's naive 'anarchist' orthodoxy.
SOUNDS

Nearly as good as its intentions.
NEW MUSICAL EXPRESS

ANGRY SAMOANS
Back From Samoa (Bad Trip)
Psycho naifs with quivering jellos for brains.
NEW MUSICAL EXPRESS

ADAM ANT
Friend Or Foe (CBS)
Never before has the sheer emptiness of his songwriting been quite so apparent.
NEW MUSICAL EXPRESS

Well short of classic.
MELODY MAKER

It makes the Anti Nowhere League sound like the Joy Strings . . . a classic in the real sense of the word.
SOUNDS

ANTENA
Camino Del Sol (Les Disques de Crepuscule)
The best so far of our nouveau beatniks because they put respect for themselves before respect for tradition.
MELODY MAKER

Just perfect for Hampstead coffee table chic . . . a late night delight, a smoocher's ideal companion.
SOUNDS

ANTI-NOWHERE LEAGUE
Live In Yugoslavia (I D Records)
A classic biker band playing dustbin rock'n'roll, they revel in foul-mouthed sewer-level ditties.
SOUNDS

In most respects, this is an appalling record.
MELODY MAKER

ANTI-NOWHERE LEAGUE
XYZ (Faulty Products)
This is a great album unleashed by a true punk band. XYZ has the raw energy of early Clash LPs.
BOSTON ROCK

ANY TROUBLE
Any Trouble (EMI America)
These songs rival anything on "Get Happy!!", say, or "East Side Story".
MELODY MAKER

Lamentably buried under six feet of sickly synthesisers, over-production and over-arrangement . . . reeks of compromise and unfulfilled potential.
RECORD MIRROR

APRIL WINE
Power Play (Capitol)
Professional but thoroughly unremarkable . . . a series of weak-kneed displays of accomplishment.
MELODY MAKER

JOAN ARMATRADING
The Key (A&M)
The type of whingeing slop you'd likely hear in an LA singles bar.
RECORD MIRROR

The best Armatrading work to date.
NEW MUSICAL EXPRESS

ARTERY
Oceans (Red Flame)
The best music I've heard all year.
SOUNDS

ADAM ANT

No redeeming qualities whatsoever . . . unbelievably pretentious thundering banality.
NEW MUSICAL EXPRESS

Evocative, stimulating, disturbing . . . better their Van Gogh than ABC's Rembrandt.
MELODY MAKER

ARTERY
One Afternoon In A Hot Air Balloon (Red Flame)
Mark Gouldthorpe is virtually unique . . . resembles the Noel Coward of post-punk modernism.
SOUNDS

BILLY MACKENZIE (THE ASSOCIATES)
THE ASSOCIATES
The Affectionate Punch (Fiction)
As contemporary as Boy George and rather more eccentric.
RECORD MIRROR

They have painstakingly polished hitherto hidden aspects of the previous work to a dazzling sheen and the results are breathtaking.
NEW MUSICAL EXPRESS

ASWAD
Not Satisfied (CBS)
We have been left with half a record — all the edges have been smoothed off . . . C'mon Aswad, tuffen up.
SOUNDS

Aswad are the toughest — the best there is . . . crucial music — beat for the feet, message for the head, and fire for the soul.
NEW MUSICAL EXPRESS

Marvellously moving pop music, "Not Satisfied" goes further than most in making satisfying music that matters!
MELODY MAKER

SWEET PEA ATKINSON
Don't Walk Away (Ze)
A concrete hard dance stormer that bulldozes even the terminally lethargic to some serious toe-tapping.
RECORD MIRROR

Sultry genius.
SOUNDS

ATTILA THE STOCKBROKER

ATTILA THE STOCKBROKER
Ranting At The Nation (Cherry Red)
This insufferably smug prat...a bunch of second rate plagiarisms...this album is bollocks.
NEW MUSICAL EXPRESS

The sound of a rank amateur drunkenly exposing his dire lack of musical ability with an unselfconsciousness that's almost spectacular.
MELODY MAKER

A maggot-ridden dead cat with a twinkle in the left eye that says 'ART'.
SOUNDS

THE AU PAIRS
Sense And Sensuality (Kamera)
Their sound takes off where the Gang of Four got grounded.
RECORD MIRROR

Its overwhelming quality is its unobtrusiveness...laidback jazzy pop so mellow and unadventurous it hardly rates above Radio One wallpaper muzak.
SOUNDS

Confidence and adventure are sadly only present sporadically. A series of promising sketches do not add up to an exciting album.
MELODY MAKER

An unwanted pest. Dull and worthy. But worthy of what?
NEW MUSICAL EXPRESS

KEVIN AYERS
Diamond Jack And The Queen Of Pain (Roadrunner)
Ayers' first album in three years and better than I would have dared hope.
MELODY MAKER

AZTEC CAMERA
High Land, Hard Rain (Rough Trade)
This is really a marvellous record.
MELODY MAKER

Worth its weight in gold.
SOUNDS

As sparkling, as profound and as essentially Scottish as Bill Forsyth's cinema.
NEW MUSICAL EXPRESS

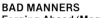

B

THE B-52'S
Whammy! (Island)
The B-52's at their worst ever.
MELODY MAKER

This is more like it!...back on artistic form.
NEW MUSICAL EXPRESS

BAD COMPANY
Rough Diamonds (Swansong)
It's a tragedy that Company have failed to come up with anything more inspiring than fatuous drivel...boring music made by bored musicians (for boring people?).
MELODY MAKER

Sounding exactly the same as they ever did.
SOUNDS

With the overall mediocrity of the material, even die-hard fans should stay away.
CREEM

Paul, for god's sake get rid of this albatross of a band, get yourself a couple of partners with a little wit, spunk, intelligence.
NEW MUSICAL EXPRESS

BAD MANNERS
Forging Ahead (Magnet)
Composed largely of poorly-paced, lightweight mock-reggae with the vocal inadequacies masked behind an irritating barrage of echo.
SOUNDS

It's time Bad Manners made a graceful exit.
NEW MUSICAL EXPRESS

BAD MANNERS
The Height Of Bad Manners (Telstar)
The epitome of loutish fun...this is where the real spirit of pop resides.
SOUNDS

TONY BANKS

TONY BANKS
The Fugitive (Charisma)
A record that throws up the past with all the unpleasantness associated with the unwelcome return of a bad Chinese meal.
MELODY MAKER

At least the lad has got something out of his system.
RECORD MIRROR

THE B-52'S

THE BARRACUDAS
Mean Time (Closer Records)
Someone should send a copy to Roger McGuinn. I'm sure he'd love to know that he hasn't been forgotten.
MELODY MAKER

All the tracks contain the same lack of imagination.
RECORD MIRROR

Seriously folks, this is a great album.
SOUNDS

One can only deplore the high-handed neglect suffered by this excellent group.
NEW MUSICAL EXPRESS

BANANARAMA
Deep Sea Skiving (London)
Entrenches Bananarama even further in the glossy rag doll mode of daffy, zany fun.
MELODY MAKER

Better than The Beverly Sisters but nowhere near as good as The Nolans.
NEW MUSICAL EXPRESS

PAUL BARRERE
On My Own Two Feet (WEA)
Should we mark his file "Retired"?
MELODY MAKER

BAUHAUS
The Sky's Gone Out (Beggars Banquet)
A massive con by musical spivs.
MELODY MAKER

They cover their ham and ignorance in a cloak of babbled incomprehensibility.
RECORD MIRROR

Comes across like David Bowie imitating Jacques Brel declaiming a pastiche of Lautreamont backed by the early Banshees. As silly as that.
NEW MUSICAL EXPRESS

BANANARAMA

The only possible excuse for not rushing out and buying this album is congenital insanity.
SOUNDS

THE BEAT
Special Beat Service (Go-Feet)
Shows the dance floor's number one salt and pepper ska team over-extending itself way beyond its creative reach.
CREEM

Pleasant, palatable, pleasing...maybe not a nourishing meal but a very tasty snack.
SOUNDS

There's something a bit listless about it, as though the band are suffering a crisis of confidence.
MELODY MAKER

A new flavour to roll around the tongue, a new taste to acquire...a transitory work rather than an arrival.
NEW MUSICAL EXPRESS

Re-affirms that The Beat are one of Britain's best bands.
RECORD MIRROR

THE BEAT
What Is Beat? (Go-Feet)
This is Beat!
NEW MUSICAL EXPRESS

A well illustrated guide through their inconsistent career to date.
MELODY MAKER

THE BEATLES
20 Greatest Hits (Parlophone)
A bright enough effort, strongly influenced by the real innovators like ABC, the Undertones and Scarlet Party.
MELODY MAKER

THE BELLE STARS
Flat Out (Stiff)
The whole set is carried off with the charm and style of Big Daddy in the wrestling ring.
SOUNDS

Good pop music.
NEW MUSICAL EXPRESS

The Belle Stars have sold out to expediency and aimed for a short cut to success...A slick, accomplished stab at danceable pop.
MELODY MAKER

PAT BENATAR
Get Nervous (Chrysalis)
There's an underlying savagery that keeps its feet firmly anchored in stack-heeled stadia-rock spaceboots.
SOUNDS

Most of the songs she sings are gross bummers of the highest order.
CREEM

THE BELLE STARS

GEORGE BENSON
In Your Eyes (Warner Bros)
Safe.
MELODY MAKER

His facility for boring listeners now fully developed, Benson is beyond all hope.
NEW MUSICAL EXPRESS

BLACK SABBATH
Live Evil (Vertigo)
An ageing and undignified iron maiden, further proof that heavy metal has irreparably cleaned up its act.
NEW MUSICAL EXPRESS

I'm proud to have "Live Evil" in my collection.
MELODY MAKER

All that's missing is a free sachet of dry ice.
RECORD MIRROR

Black Sabbath without Ozzy Osbourne is like despair without alcohol.
CREEM

BLACK SLATE
Six Plus One (Top Ranking)
Slate firmly pin their Rasta colours on their chests over a parade of musically indifferent tracks.
SOUNDS

BLACKFOOT
Highway Song Blackfoot Live (Atco)
Ageing, beer-bellied Red Injun boogie barons with a line in lyrical sensitivity that makes Coming Blood seem almost Shakespearean . . . a mostly staggering collection of shameless/clueless good time rock'n'roll.
SOUNDS

One of the best hard rock albums I've heard from an American band.
MELODY MAKER

Skiing naked down Mount Everest would only be half the experience of listening to this album.
RECORD MIRROR

BLACKFOOT

BLACKFOOT
Siogo (Atlantic)
In the great tradition of Lynyrd Skynyrd.
MELODY MAKER

BLANCMANGE

BLANCMANGE
Happy Families (London)
A calmly assured collection . . . the flaws are minor and the merits are major.
NEW MUSICAL EXPRESS

Explosive candescence . . . Blancmange set alight the dull skies of popular music.
SOUNDS

The uneasy alliance of down-home George Formby humour and more intense pretensions allows the listener little comfort beyond the conviction that something unusual is happening.
MELODY MAKER

Maybe they should get into trifle, as an element of danger would present a far more appetising dessert.
RECORD MIRROR

BOBBY BLAND
Foolin' With The Blues (Charly)
Sixteen songs and there's literally not one of them that isn't beautiful.
NEW MUSICAL EXPRESS

BLACK FLAG
Everything Went Black (SST)
Strictly amateur hour.
SOUNDS

I still think they're all nuts in LA.
NEW MUSICAL EXPRESS

THE BLASTERS
Non Fiction (Slash)
Heirs to the mantle of John Fogerty and the great legacy of Creedence . . The best from the best.
MELODY MAKER

THE BLASTERS
Over There — Live At The Venue, London (Slash/Warner Bros)
The Blasters pack more spinebending excitement into 20 minutes than most limpdicked little tarts could manage in twice the time . . . brilliant, passionate music.
MELODY MAKER

They're not full of crap.
CREEM

Their music is undeniably top-ranking.
BOSTON ROCK

BLITZ
Second Empire Justice (Future)
Reversing out of the punk cul-de-sac.
SOUNDS

In changing direction for their very survival, Blitz may have gone too far.
MELODY MAKER

BLUE RONDO A LA TURK

BLITZ
Voice Of A Generation (No Future)
Their studied sound comes from a minute dissection of what startled and provoked five years ago.
NEW MUSICAL EXPRESS

A fair sprinkling of imagination.
MELODY MAKER

The best punk debut since the Cockney Rejects...it's more on a par with the Clash's first album.
SOUNDS

KURTIS BLOW
Tough (Mercury)
Must be the worst rap album *ever*. Preposterous, boring, unimaginative, naive, repetitive, arrogant, inarticulate.
MELODY MAKER

KURTIS BLOW

BLUE ORCHIDS
Agents Of Change (Rough Trade)
Slowly, insidiously, like a creeping disease, the Orchids' tubercular melancholy contaminates the senses, weakens the resolve, gnaws at the antibodies of musical expectation and suddenly you're smitten.
MELODY MAKER

BLUE RONDO A LA TURK
Chewing The Fat (Virgin)
One of the most ambitious releases I've heard this year.
MELODY MAKER

The strength of this LP is in its belief, the assumption of some sort of musical rightness...you can stop laughing at Blue Rondo A La Turk.
SOUNDS

Perhaps I shouldn't look a clothes horse in the mouth, but all the songs sound as though they were recorded in a terrible embarrassed hurry simply so the boys could get on with the serious business of having their pictures taken.
NEW MUSICAL EXPRESS

THE BLUES BAND
Brand Loyalty (Arista)
More of the same "old white codgers can still play the blues" type material.
MELODY MAKER

THE BLUES BAND
Bye Bye Blues (Arista)
Those of us who prefer the sharper edge of R&B are only too happy to say bye bye.
MELODY MAKER

BLUE ZOO
Two By Two (Magnet)
Blue Zoo's strength lies in their aping quality.
SOUNDS

A composite of every superficial pop band that ever made "TOTP".
MELODY MAKER

BLURT
Blurt (Red Flame)
A bunch of old-enough-to-know-better, pseudo avant-garde clowns. This record is rubbish.
SOUNDS

THE BOLLOCK BROTHERS
The Last Supper (Charly)
A talent for subversion on a grand scale... the omens for future mayhem look good.
SOUNDS

An interesting and entertaining change of scenery.
MELODY MAKER

It does raise a twisted smile on first hearing, even if subsequent plays generate only profound lassitude.
NEW MUSICAL EXPRESS

GARY US BONDS
On The Line (EMI America)
It's obvious that 'da Boss' has stopped the foolish policy of giving all his best songs away for others to have hits.
RECORD MIRROR

BOW WOW WOW
I Want Candy (EMI)
The songs, great rowdy bursts of energy are irresistible...a group who wanted more than candy.
RECORD MIRROR

Sixteen tracks and a terrible cover! Who could ask for more?
NEW MUSICAL EXPRESS

Obviously shouldn't be taken too seriously.
MELODY MAKER

BOW WOW WOW
When The Going Gets Tough The Tough Get Going (RCA)
Makes for a jolly, carefree and totally meaningless half hour.
RECORD MIRROR

One mess of an album...they sound like "Not The Nine O'Clock News" piss-takes.
SOUNDS

All very brilliant...this is their moment: this is their transitory masterpiece.
NEW MUSICAL EXPRESS

A seamless, glossy slab of manufactured pop...an unflinching triumph of style over content.
CREEM

DAVID BOWIE
Let's Dance (EMI America)
Still has a useful trick or two in hand to keep the new generation of artful dodgers at bay.
MELODY MAKER

Cool, but not quite coolest.
RECORD MIRROR

This miserable ramshackle affair...like something Des O'Connor would come up with.
SOUNDS

This album just goes straight to the heart of it: it is warm, strong, inspiring and useful. Powerful, positive music that dances like a dream and makes you feel ten feet tall.
NEW MUSICAL EXPRESS

DAVID BOWIE
Rare (RCA)
Only fleetingly interesting as a series of footnotes to the various stages of Bowie's career, this haphazard, poorly-annotated collection makes more noise than sense.
MELODY MAKER

BOW WOW WOW

Neither rare nor particularly well done.
NEW MUSICAL EXPRESS

Amusing but inconsequential.
SOUNDS

Hardly essential, but it is fun to listen to.
BOSTON ROCK

Little here shows Bowie at his best.
RECORD MIRROR

THE BOX
Secrets Out (Go! Discs)
Non-outstanding music.
SOUNDS

Enough rawness, abrasion, original vision and bloody-mindedness to knock the bulk of their peers for six.
MELODY MAKER

The Box are to KajaGooGoo what Viv Richards is to Chris Tavare.
NEW MUSICAL EXPRESS

GLENN BRANCA
Symphony No 3 (Crepuscule)
Branca has superseded the art of rock guitar...a musician to be spoken of in the same breath as Cage, Reich and Glass.
SOUNDS

BRAND X
Is There Anything About? (CBS)
Organised jazz-funk flatulence...Musical masturbation which fails to reach a climax.
SOUNDS

LAURA BRANIGAN
Branigan (Atlantic)
Songs of the fallen, of divorcees and sad people singing to the memory of departed youth.
MELODY MAKER

LAURA BRANIGAN
Branigan 2 (Atlantic)
Gloria, the singing weightlifter, has the depth and passion of a cement mixer crashing through a brick wall.
RECORD MIRROR

Pack it up Laura.
MELODY MAKER

A damn lousy excuse for a singing star.
CREEM

THE BROTHERS JOHNSON
Blast! (A&M)
Axe-toting funk mercenaries trained in the Quincy Jones school of hard licks...A six-year career with all the boring bits edited out — what more could you ask?
NEW MUSICAL EXPRESS

THE BROTHERS JOHNSON

DENNIS BROWN
Love Has Found Its Way (A&M)
This kind of crawling to Middle America is as short of musical integrity as it is of the social or political equivalent.
NEW MUSICAL EXPRESS

JAMES BROWN
The Best Of James Brown (Polydor)
To represent Brown properly takes more than two sides of vinyl.
MELODY MAKER

The whole thing reeks of Pickwick or K-Tel, as small an outlay as possible to hit as many mug punters as possible.
NEW MUSICAL EXPRESS

BUCKS FIZZ
Hand Cut (RCA)
You can't despise them because every interview, every photograph seems to be desperately signalling "Help! We are hostages."
NEW MUSICAL EXPRESS

Another year, another costume change.
RECORD MIRROR

What the hell happened to the Doolies?
MELODY MAKER

BUDGIE
Deliver Us From Evil (RCA)
Somewhere between a limp Aerosmith and a heavy Supertramp.
SOUNDS

T-BONE BURNETT
Trap Door (Warner Bros)
Burnett sounds mostly strained and burned out.
MELODY MAKER

ROCKY BURNETTE
Rocky Burnette (EMI)
Boasts at least as much wit and good humour as any of the bright new poplets who regularly decorate the pages of Smash Hits. Don't dismiss a man because of his haircut.
MELODY MAKER

KATE BUSH
The Dreaming (EMI)
Ranges from the ethereal to the frankly unlistenable.
RECORD MIRROR

She's missed the boat this time.
NEW MUSICAL EXPRESS

She has to be praised for bringing in Rolf Harris on his didgeridoo, Percy Edwards with his animal noises.
SOUNDS

THE BUSINESS
Suburban Rebels (Secret)
They might have fooled us once but they ain't fooling anyone now.
SOUNDS

More an exercise in exhausting self parody than the gothic Beefheart claimed by their rabid supporters.
MELODY MAKER

JOHN CALE

THE BYRDS
The Original Singles Volume 2 (CBS)
By no means as sensational a collection as Volume 1. Worth a listen, though.
MELODY MAKER

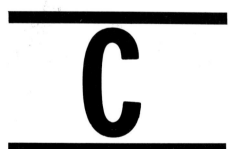

CABARET VOLTAIRE
Ha!! (Rough Trade)
Should you want something that will engage your senses through an exhausting flux of machines, muscles and ethereal flamboyance place your orders now.
MELODY MAKER

Soulless, tuneless, turgid and moronic...It reeks of putrid, self-indulgent nihilism.
SOUNDS

A six tune, live LP recorded in Japan that leaves me cold. I cannot figure out if they are singing in English or Japanese.
BOSTON ROCK

JOHN CALE
Music For A New Society (Ze/Island)
Remarkable...the only consistent commentator on these mean and bloody times, John Cale continues to thunder against the insanities that afflict our lives.
MELODY MAKER

...isn't even parody, it's just stultifyingly boring.
SOUNDS

A not very interesting, dismal and wilfully skimpy record.
CREEM

RANDY CALIFORNIA
Euro-American (Beggars Banquet)
With an open mind and a few pound notes, you could discover there are hours in your life when a little Randy comes in handy. And fact: Randy California is "red" Ken Livingstone's favourite rock performer.
NEW MUSICAL EXPRESS

CAPTAIN BEEFHEART AND THE MAGIC BAND

CAPTAIN BEEFHEART AND THE MAGIC BAND
Ice Cream For Crow (Virgin)
The Captain's back, as unbalanced by the vicissitudes of petty fashion as ever, ploughing an idiosyncratic course through the plastic wastelands like a bulldozer through so much dung.
MELODY MAKER

Living testament to the man's seemingly endless resourcefulness.
CREEM

As disappointments go, this one is serious.
NEW MUSICAL EXPRESS

It seems as though a record was due in the contract before he had quite the chance to formulate new ideas.
BOSTON ROCK

CAPTAIN SENSIBLE
Women And Captains First (A&M)
A joke of an album and not a good one.
RECORD MIRROR

The fag end of Punk doing C&W, MOR and failed 'comedy' jigs: it's really perfection itself!
SOUNDS

This is a dreadful album. Naturally. That's the point of it.
MELODY MAKER

Sensible is quite content to make records that sound dumb, but which obviously aren't. A charming and admirable bit of plastic.
NEW MUSICAL EXPRESS

CARAVAN
Back To Front (Kingdom)
Old soldiers like Caravan never die — they just make bargain bin albums.
MELODY MAKER

KIM CARNES
Voyeur (EMI America)
Tedious mundane sunbronzed Californian mutton.
RECORD MIRROR

Definitely in the running for album of the year.
SOUNDS

CARMEL
Carmel (Red Flame)
The sweet face of minimalism...what impresses most is the overall feel of sincerity.
MELODY MAKER

At certain times to certain ears this could be a novelty record.
NEW MUSICAL EXPRESS

PAUL CARRACK
Suburban Voodoo (Epic)
Strong vinyl evidence to assure his rightful place as one of Britain's finest singers.
MELODY MAKER

ROSEANNE CASH
Somewhere In The Stars (Ariola)
An unfortunate and inexplicable disappointment...a consistently lacklustre performance.
MELODY MAKER

A CERTAIN RATIO
I'd Like To See You Again (Factory)
Full of sharp city clout; snappy, alive, aware ...and, relative to their past, empty.
NEW MUSICAL EXPRESS

Scarcely stretches further than a collection of pedestrian exercises in instrumental dexterity — no doubt fun to play, but boring to listen to.
MELODY MAKER

CHARGE
Perfection (Kamera)
Average is the watchword here.
MELODY MAKER

In any normal musical era, Charge would not get beyond the John Peel Show. They would not get beyond the demo stage. The Marquee is where they would stay.
SOUNDS

CHARGED GBH
City Baby Attacked By Rats (Clay)
Forty minutes of pure hell...a wall of sound that's as fast as premature ejaculation and about as pleasing as piles.
RECORD MIRROR

Heads-down no nonsense mindless cacophony from the word go. Thirteen tracks of high-energy hardcore racket.
SOUNDS

CHARLENE
I've Never Been To Me (Motown)
Full of dime store psychology for the woman who hasn't got a mind to make up.
RECORD MIRROR

PAUL CARRACK

CHIC
Tongue In Chic (Atlantic)
Has its moments — about three in all.
NEW MUSICAL EXPRESS

Dance music for people who shower both
before and after sex.
CREEM

When I played it at a party no one danced.
SOUNDS

CHICAGO
Chicago 16 (Full Moon)
Tolkein stopped at three volumes, "Gardeners Question Time" has just reached its
1500th edition. Chicago are somewhere in
between.
MELODY MAKER

The only reason for 'Chicago 16' is to fill the
gap between 'Chicago 15' and 'Chicago 17'.
RECORD MIRROR

ALEX CHILTON
Live In London (Aura)
Chilton plundering his own past with a self-
destructive nonchalance and a sad, almost
pathetic determination to undermine the
regard of even his most devoted admirers...little more than a soiled testament
to a gutted talent.
MELODY MAKER

Coarse, simplistic, and entirely soulless...
all too typical of one's worst Dingwalls
memories.
NEW MUSICAL EXPRESS

CHINA CRISIS
**Difficult Shapes and Passive Rhythms
(Virgin)**
A thoroughly impressive debut full of poten-
tial hit singles.
MELODY MAKER

Accomplished but deplorably safe...plea-
sant, inoffensive, electrobop, as invigorating
as Depeche Mode on barbs.
NEW MUSICAL EXPRESS

THE CHURCH
The Blurred Crusade (Carrere)
I put a spike into these grooves and am intox-
icated by songs of strength and redemption.
RECORD MIRROR

The Church often become soporific and
academic from the introspective and co-
cooned nature of their idealistic pursuits,
landlocked onto an astral plane of non-
reciprocal emotions.
SOUNDS

ERIC CLAPTON
Money And Cigarettes (Duck)
A man performing his perfunctory duty with
unblinking expertise.
MELODY MAKER

The old fart has dozed his way through yet
another album.
NEW MUSICAL EXPRESS

Clapton's best post-Layla work since 461
Ocean Boulevard.
CREEM

JIMMY CLIFF
Special (CBS)
No rasta indulgence, no underprivileged bit-
terness or blinkered racial exclusion...You
won't hear a better sung, slicker played, more
boldly commercial album all year.
MELODY MAKER

There is something rather ordinary about it.
RECORD MIRROR

In the final analysis, a forward step backwards, a failure with reservations.
NEW MUSICAL EXPRESS

ERIC CLAPTON

CLIMAX BLUES BAND
Sample And Hold (Virgin)
Anti-Climax Blues band would be a better
monicker.
RECORD MIRROR

CLINT EASTWOOD AND GENERAL SAINT
Stop That Train (Greensleeves)
A critical yet comic vision of life on Maggie's
Farm.
NEW MUSICAL EXPRESS

I doubt if many better DJ albums will come
along until their next.
SOUNDS

GEORGE CLINTON
Computer Games (Capitol)
The material is generally listenable.
MELODY MAKER

Below the funk is some serious thinking.
NEW MUSICAL EXPRESS

CLOCK DVA
Advantage (Polydor)
Has good bits and bad bits...will do better
next time.
SOUNDS

Does not contain songs to remember, but it is
new and what's more important, *it is now*.
MELODY MAKER

DVA have always walked a fine line between
pomposity and genius...all too frequently
'Advantage' topples on the wrong side.
NEW MUSICAL EXPRESS

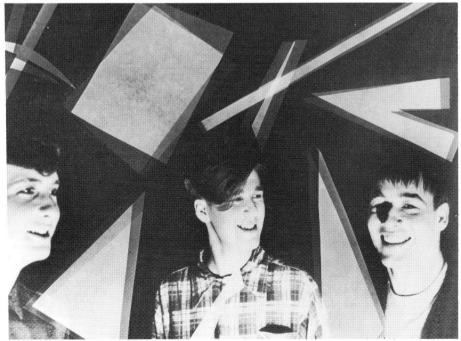
CHINA CRISIS

COATI MUNDI
The Former 12 Year Old Genius (Virgin)
An entertaining, lightweight LP that eventually stretches the jokes and the creator too far.
NEW MUSICAL EXPRESS

A short ugly man with a loud ugly voice.
MELODY MAKER

THE COCONUTS
Don't Take My Coconuts (EMI America)
Delightful deckchair music.
SOUNDS

This sort of thing was done first and best by the Bounty Bar commercials.
NEW MUSICAL EXPRESS

PHIL COLLINS
Hello, I Must Be Going (Virgin)
Collins has played it, and produced it, with a matchless skill that makes him virtually the complete rock and roll entertainer.
SOUNDS

Phil Collins has come a long way since the days when nobody ever saw him playing because Peter Gabriel's headdresses blocked him out from the audience's view.
CREEM

Glutinously stymied by the treacley self-pity of its maker.
NEW MUSICAL EXPRESS

COMATEENS
Pictures On A String (Virgin)
Blueprints for future development.
RECORD MIRROR

A stodgy amalgam of other people's trademarks and soundscapes.
NEW MUSICAL EXPRESS

COATI MUNDI

PHIL COLLINS

COMSAT ANGELS
Fiction (Polydor)
Lacks the clear focus and edge of great pop music.
RECORD MIRROR

Wall-to-wall ennui, angst for the modern sitting room — soft and spongey, nothing too disturbing.
MELODY MAKER

A thoroughly entertaining, diversified yet identifiable batch of songs. Highly recommended.
BOSTON ROCK

ALICE COOPER
Zipper Catches Skin (Warner Bros)
The pitiful sound of Alice blundering into bland mainstream HM.
MELODY MAKER

GREG COPELAND
Revenge Will Come (Geffen)
Varied and evocative...It must be unfortunate to be the only non-superstar on Geffen Records.
MELODY MAKER

JOHNNY COPELAND
Make My Home Where I Hang My Hat (Demon Records)
More emotionally compatible than most of B.B. King's current plaitings of voice and guitar.
MELODY MAKER

THE CRAMPS
Off The Bone (Illegal)
A selection of undead greats dredged from the vaults . . . a desperate power unmatched by the vast majority of the modern bone rattlers.
NEW MUSICAL EXPRESS

A drug-crazed Mansonite voodoo rite in full swing, a neanderthal bunch gorging themselves on B-movies the way most people consume Big Macs.
MELODY MAKER

A hell-fire cocktail of gutter riffing and chattering Rockabilly voodoo strum.
SOUNDS

CRASS
Christ — The Album (Crass)
Obviously, it's not pleasant listening.
NEW MUSICAL EXPRESS

A harsh, heartless drone with a vast reservoir of 'f**ks'...a truly remarkable work, perhaps even Crass's masterpiece.
SOUNDS

CRASS
Yes Sir, I Will (Crass)
Confronts you squarely with the bottom-line truths and fundamental contradictions, matters that should fill you with as much anger as they do Crass.
NEW MUSICAL EXPRESS

Unlistenable and totally bereft of anything approaching excitement or inventiveness.
SOUNDS

The same as the album before it and the one before that and the one before that.
MELODY MAKER

CHRISTOPHER CROSS

CRAZY HOUSE
They Dance Like This From As Far Off As The Crazy House (TW Records)
This could so easily have been a pathetic bedsitter-land dose of self-pity. Instead, it's an asylum of refuge for the emotionally battered.
SOUNDS

CREATION REBEL
Lows And Highs (Cherry Red)
An awesome mixture of the incredible and the incomprehensible.
SOUNDS

THE CREATURES
Feast (Polydor)
Breathlessly exotic and breathtakingly erotic.
MELODY MAKER

Siouxsie is more a cast for the Harley Street couch than the Tarzanic vine.
SOUNDS

CROWN HEIGHTS AFFAIR

The Sonny and Cher of the psychiatric ward.
NEW MUSICAL EXPRESS

MARSHALL CRENSHAW
Field Day (Warner Bros)
Only two of the songs made me consider kicking the Dansette, which has to be some kind of record.
NEW MUSICAL EXPRESS

Still has a lot to say, but he's lost his voice as well as his way here.
MELODY MAKER

More paper roses than full blooms.
SOUNDS

CROSBY, STILLS AND NASH
Allies (Atlantic)
CS&N can't hit those high notes any more.
MELODY MAKER

CHRISTOPHER CROSS
Another Page (Warner Bros)
Songs about sod all.
NEW MUSICAL EXPRESS

CROWN HEIGHTS AFFAIR
Think Positive (De-Lite)
What more is there to say about an album entitled "Think Positive" when its first track is called "Somebody Tell Me What To Do"?
NEW MUSICAL EXPRESS

CULTURE CLUB
Kissing To Be Clever (Virgin)
Culture Club are professionals.
BOSTON ROCK

Sure, sunny, joyous . . . the ultimate example and logical conclusion of the eclectic early '80s spirit of pop.
NEW MUSICAL EXPRESS

It's your loss if you ignore their emotional depth charges.
MELODY MAKER

Immensely irritating. It's like watching a gay at a party prancing around, flouting his bentness as if it's something interesting. And really boring the pants off everyone he contages.
SOUNDS

Okay when you're washing the dishes . . . you can't kiss and be clever at the same time.
CREEM

THE DAMNED
Strawberries (Polydor)
Reaches fewer goals than Hereford United.
NEW MUSICAL EXPRESS

There's little or nothing here you could find fault with; the Damned have every reason to be proud.
MELODY MAKER

If Roger Corman ever gets around to cutting a record it might well turn out like this . . . a jolt to the system. A bright and exciting treat.
SOUNDS

THE DANSE SOCIETY
Seduction (Society Records)
Exudes a sort of Teutonic precision that gives it a vague air of sado-masochism without descending to Banshee-like stridency.
NEW MUSICAL EXPRESS

Tentatively stepping towards fame and fortune, mass popularity and wide exposure. 1983 will be their year.
MELODY MAKER

Deadly dull drivel . . . it all adds up to one mammoth fart in the direction of immature bombast.
SOUNDS

THE DANCING DID
And Did Those Feet (Kamera)
What, on stage, can be vitally funny and furious seems, on record, to become merely idiosyncratic and irksome.
SOUNDS

A cultural brand of electric folk that some call perverted rockabilly . . . Ten songs, each one as wild and challenging as a favourite novel.
MELODY MAKER

THE DARK
The Living End (Fall Out)
The sound is pretty raw and the performances none too brilliant as a lot of alcohol must have been involved.
MELODY MAKER

Little more than a slap-hazard bonus for the few Dark fans still around.
SOUNDS

MILES DAVIS
Star People (CBS)
His best since the comeback...purchase at once.
MELODY MAKER

Midnight muzak for ageing hipsters.
NEW MUSICAL EXPRESS

DANIELLE DAX
Pop-Eyes (Initial)
Short, sharp pop songs that retain the idiosyncratic edge of humour and perversity.
SOUNDS

DEAD KENNEDYS

DEAD KENNEDYS
Plastic Surgery Disasters (Statik/Alternative Tentacles)
There is still a distinct necessity to hone the hysteria into a more controllable chaos.
NEW MUSICAL EXPRESS

Every song on this album is played with the fake manic intensity of Benny Hill punk.
MELODY MAKER

An indispensable addition to every home.
SOUNDS

DEAD MAN'S SHADOW
The 4 P's (Expulsion)
Possibly the last important punk album.
MELODY MAKER

A divine revelation...the second coming even.
SOUNDS

DEEP PURPLE
Live In London (Harvest)
Enough's enough already.
MELODY MAKER

DEF LEPPARD
Pyromania (Vertigo)
You'll be astonished by the new-found maturity, reeling from the soaring grandeur of the song arrangements, awestruck by the sheer brooding atmospherics.
SOUNDS

Def Leppard huff and they puff but they just cannot blow the house down.
MELODY MAKER

A good lite beer version of heavy metal.
CREEM

THE DEFECTS
Defective Breakdown (WXYZ Records)
One of the most accomplished punk LPs I've come across for a long time...imaginative, stimulating and endearing.
MELODY MAKER

Simple-minded Mickey Mouse rabble-rousing.
NEW MUSICAL EXPRESS

GABI DELGADO
Mistress (Virgin)
A dull greyness hangs over 'Mistress'. Whatever splashes of colours there are do not alter the grinding repetition or Delgado's irksome heavy breathing obscene phone call like vocals.
NEW MUSICAL EXPRESS

Simple English lyrics about complicated emotions sung in a calm, tough German accent.
BOSTON ROCK

DEMON
The Plague (Clay)
Moves from anger to melancholy and from sarcasm to sincerity in its horrific account of nuclear war.
SOUNDS

DEPECHE MODE
A Broken Frame (Mute)
Puerile infatuations papering over anonymity...merely a collection of pop hieroglyphics.
MELODY MAKER

It is possible to accept this calculated kind of blandness when it is just a three minute stab at the charts.
SOUNDS

Those who can only take the hard rusting edges that lie here and there as a reality will continue to liken Depeche Mode to a handful of sand wrapped in a handkerchief. But then, there's no need to shriek until the cows speak the language of God.
NEW MUSICAL EXPRESS

DEUTSCH AMERIKANISCHE FREUENDSCHAFT
Fur Immer (Virgin)
DAF's noise is the grime under the painted fingernail of modern pop, the stain on the silk sheet.
MELODY MAKER

Their pale constructions tick over at such speed that their luxuriance is lost to a race between singer and circuitry.
NEW MUSICAL EXPRESS

Someone's robot just died and DAF have written the funeral service.
SOUNDS

DEF LEPPARD

DEVO
Oh, No! It's Devo (Virgin)
So astoundingly average that it must deserve some kind of medal. Jesus, it's so average you'll despise it.
MELODY MAKER

Certainly enjoyable but it yields no surprises.
BOSTON ROCK

Perhaps that's the idea, presenting the superior as the ordinary so that the sub-spuds (us) can understand and maybe appreciate this integral part of DEVO's initial reversal of evolution masterplan.
SOUNDS

So merciless and supercilious it's HIGHLY enjoyable.
NEW MUSICAL EXPRESS

DEVO

DEXY'S MIDNIGHT RUNNERS
Geno (EMI)
A fine guided tour of the raging soulful power which the surly Rowland used to exude consistently back then.
MELODY MAKER

One part magic, ninety nine parts monotony.
NEW MUSICAL EXPRESS

DIRT
Never Mind Dirt — Here's The Bollocks (Crass)
This relentless barrage of complaints, warnings, worries and general discontented rantings inadvertently results in yet more misery.
SOUNDS

BUCK DHARMA
Flat Out (Portrait)
The usual smoothly-turned powerchord stuff which passes for "rack'n'rawl" in the States.
MELODY MAKER

DIAMOND HEAD
Borrowed Time (MCA)
Head and shoulders above the rest...the standard is irrepressibly high.
SOUNDS

We're talking excellence.
MELODY MAKER

RONNIE JAMES DIO
Holy Diver (Mercury)
Steaming, sizzling'n'ball-breaking...feels like being repeatedly bayoneted.
SOUNDS

DIRE STRAITS
Love Over Gold (Vertigo)
They're staggering under the weight of commercial expectations, trying to make Art.
NEW MUSICAL EXPRESS

The most adventurous and mesmeric Dire Straits album so far.
SOUNDS

Album of the year, then? No, it's worth more than that.
MELODY MAKER

Reminds me of the theme for a soap advertisement.
RECORD MIRROR

DOLL BY DOLL
Grand Passion (Magnet)
Somehow that name seems destined to be forever synonymous with broken promises and lost opportunities.
MELODY MAKER

DOLLAR
The Dollar Album (WEA)
Everything about them — from their height to their sound to their fights — is on a very small scale.
NEW MUSICAL EXPRESS

The obvious band to sell in Mothercare shops.
SOUNDS

DOME
To Speak (Uniton)
A kind of flippancy where the means of

creation are more important than the final product.
SOUNDS

DREAM SYNDICATE
The Days Of Wine And Roses (Sounds)
A living cultural epitaph to the Velvet Underground...a chain-link offensive of faultlessly observed and famously played proto-plagiarism.
SOUNDS

DR FEELGOOD
Fast Women & Slow Horses (Chiswick)
Quintessential R&B merchants with a quiet, educated savoir faire.
SOUNDS

A fine testament to the ceaseless work they've put in during the last decade.
MELODY MAKER

A whole bonanza of stuff that's been done better before.
NEW MUSICAL EXPRESS

DR JOHN
Dr John Plays Mac Rebennack (Demon)
Elegant, witty, soulful, inventive and powerful in the most relaxed manner possible... There's not much to say about this album, except that it is wonderful.
NEW MUSICAL EXPRESS

DUFFO
Lexicon (PVK Records)
A talentless lamebrain who's been allowed to inflict excruciating aural murder...it completely ruined a quiet Sunday at home.
MELODY MAKER

DIRE STRAITS

48

DOLLAR

E

EARTH, WIND AND FIRE
Powerlight (CBS)
Perhaps Earth Wind And Fire should be calling themselves Terribly Boring And Dull.
RECORD MIRROR

Strong melodies, compulsive arrangement and commendable lyrics.
MELODY MAKER

SHEENA EASTON
Madness, Money And Music (EMI)
...the worst kind of clichéd dross.
MELODY MAKER

Germ-free...meticulous in its blandness.
SOUNDS

ECHO AND THE BUNNYMEN
Porcupine (Korova)
'Porcupine' groans behind bars, an animal trapped by its own defences.
NEW MUSICAL EXPRESS

T.S. Eliot in hand, Leonard Cohen on the brain.
RECORD MIRROR

A pimply groan passing for melancholy vocals full of pain.
SOUNDS

They might climb Everest the hard way...if only they could find a map.
MELODY MAKER

EEK-A-MOUSE
Skidip (Greensleeves)
"Ben gen gen a beng-geng-geng geng." With ad-libbing like that, you know it's Eek-A-Mouse you're dealing with.
SOUNDS

EF BAND
Deep Cut (Ewita)
A load of hoary old crud.
RECORD MIRROR

ELOY
Planets (Heavy Metal Worldwide)
Probably the most cosmic and celestial piece of stupendous lyrical and narrative surrealism in the last five years.
SOUNDS

ELOY
Time To Turn (Heavy Metal Worldwide)
The scintillating sequel to the galactically far-out 'Planets' platter.
SOUNDS

Germans who take themselves far too seriously...I'd like them to stop all this as soon as possible.
MELODY MAKER

ERAZERHEAD
The Rumble Of The East (Flicknife)
...straight from the Joey Ramone School Of Yodelling Handbook.
MELODY MAKER

If you buy this LP you need full frontal surgery...a severe case of Ramones necrophilia.
SOUNDS

DAVID ESSEX
Stage Struck (Mercury)
What can you say about a man who started his public life as Jesus Christ and worked his way down?
RECORD MIRROR

EURYTHMICS
Sweet Dreams (Are Made Of This) (RCA)
The kind of record you can eat without ruining your appetite.
RECORD MIRROR

Annie Lennox is possibly the most fluid, versatile and emotional British female singer since the great Dusty Springfield.
SOUNDS

Orgasmically close to perfection, one of the most important albums of '83.
MELODY MAKER

PHIL EVERLY
Phil Everly (Capitol)
Wouldn't be out of place coming over the PA down at your local Tesco's.
RECORD MIRROR

About as much *class* as Lemmy's laundry.
SOUNDS

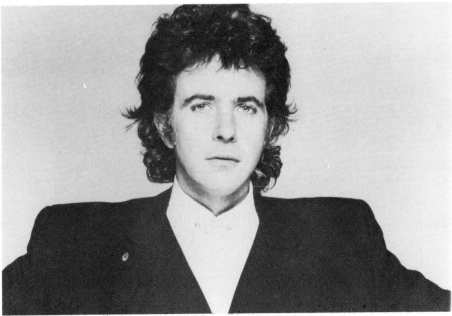
DAVID ESSEX

49

EXPLAINER
Man From The Ghetto (Sun Burst)
A tornado from Trinidad and nearby islands in the sun...as satisfying as the loudest belch you've ever done.
SOUNDS

EYELESS IN GAZA
Drumming The Beating Heart (Cherry Red)
The listener becomes transported into a cocoon of floating, pastel moods as intricate and fragile as a snowflake.
SOUNDS

The untogetherness is inspiring...the vocals have the haunting qualities of the best of folk ballad singers.
RECORD MIRROR

It's time they stopped gazing through windows and opened a few doors instead.
MELODY MAKER

FAD GADGET
Under The Flag (Mute)
A constant delight of modern electronic soundtrack with passion.
SOUNDS

Ultimately a pointless record, whose elucidations of misery and sickness is so relentless that there's no room for fondness or motivation.
NEW MUSICAL EXPRESS

...tears are not enough.
MELODY MAKER

DONALD FAGEN
The Nightfly (Warner Bros)
Musically, lyrically, spiritually and concept-wise this album's a bummer.
MELODY MAKER

A mandatory purchase for all old farts with a few Steely Dan albums stashed away at the back of the pile.
NEW MUSICAL EXPRESS

FAITH GLOBAL
The Same Mistakes (Survival)
A few arresting moments, but sadly these turn out to be false dawns.
MELODY MAKER

Somewhere between melodrama and monotony.
NEW MUSICAL EXPRESS

MARIANNE FAITHFULL
A Child's Adventure (Island)
The same sad album she's been making since 1974 — the same sad story about the same sad life.
MELODY MAKER

So long Marianne.
NEW MUSICAL EXPRESS

Bland and uninteresting.
SOUNDS

I wonder if Richard Thompson is looking for another female foil these days.
CREEM

THE FALL
Room To Live (Kamera)
Scarcely more substantial than a tawdry collection of scantily clad doodles.
NEW MUSICAL EXPRESS

...suggests he's been smoking too much dope lately.
MELODY MAKER

FASTWAY
Fastway (CBS)
An innate ability to imbue uninspired songs with sheer pace and excitement.
MELODY MAKER

It surely is a sad state of affairs that one of Britain's newest, potentially most promising rock groups seems blissfully content to ape the musical style of a band whose heyday

FAD GADGET

was all of ten years ago.
SOUNDS

FAT LARRY'S BAND
Breakin' Out (Virgin)
If things get really steaming you'll need something harder than this to keep people on their feet.
MELODY MAKER

THE FITS
You're Nothing, You're Nowhere (Rondolet)
...just a competent punk band.
SOUNDS

They tackle a wide range of subjects, from vandalism and teenage independence.
MELODY MAKER

MARIANNE FAITHFULL

THE FIXX
Reach The Beach (MCA)
Witlessly cross-fertilised pseudo-rock guaranteed to offend no-one.
MELODY MAKER

The Sad Cafe of new age pop.
SOUNDS

Prat pop at its worst.
NEW MUSICAL EXPRESS

A FLOCK OF SEAGULLS
Listen (Jive)
Patterned, pre-formed and desperately uninteresting.
MELODY MAKER

Ridiculously uneven.
SOUNDS

FOREIGNER

THE FIXX

FLUX OF PINK INDIANS
Strive To Survive Causing Least Suffering Possible (Spiderleg)
Boiling hard-rock tension and passion-racked, soul-searching sentiments.
SOUNDS

THE FLYING PICKETS
Live At The Albany Empire (AVM)
A cosily nostalgic smorgasbord of doo wop, Motown and pop standards.
NEW MUSICAL EXPRESS

PATRIK FITZGERALD
Gifts And Telegrams (Red Flame)
One of the most indulgent exercises I've ever had the misfortune to listen to. It crawls and snivels, dripping in self-pity and weak-willed defeatism.
MELODY MAKER

Fitzgerald has still got a lot of worthwhile things to say.
NEW MUSICAL EXPRESS

The little man with the huge heart is back!
SOUNDS

ELLEN FOLEY
Another Breath (Epic)
I have this theory that Pat Benatar, Joan Jett, Laura Branigan and Ellen Foley are one and the same person in different wigs.
MELODY MAKER

Floundering on the slippery face of American rock.
RECORD MIRROR

LITA FORD
Out For Blood (Mercury)
Handles her guitar with all the skill of a heart surgeon performing an operation, but without the clinical sterility.
SOUNDS

FOREIGNER
Records (Atlantic)
Well nigh faultless!...It'll fry your corpuscles to a crisp.
SOUNDS

File beside the Abba and Madness compilations for a three-ring circus of pop music.
NEW MUSICAL EXPRESS

THE FOUR TOPS
One More Mountain (Casablanca)
Not about to eclipse their Motown heyday, but coming much closer than most of us would have thought possible.
NEW MUSICAL EXPRESS

One can only assume they were hurried into making an LP that was only half-written at the time.
MELODY MAKER

ARETHA FRANKLIN
Jump To It (Arista)
A patchy affair.
NEW MUSICAL EXPRESS

Runs the fine line between genuinely moving soul and typical, Las Vegas syrup.
MELODY MAKER

FRIDA

ELLEN FOLEY

GLENN FREY
No Fun Aloud (Asylum)
If you can imagine the Eagles' limpest track, so laidback that it's supine, then you don't need to hear this to get the idea.
MELODY MAKER

FRIDA
Something's Going On (Epic)
Pop music with the pop taken out. Predictability has no place in music.
SOUNDS

THE FUNBOY THREE
Waiting (Chrysalis)
A portrait of what being British really means if you're working class.
MELODY MAKER

Rude boys don't get older, just more articulate.
SOUNDS

The fully-rounded sonic sculpture that they have ultimately always fallen short of in the past.
NEW MUSICAL EXPRESS

FAT LARRY'S BAND

G

NICK GARVEY

PETER GABRIEL
Peter Gabriel (Charisma)
A symptom of the spiritual paucity of modern life!
SOUNDS

An alienated artist trapped in Bath struggling with the contradictions of civilisation, the soul, our very existence...
NEW MUSICAL EXPRESS

Gabriel walks a fine line between brilliance and churning out a load of old cobblers.
RECORD MIRROR

PETER GABRIEL
Plays Live (Charisma)
'Biko' towers above everything else here, a giant amongst dwarves.
NEW MUSICAL EXPRESS

As dead a turkey as Mike Oldfield...a member of rock's Range Rover set.
SOUNDS

The cumulative effect is akin to eating rather too many portions of Spotted Dick — in short, indigestion.
MELODY MAKER

JERRY GARCIA
Run For The Roses (Arista)
The Grateful Dead and their many tributaries continue to produce records of little passing interest and no importance at all.
MELODY MAKER

NICK GARVEY
Blue Skies (Virgin)
Topples badly into the dense drowning world of mid-Atlantic spew-along slush that's perfectly acceptable for the Radio 2 granny market.
MELODY MAKER

MARVIN GAYE
Midnight Love (CBS)
The master is back.
RECORD MIRROR

Not a comeback but a continuation of a very special talent.
MELODY MAKER

Boldly steps where few have previously ventured.
NEW MUSICAL EXPRESS

GBH
City Baby Attacked By Rats (Clay)
A brutal physical assault with no place for things like songs or tunes.
MELODY MAKER

Yet another crass compendium of punky gobbledygook.
NEW MUSICAL EXPRESS

MARVIN GAYE

J. GEILS BAND
Showtime (EMI America)
The sickly aftertaste of stagnant recycled third rate Yankee rock'n'roll.
MELODY MAKER

Doubly shoddy when compared directly to their superb 1972 live album "Full House".
NEW MUSICAL EXPRESS

GILLAN
Magic (Virgin)
Rancid flailalong epileptic boogie...our Ian really sounds in distress here.
SOUNDS

Gillan are artisans, long-serving hacks whose brains have long since turned to Birds Eye frozen spinach. The sell-by date on most of these songs expired sometime in the Sixties.
MELODY MAKER

THE GIST
Embrace The Herd (Rough Trade)
Scarcely satisfactory.
SOUNDS

No tingles.
NEW MUSICAL EXPRESS

THE GLADIATORS
Back To Roots (L'Escargot)
Happy to jog in the shadow of their former reputations.
MELODY MAKER

Last night's smoke merely makes the room stuffy the morning after.
NEW MUSICAL EXPRESS

THE GO-BETWEENS
Before Hollywood (Rough Trade)
Trying to sound suggestive and enigmatic, the trio sounds simply vague and posturing.
MELODY MAKER

Some of the most beautiful music I've ever heard.
NEW MUSICAL EXPRESS

Australians and proud of it . . . one of the best albums this year so far.
SOUNDS

THE GO-GO'S
Vacation (IRS)
The Go-Go's act as kid sisters to Asia in the family business that shouldn't be running American music.
NEW MUSICAL EXPRESS

Only one lucky dip of ideas from first track to last.
MELODY MAKER

So simple-minded and bland it makes the gentle listener want to stand up and scream "Gonorrhoea!" even if he can't spell it.
SOUNDS

Through their cheery music, the Go-Go's have liberated us all.
CREEM

GOLDEN EARRING
Cut (Mercury)
Hippy hasbeens.
MELODY MAKER

THE GO-BETWEENS

STUART MOXHAM (THE GIST)

GRANDMASTER FLASH AND THE FURIOUS FIVE
The Message (Sugarhill)
They do have a deal more versatility than some gave them credit for.
SOUNDS

A crazy exhilarating ride, a masterful collage of noise.
MELODY MAKER

The whole thing reeks of a group mellowing their approach to suit the American mass market.
NEW MUSICAL EXPRESS

GRAND PRIX
Samurai (Chrysalis)
Spectacularly unoriginal.
MELODY MAKER

EDDY GRANT
Killer On The Rampage (Ice)
The range and eclecticism he can build on sturdy but apparently limited foundations is quite startling.
NEW MUSICAL EXPRESS

Mildly militant black music that's perfectly palatable for even the most superficial white radio programmer.
MELODY MAKER

As formularised as a 'Crossroads' programme.
RECORD MIRROR

About as dangerous as a dead wombat.
SOUNDS

AL GREEN
Precious Lord (Hi)
Oh Lordy, when they get religion, they really get it bad.
RECORD MIRROR

ZAINE GRIFF
Figvres (Polydor)
Without wishing to exaggerate, it does seem that the songs consist of a basic pair of chords.
MELODY MAKER

BILLY GRIFFIN
Be With Me (CBS)
His dull sense of the grandiose epic is hardly helped by his sounding like a whippet drowning in a vat of mollasses.
NEW MUSICAL EXPRESS

THE GUN CLUB
Miami (Animal)
Some hybrid of punk/swamp/blues/voodoo/ country / horror / rock. Love 'em to death beyond.
NEW MUSICAL EXPRESS

Every track shines like a fresh drop of blood.
CREEM

GYMSLIPS
Rocking With The Renees (Abstract)
X-Ray Spex revisited!... Ladylike they ain't. And that is their strength.
NEW MUSICAL EXPRESS

A simultaneous sense of professionalism and naivety; fabulous detail and foul play.
MELODY MAKER

Ronnie Biggs-period Pistols diluted by terrific tunes that are high on hummability and moderately ribald verbals.
SOUNDS

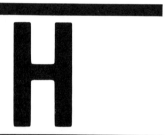

SAMMY HAGAR
Three Lock Box (Geffen)
A pulverising masterpiece of pacing and sentiment.
RECORD MIRROR

A mellowing out seems to be on hand.
SOUNDS

SAMMY HAGAR
The Very Best (Capitol)
He overshadows the likes of Blackmore and Michael Schenker to a startling degree.
MELODY MAKER

HALL AND OATES
H$_2$O (RCA)
Almost the only two people writing mature love songs.
SOUNDS

A perfect exercise in their timely synthesis.
MELODY MAKER

No sting, no bite, not even a gentle nip.
NEW MUSICAL EXPRESS

PETER HAMILL
Enter K (Naive)
While intellect holds the upper hand, instinct does not disappear without trace.
NEW MUSICAL EXPRESS

Testimony to the man's idiosyncratic tenacity.
MELODY MAKER

HERBIE HANCOCK
Quartet (CBS)
Its nearest visual equivalent would be a handful of diamonds spilled onto black velvet.
NEW MUSICAL EXPRESS

HANOI ROCKS
Back To Mystery City (Lick)
Hanoi Rocks, the Woolworths of rock'n'roll, have stepped into Harrods at last.
MELODY MAKER

Proof that there's life left yet in the Rod Stewart school of frontpersonship.
NEW MUSICAL EXPRESS

An X-rated T Rex, Mott in bondage pants, the Stones for guttersnipes.
SOUNDS

HUNTERS & COLLECTORS

HANOI ROCKS
Self Destruction Blues (Johanna Import)
A mixture of raw energy and pure genius, their talent knows no bounds.
SOUNDS

THE HAPPY FAMILY
The Man On Your Street (4AD)
It barbs your brain with a bristle of deadly hooks — its theatrical flourish underpinned with a sharp, jazzy dislocation dance.
NEW MUSICAL EXPRESS

What a disaster!... too ridiculous for words.
SOUNDS

ROY HARPER
Work Of Heart (Public)
For the faithful who have forgotten just why they started listening in the first place.
MELODY MAKER

EMMYLOU HARRIS
Last Date (Warner Bros)
So lacking in spirit that it resembles the dustiest of museums.
NEW MUSICAL EXPRESS

HAWKWIND, FRIENDS & RELATIONS
Twice Upon A Time (Flicknife)
Move over 23 Skidoo and tell P Orridge the news; the Hawkwinds are back in town.
NEW MUSICAL EXPRESS

Yet another compilation that few people really need. Garbage.
MELODY MAKER

HAYSI FANTAYZEE
Battle Hymns For Children Singing (Regard)
Imagine 2000 Zulus singing along to the Maccelsfield Brass Band in the wilds of Siberia.
RECORD MIRROR

A real stinker...rather like watching the home movies of total strangers.
NEW MUSICAL EXPRESS

A snippet of contemporary pop modes.
SOUNDS

Merely eighties equivalents of 'Chirpy chirpy cheep cheep' — banal gobbledegook.
MELODY MAKER

EMMYLOU HARRIS

NONA HENDRYX

HEADPINS
Turn It Loud (Atlantic)
No thanks, I'd rather just gently break it across my knee.
RECORD MIRROR

Headpins are not in the record business to forward any spurious theories about subtlety.
MELODY MAKER

HEAVEN 17
The Luxury Gap (Virgin)
Their early whizzkidry has matured into a sophisticated yet pointless intelligence.
NEW MUSICAL EXPRESS

Heaven 17 need to give the gadgets a break and get their hands dirty.
MELODY MAKER

A big blank nothing at the end of a very long leash. That they are named after an Anthony Burgess idea merely compounds their dreadfulness.
SOUNDS

RICHARD HELL AND THE VOIDOIDS
Destiny Street (Red Star/ID Records)
Plagiaristic, backward-looking and safe. But pretty good, all the same.
SOUNDS

A five-year-on perspective on the post-punk recession, a haphazard, breathless one-take

quality that's almost heretical in the modern nu-music marketplace.
CREEM

A dreadful cacophony.
RECORD MIRROR

JIMI HENDRIX
The Jimi Hendrix Concerts (CBS)
Exciting news indeed; an ESSENTIAL posthumous Hendrix album.
MELODY MAKER

STEVE HILLAGE

The only instrumentalist that rock music has yet produced who could legitimately be called a genius . . . this collection certainly does the man and his work no dishonour.
NEW MUSICAL EXPRESS

The best Hendrix release in eleven years.
CREEM

NONA HENDRYX
Nona Hendryx (RCA)
An unholy alliance of soul/rock/disco/reggae and pop. One of the finest, most distinguished contemporary soul voices.
NEW MUSICAL EXPRESS

In the current soul stakes there's little around to touch this record. Not Marvin Gaye, David Bowie or any of the other old pretenders.
MELODY MAKER

KEVIN HEWICK
Such Hunger For Love (Cherry Red)
Hewick's *Crossroads*-style voice and his faltering, languid projection seem to *support* the inertia he describes rather than cut a swathe of intellect through it.
SOUNDS

HIGH INERGY
So Right (Motown)
Repetitive disco pap at its most insipid.
SOUNDS

Little girls trying mummy's shoes on.
NEW MUSICAL EXPRESS

STEVE HILLAGE
For To Next (Virgin)
Still a likeably sincere hippy, but one who now makes, sadly, dreadful albums.
NEW MUSICAL EXPRESS

HUNTERS & COLLECTORS
Hunters & Collectors (Virgin)
An Australian band worth taking seriously . . . Hunt and collect.
MELODY MAKER

To those seeking the 'down' in down under, this must be heaven.
SOUNDS

Australian Gothic . . . a strung-out band from a strung-out place . . . a never-ending truck-journey through silent, arid wastes.
NEW MUSICAL EXPRESS

THE (HYPOTHETICAL) POETS
Around The World With (Hypothetical)
A second division Residents.
SOUNDS

Sounds better on paper than on a record-player.
NEW MUSICAL EXPRESS

Anyone who produces an electronic sea shanty must be worth a closer look.
MELODY MAKER

ICEHOUSE

ICEHOUSE
Love In Motion (Chrysalis)
Here it comes again like last night's onions . . . same LP of tawdry and inane crap.
NEW MUSICAL EXPRESS

ICEHOUSE
Primitive Man (Chrysalis)
A carefully-worked collection of atmosphere just waiting for a chance to invade your imagination.
MELODY MAKER

The sheer ordinariness of the tastefully monotonous music inspires nowt but sheer mental sloth.
NEW MUSICAL EXPRESS

BILLY IDOL
Billy Idol (Chrysalis)
A scoop of gutless cosmetic perjury masquerading as dancefloor dynamism, a floundering void of watered-down pop.
SOUNDS

IMAGINATION
In The Heat Of The Night (R&B)
Quality music wrapped in showbusiness, escapist music for these ha! ha! hard times.
MELODY MAKER

Once seduced, the listener is left unsatisfied.
RECORD MIRROR

So splendidly crass that they thwart analysis . . . a laid-back platter of plastic erotica, a wet dream sponge.
SOUNDS

IMAGINATION
Night Dubbing (Red Bus)
Marking time, making money, but not delivering the goods.
RECORD MIRROR

The most exciting reading of British dance music this year.
SOUNDS

THE INDIVIDUALS
Fields (Plexus)
They shoplift from only the best stores, and they wear it well.
NEW MUSICAL EXPRESS

INFRA-RIOT
Still Out Of Order (Secret)
Proves conclusively that you can be a shit-kicking, dirt-dragging, hell-raising punk band while at the same time offering thought and versatility and melody and originality.
MELODY MAKER

IRON MAIDEN
Piece Of Mind (EMI)
The strongest heavy metal band around.
MELODY MAKER

GREGORY ISAACS
Lovers Rock (Pre)
Unrivalled as reggae's foremost, charismatic ambassador.
MELODY MAKER

Guaranteed to cut a path, straight and true, to the doors of the hardest heart.
NEW MUSICAL EXPRESS

GREGORY ISAACS
Night Nurse (Island)
Seldom can a record have been made more suited to post-coital tenderness.
MELODY MAKER

More tasty than a plate of grade one oysters and cheaper to boot.
SOUNDS

THE ISLEY BROTHERS
Between The Sheets (Epic)
Recoupled to their best form, a funk record to outstrip all comers. And after all these years they've finally got themselves some decent trousers.
NEW MUSICAL EXPRESS

IMAGINATION

J

JERMAINE JACKSON
Let Me Tickle Your Fancy (Motown)
A man determined to make seamlessly crafted pop funk...the final result sits like an unavailable jewel in a neat glass case.
MELODY MAKER

MICHAEL JACKSON

MICHAEL JACKSON
Thriller (Epic)
An above-average, slick pop/soul album in today's market, it isn't impressive in the context of the Jackson(s) previous work. In some ways, it's just dull.
CREEM

The overall feeling is that of a barely developed artist being given too much artistic control.
NEW MUSICAL EXPRESS

If I was Jackson, I'd ditch everyone he's ever worked with and hunt around for some new talent.
MELODY MAKER

MILLIE JACKSON
Hard Times (Spring)
Millie Jackson's act wore extremely thin a few years ago.
NEW MUSICAL EXPRESS

THE JAM
Dig The New Breed (Polydor)
It is fitting that The Jam should bow out with a live LP...we shan't see their like again for a long time.
MELODY MAKER

Inevitably, this is more of a souvenir than an art statement.
RECORD MIRROR

DAVID SYLVIAN (JAPAN)

Sublime sound, sublime vision — The Jam were the best.
NEW MUSICAL EXPRESS

With typical flair for the dramatic, they depart not with a whimper, but with a bang!
BOSTON ROCK

RICK JAMES
Throwin' Down (Gordy/Motown)
His priorities are getting laid, getting high, getting rich.
CREEM

Judging from this, old Rick is running out of ideas.
SOUNDS

PHILIP JAP

PHILIP JAP
Philip Jap (A&M)
Tries to be new and youthful but comes over tired and ugly.
RECORD MIRROR

To anybody with any sense, Jap is as useful and as stale as rotting bread.
MELODY MAKER

JAPAN
Oil On Canvas (Virgin)
Not Japan at their best — they never achieved their potential — but at least it's the best they could do under ironic circumstances.
MELODY MAKER

All very Habitat: elegant but with simple curves, très ergonomic, adding a touch of sophistication to any colour scheme.
RECORD MIRROR

A meaningless collection of half-baked, raggedy-arsed ideas that were too asinine to have been articulated clearly.
SOUNDS

Japan's beauty really does seem to be skin deep: knee deep in stately but vapid muzak.
NEW MUSICAL EXPRESS

GARLAND JEFFREYS
Guts For Love (Epic)
A load of butch macho bollocks.
MELODY MAKER

Garland Jeffreys is a fine example of what happens when rock'n'roll grows up.
CREEM

JOAN JETT
Bad Reputation (Epic)
Cleverly blends the American version of straight ahead punk with the influence of great English eccentrics like Glitter and Marc Bolan.
MELODY MAKER

An ugly, stinking record, a clot of three-year-old demos whipped and scraped into what the producer presumably imagines is a tough rock'n'roll album.
NEW MUSICAL EXPRESS

RICHARD JOBSON
Ten Thirty On A Summer Night (Crepuscule)
A self-indulgence lovingly planned but poorly performed.
MELODY MAKER

ELTON JOHN

ELTON JOHN
Too Low For Zero (Rocket)
Simply brilliant and surprising only in its unflawed consistency...it makes you feel great to be alive!
SOUNDS

If nothing else it might help to pay for a decent midfield player, so they can cut out that long ball crap next season.
MELODY MAKER

RICKIE LEE JONES
Girl At Her Volcano (Warner Bros)
Literally the worst record I ever remember hearing in all my 50 years in the be-bop business...most people sing with more pizzazz and projection in the bath.
NEW MUSICAL EXPRESS

JOURNEY
New Frontiers (CBS)
The most coherent and complete album that Journey have released and it's virtually a flawless killer.
SOUNDS

An arthritic collection of high budget but low impact songs.
RECORD MIRROR

A rubbish album.
MELODY MAKER

JUDAS PRIEST
Screaming For Vengeance (CBS)
All the hallmarks of the second rate...it's not the tired, inflexible music that stupefies but more the gormless imagery, like Joy Division at their worst.
NEW MUSICAL EXPRESS

GRACE JONES

GRACE JONES
Living My Life (Island)
Proof that Grace Jones can cut the puppet strings from around her neck and still come up smiling.
MELODY MAKER

She's still enough to make brave men nervous in the back of a taxi.
CREEM

JUNIOR
Inside Lookin' Out (Mercury)
Comfortable and inoffensive.
RECORD MIRROR

Junior is trapped inside this chamber of horrors, looking out at what he could've been.
NEW MUSICAL EXPRESS

K

KAJAGOOGOO
White Feathers (EMI)
You have to admit that mindless trash has really come up in the world.
NEW MUSICAL EXPRESS

The lyrics and vocals seem little more than an excuse to include Limahl in the group's photo sessions.
RECORD MIRROR

These boys only SEEM like fools.
SOUNDS

An LP which makes you feel *more stupid* as you listen to it...Shove it. There's cheaper ways to be sick.
MELODY MAKER

KANSAS
Vinyl Confessions (Kirshner)
They've released 1974's Album of the Year six or seven times now and they've got it down to a skit.
CREEM

MICK KARN
Titles (Virgin)
Most of the tracks are sombre, oriental or Indian inspired instrumentals.
MELODY MAKER

Doesn't contain nearly enough revelations.
NEW MUSICAL EXPRESS

His frenetic excursions resemble the bowel movements of a constipated volcano. Although we live in the hope of pyrotechnics, we instead hear only dull farts and sickening belches.
SOUNDS

MICK KARN

KC AND THE SUNSHINE BAND
All In A Night's Work (Epic)
Dance music without frills, cumbersome brains or excessive originality.
NEW MUSICAL EXPRESS

An album with no thrust, weak rhythms, few melodies and no songs.
MELODY MAKER

KID CREOLE AND THE COCONUTS
Wise Guy (Ze/Sire)
You may not need to think when your feet just go, but if you're an intellectual stuck-in-the-mud like myself who likes to do both at the same time, Darnell and Company have just what the witch doctor ordered.
CREEM

GREG KIHN BAND
Kihnspiracy (Beserkley)
Blander than the music you get in between films at the cinema.
RECORD MIRROR

About as interesting as watching somebody mend a plug.
NEW MUSICAL EXPRESS

Vital it ain't, but pleasurably harmless it is.
SOUNDS

KILLING JOKE
Ha — Killing Joke Live (EG Records)
Captures all the excitement and power that make Killing Joke a live act of the highest calibre.
MELODY MAKER

Rock'n'roll bathed in the desperate, dark little dreams of gobbledegook.
RECORD MIRROR

The music here is miserable, underachieving garbage.
SOUNDS

KILLING JOKE
Fire Dances (EG)
Funny peculiar.
NEW MUSICAL EXPRESS

Reminded me of ritual murder in New York subways, cocaine abuse, wanking and lots of dumb, dirty kids with Magic-Marker painted faces running amok in the sewers.
SOUNDS

KING SUNNY ADE AND HIS AFRICAN BEATS
JuJu Music (Island)
Transcending all cultural complications, Ju-ju music should be enthusiastically welcomed by anyone who looks in despair for a reviving ripple in the stagnant pool of Western pop.
MELODY MAKER

KING SUNNY ADE AND HIS AFRICAN BEATS
Synchro System (Island)
The most scintillant and perfectly honed African record to be customised for European ears to date.
NEW MUSICAL EXPRESS

KID CREOLE AND THE COCONUTS

Wave after wave of talking drum reverberation. . . a pounding, infectious assault of the senses that grabs hold of your ankles and forces you to move.
SOUNDS

THE KINKS
State Of Confusion (Arista)
Energetic dross, in some cases *intelligent* dross. . . but dross all the same.
MELODY MAKER

KISS
Creatures Of The Night (Casablanca)
A dauntless, dynamite declamation. . . gritty, convincing and totally menacing.
SOUNDS

I'd prefer a dose of the crabs than listening to this bunch of monkey faces again!
MELODY MAKER

KISSING THE PINK
Naked (Magnet)
Full of clever ideas but little point.
NEW MUSICAL EXPRESS

An imitation band. . . painting-by-numbers.
SOUNDS

Could be one of the most revitalising influences on the British charts to have blessed our ears this year.
MELODY MAKER

59

EARL KLUGH
Low Ride (Capitol)
Klugh would plainly like to be George Benson when he grows up, and is doing his best to reach that plateau of complete bland-out simplicity.
NEW MUSICAL EXPRESS

MARK KNOPFLER
Local Hero (Vertigo)
A low-key score rich in melody and breadth of invention.
MELODY MAKER

Gooey in the extreme . . . save your fiver and go and see the film twice.
NEW MUSICAL EXPRESS

KOOL AND THE GANG
As One (De-Lite)
In tests, eight out of ten couldn't tell Kool And The Gang from Heatwave.
SOUNDS

Numbing banality.
NEW MUSICAL EXPRESS

"As One" boils down to hippy platitudes for the affluent, immune and the ignorant unwary, but at least these sounds sound good.
MELODY MAKER

LEO KOTTKE
Time Step (Chrysalis)
Like a draught of cool mint tea after rock's gallon of gripewater.
NEW MUSICAL EXPRESS

ROBBY KREIGER
Versions (Passport)
An album of mind-numbing blandness.
MELODY MAKER

KROKUS
Headhunter (Arista)
The world's premier pure HM outfit.
SOUNDS

L

LAUGHING CLOWNS
Laughing Clowns (Red Flame)
From Australia . . . took their spiritual guide from avant garde jazzers like Miles Davis and Pharoah Sanders.
MELODY MAKER

Seldom has the whole absurd, grinding nightmare of existence been so nakedly yet exhilaratingly expressed.
NEW MUSICAL EXPRESS

LED ZEPPELIN
Coda (Swansong)
Material that Led Zeppelin decided not to use on previous albums.
MELODY MAKER

It is a genuine collectors' item, an honest, fan-pleasin' archive release.
SOUNDS

Various warm-ups and out-takes all quite without consequence.
NEW MUSICAL EXPRESS

ALBERT LEE
Albert Lee (Polydor)
Sounds like the best Dave Edmunds album of the last six years.
CREEM

LEMON KITTENS
The Big Dentist (Illuminated)
If this album serves any useful purpose, it should be to remind would-be Bohemians of the embarrassing consequences of giving art a capital F.
NEW MUSICAL EXPRESS

JOHN LENNON
The Lennon Collection (EMI)
Gruesomely exhibits total vampirism of the dead.
SOUNDS

I cannot imagine whose collection of John Lennon's this is, unless perhaps it's EMI's accountant.
NEW MUSICAL EXPRESS

NICK LOWE

JOHN LENNON

60

LENE LOVICH

LEVEL 42
The Pursuit Of Accidents (Polydor)
Much to admire and not much to dislike.
MELODY MAKER

Pleasant enough but unsatisfying.
SOUNDS

JERRY LEE LEWIS
The Sun Years (Charly)
What a fabulous undertaking this is! A 12-record set of 209 (!) of the pumpin' piano man's Sun studio takes.
NEW MUSICAL EXPRESS

LILIPUT
Liliput (Rough Trade)
Just Switzerland's answer to the Delta Five.
NEW MUSICAL EXPRESS

Liliput deserve credit for realising the potency of minimalism.
MELODY MAKER

It's a long way away from the iciness we've come to expect from clichéd feminism and most welcome.
SOUNDS

DAVID LINDLEY AND EL-RAYO-X
Win This Record (Asylum)
Every bit as grungy and wonderful as the first.
CREEM

Totally unlike anything else available today in the commercial marketplace. One of '82's best.
BOSTON ROCK

LINX
The Last Linx (Chrysalis)

This shabbily-packaged compilation...Linx never did completely fulfil their massive potential.
NEW MUSICAL EXPRESS

LITTLE RIVER BAND
Greatest Hits (Capitol)
The poor man's Eagles release a compilation of all their non-hits...as tasty as plastic fruit.
RECORD MIRROR

LITTLE STEVEN AND THE DISCIPLES OF SOUL
Men Without Women (EMI International)
Would suggest that Van Zandt is best employed as a second banana.
NEW MUSICAL EXPRESS

JULIE LONDON
Julie Is Her Name (Edsel)
Something of a highly-desirable period icon...a debut brimming with clear artistic judgement and simple elegance.
NEW MUSICAL EXPRESS

THE LONE RANGER
Hi-Yo, Silver, Away!
(Greensleeves)
This should be a billion times better.
SOUNDS

Even Sly and Robbie playing Tonto can't disguise rusty old riffs as bright silver bullets.
MELODY MAKER

THE LORDS OF THE NEW CHURCH
The Lords Of The New Church (Illegal)
Old punks never die, they simply riff away...the Blues Band of punk.
NEW MUSICAL EXPRESS

LENE LOVICH
No Man's Land (Stiff)
Pretty turgid fare.
NEW MUSICAL EXPRESS

Another Lene Lovich album, much like the last, presumably much like the next.
MELODY MAKER

A completely triumphant return...She has the talent, the ambition, the style and imagination to create a music so vast in emotion and feeling as to engulf all rivals.
SOUNDS

NICK LOWE
The Abominable Showman (Columbia)
He's written worse songs, survived worse productions, but never sounded so half-hearted, so out of touch with himself and the elements that usually inspire his music.
MELODY MAKER

A welcome return to former glories.
SOUNDS

Lowe on particularly good form.
NEW MUSICAL EXPRESS

LEVEL 42

PHIL LYNOTT
The Philip Lynott Album (Vertigo)
An accurate aural document of Lynott's unlimited talents.
SOUNDS

Really nothing more than a bunch of out-takes...The voice creaks, the songs are weak, the imagery is out of focus.
MELODY MAKER

Highly recommended to devotees of disappointing, unimpressive albums.
NEW MUSICAL EXPRESS

PHIL LYNOTT AND JOHN SYKES

MALCOLM McLAREN
Duck Rock (Charisma)
The best album of the eighties so far...a bombardment of crazy sound, crazy style, crazy rhythm.
RECORD MIRROR

In every sense of the word, brilliant...literally makes me feel good to be alive.
MELODY MAKER

This really is a record to write home about.
NEW MUSICAL EXPRESS

Finds Malcolm beckoning to the nation's pop kids like a dirty old man with a bag full of sweets...it's a turkey of global proportions of course.
SOUNDS

MADNESS

MADNESS
Rise And Fall (Stiff)
Madness sound tired and world-weary where previously they've always been Jack The Lad with a sharp brain and a heart of gold.
MELODY MAKER

I wish Madness, like Adam, were mad instead of sad and really rather bad.
SOUNDS

Madness will be around and contributing for a hell of a lot longer than either ABC or Haircut 100...a grimly ironic title: I say Madness are strictly on the rise.
NEW MUSICAL EXPRESS

MAGNUM
The Eleventh Hour (Jet)
Combining the best of bands like Yes with the smoother, more commercial US contemporaries like Styx and Kansas.
SOUNDS

Like wading through a bowl of thick stodgy porridge.
MELODY MAKER

MAJOR ACCIDENT
Massacred Melodies (Step Forward)
Any band launching themselves on a Clockwork Orange image a la Adicts has got to be crazy.
MELODY MAKER

MALARIA!
Emotion (Les Disque Du Crepuscule)
The shared experience of five girls dressed in black and locked in a cell...music single-minded in its commitment to the notion of passion.
NEW MUSICAL EXPRESS

This is ART and all that entails...Angst-ridden to the point of claustrophobia.
MELODY MAKER

STEPHEN MALLINDER
Pow-Wow (Fetish)
Like a piece of modernist chamber music...plumbs some paranoid neurotic depths while maintaining a kind of positiveness and pleasure.
NEW MUSICAL EXPRESS

MANFRED MANN'S EARTH BAND
Somewhere In Afrika (Bronze)
Distinctive.
SOUNDS

Appalling.
NEW MUSICAL EXPRESS

MANOWAR
Battle Hymns (Liberty)
Any band that can book Orson Welles for a voice over must be in for a chance...comic book rock at its finest.
RECORD MIRROR

MARC AND THE MAMBAS
Untitled (Some Bizzare)
Four sides of erratic indulgence and Almond's most honest statement yet...a richly experimental exposé of the futile necessity of what we know as love.
MELODY MAKER

A couple of flashes of brilliance, some good efforts, and a hell of a lot of wasted time, talent and money (yours).
NEW MUSICAL EXPRESS

BOB MARLEY & THE WAILERS
Confrontation (Island)
A farewell tribute and not a sharp cash-in, the Marley finale is not, perhaps, *classic*.
MELODY MAKER

No-one who loves Bob Marley and hears this album will be disappointed.
NEW MUSICAL EXPRESS

MARILLION
Script For A Jester's Tear (EMI)
A desultory scrapbook of rags from exhausted minds...formless, straggling loops from the discarded spools of Genesis and Greenslade.
NEW MUSICAL EXPRESS

Every song is a mini-drama scripted in the florid language expected by its audience.
MELODY MAKER

A rare stunning classic of a first album...it's the coming of age of an exciting new British talent.
SOUNDS

MARTHA AND THE MUFFINS

MARINE GIRLS
Lazy Ways (Cherry Red)
While so much is good, so little is brilliant.
SOUNDS

A transitional record, pointing to a future that could be interesting.
MELODY MAKER

The Marine Girls have earned themselves a place in the lifeboat.
NEW MUSICAL EXPRESS

FRANK MARINO
Juggernaut (CBS)
This album might have the makings of a fine ashtray.
MELODY MAKER

MARTHA AND THE MUFFINS
Danseparc (RCA)
Meanders with no discernible direction or reason, it's a record that inspires neither action nor emotion.
MELODY MAKER

JOHN MARTYN
Well Kept Secret (WEA)
A class record.
NEW MUSICAL EXPRESS

Too good to remain a secret.
SOUNDS

MATCHBOX
Crossed Line (Magnet)
Second-rate Rockpile.
MELODY MAKER

MATERIAL
One Down (Elektra)
An exercise in futility . . . dispensable jive.
MELODY MAKER

MAXIMUM JOY
Station MXJY (Y Records)
Fresh and unpretentious jazzed-up funk and where it falls, it does so with honour.
SOUNDS

Whatever the potential they clearly haven't grasped it on their first album.
MELODY MAKER

MEATLOAF
Midnight At The Lost And Found (Epic)
Meat obviously doesn't realise how useless his music is . . . it is totally empty for the empty masses.
SOUNDS

Amateur hour Americana . . . music for grown ups who think they're still young.
NEW MUSICAL EXPRESS

MDC
Millions Of Dead Cops (Alternative Tentacles)
They make Discharge sound like the Spinners . . . a must for the lobotomy brigades.
SOUNDS

THE MEKONS
The Mekons Story (CNT)
Insipid MOR punk.
SOUNDS

Spanning the years from ragged punk to synthesiser escapades, it's an ambitious product and of great value to Mekons fans everywhere.
BOSTON ROCK

THE MEMBERS
Going West (Albion)
Could once have been contenders, but now they're well on their way to Palookaville.
NEW MUSICAL EXPRESS

THE MEMBERS
Uprhythm Downbeat (Arista)
At best disappointing, at worst very lame . . . I wished I loved this record but it's old and tired.
MELODY MAKER

MAXIMUM JOY

MISSING PERSONS

MEN AT WORK
Cargo (Epic)
A tidy package of hummable, inoffensive little songs...will appease the coffee table mob.
MELODY MAKER

They have no shame and no brain...Men At Work are Sting before he read Koestler.
NEW MUSICAL EXPRESS

Worthless rubbish pretending to be something important.
SOUNDS

MENTAL AS ANYTHING
If You Leave Me, Can I Come Too? (A&M)
Australian...conjures up the spirit of the late Marc Bolan (who is also 'down under' at the moment).
MELODY MAKER

THE METEORS
Wreckin' Crew (I-D Records)
Most obviously aspire to something Cramps-like but display complete lack of instinct about how this might be accomplished.
NEW MUSICAL EXPRESS

The Meteors aren't half as nasty as they'd like to think they are...a very safe album, very low-key and offering nothing new.
SOUNDS

THE MILKSHAKES
Fourteen Rhythm And Beat Greats (Big Beat)
Merciless and brilliant practitioners of the advanced voodoo garage syndrome.
SOUNDS

FRANKIE MILLER
Standing On The Edge (Capitol)
Shows old Frankie trying his best, but it just ain't good enough...it's all so predictable it's painful.
NEW MUSICAL EXPRESS

STEVE MILLER BAND
Live! (Mercury)
As expected — an immaculately recorded greatest hits package.
RECORD MIRROR

MINUTEMEN
What Makes A Man Start Fires? (SST)
The sort of gibbering, non-punctuated "poetry" that any self-respecting screwball hippy would have been proud of in 1967.
MELODY MAKER

More tension, more emotion and more musical invention than in a lifetime of Southern Death Cult.
NEW MUSICAL EXPRESS

Creative bite, energy over decibels, speed with a purpose. My album of the month.
BOSTON ROCK

MISSING PERSONS
Spring Session (Capitol)
Yet another bunch of faint-hearted LA smoothies playing the sort of timeless placeless sub-rock which keeps North America afloat.
MELODY MAKER

MISTY IN ROOTS
Earth (People Unite Records)
Shames all home-grown roots within easy memory?...eminently listenable, easily understandable and laudibly sensible.
MELODY MAKER

JONI MITCHELL
Wild Things Run Fast (Geffen)
She is making music with the realistic and graceful perception of someone who realises that this is 1982.
MELODY MAKER

There is a persistent suggestion that she's slumming in the cheapest throes of dime-novel romance, and it's ludicrous that the progenitor of the scorched skyline of the 'Hejira' set should want to settle for something so facile.
NEW MUSICAL EXPRESS

A truly menopausal record. Like a faded old tart, JM uses the cheap cosmetics of brass and hunky guitar to give her sagging musical figures a much needed lift — and the result is cheap trash.
SOUNDS

THE MOB
Let The Tribe Increase (All The Madmen Records)
Their lyrics confront the utter awful depression and degradation of modern life where alienation and isolation without love are so dwarfingly dominant.
SOUNDS

MODERN ROMANCE
Trick Of The Light (WEA)
All serving to remind us of the depths pop will sink in its obsession with trash and instant disposability.
MELODY MAKER

As a new and valid contribution to 80's music, it's a pile of used pocket handkerchiefs.
NEW MUSICAL EXPRESS

A throwback to the days when groups were put together for fun and not to change the world or deliver us from evil.
RECORD MIRROR

THE MONOCHROME SET
Eligible Bachelors (Cherry Red)
The re-birth...in blazing technicolor.
SOUNDS

Still knocking out witty ditties for whistling milkmen, the Set nonetheless seem limited: a gag in search of a punchline.
NEW MUSICAL EXPRESS

Monkees meets the Subway Sect.
RECORD MIRROR

THE MONOCHROME SET
Volume, Contrast, Brilliance (Cherry Red)
Rather like the highlights of Joe Bugner's boxing career, no hits, plenty of flops.
RECORD MIRROR

Lackadaisical cream - teas - at - high - noon drollery.
NEW MUSICAL EXPRESS

GARY MOORE
Corridors Of Power (Virgin)
A rock solid showcase of HM/HR, accentuated by fretwork of frightening superiority.
SOUNDS

THE MORELLS
Shake And Push (Borrowed)
Under any other circumstances, a group with a balding 40-year-old singer bassist, a 52-year-old female keyboard player with a short punky grey hairdo, and a popabilly guitar genius no one's ever heard of would rightly be considered a novelty act.
MELODY MAKER

VAN MORRISON
Inarticulate Speech Of The Heart (Phonogram)
Once you've scraped away the cosmic baloney it stands as a resounding, if somewhat subdued, accumulation of characteristic talents.
NEW MUSICAL EXPRESS

Morrison wouldn't know how to spell "Positive Punk" and he's about as hip as Frank Bough, but I doubt you'll hear a more complete album than this in '83.
MELODY MAKER

His third appalling album on the very rapid trot.
SOUNDS

He gets more wishy-washy album by album. This is the worst so far.
RECORD MIRROR

MOTORHEAD
Another Perfect Day (Bronze)
A 100 per cent pure beef album.
RECORD MIRROR

Typical, vintage Motorhead at their fearsome best without any evidence of the much-vaunted new melodic edge.
MELODY MAKER

It could be that this grope towards subtlety is a calumny of what Motorhead are all about.
NEW MUSICAL EXPRESS

Wooaarrrgghhh!!!
SOUNDS

MOTORHEAD
What's Words Worth (Big Beat)
Retrospectively invaluable...There's no band in the world quite as bad as Motorhead when played at a low volume.
MELODY MAKER

MUSIC FOR PLEASURE
Into The Rain (Polydor)
MFP have grown up, spread their wings and gained a soulful inner strength.
SOUNDS

It can be called modern pop but it remains light years away and ahead of the mainstream gross-outs.
MELODY MAKER

As dated and as overtly plagiaristic as the fledgling Simple Minds.
NEW MUSICAL EXPRESS

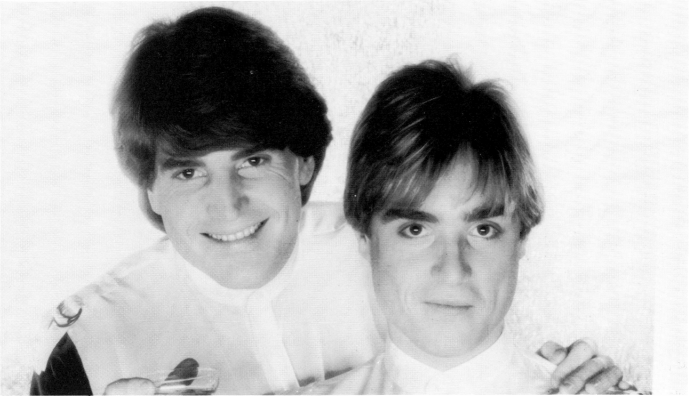

MODERN ROMANCE

MUSICAL YOUTH
The Youth Of Today (MCA)
A bright collection of cartoons...there is enough here to ward off those cynics who would have them as one-hit wonders.
MELODY MAKER

Cute, energetic, irreverent and you don't need an eleven-plus to enjoy it.
NEW MUSICAL EXPRESS

Easily digestible for mainstream appetites.
BOSTON ROCK

What do *real* Rastas make of all this junior dub?
SOUNDS

MUTABARUKA
Check It (Alligator Records)
Militant gesture combines with the harsh realities of sufferation to make Mutabaruka's first album a dynamic addition to the growing body of dub poetry.
NEW MUSICAL EXPRESS

The most invigorating and provocative reggae rage of the decade so far.
SOUNDS

N

NAKED EYES
Burning Bridges (EMI)
If you thought Tears For Fears were bad, wait till you hear their forgotten relations.
NEW MUSICAL EXPRESS

An album that repays repeated listening.
SOUNDS

BILL NELSON

MUSICAL YOUTH

NATASHA
Captured (Towerbell)
Placid pop pap, the sort Lulu would turn her nose up at.
MELODY MAKER

NATIONAL HEALTH
D.S. al Coda (Lounging Records)
Easily the most accessible of the National Health albums: fusion at its free-flowing best.
NEW MUSICAL EXPRESS

By adhering too rigidly to the dots on the paper, National Health have lost the music's fluidity.
MELODY MAKER

THE NEATS
The Monkey's Head In The Corner Of The Room (Ace of Hearts)
Excellent...American pop isn't dead. It's just living in exile in basements in places like Boston.
NEW MUSICAL EXPRESS

BILL NELSON
Chimera (Mercury)
Sublimely well-constructed electro-based tunes guaranteed to make the tiredest ears perk up.
RECORD MIRROR

A set of songs with the sort of freshness and optimism which comes only from the heart and just cannot be calculated on a royalty basis.
SOUNDS

NEW AGE STEPPERS
Foundation Steppers (On-U Sound)
A softly weaving, unavoidable seduction of rich reggae binds together a set of highly erratic foundations into a cohesive and ultimately successful end.
NEW MUSICAL EXPRESS

NEW ORDER
Power Corruption And Lies (Factory)
An exceptional album.
SOUNDS

One of the best records made in England this year...more than anything, I think, this album is final proof that New Order have arrived at an identity.
NEW MUSICAL EXPRESS

A rather sluggish journey through familiar territory.
RECORD MIRROR

NAKED EYES

RANDY NEWMAN
Trouble In Paradise (Warner Bros)
What a walloping return to form by the great Randy Newman! There isn't likely to be anything as lyrical or musically intelligent as this over the year, unless he cuts another album.
MELODY MAKER

It doesn't mark any kind of high point in Newman's output...just another West Coast album in fact.
NEW MUSICAL EXPRESS

STEVIE NICKS
The Wild Heart (WEA)
Stevie sounds as though she eats sheet metal for breakfast. I wouldn't want to meet her in a dark alley at night.
SOUNDS

NICO
Drama Of Exile (Aura)
More gloomy and self-absorbed (i.e. boring) than ever.
NEW MUSICAL EXPRESS

THE NIGHTINGALES
Pigs On Purpose (Cherry Red)
Smarter than the average bellyache. A wonderfully *humane* record.
NEW MUSICAL EXPRESS

Comical, a little shabby, but irresistible as hell.
SOUNDS

THE NITECAPS
Go To The Line (Sire)
Blue collar, bar band 'soul'...while stone sober, it's an acquired taste.
NEW MUSICAL EXPRESS

Come back Southside, somebody's walking on your grave. With hobnail boots...crude warmed-over soul and R&B with the finesse of a deranged bison.
MELODY MAKER

THE NOLANS

THE NOLANS
Altogether (Epic)
Summons up a thousand regrettable memories of Des O'Connor shows...No sign of Lemmy on this album, by the way.
MELODY MAKER

TED NUGENT
Nugent (Atlantic)
Far from having lost the old magic, Ted still has it there in abundance.
MELODY MAKER

GARY NUMAN
I, Assassin (Beggars Banquet)
Highlights Numan's basic inability to stretch away from his initial synth doodling.
SOUNDS

The whole album is one long paean to numbness...Numan still seems utterly corpse-like, a man spiritually three-fourths dead and proud of it, too.
NEW MUSICAL EXPRESS

Rarely in recording history has an artist reaped such outrageous rewards from such a paucity of imagination.
MELODY MAKER

RIC OCASEK
Beatitude (Geffen)
BOY is this LP a groaner.
NEW MUSICAL EXPRESS

Strictly yawnsville.
CREEM

OK JIVE
At The Blue Chonjo Sky Day And Night Club (Frenzy)
A fluid but effervescent sound.
SOUNDS

Often has the aroma of Hollywood back-lot fare...If Altered Images had hailed from Cameroon instead of Caledonia they might well have sounded this way.
NEW MUSICAL EXPRESS

MIKE OLDFIELD
Crises (Virgin)
If anything, his knack of writing a nifty tune has diminished.
NEW MUSICAL EXPRESS

The kind of bland, unchallenging dross which clogs up the Radio One airwaves every day...The musical equivalent of voting Tory.
SOUNDS

Arrant nonsense.
MELODY MAKER

MIKE OLDFIELD

YOKO ONO
It's Alright (I See Rainbows) (Polydor)
There is beauty here but it's the beauty of fragile ice flowers, the kind which shatter at a touch.
SOUNDS

Sounds more like the cutesy coyness of a Bananarama or a Go-Go's than a middle-aged lady who once held the weirdest art exhibitions and whose voice was famous for impersonating cat fights.
MELODY MAKER

You have to groan and wonder how anybody could be so naive in this day and age.
CREEM

ORANGE JUICE
Rip It Up (Polydor)
A minor group trying hard to be bigger and more significant than they really ought to be.
NEW MUSICAL EXPRESS

As big if not bigger a disaster than the first Josef K album...Orange squashed, if I'm any judge.
SOUNDS

ORCHESTRAL MANOEUVRES IN THE DARK
Dazzle Ships (Virgin)
OMD arrive with scalded temples, having pondered lengthily on the state of the world and the art of sound.
MELODY MAKER

Too sketchy, too unsure and wobbly to be worth much.
SOUNDS

ORANGE JUICE

OMD have bitten off more than they can (or should) chew.
BOSTON ROCK

OZZY OSBOURNE
Talk Of The Devil (Jet)
Eight sides of the most unquestionably pure and contradictory metal available today.
CREEM

A headbanger's delight. No surprises, no love songs, no ballads.
MELODY MAKER

Apparently, Oz bit the head of Arden's bulldog and pissed in his mansion so Big Don feeling unable to respond in his traditional way by suspending Ozzy out of a fifth floor window, agreed to terminate his contract with this live double album.
SOUNDS

OZZY OSBOURNE

PALLAS
Arrive Alive (Cook King)
Captures the mood of 'Nursery Cryme'-era Genesis.
SOUNDS

One big yawn.
RECORD MIRROR

ROBERT PALMER
Pride (Island)
If you think genuinely that Marillion are about "mystery" and "adventure", it will give you a heart attack.
SOUNDS

A typical Palmer LP — one part pop-soul brilliance, two parts under-achievement and one part embarrassment.
NEW MUSICAL EXPRESS

THE PARTISANS
The Partisans (No Future)
Another week, another anarchy record... essentially an unpretentious youth club band making it big.
NEW MUSICAL EXPRESS

The Partisans have captured the very essence of new punk/Oi music.
SOUNDS

THE PASSAGE
Enflame (Cherry Red)
50 per cent successful and gives a few encouraging guidelines for the future.
MELODY MAKER

Absolutely essential listening!...Stockhausen meets Al Green. Soul music for neurotics.
SOUNDS

THE PASSIONS
Sanctuary (Polydor)
Pure pleasure, elusive and ethereal...an album full of surprises.
SOUNDS

Strictly average.
MELODY MAKER

PERE UBU
Song Of The Bailing Man (Rough Trade)
Inspired, invigorating, confounding, disturbing.
MELODY MAKER

The unvarnished truth is that Pere Ubu have outlived their excellence...a giggly batch of squeaks and jingles, rhymes and noodles.
NEW MUSICAL EXPRESS

PETER AND THE TEST TUBE BABIES
Pissed And Proud (No Future)
Pissed and proud, wild and wacky, rude and skinned, cider-soaked Test Tube Babies are the Walt Disneys of punk rock.
MELODY MAKER

TOM PETTY AND THE HEARTBREAKERS

TOM PETTY AND THE HEARTBREAKERS
Long After Dark (Backstreet)
Questions Petty's ability to group together a truly challenging set of musical conceits.
NEW MUSICAL EXPRESS

All too often he's content to settle for the tried and tired trademarks of the All-American-Rock-Band.
SOUNDS

Heartbreakingly DULL...glassy-eyed, undifferentiated vervelessness.
CREEM

His best album.
MELODY MAKER

PIGBAG
Lend An Ear (Y Records)
Decisions remain unmade and directions undecided.
MELODY MAKER

They waste too much time on experimental free form drivel.
RECORD MIRROR

PINK FLOYD
The Final Cut (Harvest)
Will slip into immortality with traditional ease.
SOUNDS

Soft-headed intelligence insulting doggerel ...parts sound suspiciously like out-takes from an Alan Price album.
MELODY MAKER

The expression of a man who loathes the demands of the rock cycle yet is unable to move beyond the same linear constraints of the form.
NEW MUSICAL EXPRESS

I didn't wear safety pins for people to make records like this.
RECORD MIRROR

The idea of Waters sitting in his drawing-room reflecting on the Falklands and/or any other wars seems so ludicrous, it might be better to think of this as a comedy album.
BOSTON ROCK

Only succeeds in making Roger Waters seem as thick as a brick in the wall.
CREEM

PINK INDUSTRY
Low Technology (Zulu)
Low-budget music produced in splendid isolation...veering from the verges of brilliance to the edge of the abysmal.
NEW MUSICAL EXPRESS

THE PINKEES
Pinkees (Creole)
Like a bunch of loud Swedish tourists on an early morning rush hour tube — nauseating ...nostalgic slime.
SOUNDS

PLACEBO
Shells (Aura)
'Shells' stinks. It is woefully bad.
SOUNDS

ROBERT PLANT
Pictures At Eleven (Swansong)
It's a pleasure to hear Plant back on record again and a delight to report that he's enhanced his reputation in a situation where it could have so easily been tarnished.
MELODY MAKER

ROBERT PLANT

WENDY O. WILLIAMS (PLASMATICS)

PLASMATICS
Coup D'Etat (Capitol)
The Plasmatics have finally flipped: they want to *change the world!*
MELODY MAKER

Indifferent, shoddy, blank, thoughtless trash metal.
SOUNDS

POCO
Ghost Town (Atlantic)
By their own pathetic standards of late, not bad . . . pretty tunes which to some extent mask the banality of the lyrics.
MELODY MAKER

POISON GIRLS
Where's The Pleasure (X N Trix)
A fantastic variety of styles — disco, funk, blues, soul and rock'n'roll — all played enthusiastically and convincingly.
NEW MUSICAL EXPRESS

A near perfect statement of intent, an artistic creation that satisfies political, emotional and intellectual desires.
SOUNDS

THE POLICE
Synchronicity (A&M)
Some of the music fuses intuitive pop genius with wilfully dense orchestration so powerfully it stuns. It is occasionally sensational.
NEW MUSICAL EXPRESS

I could never fall in love with a group which plans its moves so carefully and which would never do anything just for the hell of it.
MELODY MAKER

Never has so much money been made out of so little co-ordinated talent.
SOUNDS

If Sting broke wind into the microphone the Police would still make a mint.
RECORD MIRROR

IGGY POP
Zombie Birdhouse (Animal Records)
A batch of fresh songs that combine black leather rock with everything from sea shanties to Aboriginal dronings.
MELODY MAKER

Hardly challenging like early Pop overdosed-and-on-his knees binges.
SOUNDS

Iggy needs a "collaborator" as strong as Bowie for something truly substantive to result.
BOSTON ROCK

POSITIVE NOISE
Change Of Heart (Statik)
Acceptable but not particularly original . . . has all the right ingredients but lacks the stamp of any individual style.
SOUNDS

A combination of a ridiculously overwrought and self pitying worldview and glaring plagiarism (sort of low rent Heaven 17 meets True Life Detective).
NEW MUSICAL EXPRESS

PRINCE CHARLES AND THE CITY BEAT BAND
Stone Killers (Virgin)
Obviously a serious contender for the throne George Clinton and James Brown have made their own.
RECORD MIRROR

Music born from and made for the ghetto-blasters of inner city USA, funk to defy the traffic noise and blot out the boredom.
NEW MUSICAL EXPRESS

PRINCE
1999 (Warner Bros)
1999 is an always interesting, always entertaining, masterful work.
BOSTON ROCK

One of the most inspiring dance epics known to man.
MELODY MAKER

A much more eclectic style than conventional Black American Disco.
SOUNDS

Like an interminable string of *Fame* B-sides . . . "Nothing sadder than a flasher who no one notices."
NEW MUSICAL EXPRESS

PSYCHIC TV
Force The Hand Of Chance (Some Bizzare)
A record as important to its time as 'Blonde On Blonde'.
NEW MUSICAL EXPRESS

A cynical and puerile journey to the heart of pantomime profundity . . . As music, not much. As self-promotion, bluff and pancultural plagiarism, it's brilliant in the extreme.
SOUNDS

Is this new age hippy crap or what?
MELODY MAKER

THE RAMONES

THE PSYCHEDELIC FURS
Forever Now (CBS)
In a devalued world, it sure beats Air Supply.
CREEM

As appealing and more adventurous than past efforts.
BOSTON ROCK

The secret is to take them, like all good things, in small doses or with a pinch of salt.
NEW MUSICAL EXPRESS

We're talking masterpiece here.
MELODY MAKER

JAMES T PURSEY
Revenge Is Not The Password (Who Knows)
The noose of change sits uncomfortably on the neck of Jimmy Pursey; whatever incarnation he chooses for his return, the ghost of Sham 69 will undoubtedly haunt him.
NEW MUSICAL EXPRESS

A lot more challenging than "Hurry Up Harry".
MELODY MAKER

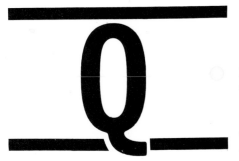

SUZI QUATRO
Main Attraction (Polydor)
Pallid pop masquerading as something more muscular.
MELODY MAKER

THE RAMONES
Subterranean Jungle (Sire)
Their third masterpiece; a record which redefines words like 'thrilling', 'redemptive' and 'direct'.
NEW MUSICAL EXPRESS

The Brudders have remained true to their skool but have also had the foresight to broaden their musical horizons.
SOUNDS

If the Clash can get to Top Ten with their worst record, so can the Ramones.
BOSTON ROCK

RANK & FILE
Sundown (Slash Records)
A Commie punk country band...a lineage which runs from Reeves and Williams down through Johnny Cash, Ernest Tubbs and Left Frizzell.
NEW MUSICAL EXPRESS

True dirt'n'guts COUNTRY, played coolly and competently with no cultural mercenary motives involved.
BOSTON ROCK

RED ALERT
We've Got The Power (No Future)
Sunderland is certainly breeding some good bands these days.
SOUNDS

LOU REED
Legendary Hearts (RCA)
Reed's seventeenth solo LP...possibly the purest, most fluid and spiritual musical unity you'll hear in rock and roll for some time to come.
NEW MUSICAL EXPRESS

In the no man's land Reed inhabits between being (musically) dead and alive, you can't help thinking that at the end he would be better off dead.
SOUNDS

Marks the definitive descent from a career that was once so in tune with reality that it was startling.
MELODY MAKER

Indicative of an artist coming into a brand new kind of prime.
CREEM

THE RESIDENTS
Residue Of The Residents (Ralph)
A collection of rarities, oddities and previously unavailable material from the last ten years...the maddest genii in the world.
SOUNDS

THE REVILLOS
Attack! (Superville)
Its attack is about as forceful as a handful of soggy tissues...The Rezillos had a z for zip — The Revillos have a v for vapid.
MELODY MAKER

Stone-age in the extreme.
SOUNDS

CLIFF RICHARD
Dressed For The Occasion (EMI)
Cliff sounding faintly uncomfortable at coming to grips with the London Philharmonic Orchestra at the Royal Albert Hall.
RECORD MIRROR

CLIFF RICHARD
Now You See Me . . . Now You Don't (EMI)
I defy even the staunchest Cliff fan to find any merit in this album . . . Give me 'Expresso Bongo' any day.
SOUNDS

RIP RIG & PANIC
Attitude (Virgin)
May not strike quite the decisive blow they have always sought to plant on the collective brainpan.
NEW MUSICAL EXPRESS

Whether much of what Rip Rig do is worth putting down for posterity, or perhaps even mass consumption, is at times debatable.
SOUNDS

Struggles vainly in the space between order and chaos.
RECORD MIRROR

SMOKEY ROBINSON
Touch The Sky (Motown)
Smokey has opted to delve further into glossy measured soul, tinged with blandness and adhesion.
NEW MUSICAL EXPRESS

One of love's greatest hunters has finally been captured by The Game.
MELODY MAKER

THE ROCHES
Keep On Doing (WEA)
They sing the ten songs like Christmas carols: flawless descants, sentimental harmonies, the scent of a gas lantern overhead.
NEW MUSICAL EXPRESS

ROCK GODDESS

They're finally beginning to figure out how to make records.
CREEM

This is a catastrophe.
MELODY MAKER

ROCK GODDESS
Rock Goddess (A&M)
So extremely bad as to attain a perversely sophisticated appeal . . . it's pathetic.
MELODY MAKER

Impresses on almost every level . . . irresistible.
SOUNDS

NILE RODGERS
Adventures In The Land Of The Good Groove (Mirage Records)
One can only hope he comes up with something more substantial for the Bowie album so this can then be viewed as a filler rather than an unfortunate requiem.
MELODY MAKER

ROSE TATTOO
Scarred For Life (Carrere)
May this be carved in letters of blazing fire: This album is an absolute MONSTER and by far the most vital vinyl perpetration yet committed by these bare-knuckle braggadocios.
SOUNDS

The best album of the year, bar none . . . a consistently brilliant album, simply reeking of quality.
MELODY MAKER

DIANA ROSS
Silk Electric (Capitol)
An exercise in slushy self indulgence.
RECORD MIRROR

Lives up to its preposterously empty title and continues the downward plunge . . . Las Vegas must be just a step away.
MELODY MAKER

KEVIN ROWLAND AND DEXYS MIDNIGHT RUNNERS
Too-Rye-Aye (Mercury)
Wildly eccentric, manically detailed . . . a crushing indictment against synth pop and modern Production.
SOUNDS

One of the best albums of this or any other recent year.
RECORD MIRROR

A cracking album — though not a patch on 'Searching For The Young Soul Rebels'.
NEW MUSICAL EXPRESS

CLIFF RICHARD

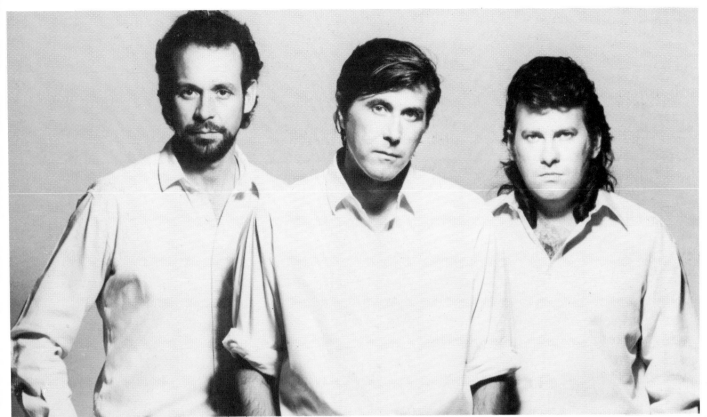
ROXY MUSIC

ROXY MUSIC
The High Road (EG)
A mini live LP recorded last year in Glasgow...from its K-Tel cover to its twee gospelly vocals, reeks of uncharacteristic haste and carelessness.
MELODY MAKER

THE RUNAWAYS
The Best Of The Runaways (Mercury)
Who the hell ever listened to the Runaways anyway?
MELODY MAKER

Mercury should pull it in and get me to put together a real 'Best Of' which might have a chance of selling more copies than this travesty.
SOUNDS

RUSH
Signals (Mercury)
Fails to match Rush's previous achievements.
SOUNDS

Could well be their best yet.
MELODY MAKER

Nothing more than a slicked-up version of such primary heavy metal groups as Budgie and Atomic Rooster.
CREEM

MIKE RUTHERFORD
Acting Very Strange (WEA)
By no means as removed from Eighties rock as you might have supposed.
SOUNDS

The bassist explores new uncharted areas well away from Genesis ground.
MELODY MAKER

Never buy a Genesis-related record unless it's splattered with P-Orridge.
NEW MUSICAL EXPRESS

RUTS DC
Rhythm Collision (Bohemian)
It'd be an injustice if this record did nothing more than raise patronising eyebrows.
NEW MUSICAL EXPRESS

S

SAMSON
Before The Storm (Polydor)
A more potent sleep inducer than Librium.
SOUNDS

Should be re-titled "Storm In A Teacup".
RECORD MIRROR

SANDII & THE SUNSETZ
Immigrants (Sire)
Perhaps the most perfect, natural and consistent blend of Eastern and Western musical skills.
SOUNDS

They manage to hit the pleasure centre with every probe.
MELODY MAKER

No reservation on the rocketship to stardom.
NEW MUSICAL EXPRESS

SANTANA
Shango (CBS)
As limp as wet haddock.
RECORD MIRROR

ALEXEI SAYLE
Cak! (Springtime)
The new series of Terry And June is far funnier.
SOUNDS

SAXON
Power And The Glory (Carrere)
Another denim and leather showcase for everything that HM stands for...a riotous rampage of rampant rhinochargin' rock.
SOUNDS

MICHAEL SCHENKER GROUP
Assault Attack (Chrysalis)
Reasonably good.
MELODY MAKER

Tragically ordinary.
SOUNDS

GIL SCOTT-HERON
Moving Target (Arista)
A brilliant record, but not perfect.
SOUNDS

A performer whose work should never be ignored.
NEW MUSICAL EXPRESS

No cocktail revolutionary, but in danger of being confused with one if he doesn't toughen up his act.
MELODY MAKER

SCRITTI POLITTI
Songs To Remember (Rough Trade)
Music for intelligent, sensitive and confused middle-class youth living in very small rooms.
NEW MUSICAL EXPRESS

Each song here is like a foam bath, luxuriously overwhelming.
SOUNDS

There's a consistency of excellence that stands out as a beacon of purity in a plagiarist climate.
MELODY MAKER

SET THE TONE

GIL SCOTT-HERON

SECTION 25
The Key Of Dreams (Factory Benelux)
It does to Pink Floyd what the Jam did to the equally mediocre Who...it makes Sun Ra seem like the Krankies.
SOUNDS

BOB SEGER AND THE SILVER BULLET BAND
The Distance (Capitol)
Very unoriginal material, very well delivered.
RECORD MIRROR

Confirmation that Bob Seger hasn't been sold to the knackers' yard for glue.
MELODY MAKER

Its heart beats loud and proud.
NEW MUSICAL EXPRESS

"The Distance" is an album that has a lot on the ball.
CREEM

WILL SERGEANT
Themes For GRIND (Ninety Two Satisfied Customers)
Suggests his home-made music is best kept for his own four walls.
NEW MUSICAL EXPRESS

SET THE TONE
Shiftin' Air Affair (Island)
What the Thompson Twins would sound like if they weren't prime, image-conscious hippy phonies.
MELODY MAKER

An adult, and perhaps more aware and therefore less dumb (who knows?), version of Haysi Fantayzee.
SOUNDS

It wouldn't matter that Set The Tone had no new ideas, if only they had a little style. They haven't and this stinks.
RECORD MIRROR

Like a vinyl chronicle of a painfully long Space Invaders game.
NEW MUSICAL EXPRESS

SEX GANG CHILDREN
Sex And Legend (Illuminated Records)
Politicians, church, bigots and deceivers are all key targets...punk has been given a 'positive' kiss of life here.
SOUNDS

A more dismal collection of third rate rock (a compliment) you'd be hard pressed to find.
NEW MUSICAL EXPRESS

SHAKATAK
Invitations (Polydor)
An almost fatal creative block.
NEW MUSICAL EXPRESS

Lots of those dinky keyboards dribbling all over the shop.
MELODY MAKER

DEL SHANNON
Drop Down And Get Me (Demon)
Sponsored and produced by Tom Petty over three years of complex contractual and logistical complications... any real romantic must go GET this album.
NEW MUSICAL EXPRESS

PETE SHELLEY
XL 1 (Genetic)
The best LP Shelley has made since the Buzzcocks' 'Another Music In A Different Kitchen' five years ago.
NEW MUSICAL EXPRESS

The work of a mature pop craftsman... an indispensable purchase if you want to hear the real pop music of 1983.
RECORD MIRROR

A formulised disco dementia.
SOUNDS

SHIVA
Firedance (Heavy Metal)
A varied mix of high quality rock.
SOUNDS

What a dire bunch of old cosmic cobblers.
RECORD MIRROR

SHOCKABILLY
Earth Versus Shockabilly (Rough Trade)
Sod the pseudo intellectual nonsense that often surrounds bands like Shockabilly, let nobody kid you, this is awful.
RECORD MIRROR

I've had more shocks on the Margate ghost train!
MELODY MAKER

SHOES
Boomerang (Elektra)
If you have even the slightest affection for adventurous, lovingly crafted pop-rock, you'll want to own it.
CREEM

SHRIEKBACK
Care (Y Records)
Magnificently quirky.
MELODY MAKER

SHAKATAK

Flashes of redemption, signals of buried treasure.
SOUNDS

Forms are beginning to emerge from the snowstorm of their sound, an overall direction behind their random explorations.
NEW MUSICAL EXPRESS

SHRIEKBACK
Tench (Y Records)
Exploring new arrays of mood and texture.
MELODY MAKER

Almost brilliant; but not quite.
SOUNDS

Ideal "unwind and lights down low" music.
BOSTON ROCK

SIMPLE MINDS
New Gold Dream (81-82-83-84) (Virgin)
Cluttered, constipated, formulated fear straining for an arty fart.
MELODY MAKER

The listener becomes immersed in the invigorating currents of the golden lake of aural showers.
SOUNDS

Whatever your preference you will find it memorable and instructed. Be swept, be drained.
NEW MUSICAL EXPRESS

SIOUXSIE AND THE BANSHEES
A Kiss In The Dreamhouse (Polydor)
When stripped of its pretence and pomposity, it reveals itself as a safe and popularised cheap novelette.
RECORD MIRROR

The Banshees are unexpectedly more valuable than they have ever been.
SOUNDS

I promise, this music will take your breath away.
NEW MUSICAL EXPRESS

Beyond all wildest hopes and dreams, beyond all past suggestion and momentum, beyond all standards set this year, "Dream House" is an intoxicating achievement.
MELODY MAKER

SHOCKABILLY

SLADE
Slade On Stage (RCA)
This sensational album goes some way towards demonstrating just why they're one of the best live rock bands in the world.
SOUNDS

MICHAEL SMITH
Mi Cyaan Believe It (Island)
Smith speaks with an authoritative love of the emotionally communicative potential of language previously unimagined in the rasta-riddled reggae vocabulary.
MELODY MAKER

Triggers intellectual and emotional turmoil but never quite manages to move the body.
SOUNDS

A strikingly individual piece of work.
NEW MUSICAL EXPRESS

SNIFF'N'THE TEARS
Ride Blue Divide (Chiswick)
Someone should confiscate his Paul Theroux novels in the hope that he might move on to some more durable thematic explorations.
MELODY MAKER

SOFT CELL
The Art Of Falling Apart (Some Bizzare)
The magnificent product of a year in the life of two very troubled souls; evidence that the best art comes out of struggle and turmoil.
SOUNDS

A stunning display of the duo's range and diversity.
NEW MUSICAL EXPRESS

A patchy streak of luck with a few magnificent moments and a number of ordinary, even tedious ones.
MELODY MAKER

THE SOUND
All Fall Down (WEA)
Not enough pioneer spirit.
MELODY MAKER

Virtually worthless.
SOUNDS

SOUTHERN DEATH CULT
The Southern Death Cult (Beggars Banquet)
This posthumous LP can charitably be described as a lash-up, though "a mess" is probably closer.
MELODY MAKER

Mickey Mouses on a pedestal.
SOUNDS

SPANDAU BALLET
True (Chrysalis)
They're further away than ever from proving what all the fuss was about . . . mutton dressed as lamb.
NEW MUSICAL EXPRESS

They set a colourful standard by which to measure the dour and meagre pop of Kaja-GooGoo, Tears For Fears and Duran Duran.
MELODY MAKER

All adding up to a longevity you'd never have expected from The Spans.
SOUNDS

A letdown . . . the songs stagnate into predictability.
BOSTON ROCK

SPARKS
In Outer Space (Atlantic)
Tacky, wacky and inevitably tedious.
SOUNDS

SPARKS
Angst In My Pants (Atlantic)
Who else but Russ and Ron could write something both jokey and metaphysical about smoking?
NEW MUSICAL EXPRESS

SPEAR OF DESTINY
Grapes Of Wrath (Burning Rome)
It fails because it's not a very good rock album . . . certainly a poor imitation of the music Kirk Brandon is presumably still capable of making.
NEW MUSICAL EXPRESS

Despite mighty aspirations, not the major album it so desperately claims to be because it is never more than the sum of its parts, it never transcends symbolic prittle prattle.
MELODY MAKER

This is the big one!
SOUNDS

SPECIAL DUTIES
77 In 82 (Rondelet)
A band with a modicum of individuality.
MELODY MAKER

Stinking rotten trash that's flat, offensive and one-dimensional.
SOUNDS

SLADE

SPIDER
Rock'n'Roll Gypsies (RCA)
Ten tracks which will wallop Quo-type wallies in the beer belly with the trouncing tenderness of an Inter-City 125.
SOUNDS

SPLODGE
In Search Of The Seven Golden Gussetts (Razor)
Public lavatory humour of the highest/lowest level.
MELODY MAKER

"Tough Shit was born in Tennessee, he was deaf and dumb, measured four foot three."
SOUNDS

RICK SPRINGFIELD

RICK SPRINGFIELD
Success Hasn't Spoiled Me Yet (RCA)
Utter bunkum...makes Bucks Fizz sound like Ozzy Osbourne.
RECORD MIRROR

BRUCE SPRINGSTEEN
Nebraska (CBS)
Tired weary old observations that tell us nothing we didn't already know.
MELODY MAKER

A valuable sideways leap.
NEW MUSICAL EXPRESS

Nobody can listen to Nebraska without figuring out that nothing's needed but a change.
CREEM

STATUS QUO

Recommended only for those who like to ponder the hopelessness of everything while drinking themselves into a lone stupor.
BOSTON ROCK

SPROUT HEAD UPRISING
Early Spring (Rocksteady)
A Radio Two version of the Residents.
SOUNDS

SQUEEZE
Singles 45s And Under (A&M)
One of the few acts who can put out a 'Best Of' without having to resort to fillers.
SOUNDS

Its relative modesty befits a group whose public projection always matches their low-life preoccupations.
NEW MUSICAL EXPRESS

A dozen golden goodies from the band with clever songwriters, strong pop sensibilities and revolving keyboard players...a nice way to say goodbye.
BOSTON ROCK

BILL SQUIER
Emotions in Motion (Capitol)
Bland, average, lacklustre Yankee rock'n'roll with consistent sexual references.
MELODY MAKER

Another collection of gutless production line songs.
RECORD MIRROR

THE STARGAZERS
Watch This Space (Epic)
Their effervescent, rock'n'roll showband personality does not translate comfortably onto plastic.
NEW MUSICAL EXPRESS

STATUS QUO
From The Makers Of (Vertigo)
Twenty years in the making, a lavish box set of three Quo compilation albums.
RECORD MIRROR

They may not represent the best of British music, but there's an honesty about them which is totally endearing.
SOUNDS

Status Quo should be recognised as the ultimate pop group, and not considered harmful in any way.
NEW MUSICAL EXPRESS

WALTER STEDING
Dancing In Heaven (Chrysalis/Animal)
East Coast 'artistry' at its most rank.
SOUNDS

STEELY DAN
Gold (MCA)
The greatest justification for 'Gold' is the hours of fun it must've provided for our two heroic dragon-chasers as they transferred the original masters.
SOUNDS

SHAKIN' STEVENS
Give Me Your Heart Tonight (Epic)
Slick but ultimately empty performance.
NEW MUSICAL EXPRESS

Mostly you admire the marketing finesse.
MELODY MAKER

ROD STEWART
Absolutely Live (Riva)
Catalogues the musical triumphs and awesome mistakes of a decade.
SOUNDS

Old songs, dutiful audience participation.
MELODY MAKER

ROD STEWART
Body Wishes (WEA)
Rod proves that he hasn't had a new idea for years and is happy to churn out the same old clap trap ad nauseam.
RECORD MIRROR

I *know* I don't have to tell you how dreadful this record is...to all intents and musical purposes, Rod Stewart died ten years ago.
MELODY MAKER

The inner sleeve depicts Rod in full tartan regalia sitting mournfully on a rocky shore. Business as usual.
NEW MUSICAL EXPRESS

An embarrassment from beginning to end...the old sod doesn't realise that *this* sort of twaddle died a death *eleven years ago.*
SOUNDS

DIDI STEWART AND THE AMPLIFIERS
Begin Here (Kirshner)
The sound is so calculated, so perfect, so commercially predictable that it's hard to get excited about.
BOSTON ROCK

STIFF LITTLE FINGERS
All The Best (Chrysalis)
Rams home just how many great tracks a band like Stiff Little Fingers amass over a period of four or five years.
SOUNDS

Let's hear it for the Bill Oddie of Airfix Kit punk. Only in a diseased economic and industrial situation could people make a living out of such utterly useless product.
NEW MUSICAL EXPRESS

STIFF LITTLE FINGERS
Now Then...(Chrysalis)
They've stopped putting two fingers up at the British system and have re-routed into ropey pop tedium.
MELODY MAKER

A very dull album.
RECORD MIRROR

A great record...This is what Stiff Little Fingers promised us all along. Brains, skill, subtlety, balls and talent.
SOUNDS

THE STRANGERS
Feline (Epic)
Will probably be dismissed as soporific, drab piffle.
MELODY MAKER

Like an untalented Steely Dan cruising through some b-sides.
SOUNDS

THE STRANGLERS
The Collection 1977-1982 (Liberty)
EMI's milk-the-past gesture.
SOUNDS

By far the greatest Stranglers album ever.
MELODY MAKER

STYX
Kilroy Was Here (A&M)
An adolescent grope through a muddled fantasy of Asimovian fatalism.
NEW MUSICAL EXPRESS

If you can divorce your consciousness from what the men of Styx mistake for lyrics you might actually enjoy some of the noise these very earnest musicians generate.
CREEM

SUBHUMANS
The Day The Country Died (Spiderleg)
It's their constant quest for variety and a brazen unwillingness to conform with usual punk processes that makes the Subhumans so special.
SOUNDS

THE STRANGLERS

NIKKI SUDDEN
The Bible Belt (Flicknife)
An unpretentious and felt record, one of the best direct hits of English rock'n'roll that I've heard in a while.
SOUNDS

This record is pure 1983 garage band . . . Who says they don't make records like this any more?
NEW MUSICAL EXPRESS

DONNA SUMMER
Donna Summer (Warner Bros)
You have to admire the architects and accountants that constructed such a masterpiece of chic soul muzak.
RECORD MIRROR

A masterpiece of funk-soul-disco offered up as heightened, tightened muzak.
NEW MUSICAL EXPRESS

Crammed with enough corn and clichés to keep someone like David Essex happy for the rest of his life.
MELODY MAKER

Forget this nauseous Americana.
SOUNDS

"Donna Summer" never really lights up.
CREEM

DONNA SUMMER
She Works Hard For The Money (Mercury)
Will lay you out on the floor and tread all over your chest with its explosion of emotions.
RECORD MIRROR

ANDY SUMMERS & ROBERT FRIPP
I Advanced Masked (A&M)
Who could fail to be charmed by this exquisite set of watercolour impression?
NEW MUSICAL EXPRESS

SUPERTRAMP
Famous Last Words (A&M)
They should call themselves Supercramp, since they've become so worn and dusty.
RECORD MIRROR

Jeez, this stuff is so soddenly bland.
CREEM

Dispensable pap — great for Supertramp fans.
MELODY MAKER

SURVIVOR
Premonition (Scotti Bros)
Disposo-pop . . . wonderful as background music when you're wallpapering a kitchen.
MELODY MAKER

SWAMP CHILDREN
So Hot (Factory)
"So Hot" manages to make you think life's worth living — because it presents the world through a shimmering kaleidoscope brightness.
MELODY MAKER

TALK TALK

T

TALKING HEADS
Speaking In Tongues (Sire)
A tough-talking return to form.
MELODY MAKER

Displays no signs of weariness, disaffection or boredom.
SOUNDS

The irony must be that in getting back to proper Talking Heads music, Byrne has all but dissolved the group's character. The tongues spoken here are all his own.
NEW MUSICAL EXPRESS

TALK TALK
The Party's Over (EMI)
A decent stab at classic modern pop.
NEW MUSICAL EXPRESS

They're living in a world where the Pleasers are household names.
SOUNDS

Somewhere between Duran Duran and The Moody Blues.
MELODY MAKER

The bland leading the bland down a foggy thoroughfare of synthesised nothingness.
RECORD MIRROR

SUPERTRAMP

TEARS FOR FEARS

TANGERINE DREAM
**Logos — Live At The Dominion, London
(Virgin)**
You could play it backwards and it would
probably make as much sense.
MELODY MAKER

There is only one thing worse than a
Tangerine Dream studio album and that's a
Tangerine Dream live album.
RECORD MIRROR

TANK
Power Of The Hunter (Kamaflage)
Raw power, with no concern for subtlety.
RECORD MIRROR

As close to Motorhead as a dray horse is to
Mill Reef.
SOUNDS

TANK
This Means War (Music For Nations)
When 2 Para took Goose Green they probably
had little idea that a year later their valiant efforts would inspire a concept album as satis-
fyingly riotous, raw-knuckled and rowdy as
this demonically paced, dynamically diamond delight.
SOUNDS

TOT TAYLOR & HIS ORCHESTRA
Playtime (Easy Listeners)
Tot Taylor is a genius out of time, a musically
cunning Woody Allen.
MELODY MAKER

My suspicion is that Tot is one of nature's
behind-the-sceners, and might most profitably remain there.
NEW MUSICAL EXPRESS

TEARS FOR FEARS
The Hurting (Mercury)
An assured masterpiece of seduction.
MELODY MAKER

Blending sizzling, memorable melodies with
sensitive, sensible lyrics, Tears For Fears bring a sense of purpose and a feeling of passion to glossy pop.
SOUNDS

The perfect group for all those fucked up,
'what are we going to do with our lives' student types who spend every moment wrapped up in their tiny problems and pathetic existence.
NEW MUSICAL EXPRESS

TECHNO TWINS
Technostalgia (PRT)
Needs less romance and more *sex*.
MELODY MAKER

The duo flopped under the monicker of Ritz,
flopped as Famous Names, and it looks as if
they'll do the same thing under this title.
RECORD MIRROR

A clothes peg on the nose is heartily recommended, the reek of quick-buck cash-in being
strong enough to induce rapid nausea.
NEW MUSICAL EXPRESS

TELEX
Birds And Bees (Interdisc)
Insanely boring electro-thud.
SOUNDS

An undistinguished piece of furniture.
NEW MUSICAL EXPRESS

Gimmick-ridden frogs...so unimportant it
doesn't even hurt.
MELODY MAKER

THIN LIZZY
Thunder And Lightning (Vertigo)
I think we've heard it all before somewhere.
SOUNDS

There is no constructive use of music
anywhere here, simply a masque of gestures
and motifs and irrelevancies.
NEW MUSICAL EXPRESS

An enormously disagreeable piece of work,
this isn't so much Thin Lizzy's last stand as
their final collapse.
MELODY MAKER

RICHARD THOMPSON
Hand Of Kindness (Hannibal)
The best British album we're likely to hear all
year...Newly aggressive, magnificently
ambitious.
MELODY MAKER

TANGERINE DREAM

80

THOMPSON TWINS
Quick Step & Side Kick (Arista)
About as interesting as a Wolverhampton bus station at two in the morning.
RECORD MIRROR

More like an exercise in industrial design than a labour of love or inspiration.
MELODY MAKER

Not only multifaceted and musically mature, but upliftingly alive as well.
NEW MUSICAL EXPRESS

They'll be around after many of today's one-hit wonders are tossed out with the next change of fashion.
CREEM

TRACY THORN

THOMPSON TWINS

TRACY THORN
A Distant Shore (Cherry Red)
A demanding record both emotionally and intellectually.
MELODY MAKER

All too rare at a time when the mechanical love-by-numbers song constructions of Martin Fry are generally considered as the ultimate in romantic songwriting.
NEW MUSICAL EXPRESS

An oasis of sense and sanity in the desperate music biz production line aridity.
SOUNDS

GEORGE THOROGOOD & THE DESTROYERS
Bad To The Bone (EMI America)
A lot of bottleneck but I don't detect too much bottle.
MELODY MAKER

JOHNNY THUNDERS
In Cold Blood (New Rose)
It's all pretty loose, grunge and grind stuff.
NEW MUSICAL EXPRESS

JOHNNY THUNDERS AND THE HEARTBREAKERS
D T K — Live At The Speakeasy (Jungle)
Thunders and the Heartbreakers at a time of promise and pandemonium, energy and tomfoolery.
MELODY MAKER

Suffers not at all from time lapse recovery. Unreservedly recommended.
SOUNDS

PETER TOSH
Mama Africa (EMI)
The set is squarely aimed at the American market with its glossy coffee-table production and a plethora of rockist guitar solos.
SOUNDS

PETE TOWNSHEND
Scoop (Atco)
More odds'n'sods from the attic of one of the oddest sods in rock music.
NEW MUSICAL EXPRESS

Nice idea, carefully packaged and annotated by the author, but really adding up to very little.
MELODY MAKER

This sorrowful piece of junk.
CREEM

THE TOY DOLLS
Dig That Groove Baby (Volume)
The best live band in North East England, if not the whole of Blighty, if not the world . . . A band this good is a rare and wonderful thing.
SOUNDS

TOYAH
Warrior Rock — Toyah On Tour (Safari)
Toyah represents a positive, adventurous spirit of rebellion.
SOUNDS

A giant leap on Toyah's unstoppable road to domination.
RECORD MIRROR

Unimaginative pomp-rock pimpled with overblown guitar solos.
NEW MUSICAL EXPRESS

PAT TRAVERS
Black Pearl (Polydor)
For someone who has enjoyed a taste of success and then fallen on his face, this is a distinctly promising re-start.
SOUNDS

TRIO
Trio (Mercury)
Original, funny, tongue in cheek and not at all your usual bleak, skeletal European sci-fi bores.
RECORD MIRROR

An immensely intelligent and many sided LP.
SOUNDS

Shan't be playing this one again.
MELODY MAKER

PETER TOSH

81

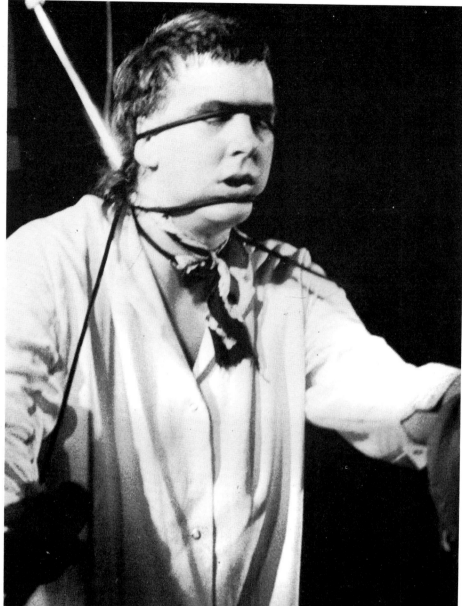

TWELFTH NIGHT

TROUBLEFUNK
Drop The Bomb (Sugarhill)
A powerhouse, non-stop and totally energised...you're bound to be hooked to the cookin' sound.
SOUNDS

Nothing wrong with it in small doses, but after the third track both muscles and brain get a little weary.
MELODY MAKER

THE TUBES
Inside/Outside (Capitol)
The Tubes have finally become what they used to lampoon: A flickering, glossy entertainment that only requires a little will-power to turn off.
SOUNDS

They should have been revealed as impostors years ago. They have nothing to say, nor anything pretty to wear.
NEW MUSICAL EXPRESS

MAUREEN TUCKER
Playin' Possum (Trash)
The first one-woman garage band in recorded history.
NEW MUSICAL EXPRESS

The sort of sad album old people make.
MELODY MAKER

TV PERSONALITIES
They Could Have Been Bigger Than The Beatles (Whaam)
Its scope is incredible, its ambition outstanding.
MELODY MAKER

Falls tantalizingly short of the standard the band has always set.
SOUNDS

It works in spurts, and wears you down over two sides.
NEW MUSICAL EXPRESS

TV SMITH
Channel Five (Expulsion)
This unexpected, unannounced gift of beauty and vitality...TV now ranks up alongside Paul Weller and the Difford/Tilbrook partnership.
SOUNDS

The sub-hermetic musical vision of TV Smith takes quite a bit of understanding.
MELODY MAKER

TWELFTH NIGHT
Fact And Fiction (Twelfth Night)
Why this lot are still going baffles me.
MELODY MAKER

They still aren't able to do much more than reproduce a style that ultimately floundered on its own pomposity.
SOUNDS

23 SKIDOO
The Culling Is Coming (Operation Twilight)
23 Skidoo remind me of a magician who has done one baffling trick with his hands and who, mystified himself by how he did it, tries to repeat it by going through fairly the same motions but without whipping out a bunny in the end.
SOUNDS

TWISTED SISTER
Under The Blade (Secret)
The cockiest cock rocker I've heard for a long time...a fabulously unsubtle piece of musical saturation bombing.
MELODY MAKER

Sheer staggering excellence...beneath all the forklift truck-loads of mascara, Twisted Sister are metal megastars.
SOUNDS

TWISTED SISTER
You Can't Stop Rock'n'Roll (Atlantic)
Cockier than a stud farm, harder than a New York street gang, more rabble-rousing than a Right To Work march, Twisted Sister are here to stay.
SOUNDS

If every successful HM platter of the last few years were fed into a computer, 'You Can't Stop Rock'n'Roll would emerge as the result. It's the perfect Identikit HM album.
NEW MUSICAL EXPRESS

TWISTED SISTER

TYGERS OF PAN TANG
The Cage (MCA)
The kind of once in a lifetime album that should see them on the path to worldwide fame.
RECORD MIRROR

Scarcely a major breakthrough either musically or commercially.
MELODY MAKER

BONNIE TYLER
Faster Than The Speed Of Night (RCA)
This is a BIG album.
SOUNDS

When Elkie Brooks at last heads for the Sunnydown Retirement home for old singing hacks, Bonnie Tyler is sure to take over.
RECORD MIRROR

TYMON DOGG
Battle Of Wills (Y Records)
It almost compensates for the drivel like ABC and Duran Duran that we've had to endure for most of the year.
MELODY MAKER

ULTRAVOX

UFO
Making Contact (Chrysalis)
About as raunchy as a twinset and pearls.
NEW MUSICAL EXPRESS

Another first class UFO album.
SOUNDS

UK SUBS
Recorded 1979-1981 (Abstract)
Contains all of the Subs' indispensable items...still one of the best-loved punk bands around.
MELODY MAKER

JAMES BLOOD ULMER
Black Rock (CBS)
Ulmer plays forgettably... Raw and raucous racket.
MELODY MAKER

ULTRAVOX
Quartet (Chrysalis)
A consistent Euro bore beat and a judicious spray of sticky hooks.
MELODY MAKER

Sounds like the last album and the next 12... makes Radio One jingles sound like the entire Velvet Underground repertoire.
NEW MUSICAL EXPRESS

What's been happening to Ultravox's music is decay. Synthetic decay.
CREEM

THE UNDERTONES
The Sin Of Pride (Ardeck)
The Undertones have grown up.
MELODY MAKER

Even better than that cracker of a debut album.
SOUNDS

URBAN DOGS
Urban Dogs (Fallout)
The slowest punk LP of all time.
NEW MUSICAL EXPRESS

URIAH HEEP

URIAH HEEP
Head First (Bronze)
This one's a gem. Heep's rebirth is continuing unabated and you should be a part of it.
SOUNDS

There's nothing to distinguish this work from any one of a dozen other mid-Atlantic metal bands.
MELODY MAKER

U2
War (Island)
U2 would do better to sign away their earnings to Amnesty International and take up posts with the Red Cross.
MELODY MAKER

Hog tied and hamfisted...another example of rock music's impotence and decay.
NEW MUSICAL EXPRESS

UB40
The Singles Album (Graduate)
Clean, inoffensive and above all, dull.
RECORD MIRROR

UB40
UB44 (Dep International)
I'm waiting for them to give a few cries of rage instead of one long lament.
RECORD MIRROR

The looming danger now is that they could become the Genesis of reggae.
MELODY MAKER

Great in parts and terminally dull at times — which is pretty much what you'd expect really.
SOUNDS

VANDENBERG
Vandenberg (Atlantic)
Unknown Dutchmen.
SOUNDS

VANITY 6
Vanity 6 (Warner Bros)
Three broody broads in scanty suspenders.
MELODY MAKER

Blatant erotica blended with irony.
SOUNDS

VARIOUS ARTISTS
Ballroom Blitz (Razor)
A timely reminder of just how effortlessly superb the best of those early Seventies glitter critters could sound.
SOUNDS

VARIOUS ARTISTS
The Batcave — Young Limbs And Numb Hymns (London)
While all the doomy gothic horror and splendour and the ripped lace and leather works to create an atmosphere there, it doesn't really transfer to vinyl.
RECORD MIRROR

Does little to convince anybody but the fervently committed that there is any purpose about it other than to promote the pose.
MELODY MAKER

VARIOUS ARTISTS
Birth Of The Y (Y Records)
Hangs on a peg of white funk and saxist bleating.
MELODY MAKER

If Y didn't release them, no one else would.
NEW MUSICAL EXPRESS

VARIOUS ARTISTS
Bullshit Detector Volume 2 (Crass)
Surely nobody could sit through this tortuous quagmire of nonsense and honestly experience any kind of pleasure.
SOUNDS

VARIOUS ARTISTS
Burning Ambitions: A History Of Punk (Cherry Red)
Only enough good songs for one disc.
SOUNDS

The most successful of the many compilations in the shops now.
MELODY MAKER

VARIOUS ARTISTS
The INDIpop CompilASIAN Album (Virgin)
It sounds "Indian" in the same way an Opal Fruit might claim to be "strawberry" or "lemon".
NEW MUSICAL EXPRESS

Takes an extremely dubious route from straight ethnic folk stuff through to piss-weak Monsoon copyism, stopping at a number of curry and kebab houses along the way.
SOUNDS

VARIOUS ARTISTS
The Kids Are United (Music For Nations)
An essential punk history lesson from 1978 to 1981 — Oi's greatest hits and more.
SOUNDS

VARIOUS ARTISTS
La Rockabilly — 14 Rockin' Hit Songs (Rhino)
Survival of the species is ensured.
SOUNDS

VARIOUS ARTISTS
Methods Of Dance Vol. 2 (Virgin)
Slapdash and thoughtless...strictly for dedicated mugs.
NEW MUSICAL EXPRESS

VARIOUS ARTISTS
Music And Rhythm (WEA)
A benefit double album for the World Of Music Arts And Dance...one of the most satisfying musical celebrations ever put together.
MELODY MAKER

A squirming bundle of musics from non-European sources, interlaced with Ethnological Forgeries by assorted pop stars.
NEW MUSICAL EXPRESS

VARIOUS ARTISTS
Oi! Oi! That's Yer Lot! (Secret)
Coming Blood steal the show with a wild stormer, ending with the great one-liner "That went down like the Belgrana".
SOUNDS

VARIOUS ARTISTS
The Original Motor Town Revue (Tamla Motown)
Poorly recorded and the backing track is often little more than a dull thud that seems to be coming from the parking lot outside.
NEW MUSICAL EXPRESS

VARIOUS ARTISTS
Original Soundtrack from Flashdance (Casablanca)
How Donna Summer, Laura Branigan and Kim Carnes could sing such dreadful songs is beyond me.
RECORD MIRROR

VARIOUS ARTISTS
Party Party (A&M)
If you get an invite don't bother going — the music's lousy.
RECORD MIRROR

VARIOUS ARTISTS
Pillows And Prayers (Cherry Red)
The perfect introduction to some of bed-sitland's more idiosyncratic young beat combos.
RECORD MIRROR

Yards ahead of any compilation this year.
NEW MUSICAL EXPRESS

VARIOUS ARTISTS
Punk And Disorderly — Further Charges (Anagram)
Every track worth its place...more than half verging on excellence!
MELODY MAKER

Pumps some clout into a fuxx-flaccid subculture.
NEW MUSICAL EXPRESS

VIRGIN PRUNES

84

HOLLY BETH VINCENT

THE VIBRATORS
Guilty (Anagram)
Don't be fooled into thinking that The Vibrators are in a time-warp or a rut.
MELODY MAKER

In a quite repulsive manner, it's brilliant.
SOUNDS

Hollow cover versions and hollower originals.
NEW MUSICAL EXPRESS

HOLLY BETH VINCENT
Holly And The Italians (Virgin)
People who still hang out at Dingwalls might take it.
MELODY MAKER

VIRGIN PRUNES
If I Die, I Die (Rough Trade)
A veneer of mannered primal angst and the portentous mystique of nostalgia de la boue.
NEW MUSICAL EXPRESS

I found it irritating just having the album in the room with me.
MELODY MAKER

VIRGIN STEELE
Virgin Steele One (Record Mirror)
Imagine Black Sabbath being played at 78 rpm with an overdub of someone smashing up a dustbin.
RECORD MIRROR

WAH!
Wah! The Maverick Years 80-81 (Wah!)
Sounds like demos and rehearsal tapes, some of it great, some atrocious.
NEW MUSICAL EXPRESS

Beg, steal, borrow or, much better, BUY a copy of "The Maverick Years" and try to remain unmoved.
MELODY MAKER

VARIOUS ARTISTS
Punk & Disorderly III — The Final Solution (Anagram)
Some of the very best street-punk releases of the last nine months.
SOUNDS

The sleeve strewn with the symbols of Nazi Germany (including Hitler) and a clutter of soldiers pointing guns at a gaggle of unfortunate blindfolded punks.
MELODY MAKER

VARIOUS ARTISTS
Rapped Uptight (Sugarhill)
Goes a long way in pinpointing the beauty and banality of rap music.
MELODY MAKER

For all practical purposes, definitive.
NEW MUSICAL EXPRESS

VARIOUS ARTISTS
Reading Rock Volume One (Mean)
Eight goodies and a dozen dustbin jobs.
MELODY MAKER

VARIOUS ARTISTS
Singles: The Great New York Singles Scene (Reach Out International)
Seminal NYC punk singles of the Seventies.
MELODY MAKER

VARIOUS ARTISTS
Summer Means Fun (CBS)
Not to me it doesn't.
RECORD MIRROR

Some of the finest rock'n'roll phenomenae America has sired.
SOUNDS

VARIOUS ARTISTS
The Whip (Kamera)
Sub-Pistollian hippy trash which draws no blood at all.
RECORD MIRROR

VENOM
Black Metal (Neat)
They make Tank and GBH sound like Sooty and Sweep.
SOUNDS

WAH!

LOUDON WAINWRIGHT III
Fame And Wealth (Demon)
The charm wears thin, as if rubbed too long against a worldly cynicism that's ossified into apathy.
NEW MUSICAL EXPRESS

The patchiest thing he's ever done.
MELODY MAKER

THE WAITRESSES
Bruiseology (Polydor)
There's only so much mileage in the true confessions of a Mid-Western female Woody Allen.
NEW MUSICAL EXPRESS

Terminal urban neurotics.
MELODY MAKER

WALL OF VOODOO
Call Of The West (Illegal)
A fearsomely assured set of songs, organised with brilliant clarity.
MELODY MAKER

A veritable bolt out of the blue that supplies a much needed shot in the arm.
SOUNDS

DIONNE WARWICK
Heartbreaker (Arista)
Hideously soupy Barry Gibb concoctions, all tremulously forgettable departure-lounge fodder.
NEW MUSICAL EXPRESS

WASTED YOUTH
The Beginning Of The End (Bridge House)
Like a primary school panto!
NEW MUSICAL EXPRESS

Never has a bunch of collective wrist artists been more aptly named.
RECORD MIRROR

A decent epitaph.
MELODY MAKER

BEN WATT
North Marine Drive (Cherry Red)
A collection of introspective confessionals that recalls nothing so much as the bedsitter images of that legion of impossibly sensitive singer-songwriters who spent the early Seventies hitching down the highways of their soulful moody minds.
MELODY MAKER

A calm pool of turbulent moods, a peaceful evocation of emotional turmoil.
SOUNDS

What we don't need is another Ralph McTell.
NEW MUSICAL EXPRESS

WEAPON OF PEACE
Rainbow Rhythm (Safari)
Could be tailor-made for Brent Cross — it has that numbing sensation: bland, sterile and boring to the point of annoyance.
MELODY MAKER

Level 42 and Shakatak spring to mind as comparisons.
NEW MUSICAL EXPRESS

WEATHER REPORT
Procession (CBS)
A show of their greatest strengths and a nosing through new quarters.
NEW MUSICAL EXPRESS

JAMES WHITE AND THE BLACKS

WEEKEND
La Variete (Rough Trade)
A masterful debut and one of the best records to emerge this year.
MELODY MAKER

It's our old friend Easy Listening — diversity and depth don't really get a look in.
NEW MUSICAL EXPRESS

Too much stylistic badge wearing, not enough sharp needles.
SOUNDS

WHAM!
Fantastic (Inner Vision)
Wham! are a period piece as surely as Darts or Mari Wilson; they sing about the early and mid-70's, last exit to boomtown.
NEW MUSICAL EXPRESS

Even at their best Wham! don't cut the cake with the same degree of sharpness as their predecessors in the white soul vocal stakes.
MELODY MAKER

The pace is a steady 100mph without a single stop for lachrymose reflection...This is white heat disco...easily the record of summer '83.
SOUNDS

WILDLIFE
Wildlife (Swansong)
Certain tracks could've done with more punch, conviction and even, dare I say, wildfire.
SOUNDS

WEEKEND

JAMES WHITE AND THE BLACKS
Sax Maniac (Animal)
Seems to have succumbed to a terminal case of tunnel vision...just looks like a spent force.
NEW MUSICAL EXPRESS

What this amounts to is "avant-funk-by-numbers" — "dance" music that makes you want to sink into a chair.
MELODY MAKER

This is the stuff of which revolutions are made. Brilliant! Just bloody brilliant.
SOUNDS

This is James White's big band record, and in my opinion, his best yet.
BOSTON ROCK

SNOWY WHITE
White Flames (Towerbell)
A varied package of rock, blues, funk and even a touch of jazz, a range of styles that illustrates Snowy's versatility well.
SOUNDS

Some people should stick to being sidemen and never step into the spotlight themselves.
MELODY MAKER

WHITESNAKE
Saints & Sinners (Liberty)
A thoroughly enjoyable album for almost any occasion, and any volume.
SOUNDS

Is it all a lucrative wind-up David?
MELODY MAKER

THE WHO
It's Hard (Polydor Deluxe)
Tired, limp, sterile and almost totally bereft of any semblance of creative spark or flair.
MELODY MAKER

Middle age has hit the Who like a ton of bricks...Me, I'd rather listen to Tony Bennett.
CREEM

MARI WILSON
Showpeople (Compact)
As piped music in some remote supermarket, it would easily blend into bland amongst the frozen peas.
SOUNDS

Can you really respect anybody whose ultimate ambition is to end up like Lulu?
MELODY MAKER

Mari Wilson sings like a boiling kettle with adenoids, and that's being kind...she is an amateur hour impersonator.
NEW MUSICAL EXPRESS

STEVE WINWOOD
Talking Back To The Night (Island)
Tender, consoling and all-embracing 'adult-oriented rock'.
SOUNDS

Winwood is this season's Gerry Rafferty.
NEW MUSICAL EXPRESS

The best album that Pete Townshend never made.
CREEM

A desultory continuation of the duller elements of Winwood's past.
MELODY MAKER

Blue-eyed MOR...Are all our cult heroes doomed to surrender to the dictates of American radio?
RECORD MIRROR

JAH WOBBLE
Jah Wobble's Bedroom Album (Logo)
Only a few notches above the meanderings of miserable dial-a-bands like Tears For Fears.
NEW MUSICAL EXPRESS

A stop-gap for the dedicated collector?
MELODY MAKER

ROY WOOD
The Singles (Speed Records)
Deserves sunshine praise born of more than just summer nostalgia.
RECORD MIRROR

MARI WILSON

XTC
Waxworks/Beeswax (Virgin)
A two-album 25-song retrospective... survey and appreciate the breathtaking breadth, vivid scope.
MELODY MAKER

The last word in uselessness...This is SDPop.
NEW MUSICAL EXPRESS

THE WHO

87

NEIL YOUNG

The World appears a better place when you see it drunk on the Yello excess.
NEW MUSICAL EXPRESS

YOUNG MARBLE GIANTS/GIST/WEEKEND
Nipped In The Bud (Rough Trade)
Rough Trade go K-Tel...20 tracks, all as short as a sliver of "Stars on 45" and fragile as the Turin Shroud.
NEW MUSICAL EXPRESS

All three groups share the same delicate feel and understatement.
RECORD MIRROR

NEIL YOUNG
Trans (Geffen)
The most imaginative, innovative and humorous electronic pop songs you've ever heard.
BOSTON ROCK

A very good Flock-of-Seagulls-meets-Kraftwerk record.
CREEM

Is a major Neil Young record.
MELODY MAKER

Offers the less than inviting spectacle of an ageing folkie rebel stumbling onto a new toy called the vocoder.
NEW MUSICAL EXPRESS

Y

YAZOO
Upstairs At Eric's (Mute)
Shows all the signs of a collaboration that's still in a promising infancy.
NEW MUSICAL EXPRESS

One hell of an album.
SOUNDS

An album of rich, dark passion, forever burying the hoary old moan that electronics and synthesisers will never be any good because they don't have a button on the front that says "emotion".
MELODY MAKER

YAZOO
You And Me Both (Mute)
Over half this record puts pop's foremost maverick duo in a superlative master class...stands as one of 1983's major achievements.
NEW MUSICAL EXPRESS

A classic example of resonant pop, fun and yet not throwaway, deep but not depressing.
SOUNDS

What a stilted, aimless mess...the pulse stopped beating long ago.
RECORD MIRROR

Shows that the duo *were* beginning to grow further apart, and perhaps it's as well they split while the going was good...*not* Yazoo's finest hour.
MELODY MAKER

YELLO
You Gotta Say Yes To Another Excess (Stiff)
In a word: brilliant. In two: brilliantly subversive.
MELODY MAKER

The most adventurous I've heard all year... mysterious, dangerous and humorous.
RECORD MIRROR

Z

WARREN ZEVON
The Envoy (Asylum)
One of our most critically overrated troubled troubadours.
CREEM

The dreariest album he's ever made.
MELODY MAKER

ZZ TOP
Eliminator (Warner Bros)
They must be patted on the back for the simple achievement of recording a completely unremarkable and eminently forgettable set of songs.
NEW MUSICAL EXPRESS

The sort of album that has given guitars a bad name. It's not the guitar that should be maligned, but the lazy, empty-hearted halfwits who think this sort of tired mediocrity is tough and dangerous.
MELODY MAKER

Good old fashioned brawl music brought right up to date...without the slightest hint of compromise or mediocrity.
MELODY MAKER

SINGLES

By July, 1983 had become the year of the Record Business Revival. The long slump (since 1978) was, it seemed, over (or had, at least, bottomed out); purring record company spokesmen were predicting a 10% increase in the year's record and tape sales. *Time* magazine had a story: New Rock On A Red-Hot Roll. Sizzling Sales Have Record Execs Dancin' In The Suites. "A diverse but irresistible mix of sounds has brought the kids back not only to the record racks, but to the clubs and the concerts as well — New Music, a blend of soul, rock, reggae and disco set to a synthesised, whipcrack beat has them buying and dancing again."

This was an American sales boom (British revival figures were less inspiring), but it was bound up with the invasion of the American charts by British pop — the "New Music" (heralded by The Human League's success last year) was mostly made in the UK. And so singles suddenly had their old purpose — not as promotional trailers for routine new LPs from routine old stars, but as the ear-grabbing way to get people to listen to new acts. For much of the last decade the US rock business has been trapped in a vicious circle: safe acts leading to dulled audiences leading to stagnant sales leading to no-risk A&R policies leading to safe acts. And so *Time*'s optimism expressed, if nothing else, the hope that risks were being taken again — risks mean excitement means the sales that justify risks. The story gave me a strong sense of an industry hyping itself up — talking risks before taking them — and for the truth of the "boom" come back next year.

Still, there are reasons why people think things are happening, why the circle can be broken. First, radio programmers have begun to realise that their traditional youth market (10-24 year olds

DURAN DURAN

89

still account for about half the American pop market) was getting decidedly bored with the Superstar format, that good pop radio still needs good *sounds* and can't rely simply on over-repeated star formulas. BBC Radio One has always understood this and so Britain's new pop successes were the obvious source of new American radio acts too — there's no doubt that more British singles were played on American radio this year than at any time since the late sixties (hence the USA's brightest new rock'n'roll band, Stray Cats, reached their audience via their British reputation).

But a conservative radio programmer like Lee Abrams doesn't change formats just because of a vague sense of boredom — he needs advance evidence that new acts really do sell and this came from a different source: 1983 was the year of Music Television. MTV started broadcasting a 24-hour-a-day video music service in August 1981 and now reaches at least 14 million subscribers. When it began the only good source of video clips were British performers — video was already an established form of UK pop promotion (on *Top of the Pops* and all those children's programmes), and it was the immediate success of such British acts as Adam Ant, The Human League and Soft Cell that made the American record industry aware of the sales possibilities of MTV. It works, in fact, as a continuous advertisement — record companies provide their clips for free — and the major record companies have benefited most from it, since they've got the stars and the video-recording resources. Indeed, MTV is half-owned by Warner Communications, and is the exact video equivalent of a mainstream AM rock station — its clips are chosen to meet the tastes of (and attract advertisers for) the 10-24 year old white music market.

It's important to stress this because in Britain, at any rate, MTV has got a mythical status, but while it can certainly be credited with British pop's American impact, it is by now (as even well-established stadium stars are video-promoted) much duller than *Top of the Pops*. My own US experience suggests that MTV is background viewing — the station's on but the sound is

THOMPSON TWINS

off, other music is playing. Boring videos seen more than once are very boring, and even good videos stand far fewer repeats than good records.

MTV is not, then, the wonder medium the record business is pretending. In television business terms it is in fact, as Dave Marsh pointed out in his newsletter, *Rock & Roll Confidential*, "a significant market failure." It is still losing money and Warners' co-owner, American Express, apparently wants out. For Warners, though, such immediate profits (from the sale of ads) are not the point. MTV is a way of boosting record sales and from this perspective MTV's effects can't be denied. For the first time since The Bay City Rollers (who also relied on TV promotion), British teen idols are crossing the Atlantic. The pop stars of the year were, I fear, Duran Duran who even,

TEARS FOR FEARS

90

bizarrely, began to preen themselves as the new Beatles (orchestrated airport hysteria, Royal Command shows, etc). Duran Duran's videos (vulgarised Martini ads) are, though, much more effective sales devices than their records (which I can't remember at all), and so the best Duran Duran record of the year was actually KajaGooGoo's unpretentiously sickly 'Too Shy', while the teeny sound of the year wasn't Duran Duran's watered down Beatlism but the more resonant angst of twitchy boys with synthesisers — Tears for Fears, Naked Eyes, Blancmange, Depeche Mode, etc. My favourite electropop hits were, though, British records that reached us via the US charts — A Flock of Seagulls' dumb 'I Ran' and Thomas Dolby's clever 'She Blinded Me With Science'.

I must confess, though, that I find this sort of New Music — programmed ditties, nursery rhymes and rhythms — much less engaging than last year's knowing New Pop (ABC etc). The pop model seems to have swung back from Roxy Music, artifice as style, to David Bowie, art as pose, and it was therefore appropriate that Bowie himself should finally bless the video pop scene with his own hit (his biggest ever). 'Let's Dance' had effortless dancefloor authority, a confidently opaque video (I never did work out what those red shoes had to do with Aboriginal Affairs) and became rapidly wearing — the very ease with which Bowie rode this market confirmed my sense of video as the ultimate capitalist fantasy. Video pop groups like Duran Duran, video pop hits like 'Let's Dance' are *pure* commercials, involve no actual product. MTV may be making record companies new profits but it seems to have no *use* value at all.

There are exceptions to all rules, though, and I can nominate the five video performers of the year; the artificers extraordinary:

Culture Club — the important point about Boy George is not the way he looks (though in the setting of MTV's sexual routines his clumsy effeminacy is definitely subversive) but that he sounds so good while looking that way. 'Do You Really Want to Hurt Me' and 'Time' are supremely elegant records.
Thompson Twins may

EURYTHMICS

have a simple formula — dribbled synthesiser lines, percussive bounce, mannered voices — but they used it to make one perfect pop single, 'Love on Your Side', and one fun follow-up, 'We Are Detective'.
Yazoo (or Yaz as they regrettably have to be called in the USA) — 'Don't Go' and 'Only You' from the beginning

of the year, 'Nobody's Diary' from the end were wonderfully simple records: Vince Clark's throwaway melodies, Alison Moyet's rounded vowels, the nagging banalities of passion.
Eurythmics are a more neurotic duo with similar obsessions — 'Love Is a Stranger' and 'Sweet Dreams' were insidious records (with sharp videos), Annie Lennox,

like Boy George, disturbing the MTV audience with the playful, furtive invention of her own sexuality.

But all these groups play games with sex, cross-cut male and female voices, electronic and human noise, disrupt the rules of video pop while meeting old ideas of pop need. See their videos against those of the mainstream and realise

PRINCE CHARLES

the stodgy conservatism of the so-called pop revival. MTV features, hour after hour, the most tedious images of masculinity and femininity, the most boring rock fantasies — glamour as tight pants, a pout, leather everywhere. In Britain, similarly, the rise of boy pop has meant a return to the old division of attention — girls as fans, boys as pin-ups. Keyboards are obvious female instruments (all those piano lessons) and there are numerous women in mixed bands (New Order, The Associates, Joe Jackson), but syn-pop is male pop and women singles-makers (Bananarama, The Belle Stars) still get packaged with a sort of big sister frothiness.

MTV has also, more controversially, systematically excluded black acts from its playlists. There are obvious (but very few) exceptions, like Prince, but it was widely reported that CBS had to threaten to withdraw all its acts to get Michael Jackson's clips shown, and this is remarkable given that Jackson was *the* superstar of the moment, *Thriller* the best-selling LP, and that his videos were the most exciting MTV had — the most dramatic, the most compulsive, the best television. **Michael Jackson** is, then, my fifth performer of the year. I sold *Thriller* (an uninteresting LP) and then rushed out to buy, one by one, the singles taken from it. 'Billie Jean', 'Beat It' and 'Wanna Be Startin' Somethin' ' had a tension, a wary energy that cut through the charts like nothing else this year.

Michael Jackson is a superstar because his music crosses all the usual market boundaries, but he's the most important star at present because his success makes it possible for other young black musicians to get major record company interest and support. Without Jackson's example A&R departments would have drifted like rock radio and MTV, into a whites-only policy, justified in terms of giving people what they want. And this isn't simply a race question but reflects a more general account of how music matters — Jackson (as his videos make brilliantly clear) places his music (slick as it is) in the experience of Reagan's (and Thatcher's) *victims* — the poor, the idle, the black, the bored. And this year such references,

MICHAEL JACKSON

exceptional on MTV, bounced recurringly round the dancefloor. The year began with The Valentine Brothers' 'Money's too Tight (to Mention)' and Grandmaster Flash's 'The Message', proceeded through a sort of hedonistic realism, pleasure as seized moments, Grace Jones' 'The Apple Stretching'/'Nipple to the Bottle', Prince's uplifting '1999', Prince Charles and The City Beat Band's 'Cash', and culminated in Gary Byrd's black pride rap, 'The Crown', a joint translation (with Stevie Wonder) of Rastafarian spiritual history into the you-can-make-it-if-you-try terms of American soul.

In Britain the dancefloor celebration of "real" emotion had a more moralistic, self-righteous ring. Making soul records meant making statements, writing manifestos. If Kevin Rowland, the original copy-writer, was kept otherwise busy by the

JOE JACKSON

GRACE JONES

international success of the folky-soul 'Come on Eileen', Paul Weller amply filled his space — The Jam's 'Beat Surrender' and Style Council's 'Money Go Round' came complete with sleeve sermons, slogans, uplift — and it became normal for would-be beat groups (JoBoxers, The Truth) to present their party music as a return to better, more manly times, though the triumph of the beat revival, Paul Young's version of 'Wherever I Lay My Hat (That's My Home)', didn't so much celebrate the old male order as brood about it.

DONNA SUMMER

Dancefloor politics is sexual politics and Paul Weller's continuing problem is that he is unsexy. The year's soul boy stars were, then, Wham!, who moved from the dole queue swagger of 'Wham Rap' via the bachelor boy boasts of 'Young Guns (Go for It)' and 'Bad Boys' to the beach-bum stroll of 'Club Tropicana' taking up more and more *Smash Hits* space as they went.

Otherwise the disco year was framed by Marvin Gaye's 'Sexual Healing' and The Isley Brothers' 'Between the Sheets' — drowsy sensuality to put the Wham! bang into its adolescent perspective. This was a good time for disco soul — Syl Johnson's bluesy 'Ms Fine Brown Frame', Denise Lasalle's urgent 'Come to Bed', Maze's laid-back 'Love Is the Key' and James Brown's cocky 'Bring It On' — and female craft — Melba Moore's 'Love's Comin' at Ya', Evelyn King's 'Love Comes Down' and Mahogany's 'Ride on the Rhythm', with Bernice

JOBOXERS

Watkins, sliding on the rhythm, gliding on the rhythm, too. Donna Summer's 'She Works Hard for the Money' (particularly in its video version) raised appropriate questions about the exploitation of women workers, while Mary Jane Girls' 'All Night Long' brought a surprisingly sweet version of stud-funk into the charts. The Weather Girls' 'It's Raining Men' and Miquel Brown's 'So Many Men — So Little Time' were hilarious gay disco records — men as fetish; but my favourite dance records were Mtume's 'Juicy Fruit' — "I'll be your lollipop — you can lick me everywhere" — and Sharon Redd's tough series of Prelude mixes, 'Never Give You Up', 'In the Name of Love', 'Beat the Street'.

The year's cult names were in the small print of these records, the new generation of New York DJs, producers, mixers, engineers — Francis Kevorkian, Shep Pettibone, John "Jellybean" Benitez. They cut up and jammed together rap and pop and scratch and funk and electronic gadgets in an agitated frenzy. The funk roots of such studio games can be traced back to George Clinton, though his own 'Loopzilla', a jokey trip around the radio dial, sounded distinctly old-fashioned compared to the computerised minimalism of the Extra Ts' 'ET Boogie', Man Parrish's 'Hip Hop Be-Bop (Don't Stop)' or the Ex Tras' 'Haven't Been Funked Enough'. This was conceptual disco — there were limits to how many times I could listen to a vocoder chant "E.T!" much as I like the idea of the phrase going on for ever. I was more comfortable with

STYLE COUNCIL

SHARON REDD

FREEEZ

Ironically enough, the most successful AOR band, the dreary Toto, also toyed with the sounds of 'Africa', while the new all-American sensation, Men at Work, were Australian — in other words the year's mainstream rock hits were as anodyne as ever. I enjoyed The Clash's 'Rock the Casbah' and Joan Armatrading's 'Drop the Pilot' — sure voices amidst the usual strained clichés, and I loved Bonnie Tyler's bemused impersonation of Meatloaf on 'Total Eclipse of the Heart', but the most intriguing chart development was the British appearance of a neo-rock sensibility. This involved punks and popsters "progressing" — Altered Images' 'Bring Me Closer' and 'Don't Talk to Me About Love' (ref: Mamas and Papas?), The Undertones' 'The Love Parade' (ref: Buffalo Springfield?). It was a matter of attitude — the self-conscious gloomy poetics of Echo and The Bunnymen's 'The Cutter' or The Cure's 'The Walk', the arrogant melodrama of Wah's 'The Story of the Blues', the stolid pretensions of Kissing the Pink's 'The Last Film'. It meant a return to guitar-driven energy — U2's 'New Year's Day', Big Country's stirring Scots adventures, 'Fields of Fire' and 'In a Big Country', Orange Juice's nervy club philosophy, 'Rip It Up'.

Meanwhile, Elton John's 'I'm Still Standing' suggested that old stars can age gracefully, Rod Stewart's 'Baby Jane' that they can't. Phil Collins' 'You Can't Hurry Love' was immaculately clean, Hot Chocolate's 'It Started With a Kiss' gloriously dirty. Dionne

BONNIE TYLER

Indeep's cornier, busier 'Last Night a DJ Saved My Life' and the Jonzun Crew's wonderfully excessive soundtracks, 'Space Is the Place' and 'Space Cowboy'. But the producer of the year was Arthur Baker, whose work on Afrika Bambaata's 'Looking for the Perfect Beat' and Rockers Revenge's 'Walking on Sunshine' made him an instant draw for all British would-be modernist funkers. And so Freeez had their simple hook line for 'I.O.U.' brilliantly shredded, and were followed into Baker's New York lab by New Order, whose own 'Blue Monday' was certainly the only British single this year with a genuinely powerful funk intelligence (for feeble funk intelligence cue Heaven 17).

Such records completed the dissolution of the distinctions between engineer and musician, recorded and live performance — what's going on when a scratch or dub mixer appears "live" with turntables as his instrument? Maybe this is why jazz funk passed me by — the appeal of even Brass

Construction's 'Walkin' the Line' and D-Train's 'Do You Wanna Ride' lay in the remixes — and this may be the reason too why, for all the live triumphs of Sunny Adé and his Afro-Beats, African singles made so little impact. The "ethnic" successes of the year were, rather, Malcolm McLaren's and Trevor Horn's scratched collages of found folk music — 'Buffalo Gals', 'Soweto' and 'Double Dutch'.

BIG COUNTRY

BUCKS FIZZ

of his 'Walking on Sunshine' began a year in which Grant's formula — exotic, bossy, crafty pop — meant number ones in both Britain ('I Don't Wanna Dance') and the USA ('Electric Avenue').

Film song of the year was, I suppose, Irene Cara's 'Flashdance' (look forward now to The Kids From Flashdance) and European record of the year was (despite Renee and Renato's Xmas efforts) F.R. David's 'Words' — timeless self-pity.

Finally, three "political" singles, records, that is, which justified pop as a way of seizing the moment, defining the time, curling sense round the usual media nonsense. Robert Wyatt's 'Shipbuilding' (words by Elvis Costello) was a profoundly sad meditation on war and work and hope, a heartening response to Falklands hysteria. Costello also emerged (as The Imposter) just before the General Election with 'Pills and Soap', a dark, swirling, passionate song which listeners knew (Costello himself had various stories) was as solid an anti-Thatcherist number as we'd get. Tom Robinson's 'War Baby' used the opposite device: personal conflict in political language, live in the combat zone. These records did what pop is supposed to do: offered public words for private use, private griefs for public use, layers of

DIONNE WARWICK

Warwick took surprising delight in the Bee Gee harmonies of 'Heartbreaker', Bucks Fizz's Abba impersonation actually made sense of 'When I Was Young', and after weeks of Spandau Ballet's stiff ballad 'True' I found I was addicted to the

"huh huh huh" bits. But the pop singles of the year were more smartly organised: Joe Jackson's 'Steppin' Out', Aztec Camera's 'Oblivious', The Police's 'Every Breath You Take' — stripped down sounds, ironic reflections, romantic disturbances.

Remaining categories. The chart successes of Bob Marley's lightweight 'Buffalo Soldier' drew attention to the lack of other reggae hits (Radio One has its own way of giving white people what they want). Musical Youth's 'Pass the Dutchie' was a lovely celebration of reggae itself, but it was a world-wide bestseller as a novelty, and there were no other overwhelming hits even in the reggae charts. My favourites thus reflect a random ignorance — Johnny Osbourne's 'One More Rub-a-Dub', heavy lovers' rock, and John Holt's 'Police and Helicopter', a wistful tale of threat and violence. And there was one remarkable Caribbean success story: Eddy Grant

ECHO AND THE BUNNYMEN

moved to Barbados just as his Ice label hit pay dirt. Rockers Revenge's smash disco version

doubt and meaning to ripple through our lives.
SIMON FRITH

HALL & OATES

A heavy fog drapes over Pennsylvania. A storm is gathering in the west; the distant sound of thunder reverberates through the stone facade of Temple University.

Just outside the building, four young men in rags cower under the eaves, shivering in the rain. Their voices rise up over the thunder, doo wopping against the tempest. The harmony is strictly American.

In the basement laboratory of the university, two students sit on high lab stools, their respectively blond and brunette heads bent over a boiling beaker. A wisp of sweat trickles down the blond's neck. The experiment is almost completed.

The translucent liquid in the beaker begins to froth madly. Strains of doo wop echo off the stone walls outside, crescendoing. A shower of smoke and fire spills ceilingwards, barely singeing the corners of the brunette's full moustache. The blond turns to face his friend.

"Eureka," he whispers hoarsely in the sudden silence. "We've found it. The formula..."

Not, perhaps, a very likely scenario. For one thing, Hall and Oates ferociously deny the accusations of adhering to a formula that follow their every record release as dependably as summer follows spring. Their music is complex, they insist. Certainly it has a rigid form, but it's thanks to that form that they have more room to improvise than other musicians. Their first three LPs (*Whole Oats, Abandoned Luncheonette* and *War Babies*), they point out, were so different that people couldn't believe they emanated from the same source. Still, their only big hit in that three album run, 'She's Gone', is echoed very effectively in the first big hit from their fourth LP, the controversial silver album. That hit was the ubiquitous 'Sara Smile', and with it Hall and Oates knew they were on to something.

How did they meet? Reports, as always in the music world, vary. The best story is that they met during a brawl in one of the clubs in which their

respective bands were playing. When the fight broke out, the story goes, Daryl and John met in the elevator, trying to escape unscathed. Other stories include the most likely one — that they met at Temple University, where John was studying journalism to avoid the Vietnam draft and Daryl was studying music. They liked each other, became roommates, and began working together when their various outside projects started to pale.

They went the usual route: building up a following in Philadelphia, showcasing for record companies in New York and finally moving there after Atlantic Records released their first album, *Whole Oats*. They credit Greenwich Village for the atmosphere of the second one, *Abandoned Luncheonette*, which, in their minds, represented the end of their lives as Pennsylvanians.

After the success of *Luncheonette*, the boys got itchy to try something new, to illustrate musically their move to the big city. So they hired Todd Rundgren as a producer and released *War Babies*.

Hall remembers wearing a leopard-skin shirt the night he and Oates, backed by art-rock heavies like Rick Laird of the Mahavishnu Orchestra, played their first hometown show after the release of their third album. "My mother came to that show," Hall laughs. "She sat down at a table for the second set, and written on the mat were the words, 'Leave! These guys suck!' " The Philly folk/doo wop fans were not happy. They'd come expecting the duo they knew and loved; instead, they were confronted with heavy metal art.

War Babies did not make them superstars. They were just about back at square one, but now, they figured, they had something to prove and not too much pressure to prove it. Enter the silver album, with a cover displaying Hall and Oates made up by Pierre La Roche, who had told them, "I'm going to immortalise you two." The album did well. And the formula was patented.

Complex is the key word in anything relating to Daryl Hall and John Oates. It is, in fact,

the word they themselves use more than any other word in the English language.

When asked if he thinks of himself as a "pop" musician, Daryl Hall replies that "We're musicians who are using pop music to do something else, and you can look at our music and perceive it on different levels. It's interesting enough, we hope, that you can look at it from all angles. And lyrically we're trying to do the same thing. The subjects of our lyrics can be looked at in a lot of different ways. Pretty complex. Especially if you should decide to spend an afternoon trying to figure out how many ways you can look at such lyrics as 'Your kiss is on my list...' "

John Oates is a little less complex on the subject. "Once you have something good, you can repeat it," he clarifies. "The problem is finding something good enough to repeat."

To make the process of writing lyrics a little less awesome, the pair often collaborate, sometimes enlisting the aid of Hall's long-time main squeeze Sara (Sandy) Allen and her kid sister Janna. They have, over the years, worked it into an almost telepathic system, Hall asserts, and now whenever one of them has trouble articulating his innermost thoughts, the other can usually help draw them out.

Bigger Than Both of Us and *Beauty on a Back Street*, both released in the mid seventies, did respectably, but the duo hit a snag with the release of *X-Static* and *Along the Red Ledge*. Hall, at this time, was busy trying to record his *Sacred Songs* solo album with Robert Fripp, struggling with the record company and fighting with producers. Not physically fighting, but struggling within. "Chris Bond used to take every song we had," Hall remembers, "and if the beat was a straight one-two-three-four, he would change it to a half-time groove. Everything! And David Foster wanted us to sound like Earth, Wind and Fire."

"I like the songs on the early albums," Oates adds, "but we

were using producers who didn't really understand us, and studio musicians, and the translation of musical ideas to these people ended up watering down the power and the vitality of our music. Also, we never really felt our recording persona was aligned with our stage persona. Now we've gotten them in line and both are more natural, much more an extension of our personalities off stage."

Outside producers now behind them, Hall and Oates have entered the eighties with a succession of hits. They are the most requested act on MTV; they were named the favourite pop group of 1983 in a recent *People* magazine readers' poll; and they were the recipients of the American Music Award for the best duo of the year. Their hits in the past few years, like 'Private Eyes', 'Your Kiss Is on My List', 'Maneater', and 'Family Man', all seem to follow the old Hall and Oates "formula", and Americans are subjected to these songs with the irritating frequency favoured by US radio programmers.

"If we have a cause or a crusade," says Oates, "it's bridging the gap — moving away from black/white polarisation and getting music itself back to the sensibilities of the late fifties and early sixties. I remember a time when you could go and see Patti Labelle and The Bluebells, The Four Tops and The Rolling Stones, all on the same bill. I guess those days are over. But some stations in the Midwest, which were formerly bastions of heavy metal, are now starting to play Michael Jackson and Prince." And, incidentally, Hall and Oates.

Whither Daryl and John? Presumably they will maintain their present routine of touring and recording for at least a while longer. The hits, now that Hall and Oates know what their hits sound like, will keep on coming. Hall will continue to spend his increasingly rare days off collecting medieval armour. Oates will go on collecting oriental art and driving his race car whenever he can. Hall may continue to have dreams that he can move

solid matter kinetically. Oates may hold fast to his day-dream of being Zeus, "the supreme heavenly honcho."

But, one wonders, can two people who work all the time, as Hall and Oates appear to, have much fun? Will Oates ever again dress up as a rat and drive his motorcycle through a ghetto in the dead of night?

The college laboratory stands empty now. Cobwebs stretch delicately over the bunsen burners. Hall and Oates have moved on to new laboratories: four-track cassette decks and rhythm machines in the convenience of their own homes.

The doo wop quartet has disbanded, the members all have straight jobs that require coats and ties. Maybe they meet once a year for a cup of coffee and memories at the corner drugstore. Philadelphia hasn't changed that much. And neither have Hall and Oates.

DREW MOSELEY

MUSICAL YOUTH

Pop stars don't often make the headlines on BBC Television News, and when they do it's most likely because some superstar claims to have broken an attendance record, got married, divorced or (commonest of all) died. One of the oddest news items of the year, then, was a broadcast in the first week of October 1982. A bunch of juvenile musicians were featured prancing up and down in front of the Houses of Parliament. Odder still, they were from the Midlands, and black. "It must be a very, very low news day," muttered one of the producers, as the item went out.

So it was that the non-record-buying public was made aware of the existence of Musical Youth, five Birmingham schoolboys who then had an average age of 13, and who that week outsold the current hits by The Jam, Shalamar and Culture Club to reach number one in the charts with a rewrite of an old Mighty Diamonds favourite, 'Pass the Dutchie'. The Diamonds (themselves borrowing a tune from Jackie Mittoo) had sung 'Pass the Kutchie', referring to the chalice in which ganja is kept. With respect for their age, and an eye on the school authorities and the conservative record-buying public, the Youth had sung instead about a Dutchie, a cooking pot.

That single, and the follow-up hit 'Don't Blame the Youth', made Musical Youth the novelty sensation of the year. No one had heard much about the band before their first single leapfrogged over 25 others to become one of the fastest-selling number ones in Britain for years. Suddenly they were being praised by everyone from *The Star* ("the happiest pop fairytale of the year") to the *NME* (with a cover announcing "Sunshine Super Youth"). Stories that unexpected and that good don't usually survive, but the Youth managed rather better than the Hitler diaries, and within a year they were scheduled to have co-headlined at the Sunsplash reggae festival in Jamaica, played in Europe and Japan, and headlined their own British tour. One-off gimmick bands can't do things like that and survive, but the Youth looked as if they deserved to last, if only because they didn't act or sound like a juvenile novelty,

just an ordinary group who happened to be quite extraordinarily young.

In the month they had their first hit, Musical Youth were all aged between 11 and 15, and all attending Duddeston Manor School in Birmingham (two of them, Dennis and Junior, have now left). The band consists of two sets of brothers, the tiny Kelvin and Michael Grant (guitars, keyboards and vocals), Junior and Patrick Waite (drums and bass), and the newest member, singer Dennis Seaton. They were brought together, outside school hours, by Junior and Patrick's father, Frederick Waite. Back in Jamaica in the sixties he had sung with a Kingston group, The Techniques.

After emigrating to England, Freddie Waite concentrated his efforts on business ventures in West Bromwich, but he kept his interest in music, playing around the local pubs and clubs in a disco band. He also started to give music lessons at the Saltley Music Workshop, a community arts centre in Nechells, Birmingham, which he ran jointly with another Jamaican musician, Tony Owens, who is now Musical Youth's manager.

Two of his earliest, most talented pupils were Michael, and later Kelvin Grant (Kelvin apparently couldn't start playing guitar for a while because his hands were still too small). Waite's own sons Junior and Patrick were encouraged to join in, and Musical Youth were born, at least as a backing band. At the start, Freddie Waite himself was the singer.

The band's first public appearances were in Birmingham pubs, The Pack Horse in Shard End, and The Crompton in Handsworth. It was a slightly difficult operation, because Kelvin was then only eight years old. As Junior remembers, "We were far too young to be in pubs, but we wanted to get some exposure. We would just play three songs." Not surprisingly, it was the juvenile backing group, rather than the distinguished singer, who got all the attention, and Freddie stepped down once a good young singer was found. Junior explains — tactfully, because the singer is his father — that there were no superstar tantrums. "It had to be done,

because we couldn't do what we wanted if a big man was in the band. If it was just youth, people would take notice. And dad was pleased to step down — he was doing it for the best."

Dennis, the new singer, remembers the hand over slightly differently. "I'd known Junior from the first year at school, and I was going to be in the band from the start, but I was told to wait until my voice improved. At first, I didn't sing, I just played percussion and watched Freddie and learned from him. He gave me hints and ideas."

With Freddie as singer, the band recorded one single for Birmingham's 021 Records, 'Political'/'Generals', and won themselves a session on John Peel's radio show. Once Dennis joined they did even better. In January 1982 they signed to MCA ("because they liked the idea of a youth band"), and by the end of the year the Birmingham schoolboys were nationwide celebrities, and threatening to be international stars. More extraordinary still, they had become the best-known, most commercial reggae band in Britain.

Their style is a blend of reggae influences, from commercial rockers through to hints of earlier Jamaican styles, crisp, commercial and tuneful reggae that compensates for the understandable lack of technical skills with sheer enthusiasm — Kelvin's style of junior toasting is simply a delight. The band's heroes are not other juveniles, but long-established reggae artists. Junior favours Gregory Isaacs, Aswad, Black Uhuru and Sly and Robbie while singer Dennis favours Isaacs and Sugar Minnot.

Their success allowed them to pay a first visit to their fathers' homeland, Jamaica, where they "made a video miming to Heartbreaker on top of a lorry on the front-line." Exposure to Jamaican reggae at first hand also posed a musical challenge "because they play in a certain way. They have a different feel that is more relaxed, more loose and spontaneous. We'd like to sound more Jamaican."

Dennis got to meet Sugar Minnot, who told him "just to keep thinking, and keep listening to music," and he noticed that "the Jamaican singers added more ad-libs on

stage and always did something a bit different or better than the records." Whatever difference the experience — and a return to Jamaica in the summer of 1983 — makes to the Youth, they say they hope the public will judge them simply in musical terms. As Junior put it, "We just see ourselves as a band, and want people to appreciate us as a band, we don't want to cash in on our age. Just do the music and not be gimmicky."

That may be a lot to ask when the band still have to take a tutor and a Birmingham school inspector around with them, but at least their plan for staying at the top doesn't involve looking cute, but trying to improve and vary their music. Junior promises "commercial reggae, dub, lovers rock, and other sounds, maybe space sounds. We've got a synthesiser and syn drums." They are also working on live shows. Having left Duddeston, Junior and Dennis (CSEs in English, Technical Drawing, Computers and Metal Work) are due for a stint at drama school "to learn dancing and improve the stage act."

After a few months of the success that other school kids can only dream of, Dennis admitted that "sometimes the pressure gets to you. At school, some of our friends were OK, and some were jealous. Some of the teachers acted the same way." His ambition was "another number one, obviously," while for Junior it was "to survive in life, to try to make enough money to try to survive. And to keep going for the love of the music."

Musical Youth may have deserved their place as a novelty on Television News, but of course they weren't the first very young band to break into the best-sellers. There's been a series of other black bands and artists who managed it, from fifties' teenage hero Frankie Lymon (who never survived his twenties) through to The Jacksons and that most recent group of singing teenies, New Edition. A perennial pop theme, perhaps, but in the words of the Jamaican pop tune that resurfaced as 'Pass the Dutchie', "this generation rules the nation with version." They deserve to survive.

Robin Denselow

DURAN DURAN

If the three hallmarks of rock'n'roll in the 1980s are stylishness, danceability and video, then Duran Duran is not simply an enormously successful chart band, but rather a perfect prototype for everyone else to follow. During its still formative career, the young quintet from Birmingham has gathered a huge world-wide following prone to fits of teen hysteria; spawned a number of popular imitators (among them KajaGooGoo, whose number one single, 'Too Shy', was produced by Duran Duran's Nick Rhodes); set expensive and impressive standards for making posh promotional videos; and helped convince the American rock business to accept new music in a big way.

If you were to sit down and imagine the ideal blend of pop, funk, glamour, romance and modernism, Duran Duran would fit the bill exactly. Where other groups emerging from the new romantic movement lacked the skill to add anything interesting to the disco drive of their music, Duran Duran has consistently come up with brilliant tunes and arrangements, hoeing close to the beat, but never wholly succumbing to it. While high-tech bands have used the sounds of synthesisers to score on the charts, Duran Duran has avoided the clichés and integrated machines into their work, creating unique textures without featuring any one instrument. In the current craze for eye-catching visuals, Duran Duran has not needed to resort to outrage, like Boy George, or costumery, like Adam Ant, yet has attracted the most style-conscious fans and always managed to present a flashy exterior.

Amazingly, Duran Duran's success has been totally on their own terms. Most would-be teen idols have to make sure their music satisfies lowest-common-denominator tastes; Duran Duran's records (especially their second album, *Rio*) are smart, sophisticated and subtle; it's difficult to imagine anyone recording 'Hungry Like the Wolf' with the same impetus as, say, 'I Love Rock'n'Roll'. Likewise, their videos. No cheap local studio knock-offs with an inexperienced cameraman for Duran Duran. They get Godley/Creme and Russell Mulcahy, and go off to such exotic lands as Sri Lanka for their five minutes of fame. But it's things like the atmospheric 'Hungry Like the Wolf', and the mildly pornographic 'Girls on Film' that have helped Duran Duran wrestle the American rock market-place to its knees.

In the last year, MTV has become America's version of a national rock station. Since much of the cable station's programming consists of promotional videos, the selection process by which groups get exposure has at least as much to do with the quality of the visual presentation as the musical content. And Duran Duran score high marks in both departments. Although unable to show the 'Girls on Film' clip without cutting out the raunchy parts, MTV has found great success with 'Rio', 'Save a Prayer', 'Hungry Like the Wolf', 'Planet Earth' and 'Careless Memories', and Duran Duran has in turn found themselves introduced to a massive audience, on top of the US record charts, mobbed during promotional appearances, and in demand as TV guests. While they're not the only band to find MTV so beneficial, they seem the most comfortable with the new video order; video seems as important in their creative lives as music.

Duran Duran was formed in 1978 by bassist John Taylor, a forgotten clarinet player, a rhythm machine and keyboardist Nick Rhodes (who had changed his name from Bates). Various additional members came and went — including Stephen Duffy (now known as Tin Tin) who's made records recently. The current line-up stabilised in 1980, with three unrelated Taylors, and no clarinetist. According to Rhodes, the original intention was "to combine the energy of punk with the danceability of disco." They took their name from a character in the movie *Barbarella* (setting off a spate of similarly double-named bands), toured to attract some attention, and went to find a label that agreed with their vision. EMI took the bait, paired them with producer Colin Thurston, and sent them off to work on conquering the world.

The world's first inkling of Duran Duran came via the single 'Planet Earth', which dented the British Top 20 upon its release in March 1981. A surprisingly slick début from a new band, the song starts with solid, subtle drumming by Roger Taylor, adds on a catchy synthesiser riff from Nick Rhodes and a scratchy guitar from Andy Taylor; Simon Le Bon's impassioned vocals and John Taylor's popping bass top off the mixture. It's structurally simplistic, but a highly effective dance number, and a fresh sound for jaded ears to behold.

Duran Duran's commercial breakthrough in England was the result of 'Girls on Film', an ace single punctuated by the sound of an autowinding camera and lyrics with a clever cinematic edge (made a bit too graphic in the video). The single went into the Top Five in August 1981, and the band's first album became a hit at around the same time. *Duran Duran* features both 'Girls on Film' and 'Planet Earth', as well as the haunting 'Is There Anyone Out There' and the generally overlooked but striking 'Friends of Mine'.

With their British pop success, Duran Duran were immediately seized upon by the local fan magazines; countless glossy posters of the serious, brooding (but exquisitely dressed and coiffed) Duran Duran were carefully removed from centrefolds and hung lovingly on bedroom walls all over Britain. The band toured their homeland and then headed for America, where the album had failed to catch on as it had in the UK. 'Planet Earth' was getting club play, and their local label, Capitol, had done its fair share of pushing the group, but it wasn't the band's time. . .yet.

That first American sojourn introduced the group to the challenge of making themselves understandable and attractive to a wholly different audience, but it was not a dispiriting experience. In fact, America proved to be an inspiration. As Simon Le Bon noted at the time, "There are some very nice things (about America) — it can be colourful, open and honest." Renaming the USA 'Rio' for the purposes of literary obscurity, the band opted to focus their second album on their reactions to America, and several of the songs on *Rio* make specific reference to things American.

As an entrée to the US market, the mid-1982 *Rio* turned the trick nicely, although it took six months for the record to transport its instant British success across the Atlantic. By the beginning of 1983, Duran Duran found themselves riding the top of the *Billboard* charts, and deservedly so. Filled with memorable, thoughtful songs like 'Save a Prayer', 'Rio', 'Hungry Like the Wolf' and 'Last Chance on the Stairway', *Rio* glides smoothly from start to finish, exposing slick but credible playing (especially by bassist John and drummer Roger Taylor), Colin Thurston's imaginative, widescreen production, and a stylish cover painting by Patrick Nagle. With the combined thrust of heavy television exposure and sudden radio play, Duran Duran exploded across America, winding up one of a select few 'new music' bands deemed acceptable by the great mass record-buying audience.

These days, the future looks rosy for Duran Duran. Their March 1983 single, 'Is There Something I Should Know', although not one of their better recordings, proved to be their biggest British hit, reaching number one only weeks after the execrable KajaGooGoo. In America, a new marketing venture by the Sony corporation resulted in a two-song commercial videocassette; a full-length video album compiling the band's promotional clips to date is also being released. MTV, which featured Duran Duran on its New Year's Eve bash/broadcast, seems unwavering in its support; American radio shows no sign of abandoning the band either.

At this stage, short of a total disaster, it would seem Duran Duran would have to do something really nightmarish to snatch defeat from such sure hands of victory.

IRA ROBBINS

TOTO

A theory was circulating during the last two or three years to the effect that the acts dominating the US album charts, and therefore the FM airways, were indistinguishable from each other and the individuals within them anonymous. Whether the first element of the contention is accurate, is down to personal taste, but there is fairly easy money to be made from fans of such acts (Journey, Styx, REO Speedwagon, Foreigner, Kansas, Quarterflash, Air Supply, Asia) by challenging the professed follower to name the group members of his favourite band.

The theory went on to suggest that the generally vague group names were deliberately chosen because of their non-specific nature, since if a group experienced huge success one or more of its members would inevitably desire greater prominence, either within the group or as a separate solo act. This, of course, would upset the chemistry of the group (and no doubt the declared democracy therein), but since some egos are such that the continuing anonymity of being a member of a group (albeit a highly rich and successful one) is insufficient, the over-ambitious would-be star is allowed to embark on a solo career and is replaced by a new anonymous face. This can be easily achieved as the copyright holder of the group name is, in most cases, their manager — fascinating, and actually occurring . . .

The newest of the megabands of this type to achieve prominence is Toto, a six-piece conglomerate of mostly ex-session musicians who would appear to conform precisely to the theory as set out above. Formed in 1978 by five distinguished session players and one virtually unknown vocalist, named (depending on who you believe) after either Dorothy's dog in *The Wizard of Oz* or the singer's surname, and immediately acclaimed by the likes of Elton John, Toto found immediate acceptance among their peers, largely because many of the biggest AOR names of the late 1970s had used one or more members of Toto on their own records.

The Porcaro brothers, Jeff on drums and Steve on keyboards, come from a musical family — their father, Joe Porcaro, is himself a session percussionist. Jeff has appeared on albums by Warren Zevon, Steely Dan, Allen Toussaint, Rickie Lee Jones, Etta James, Leo Sayer, Boz Scaggs and so on, while Steve has done sessions for such as Earth, Wind and Fire, Eddie Money and The Pointer Sisters. Fellow keyboard player David Paich also has a notable musical father, Marty Paich, a well-known Hollywood arranger/musician. Paich the younger has worked on albums by Joan Baez, Elkie Brooks and Jackson Browne, though what would appear to be his major claim to fame is his participation as writer, co-writer, arranger and even musician on Boz Scaggs' highly successful *Silk Degrees* album of 1976. Joe and Jeff Porcaro were also on that LP, and so was another Toto member, bass player David Hungate, who has also played on records by Stephen Bishop, Donovan, Barbra Streisand, Bert Jansch,

etc. The Toto guitar player is Steve Lukather, whose session credits are rather more obscure — Eric Kaz, Harvey Mason, Lee Ritenour and even some dodgy latter-day John Mayall record. One thing of which you could not accuse this quintet is lack of experience, with the possible exception of singer Bobby Kimball (or Toteaux), who did, however, appear as a backing singer on LPs by both Michael and Elliot Murphy, and was in a pre-Toto group called SS Fools.

In view of such a track record — a great advantage in America and, in 1978, the kiss of death in Britain — Toto took off quickly in the US, where their first LP, *Toto*, spent nearly a year in the album charts and made the Top Ten, no doubt sustained when it was flagging a little by the release of three hit singles which were all included on the album. 'Hold the Line', the first and best (and the only one of the three to chart in Britain, where it made the Top 20 in early 1979), was a Top Five single, an excellent US début, although the follow-up hits, 'I'll Supply the Love' and the faintly ridiculous 'Georgy Porgy' rose no higher than the mid 40s.

Strangely, a decline set in after that first album, although *Hydra*, the 1979 Toto LP, briefly made the US Top 50, and a single taken from it, '99', reached the Top 30 in the American singles chart. It need hardly be emphasised that British interest in Toto was severely limited (and that's probably overestimating it). It was not increased by *Hydra* or its 1981 follow up, *Turn Back*, whose very brief American

chart residency surely resulted from the fact that it contained no hit single; it also sounded extremely uninspired. The story was beginning to look depressingly familiar to those who had championed the group as the first session-player band that sounded as though it might have some real life and purpose: a lively first LP, followed by slow deterioration and less commitment as it becomes clear that the band member, as opposed to the session musician, makes rather less money and has to work a lot harder to get it.

This gradual decline from a start near the top is confirmed by Steve Lukather, who notes: "Success hit so fast that two months after the first LP came out, we were on stage headlining. We'd been playing together ten years, but somehow we were still feeling our way musically. Now we've had three years to mature, three years to learn how to write together as a unit. This album feels like a new birth." That's *Toto IV* he's talking about, which has not only relaunched the group with three American hit singles and given them their highest placing yet in the LP chart, but has also, even more remarkably, made Toto an increasingly big British chart name, with a pair of hit 45s in 'Africa' and 'Rosanna'.

For Britain, 'Africa' was the key, an ordinary sounding song until the classic harmonies of the chorus, although the impact of the single being available as a picture disc shaped roughly like the continent of the title cannot be underestimated. Of course, it could have been another one-off, as 'Hold the

Line' was, but fortunately there was another interesting song — 'Rosanna'.

In fact, 'Rosanna' was the track which put Toto back on the gravy train in America, all but topping the chart in the first half of 1982, but initially a failure in the UK. Its reissue in ''Grammy'' shape is a direct result both of 'Africa''s success, and the fact that Toto seemingly dominated the 1983 Grammy Awards ceremony, winning no less than seven awards — 'Rosanna' was record of the year, best pop vocal performance and best instrumental arrangement with

vocal, while *Toto IV*, although it didn't win most imaginative LP title, did make off with album of the year, best engineered recording and best producer (the album was produced by the group). Additionally, Steve Lukather won best songwriter of an R&B song for 'Turn Your Love Around', which George Benson piloted to the Top Five in the US.

It is still difficult for even the least cynical Briton to comprehend that Toto are on the verge of American superstardom (already achieved in Japan, where a ten-

day tour last year sold out two months in advance), and a quote from *Billboard* at the start of their career (''Toto specialises in music that bristles with the energy and dynamics of rock'') can only produce incredulity. Perhaps some of the other anonymous megabands in America are beginning to fade — Styx had very little chart action in 1982 — and it could be that Toto are poised to replace them as faceless heroes providing a familiar soundtrack for cruising. Ironically, perhaps, it has recently been announced that David Hungate has been

replaced in Toto by yet another of the Porcaro clan, Mike, another seasoned sessioner.

Toto's music is eminently disposable, with the occasional exception such as 'Africa', but then the same is true of all the other American bands with whom Toto are competing for music-centre and car-cassette space. It's no crime to make inoffensive music for inoffensive people. Toto, incidentally, is also the name of the major Japanese manufacturer of toilet bowls.

JOHN TOBLER

CULTURE CLUB

In the summer of 1982, with a disturbingly large number of groups scrambling toes over topknot for berths in the Funkier Than Thou Sweepstakes, Vanilla Division, critics' captiousness quotients were rising with the soaring mercury. So when from stacks of review singles out popped 'White Boy' or 'I'm Afraid of Me', Culture Club's first two singles, clothed in Virgin's typically *moderne* picture sleeves, it was no surprise to hear a chorus of groans and sniggers:

"What, more Hawaiian shirts? I thought Haircut 100 had the tropical drag market cornered!" "Speaking of drag, what's that creature under all that make-up trying to prove, and *why*?"

What a shock, then, to watch Culture Club surge to the top of the British charts — and duplicate that throughout most of the rest of the world, including the ostensibly impregnable United States on the strength of 'Do You Really Want to Hurt Me'. Those who'd set aside their

understandable prejudgments and actually *listened* to those first two 45s, however, already knew that Culture Club had more to offer than just another pose to go with a dance rhythm. 'White Boy', in fact, slams down hard on the knuckles of those who use the worst sorts of role-playing as a defensive (yet ultimately dehumanising and *off*ensive) manoeuvre, while 'I'm Afraid of Me' offers up self-doubts in a manner both charming and disarming, the former via authoritative semi-funk, the

latter cushioning its fears in sunnily infectious Caribeat.

Contrast the summer of 1982 with the summer of 1983: a bemused rock press can barely help but applaud the Club's series of international hits, the group even winning grudging admiration by coups such as anticipating — even sending up — pundit pot-shots by calling its début longplayer *Kissing to Be Clever* (not to mention making the record a balanced, durable, tough-to-fault first album). And who else had the sheer gall as well as the talent to remodel the Motown sound — with *harmonica*, yet, and a vocal harmony break straight out of the Association/Spanky & Our Gang songbook! — title it 'Church of the Poison Mind', and enjoy one of the year's stellar dance smashes with it? (Although in the US, despite it receiving heavy club and in some regions even radio play, it was passed over in favour of 'I'll Tumble 4 Ya' as the group's summer record, the latter beginning its climb up the charts even while its US predecessor, 'Time', was nestled comfortably at number three.)

Meanwhile, far from putting themselves up as melodramatic *artistes*, the combo welcomed response oozing in from all quarters, winning accolades from such diverse musical "peers" as Status Quo and Chic's Nile Rodgers. In Britain, while the group's records passed out of the domain of the in-the-know and ultra-hip, they entered that of the public at large — and *how* large! Hordes of teenage girls, many of them dressed up like Boy George clones, pack Culture Club concerts and squeal in delight when George does nothing so much as lift his shades to eye his fans between verses. Young children queue up for autographs outside TV taping sessions. Housewives — many of whom accompany their kids to Club concerts — vote George their favourite personality in a *Daily Mirror* poll.

In the US, a similar phenomenon begins to grip loads of teenage girls who bombard magazines covering the band with adulatory letters, while music biz vets scratch their brows in wonderment as trade papers show Culture Club songs even invading 'Adult Contemporary' radio. And on urban street corners, black youths who can't suppress laughter at the thought of Boy George start nonetheless to move their feet when 'Time' comes over their lunch-box radios.

A far cry it is from the days of 1978 when drummer Jon Moss can recall having walked into the offices of his then-record company, "and being asked who I was. 'I'm in the group London.' '*Who?*' 'You just *signed* us!'"

Starting in his late teens, Moss tapped the tubs for the pre-CBS Clash, London (largely neglected by manager/producer Simon Napier-Bell, then too

busy looking after the fledgling group Japan), the chaotic Damned (after which he was offered and declined the drum chair newly vacated by Tommy Ramone), The Edge (which perplexedly found itself surrendering its goal of establishing a name as an independent group in favour of virtual anonymity as Stiff Records/Jane Aire backing band The Belvederes), topped off by going uncredited (until recently) as the stick-wielder who enabled Adam Ant to turn his notions of quasi-African-cum-Gary Glitter double drumming into practice (on 'Cartrouble' and 'Kick'). By then, Moss felt battered enough to take a vacation from music-making, from which he cautiously returned when contacted by George O'Dowd out of the blue (via mutual friends). He shelved his scepticism long enough to glimpse a genuinely viable musical outlet as well as a worthy opportunity to profit from his mistakes.

O'Dowd, who'd already established himself as a "character" in the London club scene, had worked professionally in clothing (both in-store and as a model, as well as a brief spell in the make-up department of the Royal Shakespeare Company), but his only musical experience amounted to an abortive stint with Bow Wow Wow as, at different points, second lead singer and hedge against Annabella Lwin quitting/being thrown out of the band. (The sole highlight: George's lone public appearance with the group, singing the hoary Peanut Wilson Country and Western oldie 'Cast Iron Arm', as a surprise encore at a heavyweight London gig at the Hammersmith Odeon.)

It didn't take long for George and the group to part ways, but reports of the split and George's plans for another band were enough to attract bassist Michael "Mikey" Craig, an odd-jobber and sometime reggae dabbler only just returned from an unsatisfactory sojourn in Bristol and determined to try to break into the music business. Thus, In Praise of Lemmings began to take tangible, if somewhat lumpy, shape ("horrid," opines George). When Moss arrived, he cleared the way for Culture Club (out went the old name and the equally inadequate guitarist).

With the addition of guitarist/keyboardist Roy Hay, the group began to exist.

But what explains the leap from being four relative nobodies to international stardom? If anything, at least at the outset, George's androgynous image was more liability than asset, too old-hat for jaded cognoscenti yet too weird for the general populace. Superficially, the music could be classed with the rest of the young white black music bandwagon-jumpers.

Yet the Culture Club musical combine does retain, amid the ranks of lily-white would-be ethnomusicians, the novel aspect imparted by Craig; as Moss puts it, "One of us *is* black! But," he adds, "the thing is, we blend all of our influences together. We don't isolate one kind of music out and then repeat it as a formula over and over again."

Add to this eclectically synthetic approach a select crew of sidepeople, notably hornmen Terry Bailey and Steve Grainger, keyboardist Phil Picket, and erstwhile Thunderthighs vocalist Helen Terry, whose spine-tingling, bluesy belting delivery is an added *frisson* on tracks like 'Church of the Poison Mind'. Moss makes clear that while only four can belong to Culture Club, helpers like these are honorary members (respected, and not merely ancillary). The mixture is powerful and even still bursting with unrealised potential.

Temper this still further with the populism espoused by George on behalf of the whole band: "I love a good song, one that captures a scene or a feeling completely, that lots of people can relate to, no matter what the style. I mean, it sounds really corny but I really like 'Jack and Diane' by John Cougar for that reason. I think 'Do You Really Want to Hurt Me' is that kind of song, and that's the kind of thing I've always wanted to do."

Boy George is indubitably the group's visual focus as well as spokesman (the latter with occasional assistance from Moss), yet he has made every effort to avoid letting his image dominate the band's identity to the exclusion of the other members, a struggle as commendable as it is futile. Moss, Hay and Craig are content to do their (democratic) bit as writers, arrangers and musicians (although Moss often

takes on business-related duties). Says Craig, "Roy and I particularly are not good at giving interviews, and we don't need or want to.

"Besides, if we had to chase after every reporter who portrays the band as just George we'd be running around forever. George is great at handling publicity, and we don't worry about it. We know how co-operatively the band works, among ourselves. If George was going to let it go to his head, it'd probably have happened by now anyway; he hasn't, and it won't."

And despite having as sharp opinions as anyone, and an affinity for certain kinds of "message"-orientated lyrics, Boy George generally avoids preachiness, crusading, finger-pointing, or even identity-flaunting; his visual image is a strong statement in and of itself, but he prefers it to be a strictly personal one. When interviewers attempt to pin him down about it, he's evasive, yet in such a way as to indicate he's less concerned about being identified with a specific category of sexual preference than being categorised at all.

Take Culture Club, then, for what you can make of it; the quartet and its satellites see too many exciting possibilities to want to allow themselves to get painted into a corner. It's the sort of philosophy that, as long as the songs keep coming, will enable Culture Club to outlive trends and further expand an already broad-based audience.

Will 'Do You Really Want to Hurt Me' become to the eighties what 'My Way' was to the Me Decade? Will Culture Club be able to come up with another song that transcends the group itself? ('Hurt Me' has already been covered by the likes of Rita Coolidge; can it be long before we hear it in elevators?) Will Culture Club evade the destructive push-pull tensions of stardom and continue making records as delightful as they are "commercial"? Will 1984 be yet another chapter in the band's ongoing saga, or will the Club adjourn even before completing the projected celluloid autobiography (*à la* Madness's *Take It or Leave It*)? Will 'Cameo Chameleon' break the Country charts? Answers same time next year.

JIM GREEN

MEN
AT
WORK

The continent of Australia is more or less the same size as the United States. The population of Australia, however, is considerably smaller, and lately it has begun to look like just about everyone down under belongs to one band or another.

In the past, Australia used to come up with one or two generic acts every few years; Olivia Newton-John drove most sentient Americans crazy a decade ago with 'I Honestly

Love You' and 'Have You Ever Been Mellow?', and she's still pounding away with songs like 'Physical'. The Bee Gees sailed in on The Beatles' coat-tails, disappeared for a while, came back with *Saturday Night Fever*, made a mess of *Sergeant Pepper*, and are now once again on the comeback trail with the soundtrack for yet another John Travolta movie, *Staying Alive*. AC/DC and Rose Tattoo jumped on the heavy metal bandwagon a few years ago

and refuse to let it go. Split Enz rose up from New Zealand at the start of the new wave. Little River Band and Air Supply ride the AOR radio stations. And the new batch, INXS, The Divinyls and Men at Work, to name only a few, are taking over America not only musically, but visually. They're creeping into American homes via satellite on MTV.

The music industry refers to this phenomenon as "the

Australian Invasion", making reference, of course, to the British invasion of the early sixties. Optimism abounds — everyone made money on the British invasion and there's no reason to believe that the success of the music speeding over to these shores from Sydney and Melbourne means anything less. Technology has played a key part in this invasion; prior to the launching of MTV it was just about financially impossible for

Australian acts to succeed in the US. Touring costs were prohibitive and no one in the record industry wanted to spend much money promoting bands who would never be seen by the public. Thanks to MTV, it is possible for bands to be seen by an average of seven million Americans every day. And Americans are watching, and they apparently like what they see. *Business As Usual*, Men at Work's first US release, was at number one on the US charts for 15 weeks, breaking the record set 16 years ago by The Monkees (13 weeks at number one with their first album). *Business As Usual* spawned two number one singles as well: 'Who Can It Be Now' and 'Down Under'. And Men at Work has become the first act in almost a decade to place two LPs in the Top Ten simultaneously. In the week of May 9 through May 14, *Cargo*, the group's second album, jumped to number four on the charts while *Business As Usual* dropped to number seven in its 30th week on the chart. The last time one act had two albums in the Top Ten at the same time was in July of 1975, when The Rolling Stones released *Made in the Shade* and *Metamorphosis* to tie in with their first US tour in three years.

Men at Work also made news when *Cargo* made its début on the charts at number eleven, the highest entry for an act's second album since Boston's *Don't Look Back* hit the chart at number ten in September of 1978.

Clearly, Men at Work are a force to reckon with. The five piece band features Colin Hay on vocals, guitars and the lion's share of the songwriting; Greg Ham on sax, flute, vocals, keyboards, songwriting and "fiddly things"; Ron Strykert on guitars, vocals and some songwriting (not the good stuff, usually); John Rees on bass and vocals; and Jerry Speiser on drums and vocals. The album notes on *Business As Usual* also

credit manager Russell Deppeler on telephone and calculator.

The songs are fiercely Australian, and as songwriters Ham, Hay and Strykert refuse to pander to non-Australian listeners. If their new American audience doesn't know what a "fried-out combie" is, they can jolly well watch the video or look it up. It's thanks to the lyrics of 'Down Under' that any American six-year-old can now explain to his or her parents what a vegemite sandwich is and why no one would ever want to eat one. Men at Work use Australian landmarks, like Westgate Bridge in Melbourne, the way Donovan used Goodge Street and Paul McCartney used Penny Lane.

The band is getting the usual short shrift from the disbelieving US press. Jon Pareles of the *New York Times* suggests that the success of *Business As Usual* lies partly in the fact that The Police failed to release an album in 1982, leaving the field wide open for "imitators" like Men at Work. "The resemblance can't be accidental," Pareles insists. "Colin Hay copies all the inflections of the Police's Sting . . . while the band plays the rock-reggae grooves the Police perfected on 1979's *Regatta de Blanc . . .*" *Cargo*, which was completed before *Business As Usual* took off on the US charts, has been called too imitative of the first album; lines have been drawn between the two releases to demonstrate this theory, pointing out that 'Be Good Johnny' on the first LP carries the same theme as 'Settle Down My Boy' on the second, although the former was written by Ham and Hay and the latter was written by Strykert. 'It's a Mistake' on *Cargo* echoes the nuclear war story told in 'Underground' on *Business As Usual*. The list goes on. But for the American public, more is more in this case and no one seems to be complaining except the critics.

Men at Work got their start in a tiny pub called Cricketers Arms in Melbourne. "It wasn't really a rock and roll place," Greg Ham told *Circus*. "Colin had played there acoustically, and the owner really liked his music, so he told Colin to bring the whole band down. Little did he know we were going to take over a third of his barroom space."

Ham was 21 when he started playing sax, not going anywhere near the keyboards until about two years ago. He studied Law and worked in a children's theatre for three years, adding to his income by dressing in a big blue bear suit to play local shopping centres as Barney the Bear. Colin also came into the band with a theatrical background, and all of the band knows "how to think visually", according to Ham, to which fact they attribute the success of their videos and, *ipso facto*, their music.

The videos are the thing. 'Who Can It Be Now' offers the ultimate in paranoia: Colin Hay sits frozen in his easy chair as shadows climb the stairs to his apartment casting the outlines of improbable costumes in silhouette on the walls. 'Down Under' is a cartoon romp through the Australian desert. The video from *Cargo*, 'Overkill', is a moody piece which features Hay walking along a waterfront and staring at neon signs. "I can't get to sleep," he sings, and in spite of the fact that critics have suggested that he can't get to sleep because the new album echoes the first too closely, America understands. At one point or another, everyone with insomnia has wandered along a waterfront, even if only in their imaginations.

According to Greg Ham, there is at the moment an upsurge of nationalism among the people of Australia. "In the sixties," he says, "when everything happening culturally was from overseas, there was a kind of parochial

attitude there. Australians couldn't believe that they could produce stuff that was any good. But then certain things began happening, like the build up of the film industry, which in turn had an effect on the music industry. All of a sudden people said, 'Oh yeah, that's a bloody good film; it won a prize at Cannes, it must be alright.' There's a lot of latent nationalism at home, and it doesn't take much to swap from the negative to the positive. 'Down Under' attracted a variety of people — we'd get people coming to our shows just because of that one song, these big, bearded blokes who'd probably never gone to a rock show before. The Germans just went silly for it. What do you suppose *they* get out of it?"

Even David Bowie has taken the plunge and filmed some videos for his *Let's Dance* album in Australia, making a *cause célèbre* out of the Aborigines, who are to Australia what the American Indians are to the US. The Aborigines have a legend about the beginning of man, which they call the "Dream Time", when all of life slumbered while the world was created. The Dream Time was a time of magic, as was the final awakening, and one could almost say that this awakening is what Australia is now experiencing. The land down under is just beginning to come into its own musically. Instead of blindly following the American and British influences as they have done in the past, bands like Men at Work are starting to put those influences to work to create something new. Certainly, it won't all happen overnight. If *Cargo* doesn't take too many chances, the next album will, one hopes, take more.

"I think we're all a bit surprised, especially by our doing so well in America," Ham admits. "I'm prepared to be a bit more surprised yet." DREW MOSELEY

107

LIONEL RICHIE

Critics prefer their favoured soul men to occupy comfortable categories, and stay there. Lionel Richie is a frustrating and confounding case in point. Richie is slick, Los Angeles, professional; his heart, and soul, and hometown are inextricably linked to Tuskegee, Alabama. He is a former funk band member whose forte is ballads; a black man who writes not just country songs but countrypolitan ones; his own singing and writing are filled with sophisticated, jazzy licks, references to Stevie Wonder and Marvin Gaye, but he seems equally comfortable composing for a blandly unimaginative crooner like Kenny Rogers or singing a gauzy duet with Diana Ross.

Because the categories he transcends are not the correct ones — there is barely a hint of the blues in Richie's music, much less of Afro or any other polyrhythms, nor has he made any concessions to white rock — Lionel Richie has basically been ignored by serious critics. He seems too adult, too much the entertainer, far too straightforward, conventional and unaudacious for a year demarcated by Prince and Michael Jackson.

Well, maybe. Yet Richie

operates in a tradition that ranges from Nat "King" Cole to George Benson, and he's much more imaginative than the bulk of *that* breed. Big, bland (or at least, smooth) crooners are as much a part of the soul spectrum as outrageous funksters — you just read less about the crooners. And anyway, in addition to 'Endless Love' and 'My Love', Richie creates 'Serve You Right' and 'Tell Me', which are as gritty as need be.

Like the Stevie Wonder of 'You Are the Sunshine of My Life' and 'Isn't She Lovely', however, Richie's talent is never more evident, and his music is never more on-the-one, than when he's veering towards the purely maudlin. The reality is that 'Truly' (and 'My Love' and probably even 'Endless Love') are more compelling than just about anybody's funk, and that Lionel's syrupy pledges of undying sexual and spiritual fidelity aren't any more silly, in the very end, than Prince's proposition that partying down is a wise response to the imminence of Armageddon. Not as chic, of course, but you take your pleasures where you find them, and I'll take mine — guiltily if necessary.

Not that anyone in their right mind would have paid more attention to Richie's self-titled post-Commodores solo album than to *Midnight Lady, 1999* or *Thriller*. In the same way, it's silly to pay less mind to *Lionel Richie* than to less chic but less funky and romantic fare such as *Kissing to Be Clever, Rio* and *Fascination*. Much less the strained imitations like ABC. In fact, Richie is a soul light-weight only when placed in fairly élite company — matched against any but the very highest echelon of black

performers, he can easily be seen as a striking craftsman who manages to convey surprisingly deep expressiveness.

Richie is not an unprecedentedly confusing artist, of course. All those reviews that attack Motown albums for being riddled with show tune filler are inaccurate (many Motown LPs were overstocked with filler, it's true, but Berry Gordy and company usually controlled the copyrights) and miss the point anyway. The Supremes sang Rodgers and Hart for a variety of reasons, the most important being that they actually liked show tunes (who knows why?) and that this material gave them access to the mainstream entertainment business in a way that even the most brilliant rhythm and blues composition couldn't (since the entrepreneurs of legit showbiz preferred to remain ignorant of copyrights *they* did not control). This is one place where the season's best Broadway play, *Dreamgirls*, gets it absolutely right. In this, all of Lionel Richie's crossover moves are very much within the basic Motown tradition, and not much less impressive than Prince's or Michael Jackson's, even though they'll never get him any attention from FM radio or MTV.

There are other senses in which Richie is a very atypical Motown performer, and this has much to do with what makes him special. Certainly, the Motown prototype is neither Southern, nor a college-educated member of the black bourgeoisie. It's not insignificant that Richie came to the label as a core member of The Commodores, formed at the most prestigious black university in the Southern US, Tuskegee Institute. The Commodores were Motown's

first successful self-contained band to purvey the post-Sly funk styles. But partly by virtue of their lives in the South — three were from Alabama, two from Florida, one from Mississippi — The Commodores were, one and all, influenced by a wide variety of music. Richie, who was born on the Tuskegee campus, learned classical music (Bach and Beethoven) from his grandmother, the Institute's choir director; he knew something of jazz, because his uncle Bertram was an arranger for Duke Ellington; his family was church-going enough to expose him to a bit of gospel (no more than a bit, since they were Episcopals); the radio offered cosmopolitan rock and singer-songwriter soft-rock types and, at the other end of the dial, Country and Western. Lionel soaked all of this up, reasonably indiscriminately but with a special emphasis on every genre of emotive balladry; this is what he now replays in all of his songs and records, from 'Three Times a Lady' and 'Still' to 'My Love'.

The Commodores are sadly underrated as a progenitor of the current spate of black rock & roll. It's at least as hard to imagine Rick James without 'Machine Gun' as 'Tear the Roof Off the Sucker' or any of George Clinton's other hits. And The Commodores had more range than any other band of their genre, in their time. Richie has yet to create another country song as effortlessly right in its tonality as 'Sail On'. What the band does now that Richie has moved on will be fascinating and, in a way, as significant, as whatever he does on his own.

Yet it's easy to see Richie distancing himself from his past, in a way that's classically disastrous for pop performers,

especially for those pop performers who have roots in some sustaining community or tradition and are asked to deny it. While Motown's *Commodores' Anthology*, released in mid 1983, is dominated by Richie (he wrote or co-wrote 14 of its 20 songs and all but one on the final three sides), The Commodores were also the only veteran group of any significance who were not regrouped for Motown's 25th anniversary television show. Worse, Richie was the only performer who appeared exclusively on tape.

If Richie (now managed by the same people who handle Kenny Rogers) has it in mind to bolt money, he had best be cautious. In the first place, the fact that Motown's TV special got one of the highest ratings in American television history is one indication that the company, and its image, are still tremendously important. Berry Gordy still has tricks to teach even young crossover sharpies like Lionel. And who knows what a divorce from Motown might also mean — perhaps even a split with producer-arranger James Anthony Carmichael, without whom Richie has achieved nothing of importance save 'Endless Love' (not a major artwork, whatever its virtues when measured against 'Rio').

Where Richie goes from here (no matter what record label he goes with in the long run) is less significant than how much public attention he carries with him. So far, he has not written a lyric that expands beyond a basic love situation. Given the obscurantism of Maurice White, among others, this may be a blessing. But as long as Richie is breaking down categories and stereotypes, he may as well finish the job.
DAVE MARSH

109

A B C

ABC were not the most tiresome group of the year: that is an honour to be shared equally between Scritti Politti and Heaven 17. ABC even produced a really grand album, *The Lexicon of Love*. But like Scritti, Heaven 17, Altered Images and Mari Wilson, ABC showed how very complicated, self-conscious and wearying pop music had become by 1983.

Let us go back to 1981 and consider ABC's first single, 'Tears Are Not Enough'. The cover photo is an adept piece of B-movie pastiche: a freeze-frame from a melodramatic thriller, in which lead singer Martin Fry is trapped on a stairway while behind him The Girl, in evening frock, throws up her hands in alarm. Flip it over and the liner notes read like a Pinewood Studios version of Mickey Spillane:

"Marble Arch — London's richest and most fashionable quarter, but at night its more secluded streets become the centre of London's underworld. Into this jungle of terror came Martin Fry; here he constructs his kingdom with a group of musicians hand-picked for the occasion..."

This was following the Dexy's tradition of using sleeve notes, manifestos and advertisements to construct a ready-made legend. ABC's version was more obviously tongue in cheek, and it caught a neat balance. The graphic design was very Deutsche-Gramophone, classically grandiose; Fry and the girl were meant to represent 1950's glamour. But her dress was thrift shop, and she was obviously a friend of the band, while Fry looked too young and too seedy for his movie role. As for the liner notes, they were very cheeky indeed coming from a young Sheffield band that almost no one had ever seen and who had just released their first single.

So at this point, they might speculate, we should start using words like "refreshing" and "irreverent" and talk about a sharp re-working of pop's established strategies. But I found it depressing. The concept was too complete: you could almost see it giving interviews and writing its own articles. The record sleeve told us how we were meant to react to ABC, leaving no spaces for the mind and imagination to fill. Just looking at it was exhausting.

ABC represent the pop cul-de-sac that a particular way of seeing things — call it camp — found itself in the 1980s. When Susan Sontag first defined camp for intellectuals 20 years ago she called it a sensibility that "sees everything in quotation marks," a triumph of style over content, a way of being sincere and insincere simultaneously. "One is drawn to Camp when one realises that 'sincerity' is not enough." Or, presumably, tears.

Camp, as Sontag defined it in the sixties, was a way of appreciating the over-the-top, in objects that ranged from art nouveau lamps (since gone middle-brow) to Japanese horror movies (since discovered by London magazines like *City Limits*), but basically it has always been a way for people with an art sensibility to enjoy the innocent passions and extravagances of "vulgar" entertainment. "Camp is the answer to the problem: how to be a dandy in an age of mass culture." Pop music, of course, was mass culture from the beginning, and what camp did was make it possible for art students to enter the pop arena and use their fine art attitudes.

This is not to put it down. Camp was liberating, it proved that trash is neat, and it brought many new angles and subtleties into pop. It created, and was created by, Bryan Ferry. My favourite pop camp is the cover of Ferry's solo album *Another Time, Another Place* where Ferry stands by the swimming-pool in the middle of a garden party that looks like a Campari ad designed by *Harpers & Queen*. He's a lounge lizard, elegant but...so *sleazy* it throws the whole thing off kilter. It was startling at the time (in the mid seventies record covers didn't look like Martini ads); Ferry was sending up his high fashion aspirations while also celebrating them, and it seemed to open up certain

areas and poses for use, even if you didn't know what it meant. Which was the point.

ABC have been compared to Roxy Music, and Martin Fry was even awarded "The first annual Bryan Ferry Ill-Fitting Suit and Ungainly Dancer Award" by *NME* in January 1983. However, unlike Roxy, ABC spent months rather than years as cult artists. They began as a Sheffield synthesiser outfit, re-worked their strategy to become ABC, and played their first date in December 1980. By the next summer they had been written up in *The Face* and championed by *NME*. They were briefly tied in with the abortive "white funk" movement of the summer of 1981, and in the autumn had a modest (number 19) hit with their first record. A year later they had had three Top Ten singles and an album that reached number one.

The speed with which they travelled proved how well Ferry's influence had been assimilated, and how educated pop had become about itself. The camp ambiguity, in which two opposites — artifice and sincerity, parody and the real thing — operate simultaneously was now being bought and appreciated by High Street fans. Punk was the turning-point because after that nothing, apart from Bucks Fizz, was truly simple. And since then there had been so many revivals of the fifties and sixties that every pop fan could now read the references in ABC's cut-up of pop history.

Revivalism was another big thing last year (and no doubt will be next year and the year after) with everyone from Mari Wilson to a Northern cabaret act called The Maisonettes joining in. But ABC proved how many layers of association there could be in a single image: Martin Fry's gold suit came from Elvis Presley via Billy Fury through glam rock, and was actually sewn by Marc Bolan's old tailor. Ah, history! One of the pleasures, and actual selling points, in a group like ABC is the fun — and self-congratulation in spotting the references.

Then there was their handling of the press. Like the other pop successes of the year they arrived with not just a sound but an image and an attitude that would define their own coverage, dictate their own headlines in the music press ("A is for...B is for..."). Altered Images came

running down to London as *faux-naives*, Spandau Ballet bought new suits and made a manifesto out of it, Kevin Rowland forgot he was a soul boy and discovered he was Irish. As for ABC, even their name was adopted for the international market; they chose it because "the first three letters of the alphabet are known the world over." They had no personality, but what they did have was catch-phrases. Glib one-liners dropped from Martin Fry's lips like soap bubbles.

They had a manifesto before they had a record released:

"ABC represents...respect for built-in obsolescence and in-built adolescence. A techni-colour flag. Hi-tech, low-tech and discotheque. Respect for the single. Revolutions happen at 45 r.p.m. Respect for friction and fact, sophisticated boom boom and the status of the song." This was saying something about a return to well-crafted pop songs and showbusiness values, but no more than that. In the early days ABC often threw in word-play based on political rhetoric: "ABC — the radical dance faction, a democratic dance party, so vote with your feet." Presumably this meant that pop music is people's music, but like all ABC slogans it suggested more than it delivered.

The rhetoric looks like a punk hang-over; since the late seventies groups have been in the habit of talking in political terms. But ABC and their supporters seemed to really believe that they were doing something radical and challenging, presenting a truly Modern vision of romance: "acute analyses of passion's pitfalls," a "glancing acknowledgement that everything's artificial." That was in the music press. Fleet Street, the teen romance mags and the American trade papers took them straight. Camp had found its place in marketing, because the advantage of ambiguity is that you can be taken *all ways*.

When ABC talked about instituting a code of decency, pop insiders took it as tongue in cheek. The *Daily Star*, however, ran a banner headline: *GOOD MANNERS! Polite popsters find it's as easy as ABC*, with copy that read, "You don't have to be a snarling tearaway to get to the top in the pop world. It's as easy as ABC to be pleasant,

polite *and* successful." Similarly, while critics talked of irony, a girl's paper reported that "Martin believes the essential qualities of any loving relationship are tenderness and trust..." alongside their ABC pin-up.

As for any subversion of the pop process, the American trade paper *Variety* read ABC absolutely right. They weren't looking for a challenging critique, so they found none:

"ABC is to eighties' dance-rock what ELO was to seventies' AOR rock: a lushly orchestrated but torrid outfit which stretches the parameters of the form without losing its mainstream, commercial appeal...While the sound proves satisfying to the trend followers, mass appeal is abundant as well, which augurs well for the quartet's future on these shores."

In America, the music was enough. The music was always much better than the image, because Martin Fry never had *enough* style, or projected enough heart or sex appeal to break through the calculation. Great camp, after all, depends on a real tension between style (artifice) and true feeling, the make-up stained by tears. And camp, in any case, depends on uncertainty and surprise — and at the moment pop has used up its surprises.

On record, Fry's voice was enough; it had all the feeling he couldn't project on stage. The lyrics have been wildly overrated: the worst of Costello's tangled cleverness, without any of his killer lines. But the songs were wonderful melodramas, brilliantly orchestrated by Trevor Horn, whom ABC took from Dollar: "We said you make us a good record, Trevor, and we'll make you fashionable." They started the move away from funk back to old-fashioned pop/soul dramatics, later imitated by Spandau Ballet and Heaven 17.

Richard Williams wrote in *The Times* that ABC had already earned their paragraph in the history of pop. They certainly brought the Brill Building philosophy of fine pop manufacture back into the charts, but they merged this uneasily with a dependence on image and persona that could leave them locked in their own package: a package made up of relics. Last year was the year when it seemed that everything "new" had already been done.

Mary Harron

111

WHERE ARE THEY NOW?

LAST YEAR'S FAVOURITES PURSUED AND THEIR ACTIVITIES (OR LACK OF THEM) REVEALED BY IAN CRANNA

If, as Sir Harold Wilson once remarked, a week is a long time in politics, then consider the scope for changes offered by a year in contemporary music. Every year, eight of those upon whom the moon has smiled particularly broadly are selected by this volume as "Acts of the Year" — something of a double-edged compliment, initially intended to hail the achievement of the Act but usually thereafter seeing the emphasis falling ever more cruelly upon the Year.

Acts of the Year (*Rock Yearbook* style) tend to fall into two distinct categories: the Workhorses and the Inspired Amateurs. The Workhorses tend to be American beasts, dull (not to say dim) creatures of habit who prefer ploughing carefully-planned commercial furrows to running wild, and who have reached their present position by a mammoth labouring schedule broken only long enough to prepare their latest unswervingly dull excursion into the field. Private lives would seem to be as well-groomed as their careers, the sum total being about as exciting to the uninvolved as a thesis on the development of the three-pronged fork in twelfth-century Swabia.

The Inspired Amateurs, on the other hand, tend to be British, to keep a much clearer perspective on the origins and purpose of their music, and to owe their elevation as much to the challenge of fashionable theories as to following established patterns; the spur of the moment rather than the spur of the jockey. They are also generally totally unprepared for their sudden ascent to stardom, will make lots of mistakes and consequently are as likely to turn the corner into Skid Row as Easy Street. They are also much more likely to be the ones making history rather than merely repeating it.

What the two opposing styles have in common, however, is that the *modus operandi* which has led them to the now statutory 15 minutes of fame also tends to govern what happens in the following 12 months as well.

Sugar lumps, carrots and other high fashion accessories at the ready? Then follow me to the Workhorse quarters where inspection will reveal a further collection of tiresome equine metaphors. Here, and very much a rarity in these parts, is a genuine thoroughbred with splendid pedigree (J. Geils Band), there a frisky filly but temperamental dark horse (Joan Jett); over yonder is a collection of docile donkeys to give rides to the children (The Go-Go's) and last, and definitely least, is this rocking horse — wooden, going nowhere fast and strictly for the easily pleased (Journey). And so to a closer examination of the beasts themselves...

There was something more than faintly ironic about the **J. GEILS BAND** guesting on The Rolling Stones' last world stroll. It wasn't so much that they needed the break — 13 albums and 15 years of performing have taught them a thing or two about filling stadiums on their own, thank you — it was more the echoes of the old jibe about Geils and company being no more than an Americanised version of the bill-toppers.

Now, after the massive *Freeze Frame* album and hit singles on both sides of the Atlantic, you don't hear that kind of talk anymore. True, there were one or two of the hypercritical who looked askance at the inclusion of one or two instruments not actually present at the birth of the blues to give them a more radio-playable sound, but most felt that there was more than an element of justice about this reward and few would grudge them their place in the sun.

Twelve months after that burst of success, they are recording. Always a painstaking process for the band, their task has been made that much harder by having to follow their own act this time around, but their innate sense of quality control suggests that they will still be working away zealously at their beloved r'n'b as long as dignity allows, whatever the fashionable climate.

Never ones to court media popularity, the band will also doubtless remain firm advocates of that journalist's nightmare — that the music should do the talking. Interview or no interview, the result is usually the same — much stressing of the band's integrity and genuine commitment plus the musicians' own fervent belief in the band's natural development while attempting in their own understated way to make people think.

In this day and age I find it mildly astonishing that people — especially those who have laboured as long and as hard as the J. Geils Band — should still see rock music as a force for change. Me, I see rock as institutionalised rebellion and — along with similar sedatives like television — as the new opiate of the people likely to have just the opposite effect. Still, good luck to them; at least they recognise that all is not well outside those stadiums...

...which is more than can be said of the wretched **JOURNEY**, the epitome of those dinosaur bands whose adopted ideas have become more conservative than those they intended to replace. To judge by Journey, an outsider could be excused for thinking that style in rock was not some variable of recent origin but something handed down to Moses on Sinai. I mean, just look at them — grown men pulling faces like they'd just crossed the Gobi desert on a half-teaspoonful of water while producing noises that tell you your money would have been better spent getting dysentery in Spain.

Not that Journey would care. They've survived countless direct hits from a veritable battery of critical howitzers and not only lived but thrived. This year's mega-whatever-and-still-counting LP was called *Frontiers*. The title, however, as *NME* scathingly noted, was just the name of the shop; witness Neil Schon telling one reporter, "As far as the radio's concerned, I'm into whatever they want to play, because if you don't get played you don't get heard." All critical faculties thus abdicated to conservative programmers, *Frontiers*' sense of exploration was on a par with hopping blindfolded on one leg. But it sold of course — after all, no one ever lost money by underestimating the intelligence of American record buyers — though happily their success in the UK has yet to reach epidemic proportions.

But even all this was not enough. There was the usual band tour while elsewhere Schon did a second fusion LP with Jan Hammer — *Untold Passion* — and threatened to record with Sammy Hagar. Other solo projects realised or intended were Jonathan Cain's album with his wife Tane and Steve Perry's duet with the equally funky Kenny Loggins.

And then, of course, there was the Journey video game — possibly the most appropriate setting yet for the band's merchant-banking operations. In this humdinger you get to be a band member and then tackle groupies, fans, promoters, roadies, paternity suit lawyers, etc., on your way to the limo. And thence presumably to the bank, laughing all the way.

At the opposite end of the scale, there's something almost British about the way **JOAN JETT** continually flirts with disaster. Whatever it is, it's also something so ultimately endearing that the executioner's hand is always stayed, no matter how conclusive the evidence against her. Even though you cringed every time the radio gave vent to the utterly artless 'I Love Rock'n'Roll', there was still something that forced you to give a wink and a nod to someone who had been turned down by 23 labels and who still won through. She means it, ma-a-n!

And again even if the rock'n'roll in question was the bloated post-Vietnam US version instead of the original, there is still that flicker of recognition that Joan Jett at least represents the spirit of 1976. No matter how often she condemns herself, you'd have to have a heart of stone to give the thumbs down to someone who preferred baseball to the in-crowd, who openly enthused about being asked by young girls on how to start a rock band and who cried when presented with silver discs.

The past 12 months would appear to have changed little about Joan Jett. Her favourite working partnership with veteran bubblegum producer Kenny Laguna gave her another big US hit in 'Crimson and Clover' though it meant nothing at all in Britain. A financially disastrous UK tour then cleared out the coffers and Jett retired hurt to the States.

But even if she wasn't exactly top of the chart heap, Joan Jett still had the spirit to rise to the challenge elsewhere. She sued *Playboy* for a righteous $3,700,000 for claiming that a picture they had printed of a woman wearing fishnet stockings in a bathtub was her.

The lady, still on her financial uppers, also reportedly turned down an offer of a cool quarter of a million dollars to appear at a Californian festival in the company of David Bowie and The Pretenders; she objected to giving up her TV rights as she reckons TV is killing live music and she would rather beg in the gutter.

Silly girl — she should know that nothing will ever kill live music except dull shows and few things are as ultimately likely to stimulate demand for it as a sterile medium like television.

"This is my second shot at stardom," Jett said at the height of her fortunes. "It will be my last." Strange — even though her remarks have a prophetic ring to them and I'd be hard put to it to name one of her records that I really liked, I can't help hoping that it won't be.

These days Joan Jett is also reputed to be keen on avoiding being included in Women in Rock features; being lumped in with the gormless **GO-GO'S** could very well explain why.

There's one word that crops up over and over again in The Go-Go's press — "bounce". The Go-Go's are quite unnaturally bouncy; if bouncing were a crime there'd be enough on The Go-Go's to put them away for life. See them in concert, play their records and there they are — all smiles and

J. GEILS BAND

JOURNEY

JOAN JETT

113

THE GO-GO'S

KIM WILDE

wholesome as they come (though not without a certain engaging naturalness), bouncing away in what they fondly imagine to be the best Californian teenbeat tradition.

There is, however, one thing missing — tunes. Well, that's not strictly true. The Go-Go's do have two. One is 'Our Lips Are Sealed' which was co-written with Terry Hall of the Fun Boy Three. Their other tune — if only by the law of averages — is their own, 'We Got the Beat'. Sadly, that's about all they've got; the rest of their material is a variation on that theme — one-paced radio fodder, utterly lacking in depth or character, and thumpingly predictable.

The success of The Go-Go's is supposed to be an encouraging sign — a state of affairs that could only happen in America where the youth is so starved of anyone possessing youthful energy. The Go-Go's represent an improvement only when set against the dinosaur bands; the lesser of two evils, The Go-Go's have nothing to do with improvement in musical quality by any recognisable critical standards.

In short, The Go-Go's success is down to two factors. Firstly, they are an all-girl band, so relentlessly bright-eyed that you half expect them at any moment to break into a complicated song-and-dance routine.

Secondly, sheer hard work. The Go-Go's work incredibly hard, both to win over an audience and to make contact with as many audiences as possible. Look at them go, beavering away with all the avidity of stokers shovelling coal into dreadnought battleships. But it works — their second album *Vacation* (though noticeably inferior even to their first dilution of an already diluted Blondie) bounced everyone into submission except the British and the Germans.

Predictably, therefore, all the really interesting information on the girls comes from outside the musical arena. Belinda Carlisle starred in the lead role in *Grease* for the Long Beach Civic Light Opera Company and then went on to land a film part opposite Goldie Hawn and Kurt Russell in a movie called *Swing Shift*. Charlotte Coffrey recorded with Andy Summers, Gina Schock appeared on the Nona Hendrix album and Kathy Valentine collaborated on writing with Carlene Carter.

On their management front, Ginger Canzoneri teamed up with superhustler Irving Azoff who was promised "a slice of the action" in return for "help in developing projects". One "project" they will doubtless prefer to see not developed at all is the forthcoming legal battle with former member Margot Olavera who was kicked out because of supposed attitude and health problems. After all, it does promise to be more interesting than the group's music.

Perhaps the nearest thing that the Workhorses have to an overlap with the Inspired Amateurs is

KIM WILDE, whose musical direction steers a fine line between hard-nosed shiny pop and old-fashioned show business.

Personally, I have to confess that I have never understood all the fuss about Kim Wilde. She looks devastating and is also one of the most self-possessed people I have ever interviewed. But her avowed desire to be a singer is puzzling, given the unfailingly polite and passionless nature of her music.

Wilde hadn't exactly been overdoing it either in the 12 months previous to the time of writing. Interestingly she chose to close her initial period of acclaim by going on tour — as if to prove that she really did exist from the shoulders down. The concerts were by all accounts mildly interesting rather than wildly exciting affairs, suffering from the same politeness as her records and some rather forced attempts to get things moving. A long set of 18 songs was also a lot to tackle for an inexperienced newcomer and a brave move on her part. For my money, though, the highlight was when she temporarily displaced brother Ricky from the keyboards and nervously accompanied herself — a nice contrast to the unyielding stiffness elsewhere.

In other territories the march of Kim Wilde was seemingly unstoppable as number ones were racked up all round the world. Wilde embarked on the promotional swings and roundabouts to help promote, and then it seemed to stop almost as suddenly as it had begun. In public she was doing nothing for almost an entire year, though she has been in the studio for a fair amount of that time — a stay prolonged by the serious illness of her mentor Mickie Most.

The finished product of Kim's new material is rumoured to sound very American — no doubt with an eye to the one territory where her name has yet to mean anything, despite a reportedly large deal with EMI America. It will be interesting to see if she can make an impression there alongside the new British invasion, and only scarcely less interesting to see if, with the same material, she can recapture her standing in Britain after so long out of the public eye.

Also famously inactive — or at least unproductive — in the year after it was their year were **THE HUMAN LEAGUE**. Productivity records elsewhere rested untroubled as the band followed the massive success of *Dare* with precisely two singles, neither of which made it to that top slot so long the preserve of 'Don't You Want Me?'

The first one was 'Mirror Man', a skilful electronic update of classic Motown and apparently a dig at the *Daily Mirror* (one of Britain's tabloid newspapers. The Human League remain as prickly as ever). Single number two — '(Keep Feeling) Fascination' — was apparently written before its predecessor, took months to finish, went through ten mixes and

HAIRCUT 100

involved battles which actually had people leaving the room in tears. It was also notable for a switch of producers from electronics expert Martin Rushent to veteran rock producer Chris Thomas, and for the introduction of — shock, horror — *guitars* in an attempt to move away from the host of groups now operating in a territory too close for comfort.

Otherwise, not a lot occurred. Philip Oakey had his hair cut and looked much better for it. One might occasionally bump into Jo Callis in London, muttering about lack of progress, or Adrian Wright hiding at gigs pleading with inquisitive journalists not to mention his presence in case it would be interpreted as endorsing the band. Apart from that, the band wisely remained in Sheffield, trying to protect what was left of their privacy and attempting to write new songs.

Like Kim Wilde, The Human League concluded their peak period with a long tour (though not of course their first). This was judged to have been less than totally successful, accentuating the difference between the electronic precision of the band on record and the still shambolic nature of the live show where Suzanne and Joanne's featured dancing distracted from Wright's visuals, thus robbing the show of much of its presence and effectiveness.

But perhaps it was in the US — where audiences seem incapable of appreciating the spirit of amateurism, however inspired — that The Human League's newly acquired success evaporated most quickly. The follow-up to 'Don't You Want Me?' — their earlier British hit 'Love Action' — made no impression at all and relations with the American record company hit rock bottom when first the band pulled out of the *Solid Gold* TV show and then A&M licensed — without the band's knowledge or consent — one of their songs to the soundtrack of the awful *Last American Virgin* movie. A&M also declined to release either of the new singles without an album to promote but a compromise seems to have been reached with the appearance of a new mini-LP.

Whatever the current state of affairs, The Human League are a unique working aggregate of six talented, headstrong and very likeable individuals who have successfully defied both logic and the odds for years now, and it would be a foolish person who'd bet against them continuing to do so.

In an astute piece of judgement in this publication last year, John Tobler wondered whether **HAIRCUT 100** would survive the second album syndrome. At the time most of us took this for granted. After all, both singles and album were doing great business both sides of the Atlantic while British appearances were greeted by teen mania as the stage was showered with everything from marshmallows to toy tractors. But, as we all now know, Haircut 100 didn't make it — at least, not intact. Come to that, they didn't even make it to the second album.

That some sort of decline had already set in was apparent with 'Nobody's Fool' — the band's fifth UK single and the poorest to date. The problem appears to have started way back when with the addition to the original nucleus of Heyward, Nemes and Jones of the extra studio musicians — Smith, Cunningham and Fox. In particular it was percussionist Fox and Heyward who seem to have been the main protagonists, with Fox leaving at one stage for reasons that were never made clear, only to re-join shortly afterwards. A solo single, 'Bottle Run Dry', was announced but never released during Fox's spell out of ranks.

In September 1982, Heyward announced in the press that all the songs for the second album were written and ready to record, but it became clear when the planned December tour was postponed until the following February that all was not going according to plan. At first Heyward claimed this was because he wanted an album containing 12 hit singles; but as time continued to drag on rumours began to circulate of arguments in the studio — even over the choice of manager.

Finally, following a couple of very shaky and perfunctory Christmas gigs, it all came to a head. With all backing tracks long since completed but only three finished vocals in as many months, the remaining band members felt this had gone on quite long enough and summoned a band meeting to discuss the situation. Heyward in turn pre-empted the discussion by announcing his departure, citing increasing divergence in musical direction as his main reason. The remaining band members then said they were staying together, with Mark Fox taking over on lead vocals.

But why had it dragged on so long? One answer seems to lie in the way Haircut 100 recorded, with the band laying down their contribution after which Heyward would add his contribution around the foundations. Heyward apparently complained that these were too much like *Pelican West* and that nobody wanted to change.

The band, not without reason, pointed out that since Heyward had contributed no vocals — one source has it that Heyward would only sing between 5 p.m. and 6 p.m. — there was not much they could do beyond guesswork.

But it didn't stop there. The aggrieved band complained that if Heyward was going to leave he should have done it a lot earlier and accused him of wasting their money by his apparent unwillingness to complete the second album. Clearly Heyward had behaved very badly towards his former colleagues, and he is said to have made them a generous offer which they allegedly rebuffed.

And then it got nasty, and then it got legal. The band, evidently feeling hard done by, submitted a 56-page dossier of complaints against Heyward and accused Arista of encouraging Heyward to breach of contract. The result was a court injunction banning both parties from new contracts. Heyward, however, proceeded to release his first solo single — 'Whistle Down the Wind' (one of the songs originally meant for the disputed LP) which the band tried unsuccessfully to have stopped.

In the end it was settled out of court. The statement baldly stated that Haircut 100 had paid Arista a sum of money to avoid further proceedings, in return for which Arista had released the band who promptly signed to Polydor. The disputed album stayed on the shelf at Arista, and as usual only the lawyers benefited.

What will happen next is still far from clear. In an extraordinary about-turn, Heyward claimed he had had trouble remembering his lyrics and blamed everything on his commercial art background. Complaining also about his clean-cut image, which had done nothing but encourage earlier, he then seems to have gone out of his way to be particularly — and sometimes inexcusably — unpleasant about others in the pages of the music press. And while both solo singles to date had reached the Top 20, neither was exactly a revelation. In fact, as a writer of real integrity and depth, Nick Heyward makes a great commercial artist.

For Haircut 100 the future is still less clear. Now led by Mark Fox — a confident, intelligent and amusing speaker — they promise a brasher funkier sound and a move away from sixties' nostalgia. For them, however, the question is not so much about their musicianship as their ability to write a decent song. (Still, that never stopped the old Haircut 100 — the very epitome of shallow frivolity.) Polydor are clearly gambling on the fact that it is the band's name and not Heyward's that counts overseas.

But, meanwhile, the insecure Heyward is reported to be missing his original partners Jones and Nemes. Perhaps this extraordinary drama is not yet played out...

SOFT CELL, too, very nearly

SOFT CELL

became another casualty statistic. Thrown together by success and then kept in each other's pockets 24 hours a day by the non-stop exacting promotional demands created by the enormous success of 'Tainted Love', the Almond/Ball relationship became so strained that at one point they weren't on speaking terms for a week.

Fortunately, northern commonsense prevailed, and the pair decided to give more time to their individual interests for a while. In short, this meant a return to their natural habitats — for Ball, the studio, and for Almond, the stage. The result was the saving of sanities and Soft Cell, and a vastly improved working relationship.

The inadvertent cause of all these traumas, meanwhile, continued its incredible run of success, writing itself into the history books as a bona fide classic in the process. Reappearing twice more in the British charts, 'Tainted Love' also reached the Top Ten in all 17 countries of release and displaced Bill Haley's venerable 'Rock Around the Clock' as the longest running record ever in the American charts, while making its

obscure writer Ed Cobb a very happy man in the process.

Back home the flow of records continued with *Non-Stop Ecstatic Dancing* — a six-track dub mix mini-LP of dancefloor fun which thoroughly confused the critics who, having just got used to the idea of taking Soft Cell seriously, proceeded to tie themselves in knots looking for ideas where there weren't any. The run of hits also continued with 'Torch' and 'What' — another northern soul classic intended as a fond farewell to that first era of Soft Cell.

From now on, the Soft Cell material was going to be more challenging and less overtly commercial. "Why do people have to get to number one?" asked a satisfied Almond as 'Home Is Where the Heart Is' and 'Numbers' failed to make the Top 20, let alone the Top Five. Friction with the record company over this new policy visibly increased, until it all boiled over when the label, attempting to boost the sales of a struggling 'Numbers', decided on attaching a free shrink-wrapped copy of 'Tainted Love' as a marketing ploy.

Soft Cell, abroad on one of their periodic gig trips at the time, were not amused. Almond — feeling that the band, the music and the fans had all been cheapened and insulted — took himself and his manager round to the record company and gleefully avenged themselves by trashing a couple of offices. Phonogram, to their credit, bore this stoically and in good part.

Unfortunately, the corollary of lower chart positions for singles is lower chart positions for albums and the new LP clocked up appreciably fewer sales than its predecessor. Spoiled by a silly title, *The Art of Falling Apart* ('The Art of Survival' would have been more accurate and appropriate) was at once more adventurous and sophisticated. It also showed Soft Cell had well and truly arrived as a force to be reckoned with.

Workaholics both, Almond and Ball both kept up an extraordinary level of outside projects. Almond, missing the risks and rough edges of performance and finding the term "pop star" somewhat derogatory in its implied disposability, created Marc & The Mambas. Cheerfully self-indulgent,

this occasional/semi-permanent collection of musicians allowed free rein to the melodramatic in Almond who, emotions never far from going over the top, was now free to tackle writers like Scott Walker and Jacques Brel as well as some of his own more experimental material.

The resulting double 12-inch set ('Untitled') and several wonderfully informal gigs were — perhaps inevitably — uneven. Both received a decidedly mixed response from the critics, most of whom signally failed to acknowledge the spirit in which they were intended. "Spit on the purists! They're there to be trodden on!" was Almond's spirited response. A second LP *Torment and Toreros*, however, firmly establishes Almond as a talent in his own right and will come as a real eye-opener to anyone who still has him marked down as superficial, out of his depth or merely silly.

David Ball, meanwhile, also emerged in somewhat less dramatic manner, as a talent in his own right. His appearance transformed from horrendous to handsome by growing his hair and shaving off that awful moustache, he has completed a solo album and a number of production projects, including a hitherto unknown band called Sense and an album with the equally individual Virgin Prunes. He also found time in the lunch breaks of the latter task to compose a score for a West End production of the Tennessee Williams play *Suddenly Last Summer*. A multi-instrumentalist with a flair for theories as well as composition, arrangements and production, David Ball is on the verge of becoming a figure who can command considerable respect by turning his hand to a wide variety of tasks. Clearly he has a great future ahead of him.

Life with Soft Cell is evidently never going to be a quiet one. Other highlights in an incident-packed 12 months included a shock-horror-probe scandal in the gutter press over the unfinished 'Sex Dwarf' video (ironically started by the very paper from whom Almond had taken the story), a brush with Spanish mafiosi at an Iberian gig, and a cut head from Marc Almond and guitar for a beer-and-spittles Mambas gig-goer.

Lack of progress in the US after 'Tainted Love' must rank as a major source of disappointment and discontent, but otherwise their future looks healthy enough. A pleasing contrast to the vanity and arrogance which unfortunately seem to be making something of a comeback these days, Soft Cell's honesty and healthy contempt for what Ball neatly described as "government music" makes them one of the few acts whose works are consistently entertaining and challenging, and to whose releases one can look forward with a real degree of interest.

I wonder how many people that will be true of this time next year?

REDCOATS ON OVERDRIVE

RADIO ONE AND THE PERSONALITY FACTOR, BY *DAVID HEPWORTH*

Pouring scorn on Radio One is a British national sport of long standing and few indulge in it more enthusiastically than the columnists of the music press. It was significant therefore when, earlier this year, the *NME* — traditionally second-to-none among the station's critics — published an article in praise of DJ David "Kid" Jensen. As mutual back-scratching exercises go, it was a small classic; the Bible of Hip setting its seal of approval upon this formerly reviled Canadian while he punctuated the gaps in the conversation with endorsements of their editorial posture, delivered with the humility of a recent convert.

The thrust of the article was simple. This man is OK, readers, because where he used to torment us with Bay City Rollers records he now gives us Siouxsie and The Banshees in what American radio likes to call "heavy rotation". There was no suggestion that the same lack of discrimination might be at the root of both past and present policies, merely an unstated admission that, in 1983, Radio One holds sway over an area that was previously the happy hunting ground of the music papers.

Radio One enjoys the confidence of today's pop star. Radio One play doesn't just sell records; it makes names. No longer can hipsters seek refuge in the accusation that this or that oddball combo doesn't sell records because it doesn't get played on the only national pop station. The plain fact is that this or that oddball combo is probably getting more airplay than Rod Stewart these days, mainly thanks to DJs like Jensen. Whether many people are listening or not is a different matter.

Because Radio One is a division of the BBC and carries no advertising, ratings don't have the fearsome implications they do in America. It was instituted in 1967, charged with the task of replacing the recently outlawed pirate

DAVID JENSEN

stations with a national pop music service aimed at the younger listener. Great stress is placed on that word *service*.

In exchange for its monopoly of national broadcasting, Radio One must cater for the ten-year-old Bucks Fizz fan, the Motorhead maniac, the student sitting at the feet of New Order and, most importantly, millions of people who never declare their loyalties by buying a record but nevertheless like the background noise, the company. It's an impossible brief but Radio One does a remarkably good job in fulfilling it and it's their pursuit of a large and diverse audience that's largely responsible for the variety of the British chart

and the multifarious cast of characters — from Boy George to Iron Maiden — currently invading the best-selling lists of the rest of the world.

This breadth of appeal has traditionally been achieved by plotting the day's output to swing gradually through the spectrum of taste from the widely acceptable to the wilfully obscure, in recognition of the changing habits of the listeners.

Mike Read's breakfast show has the largest audience, with by far the most teenagers, and therefore the diet is predominantly chart singles. After 9 a.m. this format is broken up with oldies in recognition of the number of

young mothers (and unemployed) stranded in the home. Steve Wright's

MIKE READ

STEVE WRIGHT

PETER POWELL

enormously popular afternoon programme places great stress on listener involvement and spectacularly unfunny running gags in order to register through the clamour of the factory floor. In the late afternoon Peter Powell welcomes the returning school pupil with Spandau Ballet and Tears for Fears, playing the breathless fan for all he's worth. (Duran Duran swiftly became "Duran", but eyebrows were raised when KajaGooGoo found themselves abbreviated to "Kaj".)

Nobody is listening at 7 p.m. and so Radio One runs its quota of speech programmes; banal discussions about The Bomb or the existence of God, broken up with the new Grace Jones single. Kid Jensen turns up at eight to serenade the swotting student with The Passage and Black Uhuru and he's followed by John Peel, whose particular brand of uneasy listening goes through to the midnight closedown. Were Radio One a commercial station it's likely that its evening output would have been revamped in favour of something with more popular appeal than the half million listeners they can command at their very best. But since even these figures are far superior to those notched up by the classical Radio Three, Radio One can claim to be discharging its mission to serve the minority audience in a respectable fashion.

Ten — even five — years ago, the daytime "strip" shows seemed to exist in a different universe from the kind of esoteric "rock" programme presented by Peel. Dominated by a playlist, the strip shows dispensed Gary Glitter and The Bee Gees for singles' buyers while the rock shows played lengthy album tracks by groups who would have treated the very idea of releasing a 45 as the thin end of the commercial wedge. Over the past few years that chasm has been bridged to such an extent that the most interesting new groups are very often the most commercial and they head directly for the mainstream with carefully tailored hit singles. This results in precious little "alternative" music of consequence to fill the old slot. Indeed, when Robert Wyatt's 'Shipbuilding' turns up on Simon Bates' mid-morning show, what are the evening shift left with but Joy Division copyists and records so

perversely lacking in entertainment value that the only possible reason for listening to them can be a sense of duty?

Nowhere does the notion that an independently produced record is by definition on a higher moral plane than an EMI or CBS record die harder than in the corridors of Radio One. Punk may have caught them napping at first but it also provided them with a golden opportunity for renewal. As the simple act of making a record became easier so did the idea of getting it played on the radio. DJs are only too eager to prove how receptive and up-to-the-minute they are by leaping on a new record by a new group, often with scant regard for its quality. For every act which shows promise there are five which vary between mediocre and wretched.

In the old days A&R men were paid large salaries to listen to bad groups. These days, all too often, it's the public who have to put up with them. The A&R men tape the evening shows and listen to them in their Volvos the following morning, reeling past the tedious bits in search of something with a spark of promise, some limited pressing which got played because of a particularly heart-rending accompanying letter, some newly-formed group which won a session on the merits of a tape made in a suburban bedroom. Their chances of getting this exposure are eased by the financial implications of the BBC's agreements with the record companies. Radio One pays the music business millions of pounds a year for the privilege of broadcasting its wares, but it can play new releases free — for a limited period — on the condition that it credits the record label. This accounts for the fact that most records released will — at one time or another — get played on Radio One, leading in turn to the large number of new chart entries every week and the exceedingly low boredom threshold of the British pop fan.

Most Radio One programming is done by producers who, at least, are a more fair-minded breed than, say, the editorial staff of a music paper. A Radio One producer is unlikely to dismiss a record because of the bracket it comes from. Not for British record pluggers the horrific

JIMMY SAVILE

task of their American counterparts, trying to persuade FM stations to play Michael Jackson's 'Beat It' on the grounds that Eddie Van Halen played guitar on it. Radio One no longer has a playlist but, between the contents of the charts and the producer's perception of what *ought* to be played at this or that hour, a consensus is soon forged. And even those DJs who are too busy endorsing soft drinks to have any say in the compilation of their programmes have an effect upon the selection, purely by the nature of their radio "personalities". "It isn't right for Mike/Peter/Simon/Steve," is a rationale often employed by producers to explain programming decisions, emphasising the fact that no ornery record is going to gum up the working of this particular star vehicle. And since the majority of Radio One programmes are simply named after the people who present them, claiming no further editorial slant than that, DJs as a species are impossible to ignore.

The 1000th edition of TV's longest running music show, *Top of the Pops*, broadcast in May, provided a unique opportunity for closer examination of this curious tribe. They compèred the show *en masse*, turning up in twos and threes between songs to

jockey for position and smile with grim determination. Once again bearing out Parkinson's Law, they proliferated to fill the airtime available, eventually outnumbering the artists they were introducing. They were all there; the smoothies with their flared hair and widespread business interests; the hearties, all catchphrases and thumbs-up; the Good Sorts with their *fascinating* snippets of information gleaned from record company hand-outs. And occupying the place of honour, as befitting a man who introduced the first edition 20 years before, was Jimmy Savile. Savile is a curious case and yet, at the same time, the very definition of the British DJ.

A job description for a DJ would probably require two basic skills; a smattering of musical knowledge and the ability to introduce records correctly. On both these counts Savile is manifestly unfit. If he does know anything about pop music, he keeps it to himself and every time he introduces a group he finishes his *spiel* five seconds early and is thus forced to fill the ensuing gap with yodels and constant repetition of the words "yes, sir" and "right now". And yet for 20 years he's held down his job, achieving the average DJ's twin goals; fame and wealth. He doesn't introduce pop

118

records for a living; he introduces *himself* between pop records. He doesn't do; he *is*. And although the styles may vary with the haircuts, this is essentially what most Radio One DJs do. Understand that and you will understand the lengths many of them will go to in order to project themselves. The basic skills of the job are not transferable; they cannot be parlayed for anything but popularity. Down at the Job Centre they do not put a high premium on the proven ability to operate a couple of faders and *effervesce*.

Most of them get into the job early; running the school disco, judging knobbly knees competitions, choreographing the hokey cokey at weddings, eventually graduating to local radio. Through this school they acquire a Redcoat mentality which manifests itself in a single-minded dedication to getting everyone to cheer up, as though a listening audience who weren't permanently wreathed in beatific smiles were a slight on their professional capabilities. They start calling men "mate" and women "dear" and lying about their ages long before it's even remotely necessary. They embark on a hopeless love affair with huge numbers of people and develop a desire to be popular and famous and admired which borders on the insane.

SIMON BATES

Of course, most Radio One presenters are on the wrong side of 30 and can be excused a degree of caution about their careers. But this hale and hearty approach isn't confined to that generation. Last year it was apparent that someone in the upper echelons of Radio One was concerned about the average age of the people at the

microphone. Paul Burnett left the station and Dave Lee Travis (favourite group — Sad Cafe) moved out of prime time. New names like Steve Wright and Mike Smith were deployed in their places and into the evening and weekend slots came Janice Long, Pat Sharp and Gary Davies, amidst much publicity harping upon the fact that they were all in their twenties.

The result? No perceptible change. These young bloods — an entirely new generation — in some cases almost 20 years younger than the established staff, were almost identical in approach; cautious, responsible, cheerful, tame. The conventional wisdom of how a DJ should behave had been bred in them; the awesome responsibility of imposing themselves on a huge audience had put paid at the outset to any prospect of them behaving like individuals.

If we must have personality DJs, then we must have people with something to say about music and the wherewithal to say it. Radio One currently has two great disc jockeys,

JANICE LONG

operating at opposite ends of the day. Mike Read and John Peel are radio naturals; highly knowledgeable without feeling the need to demonstrate the fact at all times; endowed with ironic senses of humour; capable of talking on the air without reducing the English language to senseless prattle. They're also both *fans*.

Read's breakfast show is basically made up of chart records and is consequently, at the very least, listenable.

JOHN PEEL

Peel's, on the other hand, comprises the records that nobody else will play. Ten years ago this would have meant Little Feat or John Cale or The Velvet Underground; all too often these days it means The Cocteau Twins or Clock DVA or, well, just supply the name of the group who provided you with your least congenial listening experience and you're not far off. This is not to say that there isn't an audience which wants to hear this kind of thing; when I was the age of the average Peel listener I tuned in most nights and convinced myself that really I *liked* The Third Ear Band when in truth I would much rather have been listening to The Temptations. Nobody would deny today's Polytechnic students their own show, but it's fatuous to pretend that there's enough of what they'd be prepared to regard as good music released each week to fill up the eight hours a week that Peel alone commands. Particularly when Radio One can offer the disco/funk, heavy metal and jazz audiences little more than token slots in the schedule.

In my dreams I can hear a radio show and it's hosted by Peel or Read or — it doesn't really matter; any *fan* will do — and he's playing Smokey Robinson and Led Zeppelin, Steely Dan and Cliff Richard, The Drifters and Meat Loaf, Orange Juice and The Monkees, Tom Petty and The Jonzun Crew, Weather Report and The Pretenders and The Upsetters and Van Morrison and The Shadows and Elvis Costello and Hank Williams and Prince and Culture Club and whoever the hell he likes. The important point is that he sounds as if he's locked the studio door from the inside, torn up all the listeners' requests, sent the producer home and burned the BBC charter; he's brought along a pile of his favourite records and it doesn't matter whether they're new or old, whether you've heard them before or not, because you're going to *enjoy* them, you're going to be *thrilled* by them, and if not he'll want to know the reason why. Because it's that kind of honest, unbridled enthusiasm that has always provided pop radio with its most electrifying moments. And nobody ever threw a party out of duty. At least, not a good one.

ANATOMY OF A MONOPOLY

DREW MOSELEY LOOKS AT, AND BEHIND, MTV

Tenth Avenue and 33rd Street is one of the more depressed-looking areas of Manhattan. The block on the west side of the street, between 32nd and 33rd, is a wasteland of sand and wrecking crews. Further west, by the Hudson River, are the old docks and the car pound. Trucks stand abandoned in the middle of the street. At night, junkies who have strayed from the Times Square area hover in the doorways of abandoned buildings. Between 33rd and 34th, there's a seedy-looking diner and a MacDonald's, side by side. And just on the other side of the diner, there's a small building with the word "Teletronics" standing guard over the doorway. Within that building, there's a whole new world: MTV's taping centre.

It's hard to believe that in December of 1980 MTV was still only a gleam in its fathers' eyes. The final decision to go ahead with the idea wasn't made until March of 1981, with a projected first air date of August 1. Field staffs in Atlanta, Chicago, Dallas, Los Angeles and New York went out to the various cable companies and told them about the new channel. They had a demo tape floating around the country to show people what MTV would look like. And those services that had enough empty space agreed to kick off with them. MTV would be a "free" cable channel; people who already subscribed to the various cable systems would be able to watch MTV for no additional fee. Rock stars made commercials inciting viewers to write to their local cable companies and "demand" their MTV. And it worked. It worked beyond anyone's wildest dreams. It's still working.

MTV programmes rock videos 168 hours a week, 24 hours a day. It employs five VeeJays, or video jockeys, who each work an average of five hours a day, seven days a week. This means that their shows run five hours, but

LES GARLAND

because their appearances are taped 24 hours in advance of the time they're aired, the VeeJays are not sitting around doing nothing while the videos play. They're conducting interviews which will run on Sunday nights, doing voice-overs for the animated station identification breaks, looking over their scripts so they'll be ready when the camera is ready to roll, and poring over the research that is compiled for them before they sit down to talk to rock stars. They work hard; it is their job to appear cheerful whenever the camera

is on them, to be the "human touch" between their viewers and the video. They are not critics or comedians, but they are a vital link.

"Nineteen months ago, before we went on the air, no one had any idea of what a video jockey should look like, act like, dress like, what kind of information should be delivered," explains Les Garland, the Vice President of Programming for MTV. "Should they be critics? Should they just relay information? Should they be personalities? What should they be? So we

went straight arrow with it. They're good communicators — the human touch from the music to the viewer — but they don't get in the way. We fully realise that the star of this channel is the music, and the jocks realise that, too. Frankly, we're not looking for anybody to come on here and be funny and critical and say things like, 'Boy, the new Stones album sucks.' The audience can make that decision themselves. I think that's part of what happened to radio in the seventies — these stations got so opinionated, and they didn't have any idea of what they were talking about. The audience knew more about it than they did."

The reason for taping 24 hours in advance is a simple one: you can't broadcast from Manhattan 168 hours a week. It's financially impossible, according to Garland. MTV's present network operations centre is in Smithtown, New York. The day's work in the New York studio is driven out to Smithtown, shot into space some 23,000 miles, delivered back to the cable systems here on earth and sent along the cable wires to the viewers' homes.

"Not being live has hurt us on occasion," Garland admits. "But we're prepared at any given moment to either go live or do inserts. I think the best example was when Blues Brother John Belushi passed away. We were on with that within the hour. We recorded the segments immediately, the jock was called in from home, did the story, and it was helicoptered to Smithtown and put on the satellite immediately."

The most incredible thing about MTV is the way it sells records. MTV has between 1,200 and 1,300 video clips on file. At any given time, they are probably programming 900 of them, at a rate of 300 a day. "There's a difference between the oldies and the currents," says Garland. "The new ones

MTV'S VEEJAYS: (L TO R) J.J. JACKSON, MARTHA QUINN, NINA BLACKWOOD, ALAN HUNTER AND MARK GOODMAN

are chosen at the acquisitions meeting, which is held every Tuesday morning. A lot of people here come from radio, and some from the record business — most of us were all affiliated with the entertainment business in one way or another. Bob Pittman, who is the Senior Vice President of Programming for the whole company, had a very successful career in radio, as I did. John Sykes, the Director of Programming, came from the record business; Chip Racklin, Director of Acquisition, came from management and promotion and ICM, where he put in nine years as a concert promoter. Gail Sparrow, our Talent/Artist Relations Director, came from Epic Records, and her assistant, Roberta Kruger, used to be a schoolteacher. So we have a meeting of about nine people, and whatever has come in within the last seven days — submitted to us by either the record company or management or whoever — goes before the group. We sit in the conference room and look at each clip in its entirety. We get between 20 and 25 clips a week now.

"Actually, our rules are very simple. Musically, if it fits the format, we'll try it out."

The MTV format has been constantly changing. It's described as a "rock and roll" programming, but the boundaries of that label have stretched in recent months to include Kate Bush, Michael Jackson and Charlie Daniels. MTV stood up to a great deal of criticism from the black community for refusing to run clips by artists like Marvin Gaye and Lionel Richie, but that controversy should diminish somewhat when the projected black-owned counterpart to MTV, the Apollo Entertainment Network, begins its programming of mostly black,

121

R&B rooted video music. MTV does not, certainly, have any legal responsibility to play anything it doesn't want to, any more than an AOR radio station can be forced to play the Fabulous Poodles' country-and-western version of the Sex Pistols' 'Anarchy in the U.K.'

Garland continues, "We try not to judge a tape by the artist. It would be easy to sit here and say that Barbra Streisand, for example, will never make it on MTV. But who knows? It just takes the right song. After the song, we look at the video, for its technical quality — it has to be one inch and it has to be in stereo. And, as for any censorship rules, the only thing we have to worry about is that at the moment we're in about twelve and a half million homes and we have local community standards to deal with all over the country — standards which may vary from Kentucky to Los Angeles to New York — so we have to be careful about violence and frontal nudity. Other than that, it isn't too much of a problem. In 18 months we've only had to reject less than five clips because of content. Duran Duran re-edited their 'Girls on Film' video for TV. But we didn't do the editing; we let the band do the editing — we don't get involved in that kind of stuff. We actually did put Van Halen's video for 'Oh, Pretty Woman' on the air, but we got so many complaints that we had to take it off."

How big a push do all these videos give the artists who make them? "The average MTV viewer last year bought nine albums. The national average is about seven, but the MTV viewers bought nine. And of the nine they bought, four of them were purchased as a direct result of having been seen on MTV. That's almost 50%." Les Garland is understandably pleased with MTV's record.

The demographics are extraordinary. Geographically, MTV is everywhere. Of the 80 million television homes in America, 30 million homes are hooked up to cable, and MTV is available on 1,650 cable systems which run into about 12 million homes. They hope to reach 17 million homes by the end of 1983.

They're demons for research over at Warner/Amex, the parent company of MTV. "We do something like 200,000

pieces of mail a month," says Garland, "and four to six major studies a year, talking to viewers on the phone for upwards of a half hour each. 47% of the people we spoke to said the channel was more popular now than it was several months ago. 80% of the people we talked to watch every week, at least one day. The average viewer watches 4.7 days a week, and the average viewer is 25-years-old and makes $31,000 per year. Our target audience is 12 to 34, so within that group we break down into three demographic audiences: 25% of our audience is in the 12 to 17 age group; 27% is at 18 to 24; and 28% is at 25 to 34. Over 35 we have about 18% of our audience, and the rest, 2%, cues below age 12. An amazing balance. Television thrived for so many years on volume instead of quality, it's always been these 12 plus numbers — 'But the show has ten million viewers' — sure, but how old are those viewers? How much money do they make? Do they have college educations? Television has become much more sophisticated now; advertisers want to know who's watching, and whether they are likely to buy the products advertised on the programme. We deliver that kind of sophisticated audience."

The advertisers agree. Already more than 125 advertisers who represent more than 200 products have bought airtime for spots ranging from 30 to 120 seconds. MTV sells national air spots at rates of $1,500 to $6,000 with six minutes of time per hour. There are four breaks of two minutes each, but two of those minutes belong to the local cable company to allocate as it pleases.

Competition on a national level does not appear to be forthcoming. Little local channels are cropping up here and there, but Garland feels it will be difficult for these stations to go nation-wide. By MTV's calculations, anyone who might try to compete with MTV at this point would probably have to lay out about $100 million just to get in the game.

"If you think about Home Box Office, one of America's leading movie channels, you realise that the reason they're one of the leaders is that they were there seven years before anyone else. To compete with

that would cost a fortune because there is only so much cable space available around the country — a lot of the systems that are out there have only a very limited amount of space on their boxes. Very few of them can handle 54 different programming services at this time. Thank God we started when we did, because we have a very viable product that works, and had we waited another two or three years it would have been that much more difficult.

"At the same time, I'm not saying that we're going to try to monopolise this business, because I don't believe in that either. You will see the local versions pop up, and they may go from Atlanta to South Carolina to Florida, but they'll still basically be regional services."

MTV does not pay for the use of rock video — the clips are provided gratis by either the record companies, the management companies or the artists themselves. MTV does pay fees to BMI and ASCAP, just as radio does, although MTV's fees are arranged a little differently. To pay for sync licensing fees, according to Garland, or to get involved in buying the clips outright for a certain period of time, would be like killing the goose that laid the golden egg. "The record companies were in serious trouble in 1980 and 1981. *They* didn't know if this would help. But they're just now starting to see a levelling off of the drop they were in and now they're having visions of coming back; a lot of that belief has happened because of MTV. We've thrown in millions of dollars to get this thing tested, to see if it would work, and we did break a few bands last year — I think most people are aware of that. It hasn't paid off for us yet — we're still not in profits. It paid off for Duran Duran and for Men at Work and Culture Club. And *good*! Let them keep the business alive and we'll still be around in two years. We think that's wonderful. But to get into paying for videos just doesn't make any sense. It would be like radio stations paying for records."

Where is all of the money MTV is pulling in from advertisers going? At the moment it's going back into MTV. The company grew so quickly last year that when the year began there were only about 40 MTV employees.

This year there are 175.

Money is also being poured into specials which air on Saturday and Sunday nights. On Saturdays, at 11pm Eastern Time, MTV programmes concerts. On Sundays, the programming varies between *Liner Notes*, a half-hour interview/information series and *Fast Forward*, a half-hour in-depth interview with one artist. Other specials are in the planning stages.

MTV has sponsored over 15 extraordinary contests in the past two years as well. Among these are the infamous *One Night Stand* series, where winners were flown in Lear jets to spend the evening with the likes of The Who and Fleetwood Mac, and the latest *Video Star* contest, where entrants sent in postcards stating nothing more than their names and ages and one was chosen to appear in the new Loverboy video.

Money is spent on studio time for the regular jock spots, and for the more than 260 artist interviews that have been conducted over the past two years.

Basement Tapes is another exciting feature. This series gives unknown bands a chance to compete, on video tape, for an EMI recording contract. Viewers are encouraged to dial a 900 telephone number, at a cost of 50 cents, to vote for the band whose video they like best. The videos that make it to the air are chosen by a group of industry people outside of MTV.

The music industry has received a big shot in the arm from MTV in the past few years, and that boost should continue if 1983 is anything to go on. In the studio on 33rd Street, several gold and platinum albums hang on the walls, grateful gifts from bands like Aldo Nova and Duran Duran. The great surge in Australian music in the United States can be directly traced to MTV's heavy rotation of acts like Men at Work, the Divynls and INXS. People who work at MTV seem to enjoy their jobs. And the VeeJays are not too blasé about their constant contact with the superstars of the rock world. Martha Quinn reportedly finished an interview with Roger Daltrey only to discover that her knees weren't functioning properly. "His eyes are *so* blue," she whispered. Over and over.

DEATH OF THE SWIFTIAN FUNCTION

THE CHANGING FACE OF ROCK JOURNALISM, ASSESSED BY *STEVE TAYLOR*

In the early summer of 1983 a trio of people associated with the glossy monthly *The Face* went to New York at the invitation — and expense — of the hip NY club Danceteria. It was an event which drew my attention, not merely because I'd recently left a full-time job at the magazine and had thereby done myself out of a trip, but also because it seemed symptomatic of certain recent changes in the nature of rock music journalism in Britain, changes which had now been taken to the culture-obsessed city of New York. "It's just another aspect of the Anglophilia that's been here since The Beatles," my NY contact noted sagely over the transatlantic line.

But it's more than that. In the days when the good old record company freebie to the States vied with a Freddie Laker ticket as the cheapest way for a young Brit to Go West, there was a good deal of transatlantic traffic involving the old guard of rock journalists. *New Musical Express* journalists would overrun New York every other week, some like Mick Farren even moving there to live. The *NME* would entertain Lester Bangs for three weeks to write a dissertation on The Clash, paying homage to the late writer that a new generation of young people in Britain had never heard of — and cared about even less.

Now things are very different and the East Coast enthusiasm for *The Face* is a measure of that difference and the way it's begun to travel. There's still that obsession with British culture, as was indicated by the recent "Britain Salutes New York" pan-cultural binge, though the undertones of commercial graft led one colleague of mine to refer to the festival as "Britain Pollutes New York". But when more people are paying for their own tickets, there's a somewhat more democratic mix of travellers arriving at JFK, at least by the claustrophobic

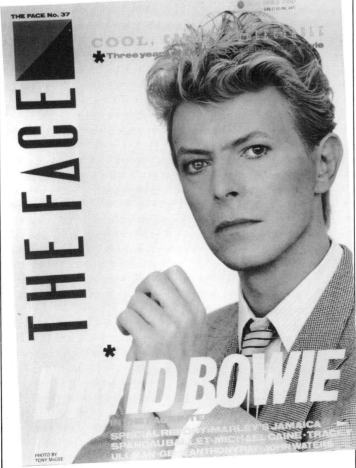

THE FACE

standards of the music world.

The record industry, if it won't pay its impromptu ambassadors, has to make do with things like the Danceteria jaunt — people gonzo enough to spend their own money — or on the continually increasing traffic in visuals that has accompanied the very successful wave of British acts hitting the US charts in the first half of 1983. Hence the interest in *The Face*; hence the feelers put out by the States' major music cable TV channel, MTV, to establish efficient links across the Atlantic; hence the way entrepreneurs in Britain are starting to package English music specially for the American cable market — as Police manager Miles Copeland is already doing.

In the United States, where much of the function of a frequent national music paper or journal is carried by cable, the effect on MTV has been to render it very schizophrenic, according to my New York correspondent: "Culture Club may be huge in the East Coast towns and in Los Angeles, but if they played Texas, they'd probably be lynched! That regionalism is why MTV is such a mess — one minute they're playing Lynyrd Skynyrd and the next it's a Duran Duran video." To be fair to MTV, at the time of writing they're in the process of rationalising their content according to genre, though the effect may be to make it look *more* rigidly divided in aims.

What they're experiencing are the knock-on effects of changes in popular music, and the media which serve them, that have already been biting deep into the established set-up in Britain. The "rock" press is becoming redundant because "rock" is a dirty word. The music it denotes and the attitudes that go with it, such as a morbid fascination with lengthy expositions of the innermost thoughts of the most banal musicians, are well on the way out.

In the vast bulk of Middle America, rock still rules, but the East Coast — with its sense of identity with Europe — and to a lesser extent the West with its terminal — yet ultimately lame — desperation to be cool, both wish to embrace the new breed of post-rock British pop.

It is typical, of course, of New York to single out *The Face*, which has the requisite visual flair and seasons its music coverage with suitably avant-garde fashion and art. Yet, in Britain, *The Face* is the tip of the iceberg of the new cool publications reflecting the glamorous, big-production-value post-rock pop. It's the up-market adult version of a publishing phenomenon that's already changed the nature of British music and youth publishing irreversibly.

Over the last 18 months, the circulation figures for music papers and magazines in this country have undergone a turnaround that is as massive numerically as it is culturally. The publication at the centre of this is not *The Face*, but the fortnightly magazine started by *The Face*'s originator Nick Logan — *Smash Hits*.

Logan's absurdly simple formula of good quality colour photographs of the new glossy pop acts, song lyrics and well written, succinctly informative features has proved to be a runaway winner. Last year *Smash Hits* trounced all the weekly tabloid music papers with a circulation of over 250,000. Since then, while the sales of the weeklies have continued to plummet, *Smash Hits*' figures have spiralled to around 350,000, consolidating an already stunning achievement.

It is a tribute to the effectiveness of the idea behind *Smash Hits* that Logan's former employers — the huge corporate British publishers IPC (for whom he established *NME* as a market leader in the seventies, as its editor) — have recently launched a formulaic competitor, *Number One*, in an attempt to capture some of the same market. At the time of writing there's no evidence of *Number One* even beginning to dent *Smash Hits*' overwhelming lead.

At the same time, the weekly papers have tried to adapt to this shifting demand. The *NME, Melody Maker* and *Sounds* try to incorporate colour into their drab monochrome layouts with the

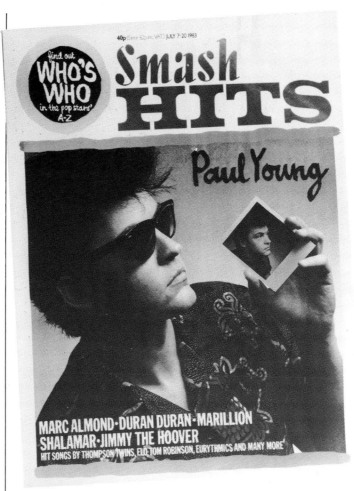

SMASH HITS

limited effect imposed by their paper quality and printing techniques. *Record Mirror* has reduced its size and slapped colour on poor paper in a half-baked attempt to bridge the gap between the weeklies and the glossies.

This is all rather limp and hasn't really addressed the essential questions that the staff behind *Smash Hits* have answered so clearly. Form and content are inseparable in this shift in publishing demand; you cannot just graft a visual emphasis and colour onto the old forms of writing and their attendant attitudes.

The majority of young record-buyers in Britain aren't taken in by self-dramatising "writers" theorising at great length about the covert significance of a particular group or individual's music. The new pop writers are anonymous and efficient: *Smash Hits* isn't run by teenage enthusiasts but by older experienced professional journalists.

The old sense of rock's cultural mission that sanctioned such excesses as the *NME*'s run of long Lester Bangs Clash travelogues simply doesn't hold any longer. And a generation of rock scribes who kept that faith has been squeezed out. In America the tradition maintains itself, albeit in a more academic, musicological form with writers such as the *New York Times*' Robert Palmer and author Greil Marcus, elder statesmen of a tendency to take rock seriously that has its more populist expression in magazines like *Creem, Crawdaddy* and *Trouser Press*.

Approval or disapproval from these cultural arbitrators can help a lawyer or manager hype a record company, but they don't popularise new acts in the way the press here used to be able to do. American rock critics like Palmer are more a part of the general critical establishment than gurus of youth culture.

In Britain, though, there is a history of a music press with pretensions to cultural arbitration *and* market manipulation. It's a history that has been irrevocably

transformed. *The Face* magazine itself went through a phase of helping force through musical and stylistic fashions. But the recognition that those cyclical changes had come to a halt meant that the kind of writers who rode them and helped define them were no longer important.

So not only have we lost the seventies' generation of serious rock journalists like Charles Shaar Murray, Nick Kent, Mick Farren, who have either shifted into editorial roles, become musicians or emigrated. We have also lost the charismatic post-punks like Paul Morley, who's now a record company A&R man; Tony Parsons — a pulp novelist; Danny Baker — television presenter.

As if to emphasise the process, even cultural spokespersons from as recent a phase as the 1980/81 Blitz/Spandau Ballet bunch — who made a brief impression on New York — have lost their impact. The most conspicuous, Robert Elms, who spread the word thickly over the pages of *The Face* and the now defunct New Romantic rag *New Sounds New Styles*, is now a general freelance for the likes of the *Mail on Sunday*.

Along with the cult of the music-writer-as-personality, the promotion of music papers by stirring up gratuitous controversy has also gone out of the window. Julie Burchill who, with her husband Tony Parsons, exemplified the rock-writer-as-thorn-in-the-nation's-flesh role, has turned her bile and dervish cynicism to imaginative reinterpretations of post-war history and book-length essays on women film stars.

Attempts to resurrect the writer's Swiftian function have singularly failed since the new pop got a grip. Gary Bushell, of the weekly *Sounds*, hoisted himself aloft as the mouthpiece for what were supposed to be the true heirs to the original punk movement, the Oi! bands. That little number floundered on the contradiction between the working-class socialist pretensions of Bushell and the blatantly fascist stance of many of the groups.

Even more recently, *The Face* tried to launch its own successor to Julie Burchill, Fiona Russell Powell, whose speciality is fey conversations with fey rock stars transcribed verbatim with the addition of an introduction — to Fiona, that is — which is varied according to circumstances each time around.

Fiona has merely come up against the shift in demand that had already cobbled Paul Morley and the *NME*. The music writer is no longer a folk figure on a par with the characters which he or she interviews. With the changeover within the *NME* from Burchill and Parsons to Morley and his cohort Ian Penman, the confrontational style of prose had already degenerated from controversy into irritation, from polemic and bite into whimsy and self-pity.

What the new pop market requires is the efficient communication of the relevant details; the individual writer is relatively unimportant in that process. It is telling that at the time of writing the *NME* does not have a single writer on its staff who is individually notorious or able to chivvy up circulation with controversy.

As if to make the role of the papers even easier, the new pop's stars tend to have their rationale laid out and ready for consumption. ABC's Martin Fry, for example, has a repertoire of aphorisms and quips which serve equally to adorn the back cover to ABC's records and "explain" the product inside, *and* to give Mr Fry a witty and trenchant persona in press or TV interviews.

In the same way, bands are effectively discouraged from getting too clever by the big emphasis on image, style and production values, musically and visually. Note that Spandau Ballet's massively increased record sales in the first half of 1983 followed a period of silence from which they reappeared *with* the back-up of mainstream new pop producers — Swain and Jolley — and *without* all the dubious guff about "white dance music" that had characterised their previous PR campaign.

The shift in musical values that underpins this corresponding shift in the role of the music press should be well documented elsewhere in this publication. At the beginning of 1983 some music commentators were anticipating a reversal of this change, perhaps getting overexcited about the third wave "punk" groups like

SPANDAU BALLET

Southern Death Cult, who were dominating the independent charts.

However, post-punk pop shows no signs of going away and a group like KajaGooGoo, which in musical style represents a distillation of ten years of "progressive" music from early Roxy Music onward, can go straight to number one with a first single. They've had no real difficulty selling this lowbrow commodity to the American chart audience, following smoothly in the wake of Duran Duran.

So where does this leave a rock press that has, it seems, to live with the new music whether it likes it or not? One big factor to take into account before speculating is the way this new pop has almost succeeded despite the press. Certainly the bands that dominate the British charts in the first half of 1983, and which also command respect for being somehow "new" or "different", came up through a combination of 12-inch singles'

CULTURE CLUB

exposure in clubs which then translated into radio play and crossover sales on the prompting of one particularly airplay-worthy song.

Wham, Thompson Twins, Tears for Fears, Blancmange, China Crisis, Yazoo, New Order and Culture Club have all pulled off this particular trick in the last 12 months and most of them are on the way to doing the same in America. One or two unfashionable British acts have leap-frogged their native charts altogether and gone straight into high-profile US chart success: Thomas Dolby and The Fixx, for example.

In the US they're staggered by the amount of power to make or break (in its true sense) bands that the British press used to wield, and even more surprised by the arbitrarily vindictive way in which it's used — the make-them-to-break-them syndrome.

The only sense Americans can make of it is that the people who run these papers must be suffering under a terrible weight of collective and individual neurosis. One New York music business lawyer compared it to the way the US press built up a political figure like Carter and then dumped on him. The inference was that music simply wasn't *that* important.

And it certainly looks as if the music press here is being shunted into a role which is *not* that crucial, even to the success of the bands themselves, let alone on any broader scale. Look at the success of Culture Club, which is based on straightforward commercial tricks like being able to write brilliant Motown knock-offs and then having the ability to arrange, play and produce them in a glossy modern manner.

Boy George's transformation from a figure of complete derision in the British music press to the front of a fully approved, chart-topping band has to be one of the most potent symbols of the diminution of the power of their disapproval. That power appears feeble too when compared to the way Radio One can push a band forward, often on the advocacy of just one DJ, as happened with Peter Powell's fervent championing of KajaGooGoo when 'Too Shy' was released in early '83. It can work equally well with someone who has been positively dropped by the music press, as in the summer of the same year when Tom Robinson's 'War Baby' revived his career on the sole basis of the quality of the song itself.

In these respects the gap between America and Britain is closing and the increasing use of the rock video has enabled a reciprocal transfer of images and recorded performances to become very easy. The advent of cable TV in this country and the growth of MTV's audience in the US are certainly going to add potency to this form of promotion.

In this climate the music publications which correspond with the new pop are servicing a demand which attaches itself to the acts as and after they become popular — it doesn't put them there. Attempts to elevate groups that can only be enjoyed if the consumer is worked up into a state of conceptual frenzy beforehand fall flat these days — look at the embarrassing number of interviews with Australian tunesmiths The Birthday Party that the *NME* ran in 1982/3. And they still never made *Top of the Pops*.

Critics of pop as consumption and consumerism will obviously not be satisfied by the existence of solely responsive publications which disseminate images and provide basic background information to satisfy curiosity and fill in the gaps. And there's no one stopping writers, who can make sense of what's happening in music, from writing in a responsible analytical way that's also witty and genuinely entertaining to read.

Yet, having worked for a substantial period of time as a features editor actively looking for such writers, it still strikes me that overwhelmingly the aspiring music writers just want to get their share of the imagined — and almost utterly non-existent — excitements of the music/music-journalism world, or they're frustrated literary types who are only killing time before a slim volume of their poetry, verse or short stories gets the proper attention from the publishers.

The talented young journalists are obviously writing about other things, probably things which they consider to be much more important. And, commercially speaking, it's interesting that in America, where there's no sign of an effective national music publication on a mass scale, they're launching a new *movie* magazine aimed at the younger audience with all the promotional pomp you'd associate with something like the benighted *Number One* here.

KAJAGOOGOO

IMPOTENCE REVISITED

JON SAVAGE **CONSIDERS EMPTY NOSTALGIA,
VIDEOS AND THE RETURN OF THE OLD ORDER**

Well, the 1983 election really showed up the pop music of the day for what it was: the Cultural Impotence of Stupid Boys — and Stupid Girls. John Maybury's happy phrase summed up the climate comprehensively: a popular culture and creaking youth market demoralised, in the pockets of the music industry, and apparently impotent — in traditional terms at least. After all, despite the obvious injustices of radical conservatism, despite the gaping holes papered over thinly by nostalgic wallpaper, despite the best intentions of an earnest youth press who, if they bothered, nailed their banners to Labour's standard, of all those newly enfranchised who reached 18 after May 1979 — under *half* voted, and many of those who did, voted Conservative. Somehow, the traditional view of youth wasn't quite working.

So here, at last, was the pretty vacancy, half celebrated, half prophesied. England was dreaming all right. The four weeks of the campaign — a short, sharp shock — had demonstrated how far a note of unreality had permeated English culture. It was not about issues, policy, even morals, but quite clearly, cynically even, about image and emotion. A campaign lived entirely in the increasingly shadowy world of complicit media — a world of polls, carefully posed photographs, and fabricated scandals. Much the same as usual, of course, but never, to many observers, quite so divorced from the things that were actually happening around the country, or the severe social and philosophical problems with which many people were trying to get to grips. Thatcherism — her central role in all of this overemphasised, if anything — was rampant, to such an extent that absolutely everything else looked silly, impotent, or just plain fringe. Just not mainstream, and therefore,

MARGARET THATCHER

simply not possible. This process had already spread as gangrene from a poisoned toe into pop's healthy limb: here, as elsewhere, any sense of genuine joy or possibility was absent. In its place, the language of calculation, conformity, and eager integration with the existing power structure.

This cultural impotence was well illustrated by one incident in election week. On that week's *Top of the Pops* — moved back to a Wednesday so the grown-ups could get on with their business on Thursday — Elvis Costello stormed and sweated his way through a generalised rant, sung with venomous conviction, called 'Pills and Soap'. Two days before, I had phoned Costello's PR — Modern Media, you know, Legoland logos and suchlike —

to try to get a clip for TV AM of Elvis performing the song. When did I intend to put it out, I was asked. On Election Day. Oh. But the song wasn't political. Oh. No, it wasn't about the election. Oh. And there had been so many phone calls on the subject that he was sick of explanation. Oh. But what *was* it about? Animal Liberation! Well I returned to my copy of the record, and to the lyric sheet in *Smash Hits*, and it still seemed pretty political to me. In not referring to anything in particular, it referred to everything; the point being that, in a climate of (at best) muted complaint, *anything* sung with such allusive spite transcended.

What was really happening in pop music was twofold: the shift of emphasis away from the classic Teenage market, and the extension of the

unreality principle that had dominated power politics into commercial culture. Harbingers: the rise and rise of *Smash Hits*, music industry awards for pop video directors, Club Culture with all its aping of the rich, and the pop video itself — the perfect vehicle for an age of packaging gone wild — the Age of Plunder.

The Teenage market bit was quite simple. Even in 1981, when I had been researching a programme on the subject, I had found that ad departments and market researchers were turning away from the classic 16-24 age group. The big new market was mini-pops — age 6, say, to 14/15 — with the older employed — say 25 to 35 — the second best. *Smash Hits* filled the junior end of the market perfectly with a glossy, irreverent mixture of words, pix, and confidences from the

127

new glitterati, while *Time Out* shed its sixties' concerns to *City Limits* and concentrated, profitably enough, on the consumerist preoccupations of those sixties' children now comfortably, if queasily, ensconced in nice media jobs.

The whole point of Teenage had been to give teenagers power: in the fifties, this had been the power of the customer, burdened by all that excess cash. And in the sixties it had spread to a national obsession — well documented in Christopher Booker's valuably dissident *The Neophiliacs* — with the Idea of Youth. Prime Ministers courted pop groups and gave them letters after their names. When the youth decided to get some of the real action — the Teen Take-over of all those trashy films like *Wild in the Streets* — by attacking the way things were actually run, they got a bloody nose. Youth wasn't quite so fab as before: in fact, it was a bloody nuisance. The political impotence that ensued took a long time to come and was only fully dramatised by punk rock — and we don't *care!* — which took the whole thing apart and watched the ashes float off into the breeze. And Punk's own cultural impotence — *never* was it as powerful as the Hippy movement — simply made the point cast-iron. What nobody had worked out was that un-employment would rocket alarmingly (although, as ever, this had been directly hinted at) and that it would attack the Teenage target area of the 16-18 year old with deadly accuracy. Thus youth was doubly disenfranchised, from "the right to work", and thus "the right to spend" — quite apart from losing their political power, they had lost that power of the penny in the pocket which had brought them into such prominence in the first place. The riots of 1981 were to mark the end of that dream of the golden youth, and Soft Cell's contemporaneous 'Bedsitter' made quite clear their understanding of these events: "I'm waiting for something/I'm only passing time/and now I'm all alone/and I don't care and I don't care. . .*and I don't care!*"

Such isolation and conscious lack of power left a vacuum into which all manner of creepy crawlies crept and made their home — a Pandora's Box in reverse. One big element was

the fetish — coincidental with the passing of the sixties', post-war even, idea of youth — of pop's wonderful heritage, indulged in by many of those still involved with youth industry. Just as it had lost real power, youth was indulged with more "rock" shows than ever before on the emergent Channel 4 — itself, as noted by Simon Frith, "the last refuge of the sixties". The producer of one of these allowed himself to be quoted as saying that the model for his epic was the famous Rediffusion show which dominated sixties' pop telly, *Ready Steady Go*. As if anything was quite so absurd! This particular strand really wound itself into a twist with the full ghastliness of a veritable television *Woodstock*: a five hour *Tube* rockathon on Midsummer Night, 1983.

Naturally, none of this meant anything — except the luxury of childhoods relived — but this all-pervasive nostalgia with pop's past really hit pay dirt in the art departments. Those who were of an age, like myself, to adore pop music as a trashy noise — its very strength in its lack of traditional "art" theory and practice — were appalled at the (self) referential garbage turned out by myriad pop groups. Design was an obvious point: virtually every brightly coloured plaything you picked up was stolen from some obscure sixties' LP, or some Constructivist poster, or from a Futurist graphics designer.

This game of spot-the-steal was fun for a while but became boring when you found the same principle applied to the artistes' image and music: naturally, it was institutionalised and made part of people's enjoyment. So you'd have a minor league supper club act like Mari Wilson promoted for a while into the second division because she had a beehive and was versed in its lore. People were expected not only to "dig" the beat but to get the references — yes, the beehive was a late fifties'/early sixties' product and had to be carried off *just so*. After the third or fourth Practical Styling photo feature, Mari Wilson cut her beehive and was revealed to be as dowdy as Koo Stark. Anything more etiolated than this process you could not imagine: Mari Wilson was only noteworthy as an obvious symptom of a disease that was

raging among England's pop kids and those who should have been old enough to know better. She didn't even sell many records.

Another symptom of cultural impotence was the ubiquity of the manifesto: you couldn't open the *NME* or turn over a Respond sleeve without tripping over some turgid piece of prose explaining how this lump of plastic (laminated, you know, just like those sixties'

covers) or pulpable newsprint was to change the world — or, at least, a corner of Kettner's, the London restaurant where "rock" journalists go to eat hamburgers. "Dance to this beat", "dig the vibes" — all that awful sub-Kerouac crap filtered through an imagined soul-speak. People who are doing it shouldn't have to talk about it. Here was the transcendence of punk's rhetoric harnessed to a poor,

ICEHOUSE

128

literal approximation of leftish theory — authenticity, struggle, the "kids", all those nice George Orwell things. The pop kids took one look, sniffed, and continued chasing Duran Duran who embodied all the qualities of the time: pliability, conventional good looks, videos shot on exotic locations, and upward social mobility. Like ABC, they came on as young squires. If ABC were slightly too neurotic (although even more calculated), Duran Duran had no such qualms. By spring 1983 they were the biggest group in Britain: their stablemates, KajaGooGoo, were a close number two. Both were, temporarily, axiomatic.

All this upward mobility — and, correspondingly, the increasing impotence of "social concern" — was directly paralleled in events outside the play-pen. In the wake of Teenage, the old order had re-established itself socially and culturally. Looking rich was a big thing. "Bright Young Things" — although nobody actually quite got that far — were back, and there was much business of baring backsides at Ascot, smart heroin addiction, and a whole old world newly described in the shiny pages of *The Tatler*. Naturally, it was nauseous, but there were not many to argue. After all, they were backed up by all the usual plus an added new ingredient: ideology. It was, simply, cool to be conservative — a stunning reversal for any sixties' and seventies' creature, but one that had to be addressed.

The year's club in the eyes of the media was not the wonderful Hacienda — where for once, promises were put into practice at least for a while — but occurred through everybody's tame entrepreneur, Simon Oates. This establishment, The Titanic, was something straight out of an Evelyn Waugh novel; while not as lively as the "Old One Hundredth" that was so lovingly displayed in Granada's fetishistic *Brideshead Revisited*, it had the same element of Boy Mulcasters meeting the *demi-monde* and being entertained by crazy niggers. Except instead of jazz bands, it was rap and scratch. Meanwhile the other half of the smart pop world nipped off to Crolla — a stone's throw away from the Sinking Ship in the heart of Mayfair — to deck their persons in Nehru suits, Raj boaters, pin-stripe shirts

BRIDESHEAD REVISITED

and whimsical ethnicity. But Oates was no Mrs Meyrick: The Titanic was perfect for the times only in that it appeared as a peculiarly cynical reaction — spraying champagne as the storm clouds gathered — masquerading as novelty.

Like the endless Sunday magazine stories about the new/old "Bright Young Things" of Oxbridge, all this said more about people's pre-conceptions than what was actually occurring. For instance, the very real psychological meat of Waugh's novel — the brilliantly acute portrait of Sebastian Flyte and Charles Ryder — was junked in favour of the book's admitted nostalgia for a golden, pre-war England. In the dramatisation, this reached the height of ickiness in one peculiarly protracted hunting scene; but this soap commercial approach to the past was, commercially, very influential. Like *Chariots of Fire*, this degutted revision of history suited the prevailing ideology well. As Mrs Thatcher's pronouncements on all things Victorian makes quite clear, the point was not an understanding of history — far from it — but the rewriting of

it, in true Orwellian style, in adspeak to suit the designs of the new/old age. The family was, suddenly, "subversive", according to Ferdinand Mount, adviser to Margaret Thatcher and her favourite ideologue. Young people dashed off to get married in an implicit condemnation of sixties' "permissiveness" — itself an irritating media creation. A war was cynically manufactured and, abetted again by a complicit news media, youth was turned into "Our Boys" and militarism was respectable. At public schools, boys fled either into the Army or

MALCOLM McLAREN 'SOWETO'

accountancy, acts virtually unthinkable a decade before, while at the other end of the social spectrum, unemployed school-leavers were faced with much the same options as the first teenagers had been back in the dear old fifties — the Army, youth clubs and street corners. The circle appeared to be closing, despite the clamour of the changes occurring in other spheres.

An ad for a potato ring broadcast frequently in June 1983 showed the rewriting of history turned down-market, in an exercise closer to the year's *real* pop scam, the promotional video. On display was the adman's dream of the fifties, rapidly becoming accepted as authentic as the awful memory faded: an archetypal "butch" rocker type parading around archetypally "feminine" rockerettes. In the background, a rewritten "classic" track chirruped: the protest and exhilaration of Eddie Cochran's 'Summertime Blues' harnessed to some chip. Here was the true banality manifest. What was remembered was the security of an accepted nostalgia image; what was forgotten, what was actually

happening then, and how our understanding of that time can shed light on the present. Suddenly, a true understanding of history was becoming subversive: was it correct that a 77-year-old historian, A.J.P. Taylor, was being written about in *The Face* like some couturier?

In the pop video, everything meshed. By mid 1983, the pop promo had become an accepted area of currency. In America, with the pre-eminence of a 24-hour video station, MTV, as an industry guide, it had caused a pop revolution. No question, vids were big. But what they were most of the time was the *Brideshead* principle of the Age of Plunder repeated ad infinitum: they were all about references, either to a mythic pop past, or a mythic social past, mere travelogues — *I know! Let's do the next one up the nose of the Sphinx! No one's done that before!* — or merely reproductions of contemporary commercial product.

Examples: A Michael Jackson song, 'Beat It', shot expertly to an updated rumble out of *West Side Story*, then copied — inexpertly — by English group Wham! for their

own 'Bad Boys'. A Spandau Ballet song shot in the style of prime TV fodder *The Professionals*. A rather good Icehouse single, 'Street Cafe' plonked in some Moroccan café, or Duran Duran poncing around, for no apparent reason, on some Sri Lankan shore for 'Save a Prayer'. The Elton John song, 'I Guess That's Why They Call It the Blues', framed by archetypally anachronistic fifties' images of Edwardian dance halls and army conscription to everyone's delight. The height of absurdity was reached by pop's great pretender, whose triumphant comeback in summer 1983 was a hollow thing which merely re-emphasised pop's apparent lack of importance: David Bowie. His videos for 'Let's Dance' and, particularly, 'China Girl' gained much publicity, but on repeated viewing were simply the state of the commercial art rather than anything else. Everything was there: references to newsreel footage, surreal juxtapositions learned from Benson and Hedges adverts, a bit of exotic travel — these foreign races are just so. . . natural — ''meaningful'' storylines, a bit of bottom (itself a much publicised reference to some over-inflated Hollywood epic), shot with an adman's eye. And so the circle was complete in this particular ritual: from ad dream to ad dream, commerce redacting commerce, as each willing pop group harnessed its heart and soul to selling soap powder.

This had other effects as well. Like the commercial selection of who had videos done, which put the artistes, even if they didn't desire it, straight into the hands of the record companies. The video meant that a total world could be constructed around the theme for the record. Groups would swap historical periods as well as costumes with each single and nobody blinked an eyelid. But these worlds had to be in a shape that was to prove acceptable to a much more severe taskmaster than the music industry: the television industry and all those IBA guidelines. Suddenly, what was ''acceptable'' was compromised even more by this collusion with yet another industry.

My favourite images of that time were about a playfulness and simple exhilaration that cut

through the general pomposity and calculation like the best pop music always did. Malcolm McLaren's bucking, weaving film for that most exhilarating of all cod-ethnic singles, 'Soweto' — where the force of what was being captured burst through any attempted soul-stealing. Soft Cell's wickedly polysexual 'Tainted Love', generally seen for the first time on a video cassette released that spring, where Marc Almond, in a bravura performance, bobbed and wreathed as Nero, wagged his finger at his latest Lolita. Haysi Fantayzee's cut-up, 'Sister Friction', admitted the chaos of what was actually occurring on those mythic ''streets'' with a confident, swaggering air. Culture Club's 'Do You Really Want to Hurt Me?', set in a thirties' gay club, put Boy George's air of androgynous splendour into another, older context. Yello achieved a stylised, brilliant pastiche of fifties' plunder in 'I Love You'. But none could beat the best video I saw at that time: an old song, 'I'm Bored', performed by a white Iggy Pop in front of a black background. There were no poxy fifties' recreations, just a simple, riveting performance well caught by a swooping, diving camera. Suddenly, almost everything else looked redundant, and all the trickery dissolved into thin air, like cultural impotence when confronted with a sense of possibility.

IGGY POP

In the end, of course, what was actually occurring underneath the surface of the time came up to the surface with great force. The rest, as they used to say, was the history of what were — in the Chinese mandarins' curse — ''interesting'' times.

TALES FROM SOPORIFIC OCEANS

ALLAN JONES RELIVES THE NIGHTMARE OF PROGRESSIVE ROCK AND DREADS ITS RECENT RESURGENCE

Of course, The Beatles were responsible for most of this muck.

As the American rock critic John Rockwell observed, *Sgt. Pepper* was "the progenitor of self-conscious experimentation . . .the album that dramatised rock's claim to artistic seriousness." It was a determined attempt to elevate pop music to the level of art: unfortunately,

inept. But their audiences were growing up and felt flattered by these conceits. Everywhere, there was a mood of seriousness; rock'n'roll was all at once upwardly mobile, moving out of the gutters and into the suburbs, relinquishing its working-class snottiness for middle-class respectability.

After a comparatively slow start around the end of the

MARILLION

it succeeded. The Beatles received the patronising taps on the head from the Establishment that they'd obviously been craving. Suddenly they were the greatest songwriters since Schubert and a lot of other dead krauts.

The vaulting ambitions of rock's aspiring young artists were switched immediately into overdrive. Inspired by the acclaim afforded *Sgt. Pepper*, previously sensible young pop songwriters like Ray Davies and Pete Townshend started grappling with the idea of

"rock operas", extended compositions that might transcend the conventions of established pop writing, legitimise rock music, present it in a manner that would have to be taken seriously. Their efforts were half-baked at best and generally quite relentlessly

sixties, there was a whole fleet of groups revving up at the start of the seventies, preparing to dominate the first half of the decade, eager to throw back the boundaries of rock, to canvas new horizons, define new territories.

Most of what they produced

was absolute tosh, and very little of it was recognisable to anyone who'd been infatuated with the primitive snap of rock'n'roll or any of its deviant offshoots. These groups were playing for what they thought were higher stakes. The comparison they were often looking for was one with classical music, and to force home the point of their aspirations, the population was made to endure their preposterous orchestral inclinations.

In 1967, The Moody Blues hauled in the London Symphony Orchestra to dignify somehow the shallow poetics and precious atmospherics of their *Days of Future Passed* LP. Lush mood music, best suited to the environments of the airport lounge or the reception area of a poodle parlour, the inflated fluff of *Days of Future Passed* was a model of sensitive creation compared to some of the vulgar outrages perpetrated by the likes of charmless oafs like ELP. As a member of The Nice, ELP's Keith Emerson was forever plundering the classics, turning pieces like Sibelius' *Karelia Suite* into the kind of popped-up drivel that usually turned up accompanying films of moon shots or tacked onto the soundtracks of current affairs documentaries about sheep-farming in Belgium. A terrible old tart, Emerson would shamelessly drag in classical composers like the gullible American Joseph Eger to lend some dubious credibility to comical symphonic pastiches like *The Five Bridges Suite*.

Encouraged by Emerson's example, dog-heads like Deep Purple's Jon Lord started knocking out blundering efforts like *Concerto for Group and Orchestra* (the latter conducted by Malcolm Arnold, who, like Eger, should have known considerably better than to get involved in the first place). More than one dead European composer must've had his eternal rest disturbed by such attempts to marry rock and the classics, mostly at the expense of the classics, but entire graveyards were probably sent spinning into orbit when Emerson formed ELP with Greg Lake (ex-King Crimson) and Carl Palmer (ex-Atomic Rooster), both musicians who shared his flair for melo-dramatic vulgarity.

ELP's début appearance at the Isle of Wight festival was

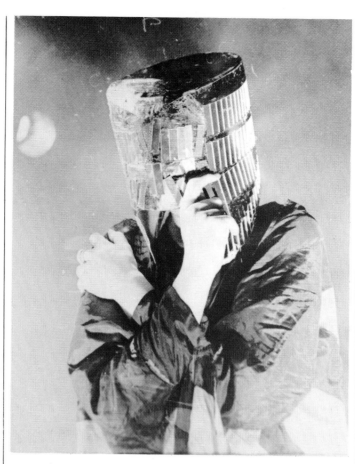

EVAN LOWSON (PALLAS)

prefaced by a thundering cannonade; an apposite fanfare for a group whose music was so definitively bombastic. Every-thing ELP did was on an extravagant scale. They thought nothing of turning Mussorgsky's *Pictures at an Exhibition* into laughable farce; they were even considerate enough to offer the original composer co-writing credits on at least half the tracks, which was very big of them. With an exaggerated flair for the colossally pompous they recorded a version of the hymn 'Jerusalem' because, they explained, *"we really dug the beauty in the melody and the words..."* ELP could never understand what some critics found so hilarious about the group: they failed to see how simple details like Greg Lake insisting upon standing on a £2,500 Persian rug during the group's concerts might reduce some observers to an advanced state of hysteria. Really quite harmlessly ludicrous, they blundered on, creating the perfect climate for the similarly crude extravagances of Rick Wakeman, like Emerson a multi-keyboard whizz with a

fatuous technique and the creative imagination of a donkey. Wakeman was an absolute buffoon who raided classical literature with the same cynically mercenary ineptitude that he brought to bear on his ravages of classical music. Recognising a public weakness for pseudo-symphonic waffle, Mike Oldfield had the novel idea of stretching one vaguely pretty theme over two sides of an album, pretending it was a coherent quasi-orchestral whole, and saw *Tubular Bells* selling in millions while boorish old hacks hailed its composer as a teenage prodigy; Mozart in a scoop-necked T-shirt and crushed velvet flares, nothing less.

Less concerned with ravishing the classics, but equally intent upon producing work of such epic proportions that one felt uncommonly obliged to bend a knee and tug a forelock in their presence, the other standard bearers of progressive rock were led from the front by Pink Floyd (who'd moved on from the vacuous experimentation of *Umma Gumma* and *Atom Heart Mother*

toward the miserable misanthropies of *Dark Side of the Moon* and the brutal cosmic puritanism of *The Wall*), Yes, Genesis, the early King Crimson and our old chums Jethro Tull.

They all shared a taste for music that was characterised by fractured melodies, instrumental virtuosity (most of these groups featured guitarists who sounded like Attila gone berserk on a fretboard), abrupt, often violent shifts of tempo, and a penchant for the kind of language whose abstract convolutions and florid metaphors were frequently carried over into the design of their album sleeves (Hipgnosis, Roger Dean and Paul Whitehead respectively illustrating the mystic drivel of the Floyd, Yes and Genesis). Pretty soon, these sleeves assumed an independent significance, the cheap symbolism and kindergarten surrealism of the art-work being scrutinised for clues to the deeper meanings of the music.

On every front, excess was encouraged; even music press interviews began to sag beneath the weight of the rhetorical line in self-analysis and windy portentousness. This is Mike Pinder of The Moody Blues describing that group's lofty musical pretensions: "We discovered music, you know — for ourselves. Ever since *Days of Future Passed*, it's been, like, continually walking along this beautiful magic garden, that we seem to have walked in forever, tasting the fruits in it and looking at the beautiful views in it...."

And here's Peter Gabriel trying to illuminate the story-line of Genesis' 'I Know What I Like (In Your Wardrobe)' to a successfully bemused hack: "...he lives a life that is preconceived by the people around him, and the only time that his identity comes out is when he's actually on the lawn, mowing the grass. I mean, I get this tremendous, physical buzz by the sensation of the cutters slicing through a whole layer of grass. There's really a sort of therapeutic ultra-violence simply in the act of mowing the lawn."

Things were clearly getting out of hand: something had to give; and it did.

Reeling from a severe critical backlash and the punk explosion of 1976/7, which

132

violently scorned everything it had represented, the progressive rock movement was as fiercely affected by the economic recession.

So absurd had the presentation of their shows become (Rick Wakeman, for instance, had the bright idea of producing his *King Arthur and the Knights of the Round Table* as an *ice-skating* spectacular at Wembley Arena) that the cost of touring was suddenly frightening. ELP's tour of America with a 60-piece orchestra was virtually scratched as overheads mounted and audiences dwindled; Gabriel quit Genesis, who soldiered on, their seemingly mythical status increasingly enhanced by the fall of casualties all around them; Jethro Tull slipped from attention and the charts, but not without loud grunts of complaint from the heavily sulking Ian Anderson; Yes split from Jon Anderson after a couple of albums that found them trying desperately to trim back on the musical fat; *re-formed*, but only the most dutiful American space cadets took any notice; most of the second division pomp rock bands — Argent, Greenslade, Camel, Gentle Giant — disappeared in the mists of their own dry ice, most of their members stomping off to open PA hire companies probably, much as footballers open pubs at the end of their careers.

Right then, it looked as if progressive rock had gone the distance, though not everyone was as happily convinced as its loudest critics who were already dancing on its grave. Jon Anderson, for instance — in the summer of 1980, Jon and I were chatting merrily away in the lounge of his villa overlooking the swaying palm fronds on the sea front at Nice when he told me that he'd just written a song anticipating the return of the spiritual impulses that had first inspired progressive music. He went so far as to quote the lyric.

" 'The children of the flower time have spread their wings and begun to fly,' " he recited huskily. " 'Those summer days are near, we breathe again...' It's a reflection of those times," he went on with a ghastly conviction. "And maybe we're going into those times again."

I hoped not; it didn't seem like it, but in the wacky world of pop there's a surprise at every turn.

Deflected by the spurious psychedelic revival hype going the usual rounds in the summer of 1982, very few people noticed that a more genuine and confident renaissance was taking place: progressive rock, as a style, an attitude, a rallying focus, was clanking back out of the shadows. A veteran rock PR who'd worked in the seventies with Yes, Keith Goodwin was in early on the action. There was a generation who'd missed out on punk, he maintains, that weren't impressed by the gory monotony of its second generation bands and felt just as disenchanted with the kind of chic fluff currently fussing up the charts in pretty trousers and cute hairlines. They were ready, Goodwin argues, to be impressed by something that was for them original and exciting, that combined elements of musicianship and a sense of purpose and a sense of showmanship that had lately been absent.

Cue Marillion.

The first of the new wave of progressive rock acts to command serious attention as a possible commercial force, Marillion had built up a formidable circuit of support by the beginning of 1983: they sold out the Hammersmith Odeon on the strength of their first single and months of Marquee headliners; *Script for a Jester's Tears*, their woofingly precious début album banged straight into the LP charts at number seven and, as I write, they're celebrating their first hit 45 with 'Garden Party'.

By almost any sane standards, *Script for a Jester's Tears* is monumental bilge, a gross, idiot duplication of early seventies' poetic bluster and instrumental verbosity. Marillion are most often compared to Genesis, and no little wonder: their album owes virtually everything to that group, whose emphasis on a kind of symphonic terrorism and taste for straining narrative excursions they share. To compound the comparison, Marillion's leader, the gangling Fish, has a vocal style whose every inflection seems to have been filched wholesale from Peter Gabriel, who has also contributed to Fish's penchant for elaborate face make-up and fancy dress.

Their admirers claim to hear echoes of punk's anger in Marillion's music, particularly in songs like 'Forgotten Sons' (a woefully misconceived epic about Northern Ireland that raids virtually every cliché in the progressive rock repertoire) and 'Garden Party', a sort of geriatric 'Eton Rifles', aimed at the privileges of a university education that bristles with a churlish, ill-tempered, quite antiquated resentment and a lot of extremely trite writing ("couples loiter in the cloisters, social leeches quoting Chaucer/ doctor's son, parson's daughter — where, why not and should they oughta..."). This equation with punk is nothing more, however, than a smokescreen.

Emotionally and temperamentally, Fish and Marillion have more in common with the spiteful disgust, wretched moral superiority and the whiff of burning martyr that surrounds Roger Waters and Pink Floyd. Marillion's music is full of grandiose suffering and glib sentimental wallowing in pain and various miseries ("Here I am... just another emotional suicide," Fish groans on the title track of their LP). Fish also runs a line in hilariously flowery poesy that might even embarrass Jon Anderson. "The rain auditions at my window, its symphony echoes in my womb/my gaze scans the walls of this apartment to rectify the confines of my tomb," Fish whinges unpleasantly on 'The Web' to the sound of stout parties collapsing in helpless mirth.

Keith Goodwin is convinced that Marillion are set to assume the same commercial status as that occupied in the seventies by Genesis and Yes; other close observers have suggested that Marillion are just a stepping stone for Fish, to be soon discarded in his bid for Bowie-style world domination. Both predictions make the flesh creep, making even a weekend in Belgium with New Order an attractive alternative.

Apocalyptic pomp rockers, Pallas, are probably Marillion's closest rivals (a recently signed five-figure record deal, an album being recorded in America with former Yes producer Eddie Offord). Pallas share a predictable theatricality, again inspired by Gabriel, and a determination to torture to death any tune that gets in the way of their violently flexing musical muscle. Lyrically, they're often full of disconsolate gloom and empty thunder. "Night-time descended on this mushroom cloud/our days have ended on a chlorine shroud," they trill unhappily on 'Heart Attack' as the music wanders off-course without a road-map. Like most of their contemporaries, Pallas tend to be woefully discursive: introductions are usually tortuous affairs, most of them taking the scenic route to the point of a song, at which junction all the instrumentalists give it maximum fuss and successfully blur the entire issue in a lot of flailing riffs and screeching solos. Predictable patterns quickly emerge, defining the various moods of the music and emotion: reflective, introspective moments are usually evoked through autumnal melodies, carried by acoustic guitars, swaying keyboards, and synthetic woodwind effects; more wintery conditions of the soul are illustrated by lashings of guitar, barman swings at the

TAMARISK

drum-kit, screaming vocals and an inconsiderate amount of stereo panning. What all these groups lack, however, is a Vasco da Gama to give them a sense of direction; they don't have the wit, themselves, of a genuine explorer, and every time they actually get somewhere, they find someone else has been there before them. The territory is littered with references to their predecessors, most obviously the Floyd, Genesis or Yes.

Following these two principals at a trot, a whole glut of new progressive groups are shaping up their acts. Twelfth Night are said to have emerged recently as heavyweight contenders, but their *Fact and Fiction* LP offers very little promise to anyone not fully enthusiastic about their indigestible mix of Genesis and Van der Graaf Generator, whose tortured, screwed-up neuroticisms are paddled out here with teeth-gritting determination. Thanks, though, to Twelfth Night for throwing up the most memorable lines discovered in this writer's recent researches: "If every time we tell a lie, a little fairy dies/they must be building death camps in the garden..."

Probably too early even to attempt to predict the fates of the other front-runners in the current field, it can safely be observed that they share a communal drabness. Most of them look like Dagaband, who look uncannily like plainclothes drug squad detectives at an open-air festival. The uniform is virtually identical: satin bomber jackets, cowboy boots, centre partings, chunky identity bracelets, digital watches, gold medallions or a variety of crucifixes around the neck, shirt slashed open to the buckle, sturdy leather belts to hold in rapidly expanding waistlines and a preference for turquoise jewellery. More ominously, I suddenly realise that this description also fits most of the A&R men on the current beat: Dagaband might've stumbled on the perfect sartorial image.

Musically, they're almost entertaining, referring not so much to the Genesis/Yes axis as The Nice and ELP, the main focus of their music being Greg Boynton's thrusting keyboard mutilations. Their music is all brassy vulgarity, surging riffs, breastbeating bravado: noisy gesticulation that engulfs the listener in lots of fanfares and hearty riffs, crunching accents and anthemic signatures. It's the kind of thing that usually accompanies hordes of Cossacks rampaging through various parts of the Ukraine with Yul Brynner at their head exchanging raw-boned banter about "Muzza Rusha" with a heavily made-up Tony Curtis. Dagaband's epic rendition of The Who's *I Can See for Miles* must be heard; a description here would barely do justice to its gargantuan wallop.

Pendragon, who are, of course, descended from Zeus Pendragon, who rather confusingly mixed Greek and Arthurian mythologies, are probably more typical of the new breed of progressive groups. They have a typical penchant for the grand gesture. Guitars sweep mountain tops, tricky time signatures abound, melodies are windswept to a man; the lyrics allude to Man and Nature, boast a pantheist vocabulary that suggests that *The Golden Bough* has recently been high on the list of approved reading, alongside the obligatory volumes of Tolkein and C.S. Lewis and all the latest SF publications; they also like flag-waving themes and betray a worrying empathy with the kind of musical patriotism popularised by Yes with the likes of 'Starship Trooper' and 'Yours Is No Disgrace'.

Tamarisk look like the survivors of a heavy metal festival in the Outer Hebrides (denim jackets with artificial sheepskin lining, chunky sweaters, long hair and sensible track shoes with soles built up out of used tractor tyres) and are obviously the type of band whose singer spends most of his time on stage perched in front of the drum rise with his eyes either shut in bogus contradiction or fixed upon some indeterminate point in the cosmic distance as the group rages and pillages around him in a sensationally mirthless fashion. Much of their time is spent plodding through the valley of the shadow of death, broadcasting mankind's imminent demise and reminding us that in the end we are all alone.

No doubt there are more bands limbering up in the cupboard (Trilogy and Solstice are already making loud grumbling noises somewhere in the woodwork), and even as I write, I have the feeling that somewhere out there, in some teenage bedroom lined with posters of Yes and Genesis, a group of lisping adolescents with chins sprouting little grassy clumps of bum-fluff are tugging at their bell-bottoms, sewing sequinned star-signs on their kaftans and leafing earnestly through well-thumbed copies of *The Hobbit* and Paramhansa Yoganda's *Autobiography of a Yogi* as they plug in their synthesiser and twiddle their plectrums, dreaming idly, perhaps, of their first album, their first gatefold sleeve, their first taped introduction (the theme from *Star Wars* replacing the theme from *2001: A Space Odyssey*, of course; one has to move with the drift of history), their first laser show, their first revolving mirror ball, the first flicker of Zippo lighters held aloft by an audience demanding encore after encore...

With U2 already confirmed as the new Led Zeppelin, Marillion as the new Genesis and Yes themselves threatening to re-form, Jon Anderson might yet be proved right: those summer days may well be here again.

Praise Gandalf! Damn Gollum! Pass the patchouli oil and *hide those Rockpile albums.*

PENDRAGON

134

BOOKS

AC/DC
Richard Bunton (Omnibus)
"The audience eats it up! You get on that stage and the more crass, gross and rowdy you sound, the more they love it!" So the late Bon Scott summed up his art, not to mention his fans. Bunton's obviously one of the latter, and although he's a terrible writer, this is more fun than most of the hack work turned out by better-known names. AC/DC are, despite their global success, often taken to task by the more sensitive elements of the pop press. Bunton rises to his heroes' cause every time he reprints a bad review. "How was it possible to encounter a rock'n'roll holocaust in-the-making and not *see* it?" he chokes at one point. Hilarious.

ALBUM COVER ALBUM — THE SECOND VOLUME
Storm Thorgerson, Roger Dean and David Howells (Paper Tiger)
The mixture pretty much as before, with an emphasis on cover design since 1977 and a liberal representation of the compiler-designers' own work. Handsomely produced but lacking any real perspective.

A-Z OF ROCK DRUMMERS
Harry Shapiro (Proteus)
Like its "Guitarists" companion volume, a collection of potted histories, with a similar shortage of technical information — lucky to get the brand of kit used, let alone a full breakdown — and most entries tell the history of the group rather than exploring the style of its percussionist. Shapiro does go into detail with a major figure like Ginger Baker, but predominantly — as in the case of Little Feat's Ritchie Hayward, to name but one — the writing falls back on cliché. A book that few non-drummers are likely to be curious about, and that most adepts (or even learners) will find more often frustrating than not.

A-Z OF ROCK GUITARISTS
Chris Charlesworth (Proteus)
Encyclopaedic in intent if not content — omissions include Lou Reed, Syd Barrett, Tom Petty, Steve Hunter and Dick Wagner . . . and so on. The rest get pocket biographies and varying amounts of detail. The only technical information on John Fogerty, for example, consists of the fact that he was lead guitarist of Creedence Clearwater Revival; others fare much better, but the overall tendency is to hide ignorance behind some of the hoariest rockprint chestnuts. Mick Jones gave The Clash their early fire thanks to his "driving lead guitar", we learn. Just the sort of helpful information would-be future heroes will find really useful!

THE BALLAD OF JOHN AND YOKO
Edited by Jonathan Cott and Christine Doudna (Rolling Stone/ Press/Michael Joseph)
Inevitably, most of the material was published in *Rolling Stone* during the 12 years or so that the magazine and Lennon had in common. Reverential and unquestioning of his genius, it makes frequently dull, occasionally revealing reading. The real meat is in six page of Harry Nilsson's recollections; the pudding you send back to the chef is in three pages of Mick Jagger's.

THE BARRY MANILOW SCRAPBOOK
Richard Peters
(Pop Universal/ Souvenir Press)
His Magical World in Words and Pictures, reads the come-on line. From then on, it follows the appropriate course of salivating worship. For anyone who likes that kind of stuff, it's here.

THE BEATLES WHO'S WHO
Bill Harry (Aurum Press)
Written in a stiff, unlovely prose and set in no particular order (not even alphabetical), these potted biographies are supposed to be a list of folks whose lives meant something to the Fab Four. Unfortunately, not many seem to fall into this category — Graham Spencer, for instance, gets in because he took some pictures of the author with Lennon amongst his early snaps of the band; Cilla Black gets a whole page to herself while Elvis Presley gets in because he spoke to the band for three hours. Once. The man who first wrote about the band in his paper *Mersey Beat*, Harry's highly personalised accounts are heavily weighted towards the group's early history (naturally) and are sorely lacking in detail from the middle-to-late eras. The rare photos have been chosen judiciously. Otherwise, dullsville.

BLACK SABBATH
Chris Welch (Proteus)
By his own admission, former *MM* stalwart Welch is a late convert to the Sabs; doubtless the resurgence of HM in the past few years has made this essential as well as inevitable. That the group were a phenomenon — particularly when in full charge, abetted by thousands of gesticulating adolescent males — was never in doubt. But does such a group's history make good reading? Welch tries hard, cutting backwards and forwards in time, allowing himself the odd humorous aside, but the crucial problem is that no Sab — not even the extrovert-plus Ozzy Osbourne — has any real facility with language. The result is that the quotes, although plentiful, are prosaic to say the least, with the group complaining about hostile press, the rigours of the road, the pains of being tax exiles . . . they only stop whining, it seems, to praise "the kids" who made it all possible. A plod.

THE BOOK OF ROCK QUOTES
Ed. Jonathon Green (Omnibus)
Revised, post-1977 edition of a rather laboured original, this version omits the lines from song lyrics and sociological pro-

nouncements in favour of a heftier dose of one-liners by assorted sages and nincompoops from the popular music racket. The utterances veer crazily from the acute to the obtuse, and Green certainly knows a patent absurdity when he hears it. Winner by a short head is Ray Davies, for the immortal "I was standing at the bar the other day and a guy came up to me and said, 'Ray, I like your songs, I think you're a very underrated songwriter, a poet really.' So I hit him over the head with a bottle."

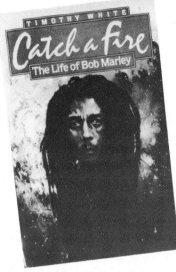

CATCH A FIRE: THE LIFE OF BOB MARLEY
Timothy White (Elm Tree)
BOB MARLEY
Stephen Davis (Arthur Barker)
It's a pity that Davis and White didn't collaborate on a single absolutely definitive biography of The Gong, since each book has its own particular strengths and weaknesses. White's book is easily superior in its re-creation of Marley's early life and in its analysis of Ras Tafari, while Davis' area of expertise is Marley's business affairs and the economics of reggae music in Jamaica. The White book can also claim a far better selection of photographs and a discography, the latter feature being a rather glaring omission from Davis' effort. However, Davis' account of Marley's break from his manager Don Taylor (who stopped five bullets intended for Marley during the pre-Peace Concert assassination attempt) makes scarifying reading, and his book ends with a touching description of the concert held to mark the first anniversary of Marley's death. The world badly needs a serious biography of Bob Marley, and these two provide an embarrassment of riches even though neither is a *Hellfire* or *'Scuse Me While I Kiss the Sky*. Devotees should check both, but

in a straight fight Timothy White has the edge.

BRYAN FERRY & ROXY MUSIC
Barry Lazell and Dafydd Rees (Proteus)
An uncluttered, easy-flowing account which highlights the major events without too much of the analytical breast-beating the group tends to engender. Unlike Johnny Rogan's biography last year, this is slim, glossy and lavishly illustrated with, not unexpectedly from a duo who make their living out of compiling pop charts, a ludicrously detailed discography.

CHUCK BERRY: MR ROCK'N' ROLL
Krista Reese (Proteus)
The legend of Chuck Berry pivots around the essential contradiction between the extraordinary warmth and generosity of his greatest music and the equally extraordinary stinginess and paranoia of the man himself. Krista Reese, fresh from a cautious walk around the perimeters of another fairly private

man, Elvis Costello, collates a fair amount of the existing information about Berry, but his personal walls remain unbroached and the book has an alarmingly perfunctory air to it. It is, after all, the only book about one of rock and roll's first key figures, but its lack of real penetration — either musicological or psychological — into its subject renders it irritating and dissatisfying.

DAVID BOWIE: THE ILLUSTRATED DISCOGRAPHY
Stuart Hoggard (Omnibus)
Revised and updated edition of a book which appeared useful a few years ago (when Bowie's discography had not yet been chronicled to the point of tedium) but now seems utterly redundant, its sketchy commentary merely adding to the irritant factor.

DAVID BOWIE: THE PITT REPORT
Kenneth Pitt (Design)
The early years, chronicled by his manager of the time. Full of dates, times, places, costs and correspondence, but reading as little more than a very time-consuming flick through a filing cabinet.

DEATH OF A ROLLING STONE: THE BRIAN JONES STORY
Mandy Aftel (Sidgwick & Jackson)
Even the most abject Rolling Stones devotee would be hard put to dredge up more than a few crumbs of interest in this sycophantic tale of a very pretty and gifted boy who just happened to be a self-indulgent, callous and spineless little Nero and the first big-name rock casualty of the sixties. Execrably written and mind-numbingly sentimental, it's pop hagiography at its all too frequent worst.

DOLLY CLOSE UP/UP CLOSE
Ed Caraeff (Delilah/Sidgwick & Jackson)
Caraeff did the cover photography for *Here You Come Again*, the LP with which Parton successfully "crossed over" from country to pop, and continued to take her picture for a couple of years after that. The results are reproduced here. The photos are fine, the gushy text barely tolerable.

DURAN DURAN: THEIR STORY
Kasper de Graaf/Malcolm Garrett (Proteus)
DURAN DURAN: THE OFFICIAL LYRIC BOOK (Music Sales)
Better-than-average slim biography by the former editor of the now defunct *New Sounds New Styles*, hampered by the fact that, as far as a real story is concerned, Duran Duran don't have one. Beefed up with an appendix of each member's personal file, the

sort beloved of *Smash Hits* readers, it's well-designed with more imaginative flair than the Lyric Book which numbers a mere 17 songs. A pull-out colour poster bulks out the otherwise meagre fare.

EARLY ROCKERS
Howard Elson (Proteus)
Ignoring 'Burnin' Love', to mention just one of several, Elson dismisses Presley's work in the seventies as "an all-time low." Fairly typical of a book consisting of 13 slim biographies. The overall lack of care (no discographies etc.) reaches a telling nadir with the piece on Little Richard — the lay-out team were in such a hurry that they didn't even notice they'd got the copy mixed up, resulting in a "cut-up" Bill Burroughs would be proud of but that will probably have young rockabillies scratching their DAs in confusion.

ELVIS
Dave Marsh (Rolling Stone Press/ Elm Tree)
The ultimate picture book on Presley, beautifully illustrated and supplemented by a critical and concise career analysis. Simply the best volume to date on the subject.

ELVIS: THE ILLUSTRATED RECORD
Roy Carr and Mick Farren (Eel Pie)
Like its Beatles / Stones / Bowie predecessors, this is the sort of rock book that makes all the quickie rubbish worth wading through: glorious design, mountains of information, everything you want to know at the flick of a wrist. So good that when one does find a mistake — attributing the soundtrack of *A Fistful of Dollars* to Hugo Montenegro (it was, of course, Ennio Morricone) — one leaps for joy. A beauty of a book, no argument.

THE FRANK SINATRA SCRAPBOOK
Richard Peters
(Pop Universal/Souvenir Press)
FRANK SINATRA: OL' BLUE EYES
Norm Goldstein
(Holt, Rinehart and Winston)

The first, which claims to be a scrapbook, is precisely that: a brief career history, a bunch of articles, a detailed discography, liquidised facts made effortless to read. The second masquerades as "the definitive book" but is instead a weary action replay of already over familiar details, tarted up with some good pictures. The sheer tameness of all the biographies on him — including, surprisingly, Scaduto's some years back — is a tribute to Sinatra's discretion, the loyalty of his friends and the power of the mohair suit.

GIRL GROUPS: THE STORY OF A SOUND
Alan Betrock (Delilah/Omnibus)

In his preface, Alan Betrock is at pains to point out that this is "not a book about women in rock and it is not even a book about girls in rock," but his affectionate and intimidatingly detailed look at the history of the Brill Building, and its spiritual neighbours throughout the USA, does tend to emphasise the domination and manipulation of the dispensable teendreams by their managers and producers, while largely sidestepping the implications of the "innocent victim" role which these wonderful musical confectioners laid down as proper for adolescent females. The chapters on Motown (contributed by Aaron Fuchs) are notable exceptions, and anybody who ever felt that The Marvellettes' lead singer Gladys Horton could out-sing Diana Ross in her sleep will cheer Fuchs on. Betrock's energy and enthusiasm for his subject win the day despite the ideological cop-out, but the many excellent

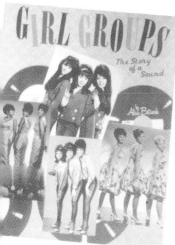

photographs are singularly ill-served by picture reproduction only just above fanzine quality.

GUITAR GREATS
John Tobler and Stuart Grundy
(BBC)

Fourteen of them, anyway, as featured in the radio series of the same name. Living up to that name is something else. Obviously Jimi Hendrix was unavailable for interview. But why no Keith Richard? Some good photos (but not enough) and solidly authoritative text, quotes by the ton, discographies — albeit without labels or catalogue numbers — and writing that betrays its origins as radio material: a tendency to talk down that's counterbalanced by a necessary lack of waffle, something to which Mr Tobler, sincere though he may be, has been no stranger to in the past. Oh, and the cover's crap.

HELLFIRE:
The Jerry Lee Lewis Story
Nick Tosches (Plexus)
GREAT BALLS OF FIRE:
The True Story of Jerry Lee Lewis
Myra Lewis with Murray Silver
(Virgin)

Tosches' book is utterly appropriate to its subject: sprawling, apocalyptic, sly, vicious and sentimental by turns. It dwarfs Myra Lewis' warm, witty and surprisingly unvindictive memoir almost without meaning to, but this is inevitable: Tosches deals with the relationship between Lewis and God, while Myra deals principally with the relationship between Lewis and herself. *Hellfire* depicts with hallucinatory clarity the kind of authority that the Louisiana Wild Man brought to his music: that of a man who believes that by playing what he plays he is eternally damned and therefore the moment is all. Tosches' book is — in its finest passages — as steamy and demented as its subject's greatest performances, and cannot be recommended too highly. Myra Lewis' book is admirable

supplementary reading for anyone who still wants more after reading Tosches and it demonstrates both her affection for this magnificent loony and the extent to which he must have been completely intolerable as a husband.

HUMAN LEAGUE
Alaska Ross
MADNESS
Mark Williams
TOYAH
Gayna Evans (Proteus)

Thirty two-page microbiographies with the emphasis on design and pictures, the texts serving merely as a familiar litany of facts. Presumably aimed at fans of the people in question, none of these inflated magazines reveal anything they're not likely to know already.

THE ILLUSTRATED COUNTRY ALMANAC
Richard Wootton (Virgin)

The almanac format is a great "dip" no matter what the subject, and this is no exception. Of course, it's just a deft way of rearranging familiar material, but in this case the fascinating facts are both reliable and well-assembled, including anyone who's anyone in this broad soundscape, from Parsons to Parton, Kenny Rogers to Roy Rogers. Poor old Roy — fancy being born Leonard Slye! Taking this into account, his later intense relationships with a dog and a horse begin to make a great deal of sense. If the hideous cover looks familiar, it's because it's a cousin of the spangled posters that advertise the annual Country bashes at Wembley. This minor blemish apart, a most engrossing volume.

THE ILLUSTRATED POP QUIZ BOOK
Barry Lazell and Dafydd Rees
(Proteus)

Spanning the history of rock from the early fifties to the present day, this addition to the already prodigious output from the chart-compiling duo is aimed fairly at the average fan's ken. Devoting 20 or so questions to each section, this is an irresistible and very disposable slim volume that earns its "illustrated" title from its sparse scattering of pix. Fairly commonplace questions, but accurate and guaranteed fun for one afternoon, at least.

JAH REVENGE
Michael Thomas & Adrian Boot
(Eel Pie)

Thomas and Boot's *Babylon on a Thin Wire* was the first and most important book-length report on

contemporary Jamaican culture, music and politics, and *Jah Revenge* continues the story of an island under heavy pressure. Thomas' text is tense, slangy and wry, reminiscent of the Tom Wolfe of *Radical Chic and Mau-Mauing the Flak-Catchers,* and Boot's photographs convey the division most eloquently: the juxtaposition of faded colonial pomp and Rasta culture and militancy renders the text almost superfluous. Alternately funny, frightening and moving, this slice of contemporary political history provides a perfect backdrop for today's reggae music.

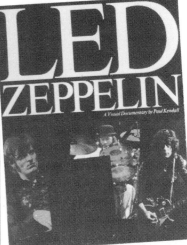

LED ZEPPELIN —
A Visual Documentary
Paul Kendall (Omnibus)

Large format, glossy, day-by-day history peppered with pics, posters, mementos and quotes. The busy-busy, highly colourful layout recalls the "Illustrated Record" series, and that's no bad thing. The fact that the band is no more (the book is already out of date, failing to note Robert Plant's solo LP) will doubtless affect sales but those die-hards who want to see the scrapbook of their dreams need look no further.

THE LONG AND WINDING ROAD
Neville Stannard (Virgin)

Subtitled *A History of the Beatles on Record,* this certainly lives up to its title, taking the reader through The Beatles' discography with an utterly monomaniacal devotion to detail. Every single fact about every single recording is here, everything you could want to know and everything that you would never dream of thinking about, every single disparity between British, American and continental releases...the thin line between exhaustive and exhausting is crossed and re-crossed countless times. Neville Stannard isn't that much of a critic, and his prose is little more than serviceable, but then this book fulfils a different function to the more lavish and literary Carr/Tyler *Beatles Illustrated Record*. The ultimate reference book designed to settle all Beatle arguments with but a flip of the pages, *The Long and Winding Road* is for looking things up in rather than curling up and reading. As such, it cannot be faulted.

LOU REED & THE VELVET UNDERGROUND
Diana Clapton (Proteus)
"Its intimacy and hints of salvation made a wonderful accompaniment to acid trips." So does the author attempt to communicate the delights of the third Velvet Underground LP. No wonder Lou Reed hates the music press. The author doesn't appear to have met Mr Reed himself, but she does have interesting reminiscences from everyone else in the band. Hence some of the story of this most intriguing of combos finally sees the light, no thanks to the writer (as opposed to the interviewer) in Ms Clapton. The former keeps butting in with gems like this one: "Lou tucked his dragon's tail into his leather jeans and headed out on tour, ready to give his fans the fearsome rock and roll they clearly desired above all else." *Exterminate!*

MAKING MUSIC
Ed. George Martin (Pan)
Subtitled "The Guide to Writing, Performing and Recording", with contributions from numerous writers, performers, producers and moguls. Useful, wide-ranging and informative, its generally avuncular tone somehow manages to make all the activities described therein sound rather dull.

MARC BOLAN —
BORN TO BOOGIE
Chris Welch/Simon Napier-Bell (Eel Pie)
ELECTRIC WARRIOR —
THE MARC BOLAN STORY
Paul Sinclair (Omnibus)
Two histories of the Bopping Elf, one by a long-time fan, the other by a couple of old pop tarts who also happen to be fans (Napier-Bell, as both books note, managed Bolan in his John's Children days). Sympathies usually go to the underdog in cases like these, but this time out it's the old pros who do the best job on all counts: the Welch/Napier-Bell book has the best design, most information, richest quotes. However, it's a pity that such a colourful figure should be represented in dull monochrome.

MEET ON THE LEDGE —
A HISTORY OF FAIRPORT CONVENTION
Patrick Humphries (Eel Pie)
In the eighties, a pop group has roots if one member remembers Bolan or The Beatles, and Folk has once more become a sub-genre with its own *aficionados*. The late sixties were far more eclectic times and the Fairports, like Dylan and The Byrds across the Atlantic, welded their country's traditional musics with the electric instrumentation of the day, often with results that were frequently inspiring, as well as being commercial successes in their own right. Humphries' history has leanings towards the minutiae of the old *Zig Zag*, as well as the "fan's notes" enthusiasm and leisurely, colloquial style of that organ. The result's a virtual history of UK folk/rock, its many branchings helpfully clarified by a Pete Frame family tree. Scholarly and illuminating.

THE NAME OF THIS BOOK IS TALKING HEADS
Krista Reese (Proteus)
Bloated account of the Heads'

career garnered from second-hand sources; forgiveable if given a new interpretation, but Reese merely repeats without re-appraisal. Just how the author manages to make such a fascinating group of personalities so dreadfully boring is a marvel in itself.

THE OCEAN VIEW
Humphrey Ocean (MPL)
The Wings tour of America in the summer of 1976 chronicled in drawings and diary entries. An agreeable enough flick as slim volumes go, with some attractive colour material, but it's difficult to work out who might care about this kind of stuff seven years after the event, particularly when the group hasn't existed for almost as long.

ORCHESTRAL MANOEUVRES IN THE DARK
Mike West (Omnibus)
Author of the magnificently appalling *Toyah*, West has managed to do an equally turgid job on OMD, full of inordinately long sentences, stuffed with ponderous clichés and tedious snippets from press reviews. At least this time he has remembered to include a few quotes, seven to be precise. According to the accompanying press release, this book is illuminating — something I found to be true only after I had set it on fire.

THE PERFECT COLLECTION
Ed. Tom Hibbert (Proteus)
Hibbert and an assorted bunch of music biz people (some of whom deserve to be there, some of whom probably don't even exist) choose a selection of over 200 albums, spanning the fifties to the eighties, and considered essential for the newcomer. Daft idea, as the editor admits, since it's always a matter of taste. Listed under each are the comments made by the contributors — some pithy, some portentous.

THE PRETENDERS
Chris Salewicz (Proteus)
More articulate and conscientious than the average hack, Salewicz is particularly good when illuminating Chrissie Hynde's formative years on the fringes of the London and Paris rock scene. Unfortunately, all the photographs are from the far more familiar era of the established Pretenders line-up. Ironically, Hynde became less accessible as she became more famous, and the latter part of the book is somewhat undernourished as a result. Still, considering the group's brief lifetime, an entertaining and well-researched read.

RARE RECORDS
Tom Hibbert (Proteus)
Want to know how much your mint condition copy of Tich and Quackers singing 'Santa Bring Me Ringo' is worth? Hibbert's guide to collectable "Wax Trash and Vinyl Treasures" tells you. Not a scholarly tome that attempts to catalogue exhaustively, but a highly amusing and entertaining guide to the weird and generally awful. Only grumble is that each chapter is accompanied by a list of records key-coded for price, requiring constant reference to the front of the book to find the legend. Otherwise, it's silly, and maybe even profitable, fun.

REGGAE: DEEP ROOTS MUSIC
Howard Johnson & Jim Pines (Proteus)
A companion piece to the recent Channel 4 series of the same name (though, unfortunately, lacking the Mikey Dread voice-overs), this book scores for its lengthy history of the oppression of the black man in Jamaica, its examination of the origins of Rasta and its excellent illustration and design. Expensively produced and exhaustively researched, its most serious flaw is the persistent dryness of the text, which is written in the kind of poker-faced academese which seems more appropriate for discussing the blues singers of the 1920s. This is an almost inevitable side-effect of the historical approach, and one which — again, inevitably — fails to convey the energy and the passion of reggae music.

REGGAE INTERNATIONAL
Stephen Davis and Peter Simon (Thames & Hudson)
This sequel to the same authors' 1977 *Reggae Bloodlines* is certainly the most comprehensive (not to say exhaustive) of the coffee-table reggae books simply

because it manages to cover just about everything that it needs to, and also because it is absolutely jam-up with crucial photographs. The first Simon/Davis book depended heavily on the authors' jokey self-portraits as well-meaning and eager Babylonian tourists, but here they've opted for contributions by an assortment of different reggae pundits, and the entries range from the specious (Lenny Kaye on white reggae) to the overly dry and academic (Luke Erlich on dub) and the genuinely eloquent and revealing (Carl Gayle on deejay music and Timothy White and Davis himself on Bob Marley). Despite the genuine love and energy which has gone into this book, much of it comes over as the kind of historical exercise more usually found documenting Delta Blues in the twenties, but even the most ital reggae élitist would be happy to spend an evening flipping through it.

THE ROAD GOES ON FOREVER
Philip Norman (Elm Tree)
A collection of articles Norman wrote for *The Times* and *Sunday Times* when, for a decade or so, he provided their link with the pop world. The passing of time has dulled some of the insights, of course — the brief portrait of Bryan Ferry now reads as little more than a gossip column puff — but the style remains witty, pointed and endlessly readable.

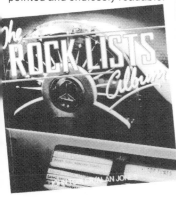

THE ROCK LISTS ALBUM
John Tobler and Alan Jones (Plexus)
Unswervingly infatuated with the notion of trivia as a legitimate obsession for people with time on their hands, this one, amongst a tidal wave of really preposterous minutiae, even manages to list Cliff Richard's seven British flops. Well designed, enjoyable to read, even better to flick through, this blow-out among list books must surely be the end of the line.

ROCK'N'ROLL BABYLON
Gary Herman (Plexus)
The problem with this kind of

book, of course, is just one word with two syllables: libel. Consequently, all the tales of excess and self-immolation around which such volumes are constructed — and this one is entertaining if rather familiar — reflect more the blue pencil than the fearless quill. As a digest of debauchery, though, it doesn't miss too much that's printable.

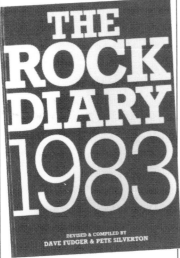

ROCK CHRONICLE
Dan Formento
(Delilah/Sidgwick & Jackson)
THE ROCK DIARY 1983
Dave Fudger and Pete Silverton
(Proteus)
Two books which apparently duplicate each other's functions — to outline events in rock history in diary form — end up, by virtue of their different countries of origin and the concomitant bias, as companion volumes for the really tireless fact fetishist. The entries for January 1, for example — nine in both cases — have only two in common. Some cross-pilfering is recommended for the second editions.

RUSH
Brian Harrigan (Omnibus)
Harrigan is one of the few HM chroniclers who's entertaining even to non-fans, chiefly because the necessary devotion to the genre is overlaid by a distinctive humorous accent. Unfortunately, he appears to have forgotten his tickling-stick whilst composing this brief, overnight history of the Canadian "pomp" behemoths. Plenty of facts and quotes (Harrigan was the group's press officer at one time, hence much access) but there's no evidence of wit, personality or any other distinguishing mark among the threesome's familiar we-love-our-fans manifesto. Non-Rush people will, despite Harrigan's sturdy clean-up and vindication, doubtless continue to think of the

group as noisy crypto-Fascists with a soft spot for the ludicrous Ayn Rand.

SILVER CLIFF
Tony Jasper
(Sidgwick & Jackson)
Twenty five years of Cliff Richard, written, the cover emphasises with some pride, in co-operation with the subject himself. Fine if you're content with fab pix and a litany of accomplishments masquerading as prose; devoid of interest otherwise.

SKINHEAD
Nick Knight (Omnibus)
This sullen little brother to Richard Barnes' *Mods* book very nearly achieves the impossible: to speak for and represent skinheads without getting sucked in by their collective prejudices, while simultaneously remaining sufficiently detached to take a hard look at the quality of the skinhead response to the environment which produced it. Containing a detailed and fascinating look at the rudiments and ephemera of skinhead style, a penetrating and concise essay by Dick Hebdige and many highly eloquent photographs by Knight himself and others, *Skinhead* illuminates its subject without glorifying it or condescending to it. As cultural history, it fills a very real need, and — among other things — throws into fascinating relief the vexed question of skins' relationship to Jamaican music, and their alliance with punk.

SMALL FACES:
ALL OUR YESTERDAYS
Terry Rawlings (Riot Stories)
An enthusiastic and workmanlike account of the lives and times of the most authentic London mod band of the sixties, Rawlings' lovingly researched and generously illustrated pamphlet traces the eventual psychedelicisation and dissolution of the most unselfconsciously enjoyable band of their time. More of a pamphlet than a book, *Small Faces* neither inflates its subject to squeeze out more juice nor shortchanges the reader, but plugs a small and significant hole in sixties pop bibliography. Rawlings has a fine suss on what made the Small Faces a far more enjoyable and rewarding band than the seventies Ronnie-and-Rod Faces ever were, and the pictures are a definitive treat.

SWING AND GO
Aidan Cant (Riot Stories)
Bright, angry and derivative young rock-poet with appalling sixties haircut emerges from the

Paul Weller stable with more than a few good licks, not to mention nods to Dylan, Orwell, John Cooper Clarke, Shakespeare and Marvel Comics. Much better than the cover would suggest, and unlikely to bankrupt the purchaser.

THE WHO: MAXIMUM R&B
Richard Barnes (Eel Pie)
A soundly assembled, moderately revealing pictorial history which, correctly, allows the photos to do most of the talking.

WHOLE LOTTA SHAKIN'
Ian Whitcomb (Arrow)
Large-format paperback subtitled "a rock'n'roll scrapbook." Whitcomb's personal pop history, from eavesdropping youngster to five-minute-wonder with the one-off 'You Turn Me On' in 1965, is intercut with contemporary press clippings from the pop and national press. The cuttings are fascinating, Whitcomb wields a mean (well, fetchingly whimsical) quill. Opportunistic and frothy, but worth checking the remainder bins for all the same.

WITH THE BEATLES
Dezo Hoffman (Omnibus)
Photographs from the not-so-recent past always convey the illusion that life must have been simpler way-back-then, but this collection of early Beatles snaps by the first photographer to understand their importance and respond to their charm displays a lack of self-consciousness that has completely vanished from pop music. Hoffman followed The Beatles — literally — from the audition at Abbey Road studios that got them their deal with EMI to Paul's dad's back garden to the London Palladium and their conquest of America. The freshness and vitality of the band and their openness to experience comes through with devastating clarity. An elegant, elegiac volume that nobody with any interest whatsoever in its subject can afford to be without.

YOU'RE SO COLD I'M TURNING BLUE
Martha Hume (Viking Press/Penguin)
A simplistic but informative and entertaining guided tour around the perimeter of country music, with an outline of its subdivisions, a chronology of important events, a section on musical families, plus, of course, plenty of quizzes, lists and impressions.

V I D E O S

ABBA
The Movie (MGM/UA)

ADAM & THE ANTS
Prince Charming Review
(CBS/Fox)

AMERICA
Live In Central Park (EMI Music)

APRIL WINE
Live In London (EMI)

ASHFORD & SIMPSON
The Ashford & Simpson Video Tape (Thorn EMI)
There's got to be a way of conveying visually the music of soul stars like Nick Ashford and Valerie Simpson, but despite the constant injunctions to "git down" and demands to know "what's goin' on?", this ain't it. Black folks might think differently, but the move out of spangles into dungarees (still with the odd spot of glitter on the olive drab) for the five-part 'Street Opera' lacked, how you say, credibility.

BARCLAY JAMES HARVEST
A Concert For The People
(Polygram Spectrum, also on LaserVision disc)

BEATLES
The Compleat Beatles
(MGM/UA)
Dir: Patrick Montgomery
The sales prove the curiosity demand there must be for authentic footage to explain to later generations what the fuss was all about, but do we really need fatuous intrusions like "The Beatles! Poets of a generation!" over the music, even if they are spoken by Malcolm McDowell? In addition to The Moptops doing 57 tunes, everything from 'Rock and Roll Music' to 'Blackbird', there are brief clips from Bill Haley, Chuck Berry, Lonnie Donegan, Gerry Marsden, Eddie Dixon, Frankie Avalon, Cliff Richard and Tony Sheridan. Necessarily, a lot of the early history is covered by stills with background music, and people like George Martin and Bill Harry remembering what it was like way back then, though they've got the legendary Granada footage from The Cavern.

The archives start to get into colour with 'Nowhere Man', but while the soundtrack talks about the "failure" of *Magical Mystery Tour* and the comparative success of *Yellow Submarine*, no clips are included to allow us to enjoy, for instance, the wonderful animation for 'Lucy in the Sky With Diamonds' in the latter movie. As a documentary, it's a workmanlike-enough job. The tragedy is that a music-only tape, with the relevant extracts from the movies, would presumably have been no harder to clear in terms of copyright but would have been better than this missed opportunity.

BLACK SABBATH
In Concert (VCL)

BLACK SABBATH/BLUE OYSTER CULT
Black And Blue
(Polygram Music Video)

BLANCMANGE

BLANCMANGE
The Videosingles (Polygram)
'Living on the Ceiling', 'Waves', 'Blind Vision'.

BLUE SUEDE SHOWS
(Atlantis)
Gene Vincent, Cliff Richard, Tommy Steele, Billy Fury, Bill Haley, Eddie Cochran and many lesser mortals (bands and fans) in a really good evocation of the roots of British rock, with intriguing clips. Highly recommended.

BROOKS, ELKIE
Pearl, The Video (A&M, also on LaserVision disc)

CALIFORNIA GIRLS (VCL)
If you enjoy watching pneumatic Californians doing athletic things (tennis, hang-gliding, aerobics) to familiar songs from the likes of 10CC, Queen, Kool and The Gang, The Police, Blondie and many others, you'll be able to ignore the tenuous story-line about a failing DJ's wheeze to offer $10,000 to the West Coast's most exciting female, and three damsels who resolve to win it, come what may, including (shock, horror) even nudity. As the blurb says, "Their antics are hilarious — and outrageous — guaranteeing laughs (and thrills) all the way!"

CASH, JOHNNY
I Walk The Line (RCA/Columbia)

CHEECH AND CHONG
Nice Dreams (RCA/Columbia)

CLIFF, JIMMY
Bongo Man (Films International)

COMEALOT — THE MOTOR-BIKE ROCK OPERA
(Champagne)

COMEBACK
(World of Video 2000)

CONCERT FOR BANGLADESH
(Thorn EMI)

COOPER, ALICE
Welcome To My Nightmare
(Universal Video)

ELKIE BROOKS

DEXY'S MIDNIGHT RUNNERS
The Bridge (Polygram)
Shot and lit with a gritty intimacy which is remarkable for concert material, and entirely appropriate to the Celtic soul brothers, this was filmed at the Shaftesbury Theatre, London, in October 1982. Interesting to compare what the band's really like with the romantic images of the 'Eileen' promo, especially when the tune comes round towards the end of the show, and also to compare their version of 'Jackie Wilson Said' with recollections of Van Morrison's own.

DIRT BAND
Tonite (Thorn EMI)
Just a concert movie (Denver, autumn 1981) with no fancy stuff, directed by the concert footage master, Derek Burbidge. Fans of the great country rock outfit will love it, but it will leave the uncommitted severely unmoved, even by the climactic 'Will the Circle Be Unbroken', the old tune they have made so much their own, which of course closes the show. Rosemary Butler guests.

DURAN DURAN
Duran Duran (EMI)
For sheer triumph of form over content, these promo videos — eight out of eleven directed by the promo king, Russell Mulcahy — have caught the spirit of their subject perfectly. One wonders (sincerely) at what a generation raised on these images of conspicuous consumption ('Rio', 'Hungry Like the Wolf', 'Nightboat'), eroticism, sexism and female degradation ('Girls on Film', 'The Chauffeur' — the latter never made it to *TOTP*, presumably because of its rather dodgy subject matter) will grow up like, especially the little girls. Also, what kind of feature films people like Mulcahy could produce, given the chance.

EASTON, SHEENA
(EMI)
Before you turn off in disgust, give it a listen and a look, not merely because the whole production is an ideal example of how a straightforward no-non-

sense in-concert video can be faithful to its subject without being boring, but also because the young lady clearly has a genuine talent. The lyrical material is fairly trivial, never rising above the superficialities of her 'Modern Girl' — and notice the way she empathises with the blasé response of the Hollywood audience when she announces it. She's got the voice, the stagecraft, and the basic talent: with maturity that could find itself greening into something really significant.

ECHO & THE BUNNYMEN
Porcupine (Kace)
Six tunes, photographed in Liverpool and Iceland, in a low-key manner which entirely suits the band's 1978 version of Merseybeat. The Iceland photography is inconspicuous by its presence.

ELECTRIC LIGHT VOYAGE
(Media)
Computer graphic images matched to electronic muzak. No connection with ELO.

EMERSON LAKE & PALMER
Pictures At An Exhibition (Imagination, re-issue in simulated stereo)

FIRST NUDIE MUSICAL, THE
(Temple)

FLEETWOOD MAC

FLEETWOOD MAC IN CONCERT
(Polygram)

GENESIS
Three Sides Live (EMI)
One of the first rock stereo videos to be released, with a crystal clear Dolby soundtrack, this did remarkably well in the video charts when it first came out, which is a little surprising, because it isn't really a very good representation of how exciting the band can still be, even though its greatest days are clearly behind it now, as Phil Collins concentrates upon his solo career.

GRANT, EDDY
At Notting Hill (re-released in stereo, VCL)

Roxy and The Vortex, its hour come round at last.

HOT GOSSIP
The Video Show (EMI)

HUMAN LEAGUE
The Singles Video (Virgin)

HUNTER, IAN
Rocks (Chrysalis)

IMAGINATION
Music And Lights (Precision)
Judging by the video evidence, British funk seems to have its act together rather better than the original, Stateside product, for while Imagination may not be the best representatives of the genre internationally, this tape is vastly more entertaining than others of whom we might have hoped more. Of course, director Mike Mansfield knows what he's doing, and the show is so well mounted that even if the music wasn't up to scratch, it would still impress for its sheer professionalism. And the stereo sound is perfect.

IRON MAIDEN
(EMI)

IRON MAIDEN
Video Pieces (EMI)
Lots of dry ice and flying hair in

PHIL OAKEY (THE HUMAN LEAGUE)

are here. Got to be a winner.

JACKSONS
In Concert (VCL)

JAM
Trans-Global Unity Express (Polygram/Spectrum)
It's a real tragedy that a band as significant, in its time, as The Jam, should have been commemorated by such a limping, lack-lustre video as this. The guilty man is director Gordian P. Troeller, who is capable of better, as his track record as an album producer of some distinction (Van Der Graf Generator) and the better Jam footage on 'Kids Like You and Me' (which see) should indicate. Definitely for addicts only.

JAPAN
Oil On Canvas (Virgin)
Hammersmith Odeon live footage is intercut with location shooting in Thailand and Hong

DURAN DURAN

FLACK, ROBERTA
In Concert (3M)
Middle-class soul, in Edmonton, Canada, with the local symphony orchestra. Naturally, she does 'Killing Me Softly' and 'First Time Ever I Saw Your Face'.

FLAME (3M)

GREAT ROCK'N'ROLL SWINDLE
(Virgin)
Dir: Julian Temple
And so a legend is created: punk as a situationist joke on the rock'n'roll establishment, a verdict which is a damn sight less subversive than the gritty, vigorous reality of the music that slouched out of clubs like The

Video EP, featuring 'Number of the Beast', 'Run to the Hills', 'Flight of the Icarus', 'The Trooper'. The concessions to "art" (Lon Chaney lookalike in 'Beast', *Charge of the Light Brigade* clips in 'The Trooper') are really not necessary, as long as the power chords come over loud and clear, and the lyrics are more or less incomprehensible, as they

IRON MAIDEN

Kong to provide the necessary Oriental validation for the band's name. Appropriately, the colour has a rather washed-out look, and anyone seeking a reason for Japan's huge international status would find it hard to discover here.

JETHRO TULL
Slipstream (Chrysalis)
Sandwiched between some

pretty nonsensical shots of Ian Anderson looning around like the Fool in *King Lear* (looks like his native loch, treated with chroma-key) is some fiery concert footage. Though the animations and other interpolated material is well enough done, one wonders if it is really necessary. And things like the dramatisation of the anti-nuclear 'Flyingdale Flyer' actually get in the way of the message.

JOHN, ELTON
In Central Park, N.Y.
(re-released in stereo, VCL)

JOHN, ELTON
The Fox (Rank)

JOHN, ELTON
The Videosingles (Polygram)
'I Guess That's Why They Call It the Blues', 'Empty Garden' and 'Blue Eyes' (both dir: ECV Australia).

GRACE JONES

JONES, GRACE
A One-Man Show (Island)

KAJAGOOGOO
Video EP (EMI)
Three video promos, 'Too Shy', 'Ooh to Be Ah', 'Hang on Now', illustrating the strengths and weaknesses of the medium applied to an act like this. Fans will probably have recorded them already from *TOTP*, and the images are really too strong for the fairly vacuous music.

KID CREOLE & THE COCONUTS
Live In Concert "At The Ritz"
New York (Island)
Still a model of what a concert video should be, this is unsurpassed nearly 12 months after release.

KIDS LIKE ME AND YOU
(3M)
The Jam: 'In the City', 'Mr Clean', 'A-Bomb in Wardour St'; *Sham 69:* 'Borstal Breakout', 'Angels With

Dirty Faces', 'If the Kids Are United'; *Ultravox:* 'Slow Motion', 'Quiet Man', 'Slip Away'; *Penetration:* 'Lovers of Outrage', 'Life's a Gamble'; *The Pirates:* 'Johnny B. Goode's Good', 'Shakin' All Over'.

It sounds like a terrible mish-mash of groups (a typical Reading Festival, in fact) but in attempting to get into the nature of the phenomenon (don't yawn), the director and his assistant, the same Gordian Troeller responsible for the dreadful 'Trans-Global Unity Express', have produced a worthwhile show, possibly despite themselves. It's a bit historical, of course: Ultravox Mk I included John Foxx, and the Sham 69 sequences merely point up how much we miss the energy of Jimmy Pursey, whose celebrated tearful end to 'If the Kids Are United' is enshrined on tape, for the embarrassment of all. But though it's five years old, it's far from being only ancient history. More a recollection of what we've lost in the self-assured sharpness of much contemporary pop.

KIDS ARE ALRIGHT, THE
(Re-released on LaserVision disc, Polygram)

KIDS FROM FAME
At The Royal Albert Hall
(MGM/UA)

LADD, CHERYL
Fascinated (EMI Music)
Does anyone bother to watch junk like this, even in its homeland? Ladd plays a photographer who fantasises herself into a lead singer in a rock band in the studio: lots of rim lighting round Varuschka hair-do's, a pleasant enough voice for an ex-Angel, but really, why bother?

MADNESS
Take It Or Leave It (Stiff)

MADNESS
Complete (Stiff)

MARTYN, JOHN
In Vision 1973-81 (BBC)
Now that the BBC has sorted out matters with the MU, one of the last obstacles to making accessible the wealth of BBC archive material on video — if they haven't wiped it already — has been removed, and this first result promises marvellous things ahead. Actually, they couldn't be much more marvellous than this, which is not merely a superlative overview of one of British rock's great originals, but is almost perfectly presented, with good sleeve notes, timings of tunes, all

the sort of stuff they used to put on LP covers but don't any more. The dreaded deaf-and-dumb BBC sound engineer seems to have taken leave of absence on most of these gigs, including the later super-session when the presence of Phil Collins on drums and back-up vocals might have been thought to guarantee they'd blow it.

MAZE
Happy Feelin's Live In New Orleans (EMI)
Workmanlike mellow funk, well played and competently shot in concert in November 1980, which nevertheless fails to convey any reason why the audience should get so excited. But then the sound of Philadelphia, West Coast-style, always was rather laid-back.

MINK DE VILLE
Live At The Savoy
(Polygram/Spectrum)

MORRISON, VAN
In Ireland (Narrowcast)
The Lion of Caledonia does not sleep tonight: though Morrison's laid-back style doesn't generate as much excitement as once it did, there is no doubting the man's charisma still, even if the tear-up finale, including James Brown-like collapse backwards on to the floor and the rally cry, "It's too late to stop now," seems like a mere going through of motions. But is anyone interested, any more, in those shots of bands in buses? What mystery there may once have been in life on the road has been dispelled by the definitive studies of Pennebaker & Co.

NAZARETH
The Loudest And The Proudest
Live (VCL)
A really powerful evocation of what all those power chords can mean for an audience, interspersed with the usual boring interviews.

NEWTON-JOHN, OLIVIA
Live (Embassy, also LaserVision disc)
After the glossy expertise of 'Physical', which was undoubtedly one of the best videos of the year, this live concert (Weber State University, Ogden, Utah, October 12/13 1982) brings us back to earth with a bump, and the realisation that the lady doesn't really make it as a concert artist. Director Brian Grant tries hard, opening with a sort of overture of her hit tunes to back a collage of her career, cuttings

and pix with the famous (including a bit of 'You're the One That I Want' with Travolta in *Grease*), but then the lady appears, and it's a bit like those Petula Clark/Cilla Black variety shows the BBC always used to screen when their planners ran out of inspiration.

NEW SEEKERS
In Concert (Champion Video)

NEW SENSATION
(Merlin)

NO NUKES
The MUSE concert (CBS/Fox)
The "boring old hippies reunion enlivened by the Bruce Springsteen sequence" reviews which the movie got a couple of years back seemed to be more of an anti-Woodstock backlash than a considered verdict on the film as a film, as a sequence of musical items, or as a commentary on the anti-nuclear movement. In many respects, it is rather better put together than most of its ilk (much better, for instance, than Martin Scorsese's *The Last Waltz*, which lapses into tedium in the interviews), and the backstage and press conference sequences mesh together with the music. Catch the way that Crosby, Stills and Nash's rehearsal of 'Suite: Judy Blue-Eyes' jump cuts to the stage performance so neatly that you can't see the join, concluding with Stills' own comment on the way in which the backstage confusion resulted in onstage magic. You cannot object that pop music is not a suitable way of making the anti-nuclear case, because there is plenty of discussion of the issues involved. The critics were right about one thing: the Bruce Springsteen sequence is truly amazing.

NUMAN, GARY
Micromusic (Palace)

NUMAN, GARY
New Man Numan (Palace)
Videos like these are the visual equivalent of those classic pop singles which we all treasure: ephemeral as they are, they have a unique timelessness at the same time which transcends the trashiness of music and concept.

ORCHESTRAL MANOEUVRES IN THE DARK
(Virgin)

PENDERGRASS, TEDDY
Live In London (CBS/Fox)
Just a month before the horrific road accident which seemed as if it was going to retire him perman-

ently, the former Blue Notes lead singer recorded this concert in London in February 1982. Songs include 'Close the Door' and 12 others. No underwear is thrown on to the stage (despite the chorus of female affirmatives following his question: "Are we friends?") but after all this *is* England, dammit.

PINK FLOYD
Live At Pompeii
(re-released in stereo, Polygram)
A pity they didn't put back the deleted footage, including some rather inconsequential interview material and interesting "work in progress" which ended up as *Dark Side of the Moon*, shot in Abbey Road studios, while they were at it, to make it up to its full theatrical length.

PINK FLOYD
The Wall (EMI)
A crystal-clear stereo soundtrack and Gerry Scarfe's animations, plus Roger Waters' melancholic vision of rock star as paradigm of contemporary alienation, works remarkably well in the home, possibly because the domestic environment turns down the over-kill of Parker's Ken Russell-like sensationalism. Over the top it may be, and Waters and Parker may no longer be talking, but it's remarkably true to the writer's original concept. Recommended.

PINK FLOYD
Crystal Voyager (IFS)
Drippy soundtrack, plus enthralling shots of the construction of a boat in a million, concluded by staggering slow-motion sequence of surfing within "the curl" or a big wave, to the music of Floyd's 'Echoes'.

PINK FLOYD
Video EP (EMI)
'Not Now John', 'Fletcher Memorial Home', 'The Final Cut', 'The Gunner's Dream'. From *The Final Cut* album. Whatever reservations Roger Waters might have about Alan Parker's work on *The Wall*, Parker is never boring, and there are long stretches of this four-part distillation of *The Final Cut*, especially the promo for the single, 'Not Now John', which really drag. The four items are given a spurious unity by being all viewed by Alex McAvoy (who played the teacher in *The Wall*) on a family TV set, intercut with shots from the Falklands War.

POLICE
Police Around The World (EMI)
More Derek Burbidge direction, interspersed with rather obvious travelogue footage. You know the

THE POLICE

sort of thing: if this is Japan, Andy Summers has to dress up as a sumo wrestler and take a fall or two; in Hong Kong, Sting takes a rickshaw, and ends up giving the operator a ride; in India, Summers has a go at playing 'Walking on the Moon' on the sitar; up the Parthenon in Greece (for 'Canary in a Coalmine'?); in South America the lads dress up as gauchos and ride around an estancia. We are spared the Eiffel Tower in the French sequence, mercifully, and the American material is enlivened by Jools Holland developing the interview techniques he has since made peculiarly his own on *The Tube*. Generally nothing is revealed, especially about what makes this very traditional three-piece such international superstars in the post-punk era, except that only superstars would have the gall to unload this kind of material on to a gullible public. The Montserrat TV programme was better than this.

ELVIS PRESLEY

PRESLEY, ELVIS
Comeback Special (Mountain)

PRESLEY, ELVIS
Live In Hawaii (WWV1 Corp)

PRESLEY, ELVIS
Elvis, King Of Rock & Roll
(World of Video 2000)

PRESLEY, ELVIS
Elvis In Concert (World of Video)

PRINCE'S ROCK TRUST GALA
(MGM/UA)
Roughly in order of appearance: Madness, Ian Anderson, Unity (contest prizewinners), Joan Armatrading, Phil Collins, Midge Ure, Pete Townshend, Gary Brooker (who does 'Whiter Shade of Pale', what else?), Kate Bush (looking less glamorous than on her own video), Robert Plant, concluding with a superstar jam on Sly Stone's 'I Want to Take You Higher', of all things, which works as well as might be expected.

QUEEN
Greatest Flix (EMI)

QUEEN
Royal Philharmonic Orchestra
Plays (EMI Music)
The idea of getting a symphony orchestra to play Queen's greatest hits is just crazy enough to work — and if you want to check out the capabilities of any stereo video machine, then you don't need to go much further than this one, because the stereo is great. Jacques Loussier and Elena Duran are among the distinguished musicians getting involved with this farrago.

RAINBOW
Live Between The Eyes
(Polygram)
Ritchie Blackmore's boys filmed in San Antonio, Texas, in an undistinguished but reasonably competent examination of the contemporary example of how sixties' super-rock has become heavy metal.

REGGAE SUNSPLASH PART I
(VCL)
Chalice: 'This Is Reggae Music', 'Roadblock'; *Steel Pulse:* 'Blues Dance Raid'; *Eek-a-Mouse:* 'Ghetto Living'; *Lloyd Parkes & We the People:* 'Redemption Song', 'What More Can I Do'; *Aswad:* 'African Children'; *Burning Spear:* 'Slavery Days'; *Mutabaruka:* 'It No Good to Live in a White Man's Country'; *Big Youth:* 'Ten Against One'; *Home T Four:* 'Cool Running'; *Mighty Diamonds:* 'Pass the Kutchie'; *Blue Riddim Band:* 'My Name Is Nancy'.

Not the mediocre 1979 film, which featured Bob Marley, but the 1982 Montego Bay festival, a gentle, melodic day in the sun that almost gives you a suntan. 'Kutchie' is the Mighty Diamonds hit

which Musical Youth parlayed into a UK chart-topper, by turning it into 'Dutchie' (cooking pot) and changing "'ow do you feel when you got no 'erb?" to "got no food."

REGGAE SUNSPLASH PART II
(VCL)

REO SPEEDWAGON
In Concert (CBS/Fox)
If you've ever felt inclined to yell the magic imperative "Boogie" at your video, then come with us to the McNichols Arena, Denver, Colorado, for an hour and a half of the stuff of which headaches are made. For the non-fan, it's a bit like living next door to a rather noisy party-goer: everyone seems to be having a good time, but to you it's just a pain.

ROCK ROCK ROCK
(Derann)

ROLLING STONES
The Stones In The Park (Granada)
Fourteen years later, and at last one of the great epochal events of the sixties, created in its entirety for television, whatever myth might recall, comes out on video. Can The Doors be far behind? Brian Jones is barely laid in his grave, Jagger reads 'Endymion' in his memory, wearing that pretty little Mr Fish dress as if it was made for him, and thousands of butterflies are released over Hyde Park. And The Stones play atrociously! Ginger Johnson's African drummers are good, though.

ROXY MUSIC
The High Road
(Polygram/Spectrum)
Bryan Ferry and the boys recorded in Frejus, France, in summer 1982, running through the Roxy songbook from 'The Main Thing' to 'Jealous Guy', while Ferry does his well-known deterioration from neat lounge lizard at the opening to coatless, tieless sweaty slob for the concluding number.

RUSH

RUSH
Exit Stage Left (Polygram)

SECRET POLICEMAN'S BALL
(Hokushin)

SIMON & GARFUNKEL
The Concert In The Park
(Warner Home Video)
Video can be cruel. Take a look at Paul Simon's eyes every time he glances at the camera, and you'll see the born-again Brill Building hack who switched his act to folk and became platinum. Compared with Art Garfunkel's passionate dedication to what he is performing, this is definitely the old pro going through the motions for the fans, and doing it all superbly. Director Michael Lindsay-Hogg (*Let It Be*, The Rolling Stones' *Rock'n'Roll Circus*) is the sort of man who can shoot a concert so it's never boring, not missing the crazed fan who almost puts Simon off his stroke (but not, of course, quite succeeding). There's one new song, 'Johnny Ace', linking the death of the fifties' rocker of that name with the death of Lennon, which he sings as if it really means something to him, and they're backed by an almost perfect band of Big Apple sessioneers (get Steve Gadd's tight press-drum rolls on 'Fifty Ways to Leave Your Lover' which really deserve the acknowledgement they get from the stage). Perhaps you got this already from the TV transmission, but the tape (rental only) has the advantage of a superlatively crisp stereo soundtrack.

SIOUXSIE & THE BANSHEES
Once Upon A Time (Polygram)
Once upon a time, between August 1978 and July 1981, to be precise, Siouxsie Sue was the Queen of Punk, and the directors of her single video promos did her proud. Here are nine of the results, but the soundtrack's a bit muddy.

SKY
At Westminster Abbey (BBC)
As is so often the case, the band seems overpowered by the setting, and this is a disadvantage when they are better at playing than jumping about, as here. The stereo sound is fine and some of the profits go to Amnesty, and unless you hate what they've done to J.S. Bach's 'Toccata and Fugue in D Minor', you'll enjoy it best if you close your eyes.

SOFT CELL
The Non-Stop Exotic Video Show (EMI)
An engaging, deliberately amateurish sort of video fanzine, introduced and linked by Marc Almond himself, with various lunacies *en passant*, between the

SOFT CELL

clips of 'Entertain Me' and 'Say Hello Wave Goodbye', and nine other tunes. Any classicist rock fans spot the Latin boob in the 'Frustration' bit?

STATUS QUO
Live In Concert At The NEC, Birmingham (Polygram)

STEWART, ROD
Tonight I'm Yours
(Embassy, also LaserVision disc)
Oh dear. There have been great TV shows by Rod the Mod (as we Steam Packet fans will ever remember him) in his heyday, but this isn't one, despite a 100-piece gospel choir and Tina Turner on two numbers ('Get Back', 'Hot Legs').

STIFF VISIONS
Vol. 1 (Stiff)

STRANGLERS
The Video Collection 1977-82 (EMI)
Lindsey Clennell has gathered together several different directors' differing approaches to one of the great seventies' bands, including five of his own, and three co-directed by Hugh Cornwell, including the unpleasant (and apt) live strip on 'Nice'n'Sleazy'. Russell Mulcahy's 'Duchess' was banned as blasphemous by *TOTP*, just because the band was dressed in cassock and surplice and shot in a church. Collectively, one of the best videos of the year.

TEARS FOR FEARS
The Videosingle
(Polygram/Spectrum)

TOYAH
Good Morning Universe (BBC)
The acceptable face of punk, looking like a Kenny Everett take-off, recorded by BBC's *Old Grey Whistle Test* from the Theatre Royal, Drury Lane, on Christmas Eve, 1981. It was transmitted live at the time, and there's an urgency about the editing that suggests there have been no second thoughts.

TURNER, TINA
The Queen Of Rock And Roll
(re-released in stereo, VCL)

TURNER, TINA
Nice'n'Rough (Thorn EMI)
Anyone who remembers the

Turner revue at Tiles in the sixties, which got Tina's garter belt on the front page of the *MM* and had all the young dudes wiping the drool from their chins, will find it incredible that the lady is ageing as gracelessly as this. She seems never to have got over the experience of being encouraged to overplay her role as the Acid Queen (which she sings here, histrionically as ever) in Ken Russell's *Tommy*.

URGH! A MUSIC WAR
(re-released on LaserVision disc, Guild)

UK/DK
(Cherry Red)
At last a real punk movie, designed to support the proposition that punk is alive and well and living outside the Metropolis, propounded sensibly by *MM* punkette Carol Clerk and rather ponderously by *Sounds'* Gary Bushell, supported by music from The Exploited, Vice Squad, Blitz, New Age, The Business, Chaos UK, and Disorder, and some irrelevant studio footage of The Damned, including Captain Sensible miming to Jimi Hendrix.

There are also interview clips and a sequence in a Bristol squat which conveys the authentic squalor of such habitations disturbingly accurately. The cameras went to places like The Red Lion, Gravesend, Drifters, USA, as well as London's 100 Club (complete with genuine Kenny Ball poster behind the band), and spent almost as much time being pointed at the good-natured but not always bloodless violence of the audiences, so got the flavour exactly right as a consequence. Masterful, and recommended.

VIDEOTHEQUE
(EMI)
Dexy's Midnight Runners: 'Come on Eileen'; *Yazoo:* 'Don't Go'; *Imagination:* 'Just an Illusion'; *Roxy Music:* 'Avalon'; *Fat Larry's Band:* 'Zoom'; *Fashion:* 'Love Shadow'; *Japan:* 'I Second That Emotion'; *Depeche Mode:* 'Leave in Silence'; *Eddy Grant:* 'I Don't Wanna Dance'; *Bananarama:* 'Shy Boy'; *Tight Fit:* 'Fantasy Island'; *Toto Coelo:* 'I Eat Cannibals'; *Bow Wow Wow:* 'I Want Candy'; *Natasha:* 'Iko Iko'; *John Cougar:* 'Jack and Diane'; *Tony Basil:* 'Mickey'; *Nikka Costa:* 'On My Own'; *Prelude:* 'After the Goldrush'; *Bucks Fizz:* 'Now These Days Are Gone'; *Elton John:* 'Blue Eyes'; *Phil Collins:* 'Thru These Walls'; *Dire Straits:* 'Private Investigations'.

A collection of 1982 video promos, sandwiched between

commercials for Sanyo and the 'Don't Stand So Close to Me' Body Mist 2 spot which upset The Police so, which are evidence (if any be needed) to prove that *Top of the Pops* is responsible for the most creative use of the video image to date. Almost every technique in the book — solarisation, colour key, bleach out, slow motion, the lot — is employed. I suspect buyers will be more fascinated, in future years, to remind themselves of the true identity of some of the one-hit wonders to be found there, among the genuine talent.

VIDEO ROCK ATTACK
(Spectrum)
Roxy Music: 'More Than This'; *Soft Cell:* 'Say Hello Wave Goodbye'; *Level 42:* 'Are You Hearing (What I Hear)?'; *Junior:* 'Mama Used to Say'; *Steve Miller:* 'Abracadabra'; *Shakatak:* 'Nightbirds'; *Dire Straits:* 'Private Investigations'; *Rainbow:* 'Death Alley Driver'; *King Crimson:* 'Heartbeat'; *Dexy's Midnight Runners:* 'Come on Eileen'; *Tears for Fears:* 'Mad World'; *Trio:* 'Da Da Da'; *Junior:* 'Too Late'; *Golden Earring:* 'Twilight Zone'.
One of the first of the video compilations, and it shows, slightly. The computer-generated graphics are smart, but a little intrusive, and none of the promos are credited to their directors, who in some cases are now more famous than their subjects. The Dire Straits isn't the same as on *Videotheque*, but the Dexy's 'Eileen' is.

WASHINGTON, GROVER
Live (Pioneer Laser Disc)
A really smart inter-active disc (meaning you can go directly to any chapter, which is what Laser Disc tracks are called), directed by Donny Osmond, of all people, but while the music may be smooth, it's not exactly Salt Lake City squeaky clean. In the band are guitar virtuoso Eric Gale and New York supersessioneer drummer Steve Gadd.

XTC
Look Look (Virgin)
Eleven hits from the history of power pop, from 'This Is Pop' in April 1978 to 'Senses Working Overtime' in January 1982. None of the directors of the individual sequences is credited, which is hardly fair, since whoever he/they is/are, a perfect amalgam of sound and image has been achieved to make these models of what a rock video ought to be.

YOUNG, NEIL
Rust Never Sleeps (VTC)

BEST & WORST

A section in which our contributors, camouflaged by anonymity, are encouraged to make all kinds of opinionated and boorish judgements about album covers, people they think are going to be successful, if they aren't already, people they'd rather just went away and what they remember best from the year. Some are included as a result of unanimous voting; others are just petty prejudices.

ALBUM COVERS OF THE YEAR

IN ONE WAY OR ANOTHER

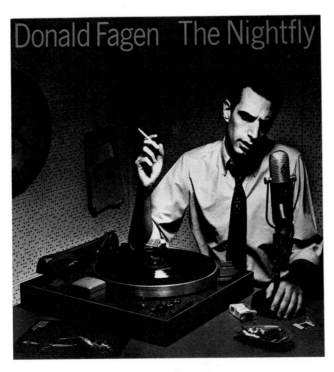

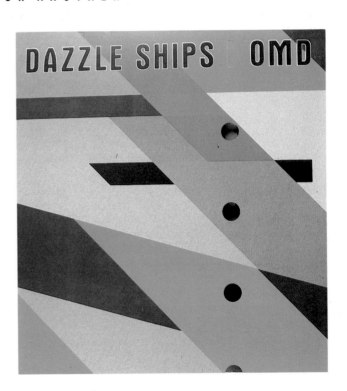

DONALD FAGEN
THE NIGHTFLY (WARNER BROTHERS)
Art Direction:
GEORGE DELMERICO
Photography:
JAMES HAMILTON
A simple idea perfectly executed, its rather mannered air on the right side of pretentiousness. Might even have brought back untipped Chesterfields.

ORCHESTRAL MANOEUVRES IN THE DARK
DAZZLE SHIPS (VIRGIN)
Design:
M. GARRETT, K. KENNEDY,
P. PENNINGTON, P. SAVILLE,
B. WICKENS
Excessively complicated, as befits a cover involving no less than five designers, and a bit desperate in its attempt to impress, but beautifully produced and extremely striking.

JAPAN
OIL ON CANVAS (VIRGIN)
'Cover concept:
SYLVIAN
Cover painting:
FRANK AUERBACH
Fey, but effective in its choice of colours and general presentation. Japan is a good example of a group that knows exactly what its audience wants in terms of trappings.

DEAD KENNEDYS
PLASTIC SURGERY DISASTERS (STATIK)
Sleeve Concept:
JELLO BIAFRA
Photography:
MIKE WELLS
One of the few groups which still enjoy causing as much offence as possible, The Kennedys — or, just as easily, The Deads — always take the risk of simply being a cheap joke, but often come up with strong, memorable covers. This is one.

BLANCMANGE
HAPPY FAMILIES (LONDON)
Painting:
MICHAEL BROWNLOW AFTER LOUIS WAIN
Good to see a supposedly solemn synthesiser duo dressing up their first LP in such a frivolous way. The intellectual irony, if there is any, is lost.

THE GO-GO'S
VACATION (A&M)
Design and Photography:
MICK HAGGERTY
Art Direction:
MICK HAGGERTY, GINGER CANZONERI
Effective and appropriate. An easy group to sell — to Americans at least — but accomplished with some style.

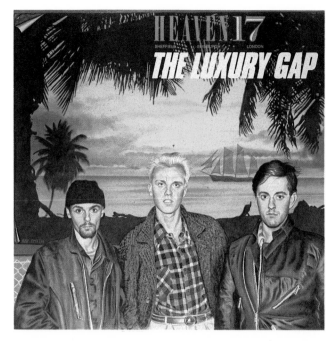

NEW ORDER
FACTUS 8 (FACTORY)
Design:
PETER SAVILLE
Painting:
MARTHA LADLY
One of the consistently impressive things about Saville's covers is that regardless of how routine (and often borrowed) the central idea may be, the finish is always impeccable.

PETE TOWNSHEND
SCOOP (ATCO)
Art direction:
JB
Illustration:
IAN WRIGHT
Covers connected with Townshend tend to be either self-consciously naturalistic or hideously arty. This one is neither. A bit "modern" perhaps, but an excellent illustration with effective results.

HEAVEN 17
THE LUXURY GAP (VIRGIN)
Cover concept and painting:
RAY SMITH
A high-risk cover painting which works very well, conveying the group's general sense of irony with subtle effectiveness. Even if it is part of the same "attitude", one wishes they'd drop the weary sub-Dunhill Sheffield-Edinburgh-London subtitle.

ROBERT WYATT
NOTHING CAN STOP US (ROUGH TRADE)
Drawing:
ALFREDA BENGE
Simple and direct, complementing perfectly the playful subversion of the music.

MARI WILSON
SHOWPEOPLE (COMPACT)
Design:
JB
Photography:
BRIAN GRIFFIN
Allowing for the fact that it's unlikely
Mari Wilson would be mistaken by
anyone for a member of Motorhead, it's
a pity that the record company didn't go
through with avoiding all type on the
cover but added a sticker for the shops.
No identification = commendable
arrogance (for the time being).

NEW ORDER
POWER, CORRUPTION & LIES (FACTORY)
Painting:
FANTIN-LATOUR
Playing a perverse game with the
potential purchaser, and defining new
complexities in sleeve design, this is one
of those sleeves on which you can't find
out what you want to know. Stylish stuff,
though, if a bit gratuitous in the use of
holes and colour bars.

MALCOLM McLAREN
DUCK ROCK (CHARISMA)
Design:
NICK EGAN
Illustration:
KEITH HARING
Loud and comic and unarty, unimpaired
by any self-conscious ''tastefulness'' —
the perfect McLaren sales pitch.

RICKIE LEE JONES
GIRL AT HER VOLCANO
(WARNER BROTHERS)
Design:
RICKIE LEE JONES AND JERRY
McMANUS
Painting:
RICKIE LEE JONES
Sophisticated, cool and imaginative,
particularly exceptional when one
considers how few American AOR
records have interesting sleeves.

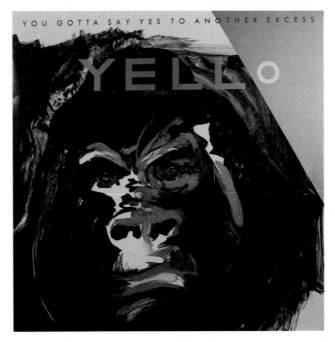

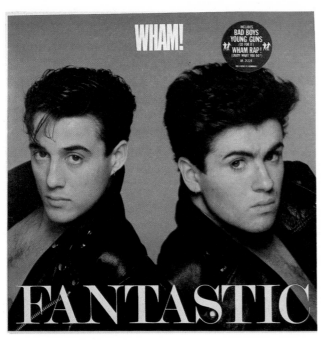

MOTOR BOYS MOTOR
MOTOR BOYS MOTOR (ALBION)
(Uncredited)
As repulsive but captivating images go, this is a picture that positively defies you not to notice it. When you have, playing the record seems to follow naturally.

WHAM!
FANTASTIC (CBS)
Design:
''SHOOT THAT TIGER'' AND WHAM!
Photography:
CHRIS CRAMER
Has its comical element in that the two chaps are both looking so doggedly mean, moody and magnificent. But the audience at which they're aiming wouldn't question it, and it's an effective bit of face selling.

YELLO
YOU GOTTA SAY YES TO ANOTHER EXCESS (STIFF)
Design:
ERNST GAMPER
Photography:
RAY PHOTOGRAPHY
Best album title of the year, too.

ELTON JOHN
TOO LOW FOR ZERO (ROCKET)
Design:
CLIVE PIERCY, DYER/KHAN, INC.
Art Direction:
DOD DYER
Not extraordinary, but like the LP inside a considerable step towards snatching victory from the jaws of defeat.

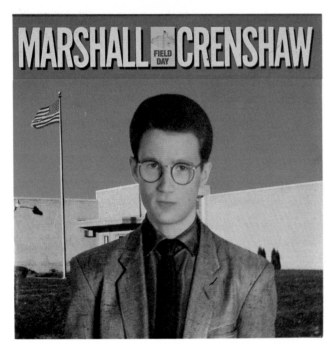

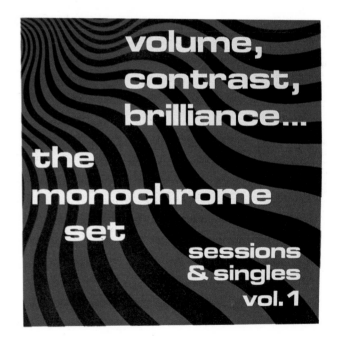

DEPECHE MODE
A BROKEN FRAME (MUTE)
(Uncredited)
A bit precious, but a lovely photograph
that imbues the album with a good deal
more weight than the music does.

MARSHALL CRENSHAW
FIELD DAY (WARNER BROTHERS)
Design:
M & CO, NEW YORK
Photography:
LARRY WILLIAMS
Ever since American rock musicians
started getting their hair cut, their
record covers have been getting more
tiresomely ''modern''. This is one of the
more acceptable ones.

ALTERED IMAGES
BITE (EPIC)
Design:.
MARTYN ATKINS AND ALTERED IMAGES
Photography:
NEIL KIRK
A bit too art directed, to go with the
group's rather self-conscious change of
gear, but a clever step forward in terms
of image.

THE MONOCHROME SET
VOLUME, CONTRAST,
BRILLIANCE . . .(CHERRY RED)
Design:
THOMAS W.B. HARDY
Skilfully imitative of old jazz covers, it
has all the qualities of the title.

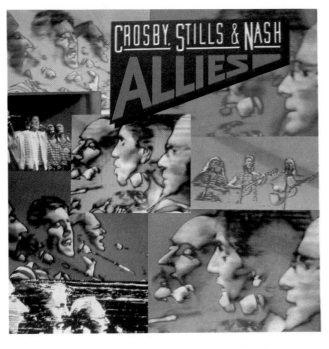

THIN LIZZY
THUNDER AND LIGHTNING (VERTIGO)
Design:
ANDREW PREWETT
Photography:
BOB ELSDALE
Two of the elements which characterise heavy rock are pomposity and a lack of taste. This cover incorporates them both.

CROSBY, STILLS & NASH
ALLIES (ATLANTIC)
Design:
JIMMY WATCHEL, DAWN PATROL
Photography and Concept:
DAVID PETERS
This is clearly an attempt to give some contemporary emphasis to their weary and tiresome music. The graphic equivalent of Neil Young's silly microphone.

PSYCHIC TV
FORCE THE HAND CHANCE
(SOME BIZARRE)
Design:
PSYCHIC TV
Skull:
JOHN HARWOOD
Artwork:
NEVILLE BRODY
A good example of a cover which strives hard for its effect, works overtime to accomplish it and still falls flat.

KATE BUSH
KATE BUSH (EMI-AMERICA MINI LP)
Design:
MICHAEL DIEHL
Photography:
KIND LIGHT
Art Direction:
HENRY MARQUEZ
Extraordinarily grotesque to the point of being comic. Difficult to determine even the intention with this one.

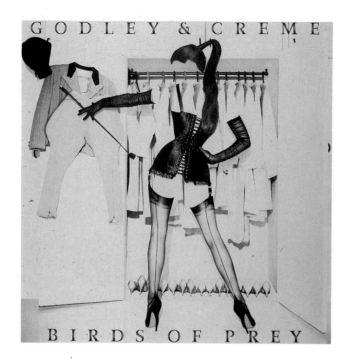

GODLEY & CREME
BIRDS OF PREY (POLYDOR)
Design and photography:
GEOFF HAPLIN
Outdated, offensive, a weary idea
begging to be put out of its misery.

FRANKIE & THE KNOCKOUTS
BELOW THE BELT (MILLENIUM)
Art Direction:
SPENCER DRATE
Illustration:
BRIAN ZICK
One has to concede grudgingly that this
wizened old idea has been executed
with a certain amount of wit.

DAVID ESSEX
STAGE STRUCK (MERCURY)
(Uncredited)
An uninteresting record wrapped in
dreary banality.

BUCKS FIZZ
HAND CUT (RCA)
Design and Art Direction:
ANDREW CHRISTIAN
Concept and photography:
JOHN THORNTON
Comically self-aggrandising, classically
awful.

STEVE HACKETT

HIGHLY STRUNG

STEVE HACKETT
HIGHLY STRUNG (CHARISMA)
Painting:
KIM POOR
Traditional guitarist goes ''modern''.
Sense of judgement highly suspect
where concomitant album sleeve is
concerned.

MEN AT WORK
BUSINESS AS USUAL (EPIC)
Illustration:
JOHN DICKSON
Even by the standards of the genre,
simply hideous.

IRON MAIDEN
PIECE OF MIND (EMI)
Design and Concept:
IRON MAIDEN,
ROD SMALLWOOD,
DEREK RIGGS
Illlustration:
DEREK ''MR DEATH'' RIGGS
Photography:
SIMON ''BULLSEYE'' FOWLER
Proof that one of the most commercially
successful LPs of the year can still have
one of the dullest and most amateurish
covers.

IMAGINATION
NIGHT DUBBING (R&B)
Concept and Art Direction:
DIANE WALLER, TIM GATES
Photography:
PHIL SURBEY
Inexplicably dull, it sells nothing, least
of all the group.

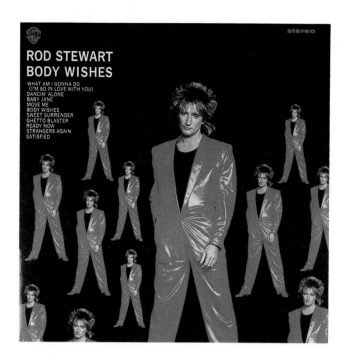

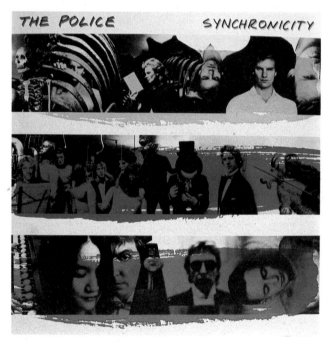

ROD STEWART
BODY WISHES (WARNER BROTHERS)
Design and Art Direction:
KOSH & RON LARSON
Photography:
BOB BLAKEMAN
An acknowledged steal from 'Elvis' Gold Records Vol. 2', down to the positioning of the typography it ends up looking like a thoroughly inferior compilation album.

THE POLICE
SYNCHRONICITY (A&M)
Design and Art Direction:
JEFF AYEROFF WITH NORMAN MOORE
Photography:
DUANE MICHALS
Super-attentive to detail in most other respects, The Police still have trouble with their record sleeves. This is their most ineffectual to date.

STEVIE NICKS
THE WILD HEART (MODERN)
Design, Photography,
Art Direction:
HERBERT WHEELER WORTHINGTON III
Given the number of people who must have a voice in the marketing of Stevie Nicks, it's difficult to imagine how a cover so clearly devoid of anything attractive or interesting could have passed the corporate test.

CHRISTOPHER CROSS
ANOTHER PAGE (WARNER BROTHERS)
Design and Art Direction:
CHRISTINE SAUERS
Illustration:
LOUISE SCOTT
The flamingo motif makes its reappearance, bigger and more uncomfortable looking. Cross looks big and uncomfortable inside, but at least he's shaved off that silly little beard.

THE BEAT
WHAT IS BEAT? (ARISTA-GO-FEET)
Design:
C. MORE TONY
Illustration:
IAN WRIGHT
"They have a hit. Let's get a compilation out. Something fragmented, something ska, something Ian Wright for the cover. How about a jigsaw concept? Love it. Can we get it out in a week?"

THE KINKS
STATE OF CONFUSION (ARISTA)
Design:
HOWARD FRITZSON
Photography:
ROBERT ELLIS
Terribly uninteresting in every respect.

THE ISLEY BROTHERS
BETWEEN THE SHEETS (EPIC)
Photography:
DAVID KENNEDY
A person with no taste's idea of romance and sensuality.

DEMON
THE PLAGUE (DEMON)
Drawings:
MIKE HANNAN
Devoid of anything that makes sleeves interesting.

HAYSI FANTAYSEE
BATTLE HYMNS (REGARD)
Photography:
SIMON FOWLER
Graphics:
GRAHAM SMITH
Cartoons:
DAVID THOMAS
Extraordinarily bad cover for a band that
puts so much emphasis on style.

DIO
HOLY DIVER (VERTIGO)
Design and Art Direction:
SIMON LEVY AND JERI McMANUS
Concept:
WENDY DIO
Illustration:
RANDY BERRETT
The precise point at which pomposity
meets stupidity.

YOKO ONO
IT'S ALRIGHT (I SEE RAINBOWS)
(POLYDOR)
Design:
YOKO ONO
Photography:
BOB GRUEN
Artwork:
BILL LEVY/BOB HEIMALL
The back cover, on display here, is
flabbergastingly tasteless, the kind of
thing a bootleg competition might at
least do with some style.

BOB MARLEY AND THE WAILERS
CONFRONTATION (ISLAND)
Illustration and Art Direction:
NEVILLE GARRICK
Irrelevant, dated, undignified, risible.

THANKS . . .

David Bowie: Returned, more popular than ever, shrewdly anticipating what his audience wants.

Elvis Costello: General excellence.

Malcolm McLaren: Plunder leading to pleasure, with one of the year's most entertaining LPs.

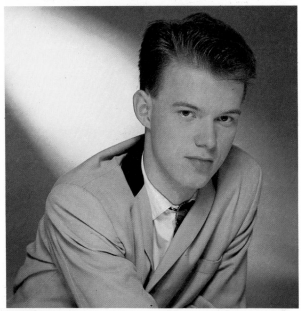

Edwyn Collins of Orange Juice: An acute view of pop's absurdities.

Marc Almond: Still full of surprises.

King Sunny Ade: Livened everything up.

Marvin Gaye: Resurgence with a vengeance.

Wynton Marsalis: Trumpeter of the year.

Wham!: Make other "dance" groups look gauche.

Eurythmics: A series of terrific records.

Squeeze: Unswerving entertainment over the years, to be continued no doubt by Difford and Tilbrook.

Blondie: It was time to throw in the towel and they did. The empty venues said the rest.

The Police: One dazzling single, 'Every Breath You Take', from a lacklustre LP.

Robert Wyatt: A wonderful voice, back in the foreground.

Aztec Camera: Best new(ish) group.

Renee & Renato: The year's most entertaining video.

Madness: Finally cracking America after four years.

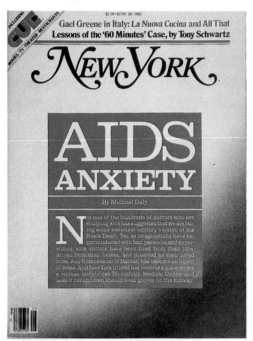

AIDS: Just as everybody was getting bored with herpes.

KajaGooGoo: The year's flimsiest successful group.

Boring interviewee 1: **Pete Wylie** of Wah!

Boring interviewee 2: **Bono** of U2

Overused instrument of the year (and the one before that): **The Linndrum**

Video Nasty 1: Promo films in which the (male) singer is pawed by a scantily clad model (here, **David Bowie**).

Video Nasty 2: Promo films shot in Sri Lanka (principal exponents: **Duran Duran**).

Kids From Fame: Popularisers of leg warmers and homilies about hoofing.

Must You Reform? 1: **Crosby, Stills and Nash**

Must You Reform? 2: **Yes.**

Rod Stewart: The most tedious LP of his career.

Style Council: Crown princes of pretentious manifestos.

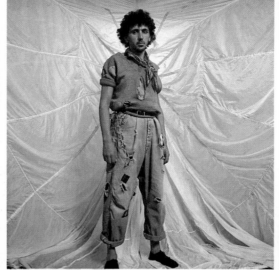

Depression Chic 1: **Kevin Rowland** with backdrop.

Depression Chic 2: **Jo Boxers** al fresco.

Supertramp: Still the world's most boring group.

Intense Young Men of the Year: **Tears for Fears.**

Rock Stars in Ropey Movies: **Sting** in 'Brimstone and Treacle'.

Neil Young and his vocoder: Remember what it did for Peter Frampton.

Can We Have It In Writing This Time?: The break-up of **Thin Lizzy.**

Duck You Sucker Dept: Disco Mixes, Dance Mixes, Party Mixes.

THE BUSINESS YEAR/UK

How long can this go on? A further 10% decline in album sales during 1982 when the figures were finally, with many a wince, totted up by the BPI. The previously trenchant singles' market had declined by a couple of percentage points and the value of pre-recorded cassettes, although up again, was offset by an even bigger rise in sales of blank tape. This is no business for the faint-hearted, but results like these are scaring a music business already chopped back to the minimum possible manpower more than might be divined by the casual viewer of £50,000 promo videos on *Top of the Pops*.

A hint of the behind-the-scenes alarm emerges now and again in the football manager-style chopping and changing of managing directors of major record companies — and there have been plenty of them this past 12 months. Some have done such a good job they have been head-hunted in the hope that some of their magic will rub off at the new location. Others have been exhausted by the strain and moved gently sideways out of the limelight. They also drop from sight totally if things have fared particularly badly. At WEA, for instance, the year has seen the end of the Charles Levison and Tarquin Gotch reign, which over 30 months produced barely a worthwhile new British signing, and more importantly, a diminishing number of American hits, which always displeases the Warner Communications moguls over in Burbank.

Levison has been replaced by the 32-year-old Rob Dickins, who has been finding new talent for the Warner Brothers Music UK publishing company for the past eight years or so, and equally consistently steering the firm to the top publisher's position. He signed the Sex Pistols as songwriters and stuck with them while faint-hearted record companies shook in their shoes. He saw

ROB DICKINS

something in ramshackle ska-crazies Madness and fronted up enough money for their initial demos. Needless to say he has hung on to their vastly profitable publishing interests too. Wah!, Whitesnake, Vangelis and Echo and The Bunnymen are all Dickins captures — the last-named also signed to his Korova label and reached the Top Five with *The Cutter*. He immediately brought in former Stiff general manager Paul Conroy to look after sales and marketing, and with a new A&R team installed, WEA is obviously going to be a force in the new acts market. The company's singular failure to provide the Americans with a now-fashionable English band to join the invasion of the US

charts in the past 12 months must have contributed to the old regime's departure.

In fact, the recent success story of new Brit-rock in America is just about the only positive factor to come out of the UK business this year, and A&R-led operations like Phonogram and Virgin are reaping the benefits of taking a few risks. As this is being prepared, there are 17 British artists in the American Top 40.

Having overseen the revitalisation of the PolyGram group in the UK, South African David Fine was promoted to the main board of the giant PolyGram leisure conglomerate which is jointly-owned by Dutch Philips and German Seimens. His place was filled

by the talented Ramon Lopez. How far were these two powerful men responsible for what turned out to be the biggest record industry story of 1983?

The whole business was amazed back in early July when plans were announced to create a vast new company that would bring together the European might of PolyGram and the American mega-muscle of WEA. For some months there had been speculation that the Seimens arm of PolyGram was anxious to see the back of its loss-making music interests and the company's statement admitted that it would be Philips that would be the principal partner in the merger. Seimens would substantially decrease its share in the music field. After reading the financial bottom lines in Burbank and Baarn, Holland, it seems pretty obvious that the "new structure that will enable the companies to deal more efficiently with the problems confronting the recorded music industry" has been forced upon the prospective partners by a business downturn that has hit the whole world.

More to the point, although the statement stressed that the separate identity and artistic integrity of each party's major labels would be preserved, hundreds, or possibly thousands, of jobs will be lost in the inevitable rationalisation of sales, distribution and service departments. Britain could lose even more of its disc pressing capacity — plants are already under pressure from the steady outflow of album pressing work to slick new factories in France and Germany with plenty of spare capacity and lower overheads than their ageing British rivals. In the UK and Europe the "PolyWarner" behemoth will be a 50-50 arrangement and will command vast resources of both finance and repertoire. Meanwhile Britain will be left with four major record companies — CBS, EMI, RCA and PolyWarner — if anti-trust lobbying by their rivals in the USA and Europe does not succeed in keeping the hopeful pair apart. And what of the poor artists who might well be frightened away from the company because of its sheer size? Time will tell.

RCA, meanwhile, has also experienced a change at the top. This time it was cheery American managing director Don Ellis who was wooed back to New York for succeeding so well in London. An absurd wait for the announcement of his successor followed...absurd because everyone in town knew that Regard Records boss David Betteridge was already occupying a floor at RCA HQ with his (so far) disappointing little record company and was just about the only man with the right credentials to take over the helm. Nobody was surprised when he took the job in April, although one or two eyebrows were raised when A&R chief Bill Kimber quit the same week.

Neither was EMI immune from the epidemic of musical chairs. Long-serving Cliff Busby — a former sales rep with the common touch and the true record man's feel for a hit coupled with a hint of low cunning — was taken out of the firing line having seen the slumbering giant of Manchester Square back among the biggies. He went off to look after international sales for EMI Music, and in flew young Peter Jamieson from Australia having just missed one of EMI's newest hopes, KajaGooGoo, hit the top of the singles charts. Out went regional UK director and acknowledged troubleshooter Richard Robinson, his hatchet-man tasks completed. Jamieson quickly imposed his authority with the wholesale clear-out of EMI's promotion department.

No such upheavals at CBS, however. Maurice Oberstein is now regarded as the grand old man of the British record industry, despite his New York antecedents, and his status was confirmed early in the year when he was voted, unopposed, to chair the British Phonographic Industry (BPI) to replace the popular and respected Chrysalis chief Chris Wright who stood down in order to concentrate more heavily on problems closer to home. CBS and Epic consistently came up with winners — perhaps fewer than

MAURICE OBERSTEIN

DAVID BETTERIDGE

they have become accustomed to — but nonetheless Men at Work, a revitalised Bonnie Tyler, the wealth of major talent that flows through its release schedules from America, all kept record store tills ringing, while distributed labels like A&M and Virgin filled in the rare gaps.

Only months before he took up his chairmanship of the BPI, though, Oberstein demonstrated one of his other talents — the one for setting cats among pigeons. For months the BPI-sponsored and BBC-broadcast charts had been in a complete mess. The old research contract with the British Market Research Bureau came to an end on December 31, 1982, and for the previous few months what were officially termed "odd things" had been happening. Singles lacking in even the most cursory national airplay were suddenly in the Top 20, and it was plain that something had gone badly wrong in BMRB's normally reasonably sensitive anti-hyping system. It turned out that a top executive had been taking bribes from an interested party — probably an independent promo man who wanted to load the dice — thus cutting out all that expensive "impact marketing" (giving away vast quantities of freebies), "ticking up" (putting your own sales figures into the supposedly sacrosanct diaries in the 750 or so chart shops) or "buying in" (sending teams of housewives around the chart stores to purchase enough copies of a single for it to register in the lower reaches). The miscreant was BMRB's final security checker. He vanished as soon as the spotlight was shone his way amid lurid tales of Volvo cars changing hands at the dead of night. The police were called in, and all parties concerned promised their utmost co-operation. Still no charges as this is written, though.

The replacement chart was the all-new, super hi-tech, computerised data capturing system developed by well-known pollsters Gallup. It came on-stream with less than half the projected 250 stores hooked into the system, which automatically records every record sold. With such a tiny sample, and the special data-capture tills an easy identification pointer, the new lists of chart shops was known to every record label in London

DON ELLIS

CLIFF BUSBY

Companies were told to report any special offers to Gallup, which was given full backing to remove suspect records from the chart. Since February several singles, some by major artists, have been dumped from the Top 100, and while the Gallup sample remains pitifully small, hyping the chart is now back within manageable parameters.

The majors cleaned up in the TV-advertised album stakes over the past year too, although not without having to deal with an alarming proliferation of independent televised merchandisers. First K-tel's managing director, Colin Ashby, split away to set up TV Records, heavily backed by Virgin's Richard Branson. . Then, his opposite number at Ronco, Sean O'Brien, struck out on his own with a label called TelStar, and before the lucrative run-up to Christmas 1982 was in full swing, yet a third operator — Starblend — set up shop. Before the year was out the British public had not less than 55 TV-advertised LPs to choose from, and predictably went for the stars and labels it knew. The result was that *The John Lennon Collection* on EMI outsold everything in sight and by mid January 1983, Colin Ashby was fighting a desperate battle to save his TV Records after Branson summarily cut off the cash flow. In four months Ashby had spent more than £1 million on TV advertising. "It may be that there are too many TV merchandised record companies," said Branson. A rare understatement.

Private Eye's favourite teenage millionaire was also, rather less directly, involved in the big publishing hoo-hah of the year, which at one stage threatened to change the face of pop music publishing. One Gordon Sumner had sued Virgin Music in a bid to end a publishing contract he alleged to be unfair. At the time he signed to Virgin he claimed he had been ignorant of the wily ways of the music publishing world and that the initial revenue split between him and Virgin, under which he received only 50% of the gross earnings of his song copyrights, was so unfair that he wanted a High Court judge to make Virgin return all £700,000 it had earned from his songs since 1976 plus the immediate return of his copyrights. Eleven days in court and about

£200,000-worth of court costs later, a new deal was thrashed out which gave Sting a significant improvement in the retrospective royalty rate, and 75%, rising to 80%, of all future earnings. By 1990 he will own all his copyrights too, an advantage even Paul McCartney cannot claim.

Sting was suing retrospectively, on the grounds that a 50-50 royalty split was unfair to the artist, and that he had not been properly legally advised. Only months before Gilbert O'Sullivan had

GILBERT O'SULLIVAN

managed to convince another High Court judge that his MAM publishing deal was unfair — although he had been able to prove a number of instances of chicanery. The judge agreed that the singer had been swindled and awarded him a vast sum in damages plus the return of his copyrights. Hard on the heels of the Sting case, Elton John decided to sue Dick James Music on similar grounds. By settling out of court, Sting's contract was not really tested, but as manager Miles Copeland remarked afterwards: "Music publishers will now think twice before signing a songwriter to a 50-50 deal without allowing the artist to see a skilled music business lawyer and without helping him find a record deal." Indeed, he was right, for only weeks afterwards, the Music Publishers Association recommended all its members

to insert a clause in standard publishing contracts demanding proper legal advice.

Branson pointed out that it was Sting's counsel's decision to settle, and that the singer had been advised by a lawyer at contract stage. "If he had won, no publishing contract in the country would have survived," said the relieved mogul, who also pointed out that the aggrieved Sting had, after all, received upwards of £900,000 under the "unfair" agreement in five years, with plenty more to come.

On the hardware front, the Philips Compact Audio Disc (CD) was born and was an immediate success. At first only the PolyGram companies were providing repertoire, to be followed into the format by Arista/Ariola, Chrysalis and CBS, but WEA and EMI held off for a while. New carrier formats have had a poor track record in the UK ever since the quad débâcle of the early seventies, and Thorn-EMI had only last year been forced to write off £25 million development costs when it pulled out of the doomed JVC video disc. The remarkable sound quality of the laser-read mini-discs and the widespread public enthusiasm for them quickly overcame entrenched attitudes, though, and the two companies were soon providing digitally-recorded music for the CD market. Start-up costs for Philips had been huge — the

within a matter of a fortnight, and more "odd things" were happening than ever before. Then Oberstein stepped in.

To promote singles by Men at Work, Toto and The Stranglers CBS offered cheap cut-out and picture discs through 100 named disc outlets via national newspaper advertising. Most of the shops turned out to be on the allegedly secret Gallup list and the BPI was swift to react this time.

Concern had been building up for some time about this particular method of influencing chart entries, ever since WEA pioneered the concept of giving away a copy of Elvis Costello's *Get Happy!!* album for every 'Head to Toe' single bought through nominated (chart) shops. But once Oberstein had shown up the faults in the system with his direct action — and there is little doubt that this was a deliberate ploy on CBS's part — the BPI pledged firm action to stamp out similar promotions within seven days.

CD was a spin-off from the tremendously expensive research for the LaserVision video disc — and may well have been one of the underlying causes of the "PolyWarner" amalgamation plans.

Of the smaller labels, Chrysalis was in the poorest shape at the outset of 1983. The once-easy route to the top via Blondie had long since vanished and nothing seemed to be going right. Then along came Spandau Ballet with their best song in ages — 'True' — and everything started to look rosy once more.

Island's tradition of breaking one big act a year was continued by the emergence as a mega-seller of U2, while its more esoteric approach to music paid off with the establishment of King Sunny Adé as the leading African performer here. Virgin's bout of "cheque-book A&R" of the previous years was continuing to pay off in a big way — Human League, Culture Club, Heaven 17, China Crisis, are consistently shifting units as well as spearheading the British invasion of the American charts.

A&M remains strong as long as Police are making records, but can't really count on Joan Armatrading, Supertramp and Joe Jackson to garner huge profits. The company, like MCA, is out on a talent search right now. Stiff was without a Madness disc for far too long, although the band is now committed long term to the label again, but made up with

THE BELLE STARS

novelty hits like Tracy Ullman's 'Breakaway' and a whole bunch from The Belle Stars. Beggars Banquet has managed to replace the fast-fading Gary Numan with bright acts like Freeez. Arista/Ariola went through a bad spell, losing Haircut 100 and scoring retrospective hits with The Beat, only to see the band leave. Bright spots were the Dionne Warwick singles and LP.

The year ends with copyright in a terrible mess. There is no sign that the Tory government wants to protect the record industry from the ravages of home taping, despite its moves to protect the video industry from piracy. Profit margins are still too low and there is a shortage of investment funds. A Mintel Market Intelligence Report on Records and Tapes reported that the price of records in the UK has been falling in real terms since 1978, and predicted the beginning of the end of pure audio as a mass entertainment medium. The new media are here already in the form of video, and embryonic cable, which will certainly become a major music carrier. The bulk of record companies now place heavy emphasis on audio-visual aspects of their business, and MTV in America has begun to pick up big advertisers. Perhaps, as even more adventurous plans are hatched to provide non-stock rock via satellite, the British record business will begin to change course and become more like the publishing industry — serving as a creative centre and catalyst for the world market, and collecting its revenue via exploitation of its copyrights rather than the direct selling of black pvc discs to punters. The industry's brighter brains are already considering these routes. Whatever happens, something must change. How long can this go on?
JOHN HAYWARD

THE BUSINESS YEAR/US

The password at record companies in the US this year must be "The Australian Invasion". That, or "MTV", or some combination of the two. From the outside, it would appear that optimism is abounding. Sales are up thanks to video; new acts, though predominantly Australian and British, are being broken; but a cold sliver of fear still lurks in the hearts of US record company executives, particularly when it concerns

signing new American acts.

Talent scouting, the true vocation of any A&R person, has fallen by the wayside over the past few years. The results of this are being seen this year in all the non-American acts topping the charts. According to Paul Turner, the head of WEA Australia and president of that country's Record Industry Association, "US record companies have panicked. They're not signing new acts as they used to, and

they're not taking any chances." This is not to suggest that US record companies should be out on the streets, as they were in the sixties, signing anyone who could play three chords on the guitar and knew the words to 'Blowin' in the Wind', but there is such a thing as too much caution. Reorganisation within the industry is certainly called for.

Clearly, record companies in the US became a little too

accustomed to putting out very little money and making a lot, which is no longer possible. Costs for recording, promotion (including pay-offs to radio, etc.), industry salaries, and so forth have in no way reflected the true state of the economy in this country over the past few years. With foreign product, the original recording and advance costs are negligible, and more money is therefore available for "promotion". US record companies have set themselves up so as to make it nearly impossible to break new American acts.

Chrysalis, this past year riding high on Toni Basil's number one single, 'Mickey', closed a deal with CBS for distribution, thus ending the label's six-year run as an independent. This year, too, RCA "acquired interest" in Arista records. The press release from Arista reads, "Under the agreement, Arista will remain a fully independent company, with product distributed by RCA Records National Sales Branch Organisation." Arista president Clive Davis is quoted as saying, 'As the industry changes, we have been looking into means by which we can continue to develop as a trend-setting, viable company in the pre-recorded music industry." Mr Davis' lofty aspirations did not completely discourage a suit filed by independent distributors the Schwartz Brothers, who filed against both Arista and RCA in April of this year. However, the suit was finally settled out of court for an undisclosed sum. Nor can the US have much confidence in a company whose two top-selling acts this year were not American but British (A Flock of Seagulls and The Kinks). Are we doomed to watch all the US-based record companies swallow each other up in distribution deals for the next decade?

Record companies continue to fume over home taping and video games. Stanley Gornkov, the president of the Recording Industry Association of America (RIAA) was once again unable to persuade Congress to pass the Mathias Amendment, which would have added a royalty tax on the sale of blank tape. Glen Boyd, manager of Penny Lane Records and Tapes in Tacoma, Washington, wrote a commentary article in *Billboard* this past year entitled "Taping: Cause or Symptom", which effectively addresses the home taping issue. "Where sales are being lost," he points out, "is in pre-recorded tape. The reason is simple economics. A pre-recorded cassette which I sell for $7.79 will provide approximately 45 minutes of music on a tape of fair quality. A blank UDXL II cassette, which I sell for $5.19, will yield 90 minutes of music on a tape of superior quality."

Meanwhile, CBS engineers claim to have developed a hardware-dependent spoiler system to prevent home taping, although there are no plans to introduce the system to the US any time in the near future, due to "political considerations". CBS has made no official comment on this rumour, although "insiders" claim that CBS has indeed come up with a system where recorders equipped with a special device would be prevented from recording discs or tapes containing an electronic signal that would activate the device and de-activate the recorder. Naturally, this is not the kind of device consumers are going to be insisting to have added to their tape recorders, so in order for the system to work the US government would have to mandate that all recorders sold contain the anti-tape device. The chances of Congress passing such legislation, unpopular with their constituents, is more than slim. CBS is hoping, according to these same unidentified insiders, to manufacture this device in other countries, notably Britain, where home taping is already illegal, before trying to bring the technology home.

Another phrase being bandied about this year is "compact disc". CDs are being touted as the closest thing to being in the recording studio. These laser-etched mini discs are reported to be virtually indestructible, so that no amount of dust, dropping or casual use will affect the quality of their sound. CD players do not use needles, so the records cannot skip. CDs do not warp. The problem with CDs is that they will cost upwards of $20 and the CD player (not counting amp, pre-amp and speakers) will cost anywhere from $800 to $1,500. Will America trade in its stereo systems and albums and start all over again? At this juncture it seems unlikely. Those who listen to records often have extensive collections and will not take kindly to rebuilding from scratch. It is not at all the same as going from victrolas and 78 r.p.m records to mono and 33⅓ r.p.m, however much the industry would like to look at it that way. For the same reason that laser video discs have not taken off to the same degree as video recorders, CDs will have trouble competing with technology in cassette taping.

This brings us to the question of video — perhaps not really a question, because almost everyone in the industry will tell you that video is saving the market-place. MTV has sold more new music to consumers this year than radio has in the last five years, if only because MTV reaches its audience on a national level while radio reaches a more localised group of people. Still, Steve Kahn, the former director of the video department at RCA, contributed an interesting commentary for *Billboard* this year called "Video and the Bottom Line". "Record companies," he wrote, "will have to rethink what they are doing and what they can do with video. Because the money spent on videos is non-recoupable, record companies tend to be careful about how they spend their dollars... You can't spend $200,000 on a clip that's going to be shown for nothing... I don't think the recording industry can afford to support another art form. The industry has to support selling records, period."

To this end, the marketing of the video single has begun. The Sony Corporation recently released three 10-to-15 minute video cassettes which retail for $15.95 in Beta format and $19.95 in VHS. Full-length music videos have not sold well in the past, according to Sony executive John O'Donnell, because of three problems. "One, sound quality. To get the video at that length, you have to give up good sound. Two, they're too expensive. And three, the length is a problem... video demands closer attention, and rather than watch it over and over, people would say, 'I don't have an hour and a half, and besides, some of the songs are boring.' People bought 60 million video games last year. We think that if they're willing to pay $29 for a game, they'll spend half that for a cassette they can play over and over." The votes are still out on that rather convoluted bit of reasoning.

The music news story that received the greatest amount of press in the US this year was the second annual US Festival, staged once again by computer whiz-kid Stephen Wozniak. The festival was held over Memorial Day weekend (May 28-30) in Devore, California, in the San Bernardino Valley. At this stage, it has lost several million dollars (there are

possible ways to recoup the lost money through film rights and so forth). It also resulted in two deaths, 26 injuries and 137 arrests. The two people who died at the event were both young men: one murdered with a piece of piping during an apparent drug dispute, the other found dead in the parking lot due to natural causes or a drug overdose. The most serious injury was incurred by a 12-year-old girl who was run over by a car while in her sleeping bag in the parking lot.

The tussles between the featured acts were few but interesting. A Flock of Seagulls and The English Beat had a brief argument over who would follow whom on the bill. John Cougar pulled out early because he didn't want to give up his video rights, according to a Cougar aide. According to Unison president Peter Ellis, the problem was that Cougar asked for an additional $50,000 to appear at the Festival and pulled out when he didn't get it.

The most widely publicised débâcle was The Clash's press conferences, the first of which was held in Los Angeles right before the Festival. During this conference, Joe Strummer compared the Festival to "cat food", explaining, "it's being marketed as such." The second press conference was held just before The Clash took the stage, and the band once again denounced the Festival, sneering that the money would have been better spent helping the unemployed in California. They then said they would use their money to help new English bands. The Clash's press agent, Cosmo Vinyl, got into a fist fight with the Festival stage crew when they pulled the plug after waiting 15 minutes for the band to come back for a second encore. By this time, it must be added, most of the fans were already heading for the exits. Ellis, in an understandably ungracious moment, was heard to snarl, "I bet they can't even *spell* socialism."

There have been some amusing news items this year as well. For example, The Bee Gees lost their much ballyhooed lawsuit over the copyright to 'How Deep Is Your Love', from *Saturday Night Fever*, to an amateur suburban musician named Ronald H. Selle. Selle, an antique dealer and church choir director, has sued the brothers Gibb on the basis that they had infringed on 12 bars of his song, 'Let It End', and worked the bars into their hit. The Bee Gees had won their first Grammy award in 1977 for their performance of 'How Deep', which Selle claimed he wrote one morning while shaving. Selle copyrighted the song but never published or produced it commercially. He testified that he had sent 14 demo tapes to record and music publishing companies and that only eleven of those tapes were returned. Robin Gibb was last heard screaming, ''It's lies!'' proving once again that grammar is not a necessary tool for songwriters.

A former Hell's Angel turned Government informer claimed that the Angels have had a contract out on Mick Jagger's life since Altamont. Altamont, you will recall, was the scene of the famous Rolling Stones concert-film-cum-snuff-film, wherein movie-goers everywhere were treated to the sight of a Hell's Angel stabbing a member of the audience to death. According to ''Chuck'', a former member of the Oakland, California Angels chapter, the boys with big bikes didn't like the way Jagger dismissed them after the concert, and they've been holding a grudge for 14 years. The Hell's Angels naturally denied this allegation, pointing out that if they'd really wanted Jagger dead they certainly could have had the job done in the 14 years since the occasion.

Jovan, who supported last year's Stones' tour, has now turned its mega-conglomerate eyes to country crooner Kenny Rogers. They have reportedly put together a line of fragrances named after two of Rogers' biggest hits: 'Lady' and 'The Gambler'.

''The Stones tour gave us a chance to reach our audience in a different way,'' explains Mitch Berk, Jovan's Director of Advertising. With Kenny Rogers, we're supporting a product launch, at the same time making possible a tour of one of the greatest names in music.'' A good thing for Kenny, too, because a blind item in gossip maven Liz Smith's recent column claims that a famous singer whose wealth has been reckoned in the several millions and whose homes have been photographed left and right is bouncing checks all over Los Angeles. Is that *you*, Kenny? You do have a lot of real estate . . .

Finally, one of the best lines of the year came not from anyone remotely concerned with the music business, but from our own New York State Senator Daniel P. Moynihan. Upon hearing that Secretary of the Interior James Watt had banned The Beach Boys from this year's Fourth of July festivities on the Washington Mall because they ''attract an undesirable element,'' Moynihan was quoted as saying, ''If I understand correctly, The Monkees, The Turtles, The Beatles — indeed, The Animals — are already extinct without any assist from Mr Watt.'' Indeed, many Americans wondered why The Beach Boys were considered un-American by Mr Watt while glittery, sequin-smothered Wayne Newton is comparable in Watt's mind only to apple pie. Ah well. As Dick Clark always says, the beat goes on. DREW MOSELEY

UK INDEPENDENT

*"Money! It's a hit
Don't give me that do goody good
    bullshit . . ."*

I begin with a quote from Pink Floyd not as some sort of grotesque financial irony, nor even to introduce my pet theory of Roger Waters as a lyrical visionary (it's true; check any year for social comment and you'll find that theme on the previous year's Pink Floyd LP) but simply because if there was one consistent thread to the independents' year then Money (or lack of same) was definitely it.

The optimism of last year's independent planners was based to a large degree on the naive assumption that the major record companies would be content to allow themselves to wither on the vine. They weren't, of course, and with the continued blurring of the fine line between upwardly mobile independents and belatedly awakening majors, the Goliaths now exploited to the full their one resource not available to — indeed previously a taboo subject to — the would-be Davids: money.

FARMERS BOYS

Why, came the sirens' call, should ambitious bands have to hang around with those seven stone commercial weaklings, the independents? Why not come with us and our muscular marketing budgets? To those inexperienced in the joys of the Sisyphean task of trying to wrestle the uncoordinated (and frequently apparently totally unconnected) departmental limbs of a major record company into something approaching concerted action, this wonderfully uncomplicated view must seem an attractive proposition and inevitably there were those who took the bait.

Dead or Alive went to CBS, Mari Wilson and Carmel linked arms with the Phonogram group and The Farmers Boys left Backs Records of Norwich for EMI who also signed that tireless self-publicist Chris Sievey, fresh from The Freshies. Cabaret Voltaire finally decided to seek pastures new and quit Rough Trade for Some Bizzare and subsequent British release through Virgin for some of their most direct and commercial material to date. Scritti Politti and Aztec Camera, too, were the objects of cynical poaching attempts by majors who earlier on wouldn't have given them the time of day let alone demo time.

And if Rough Trade couldn't hang on to their acts, then what hope had anybody else? With the exception of the fanatical or strong-willed like Crass or Factory, were independents now doomed to become nothing more than cheap A&R breeding grounds for wealthy multinationals? Last year Island Records signed more labels (including Belgian art factory Crepuscule) than they did bands. Was satellite status the best the future could offer an independent label?

There was even an alarming point in the year when it seemed as if Rough Trade itself — the textbook case of a small business that had expanded too quickly — might fold. With the crisis now past, Rough Traders are now naturally keen to minimise its importance, preferring to see it as a rationalisation and upgrading of certain unsatisfactory departments. While in retrospect there was never any real danger that Rough Trade would go under, the problems highlighted are relevant to the independent scene as a whole.

Money, perhaps predictably, was the root of the problem. So, given the problems of cash flow of any under-capitalised business, how do you compete with the financial muscle of the majors?

One answer came from the USA, where the steady progression of New Wave standards of musicianship now coincided with the natives' rediscovery of life before stadiums to give rise to that nebulous entity called New Music. In their desperation to acquire their piece of the new

CARMEL

AZTEC CAMERA

philosophers' stone, the American majors unwittingly threw the struggling British independents a financial lifeline. A US deal with US dollars for the likes of Aztec Camera or Modern English could now provide the cash necessary for the likes of Rough Trade or 4AD to compete with the majors for new talent. Thus Rough Trade were able to secure the highly-rated Manchester band The Smiths to a long-term deal in the face of huge advances dangled by majors in what was termed "a conscious decision of preference." One hopes this will herald a significant reversal of fortunes for the depleted independents.

Secondly, independent labels were now finding that their records were selling all over the world. Individual bands aside, on a larger scale this was either through the success of sister companies like RTD (Rough Trade Deutschland) or Boudisque in The Netherlands, or through label deals as in Rough Trade's link up with WEA in Canada. This was hailed in some quarters as a triumph for the policy of seeking — and waiting for, if necessary — like-minded people and working closely with them, but either way the welcome end result was extra cash at base camp.

Another major factor in the independents' battle to compete with the majors was the arrival on the domestic scene of IDS (Independent Distribution Services) who provided the non-aligned companies with access to a sales force they could afford. Where previously the established independent national distributors — Spartan, Pinnacle and The Cartel — were content in the main simply to distribute, IDS (the brainchild of former major employees) broke new ground by introducing the marketing techniques of the majors to the independent sector.

And certainly, in terms of breaking that all-important Top 75 barrier, IDS have been very successful very quickly. Among their "assists" can be chalked up Top 20 entries for Tom Robinson's 'War Baby' (Panic Records), Flash & The Pan's 'Waiting for a Train' (Ensign) and Elvis Costello's between-majors disguise as The Imposter with 'Pills and Soap' (Imp). Even Rough Trade used them to advantage to breathe chart life into Aztec Camera and Robert Wyatt.

This, you might think, would be the answer to every independent label's prayers. IDS' techniques in achieving such results, however, have been viewed with mounting apprehension in certain quarters of the independent sector and have raised a big question mark over the independents' attitudes towards such thorny questions as hyping and free records.

Traditionally, the independent labels have always walked a very thin line in terms of profitability on small-scale sales, but IDS' tactics of giving away large quantities of records and of giving very high rates of discount have meant that record shops have now come to expect this kind of service from all the other independents as well. These expectations are causing a lot of financial headaches among smaller operations. At what point, they question, does a record become self-sufficient? Are these tactics really good for business? The problem of whether the independents can really afford an IDS in the long term is one to which there is no evident easy solution.

One immediate effect these tactics have had, however, is that The Cartel have been forced to bring forward their much discussed central administration, which will include their own sales force in direct opposition. It will be interesting to see how labels and distributors alike respond to this new challenge.

Progress for The Cartel —the independent national distribution network formed by six regional distribution set-ups, Backs of Norwich, Fast Product of Edinburgh, Probe of Liverpool, Red Rhino of York, Revolver of Bristol and Rough Trade in London — has been slower than hoped for. Again restricted by lack of capital, the six — most of whom have also had own label operations to contend with — have concentrated on keeping their heads above water. Inevitably there have been problems in keeping six unequal partners headed in the same direction but Red Rhino at least thrived enough to open a second outlet in the English Midlands.

Yet while the independents' share of the market continues to increase, this year's optimism is distinctly guarded. Richard Scott of Rough

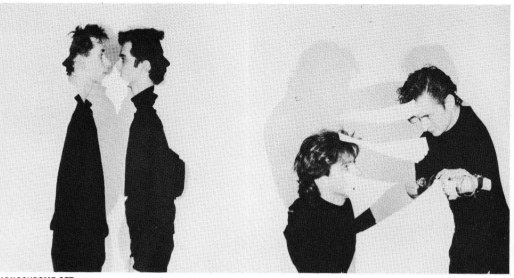

MONOCHROME SET

Trade's distribution department — in optimistic mood last year and a man whose predictions are generally fairly accurate — now views the rise of computer software and the approach of cable as heralding the decline of the vinyl record into a specialist market only. Scott also voices considerable reservations about the escalating costs and potentially fatal results of joining the majors in the Top 75 Entry poker game. Last year's dreams of exclusive distribution for certain labels have also gone — it is now considered potentially dangerous to grow dependent on labels like Mute or Y — and capturing this reduced specialist market on a sensible set of overheads is now seen as a more realistic alternative.

And so, as the distinction between what is "independent" and what isn't grows increasingly academic and hence ceases to be at all telling, future distinctions would now seem to lie in attitudes and ways of working rather than generalised labels like "independent". That is to say, between those trying to encourage base sales of new acts and those trying to attack the top end of the market in the same way as the majors. (It is interesting to note, incidentally, that these comments are in themselves a comment on how far the independents have come in the past couple of years.)

Movement of the year — in theory at least — was "Positive Punk": a banner invented by the exclusively Southern music press to describe the rise of an assortment of mainly Northern bands, most of whom promptly

disassociated themselves from such an unwelcome trendy-type label. The genre's flagship, Southern Death Cult, hit the rocks after only one single — the impressive 'Fat Man' on Situation 2 — though leader Ian Lindsay retains the Death Cult tag for future use. A posthumous album of radio sessions also appeared, this time through the offices of Beggars Banquet — a good idea.

Hardcore (i.e. negative) punk showed no signs of abating and kept the flag flying for individual labels, enlightened occasionally by some like The Newtown Neurotics who can actually write good songs. The more up-market, quality orientated labels — such as Dave Kitson's Red Flame (Artery, The Decorators, The Room) — in contrast found the going difficult for their more tasteful but less urgent music. Mention should also be given round about here for those two venerable institutions — Crass (and their many disciples) and The Cramps, both of whom deserve a medal for long service if nothing else.

Sales of imports were well up this year, mostly due to the initiative of the distributors, with items from Germany and Africa selling particularly well. Reggae too moved more and more into the limelight. Greensleeves Records in particular gave the lie to the popular impression that Rastas cannot handle business with total sales now over a million from some two hundred releases. With a good balance between Caribbean charismatics (such as Yellow-man and the wonderfully-

named Eek-a-Mouse) and home grown talent (like Clint Eastwood and General Saint, who even made it to daytime Radio One airplay), Greensleeves' rising star will be one to watch with interest.

Eastwood and Saint are on a long-term contract at Greensleeves but reggae remains something that the majors still have clearly no idea how to handle. Leading lights Aswad finally left CBS to return to the more sympathetic and in-touch independent network with their own Simba label.

Best placed amongst Class of '83 for labels were undoubtedly self-effacing Mute Records who wisely chose to consolidate instead of trying to expand. Proprietor Daniel Miller's quality control and regular chart entries from Depeche Mode and Yazoo kept integrity and cash flow healthy, with Yazoo notching up the noteworthy achievement of the first ever independent number one in the LP charts — something even UB40 hadn't managed.

Sadly Yazoo parted company as their record was released and then — unbelievably in view of their achievements with Mute and the independent distributors — assigned their individual futures to majors, with Alf going to CBS and Vince Clarke's fledgeling Reset label to RCA. Clarke himself, however, will continue to work with Mute, whose other forthcoming projects include persevering with the talents of Fad Gadget, Robert Rental and ex-DAF man Robert Gorl (amongst others), presenting the final burnt offering from

The Birthday Party and licensing the Throbbing Gristle back catalogue. More power to them.

Rough Trade had mixed fortunes but continued their general upward climb with hit singles and albums from Robert Wyatt — whose 'Shipbuilding' was one of the most welcome successes of the year — Aztec Camera and the Soweto compilation. Weekend, Chris & Cosey and The Go-Betweens proved hard work, but interesting acquisitions for the future have been The Smiths, hardy annuals The Fall, Ivor Cutler and a close relationship with American semi-independent Slash's offshoot Ruby Records. This has already produced a belated release for The Dream Syndicate's *Days of Wine and Roses* LP and promises the Violent Femmes' album which Geoff Travis sees as "one of the greatest American records for a long time."

Factory, dozing gently through their Section 25 *et al* releases, were given a real boost when New Order suddenly emerged from the slough of despond with a superb dance single in 'Blue Monday' and an at times quite brilliant LP in *Power, Corruption and Lies*. Y had a quiet year — a burst of releases followed by a long silence as Shriekback failed to make the

progress expected and Pigbag fell victim to the differing pressures of success and too much democracy. The core of Pigbag regrouped as Instinct, and the birth of the New York Connexion label was announced to license American funk, but lack of identity remains Y's main problem.

4AD and stablemates Situation 2 look set to continue on a steady course despite the loss of The Birthday Party and Southern Death Cult. The Cocteau Twins and Bauhaus-offshoot Tones on Tail sold healthily as did German newcomers Xmal Deutschland, while in The Icicle Works they could well have found their commercial crossover follow-up to The Associates. Colour Box also look a likely crew for the future.

Cherry Red, however, had problems with The Passage, Attila the Stockbroker, The Nightingales and Thomas Leer all leaving the label in disputes over promotion — or lack of it. Some of those remaining were also reported unhappy with the lack of commercial muscle. On the other hand, Cherry Red also continued their welcome (and cost effective) sideline in historical esoterica with archive releases from The Misunderstood, Can and a Monochrome Set compilation. Sales success came with Ben Watt and The Marine Girls in

various permutations and with a best-selling budget sampler album (*Pillows and Prayers*, cost just 99p). With their minimal recording costs and no great ambitions these projects seem ideal for the cost-conscious label, but are Cherry Red no more ambitious than to become a haven for the new folkies?

Cherry Red's MD Ian McNay also succeeded in getting himself elected to the industry's governing body, the BPI. Whether he can achieve any of his anti-hyping/marketing aims and thus give smaller labels a fairer chance in the chart stakes or whether he ends up talking to himself remains to be seen.

Casualties of the year included the Kamera and Fetish labels, while missing presumed hibernating were Fast Product and Charlie Gillett's Oval. Also apparently disappearing into limbo, after a much trumpeted entry as the new Postcard, were Kitchenware Records of Newcastle. Amongst other notable newcomers were Kabuki (attempting to nurture native Irish talent) and Go! Discs who showed style if indifferent taste with The Box, a pretentious crew of ex-ClockDVAtes from Sheffield who briefly became flavour of the month among people who ought to know better.

Other curiosities of note

included successful albums from veteran folkie Richard Thompson (*Hand of Kindness* on Joe Boyd's Hannibal label) and Bunnyman guitarist Will Sergeant (*Themes From Grind* on 92 Happy Customers — an outlet not entirely unconnected with Zoo). The Spirit of Garageland Memorial Award went to The Gymslips for their cheerful, cheeky *Rockin' With the Renees* LP (Abstract), and finally no survey would be complete without mentions of The Sisters of Mercy (on Merciful Release) and Cook Da Books (on Kiteland) for no other reason than that they're good.

And as for who's still alive and competing this time next year, that will depend on how well the labels can develop the ability to nurture the careers of their artists; and, where those artists who are making commercial records are concerned, on ensuring that they have enough money to make them work, even if it means not undertaking other projects. The result should be that they should be able to enjoy more of the fruits of their hard labours over the past couple of years.

"New car, caviar, four star daydream
Think I'll buy me a football team . . ."
IAN CRANNA

US INDEPENDENT

Meanwhile, over on the other side of the Atlantic, these are stirring times for independents. At the end of June 1983, Motown (the last label of any real size and consequence to have its records independently distributed) linked up with a revitalised MCA to have its product branch distributed by that major. Following as it did similar deals by Arista (with RCA) and Chrysalis (with CBS) within the previous six months, this move effectively turned the world of independent distribution on its head.

Cushioned for so long from having to know their business by the big accounts, the

independent distributors were now faced with the stark choice of coming to terms with independent labels of a size more popularly associated with the UK (and with the odds far more effectively stacked against them) or going out of business. And choices don't come much more fundamental than that.

Distribution in the US, it is worth recalling here, is a very different beast from that found in Britain. In the UK, one company can reach the length and breadth of the country. In the US — leaving aside the question of regional and demographic variations in taste

— sheer distances dictate otherwise, unless you happen to have the resources of a major. American distributors thus tend to fall into two groups — local distributors concentrating on a smaller range of labels (such as Motown, Arista, Chrysalis) and possibly specialist markets like Urban Contemporary, and the bigger boys who cover bigger territories and carry a greater range of smaller labels. In the end, of course, it is the stores which dictate who stays in business, usually by buying cheapest.

Inevitably there will now be rationalisations and mergers

with the independent distributors, and some have already thrown in the towel. With Motown gone, the remaining distributors will *have* to listen to the small labels if they want to stay around, and so for the independent labels there now arises a very real opportunity to harness the energy of change and make their views count. With the numbers of the majors steadily contracting by mergers and buy-outs, the consequences for the future of American music could be far reaching indeed.

In trying to assess the future for American independents in this highly volatile situation, it

169

is hard to see past the figure of Tom Silverman. Owner of the successful independent Tommy Boy label and the in-touch tipsheet *Dance Music Report* as well as being co-promoter of the extremely influential New Music Seminars, Silverman is an energetic, discriminating and successful entrepreneur. But even more significant, especially for an American, is that his field of vision extends beyond worship of the almighty dollar. Tom Silverman is independent because he likes it that way and this attitude will be a key factor in determining the future of the American independents.

Likeable and forthright without being overbearing, Silverman seems to thrive on tackling problems. He is even determined enough to question whether independent distributors are necessarily crucial to his operation. Left nursing a $90,000 debt by the bankruptcy of two of his Californian distributors, he promptly started selling direct (as the majors do) some 3,000 miles away from his New York base. The result was a 50% increase in his market share in the state, plus he was getting paid more per record, plus he was getting paid! He also gained the invaluable ground knowledge of where his records were selling and where work needed to be done.

Amost inevitably, Silverman is also involved in setting up the Independent Label Coalition. Formed to protect the interests of the independents — there will be no truck with major-affiliates like Slash or 415 — the ILC is a very diverse group. Headed by a council of nine, its members range from the established

Roulette group to committed individual projects like the acidic Rick Harte's Ace of Hearts label, while the music covered ranges from soul right through the spectrum to MOR.

At the time of writing, the fledgeling ILC comprised some 40% of the US independent labels which together represented a good 90% of the independent volume. By pooling their various skills and specialist knowledge, they hope to speak with one voice and act as a pressure group to get established institutions to become more responsive to their needs. They will also, Silverman enthuses, have street level resources that the majors can't even fathom, if they knew what the street was in the first place.

One aim high on the list of ILC priorities is to put pressure on *Billboard* magazine to redefine its methods of chart compilation away from its present heavy bias towards airplay (still the exclusive preserve of the majors) towards a sales-only basis. In the past year, records like New Edition's 'Candy Girl' and Afrika Bambaata's Soul Sonic Force's 'Planet Rock' have made the charts in Britain. In America this could never happen — even though they were outselling most acts listed in the Top 40 — simply because of this airplay weighting. Radio stations, Silverman complains, still hide behind the smokescreen of a record's supposed availability and take the attitude that only majors can make records for radio.

The other main objective for the ILC, Silverman believes, is to secure more responsive reporting and more upfront promotion from their

distributors. Since not everyone can — or even wants to — match Silverman's tireless energy and resourcefulness, there remains a definite role to be filled by an active independent distributor, especially in a land where there is no national TV, radio or music press to speak of.

For the independent labels this means not only being able to find out which stores are buying their records and which are not, but also the infiltration of discos and clubs, of all kinds of radio (pop included) to bring about crossover, the securing of in-store displays and turntable plays — the whole works. Since the labels themselves do not have the resources or the finesse to realise fully their marketing ideas, they now look to their distributors to resume this active role, much neglected in recent years.

The distributors are, after all, well paid for it. On the average $4.98 twelve-inch, they receive approximately 40 cents more per record from an independent than they do from a major. For the independent distributors, the target is now fairly clear: within the next five years they have to develop (and keep) the next Motown, Arista, Chrysalis from the ranks of the present independents if they want to stay in business. Some of them, Silverman notes acidly, might be happier in real estate.

Much has been made of the use of video in the development of a new musical climate — however uncertain — in America through the clubs and cable TV. Could this too be used as an effective mouthpiece for the independents? Silverman, however, pours scorn on the pioneer MTV for

being blinkered and close-minded, to the extent that their so-called "demographic targeting" popularly passes for racism by using black music only when it crosses over sufficiently (i.e. Michael Jackson) to appeal to white values. As soon as they have a rival, Silverman fervently hopes that MTV will pay dearly for targeting white audiences instead of mass appeal. Clearly many doors have yet to be opened before video can be an effective tool for the independents.

By using his resources properly and by restricting his releases to those which stand a working chance of success, Tom Silverman has turned Tommy Boy Records into a stable and successful market leader. Such success has naturally brought eager majors to his door in search of buying success. While every man has his price, Tom Silverman continues to pitch his asking price for Tommy Boy sufficiently high to deter all but the most infatuated of his suitors amongst the majors. "I'm just not interested," he says. "They can't do anything for me except take away my marketing freedom and I'm not really interested in that. Maybe they'll help crossover if it happens to be their priority that week, but I don't want to be at the mercy of some whitebeard's priorities for the week."

While their leadership remains with entrepreneurs like Tom Silverman, the future of the American independents is in good hands.
IAN CRANNA

EUROPE

Two events and the surfacing of an until-now underground cultural "movement", which in themselves stand for all that's good in Europe, sprang immediately to mind as soon as I switched on my ailing Smith-Corona. The events were, firstly, the week-long Tone &

Gegentone Festival held in Vienna early in June, and the riotous assembly of Gilbert Artman's 50-strong saxophone squadron, Urban Sax, in the theatres, on the streets, up the lamp-posts and on a variety of municipal vehicles, from flatbed trucks to hospital

stretchers, at the annual Bath Festival. Perhaps unsurprisingly, the "surfacing" was that of the Geniale Dilletanten group in Berlin, led by Einsturzende Neubauten.

The Tone & Gegentone (roughly, "Music & Anti-Music") Festival was held at

Vienna's Sezession Club, a big, airy place founded in the 1900s by Gustav Klimt and others of the Austrian "Sezession" Art Nouveau movement (a modern Sezession "school" still uses it as a gallery and club). The bill included The Residents, Glenn Branca, Terry Riley, Lydia

Lunch, Z'ev, showcases for local post-wave groups and a visiting posse of New York No Wavers, among them the promising Sonic Youth, and others. All but one of the evenings sold out, and that one was a near thing. Striking "post-constructivist" posters for the festival were all over Vienna, and on first sighting one I was dumbfounded that such an exotic event could not only occur but flourish, albeit with assistance from a state grant, when state aid in Britain is directed primarily at safe, traditional and essentially mainstream arts, with events like the ICA Rock Weeks and WOMAD festival not only having to seek private support (Capital Radio) but also break even or else. (I should also add, on a sober note, that the last ICA Rock Week did not do too well at all.) As with their licensing laws, I left Vienna envying its inhabitants what seemed to be an outward sign of State largesse towards the less populist arts...

The continued existence of Urban Sax also suggests a level of state support unseen in this country. From their two (now hard-to-unearth) albums on the defunct French label Cobra, Artman conceived the group as a reeds-dominated Magma boosted up to orchestral size, but from reports of their live appearances (the author having been elsewhere with a group of people wearing fibreglass eyeballs on their heads) these pale into insignificance alongside outrageously-conceived macro-theatre events where the group have been known to take over railway stations, hotels, large squares, even whole towns, each individual or unit of players "conducted" over walkie-talkie by Artman as he stood at the point where the orchestra would converge. Apart from the brilliance of Artman's concept (somewhere between the numerous mountain-top orchestras in Charles Ives' *Universal Symphony* and the somewhat more modest street performances of our own Mike Westbrook Band), that so enormous a "rock" group can come together for performances involving thousands of non-specialist punters in any city they play says there's something very healthy about parts of European music — even if much of it is looking decidedly sickly. It's said that, after the

Bath Festival and if enough funds can be found, Artman will be bringing the group to London in the late summer for an invasion of the Covent Garden Piazza and environs.

The most boisterous, and probably wide-ranging, event was undoubtedly the half-jokily termed "die Neue Deutsche Welle" (New German Wave), led by EN ("Collapsing New Buildings", after the new government building in Berlin that fell down promptly on completion), Abwarts, X-Mal Deutschland, Malaria! (née Kleenex) and others. Initial press coverage was so laudatory that even the multinational Phonogram/Mercury Records saw fit to release a compilation of "die Neue Deutsche Welle" bands, including, strangely, the ghastly minimal-schlager band Trio, who thankfully haven't been heard of since the unsuccessful follow-up to 'Da Da Da', 'Anna Letmein Letmeout'. Phonogram would now appear to have had second thoughts about the potential of The New Wave of German Bands — in its own small way, a self-fulfilment of their own prophecy.

Similar to but far more extreme than the British "industrial" bands, Einsturzende Neubauten and cohorts launch-off from a celebration of cultural atrophy, but unlike the British industrialist, who later claimed to be warning of collapse, they're actually cheering it on — and what better place to locate and date the closedown than in the heavily loaded metaphor of Berlin?

Beyond their extravagant manifestos, Einsturzende Neubauten certainly have the looks, and the noise. Their 12-inch EP, live tape and ZickZack album (aptly titled *Kollaps* and, perhaps not so aptly, featuring a visual echo of the *UmmaGumma* centrespread on the sleeve) have made them *the* hip thing to see in London and, recently, New York; gaunt young self-immolationists wielding a variety of found instruments (lumps of metal, cans, hammers) and industrial machinery over painful free and rhythmic anti-music, sometimes getting carried away and trying out road drills and monster wire cutters on the fabric on the auditorium they happen to be playing in. I get the impression that their

best performance would be one where they were accompanied by the sound of Russian tanks rolling over Berlin before setting off at a lick towards the Ruhr.

While no less grim, Abwarts (who share bassist Marc Chung with EN) are at least considerate enough to employ kinder rock structures; from their ZickZack releases and latest album for Mercury, *Der Westen Ist Einsam* ("The West Is Alone") they mix giddyingly ferocious post-punk swing with improvisations and electronics, topped off with sour political comment. Of the lot — because of their considerable power and root accessibility — they are the ones Most Likely To Win. Or should that be Lose?

Both Malaria! and X-Mal Deutschland started as feminist punks in the late 1970s. The former have progressed considerably — from recent outings, moving on to an experimental, Factory-style sound coupled with a bleak political/sexual outlook usually encountered among only the most cynical of German film directors. X-Mal Deutschland now sport a Token Male, and from their latest album, *Fetisch*, for Britain's 4-AD label, have the intent but none of the wild, bridling style of their compatriots in the Grim Zone. And after last year's promising David Cunningham-produced début, Palais Schaumburg's follow-up, *Lupa* — produced by, of all people, Sugar-Coated Andy Hernandez — was a bemusing, often inexplicable, fusion of their adventurous improvisations and Hernandez's American funk; the joins showed.

The subject is wide open to lengthy and pretentious armchair theorising, but these and other, lesser-known bands appearing on indie tape and vinyl labels, have picked up on an atmosphere that's been around in German cinema, literature and politics for some years now: the end is coming, our instinctive barbarism is beginning to show through, and the best you can do is help yourself to whatever's in sight while you sit it out. It would also seem to be more than just a punk flashback; older musicians I've spoken to, like Edgar Froese and Chris Franke of The Tangs, Can's Irmin Schmidt (who scored Reinhard Hauff's hopelessly depressing *Messer Im Kopf*) and Kraftwerk's Ralf Hutter have

all expressed similar opinions to varying degrees. Movie-critic friends say they've seen the same in German cinema, from "old wavers" like Fassbinder to the young bucks in their late teens who think anything more than a hand-held camera is bourgeois. The point, perhaps, is whether you consider it to be poseur scaremongering or the sharp end of realism. I wonder, as far as the music is concerned, if Deutsche Amerikanische Freundschaft realised what they started?

Tellingly, of that first wave of German music, both Irmin Schmidt and Micky Karoli have fled Cologne for the gentler climes of Southern France, and, although he refused to be drawn on the subject when last in London, rumour had it that Edgar Froese is/was considering disbanding Tangerine Dream and — echoes of *On the Beach* — taking his family to Australia. (He *would* admit that there were a number of groups in the swelling Australian electronics scene he wanted to collaborate with, but no more.)

Little of this shows up in the commercial German scene — like the rest of Europe, dominated by the 1,001 dialects of schlagermusik — although in a knock-on effect from the likes of DAF, intelligent young electropop bands like Die Krupps, Fehlfarben and Rheingold are now enjoying some success in the shops. A visit to the massive Saturn Records in Cologne (which dwarfs the London HMV store) found a healthy Can section, naturally, but a woefully unrepresentative selection of German new wave bands. Transatlantic dinosaur bands dominated the album charts, but one notable phenomenon is that some British bands of the Factory/Rough Trade/Cherry Red axis are releasing EPs and albums on small German labels that rarely, if ever, appear in Britain. As is happening elsewhere, Kitaro is now the biggest seller in the mood-electronics market, with over half a dozen albums loudly displayed. But alas, not one Einsturzende Neubauten or Abwarts album to be had for love or money...

To commit the unforgivable sin of lapsing into businessman's jargon, the Lowlands (to lump them into that rudely arbitrary region) seemed to develop a strong

171

"power base" over the last year. Les Disques du Crepuscule continued to expand, releasing solo and group works from Tuxedomoon (who, incidentally, visiting friends said were in a state of some depression having chosen self-imposed exile from America), Mania D, Hillcrest Club and other bands from across Europe. Crammed Discs, run by Marc Hollander, released a dub mix of the quirky Honeymoon Killers' album *Les Tueurs,* a moody Gilbert/Lewis-style album from Tuxmoon's Steven Brown duetting with Benjamin Louw, and a delightful, if very odd, duet EP from Hector Zazou, once of French filigree composing duo ZNR, and African percussionist Papa Wembou. And Holland's splendid Nasmak got as far as winning a British deal with the Aura label for their album *Duel,* full of taut, exploratory funk rhythms and strange Chinesey melodies. Keep an eye peeled, too, for Holland's Exploiting the Prophets, whose *The Thin King Man* frequently attains that level of eerie surprise of early Tuxedomoon.

As ever, with the commercial sector still panting along behind their British and American counterparts, it was the work of the likes of the excellent international Recommended Records network to keep the flow of information up about the forefront of European music. Most importantly, perhaps, the year marked the long-awaited return of ZNR, quiet for some years now. Their *Les Flots Bleus* continues the line of eccentric, humorous neo (cod?) classical vignettes, and if the mood was rather more sombre than their first two albums, at least the classical-quality pressing (after the glue-covered earlier albums) allowed a proper appreciation of what the duo are up to. Earlier in the year covered by this edition, Recommended released a splendid two-hour long double-album sampler (the duration achieved by the pressing process) featuring most, if not all, the bands from France, Germany, Holland, Spain, Italy, America and Scandinavia who distribute through their network — notables like The Residents, Henry Cow/Art Bears, Univers Zero, Stormy Six, Robert Wyatt, Faust, This Heat, Italy's brilliant and still

unrivalled Stormy Six as well as others who are but shouldn't be less well known. As well as pioneering European music, the label serves to make available albums from British notables Henry Cow/Art Bears in their various permutations: Chris Cutler and Fred Frith improvising live in Prague and Washington; singles and EPs from the likes of Lindsay Cooper, Cutler, Frith *et al*; and *Winter Comes Home,* an unlikely series of improvisations around 'Stormy Weather', *West Side Story* and others on which the above join the Pere Ubu singer to become David Thomas & His Legs. Packaged more like artworks than albums — glitter sleeves, see-through and picture discs, all manner of art inserts, fold-outs, booklets and so on — the *objects* themselves are often as fascinating as their contents. A very recommended, if you'll forgive the pun, s.a.e. to Recommended Records, 387 Wandsworth Road, London SW8, will put you in immediate touch with the most important music coming out of Europe.

A major arrival from Scandinavia — Norway to be precise — is that of the Strawberry label, being distributed here alongside its fellow countryperson, Uniton Records. Possibly conceived as a bridge between ECM and Sky, Strawberry has plugged into a strange vein of not-quite-avant-garde, not-quite-Mike Oldfield, contemporary rock composers — not all of them Norwegian — like Pluto, Hideaway, Bruce Stephens and Kit Watkins. The likes of Hideaway and Watkins produce a polite, mellow "progressive" sound, not too divorced from the likes of the late Tasavallan Presidentii. Stephens sticks out for being a recidivist Rock and Roll singer-songwriter.

Uniton is by far the most experimental of the two. Apart from *Will You Speak This Word,* the Gilbert/Lewis album mentioned elsewhere in this edition, they've signed Berlin composer Rolf Trostel and the very promising young post-punk electronic band, Holy Toy. Trostel stands on the periphery of the Schulze/Hoenig/Baumann area, but his *Der Prophet* is at the very least possessed of an engaging spirit in that context. Holy Toy are the most promising young band in Norway; a quartet led by a Polish refugee, Andrei Nebb,

whose début EP, 'Perfect Day', and follow-up, the 12-inch 'Soldier Toy', display a very strong, very unusual variant on the Mute school of electronics; at times even recalling the playful lunacy of The Residents, but always linked to a hard dance pulse. Watch out for them.

France provided little that caught my attention over the year. Handsome Dick Pinhas was silent — perhaps due to the disaster his London début the previous year turned out to be. So were Magma, and unless the nurse has been keeping their albums hidden because of my blood pressure, so were Tim Blake and Jean-Michel Jarre. Thank God.

However, the year in France was notable for the ascendance of Parisian electronic composer Bernard Szajner, the most engaged composer/performer in French rock today. Signed to Island, he put together a touring band — including ex-Magma bassist Bernard Paganotti — and surprised everyone by luring Howard Devoto onto the tour as guest vocalist. Like the previous, harrowing *Some Deaths Take Forever,* for a non-musician Szajner's compositions have sharp teeth and firm muscles, and lean towards the avant-garde rather than electronic mood-doodlings. A show I caught in Bordeaux was spectacular: hard, worrying electronic lead backed by an explosive rhythm section, occasionally graced by Devoto's enigmatic, oblique and sometimes vocal delivery. The tour also saw the début from Szajner's two new inventions: the Oestre, a stick-shaped ribbon-sensitive instrument which fires a green laser beam out of each end, scything through the roof and floor (*not* literally) as Szajner moved around on stage; and the Syeringe, the extraordinary laser-harp, shaped like an abstract sculpture, containing a field of laser beams which, when interrupted by Szajner's hand, triggered off notes on his synthesiser. Unsurprisingly, the London press — if not the audience — fell adoringly at Devoto's feet, much to his dislike, and slagged off this upstart Frog who dared to play with the godhead who had brought them The Buzzcocks and Magazine.

If to a lesser degree, Switzerland is experiencing the same upheavals as Germany;

street riots are regular occurrences — one happened outside the doors of the Zurich theatre in which The Residents played on their tour and led to their audience being tear-gassed — and at least one young demonstrator has followed Jan Palach and torched themselves on the street. Much of the musical accompaniment to this ruckus in (consumer) Paradise is bad, derivative punk, but the rise of Yello has given a sense of direction to a number of young post-punk bands, and the next band to watch out for are Zurich's Mort à Venise (which, apparently, in the vernacular can mean either Death in Venice or Dead Venice). They owe something to Yello in their style of devious electropop — perhaps understandably so, since they're being produced by Boris Blank — but from what I hear, they may have already been signed and released an album by the time this appears.

I doubt if mainstream Europe will ever catch up with Britain (maybe I mean overloaded London) — but then I long ago gave up on mainstream America getting anywhere close. Considering their media, the market and the way people use their entertainment, it's very probable that Britain is in fact the odd one out with its wide-ranging media, incestuous cults, high fad turnover, and the quaint notion that even business can involve a modicum of creativity (something no European businessman I met seems to have ever considered — perhaps, when it comes to doing the accounts, quite sensibly). But the European vanguard is capable, each year, of throwing up such forward-looking bands — often involving a quantum jump in terms of stylistic progression — that Britain and America rush to at best applaud and at worst copy them. For that I personally am eternally grateful. Doubly so in the case of Dieter Meier.

And did anyone notice that this year's Eurovision Song Contest featured two sanitised punk/electronics groups? It had to come.
JOHN GILL

THE YEAR'S CHARTS

FEATURING THE
BILLBOARD
AND MUSIC WEEK
CHARTS

U S   S I N G L E S

1. **EYE OF THE TIGER**
   Survivor-Scotti Bros
2. **ROSANNA**
   Toto-Columbia
3. **HURTS SO GOOD**
   John Cougar-Polygram
4. **HOLD ME**
   Fleetwood Mac-Warner Bros.
5. **ABRACADABRA**
   Steve Miller Band-Capitol
6. **HARD TO SAY I'M SORRY**
   Chicago-Warner Bros.
7. **DON'T YOU WANT ME**
   Human League-A&M Virgin
8. **THE NIGHTS ARE BETTER**
   Air Supply-Arista
9. **ONLY THE LONELY**
   Motels-Capitol
10. **KEEP THE FIRE BURNIN'**
    Reo Speedwagon-Epic
11. **LET IT WHIP**
    Dazz Band-Motown
12. **TAINTED LOVE**
    Soft Cell-Warner Bros.
13. **WASTED ON THE WAY**
    Crosby, Stills & Nash-Atlantic
14. **LOVE'S BEEN A LITTLE BIT...**
    Juice Newton-Capitol
15. **VACATION**
    The Go-Gos-I.R.S.
16. **DO I DO**
    Stevie Wonder-Motown
17. **CAUGHT UP IN YOU**
    .38 Special-A&M
18. **TAKE IT AWAY**
    Paul McCartney-Columbia
19. **STILL THEY RIDE**
    Journey-Columbia
20. **PERSONALLY**
    Karla Bonoff-Columbia

U S   A L B U M S

1. **ASIA**
   Asia-Geffen
2. **ALWAYS ON MY MIND**
   Willie Nelson-Columbia
3. **MIRAGE**
   Fleetwood Mac-Warner Bros.
4. **TOTO IV**
   Toto-Columbia
5. **STILL LIFE**
   Rolling Stones-Rolling Stones Records
6. **AMERICAN FOOL**
   John Cougar-Riva/Mercury
7. **EYE OF THE TIGER**
   Survivor-Scotti Bros.
8. **PICTURES AT ELEVEN**
   Robert Plant-Swansong
9. **GOOD TROUBLE**
   Reo Speedwagon-Epic
10. **SPECIAL FORCES**
    .38 Special-A&M
11. **GET LUCKY**
    Loverboy-Columbia
12. **ABRACADABRA**
    Steve Miller Band-Capitol
13. **THROWIN' DOWN**
    Rick James-Gordy
14. **KEEP IT ALIVE**
    Dazz Band-Motown
15. **THREE SIDES LIVE**
    Genesis-Atlantic
16. **DARE**
    Human League-A&M/Virgin
17. **ESCAPE**
    Journey-Columbia
18. **DREAMGIRLS**
    Original Cast-Geffen
19. **ALL FOUR ONE**
    Motels-Capitol
20. **TUG OF WAR**
    Paul McCartney-Columbia

U K   S I N G L E S

1. **FAME**
   Irene Cara-RSO
2. **COME ON EILEEN**
   Dexys Midnight Runners/EM Exp-Mercury
3. **DON'T GO**
   Yazoo-Mute
4. **DRIVING IN MY CAR**
   Madness-Stiff
5. **DA DA DA**
   Trio-Mobile/Phonogram
6. **SHY BOY**
   Bananarama-London
7. **IT STARTED WITH A KISS**
   Hot Chocolate-RAK
8. **ABRACADABRA**
   Steve Miller Band-Mercury/Phonogram
9. **I SECOND THAT EMOTION**
   Japan-Hansa
10. **A NIGHT TO REMEMBER**
    Shalamar-Solar
11. **STOOL PIGEON**
    Kid Creole & The Coconuts-Ze/Island
12. **NIGHT TRAIN**
    Visage/Polydor
13. **INSIDE OUT**
    Odyssey-RCA
14. **THE ONLY WAY OUT**
    Cliff Richard-EMI
15. **ME AND MY GIRL**
    David Essex-Mercury/Phonogram
16. **NOW THOSE DAYS ARE GONE**
    Bucks Fizz-RCA
17. **VIDEOTHEQUE**
    Dollar-WEA
18. **MUSIC AND LIGHTS**
    Imagination-R&B
19. **STRANGE LITTLE GIRL**
    Stranglers-Liberty
20. **TAKE IT AWAY**
    Paul McCartney-Parlophone

U K   A L B U M S

1. **FAME**
   Original Soundtrack-Various-RSO
2. **THE KIDS FROM FAME**
   Various-BBC
3. **THE LEXICON OF LOVE**
   ABC-Neutron/Phonogram
4. **LOVE AND DANCING**
   League Unlimited Orchestra-Virgin
5. **AVALON**
   Roxy Music-EG(Polydor)
6. **COMPLETE MADNESS**
   Madness-Stiff
7. **TROPICAL GANGSTERS**
   Kid Creole & The Coconuts-Ze/Island
8. **PICTURES AT ELEVEN**
   Robert Plant-Swansong
9. **CONCERT IN CENTRAL PARK**
   Simon & Garfunkel-Geffen
10. **ABRACADABRA**
    Steve Miller Band-Mercury/Phonogram
11. **MIRAGE**
    Fleetwood Mac-Warner Bros.
12. **STILL LIFE**
    Rolling Stones-Rolling Stones Records
13. **TUG OF WAR**
    Paul McCartney-Parlophone
14. **ASIA**
    Asia-Geffen
15. **OVERLOAD**
    Various-Ronco
16. **FRIENDS**
    Shalamar-Solar
17. **IMPERIAL BEDROOM**
    Elvis Costello & The Attractions-F.Beat
18. **SCREAMING FOR VENGEANCE**
    Judas Priest-CBS
19. **RIO**
    Duran Duran-EMI
20. **NON-STOP ECSTATIC DANCING**
    Soft Cell-Some Bizzare/Phonogram

U S   S I N G L E S

1. **EYE OF THE TIGER**
   Survivor-Scotti Bros.
2. **HURTS SO GOOD**
   John Cougar-Riva
3. **ABRACADABRA**
   The Steve Miller Band-Capitol
4. **HOLD ME**
   Fleetwood Mac-Warner Bros.
5. **HARD TO SAY I'M SORRY**
   Chicago-Full Moon/Warner Bros.
6. **ROSANNA**
   Toto-Columbia
7. **THE NIGHTS ARE BETTER**
   Air Supply-Arista
8. **KEEP THE FIRE BURNIN'**
   REO Speedwagon-Epic
9. **ONLY THE LONELY**
   The Motels-Capitol
10. **DON'T YOU WANT ME**
    The Human League-A&M/Virgin
11. **WASTED ON THE WAY**
    Crosby, Stills & Nash-Atlantic
12. **VACATION**
    The Go-Go's-I.R.S.
13. **LET IT WHIP**
    Dazz Band-Motown
14. **TAKE IT AWAY**
    Paul McCartney-Columbia
15. **YOU SHOULD HEAR HOW ...**
    Melissa Manchester-Arista
16. **LOVE IS IN CONTROL**
    Donna Summer-Geffen
17. **TAINTED LOVE**
    Soft Cell-Sire
18. **LOVE'S BEEN A LITTLE BIT ...**
    Juice Newton-Capitol
19. **PERSONALLY**
    Karla Bonoff-Columbia
20. **DO I DO**
    Stevie Wonder-Tamla

U S   A L B U M S

1. **MIRAGE**
   Fleetwood Mac-Warner Bros.
2. **ASIA**
   Asia-Geffen
3. **EYE OF THE TIGER**
   Survivor-Scotti Bros.
4. **AMERICAN FOOL**
   John Cougar-Riva/Mercury
5. **PICTURES AT ELEVEN**
   Robert Plant-Swan Song
6. **ABRACADABRA**
   The Steve Miller Band-Capitol
7. **GOOD TROUBLE**
   REO Speedwagon-Epic
8. **TOTO IV**
   Toto-Columbia
9. **ALWAYS ON MY MIND**
   Willie Nelson-Columbia
10. **DAYLIGHT AGAIN**
    Crosby, Stills & Nash-Atlantic
11. **STILL LIFE**
    Rolling Stones-Rolling Stones Records
12. **GET LUCKY**
    Lover Boy-Columbia
13. **THREE SIDES LIVE**
    Genesis-Atlantic
14. **SPECIAL FORCES**
    .38 Special-A&M
15. **DREAMGIRLS**
    Original Cast-Geffen
16. **DARE**
    The Human League-A&M/Virgin
17. **ESCAPE**
    Journey-Columbia
18. **ALL FOUR ONE**
    The Motels-Capitol
19. **GAP BAND IV**
    Gap Band-Total Experience
20. **COMBAT ROCK**
    The Clash-Epic

U K   S I N G L E S

1. **COME ON EILEEN**
   Dexys Midnight Runners-Mercury
2. **FAME**
   Irene Cara-Polydor
3. **DON'T GO**
   Yazoo-Mute
4. **DRIVING IN MY CAR**
   Madness-Stiff
5. **IT STARTED WITH A KISS**
   Hot Chocolate-RAK
6. **DA DA DA**
   Trio-Mobile Suit/Phonogram
7. **SHY BOY**
   Bananarama-London
8. **STOOL PIGEON**
   Kid Creole & The Coconuts-Ze/Island
9. **I SECOND THAT EMOTION**
   Japan-Hansa
10. **THE ONLY WAY OUT**
    Cliff Richard-EMI
11. **STRANGE LITTLE GIRL**
    The Stranglers-Liberty
12. **ABRACADABRA**
    The Steve Miller Band-Mercury
13. **ME AND MY GIRL**
    David Essex-Mercury
14. **A NIGHT TO REMEMBER**
    Shalamar-Solar
15. **TAKE IT AWAY**
    Paul McCartney-Parlophone
16. **NIGHT TRAIN**
    Visage-Polydor
17. **ARTHUR DALEY**
    The Firm-Bark/Stiff
18. **VIDEOTHEQUE**
    Dollar-WEA
19. **THE CLAPPING SONG**
    The Belle Stars-Stiff
20. **CHALK DUST ...**
    The Brat-Hansa

U K   A L B U M S

1. **THE KIDS FROM FAME**
   Various-BBC
2. **TOO-RYE-AY**
   Dexys Midnight Runners-Mercury
3. **FAME**
   Original Soundtrack/Various-Polydor
4. **LOVE AND DANCING**
   The League Unlimited Orchestra-Virgin
5. **THE LEXICON OF LOVE**
   ABC-Neutron/Phonogram
6. **TROPICAL GANGSTERS**
   Kid Creole & The Coconuts-Ze/Island
7. **AVALON**
   Roxy Music-EG (Polydor)
8. **COMPLETE MADNESS**
   Madness-Stiff
9. **CONCERT IN CENTRAL PARK**
   Simon & Garfunkel-Geffen
10. **STILL LIFE**
    Rolling Stones-Rolling Stones Records
11. **MIRAGE**
    Fleetwood Mac-Warner Bros.
12. **ABRACADABRA**
    The Steve Miller Band-Mercury
13. **CAN'T STOP THE CLASSICS**
    Louis Clark/Royal Philharmonic-K-tel
14. **PICTURES AT ELEVEN**
    Robert Plant-SwanSong
15. **DONNA SUMMER**
    Donna Summer-Warner Bros.
16. **TUG OF WAR**
    Paul McCartney-Parlophone
17. **ASIA**
    Asia-Geffen
18. **FRIENDS**
    Shalamar-Solar
19. **CONCERT FOR THE PEOPLE**
    Barclay James Harvest-Polydor
20. **RIO**
    Duran Duran-EMI

US SINGLES

1. **EYE OF THE TIGER**
   Survivor-Scotti Bros.
2. **HURTS SO GOOD**
   John Cougar-Riva
3. **ABRACADABRA**
   The Steve Miller Band-Capitol
4. **HOLD ME**
   Fleetwood Mac-Warner Bros.
5. **HARD TO SAY I'M SORRY**
   Chicago-Full Moon/Warner Bros.
6. **THE NIGHTS ARE BETTER**
   Air Supply-Arista
7. **KEEP THE FIRE BURNIN'**
   REO Speedwagon-Epic
8. **ROSANNA**
   Toto-Columbia
9. **VACATION**
   The Go-Go's-I.R.S.
10. **WASTED ON THE WAY**
    Crosby, Stills & Nash-Atlantic
11. **ONLY THE LONELY**
    The Motels-Capitol
12. **TAKE IT AWAY**
    Paul McCartney-Columbia
13. **YOU SHOULD HEAR HOW ...**
    Melissa Manchester-Arista
14. **LOVE IS IN CONTROL**
    Donna Summer-Geffen
15. **DON'T YOU WANT ME**
    The Human League-A&M/Virgin
16. **LET IT WHIP**
    Dazz Band-Motown
17. **TAINTED LOVE**
    Soft Cell-Sire
18. **LOVE WILL TURN YOU ...**
    Kenny Rogers-Liberty
19. **PERSONALLY**
    Karla Bonoff-Columbia
20. **AMERICAN MUSIC**
    Pointer Sisters-Planet

US ALBUMS

1. **MIRAGE**
   Fleetwood Mac-Warner Bros.
2. **EYE OF THE TIGER**
   Survivor-Scotti Bros.
3. **ASIA**
   Asia-Geffen
4. **AMERICAN FOOL**
   John Cougar-Riva/Mercury
5. **PICTURES AT ELEVEN**
   Robert Plant-Swan Song
6. **ABRACADABRA**
   The Steve Miller Band-Capitol
7. **GOOD TROUBLE**
   REO Speedwagon-Epic
8. **DAYLIGHT AGAIN**
   Crosby, Stills & Nash-Atlantic
9. **TOTO IV**
   Toto-Columbia
10. **ALWAYS ON MY MIND**
    Willie Nelson-Columbia
11. **THREE SIDES LIVE**
    Genesis-Atlantic
12. **GET LUCKY**
    Loverboy-Columbia
13. **DREAMGIRLS**
    Original Cast-Geffen
14. **CHICAGO 16**
    Chicago-Full Moon/Warner Bros.
15. **DARE**
    The Human League-A&M/Virgin
16. **ALL FOUR ONE**
    The Motels-Capitol
17. **ESCAPE**
    Journey-Columbia
18. **GAP BAND IV**
    Gap Band-Total Experience
19. **ROCKY III**
    Soundtrack-Liberty
20. **COMBAT ROCK**
    The Clash-Epic

UK SINGLES

1. **COME ON EILEEN**
   Dexys Midnight Runners-Mercury
2. **FAME**
   Irene Cara-Polydor
3. **DON'T GO**
   Yazoo-Mute
4. **DRIVING IN MY CAR**
   Madness-Stiff
5. **IT STARTED WITH A KISS**
   Hot Chocolate-RAK
6. **EYE OF THE TIGER**
   Survivor-Scotti Bros.
7. **STOOL PIGEON**
   Kid Creole & The Coconuts-Ze/Island
8. **STRANGE LITTLE GIRL**
   The Stranglers-Liberty
9. **MY GIRL LOLLIPOP**
   Bad Manners-Magnet
10. **SHY BOY**
    Bananarama-London
11. **I SECOND THAT EMOTION**
    Japan-Hansa
12. **THE CLAPPING SONG**
    The Belle Stars-Stiff
13. **DA DA DA**
    Trio-Mobile Suit /Phonogram
14. **THE ONLY WAY OUT**
    Cliff Richard-EMI
15. **TAKE IT AWAY**
    Paul McCartney-Parlophone
16. **ARTHUR DALEY**
    The Firm-Bark/Stiff
17. **ME AND MY GIRL**
    David Essex-Mercury
18. **LOVE IS IN CONTROL**
    Donna Summer-Warner Bros.
19. **CHALK DUST ...**
    The Brat-Hansa
20. **TOO LATE**
    Junior-Mercury

UK ALBUMS

1. **THE KIDS FROM FAME**
   Various-BBC
2. **TOO-RYE-AY**
   Dexys Midnight Runners-Mercury
3. **FAME**
   Original Soundtrack/Various-Polydor
4. **LOVE AND DANCING**
   The League Unlimited Orchestra-Virgin
5. **THE LEXICON OF LOVE**
   ABC-Neutron/Phonogram
6. **TROPICAL GANGSTERS**
   Kid Creole & The Coconuts-Ze/Island
7. **COMPLETE MADNESS**
   Madness-Stiff
8. **TALKING BACK ...**
   Steve Winwood-Island
9. **AVALON**
   Roxy Music-EG (Polydor)
10. **MIRAGE**
    Fleetwood Mac-Warner Bros.
11. **CONCERT IN CENTRAL PARK**
    Simon & Garfunkel-Geffen
12. **ABRACADABRA**
    The Steve Miller Band-Mercury
13. **STILL LIFE**
    Rolling Stones-Rolling Stones Records
14. **DONNA SUMMER**
    Donna Summer-Warner Bros.
15. **CONCERT FOR THE PEOPLE**
    Barclay James Harvest-Polydor
16. **CAN'T STOP THE CLASSICS**
    Louis Clark/Royal Philharmonic-K-tel
17. **TUG OF WAR**
    Paul McCartney-Parlophone
18. **PICTURES AT ELEVEN**
    Robert Plant-SwanSong
19. **FRIENDS**
    Shalamar-Solar
20. **ASIA**
    Asia-Geffen

US SINGLES

1. **EYE OF THE TIGER**
   Survivor-Scotti Bros.
2. **HURTS SO GOOD**
   John Cougar-Riva
3. **ABRACADABRA**
   The Steve Miller Band-Capitol
4. **HOLD ME**
   Fleetwood Mac-Warner Bros.
5. **HARD TO SAY I'M SORRY**
   Chicago-Full Moon/Warner Bros.
6. **THE NIGHTS ARE BETTER**
   Air Supply-Arista
7. **KEEP THE FIRE BURNIN'**
   REO Speedwagon-Epic
8. **VACATION**
   The Go-Go's-I.R.S.
9. **WASTED ON THE WAY**
   Crosby, Stills & Nash-Atlantic
10. **TAKE IT AWAY**
    Paul McCartney-Columbia
11. **YOU SHOULD HEAR HOW ...**
    Melissa Manchester-Arista
12. **LOVE IS IN CONTROL**
    Donna Summer-Geffen
13. **ONLY THE LONELY**
    The Motels-Capitol
14. **LOVE WILL TURN YOU ...**
    Kenny Rogers-Liberty
15. **ROSANNA**
    Toto-Columbia
16. **JACK AND DIANE**
    John Cougar-Riva/Mercury
17. **EYE IN THE SKY**
    The Alan Parsons Project-Arista
18. **AMERICAN MUSIC**
    Pointer Sisters-Planet
19. **THINK I'M IN LOVE**
    Eddie Money-Columbia
20. **WHO CAN IT BE NOW?**
    Men at Work-Columbia

US ALBUMS

1. **MIRAGE**
   Fleetwood Mac-Warner Bros.
2. **EYE OF THE TIGER**
   Survivor-Scotti Bros.
3. **ASIA**
   Asia-Geffen
4. **AMERICAN FOOL**
   John Cougar-Riva/Mercury
5. **PICTURES AT ELEVEN**
   Robert Plant-Swan Song
6. **ABRACADABRA**
   The Steve Miller Band-Capitol
7. **GOOD TROUBLE**
   REO Speedwagon-Epic
8. **DAYLIGHT AGAIN**
   Crosby, Stills & Nash-Atlantic
9. **VACATION**
   The Go Go's-I.R.S.
10. **THREE SIDES LIVE**
    Genesis-Atlantic
11. **DREAMGIRLS**
    Original Cast-Geffen
12. **ALWAYS ON MY MIND**
    Willie Nelson-Columbia
13. **CHICAGO 16**
    Chicago-Full Moon/Warner Bros.
14. **GET LUCKY**
    Loverboy-Columbia
15. **ROCKY III**
    Soundtrack-Liberty
16. **ALL FOUR ONE**
    The Motels-Capitol
17. **GAP BAND IV**
    Gap Band-Total Experience
18. **EMOTIONS IN MOTION**
    Billy Squier-Capitol
19. **EYE IN THE SKY**
    Alan Parsons Project-Arista
20. **COMBAT ROCK**
    The Clash-Epic

UK SINGLES

1. **COME ON EILEEN**
   Dexys Midnight Runners-Mercury
2. **EYE OF THE TIGER**
   Survivor-Scotti Bros.
3. **FAME**
   Irene Cara-Polydor
4. **DON'T GO**
   Yazoo-Mute
5. **IT STARTED WITH A KISS**
   Hot Chocolate-RAK
6. **CAN'T TAKE MY EYES ...**
   Boystown Gang-ERC
7. **STRANGE LITTLE GIRL**
   The Stranglers-Liberty
8. **DRIVING IN MY CAR**
   Madness-Stiff
9. **STOOL PIGEON**
   Kid Creole & The Coconuts-Ze/Island
10. **MY GIRL LOLLIPOP**
    Bad Manners-Magnet
11. **THE CLAPPING SONG**
    The Belle Stars-Stiff
12. **I EAT CANNIBALS Part 1**
    Toto Coelo-Radialchoice/Virgin
13. **WHAT**
    Soft Cell-Some Bizarre/Phonogram
14. **ARTHUR DALEY**
    The Firm-Bark/Stiff
15. **BIG FUN**
    Kool & The Gang-De-Lite/Phonogram
16. **JOHN WAYNE IS BIG LEGGY**
    Haysi Fantayzee-Regard
17. **HURRY HOME**
    Wavelength-Ariola
18. **SUMMERTIME**
    The Fun Boy Three-Chrysalis
19. **SHY BOY**
    Bananarama-London
20. **I SECOND THAT EMOTION**
    Japan-Hansa

UK ALBUMS

1. **THE KIDS FROM FAME**
   Various-BBC
2. **TOO-RYE-AY**
   Dexys Midnight Runners-Mercury
3. **LOVE AND DANCING**
   The League Unlimited Orchestra-Virgin
4. **FAME**
   Original Soundtrack/Various-Polydor
5. **TROPICAL GANGSTERS**
   Kid Creole & The Coconuts-Ze/Island
6. **TALKING BACK ...**
   Steve Winwood-Island
7. **THE LEXICON OF LOVE**
   ABC-Neutron/Phonogram
8. **LOVE SONGS**
   Commodores-K-tel
9. **COMPLETE MADNESS**
   Madness-Stiff
10. **MIRAGE**
    Fleetwood Mac-Warner Bros.
11. **AVALON**
    Roxy Music-EG (Polydor)
12. **CONCERT IN CENTRAL PARK**
    Simon & Garfunkel-Geffen
13. **DONNA SUMMER**
    Donna Summer-Warner Bros.
14. **ABRACADABRA**
    The Steve Miller Band-Mercury
15. **RIO**
    Duran Duran-EMI
16. **JIMI HENDRIX CONCERTS**
    Jimi Hendrix-CBS
17. **CITY BABY ATTACKED ...**
    Charge G.B.H.-Clay
18. **TUG OF WAR**
    Paul McCartney-Parlophone
19. **ASIA**
    Asia-Geffen
20. **STILL LIFE**
    Rolling Stones-Rolling Stones Records

WEEK ENDING AUGUST 28 1982

US SINGLES

1. **EYE OF THE TIGER**
   Survivor-Scotti Bros.
2. **HURTS SO GOOD**
   John Cougar-Riva
3. **ABRACADABRA**
   The Steve Miller Band-Capitol
4. **HOLD ME**
   Fleetwood Mac-Warner Bros.
5. **HARD TO SAY I'M SORRY**
   Chicago-Full Moon/Warner Bros.
6. **THE NIGHTS ARE BETTER**
   Air Supply-Arista
7. **KEEP THE FIRE BURNIN'**
   REO Speedwagon-Epic
8. **VACATION**
   The Go-Go's-I.R.S.
9. **WASTED ON THE WAY**
   Crosby, Stills & Nash-Atlantic
10. **TAKE IT AWAY**
    Paul McCartney-Columbia
11. **YOU SHOULD HEAR HOW ...**
    Melissa Manchester-Arista
12. **LOVE IS IN CONTROL**
    Donna Summer-Geffen
13. **LOVE WILL TURN YOU ...**
    Kenny Rogers-Liberty
14. **JACK AND DIANE**
    John Cougar-Riva/Mercury
15. **EYE IN THE SKY**
    The Alan Parsons Project-Arista
16. **AMERICAN MUSIC**
    Pointer Sisters-Planet
17. **THINK I'M IN LOVE**
    Eddie Money-Columbia
18. **WHO CAN IT BE NOW?**
    Men at Work-Columbia
19. **ONLY THE LONELY**
    The Motels-Capitol
20. **ROSANNA**
    Toto-Columbia

US ALBUMS

1. **MIRAGE**
   Fleetwood Mac-Warner Bros.
2. **EYE OF THE TIGER**
   Survivor-Scotti Bros.
3. **AMERICAN FOOL**
   John Cougar-Riva/Mercury
4. **ASIA**
   Asia-Geffen
5. **PICTURES AT ELEVEN**
   Robert Plant-Swan Song
6. **ABRACADABRA**
   The Steve Miller Band-Capitol
7. **GOOD TROUBLE**
   REO Speedwagon-Epic
8. **DAYLIGHT AGAIN**
   Crosby, Stills & Nash-Atlantic
9. **VACATION**
   The Go Go's-I.R.S.
10. **THREE SIDES LIVE**
    Genesis-Atlantic
11. **DREAMGIRLS**
    Original Cast-Geffen
12. **CHICAGO 16**
    Chicago-Full Moon/Warner Bros.
13. **EMOTIONS IN MOTION**
    Billy Squier-Capitol
14. **GET LUCKY**
    Loverboy-Columbia
15. **ROCKY III**
    Soundtrack-Liberty
16. **ALWAYS ON MY MIND**
    Willie Nelson-Columbia
17. **GAP BAND IV**
    Gap Band-Total Experience
18. **EYE IN THE SKY**
    Alan Parsons Project-Arista
19. **ALL FOUR ONE**
    The Motels-Capitol
20. **COMBAT ROCK**
    The Clash-Epic

UK SINGLES

1. **COME ON EILEEN**
   Dexys Midnight Runners-Mercury
2. **EYE OF THE TIGER**
   Survivor-Scotti Bros.
3. **WHAT!**
   Soft Cell-Some Bizarre/Phonogram
4. **CAN'T TAKE MY EYES ...**
   Boystown Gang-ERC
5. **SAVE A PRAYER**
   Duran Duran-EMI
6. **FAME**
   Irene Cara-Polydor
7. **HI-FIDELITY**
   The Kids From "Fame"-RCA
8. **DON'T GO**
   Yazoo-Mute
9. **I EAT CANNIBALS Part 1**
   Toto Coelo-Radialchoice/Virgin
10. **NOBODY'S FOOL**
    Haircut One Hundred-Arista
11. **JOHN WAYNE IS BIG LEGGY**
    Haysi Fantayzee-Regard
12. **IT STARTED WITH A KISS**
    Hot Chocolate-RAK
13. **STRANGE LITTLE GIRL**
    The Stranglers-Liberty
14. **BIG FUN**
    Kool & The Gang-De-Lite/Phonogram
15. **MY GIRL LOLLIPOP**
    Bad Manners-Magnet
16. **THE CLAPPING SONG**
    The Belle Stars-Stiff
17. **STOOL PIGEON**
    Kid Creole & The Coconuts-Ze/Island
18. **DRIVING IN MY CAR**
    Madness-Stiff
19. **WALKING ON SUNSHINE**
    Rockers Revenge-London
20. **WHITE BOYS AND HEROES**
    Gary Numan-Beggars Banquet

UK ALBUMS

1. **THE KIDS FROM FAME**
   Various-BBC
2. **TOO-RYE-AY**
   Dexys Midnight Runners-Mercury
3. **TROPICAL GANGSTERS**
   Kid Creole & The Coconuts-Ze/Island
4. **LOVE AND DANCING**
   The League Unlimited Orchestra-Virgin
5. **LOVE SONGS**
   Commodores-K-tel
6. **THE LEXICON OF LOVE**
   ABC-Neutron/Phonogram
7. **FAME**
   Original Soundtrack/Various-Polydor
8. **RIO**
   Duran Duran-EMI
9. **COMPLETE MADNESS**
   Madness-Stiff
10. **TALKING BACK ...**
    Steve Winwood-Island
11. **AVALON**
    Roxy Music-EG (Polydor)
12. **EYE OF THE TIGER**
    Survivor-Scotti Bros.
13. **THE CAGE**
    Tygers of Pan Tang-MCA
14. **DONNA SUMMER**
    Donna Summer-Warner Bros.
15. **ROUGH DIAMONDS**
    Bad Company-SwanSong
16. **MIRAGE**
    Fleetwood Mac-Warner Bros.
17. **JIMI HENDRIX CONCERTS**
    Jimi Hendrix-CBS
18. **CAN'T STOP THE CLASSICS**
    Louis Clark/Royal Philharmonic-K-tel
19. **CONCERT IN CENTRAL PARK**
    Simon & Garfunkel-Geffen
20. **CITY BABY ATTACKED ...**
    Charge G.B.H.-Clay

WEEK ENDING SEPTEMBER 4 1982

US SINGLES

1. **ABRACADABRA**
   The Steve Miller Band-Capitol
2. **EYE OF THE TIGER**
   Survivor-Scotti Bros.
3. **HARD TO SAY I'M SORRY**
   Chicago-Full Moon/Warner Bros.
4. **HOLD ME**
   Fleetwood Mac-Warner Bros.
5. **THE NIGHTS ARE BETTER**
   Air Supply-Arista
6. **YOU SHOULD HEAR HOW ...**
   Melissa Manchester-Arista
7. **HURTS SO GOOD**
   John Cougar-Riva
8. **VACATION**
   The Go-Go's-I.R.S.
9. **WASTED ON THE WAY**
   Crosby, Stills & Nash-Atlantic
10. **TAKE IT AWAY**
    Paul McCartney-Columbia
11. **JACK AND DIANE**
    John Cougar-Riva/Mercury
12. **LOVE IS IN CONTROL**
    Donna Summer-Geffen
13. **LOVE WILL TURN YOU ...**
    Kenny Rogers-Liberty
14. **EYE IN THE SKY**
    The Alan Parsons Project-Arista
15. **WHO CAN IT BE NOW?**
    Men at Work-Columbia
16. **AMERICAN MUSIC**
    Pointer Sisters-Planet
17. **THINK I'M IN LOVE**
    Eddie Money-Columbia
18. **KEEP THE FIRE BURNIN'**
    REO Speedwagon-Epic
19. **ONLY THE LONELY**
    The Motels-Capitol
20. **YOU CAN DO MAGIC**
    America-Capitol

US ALBUMS

1. **MIRAGE**
   Fleetwood Mac-Warner Bros.
2. **EYE OF THE TIGER**
   Survivor-Scotti Bros.
3. **AMERICAN FOOL**
   John Cougar-Riva/Mercury
4. **ASIA**
   Asia-Geffen
5. **PICTURES AT ELEVEN**
   Robert Plant-Swan Song
6. **ABRACADABRA**
   The Steve Miller Band-Capitol
7. **GOOD TROUBLE**
   REO Speedwagon-Epic
8. **DAYLIGHT AGAIN**
   Crosby, Stills & Nash-Atlantic
9. **VACATION**
   The Go Go's-I.R.S.
10. **THREE SIDES LIVE**
    Genesis-Atlantic
11. **DREAMGIRLS**
    Original Cast-Geffen
12. **CHICAGO 16**
    Chicago-Full Moon/Warner Bros.
13. **EMOTIONS IN MOTION**
    Billy Squier-Capitol
14. **GET LUCKY**
    Loverboy-Columbia
15. **ROCKY III**
    Soundtrack-Liberty
16. **GAP BAND IV**
    Gap Band-Total Experience
17. **EYE IN THE SKY**
    Alan Parsons Project-Arista
18. **ALWAYS ON MY MIND**
    Willie Nelson-Columbia
19. **COMBAT ROCK**
    The Clash-Epic
20. **A FLOCK OF SEAGULLS**
    A Flock of Seagulls-Jive/Arista

UK SINGLES

1. **EYE OF THE TIGER**
   Survivor-Scotti Bros.
2. **COME ON EILEEN**
   Dexys Midnight Runners-Mercury
3. **SAVE A PRAYER**
   Duran Duran-EMI
4. **WHAT!**
   Soft Cell-Some Bizarre/Phonogram
5. **HI-FIDELITY**
   The Kids From "Fame"-RCA
6. **CAN'T TAKE MY EYES ...**
   Boystown Gang-ERC
7. **WALKING ON SUNSHINE**
   Rockers Revenge-London
8. **I EAT CANNIBALS Part 1**
   Toto Coelo-Radialchoice/Virgin
9. **NOBODY'S FOOL**
   Haircut One Hundred-Arista
10. **FAME**
    Irene Cara-Polydor
11. **JOHN WAYNE IS BIG LEGGY**
    Haysi Fantayzee-Regard
12. **GIVE ME YOUR HEART ...**
    Shakin' Stevens-Epic
13. **PRIVATE INVESTIGATIONS**
    Dire Straits-Vertigo/Phonogram
14. **BIG FUN**
    Kool & The Gang-De-Lite/Phonogram
15. **TODAY**
    Talk Talk-EMI
16. **CHERRY PINK ...**
    Modern Romance/John Du Prez-WEA
17. **IT STARTED WITH A KISS**
    Hot Chocolate-RAK
18. **SPREAD A LITTLE ...**
    Sting-A&M
19. **THE MESSAGE**
    Grand Master Flash-Sugar Hill
20. **WHITE BOYS AND HEROES**
    Gary Numan-Beggars Banquet

UK ALBUMS

1. **THE KIDS FROM FAME**
   Various-BBC
2. **UPSTAIRS AT ERIC'S**
   Yazoo-Mute
3. **TOO-RYE-AY**
   Dexys Midnight Runners-Mercury
4. **NOW YOU SEE ME ...**
   Cliff Richard-EMI
5. **RIO**
   Duran Duran-EMI
6. **THE LEXICON OF LOVE**
   ABC-Neutron/Phonogram
7. **LOVE AND DANCING**
   The League Unlimited Orchestra-Virgin
8. **LOVE SONGS**
   Commodores-K-tel
9. **TROPICAL GANGSTERS**
   Kid Creole & The Coconuts-Ze/Island
10. **COMPLETE MADNESS**
    Madness-Stiff
11. **FAME**
    Original Soundtrack/Various-Polydor
12. **EYE OF THE TIGER**
    Survivor-Scotti Bros.
13. **THE CAGE**
    Tygers of Pan Tang-MCA
14. **TALKING BACK ...**
    Steve Winwood-Island
15. **AVALON**
    Roxy Music-EG (Polydor)
16. **CAN'T STOP THE CLASSICS**
    Louis Clark/Royal Philharmonic-K-tel
17. **THE SINGLES ALBUM**
    UB40-Graduate
18. **ROUGH DIAMONDS**
    Bad Company-SwanSong
19. **JIMI HENDRIX CONCERTS**
    Jimi Hendrix-CBS
20. **MIRAGE**
    Fleetwood Mac-Warner Bros.

US SINGLES

1. **HARD TO SAY I'M SORRY**
   Chicago-Full Moon/Warner Bros.
2. **EYE OF THE TIGER**
   Survivor-Scotti Bros.
3. **ABRACADABRA**
   The Steve Miller Band-Capitol
4. **JACK AND DIANE**
   John Cougar-Riva/Mercury
5. **THE NIGHTS ARE BETTER**
   Air Supply-Arista
6. **YOU SHOULD HEAR HOW ...**
   Melissa Manchester-Arista
7. **HOLD ME**
   Fleetwood Mac-Warner Bros.
8. **HURTS SO GOOD**
   John Cougar-Riva
9. **WASTED ON THE WAY**
   Crosby, Stills & Nash-Atlantic
10. **TAKE IT AWAY**
    Paul McCartney-Columbia
11. **VACATION**
    The Go Go's-I.R.S.
12. **LOVE IS IN CONTROL**
    Donna Summer-Geffen
13. **LOVE WILL TURN YOU ...**
    Kenny Rogers-Liberty
14. **EYE IN THE SKY**
    The Alan Parsons Project-Arista
15. **WHO CAN IT BE NOW?**
    Men at Work-Columbia
16. **AMERICAN MUSIC**
    Pointer Sisters-Planet
17. **THINK I'M IN LOVE**
    Eddie Money-Columbia
18. **YOU CAN DO MAGIC**
    America-Capitol
19. **ONLY TIME WILL TELL**
    Asia-Geffen
20. **SOMEBODY'S BABY**
    Jackson Browne-Asylum

US ALBUMS

1. **AMERICAN FOOL**
   John Cougar-Riva/Mercury
2. **MIRAGE**
   Fleetwood Mac-Warner Bros.
3. **EYE OF THE TIGER**
   Survivor-Scotti Bros.
4. **ABRACADABRA**
   The Steve Miller Band-Capitol
5. **PICTURES AT ELEVEN**
   Robert Plant-Swan Song
6. **ASIA**
   Asia-Geffen
7. **GOOD TROUBLE**
   REO Speedwagon-Epic
8. **DAYLIGHT AGAIN**
   Crosby, Stills & Nash-Atlantic
9. **VACATION**
   The Go Go's-I.R.S.
10. **CHICAGO 16**
    Chicago-Full Moon/Warner Bros.
11. **EMOTIONS IN MOTION**
    Billy Squier-Capitol
12. **DREAMGIRLS**
    Original Cast-Geffen
13. **GET LUCKY**
    Loverboy-Columbia
14. **GAP BAND IV**
    Gap Band-Total Experience
15. **ROCKY III**
    Soundtrack-Liberty
16. **EYE IN THE SKY**
    Alan Parsons Project-Arista
17. **BUSINESS AS USUAL**
    Men at Work-Columbia
18. **A FLOCK OF SEAGULLS**
    A Flock of Seagulls-Jive/Arista
19. **COMBAT ROCK**
    The Clash-Epic
20. **THREE SIDES LIVE**
    Genesis-Atlantic

UK SINGLES

1. **EYE OF THE TIGER**
   Survivor-Scotti Bros.
2. **SAVE A PRAYER**
   Duran Duran-EMI
3. **COME ON EILEEN**
   Dexys Midnight Runners-Mercury
4. **PRIVATE INVESTIGATIONS**
   Dire Straits-Vertigo/Phonogram
5. **WALKING ON SUNSHINE**
   Rockers Revenge-London
6. **HI-FIDELITY**
   The Kids From "Fame"-RCA
7. **WHAT!**
   Soft Cell-Some Bizarre/Phonogram
8. **ALL OF MY HEART**
   ABC-Neutron/Phonogram
9. **I EAT CANNIBALS Part 1**
   Toto Coelo-Radialchoice/Virgin
10. **CAN'T TAKE MY EYES ...**
    Boystown Gang-ERC
11. **GIVE ME YOUR HEART ...**
    Shakin' Stevens-Epic
12. **NOBODY'S FOOL**
    Haircut One Hundred-Arista
13. **THE MESSAGE**
    Grand Master Flash-Sugar Hill
14. **TODAY**
    Talk Talk-EMI
15. **CHERRY PINK ...**
    Modern Romance/John Du Prez-WEA
16. **SPREAD A LITTLE ...**
    Sting-A&M
17. **THERE IT IS**
    Shalamar-Solar
18. **JOHN WAYNE IS BIG LEGGY**
    Haysi Fantayzee-Regard
19. **SADDLE UP**
    David Christie-KR
20. **FAME**
    Irene Cara-Polydor

UK ALBUMS

1. **THE KIDS FROM FAME**
   Various-BBC
2. **UPSTAIRS AT ERIC'S**
   Yazoo-Mute
3. **TOO-RYE-AY**
   Dexys Midnight Runners-Mercury
4. **RIO**
   Duran Duran-EMI
5. **THE LEXICON OF LOVE**
   ABC-Neutron/Phonogram
6. **NOW YOU SEE ME ...**
   Cliff Richard-EMI
7. **BREAKOUT**
   Various-Ronco
8. **IN THE HEAT OF THE NIGHT**
   Imagination-R&B
9. **LOVE SONGS**
   Commodores-K-tel
10. **LOVE AND DANCING**
    The League Unlimited Orchestra-Virgin
11. **IT'S HARD**
    The Who-Polydor
12. **SONGS TO REMEMBER**
    Scritti Politti-Rough Trade
13. **COMPLETE MADNESS**
    Madness-Stiff
14. **HIGHWAY SONG**
    Blackfoot-Atco
15. **EYE OF THE TIGER**
    Survivor-Scotti Bros.
16. **TROPICAL GANGSTERS**
    Kid Creole & The Coconuts-Ze/Island
17. **FAME**
    Original Soundtrack/Various-Polydor
18. **JIMI HENDRIX CONCERTS**
    Jimi Hendrix-CBS
19. **MIRAGE**
    Fleetwood Mac-Warner Bros.
20. **WELL KEPT SECRET**
    John Martyn-WEA

US SINGLES

1. **HARD TO SAY I'M SORRY**
   Chicago-Full Moon/Warner Bros.
2. **ABRACADABRA**
   The Steve Miller Band-Capitol
3. **EYE OF THE TIGER**
   Survivor-Scotti Bros.
4. **JACK AND DIANE**
   John Cougar-Riva/Mercury
5. **YOU SHOULD HEAR HOW ...**
   Melissa Manchester-Arista
6. **THE NIGHTS ARE BETTER**
   Air Supply-Arista
7. **HOLD ME**
   Fleetwood Mac-Warner Bros.
8. **HURTS SO GOOD**
   John Cougar-Riva
9. **EYE IN THE SKY**
   The Alan Parsons Project-Arista
10. **TAKE IT AWAY**
    Paul McCartney-Columbia
11. **LOVE IS IN CONTROL**
    Donna Summer-Geffen
12. **WHO CAN IT BE NOW?**
    Men at Work-Columbia
13. **LOVE WILL TURN YOU ...**
    Kenny Rogers-Liberty
14. **YOU CAN DO MAGIC**
    America-Capitol
15. **BLUE EYES**
    Elton John-Geffen
16. **THINK I'M IN LOVE**
    Eddie Money-Columbia
17. **ONLY TIME WILL TELL**
    Asia-Geffen
18. **SOMEBODY'S BABY**
    Jackson Browne-Asylum
19. **WASTED ON THE WAY**
    Crosby, Stills & Nash-Atlantic
20. **LET ME TICKLE YOUR ...**
    Jermaine Jackson-Motown

US ALBUMS

1. **AMERICAN FOOL**
   John Cougar-Riva/Mercury
2. **MIRAGE**
   Fleetwood Mac-Warner Bros.
3. **ABRACADABRA**
   The Steve Miller Band-Capitol
4. **ASIA**
   Asia-Geffen
5. **EMOTIONS IN MOTION**
   Billy Squier-Capitol
6. **PICTURES AT ELEVEN**
   Robert Plant-Swan Song
7. **GOOD TROUBLE**
   REO Speedwagon-Epic
8. **VACATION**
   The Go Go's-I.R.S.
9. **CHICAGO 16**
   Chicago-Full Moon/Warner Bros.
10. **EYE OF THE TIGER**
    Survivor-Scotti Bros.
11. **DAYLIGHT AGAIN**
    Crosby, Stills & Nash-Atlantic
12. **EYE IN THE SKY**
    Alan Parsons Project-Arista
13. **GET LUCKY**
    Loverboy-Columbia
14. **GAP BAND IV**
    Gap Band-Total Experience
15. **ROCKY III**
    Soundtrack-Liberty
16. **BUSINESS AS USUAL**
    Men at Work-Columbia
17. **A FLOCK OF SEAGULLS**
    A Flock of Seagulls-Jive/Arista
18. **COMBAT ROCK**
    The Clash-Epic
19. **HEY RICKY**
    Melissa Manchester-Arista
20. **DONNA SUMMER**
    Donna Summer-Geffen

UK SINGLES

1. **EYE OF THE TIGER**
   Survivor-Scotti Bros.
2. **PRIVATE INVESTIGATIONS**
   Dire Straits-Vertigo/Phonogram
3. **SAVE A PRAYER**
   Duran Duran-EMI
4. **WALKING ON SUNSHINE**
   Rockers Revenge-London
5. **THE BITTEREST PILL**
   The Jam-Polydor
6. **ALL OF MY HEART**
   ABC-Neutron/Phonogram
7. **HI-FIDELITY**
   The Kids From "Fame"-RCA
8. **THE MESSAGE**
   Grand Master Flash-Sugar Hill
9. **COME ON EILEEN**
   Dexys Midnight Runners-Mercury
10. **THERE IT IS**
    Shalamar-Solar
11. **GIVE ME YOUR HEART ...**
    Shakin' Stevens-Epic
12. **SADDLE UP**
    David Christie-KR
13. **I EAT CANNIBALS Part 1**
    Toto Coelo-Radialchoice/Virgin
14. **TODAY**
    Talk Talk-EMI
15. **WHAT!**
    Soft Cell-Some Bizarre/Phonogram
16. **NOBODY'S FOOL**
    Haircut One Hundred-Arista
17. **WHY**
    Carly Simon-WEA
18. **LOVE COME DOWN**
    Evelyn King-RCA
19. **CAN'T TAKE MY EYES ...**
    Boystown Gang-ERC
20. **CHERRY PINK ...**
    Modern Romance/John Du Prez-WEA

UK ALBUMS

1. **THE KIDS FROM FAME**
   Various-BBC
2. **UPSTAIRS AT ERIC'S**
   Yazoo-Mute
3. **SIGNALS**
   Rush-Mercury/Phonogram
4. **BREAKOUT**
   Various-Ronco
5. **THE LEXICON OF LOVE**
   ABC-Neutron/Phonogram
6. **PETER GABRIEL**
   Peter Gabriel-Charisma
7. **CHART BEAT/CHART HEAT**
   Various-K-tel
8. **I, ASSASSIN**
   Gary Numan-Beggars Banquet
9. **IN THE HEAT OF THE NIGHT**
   Imagination-R&B
10. **RIO**
    Duran Duran-EMI
11. **TOO-RYE-AY**
    Dexys Midnight Runners-Mercury
12. **NOW YOU SEE ME ...**
    Cliff Richard-EMI
13. **SONGS TO REMEMBER**
    Scritti Politti-Rough Trade
14. **LOVE SONGS**
    Commodores-K-tel
15. **LOVE AND DANCING**
    The League Unlimited Orchestra-Virgin
16. **IT'S HARD**
    The Who-Polydor
17. **HIGHWAY SONG**
    Blackfoot-Atco
18. **SOMETHING'S GOING ON**
    Frida-Epic
19. **EYE OF THE TIGER**
    Survivor-Scotti Bros.
20. **TROPICAL GANGSTERS**
    Kid Creole & The Coconuts-Ze/Island

US SINGLES

1. **ABRACADABRA**
   The Steve Miller Band-Capitol
2. **JACK AND DIANE**
   John Cougar-Riva/Mercury
3. **HARD TO SAY I'M SORRY**
   Chicago-Full Moon/Warner Bros.
4. **EYE OF THE TIGER**
   Survivor-Scotti Bros.
5. **YOU SHOULD HEAR HOW ...**
   Melissa Manchester-Arista
6. **EYE IN THE SKY**
   The Alan Parsons Project-Arista
7. **WHO CAN IT BE NOW?**
   Men at Work-Columbia
8. **SOMEBODY'S BABY**
   Jackson Browne-Asylum
9. **HURTS SO GOOD**
   John Cougar-Riva
10. **LOVE IS IN CONTROL**
    Donna Summer-Geffen
11. **TAKE IT AWAY**
    Paul McCartney-Columbia
12. **YOU CAN DO MAGIC**
    America-Capitol
13. **LOVE WILL TURN YOU ...**
    Kenny Rogers-Liberty
14. **BLUE EYES**
    Elton John-Geffen
15. **I KEEP FORGETTIN'**
    Michael McDonald-Warner Bros.
16. **THINK I'M IN LOVE**
    Eddie Money-Columbia
17. **ONLY TIME WILL TELL**
    Asia-Geffen
18. **LET ME TICKLE YOUR ...**
    Jermaine Jackson-Motown
19. **HOLD ON**
    Santana-Columbia
20. **DO YOU WANNA TOUCH ME**
    Joan Jett & The Blackhearts-Boardwalk

US ALBUMS

1. **AMERICAN FOOL**
   John Cougar-Riva/Mercury
2. **MIRAGE**
   Fleetwood Mac-Warner Bros.
3. **ABRACADABRA**
   The Steve Miller Band-Capitol
4. **ASIA**
   Asia-Geffen
5. **EMOTIONS IN MOTION**
   Billy Squier-Capitol
6. **PICTURES AT ELEVEN**
   Robert Plant-Swan Song
7. **GOOD TROUBLE**
   REO Speedwagon-Epic
8. **VACATION**
   The Go Go's-I.R.S.
9. **CHICAGO 16**
   Chicago-Full Moon/Warner Bros.
10. **EYE OF THE TIGER**
    Survivor-Scotti Bros.
11. **EYE IN THE SKY**
    Alan Parsons Project-Arista
12. **IF THAT'S WHAT IT TAKES**
    Michael McDonald-Warner Bros.
13. **GET LUCKY**
    Loverboy-Columbia
14. **GAP BAND IV**
    Gap Band-Total Experience
15. **BUSINESS AS USUAL**
    Men at Work-Columbia
16. **DAYLIGHT AGAIN**
    Crosby, Stills & Nash-Atlantic
17. **A FLOCK OF SEAGULLS**
    A Flock of Seagulls-Jive/Arista
18. **COMBAT ROCK**
    The Clash-Epic
19. **HEY RICKY**
    Melissa Manchester-Arista
20. **DONNA SUMMER**
    Donna Summer-Geffen

UK SINGLES

1. **EYE OF THE TIGER**
   Survivor-Scotti Bros.
2. **THE BITTEREST PILL**
   The Jam-Polydor
3. **PRIVATE INVESTIGATIONS**
   Dire Straits-Vertigo/Phonogram
4. **WALKING ON SUNSHINE**
   Rockers Revenge-London
5. **ALL OF MY HEART**
   ABC-Neutron/Phonogram
6. **THERE IT IS**
   Shalamar-Solar
7. **SAVE A PRAYER**
   Duran Duran-EMI
8. **THE MESSAGE**
   Grand Master Flash-Sugar Hill
9. **SADDLE UP**
   David Christie-KR
10. **FRIEND OR FOE**
    Adam Ant-CBS
11. **GIVE ME YOUR HEART ...**
    Shakin' Stevens-Epic
12. **WHY**
    Carly Simon-WEA
13. **HI-FIDELITY**
    The Kids From "Fame"-RCA
14. **COME ON EILEEN**
    Dexys Midnight Runners-Mercury
15. **LOVE COME DOWN**
    Evelyn King-RCA
16. **TODAY**
    Talk Talk-EMI
17. **ZOOM**
    Fat Larry's Band-WMOT/Virgin
18. **LEAVE IN SILENCE**
    Depeche Mode-Mute
19. **JUST WHAT I ALWAYS ...**
    Mari Wilson-Compact
20. **CAN'T TAKE MY EYES ...**
    Boystown Gang-ERC

UK ALBUMS

1. **THE KIDS FROM FAME**
   Various-BBC
2. **CHART BEAT/CHART HEAT**
   Various-K-tel
3. **THE DREAMING**
   Kate Bush-EMI
4. **UPSTAIRS AT ERIC'S**
   Yazoo-Mute
5. **THE LEXICON OF LOVE**
   ABC-Neutron/Phonogram
6. **NEW GOLD DREAM**
   Simple Minds-Virgin
7. **IN THE HEAT OF THE NIGHT**
   Imagination-R&B
8. **RIO**
   Duran Duran-EMI
9. **BREAKOUT**
   Various-Ronco
10. **SIGNALS**
    Rush-Mercury/Phonogram
11. **PETER GABRIEL**
    Peter Gabriel-Charisma/Phonogram
12. **TOO-RYE-AY**
    Dexys Midnight Runners-Mercury
13. **THE COLLECTION 1977-1982**
    The Stranglers-Liberty
14. **LOVE SONGS**
    Commodores-K-tel
15. **SONGS TO REMEMBER**
    Scritti Politti-Rough Trade
16. **I, ASSASSIN**
    Gary Numan-Beggars Banquet
17. **PURSUIT OF ACCIDENTS**
    Level 42-Polydor
18. **LOVE AND DANCING**
    The League Unlimited Orchestra-Virgin
19. **NOW YOU SEE ME ...**
    Cliff Richard-EMI
20. **SOMETHING'S GOING ON**
    Frida-Epic

US SINGLES

1. **JACK AND DIANE**
   John Cougar-Riva/Mercury
2. **ABRACADABRA**
   The Steve Miller Band-Capitol
3. **HARD TO SAY I'M SORRY**
   Chicago-Full Moon/Warner Bros.
4. **EYE OF THE TIGER**
   Survivor-Scotti Bros.
5. **YOU SHOULD HEAR HOW ...**
   Melissa Manchester-Arista
6. **EYE IN THE SKY**
   The Alan Parsons Project-Arista
7. **WHO CAN IT BE NOW?**
   Men at Work-Columbia
8. **SOMEBODY'S BABY**
   Jackson Browne-Asylum
9. **I KEEP FORGETTIN'**
   Michael McDonald-Warner Bros.
10. **HURTS SO GOOD**
    John Cougar-Riva
11. **YOU CAN DO MAGIC**
    America-Capitol
12. **BLUE EYES**
    Elton John-Geffen
13. **HEART ATTACK**
    Olivia Newton-John-MCA
14. **I RAN**
    A Flock of Seagulls-Jive/Arista
15. **BREAK IT TO ME GENTLY**
    Juice Newton-Capitol
16. **THINK I'M IN LOVE**
    Eddie Money-Columbia
17. **ONLY TIME WILL TELL**
    Asia-Geffen
18. **LET ME TICKLE YOUR ...**
    Jermaine Jackson-Motown
19. **HOLD ON**
    Santana-Columbia
20. **DO YOU WANNA TOUCH ME**
    Joan Jett & The Blackhearts-Boardwalk

US ALBUMS

1. **AMERICAN FOOL**
   John Cougar-Riva/Mercury
2. **MIRAGE**
   Fleetwood Mac-Warner Bros.
3. **ABRACADABRA**
   The Steve Miller Band-Capitol
4. **ASIA**
   Asia-Geffen
5. **EMOTIONS IN MOTION**
   Billy Squier-Capitol
6. **IF THAT'S WHAT IT TAKES**
   Michael McDonald-Warner Bros.
7. **GOOD TROUBLE**
   REO Speedwagon-Epic
8. **VACATION**
   The Go Go's-I.R.S.
9. **CHICAGO 16**
   Chicago-Full Moon/Warner Bros.
10. **EYE IN THE SKY**
    Alan Parsons Project-Arista
11. **EYE OF THE TIGER**
    Survivor-Scotti Bros.
12. **IT'S HARD**
    The Who-Warner Bros.
13. **GET LUCKY**
    Loverboy-Columbia
14. **GAP BAND IV**
    Gap Band-Total Experience
15. **BUSINESS AS USUAL**
    Men at Work-Columbia
16. **PICTURES AT ELEVEN**
    Robert Plant-Swan Song
17. **A FLOCK OF SEAGULLS**
    A Flock of Seagulls-Jive/Arista
18. **COMBAT ROCK**
    The Clash-Epic
19. **HEY RICKY**
    Melissa Manchester-Arista
20. **DONNA SUMMER**
    Donna Summer-Geffen

UK SINGLES

1. **PASS THE DUTCHIE**
   Musical Youth-MCA
2. **THE BITTEREST PILL**
   The Jam-Polydor
3. **ZOOM**
   Fat Larry's Band-WMOT/Virgin
4. **EYE OF THE TIGER**
   Survivor-Scotti Bros.
5. **THERE IT IS**
   Shalamar-Solar
6. **WALKING ON SUNSHINE**
   Rockers Revenge-London
7. **LOVE COME DOWN**
   Evelyn King-RCA
8. **PRIVATE INVESTIGATIONS**
   Dire Straits-Vertigo/Phonogram
9. **FRIEND OR FOE**
   Adam Ant-CBS
10. **WHY**
    Carly Simon-WEA
11. **HARD TO SAY I'M SORRY**
    Chicago-Full Moon
12. **ALL OF MY HEART**
    ABC-Neutron/Phonogram
13. **SADDLE UP**
    David Christie-KR
14. **JUST WHAT I ALWAYS ...**
    Mari Wilson-Compact
15. **DO YOU REALLY WANT ...**
    Culture Club-Virgin
16. **THE MESSAGE**
    Grand Master Flash-Sugar Hill
17. **GLITTERING PRIZE**
    Simple Minds-Virgin
18. **SAVE A PRAYER**
    Duran Duran-EMI
19. **LEAVE IN SILENCE**
    Depeche Mode-Mute
20. **COME ON EILEEN**
    Dexys Midnight Runners-Mercury

UK ALBUMS

1. **LOVE OVER GOLD**
   Dire Straits-Vertigo/Phonogram
2. **THE KIDS FROM FAME**
   Various-BBC
3. **NEW GOLD DREAM**
   Simple Minds-Virgin
4. **CHART BEAT/CHART HEAT**
   Various-K-tel
5. **NEBRASKA**
   Bruce Springsteen-CBS
6. **UPSTAIRS AT ERIC'S**
   Yazoo-Mute
7. **THE LEXICON OF LOVE**
   ABC-Neutron/Phonogram
8. **THE DREAMING**
   Kate Bush-EMI
9. **RIO**
   Duran Duran-EMI
10. **IN THE HEAT OF THE NIGHT**
    Imagination-R&B
11. **FRIENDS**
    Shalamar-Solar
12. **THE COLLECTION 1977-1982**
    The Stranglers-Liberty
13. **TOO-RYE-AY**
    Dexys Midnight Runners-Mercury
14. **PETER GABRIEL**
    Peter Gabriel-Charisma/Phonogram
15. **LOVE SONGS**
    Commodores-K-tel
16. **BREAKOUT**
    Various-Ronco
17. **SIGNALS**
    Rush-Mercury/Phonogram
18. **MAGIC**
    Gillan-Virgin
19. **SOMETHING'S GOING ON**
    Frida-Epic
20. **LOVE AND DANCING**
    The League Unlimited Orchestra-Virgin

US SINGLES

1. **JACK AND DIANE**
   John Cougar-Riva/Mercury
2. **ABRACADABRA**
   The Steve Miller Band-Capitol
3. **HARD TO SAY I'M SORRY**
   Chicago-Full Moon/Warner Bros.
4. **EYE IN THE SKY**
   The Alan Parsons Project-Arista
5. **WHO CAN IT BE NOW?**
   Men at Work-Columbia
6. **EYE OF THE TIGER**
   Survivor-Scotti Bros.
7. **I KEEP FORGETTIN'**
   Michael McDonald-Warner Bros.
8. **SOMEBODY'S BABY**
   Jackson Browne-Asylum
9. **YOU CAN DO MAGIC**
   America-Capitol
10. **I RAN**
    A Flock of Seagulls-Jive/Arista
11. **HEART ATTACK**
    Olivia Newton-John-MCA
12. **BLUE EYES**
    Elton John-Geffen
13. **BREAK IT TO ME GENTLY**
    Juice Newton-Capitol
14. **YOU SHOULD HEAR HOW ...**
    Melissa Manchester-Arista
15. **HURTS SO GOOD**
    John Cougar-Riva
16. **HOLD ON**
    Santana-Columbia
17. **UP WHERE WE BELONG**
    Joe Cocker & Jennifer Warnes-Island
18. **GLORIA**
    Laura Branigan-Atlantic
19. **WHAT'S FOREVER FOR**
    Michael Murphey-Liberty
20. **DO YOU WANNA TOUCH ME**
    Joan Jett & The Blackhearts-Boardwalk

US ALBUMS

1. **AMERICAN FOOL**
   John Cougar-Riva/Mercury
2. **MIRAGE**
   Fleetwood Mac-Warner Bros.
3. **ABRACADABRA**
   The Steve Miller Band-Capitol
4. **ASIA**
   Asia-Geffen
5. **EMOTIONS IN MOTION**
   Billy Squier-Capitol
6. **IF THAT'S WHAT IT TAKES**
   Michael McDonald-Warner Bros.
7. **EYE IN THE SKY**
   Alan Parsons Project-Arista
8. **VACATION**
   The Go Go's-I.R.S.
9. **CHICAGO 16**
   Chicago-Full Moon/Warner Bros.
10. **IT'S HARD**
    The Who-Warner Bros.
11. **BUSINESS AS USUAL**
    Men at Work-Columbia
12. **A FLOCK OF SEAGULLS**
    A Flock of Seagulls-Jive/Arista
13. **GET LUCKY**
    Loverboy-Columbia
14. **GAP BAND IV**
    Gap Band-Total Experience
15. **EYE OF THE TIGER**
    Survivor-Scotti Bros.
16. **GOOD TROUBLE**
    REO Speedwagon-Epic
17. **HIGH ADVENTURE**
    Kenny Loggins-Columbia
18. **COMBAT ROCK**
    The Clash-Epic
19. **HEY RICKY**
    Melissa Manchester-Arista
20. **DONNA SUMMER**
    Donna Summer-Geffen

UK SINGLES

1. **PASS THE DUTCHIE**
   Musical Youth-MCA
2. **ZOOM**
   Fat Larry's Band-WMOT/Virgin
3. **DO YOU REALLY WANT ...**
   Culture Club-Virgin
4. **HARD TO SAY I'M SORRY**
   Chicago-Full Moon
5. **JACKIE WILSON SAID**
   Dexys Midnight Runners-Mercury
6. **THERE IT IS**
   Shalamar-Solar
7. **LOVE COME DOWN**
   Evelyn King-RCA
8. **JUST WHAT I ALWAYS ...**
   Mari Wilson-Compact
9. **FRIEND OR FOE**
   Adam Ant-CBS
10. **THE BITTEREST PILL**
    The Jam-Polydor
11. **EYE OF THE TIGER**
    Survivor-Scotti Bros.
12. **WALKING ON SUNSHINE**
    Rockers Revenge-London
13. **WHY**
    Carly Simon-WEA
14. **STARMAKER**
    The Kids From "Fame"-RCA
15. **SADDLE UP**
    David Christie-KR
16. **GLITTERING PRIZE**
    Simple Minds-Virgin
17. **ALL OF MY HEART**
    ABC-Neutron/Phonogram
18. **PRIVATE INVESTIGATIONS**
    Dire Straits-Vertigo/Phonogram
19. **HOUSE OF THE RISING SUN**
    The Animals-RAK
20. **THE MESSAGE**
    Grand Master Flash-Sugar Hill

UK ALBUMS

1. **LOVE OVER GOLD**
   Dire Straits-Vertigo/Phonogram
2. **THE KIDS FROM FAME**
   Various-BBC
3. **NEBRASKA**
   Bruce Springsteen-CBS
4. **UB44**
   UB40-DEP International
5. **THE LEXICON OF LOVE**
   ABC-Neutron/Phonogram
6. **UPSTAIRS AT ERIC'S**
   Yazoo-Mute
7. **CHART BEAT/CHART HEAT**
   Various-K-tel
8. **NEW GOLD DREAM**
   Simple Minds-Virgin
9. **TOO-RYE-AY**
   Dexys Midnight Runners-Mercury
10. **A BROKEN FRAME**
    Depeche Mode-Mute
11. **LOVE SONGS**
    Commodores-K-tel
12. **GIVE ME YOUR HEART ...**
    Shakin' Stevens-Epic
13. **IN THE HEAT OF THE NIGHT**
    Imagination-R&B
14. **FRIENDS**
    Shalamar-Solar
15. **THE DREAMING**
    Kate Bush-EMI
16. **RIO**
    Duran Duran-EMI
17. **MAGIC**
    Gillan-Virgin
18. **THE COLLECTION 1977-1982**
    The Stranglers-Liberty
19. **AVALON**
    Roxy Music-EG (Polydor)
20. **FOREVER NOW**
    Psychedelic Furs-CBS

US SINGLES

1. **JACK AND DIANE**
   John Cougar-Riva/Mercury
2. **WHO CAN IT BE NOW?**
   Men at Work-Columbia
3. **EYE IN THE SKY**
   The Alan Parsons Project-Arista
4. **HARD TO SAY I'M SORRY**
   Chicago-Full Moon/Warner Bros.
5. **ABRACADABRA**
   The Steve Miller Band-Capitol
6. **I KEEP FORGETTIN'**
   Michael McDonald-Warner Bros.
7. **SOMEBODY'S BABY**
   Jackson Browne-Asylum
8. **YOU CAN DO MAGIC**
   America-Capitol
9. **HEART ATTACK**
   Olivia Newton-John-MCA
10. **I RAN**
    A Flock of Seagulls-Jive/Arista
11. **UP WHERE WE BELONG**
    Joe Cocker & Jennifer Warnes-Island
12. **BLUE EYES**
    Elton John-Geffen
13. **BREAK IT TO ME GENTLY**
    Juice Newton-Capitol
14. **EYE OF THE TIGER**
    Survivor-Scotti Bros.
15. **GYPSY**
    Fleetwood Mac-Warner Bros.
16. **HOLD ON**
    Santana-Columbia
17. **GLORIA**
    Laura Branigan-Atlantic
18. **HEARTLIGHT**
    Neil Diamond-Columbia
19. **WHAT'S FOREVER FOR**
    Michael Murphey-Liberty
20. **DON'T FIGHT IT**
    Kenny Loggins & Steve Perry-Columbia

US ALBUMS

1. **AMERICAN FOOL**
   John Cougar-Riva/Mercury
2. **MIRAGE**
   Fleetwood Mac-Warner Bros.
3. **ABRACADABRA**
   The Steve Miller Band-Capitol
4. **NEBRASKA**
   Bruce Springsteen-Columbia
5. **EMOTIONS IN MOTION**
   Billy Squier-Capitol
6. **IT THAT'S WHAT IT TAKES**
   Michael McDonald-Warner Bros.
7. **EYE IN THE SKY**
   Alan Parsons Project-Arista
8. **VACATION**
   The Go Go's-I.R.S.
9. **CHICAGO 16**
   Chicago-Full Moon/Warner Bros.
10. **IT'S HARD**
    The Who-Warner Bros.
11. **BUSINESS AS USUAL**
    Men at Work-Columbia
12. **A FLOCK OF SEAGULLS**
    A Flock of Seagulls-Jive/Arista
13. **SIGNALS**
    Rush-Mercury
14. **GET LUCKY**
    Loverboy-Columbia
15. **HIGH ADVENTURE**
    Kenny Loggins-Columbia
16. **ASIA**
    Asia-Geffen
17. **EYE OF THE TIGER**
    Survivor-Scotti Bros.
18. **COMBAT ROCK**
    The Clash-Epic
19. **HEY RICKY**
    Melissa Manchester-Arista
20. **DONNA SUMMER**
    Donna Summer-Geffen

UK SINGLES

1. **PASS THE DUTCHIE**
   Musical Youth-MCA
2. **DO YOU REALLY WANT ...**
   Culture Club-Virgin
3. **ZOOM**
   Fat Larry's Band-WMOT/Virgin
4. **STARMAKER**
   The Kids From "Fame"-RCA
5. **HARD TO SAY I'M SORRY**
   Chicago-Full Moon
6. **JACKIE WILSON SAID**
   Dexys Midnight Runners-Mercury
7. **LOVE COME DOWN**
   Evelyn King-RCA
8. **JUST WHAT I ALWAYS ...**
   Mari Wilson-Compact
9. **THERE IT IS**
   Shalamar-Solar
10. **LIFELINE**
    Spandau Ballet-Reformation/Chrysalis
11. **FRIEND OR FOE**
    Adam Ant-CBS
12. **WHY**
    Carly Simon-WEA
13. **HOUSE OF THE RISING SUN**
    The Animals-RAK
14. **LOVE ME DO**
    The Beatles-Parlophone
15. **ANNIE, I'M NOT YOUR ...**
    Kid Creole & The Coconuts-Ze/Island
16. **THE BITTEREST PILL**
    The Jam-Polydor
17. **WALKING ON SUNSHINE**
    Rockers Revenge-London
18. **GLITTERING PRIZE**
    Simple Minds-Virgin
19. **EYE OF THE TIGER**
    Survivor-Scotti Bros.
20. **REAP THE WILD WIND**
    Ultravox-Chrysalis

UK ALBUMS

1. **LOVE OVER GOLD**
   Dire Straits-Vertigo/Phonogram
2. **THE KIDS FROM FAME**
   Various-BBC
3. **GIVE ME YOUR HEART ...**
   Shakin' Stevens-Epic
4. **UB44**
   UB40-DEP International
5. **UPSTAIRS AT ERIC'S**
   Yazoo-Mute
6. **TOO-RYE-AY**
   Dexys Midnight Runners-Mercury
7. **THE LEXICON OF LOVE**
   ABC-Neutron/Phonogram
8. **A BROKEN FRAME**
   Depeche Mode-Mute
9. **REFLECTIONS**
   Various-CBS
10. **NEBRASKA**
    Bruce Springsteen-CBS
11. **LOVE SONGS**
    Commodores-K-tel
12. **KISSING TO BE CLEVER**
    Culture Club-Virgin
13. **NEW GOLD DREAM**
    Simple Minds-Virgin
14. **IN THE HEAT OF THE NIGHT**
    Imagination-R&B
15. **FRIENDS**
    Shalamar-Solar
16. **CHART ATTACK**
    Various-Telstar
17. **CHART BEAT/CHART HEAT**
    Various-K-tel
18. **THE DREAMING**
    Kate Bush-EMI
19. **RIO**
    Duran Duran-EMI
20. **AVALON**
    Roxy Music-EG (Polydor)

US SINGLES

1. JACK AND DIANE
   John Cougar-Riva/Mercury
2. WHO CAN IT BE NOW?
   Men at Work-Columbia
3. EYE IN THE SKY
   The Alan Parsons Project-Arista
4. I KEEP FORGETTIN'
   Michael McDonald-Warner Bros.
5. UP WHERE WE BELONG
   Joe Cocker & Jennifer Warnes-Island
6. HEART ATTACK
   Olivia Newton-John-MCA
7. SOMEBODY'S BABY
   Jackson Browne-Asylum
8. YOU CAN DO MAGIC
   America-Capitol
9. I RAN
   A Flock of Seagulls-Jive/Arista
10. ABRACADABRA
    The Steve Miller Band-Capitol
11. BREAK IT TO ME GENTLY
    Juice Newton-Capitol
12. GYPSY
    Fleetwood Mac-Warner Bros.
13. HEARTLIGHT
    Neil Diamond-Columbia
14. GLORIA
    Laura Branigan-Atlantic
15. HOLD ON
    Santana-Columbia
16. HARD TO SAY I'M SORRY
    Chicago-Full Moon/Warner Bros.
17. DON'T FIGHT IT
    Kenny Loggins & Steve Perry-Columbia
18. EYE OF THE TIGER
    Survivor-Scotti Bros.
19. WHAT'S FOREVER FOR
    Michael Murphey-Liberty
20. THE ONE YOU LOVE
    Glenn Frey-Asylum

US ALBUMS

1. AMERICAN FOOL
   John Cougar-Riva/Mercury
2. MIRAGE
   Fleetwood Mac-Warner Bros.
3. ABRACADABRA
   The Steve Miller Band-Capitol
4. NEBRASKA
   Bruce Springsteen-Columbia
5. EMOTIONS IN MOTION
   Billy Squier-Capitol
6. IF THAT'S WHAT IT TAKES
   Michael McDonald-Warner Bros.
7. EYE IN THE SKY
   Alan Parsons Project-Arista
8. IT'S HARD
   The Who-Warner Bros.
9. BUSINESS AS USUAL
   Men at Work-Columbia
10. A FLOCK OF SEAGULLS
    A Flock of Seagulls-Jive/Arista
11. SIGNALS
    Rush-Mercury
12. THE NYLON CURTAIN
    Billy Joel-Columbia
13. HIGH ADVENTURE
    Kenny Loggins-Columbia
14. GET LUCKY
    Loverboy-Columbia
15. HEARTLIGHT
    Neil Diamond-Columbia
16. COMBAT ROCK
    The Clash-Epic
17. EYE OF THE TIGER
    Survivor-Scotti Bros.
18. BUILT FOR SPEED
    Stray Cats-EMI America
19. SCREAMING FOR VENGEANCE
    Judas Priest-Columbia
20. NO CONTROL
    Eddie Money-Columbia

UK SINGLES

1. DO YOU REALLY WANT ...
   Culture Club-Virgin
2. PASS THE DUTCHIE
   Musical Youth-MCA
3. STARMAKER
   The Kids From "Fame"-RCA
4. ZOOM
   Fat Larry's Band-WMOT/Virgin
5. LOVE ME DO
   The Beatles-Parlophone
6. HARD TO SAY I'M SORRY
   Chicago-Full Moon
7. LIFELINE
   Spandau Ballet-Reformation/Chrysalis
8. DANGER GAMES
   The Pinkees-Creole
9. ANNIE, I'M NOT YOUR ...
   Kid Creole & The Coconuts-Ze/Island
10. JACKIE WILSON SAID
    Dexys Midnight Runners-Mercury
11. HOUSE OF THE RISING SUN
    The Animals-RAK
12. REAP THE WILD WIND
    Ultravox-Chrysalis
13. I WANNA DO IT WITH YOU
    Barry Manilow-Arista
14. JUST WHAT I ALWAYS ...
    Mari Wilson-Compact
15. LOVE COME DOWN
    Evelyn King-RCA
16. MAD WORLD
    Tears For Fears-Mercury
17. SHOULD I STAY ...
    The Clash-CBS
18. ZIGGY STARDUST
    Bauhaus-Beggars Banquet
19. THERE IT IS
    Shalamar-Solar
20. I'LL BE SATISFIED
    Shakin' Stevens-Epic

UK ALBUMS

1. LOVE OVER GOLD
   Dire Straits-Vertigo/Phonogram
2. KIDS FROM FAME
   Various-BBC
3. KIDS FROM 'FAME' AGAIN
   The Kids From 'Fame'-RCA
4. REFLECTIONS
   Various-CBS
5. FRIEND OR FOE
   Adam Ant-CBS
6. QUARTET
   Ultravox-Chrysalis
7. CHART ATTACK
   Various-Telstar
8. KISSING TO BE CLEVER
   Culture Club-Virgin
9. GIVE ME YOUR HEART ...
   Shakin' Stevens-Epic
10. UPSTAIRS AT ERIC'S
    Yazoo-Mute
11. UB44
    UB40-DEP International
12. TOO-RYE-AY
    Dexys Midnight Runners-Mercury
13. THE LEXICON OF LOVE
    ABC-Neutron/Phonogram
14. A BROKEN FRAME
    Depeche Mode-Mute
15. STRAWBERRIES
    The Damned-Bronze
16. NEBRASKA
    Bruce Springsteen-CBS
17. TROPICAL GANGSTERS
    Kid Creole & The Coconuts-Ze/Island
18. LOVE SONGS
    Commodores-K-tel
19. IN THE HEAT OF THE NIGHT
    Imagination-R&B
20. NEW GOLD DREAM
    Simple Minds-Virgin

US SINGLES

1. WHO CAN IT BE NOW?
   Men at Work-Columbia
2. JACK AND DIANE
   John Cougar-Riva/Mercury
3. EYE IN THE SKY
   The Alan Parsons Project-Arista
4. I KEEP FORGETTIN'
   Michael McDonald-Warner Bros.
5. UP WHERE WE BELONG
   Joe Cocker & Jennifer Warnes-Island
6. HEART ATTACK
   Olivia Newton-John-MCA
7. SOMEBODY'S BABY
   Jackson Browne-Asylum
8. YOU CAN DO MAGIC
   America-Capitol
9. I RAN
   A Flock of Seagulls-Jive/Arista
10. HEARTLIGHT
    Neil Diamond-Columbia
11. BREAK IT TO ME GENTLY
    Juice Newton-Capitol
12. GYPSY
    Fleetwood Mac-Warner Bros.
13. GLORIA
    Laura Branigan-Atlantic
14. TRULY
    Lionel Richie-Motown
15. HOLD ON
    Santana-Columbia
16. THE ONE YOU LOVE
    Glenn Frey-Asylum
17. DON'T FIGHT IT
    Kenny Loggins & Steve Perry-Columbia
18. MUSCLES
    Diana Ross-RCA
19. WHAT'S FOREVER FOR
    Michael Murphey-Liberty
20. LOVE COME DOWN
    Evelyn King-RCA

US ALBUMS

1. AMERICAN FOOL
   John Cougar-Riva/Mercury
2. MIRAGE
   Fleetwood Mac-Warner Bros.
3. NEBRASKA
   Bruce Springsteen-Columbia
4. BUSINESS AS USUAL
   Men at Work-Columbia
5. EMOTIONS IN MOTION
   Billy Squier-Capitol
6. IF THAT'S WHAT IT TAKES
   Michael McDonald-Warner Bros.
7. EYE IN THE SKY
   Alan Parsons Project-Arista
8. IT'S HARD
   The Who-Warner Bros.
9. THE NYLON CURTAIN
   Billy Joel-Columbia
10. A FLOCK OF SEAGULLS
    A Flock of Seagulls-Jive/Arista
11. SIGNALS
    Rush-Mercury
12. HEARTLIGHT
    Neil Diamond-Columbia
13. HIGH ADVENTURE
    Kenny Loggins-Columbia
14. ABRACADABRA
    The Steve Miller Band-Capitol
15. COMBAT ROCK
    The Clash-Epic
16. BUILT FOR SPEED
    Stray Cats-EMI America
17. SCREAMING FOR VENGEANCE
    Judas Priest-Columbia
18. GREATEST HITS VOL. 2
    Olivia Newton-John-MCA
19. GET LUCKY
    Loverboy-Columbia
20. NO CONTROL
    Eddie Money-Columbia

UK SINGLES

1. DO YOU REALLY WANT ...
   Culture Club-Virgin
2. ANNIE, I'M NOT YOUR ...
   Kid Creole & The Coconuts-Ze/Island
3. STARMAKER
   The Kids From "Fame"-RCA
4. LOVE ME DO
   The Beatles-Parlophone
5. PASS THE DUTCHIE
   Musical Youth-MCA
6. MAD WORLD
   Tears For Fears-Mercury
7. LIFELINE
   Spandau Ballet-Reformation/Chrysalis
8. ZOOM
   Fat Larry's Band-WMOT/Virgin
9. HARD TO SAY I'M SORRY
   Chicago-Full Moon
10. I WANNA DO IT WITH YOU
    Barry Manilow-Arista
11. I DON'T WANNA DANCE
    Eddy Grant-Ice
12. DANGER GAMES
    The Pinkees-Creole
13. REAP THE WILD WIND
    Ultravox-Chrysalis
14. HOUSE OF THE RISING SUN
    The Animals-RAK
15. ZIGGY STARDUST
    Bauhaus-Beggars Banquet
16. OOH LA, LA, LA
    Kool & The Gang-De-Lite/Phonogram
17. JACKIE WILSON SAID
    Dexys Midnight Runners-Mercury
18. SHOULD I STAY ...
    The Clash-CBS
19. I'LL BE SATISFIED
    Shakin' Stevens-Epic
20. LOVE COME DOWN
    Evelyn King-RCA

UK ALBUMS

1. THE KIDS FROM FAME
   Various-BBC
2. KIDS FROM 'FAME' AGAIN
   The Kids From 'Fame'-RCA
3. LOVE OVER GOLD
   Dire Straits-Vertigo/Phonogram
4. THE SKY'S GONE OUT
   Bauhaus-Beggars Banquet
5. KISSING TO BE CLEVER
   Culture Club-Virgin
6. REFLECTIONS
   Various-CBS
7. QUARTET
   Ultravox-Chrysalis
8. GIVE ME YOUR HEART ...
   Shakin' Stevens-Epic
9. FRIEND OR FOE
   Adam Ant-CBS
10. TROPICAL GANGSTERS
    Kid Creole & The Coconuts-Ze/Island
11. GREATEST HITS
    Olivia Newton-John-EMI
12. CHART ATTACK
    Various-Telstar
13. THE LEXICON OF LOVE
    ABC-Neutron/Phonogram
14. UPSTAIRS AT ERIC'S
    Yazoo-Mute
15. AMOR
    Julio Iglesias-CBS
16. LOVE SONGS
    Commodores-K-tel
17. 20 GREATEST HITS
    The Beatles-Parlophone
18. TOO-RYE-AY
    Dexys Midnight Runners-Mercury
19. ASSAULT ATTACK
    Michael Schenker Group-Chrysalis
20. STRAWBERRIES
    The Damned-Bronze

US SINGLES

1. **UP WHERE WE BELONG**
   Joe Cocker & Jennifer Warnes-Island
2. **WHO CAN IT BE NOW?**
   Men at Work-Columbia
3. **HEART ATTACK**
   Olivia Newton-John-MCA
4. **I KEEP FORGETTIN'**
   Michael McDonald-Warner Bros.
5. **JACK AND DIANE**
   John Cougar-Riva/Mercury
6. **EYE IN THE SKY**
   The Alan Parsons Project-Arista
7. **HEARTLIGHT**
   Neil Diamond-Columbia
8. **YOU CAN DO MAGIC**
   America-Capitol
9. **GLORIA**
   Laura Branigan-Atlantic
10. **TRULY**
    Lionel Richie-Motown
11. **BREAK IT TO ME GENTLY**
    Juice Newton-Capitol
12. **GYPSY**
    Fleetwood Mac-Warner Bros.
13. **SOMEBODY'S BABY**
    Jackson Browne-Asylum
14. **MUSCLES**
    Diana Ross-RCA
15. **THE ONE YOU LOVE**
    Glenn Frey-Asylum
16. **I RAN**
    A Flock of Seagulls-Jive/Arista
17. **LOVE COME DOWN**
    Evelyn King-RCA
18. **YOU DON'T WANT ME ...**
    Steel Breeze-RCA
19. **WHAT'S FOREVER FOR**
    Michael Murphey-Liberty
20. **AMERICAN HEARTBEAT**
    Survivor-Scotti Bros.

US ALBUMS

1. **AMERICAN FOOL**
   John Cougar-Riva/Mercury
2. **MIRAGE**
   Fleetwood Mac-Warner Bros.
3. **NEBRASKA**
   Bruce Springsteen-Columbia
4. **BUSINESS AS USUAL**
   Men at Work-Columbia
5. **EMOTIONS IN MOTION**
   Billy Squier-Capitol
6. **IF THAT'S WHAT IT TAKES**
   Michael McDonald-Warner Bros.
7. **EYE IN THE SKY**
   Alan Parsons Project-Arista
8. **IT'S HARD**
   The Who-Warner Bros.
9. **THE NYLON CURTAIN**
   Billy Joel-Columbia
10. **A FLOCK OF SEAGULLS**
    A Flock of Seagulls-Jive/Arista
11. **SIGNALS**
    Rush-Mercury
12. **HEARTLIGHT**
    Neil Diamond-Columbia
13. **HIGH ADVENTURE**
    Kenny Loggins-Columbia
14. **COMBAT ROCK**
    The Clash-Epic
15. **BUILT FOR SPEED**
    Stray Cats EMI-America
16. **LIONEL RICHIE**
    Lionel Richie-Motown
17. **SCREAMING FOR VENGEANCE**
    Judas Priest-Columbia
18. **GREATEST HITS VOL. 2**
    Olivia Newton-John-MCA
19. **NIGHT AND DAY**
    Joe Jackson-A&M
20. **NO CONTROL**
    Eddie Money-Columbia

UK SINGLES

1. **DO YOU REALLY WANT ...**
   Culture Club-Virgin
2. **I DON'T WANNA DANCE**
   Eddy Grant-Ice
3. **MAD WORLD**
   Tears For Fears-Mercury
4. **STARMAKER**
   The Kids From "Fame"-RCA
5. **HEARTBREAKER**
   Dionne Warwick-Arista
6. **ANNIE, I'M NOT YOUR ...**
   Kid Creole & The Coconuts-Ze/Island
7. **LOVE ME DO**
   The Beatles-Parlophone
8. **I WANNA DO IT WITH YOU**
   Barry Manilow-Arista
9. **LIFELINE**
   Spandau Ballet-Reformation/Chrysalis
10. **I'LL BE SATISFIED**
    Shakin' Stevens-Epic
11. **OOH, LA, LA, LA**
    Kool & The Gang-De-Lite/Phonogram
12. **HARD TO SAY I'M SORRY**
    Chicago-Full Moon
13. **CAROLINE**
    Status Quo-Vertigo/Phonogram
14. **PASS THE DUTCHIE**
    Musical Youth-MCA
15. **LOVE'S COMIN' AT YA**
    Melba Moore-EMI America
16. **ZOOM**
    Fat Larry's Band-WMOT/Virgin
17. **BACK ON THE CHAIN GANG**
    Pretenders-Real
18. **(SEXUAL) HEALING**
    Marvin Gaye-CBS
19. **ZIGGY STARDUST**
    Bauhaus-Beggars Banquet
20. **MANEATER**
    Daryl Hall & John Oates-RCA

UK ALBUMS

1. **THE KIDS FROM FAME**
   Various-BBC
2. **KIDS FROM 'FAME' AGAIN**
   The Kids From 'Fame'-RCA
3. **LOVE OVER GOLD**
   Dire Straits-Vertigo/Phonogram
4. **REFLECTIONS**
   Various-CBS
5. **KISSING TO BE CLEVER**
   Culture Club-Virgin
6. **'...FAMOUS LAST WORDS...'**
   Supertramp-A&M
7. **THE SKY'S GONE OUT**
   Bauhaus-Beggars Banquet
8. **SINGLES-45's AND UNDER**
   Squeeze-A&M
9. **GREATEST HITS**
   Olivia Newton-John-EMI
10. **20 GREATEST HITS**
    The Beatles-Parlophone
11. **TROPICAL GANGSTERS**
    Kid Creole & The Coconuts-Ze/Island
12. **GIVE ME YOUR HEART ...**
    Shakin' Stevens-Epic
13. **HEARTBREAKER**
    Dionne Warwick-Arista
14. **AMOR**
    Julio Iglesias-CBS
15. **QUARTET**
    Ultravox-Chrysalis
16. **LOVE SONGS**
    Commodores-K-tel
17. **UPSTAIRS AT ERIC'S**
    Yazoo-Mute
18. **THE DOLLAR ALBUM**
    Dollar-WEA
19. **THE LEXICON OF LOVE**
    ABC-Neutron/Phonogram
20. **FRIEND OR FOE**
    Adam Ant-CBS

US SINGLES

1. **UP WHERE WE BELONG**
   Joe Cocker & Jennifer Warnes-Island
2. **TRULY**
   Lionel Richie-Motown
3. **HEART ATTACK**
   Olivia Newton-John-MCA
4. **GLORIA**
   Laura Branigan-Atlantic
5. **HEARTLIGHT**
   Neil Diamond-Columbia
6. **WHO CAN IT BE NOW?**
   Men at Work-Columbia
7. **JACK AND DIANE**
   John Cougar-Riva/Mercury
8. **YOU CAN DO MAGIC**
   America-Capitol
9. **I KEEP FORGETTIN'**
   Michael McDonald-Warner Bros.
10. **MUSCLES**
    Diana Ross-RCA
11. **EYE IN THE SKY**
    The Alan Parsons Project-Arista
12. **MANEATER**
    Daryl Hall & John Oates-RCA
13. **MICKEY**
    Toni Basil-Radialchoice/Virgin/Chrys.
14. **STEPPIN' OUT**
    Joe Jackson-A&M
15. **THE ONE YOU LOVE**
    Glenn Frey-Asylum
16. **YOU DON'T WANT ME ...**
    Steel Breeze-RCA
17. **LOVE COME DOWN**
    Evelyn King-RCA
18. **AMERICAN HEARTBEAT**
    Survivor-Scotti Bros.
19. **NOBODY**
    Sylvia-RCA
20. **SOUTHERN CROSS**
    Crosby, Stills & Nash-Atlantic

US ALBUMS

1. **BUSINESS AS USUAL**
   Men at Work-Columbia
2. **MIRAGE**
   Fleetwood Mac-Warner Bros.
3. **NEBRASKA**
   Bruce Springsteen-Columbia
4. **AMERICAN FOOL**
   John Cougar-Riva/Mercury
5. **LIONEL RICHIE**
   Lionel Richie-Motown
6. **BUILT FOR SPEED**
   Stray Cats-EMI America
7. **EYE IN THE SKY**
   Alan Parsons Project-Arista
8. **IT'S HARD**
   The Who-Warner Bros.
9. **THE NYLON CURTAIN**
   Billy Joel-Columbia
10. **EMOTIONS IN MOTION**
    Billy Squier-Capitol
11. **SIGNALS**
    Rush-Mercury
12. **HEARTLIGHT**
    Neil Diamond-Columbia
13. **COMBAT ROCK**
    The Clash-Epic
14. **IF THAT'S WHAT IT TAKES**
    Michael McDonald-Warner Bros.
15. **NIGHT AND DAY**
    Joe Jackson-A&M
16. **GREATEST HITS VOL. 2**
    Olivia Newton-John-MCA
17. **SCREAMING FOR VENGEANCE**
    Judas Priest-Columbia
18. **THE NIGHTFLY**
    Donald Fagen-Warner Bros.
19. **LOVE OVER GOLD**
    Dire Straits-Warner Bros.
20. **A FLOCK OF SEAGULLS**
    A Flock of Seagulls-Jive/Arista

UK SINGLES

1. **I DON'T WANNA DANCE**
   Eddy Grant-Ice
2. **HEARTBREAKER**
   Dionne Warwick-Arista
3. **MAD WORLD**
   Tears For Fears-Mercury
4. **DO YOU REALLY WANT ...**
   Culture Club-Virgin
5. **(SEXUAL) HEALING**
   Marvin Gaye-CBS
6. **OOH LA, LA, LA**
   Kool & The Gang-De-Lite/Phonogram
7. **STARMAKER**
   The Kids From "Fame"-RCA
8. **I WANNA DO IT WITH YOU**
   Barry Manilow-Arista
9. **THE GIRL IS MINE**
   Michael Jackson/Paul McCartney-Epic
10. **MANEATER**
    Daryl Hall & John Oates-RCA
11. **THEME FROM HARRY'S...**
    Clannad-RCA
12. **ANNIE, I'M NOT YOUR ...**
    Kid Creole & The Coconuts-Ze/Island
13. **I'LL BE SATISFIED**
    Shakin' Stevens-Epic
14. **CAROLINE**
    Status Quo-Vertigo/Phonogram
15. **LOVE ME DO**
    The Beatles-Parlophone
16. **LOVE'S COMIN' AT YA**
    Melba Moore-EMI
17. **ZAMBEZI**
    The Piranhas-Dakota
18. **LIFELINE**
    Spandau Ballet-Reformation/Chrysalis
19. **LIVING ON THE CEILING**
    Blancmange-London
20. **NEVER GIVE YOU UP**
    Sharon Redd-Prelude

UK ALBUMS

1. **THE KIDS FROM FAME**
   Various-BBC
2. **HELLO, I MUST BE GOING!**
   Phil Collins-Virgin
3. **SINGLES-45's AND UNDER**
   Squeeze-A&M
4. **KIDS FROM 'FAME' AGAIN**
   The Kids From 'Fame'-RCA
5. **HEARTBREAKER**
   Dionne Warwick-Arista
6. **LOVE OVER GOLD**
   Dire Straits-Vertigo/Phonogram
7. **'...FAMOUS LAST WORDS...'**
   Supertramp-A&M
8. **REFLECTIONS**
   Various-CBS
9. **KISSING TO BE CLEVER**
   Culture Club-Virgin
10. **'FROM THE MAKERS OF ...'**
    Status Quo-Vertigo/Phonogram
11. **KISS IN THE DREAMHOUSE**
    Siouxsie & The Banshees-Polydor
12. **GIVE ME YOUR HEART ...**
    Shakin' Stevens-Epic
13. **THE RISE & FALL**
    Madness-Stiff
14. **PETER GABRIEL**
    Peter Gabriel-Charisma/Phonogram
15. **GREATEST HITS**
    Olivia Newton-John-EMI
16. **TROPICAL GANGSTERS**
    Kid Creole & The Coconuts-Ze/Island
17. **CHART HITS '82**
    Various-K-tel
18. **20 GREATEST HITS**
    The Beatles-Parlophone
19. **FLASH TRACKS**
    Various-TV Records
20. **WARRIOR ROCK**
    Toyah-Safari

US SINGLES

1 UP WHERE WE BELONG
Joe Cocker & Jennifer Warnes-Island
2 TRULY
Lionel Richie-Motown
3 HEART ATTACK
Olivia Newton-John-MCA
4 GLORIA
Laura Branigan-Atlantic
5 HEARTLIGHT
Neil Diamond-Columbia
6 WHO CAN IT BE NOW?
Men at Work-Columbia
7 MICKEY
Toni Basil-Radialchoice/Virgin/Chrys
8 MANEATER
Daryl Hall & John Oates-RCA
9 STEPPIN' OUT
Joe Jackson-A&M
10 MUSCLES
Diana Ross-RCA
11 JACK AND DIANE
John Cougar-Riva/Mercury
12 ROCK THIS TOWN
Stray Cats-EMI America
13 DIRTY LAUNDRY
Don Henley-Asylum
14 THE GIRL IS MINE
Michael Jackson/Paul McCartney-Epic
15 NOBODY
Sylvia-RCA
16 YOU DON'T WANT ME ...
Steel Breeze-RCA
17 AMERICAN HEARTBEAT
Survivor-Scotti Bros.
18 SOUTHERN CROSS
Crosby, Stills & Nash-Atlantic
19 SEXUAL HEALING
Marvin Gaye-Columbia
20 PRESSURE
Billy Joel-Columbia

US ALBUMS

1 BUSINESS AS USUAL
Men at Work-Columbia
2 MIRAGE
Fleetwood Mac-Warner Bros.
3 NEBRASKA
Bruce Springsteen-Columbia
4 LIONEL RICHIE
Lionel Richie-Motown
5 BUILT FOR SPEED
Stray Cats-EMI America
6 NIGHT AND DAY
Joe Jackson-A&M
7 THE NYLON CURTAIN
Billy Joel-Columbia
8 IT'S HARD
The Who-Warner Bros.
9 AMERICAN FOOL
John Cougar-Riva/Mercury
10 HEARTLIGHT
Neil Diamond-Columbia
11 SIGNALS
Rush-Mercury
12 COMBAT ROCK
The Clash-Epic
13 THE NIGHTFLY
Donald Fagen-Warner Bros.
14 FAMOUS LAST WORDS
Supertramp-A&M
15 H2O
Daryl Hall & John Oates-RCA
16 GREATEST HITS VOL. 2
Olivia Newton-John-MCA
17 SCREAMING FOR VENGEANCE
Judas Priest-Columbia
18 DAYLIGHT AGAIN
Crosby, Stills & Nash-Atlantic
19 LOVE OVER GOLD
Dire Straits-Warner Bros.
20 A FLOCK OF SEAGULLS
A Flock of Seagulls-Jive/Arista

UK SINGLES

1 I DON'T WANNA DANCE
Eddy Grant-Ice
2 HEARTBREAKER
Dionne Warwick-Arista
3 MAD WORLD
Tears For Fears-Mercury
4 (SEXUAL) HEALING
Marvin Gaye-CBS
5 THEME FROM HARRY'S ...
Clannad-RCA
6 MANEATER
Daryl Hall & John Oates-RCA
7 DO YOU REALLY WANT ...
Culture Club-Virgin
8 THE GIRL IS MINE
Michael Jackson/Paul McCartney-Epic
9 MIRROR MAN
The Human League-Virgin
10 YOUNG GUNS (GO FOR IT)
Wham!-Innervision
11 OOH LA, LA, LA
Kool & The Gang-De-Lite/Phonogram
12 LIVING ON THE CEILING
Blancmange-London
13 RIO
Duran Duran-EMI
14 STATE OF INDEPENDENCE
Donna Summer-Warner Bros.
15 MUSCLES
Diana Ross-Capitol
16 I WANNA DO IT WITH YOU
Barry Manilow-Arista
17 CAROLINE
Status Quo-Vertigo/Phonogram
18 DO IT TO THE MUSIC
Raw Silk-KR
19 STARMAKER
The Kids From "Fame"-RCA
20 ZAMBEZI
The Piranhas-Dakota

UK ALBUMS

1 THE KIDS FROM FAME
Various-BBC
2 HELLO, I MUST BE GOING!
Phil Collins-Virgin
3 HEARTBREAKER
Dionne Warwick-Arista
4 SINGLES-45's AND UNDER
Squeeze-A&M
5 'FROM THE MAKERS OF ...'
Status Quo-Vertigo/Phonogram
6 SINGLES-FIRST TEN YEARS
Abba-Epic
7 REFLECTIONS
Various-CBS
8 '...FAMOUS LAST WORDS...'
Supertramp-A&M
9 KIDS FROM 'FAME' AGAIN
The Kids From 'Fame'-RCA
10 THE RISE & FALL
Madness-Stiff
11 CHART HITS '82
Various-K-tel
12 GIVE ME YOUR HEART ...
Shakin' Stevens-Epic
13 LOVE OVER GOLD
Dire Straits-Vertigo/Phonogram
14 KISS IN THE DREAMHOUSE
Siouxsie & The Banshees-Polydor
15 LIVING MY LIFE
Grace Jones-Island
16 RIO
Duran Duran-EMI
17 MIDNIGHT LOVE
Marvin Gaye-CBS
18 KISSING TO BE CLEVER
Culture Club-Virgin
19 PEARLS II
Elkie Brooks-A&M
20 JOHN LENNON COLLECTION
John Lennon-Parlophone

US SINGLES

1 TRULY
Lionel Richie-Motown
2 GLORIA
Laura Branigan-Atlantic
3 HEART ATTACK
Olivia Newton-John-MCA
4 UP WHERE WE BELONG
Joe Cocker & Jennifer Warnes-Island
5 HEARTLIGHT
Neil Diamond-Columbia
6 MICKEY
Toni Basil-Radialchoice/Virgin/Chrys
7 MANEATER
Daryl Hall & John Oates-RCA
8 STEPPIN' OUT
Joe Jackson-A&M
9 THE GIRL IS MINE
Michael Jackson/Paul McCartney-Epic
10 MUSCLES
Diana Ross-RCA
11 DIRTY LAUNDRY
Don Henley-Asylum
12 ROCK THIS TOWN
Stray Cats-EMI America
13 SEXUAL HEALING
Marvin Gaye-Columbia
14 IT'S RAINING AGAIN
Supertramp-A&M
15 NOBODY
Sylvia-RCA
16 SHADOWS OF THE NIGHT
Pat Benatar-Chrysalis
17 AMERICAN HEARTBEAT
Survivor-Scotti Bros.
18 SOUTHERN CROSS
Crosby, Stills & Nash-Atlantic
19 HEARTBREAKER
Dionne Warwick-Arista
20 PRESSURE
Billy Joel-Columbia

US ALBUMS

1 BUSINESS AS USUAL
Men at Work-Columbia
2 BUILT FOR SPEED
Stray Cats-EMI America
3 LIONEL RICHIE
Lionel Richie-Motown
4 NIGHT AND DAY
Joe Jackson-A&M
5 FAMOUS LAST WORDS
Supertramp-A&M
6 H2O
Daryl Hall & John Oates-RCA
7 THE NYLON CURTAIN
Billy Joel-Columbia
8 NEBRASKA
Bruce Springsteen-Columbia
9 HEARTLIGHT
Neil Diamond-Columbia
10 SIGNALS
Rush-Mercury
11 THE NIGHTFLY
Donald Fagen-Warner Bros.
12 COMBAT ROCK
The Clash-Epic
13 MIRAGE
Fleetwood Mac-Warner Bros.
14 AMERICAN FOOL
John Cougar-Riva/Mercury
15 MIDNIGHT LOVE
Marvin Gaye-Columbia
16 GREATEST HITS VOL. 2
Olivia Newton-John-MCA
17 SCREAMING FOR VENGEANCE
Judas Priest-Columbia
18 DAYLIGHT AGAIN
Crosby, Stills & Nash-Atlantic
19 LOVE OVER GOLD
Dire Straits-Warner Bros.
20 A FLOCK OF SEAGULLS
A Flock of Seagulls-Jive/Arista

UK SINGLES

1 I DON'T WANNA DANCE
Eddy Grant-Ice
2 MIRROR MAN
The Human League-Virgin
3 HEARTBREAKER
Dionne Warwick-Arista
4 YOUNG GUNS (GO FOR IT)
Wham!-Innervision
5 (SEXUAL) HEALING
Marvin Gaye-CBS
6 MAD WORLD
Tears For Fears-Mercury
7 LIVING ON THE CEILING
Blancmange-London
8 THEME FROM HARRY'S ...
Clannad-RCA
9 SAVE YOUR LOVE
Renée & Renato-Hollywood
10 MANEATER
Daryl Hall & John Oates-RCA
11 RIO
Duran Duran-EMI
12 THE GIRL IS MINE
Michael Jackson/Paul McCartney-Epic
13 CRY BOY CRY
Blue Zoo-Magnet
14 WISHING
A Flock of Seagulls-Jive
15 STATE OF INDEPENDENCE
Donna Summer-Warner Bros.
16 YOUTH OF TODAY
Musical Youth-MCA
17 TRULY
Lionel Richie-Motown
18 DO YOU REALLY WANT ...
Culture Club-Virgin
19 MUSCLES
Diana Ross-Capitol
20 THE OTHER SIDE OF LOVE
Yazoo-Mute

UK ALBUMS

1 SINGLES-FIRST TEN YEARS
Abba-Epic
2 THE KIDS FROM FAME
Various-BBC
3 HEARTBREAKER
Dionne Warwick-Arista
4 'FROM THE MAKERS OF...'
Status Quo-Vertigo/Phonogram
5 HELLO, I MUST BE GOING!
Phil Collins-Virgin
6 RIO
Duran Duran-EMI
7 I WANNA DO IT WITH YOU
Barry Manilow-Arista
8 REFLECTIONS
Various-CBS
9 SAINTS AN' SINNERS
Whitesnake-Liberty
10 MIDNIGHT LOVE
Marvin Gaye-CBS
11 SINGLES-45's AND UNDER
Squeeze-A&M
12 20 GREATEST LOVE SONGS
Nat King Cole-Capitol
13 PEARLS II
Elkie Brooks-A&M
14 JOHN LENNON COLLECTION
John Lennon-Parlophone
15 GIVE ME YOUR HEART ...
Shakin' Stevens-Epic
16 KIDS FROM 'FAME' AGAIN
The Kids From 'Fame'-RCA
17 LOVE OVER GOLD
Dire Straits-Vertigo/Phonogram
18 '...FAMOUS LAST WORDS...'
Supertramp-A&M
19 THE RISE & FALL
Madness-Stiff
20 CHART HITS '82
Various-K-tel

US SINGLES

1. **TRULY**
   Lionel Richie-Motown
2. **GLORIA**
   Laura Branigan-Atlantic
3. **MICKEY**
   Toni Basil-Radialchoice/Virgin/Chrys
4. **MANEATER**
   Daryl Hall & John Oates-RCA
5. **HEARTLIGHT**
   Neil Diamond-Columbia
6. **UP WHERE WE BELONG**
   Joe Cocker & Jennifer Warnes-Island
7. **STEPPIN' OUT**
   Joe Jackson-A&M
8. **THE GIRL IS MINE**
   Michael Jackson/Paul McCartney-Epic
9. **DIRTY LAUNDRY**
   Don Henley-Asylum
10. **MUSCLES**
    Diana Ross-RCA
11. **ROCK THIS TOWN**
    Stray Cats-EMI America
12. **SEXUAL HEALING**
    Marvin Gaye-Columbia
13. **IT'S RAINING AGAIN**
    Supertramp-A&M
14. **SHADOWS OF THE NIGHT**
    Pat Benatar-Chrysalis
15. **NOBODY**
    Sylvia-RCA
16. **HEART ATTACK**
    Olivia Newton-John-MCA
17. **HEARTBREAKER**
    Dionne Warwick-Arista
18. **SOUTHERN CROSS**
    Crosby, Stills & Nash-Atlantic
19. **DOWN UNDER**
    Men at Work-Columbia
20. **PRESSURE**
    Billy Joel-Columbia

US ALBUMS

1. **BUSINESS AS USUAL**
   Men at Work-Columbia
2. **BUILT FOR SPEED**
   Stray Cats-EMI America
3. **LIONEL RICHIE**
   Lionel Richie-Motown
4. **NIGHT AND DAY**
   Joe Jackson-A&M
5. **FAMOUS LAST WORDS**
   Supertramp-A&M
6. **H2O**
   Daryl Hall & John Oates-RCA
7. **THE NYLON CURTAIN**
   Billy Joel-Columbia
8. **MIDNIGHT LOVE**
   Marvin Gaye-Columbia
9. **HEARTLIGHT**
   Neil Diamond-Columbia
10. **GET NERVOUS**
    Pat Benatar-Chrysalis
11. **THE NIGHTFLY**
    Donald Fagen-Warner Bros.
12. **COMBAT ROCK**
    The Clash-Epic
13. **NEBRASKA**
    Bruce Springsteen-Columbia
14. **MIRAGE**
    Fleetwood Mac-Warner Bros.
15. **LONG AFTER DARK**
    Tom Petty-Backstreet
16. **GREATEST HITS VOL. 2**
    Olivia Newton-John-MCA
17. **SCREAMING FOR VENGEANCE**
    Judas Priest-Columbia
18. **DAYLIGHT AGAIN**
    Crosby, Stills & Nash-Atlantic
19. **SIGNALS**
    Rush-Mercury
20. **EMOTIONS IN MOTION**
    Billy Squier-Capitol

UK SINGLES

1. **BEAT SURRENDER**
   The Jam-Polydor
2. **MIRROR MAN**
   The Human League-Virgin
3. **YOUNG GUNS (GO FOR IT)**
   Wham!-Innervision
4. **I DON'T WANNA DANCE**
   Eddy Grant-Ice
5. **SAVE YOUR LOVE**
   Renée & Renato-Hollywood
6. **TRULY**
   Lionel Richie-Motown
7. **LIVING ON THE CEILING**
   Blancmange-London
8. **HEARTBREAKER**
   Dionne Warwick-Arista
9. **TIME**
   Culture Club-Virgin
10. **RIO**
    Duran Duran-EMI
11. **WISHING**
    A Flock of Seagulls-Jive
12. **(SEXUAL) HEALING**
    Marvin Gaye-CBS
13. **YOUTH OF TODAY**
    Musical Youth-MCA
14. **THE OTHER SIDE OF LOVE**
    Yazoo-Mute
15. **MAD WORLD**
    Tears For Fears-Mercury
16. **HYMN**
    Ultravox-Chrysalis
17. **OUR HOUSE**
    Madness-Stiff
18. **BEST YEARS OF OUR LIVES**
    Modern Romance-WEA
19. **STATE OF INDEPENDENCE**
    Donna Summer-Warner Bros.
20. **THEME FROM HARRY'S ...**
    Clannad-RCA

UK ALBUMS

1. **JOHN LENNON COLLECTION**
   John Lennon-Parlophone
2. **SINGLES-FIRST TEN YEARS**
   Abba-Epic
3. **THE KIDS FROM FAME**
   Various-BBC
4. **CODA**
   Led Zeppelin-SwanSong
5. **RIO**
   Duran Duran-EMI
6. **'FROM THE MAKERS OF...'**
   Status Quo-Vertigo/Phonogram
7. **20 GREATEST LOVE SONGS**
   Nat King Cole-Capitol
8. **PEARLS II**
   Elkie Brooks-A&M
9. **HEARTBREAKER**
   Dionne Warwick-Arista
10. **I WANNA DO IT WITH YOU**
    Barry Manilow-Arista
11. **SAINTS AN' SINNERS**
    Whitesnake-Liberty
12. **HELLO, I MUST BE GOING!**
    Phil Collins-Virgin
13. **SINGLES-45's AND UNDER**
    Squeeze-A&M
14. **MIDNIGHT LOVE**
    Marvin Gaye-CBS
15. **REFLECTIONS**
    Various-CBS
16. **GIVE ME YOUR HEART ...**
    Shakin' Stevens-Epic
17. **CHART HITS '82**
    Various-K-tel
18. **KIDS FROM 'FAME' AGAIN**
    The Kids From 'Fame'-RCA
19. **LOVE OVER GOLD**
    Dire Straits-Vertigo/Phonogram
20. **'...FAMOUS LAST WORDS...'**
    Supertramp-A&M

US SINGLES

1. **MICKEY**
   Toni Basil-Radialchoice/Virgin/Chrys
2. **GLORIA**
   Laura Branigan-Atlantic
3. **MANEATER**
   Daryl Hall & John Oates-RCA
4. **TRULY**
   Lionel Richie-Motown
5. **THE GIRL IS MINE**
   Michael Jackson/Paul McCartney-Epic
6. **STEPPIN' OUT**
   Joe Jackson-A&M
7. **DIRTY LAUNDRY**
   Don Henley-Asylum
8. **SEXUAL HEALING**
   Marvin Gaye-Columbia
9. **ROCK THIS TOWN**
   Stray Cats-EMI America
10. **MUSCLES**
    Diana Ross-RCA
11. **IT'S RAINING AGAIN**
    Supertramp-A&M
12. **UP WHERE WE BELONG**
    Joe Cocker & Jennifer Warnes-Island
13. **SHADOWS OF THE NIGHT**
    Pat Benatar-Chrysalis
14. **DOWN UNDER**
    Men at Work-Columbia
15. **HEARTBREAKER**
    Dionne Warwick-Arista
16. **HEART ATTACK**
    Olivia Newton-John-MCA
17. **HEARTLIGHT**
    Neil Diamond-Columbia
18. **AFRICA**
    Toto-Columbia
19. **ROCK THE CASBAH**
    The Clash-Epic
20. **THE LOOK OF LOVE**
    ABC-Mercury

US ALBUMS

1. **BUSINESS AS USUAL**
   Men at Work-Columbia
2. **BUILT FOR SPEED**
   Stray Cats-EMI America
3. **LIONEL RICHIE**
   Lionel Richie-Motown
4. **NIGHT AND DAY**
   Joe Jackson-A&M
5. **FAMOUS LAST WORDS**
   Supertramp-A&M
6. **H2O**
   Daryl Hall & John Oates-RCA
7. **THE NYLON CURTAIN**
   Billy Joel-Columbia
8. **MIDNIGHT LOVE**
   Marvin Gaye-Columbia
9. **HEARTLIGHT**
   Neil Diamond-Columbia
10. **GET NERVOUS**
    Pat Benatar-Chrysalis
11. **THE NIGHTFLY**
    Donald Fagen-Warner Bros.
12. **COMBAT ROCK**
    The Clash-Epic
13. **LONG AFTER DARK**
    Tom Petty-Backstreet
14. **HELLO, I MUST BE GOING**
    Phil Collins-Atlantic
15. **NEBRASKA**
    Bruce Springsteen-Columbia
16. **DAYLIGHT AGAIN**
    Crosby, Stills & Nash-Atlantic
17. **SCREAMING FOR VENGEANCE**
    Judas Priest-Columbia
18. **GREATEST HITS**
    Dan Fogelberg-Full Moon/Epic
19. **EMOTIONS IN MOTION**
    Billy Squier-Capitol
20. **FOREVER, FOR ALWAYS...**
    Luther Vandross-Epic

UK SINGLES

1. **BEAT SURRENDER**
   The Jam-Polydor
2. **MIRROR MAN**
   The Human League-Virgin
3. **SAVE YOUR LOVE**
   Renée & Renato-Hollywood
4. **YOUNG GUNS (GO FOR IT)**
   Wham!-Innervision
5. **TIME**
   Culture Club-Virgin
6. **TRULY**
   Lionel Richie-Motown
7. **LIVING ON THE CEILING**
   Blancmange-London
8. **I DON'T WANNA DANCE**
   Eddy Grant-Ice
9. **RIO**
   Duran Duran-EMI
10. **WISHING**
    A Flock of Seagulls-Jive
11. **BEST YEARS OF OUR LIVES**
    Modern Romance-WEA
12. **OUR HOUSE**
    Madness-Stiff
13. **THE OTHER SIDE OF LOVE**
    Yazoo-Mute
14. **HYMN**
    Ultravox-Chrysalis
15. **HEARTBREAKER**
    Dionne Warwick-Arista
16. **YOUTH OF TODAY**
    Musical Youth-MCA
17. **(SEXUAL) HEALING**
    Marvin Gaye-CBS
18. **LET'S GET THIS STRAIGHT**
    Dexys Midnight Runners-Mercury
19. **FRIENDS**
    Shalamar-Solar
20. **STATE OF INDEPENDENCE**
    Donna Summer-Warner Bros.

UK ALBUMS

1. **JOHN LENNON COLLECTION**
   John Lennon-Parlophone
2. **SINGLES-FIRST TEN YEARS**
   Abba-Epic
3. **RIO**
   Duran Duran-EMI
4. **THE KIDS FROM FAME**
   Various-BBC
5. **PEARLS II**
   Elkie Brooks-A&M
6. **CODA**
   Led Zeppelin-SwanSong
7. **20 GREATEST LOVE SONGS**
   Nat King Cole-Capitol
8. **HEARTBREAKER**
   Dionne Warwick-Arista
9. **'FROM THE MAKERS OF...'**
   Status Quo-Vertigo/Phonogram
10. **LOVE SONGS**
    Diana Ross-K-tel
11. **I WANNA DO IT WITH YOU**
    Barry Manilow-Arista
12. **CHART HITS '82**
    Various-K-tel
13. **HELLO, I MUST BE GOING!**
    Phil Collins-Virgin
14. **GIVE ME YOUR HEART ...**
    Shakin' Stevens-Epic
15. **RICHARD CLAYDERMAN**
    Richard Clayderman-Delphine/Decca
16. **KISSING TO BE CLEVER**
    Culture Club-Virgin
17. **KIDS FROM 'FAME' AGAIN**
    The Kids From 'Fame'-RCA
18. **THE RISE & FALL**
    Madness-Stiff
19. **QUARTET**
    Ultravox-Chrysalis
20. **LOVE OVER GOLD**
    Dire Straits-Vertigo/Phonogram

US SINGLES

1. **MANEATER**
Daryl Hall & John Oates-RCA
2. **MICKEY**
Toni Basil-Radialchoice/Virgin/Chrys
3. **GLORIA**
Laura Branigan-Atlantic
4. **THE GIRL IS MINE**
Michael Jackson/Paul McCartney-Epic
5. **TRULY**
Lionel Richie-Motown
6. **STEPPIN' OUT**
Joe Jackson-A&M
7. **DIRTY LAUNDRY**
Don Henley-Asylum
8. **SEXUAL HEALING**
Marvin Gaye-Columbia
9. **ROCK THIS TOWN**
Stray Cats-EMI America
10. **MUSCLES**
Diana Ross-RCA
11. **IT'S RAINING AGAIN**
Supertramp-A&M
12. **DOWN UNDER**
Men at Work-Columbia
13. **SHADOWS OF THE NIGHT**
Pat Benatar-Chrysalis
14. **HEARTBREAKER**
Dionne Warwick-Arista
15. **UP WHERE WE BELONG**
Joe Cocker & Jennifer Warnes-Island
16. **AFRICA**
Toto-Columbia
17. **ROCK THE CASBAH**
The Clash-Epic
18. **YOU AND I**
Eddie Rabbitt/Crystal Gayle-Elektra
19. **THE LOOK OF LOVE**
ABC-Mercury
20. **BABY, COME TO ME**
Patti Austin-Qwest

US ALBUMS

1. **BUSINESS AS USUAL**
Men at Work-Columbia
2. **BUILT FOR SPEED**
Stray Cats-EMI America
3. **LIONEL RICHIE**
Lionel Richie-Motown
4. **NIGHT AND DAY**
Joe Jackson-A&M
5. **FAMOUS LAST WORDS**
Supertramp-A&M
6. **H2O**
Daryl Hall & John Oates-RCA
7. **MIDNIGHT LOVE**
Marvin Gaye-Columbia
8. **GET NERVOUS**
Pat Benatar-Chrysalis
9. **CODA**
Led Zeppelin-Swan Song
10. **COMBAT ROCK**
The Clash-Epic
11. **THE NIGHTFLY**
Donald Fagen-Warner Bros.
12. **THE NYLON CURTAIN**
Billy Joel-Columbia
13. **LONG AFTER DARK**
Tom Petty-Backstreet
14. **HELLO, I MUST BE GOING**
Phil Collins-Atlantic
15. **GREATEST HITS**
Dan Fogelberg-Full Moon/Epic
16. **DAYLIGHT AGAIN**
Crosby, Stills & Nash-Atlantic
17. **SCREAMING FOR VENGEANCE**
Judas Priest-Columbia
18. **HEARTLIGHT**
Neil Diamond-Columbia
19. **EMOTIONS IN MOTION**
Billy Squier-Capitol
20. **FOREVER, FOR ALWAYS...**
Luther Vandross-Epic

UK SINGLES

1. **SAVE YOUR LOVE**
Renée & Renato-Hollywood
2. **BEAT SURRENDER**
The Jam-Polydor
3. **TIME**
Culture Club-Virgin
4. **THE SHAKIN' STEVENS EP**
Shakin' Stevens-Epic
5. **OUR HOUSE**
Madness-Stiff
6. **TRULY**
Lionel Richie-Motown
7. **MIRROR MAN**
The Human League-Virgin
8. **YOUNG GUNS (GO FOR IT)**
Wham!-Innervision
9. **BEST YEARS OF OUR LIVES**
Modern Romance-WEA
10. **PEACE ON EARTH**
David Bowie & Bing Crosby-RCA
11. **LIVING ON THE CEILING**
Blancmange-London
12. **FRIENDS**
Shalamar-Solar
13. **HYMN**
Ultravox-Chrysalis
14. **RIO**
Duran Duran-EMI
15. **WISHING**
A Flock of Seagulls-Jive
16. **THE OTHER SIDE OF LOVE**
Yazoo-Mute
17. **YOU CAN'T HURRY LOVE**
Phil Collins-Virgin
18. **LET'S GET THIS STRAIGHT**
Dexys Midnight Runners-Mercury
19. **BUFFALO GALS**
Malcolm McLaren-Charisma
20. **IF YOU CAN'T STAND ...**
Bucks Fizz-RCA

UK ALBUMS

1. **JOHN LENNON COLLECTION**
John Lennon-Parlophone
2. **DIG THE NEW BREED**
The Jam-Polydor
3. **SINGLES-FIRST TEN YEARS**
Abba-Epic
4. **HEARTBREAKER**
Dionne Warwick-Arista
5. **RIO**
Duran Duran-EMI
6. **PEARLS II**
Elkie Brooks-A&M
7. **THE KIDS FROM FAME**
Various-BBC
8. **LOVE SONGS**
Diana Ross-K-tel
9. **20 GREATEST LOVE SONGS**
Nat King Cole-Capitol
10. **THE RISE & FALL**
Madness-Stiff
11. **FRIENDS**
Shalamar-Solar
12. **RICHARD CLAYDERMAN**
Richard Clayderman-Delphine/Decca
13. **'FROM THE MAKERS OF...'**
Status Quo-Vertigo/Phonogram
14. **KISSING TO BE CLEVER**
Culture Club-Virgin
15. **THRILLER**
Michael Jackson-Epic
16. **I WANNA DO IT WITH YOU**
Barry Manilow-Arista
17. **MIDNIGHT LOVE**
Marvin Gaye-CBS
18. **CHART HITS '82**
Various-K-tel
19. **CODA**
Led Zeppelin-SwanSong
20. **GIVE ME YOUR HEART ...**
Shakin' Stevens-Epic

US SINGLES

1. **MANEATER**
Daryl Hall & John Oates-RCA
2. **MICKEY**
Toni Basil-Radialchoice/Virgin/Chrys
3. **THE GIRL IS MINE**
Michael Jackson/Paul McCartney-Epic
4. **DIRTY LAUNDRY**
Don Henley-Asylum
5. **GLORIA**
Laura Branigan-Atlantic
6. **STEPPIN' OUT**
Joe Jackson-A&M
7. **SEXUAL HEALING**
Marvin Gaye-Columbia
8. **DOWN UNDER**
Men at Work-Columbia
9. **ROCK THIS TOWN**
Stray Cats-EMI America
10. **TRULY**
Lionel Richie-Motown
11. **IT'S RAINING AGAIN**
Supertramp-A&M
12. **HEARTBREAKER**
Dionne Warwick-Arista
13. **SHADOWS OF THE NIGHT**
Pat Benatar-Chrysalis
14. **AFRICA**
Toto-Columbia
15. **ROCK THE CASBAH**
The Clash-Epic
16. **YOU AND I**
Eddie Rabbitt/Crystal Gayle-Elektra
17. **BABY, COME TO ME**
Patti Austin-Qwest
18. **THE OTHER GUY**
Little River Band-Capitol
19. **THE LOOK OF LOVE**
ABC-Mercury
20. **YOU CAN'T HURRY LOVE**
Phil Collins-Atlantic

US ALBUMS

1. **BUSINESS AS USUAL**
Men at Work-Columbia
2. **BUILT FOR SPEED**
Stray Cats-EMI America
3. **LIONEL RICHIE**
Lionel Richie-Motown
4. **NIGHT AND DAY**
Joe Jackson-A&M
5. **FAMOUS LAST WORDS**
Supertramp-A&M
6. **H2O**
Daryl Hall & John Oates-RCA
7. **MIDNIGHT LOVE**
Marvin Gaye-Columbia
8. **GET NERVOUS**
Pat Benatar-Chrysalis
9. **CODA**
Led Zeppelin-Swan Song
10. **COMBAT ROCK**
The Clash-Epic
11. **THRILLER**
Michael Jackson-Epic
12. **LONG AFTER DARK**
Tom Petty-Backstreet
13. **THE NYLON CURTAIN**
Billy Joel-Columbia
14. **HELLO, I MUST BE GOING**
Phil Collins-Atlantic
15. **GREATEST HITS**
Dan Fogelberg-Full Moon/Epic
16. **DAYLIGHT AGAIN**
Crosby, Stills & Nash-Atlantic
17. **SPEAK OF THE DEVIL**
Ozzy Osbourne-Jet
18. **EMOTIONS IN MOTION**
Billy Squier-Capitol
19. **THE NIGHTFLY**
Donald Fagen-Warner Bros.
20. **FOREVER, FOR ALWAYS...**
Luther Vandross-Epic

UK SINGLES

1. **SAVE YOUR LOVE**
Renée & Renato-Hollywood
2. **THE SHAKIN' STEVENS EP**
Shakin' Stevens-Epic
3. **PEACE ON EARTH**
David Bowie & Bing Crosby-RCA
4. **TIME**
Culture Club-Virgin
5. **OUR HOUSE**
Madness-Stiff
6. **YOU CAN'T HURRY LOVE**
Phil Collins-Virgin
7. **A WINTER'S TALE**
David Essex-Mercury
8. **BEST YEARS OF OUR LIVES**
Modern Romance-WEA
9. **TRULY**
Lionel Richie-Motown
10. **BEAT SURRENDER**
The Jam-Polydor
11. **LITTLE TOWN**
Cliff Richard-EMI
12. **MIRROR MAN**
The Human League-Virgin
13. **YOUNG GUNS (GO FOR IT)**
Wham!-Innervision
14. **ALL THE LOVE ...**
Dionne Warwick-Arista
15. **FRIENDS**
Shalamar-Solar
16. **HYMN**
Ultravox-Chrysalis
17. **LET'S GET THIS STRAIGHT**
Dexys Midnight Runners-Mercury
18. **BUFFALO GALS**
Malcolm McLaren-Charisma
19. **SINGALONG-A-SANTA**
Santa Claus-Polydor
20. **IF YOU CAN'T STAND ...**
Bucks Fizz-RCA

UK ALBUMS

1. **JOHN LENNON COLLECTION**
John Lennon-Parlophone
2. **SINGLES-FIRST TEN YEARS**
Abba-Epic
3. **DIG THE NEW BREED**
The Jam-Polydor
4. **RIO**
Duran Duran-EMI
5. **LOVE SONGS**
Diana Ross-K-tel
6. **PEARLS II**
Elkie Brooks-A&M
7. **20 GREATEST LOVE SONGS**
Nat King Cole-Capitol
8. **THE KIDS FROM FAME**
Various-BBC
9. **HEARTBREAKER**
Dionne Warwick-Arista
10. **'FROM THE MAKERS OF...'**
Status Quo-Vertigo/Phonogram
11. **THE RISE & FALL**
Madness-Stiff
12. **FRIENDS**
Shalamar-Solar
13. **KISSING TO BE CLEVER**
Culture Club-Virgin
14. **RICHARD CLAYDERMAN**
Richard Clayderman-Delphine/Decca
15. **HELLO, I MUST BE GOING!**
Phil Collins-Virgin
16. **I WANNA DO IT WITH YOU**
Barry Manilow-Arista
17. **CHART HITS '82**
Various-K-tel
18. **LIONEL RICHIE**
Lionel Richie-Motown
19. **THRILLER**
Michael Jackson-Epic
20. **GIVE ME YOUR HEART ...**
Shakin' Stevens-Epic

US SINGLES

1. **MANEATER** — Daryl Hall & John Oates-RCA
2. **THE GIRL IS MINE** — Michael Jackson/Paul McCartney-Epic
3. **DIRTY LAUNDRY** — Don Henley-Asylum
4. **DOWN UNDER** — Men at Work-Columbia
5. **SEXUAL HEALING** — Marvin Gaye-Columbia
6. **MICKEY** — Toni Basil-Radialchoice/Virgin/Chrys
7. **GLORIA** — Laura Branigan-Atlantic
8. **STEPPIN' OUT** — Joe Jackson-A&M
9. **ROCK THIS TOWN** — Stray Cats-EMI America
10. **TRULY** — Lionel Richie-Motown
11. **HEARTBREAKER** — Dionne Warwick-Arista
12. **AFRICA** — Toto-Columbia
13. **BABY, COME TO ME** — Patti Austin-Qwest
14. **ROCK THE CASBAH** — The Clash-Epic
15. **YOU AND I** — Eddie Rabbitt/Crystal Gayle-Elektra
16. **THE OTHER GUY** — Little River Band-Capitol
17. **YOU CAN'T HURRY LOVE** — Phil Collins-Atlantic
18. **THE LOOK OF LOVE** — ABC-Mercury
19. **IT'S RAINING AGAIN** — Supertramp-A&M
20. **HEART TO HEART** — Kenny Loggins-Columbia

US ALBUMS

1. **BUSINESS AS USUAL** — Men at Work-Columbia
2. **BUILT FOR SPEED** — Stray Cats-EMI America
3. **LIONEL RICHIE** — Lionel Richie-Motown
4. **H2O** — Daryl Hall & John Oates-RCA
5. **FAMOUS LAST WORDS** — Supertramp-A&M
6. **GET NERVOUS** — Pat Benatar-Chrysalis
7. **MIDNIGHT LOVE** — Marvin Gaye-Columbia
8. **CODA** — Led Zeppelin-Swan Song
9. **THRILLER** — Michael Jackson-Epic
10. **COMBAT ROCK** — The Clash-Epic
11. **LONG AFTER DARK** — Tom Petty-Backstreet
12. **HELLO, I MUST BE GOING** — Phil Collins-Atlantic
13. **THE NYLON CURTAIN** — Billy Joel-Columbia
14. **NIGHT AND DAY** — Joe Jackson-A&M
15. **GREATEST HITS** — Dan Fogelberg-Full Moon/Epic
16. **SPEAK OF THE DEVIL** — Ozzy Osbourne-Jet
17. **DAYLIGHT AGAIN** — Crosby, Stills & Nash-Atlantic
18. **EMOTIONS IN MOTION** — Billy Squier-Capitol
19. **HEARTLIGHT** — Neil Diamond-Columbia
20. **FOREVER, FOR ALWAYS...** — Luther Vandross-Epic

UK SINGLES

1. **SAVE YOUR LOVE** — Renée & Renato-Hollywood
2. **YOU CAN'T HURRY LOVE** — Phil Collins-Virgin
3. **A WINTER'S TALE** — David Essex-Mercury
4. **BEST YEARS OF OUR LIVES** — Modern Romance-WEA
5. **OUR HOUSE** — Madness-Stiff
6. **TIME** — Culture Club-Virgin
7. **THE SHAKIN' STEVENS EP** — Shakin' Stevens-Epic
8. **ORVILLE'S SONG** — Keith Harris & Orville-BBC
9. **PEACE ON EARTH** — David Bowie & Bing Crosby-RCA
10. **ALL THE LOVE ...** — Dionne Warwick-Arista
11. **BUFFALO GALS** — Malcolm McLaren-Charisma
12. **HYMN** — Ultravox-Chrysalis
13. **IF YOU CAN'T STAND ...** — Bucks Fizz-RCA
14. **YOUNG GUNS (GO FOR IT)** — Wham!-Innervision
15. **BEAT SURRENDER** — The Jam-Polydor
16. **CACHARPAYA** — Incantation-Beggars Banquet
17. **TRULY** — Lionel Richie-Motown
18. **LITTLE TOWN** — Cliff Richard-EMI
19. **FRIENDS** — Shalamar-Solar
20. **MIRROR MAN** — The Human League-Virgin

UK ALBUMS

1. **JOHN LENNON COLLECTION** — John Lennon-Parlophone
2. **SINGLES-FIRST TEN YEARS** — Abba-Epic
3. **RAIDERS OF POP CHARTS** — Various-Ronco
4. **RIO** — Duran Duran-EMI
5. **HEARTBREAKER** — Dionne Warwick-Arista
6. **PEARLS II** — Elkie Brooks-A&M
7. **THE KIDS FROM FAME** — Various-BBC
8. **LOVE SONGS** — Diana Ross-K-tel
9. **FRIENDS** — Shalamar-Solar
10. **'FROM THE MAKERS OF...'** — Status Quo-Vertigo/Phonogram
11. **THE RISE & FALL** — Madness-Stiff
12. **DIG THE NEW BREED** — The Jam-Polydor
13. **HELLO, I MUST BE GOING!** — Phil Collins-Virgin
14. **RICHARD CLAYDERMAN** — Richard Clayderman-Delphine/Decca
15. **GREATEST HITS** — Olivia Newton-John-EMI
16. **KISSING TO BE CLEVER** — Culture Club-Virgin
17. **20 GREATEST LOVE SONGS** — Nat King Cole-Capitol
18. **20 GREATEST HITS** — The Beatles-Parlophone
19. **LIONEL RICHIE** — Lionel Richie-Motown
20. **COMPLETE MADNESS** — Madness-Stiff

US SINGLES

1. **DOWN UNDER** — Men at Work-Columbia
2. **THE GIRL IS MINE** — Michael Jackson/Paul McCartney-Epic
3. **DIRTY LAUNDRY** — Don Henley-Asylum
4. **MANEATER** — Daryl Hall & John Oates-RCA
5. **SEXUAL HEALING** — Marvin Gaye-Columbia
6. **MICKEY** — Toni Basil-Radialchoice/Virgin/Chrys
7. **AFRICA** — Toto-Columbia
8. **BABY, COME TO ME** — Patti Austin-Qwest
9. **ROCK THE CASBAH** — The Clash-Epic
10. **HEARTBREAKER** — Dionne Warwick-Arista
11. **GLORIA** — Laura Branigan-Atlantic
12. **YOU AND I** — Eddie Rabbitt/Crystal Gayle-Elektra
13. **STEPPIN' OUT** — Joe Jackson-A&M
14. **THE OTHER GUY** — Little River Band-Capitol
15. **YOU CAN'T HURRY LOVE** — Phil Collins-Atlantic
16. **SHAME ON THE MOON** — Bob Seger-Capitol
17. **HEART TO HEART** — Kenny Loggins-Columbia
18. **THE LOOK OF LOVE** — ABC-Mercury
19. **GOODY TWO SHOES** — Adam Ant-Epic
20. **HAND TO HOLD ON TO** — John Cougar-Riva

US ALBUMS

1. **BUSINESS AS USUAL** — Men at Work-Columbia
2. **BUILT FOR SPEED** — Stray Cats-EMI America
3. **H2O** — Daryl Hall & John Oates-RCA
4. **GET NERVOUS** — Pat Benatar-Chrysalis
5. **LIONEL RICHIE** — Lionel Richie-Motown
6. **CODA** — Led Zeppelin-Swan Song
7. **MIDNIGHT LOVE** — Marvin Gaye-Columbia
8. **THRILLER** — Michael Jackson-Epic
9. **COMBAT ROCK** — The Clash-Epic
10. **LONG AFTER DARK** — Tom Petty-Backstreet
11. **HELLO, I MUST BE GOING** — Phil Collins-Atlantic
12. **FAMOUS LAST WORDS** — Supertramp-A&M
13. **THE NYLON CURTAIN** — Billy Joel-Columbia
14. **SPEAK OF THE DEVIL** — Ozzy Osbourne-Jet
15. **EMOTIONS IN MOTION** — Billy Squier-Capitol
16. **THE DISTANCE** — Bob Seger-Capitol
17. **HEARTLIGHT** — Neil Diamond-Columbia
18. **NIGHT AND DAY** — Joe Jackson-A&M
19. **GREATEST HITS** — Dan Fogelberg-Full Moon/Epic
20. **SPRING SESSION M** — Missing Persons-Capitol

UK SINGLES

1. **YOU CAN'T HURRY LOVE** — Phil Collins-Virgin
2. **A WINTER'S TALE** — David Essex-Mercury
3. **SAVE YOUR LOVE** — Renée & Renato-Hollywood
4. **ORVILLE'S SONG** — Keith Harris & Orville-BBC
5. **BEST YEARS OF OUR LIVES** — Modern Romance-WEA
6. **THE STORY OF THE BLUES** — Wah!-Eternal
7. **DOWN UNDER** — Men at Work-Epic
8. **TIME** — Culture Club-Virgin
9. **BUFFALO GALS** — Malcolm McLaren-Charisma
10. **IF YOU CAN'T STAND ...** — Bucks Fizz-RCA
11. **HYMN** — Ultravox-Chrysalis
12. **ALL THE LOVE ...** — Dionne Warwick-Arista
13. **OUR HOUSE** — Madness-Stiff
14. **CACHARPAYA** — Incantation-Beggars Banquet
15. **HEARTACHE AVENUE** — The Maisonettes-Ready Steady Go!
16. **EUROPEAN FEMALE** — The Stranglers-Epic
17. **THEME FROM E.T.** — John Williams-MCA
18. **YOUNG GUNS (GO FOR IT)** — Wham!-Innervision
19. **STEPPIN' OUT** — Joe Jackson-A&M
20. **FRIENDS** — Shalamar-Solar

UK ALBUMS

1. **RAIDERS OF POP CHARTS** — Various-Ronco
2. **JOHN LENNON COLLECTION** — John Lennon-Parlophone
3. **RIO** — Duran Duran-EMI
4. **HEARTBREAKER** — Dionne Warwick-Arista
5. **HELLO, I MUST BE GOING!** — Phil Collins-Virgin
6. **FRIENDS** — Shalamar-Solar
7. **RICHARD CLAYDERMAN** — Richard Clayderman-Delphine/Decca
8. **GREATEST HITS** — Olivia Newton-John-EMI
9. **SINGLES-FIRST TEN YEARS** — Abba-Epic
10. **KISSING TO BE CLEVER** — Culture Club-Virgin
11. **CACHARPAYA** — Incantation-Beggars Banquet
12. **BUSINESS AS USUAL** — Men at Work-Epic
13. **PEARLS II** — Elkie Brooks-A&M
14. **THE KIDS FROM FAME** — Various-BBC
15. **COMPLETE MADNESS** — Madness-Stiff
16. **DIG THE NEW BREED** — The Jam-Polydor
17. **QUARTET** — Ultravox-Chrysalis
18. **LOVE SONGS** — Diana Ross-K-tel
19. **TOO-RYE-AY** — Dexys Midnight Runners-Mercury
20. **THE LEXICON OF LOVE** — ABC-Neutron/Phonogram

WEEK ENDING JANUARY 22 1983

US SINGLES	US ALBUMS	UK SINGLES	UK ALBUMS
1 DOWN UNDER *Men at Work-Columbia*	1 BUSINESS AS USUAL *Men at Work-Columbia*	1 YOU CAN'T HURRY LOVE *Phil Collins-Virgin*	1 RAIDERS OF POP CHARTS *Various-Ronco*
2 THE GIRL IS MINE *Michael Jackson/Paul McCartney-Epic*	2 BUILT FOR SPEED *Stray Cats-EMI America*	2 DOWN UNDER *Men at Work-Epic*	2 BUSINESS AS USUAL *Men at Work-Epic*
3 DIRTY LAUNDRY *Don Henley-Asylum*	3 H2O *Daryl Hall & John Oates-RCA*	3 THE STORY OF THE BLUES *Wah!-Eternal*	3 HELLO, I MUST BE GOING! *Phil Collins-Virgin*
4 SEXUAL HEALING *Marvin Gaye-Columbia*	4 GET NERVOUS *Pat Benatar-Chrysalis*	4 ELECTRIC AVENUE *Eddy Grant-Ice*	4 JOHN LENNON COLLECTION *John Lennon-Parlophone*
5 AFRICA *Toto-Columbia*	5 THRILLER *Michael Jackson-Epic*	5 ORVILLE'S SONG *Keith Harris & Orville-BBC*	5 ART OF FALLING APART *Soft Cell-Some Bizarre/Phonogram*
6 MANEATER *Daryl Hall & John Oates-RCA*	6 CODA *Led Zeppelin-Swan Song*	6 A WINTER'S TALE *David Essex-Mercury*	6 HEARTBREAKER *Dionne Warwick-Arista*
7 BABY, COME TO ME *Patti Austin-Qwest*	7 COMBAT ROCK *The Clash-Epic*	7 HEARTACHE AVENUE *The Maisonettes-Ready Steady Go!*	7 FELINE *The Stranglers-Epic*
8 ROCK THE CASBAH *The Clash-Epic*	8 THE DISTANCE *Bob Seger-Capitol*	8 STEPPIN' OUT *Joe Jackson-A&M*	8 GREATEST HITS *Olivia Newton-John-EMI*
9 MICKEY *Toni Basil-Radialchoice/Virgin/Chrys*	9 LONG AFTER DARK *Tom Petty-Backstreet*	9 EUROPEAN FEMALE *The Stranglers-Epic*	9 FRIENDS *Shalamar-Solar*
10 HEARTBREAKER *Dionne Warwick-Arista*	10 HELLO, I MUST BE GOING *Phil Collins-Atlantic*	10 OUR HOUSE *Madness-Stiff*	10 RICHARD CLAYDERMAN *Richard Clayderman-Delphine/Decca*
11 YOU AND I *Eddie Rabbitt/Crystal Gayle-Elektra*	11 LIONEL RICHIE *Lionel Richie-Motown*	11 BUFFALO GALS *Malcolm McLaren-Charisma*	11 RIO *Duran Duran-EMI*
12 SHAME ON THE MOON *Bob Seger-Capitol*	12 FAMOUS LAST WORDS *Supertramp-A&M*	12 CACHARPAYA *Incantation-Beggars Banquet*	12 CACHARPAYA *Incantation-Beggars Banquet*
13 YOU CAN'T HURRY LOVE *Phil Collins-Atlantic*	13 THE NYLON CURTAIN *Billy Joel-Columbia*	13 SAVE YOUR LOVE *Renée & Renato-Hollywood*	13 LIVE EVIL *Black Sabbath-Vertigo/Phonogram*
14 THE OTHER GUY *Little River Band-Capitol*	14 SPEAK OF THE DEVIL *Ozzy Osbourne-Jet*	14 BEST YEARS OF OUR LIVES *Modern Romance-WEA*	14 SINGLES-FIRST TEN YEARS *Abba-Epic*
15 GLORIA *Laura Branigan-Atlantic*	15 EMOTIONS IN MOTION *Billy Squier-Capitol*	15 ALL THE LOVE ... *Dionne Warwick-Arista*	15 PEARLS II *Elkie Brooks-A&M*
16 HEART TO HEART *Kenny Loggins-Columbia*	16 MIDNIGHT LOVE *Marvin Gaye-Columbia*	16 IF YOU CAN'T STAND ... *Bucks Fizz-RCA*	16 LOVE SONGS *Diana Ross-K-tel*
17 GOODY TWO SHOES *Adam Ant-Epic*	17 HEARTLIGHT *Neil Diamond-Columbia*	17 TIME *Culture Club-Virgin*	17 COMPLETE MADNESS *Madness-Stiff*
18 THE LOOK OF LOVE *ABC-Mercury*	18 AMERICAN FOOL *John Cougar-Riva/Mercury*	18 HYMN *Ultravox-Chrysalis*	18 'FROM THE MAKERS OF...' *Status Quo-Vertigo/Phonogram*
19 HAND TO HOLD ON TO *John Cougar-Riva*	19 SPRING SESSION M *Missing Persons-Capitol*	19 SIGN OF THE TIMES *The Belle Stars-Stiff*	19 KISSING TO BE CLEVER *Culture Club-Virgin*
20 ALLENTOWN *Billy Joel-Columbia*	20 TOTO IV *Toto-Columbia*	20 GLORIA *Laura Branigan-Atlantic*	20 QUARTET *Ultravox-Chrysalis*

WEEK ENDING JANUARY 29 1983

US SINGLES	US ALBUMS	UK SINGLES	UK ALBUMS
1 DOWN UNDER *Men at Work-Columbia*	1 BUSINESS AS USUAL *Men at Work-Columbia*	1 DOWN UNDER *Men at Work-Epic*	1 BUSINESS AS USUAL *Men at Work-Epic*
2 AFRICA *Toto-Columbia*	2 BUILT FOR SPEED *Stray Cats-EMI America*	2 YOU CAN'T HURRY LOVE *Phil Collins-Virgin*	2 RAIDERS OF POP CHARTS *Various-Ronco*
3 SEXUAL HEALING *Marvin Gaye-Columbia*	3 H2O *Daryl Hall & John Oates-RCA*	3 ELECTRIC AVENUE *Eddy Grant-Ice*	3 HELLO, I MUST BE GOING! *Phil Collins-Virgin*
4 DIRTY LAUNDRY *Don Henley-Asylum*	4 GET NERVOUS *Pat Benatar-Chrysalis*	4 THE STORY OF THE BLUES *Wah!-Eternal*	4 FELINE *The Stranglers-Epic*
5 THE GIRL IS MINE *Michael Jackson/Paul McCartney-Epic*	5 THRILLER *Michael Jackson-Epic*	5 SIGN OF THE TIMES *The Belle Stars-Stiff*	5 RICHARD CLAYDERMAN *Richard Clayderman-Delphine/Decca*
6 MANEATER *Daryl Hall & John Oates-RCA*	6 CODA *Led Zeppelin-Swan Song*	6 STEPPIN' OUT *Joe Jackson-A&M*	6 JOHN LENNON COLLECTION *John Lennon-Parlophone*
7 BABY, COME TO ME *Patti Austin-Warner Bros.*	7 COMBAT ROCK *The Clash-Epic*	7 HEARTACHE AVENUE *The Maisonettes-Ready Steady Go!*	7 HEARTBREAKER *Dionne Warwick-Arista*
8 ROCK THE CASBAH *The Clash-Epic*	8 THE DISTANCE *Bob Seger-Capitol*	8 GLORIA *Laura Branigan-Atlantic*	8 ART OF FALLING APART *Soft Cell-Some Bizarre/Phonogram*
9 SHAME ON THE MOON *Bob Seger-Capitol*	9 LONG AFTER DARK *Tom Petty-Backstreet*	9 ORVILLE'S SONG *Keith Harris & Orville-BBC*	9 CACHARPAYA *Incantation-Beggars Banquet*
10 YOU AND I *Eddie Rabbitt/Crystal Gayle-Elektra*	10 HELLO, I MUST BE GOING *Phil Collins-Atlantic*	10 TOO SHY *Kajagoogoo-EMI*	10 GREATEST HITS *Olivia Newton-John-EMI*
11 YOU CAN'T HURRY LOVE *Phil Collins-Atlantic*	11 LIONEL RICHIE *Lionel Richie-Motown*	11 THE CUTTER *Echo & The Bunnymen-Korova*	11 'FROM THE MAKERS OF...' *Status Quo-Vertigo/Phonogram*
12 THE OTHER GUY *Little River Band-Capitol*	12 TOTO IV *Toto-Columbia*	12 NEW YEAR'S DAY *U2-Island*	12 RIO *Duran Duran-EMI*
13 MICKEY *Toni Basil-Radialchoice/Virgin/Chrys*	13 THE NYLON CURTAIN *Billy Joel-Columbia*	13 EUROPEAN FEMALE *The Stranglers-Epic*	13 LIVE EVIL *Black Sabbath-Vertigo/Phonogram*
14 GOODY TWO SHOES *Adam Ant-Epic*	14 SPEAK OF THE DEVIL *Ozzy Osbourne-Jet*	14 CACHARPAYA *Incantation-Beggars Banquet*	14 FRIENDS *Shalamar-Solar*
15 HEART TO HEART *Kenny Loggins-Columbia*	15 EMOTIONS IN MOTION *Billy Squier-Capitol*	15 A WINTER'S TALE *David Essex-Mercury*	15 NIGHT AND DAY *Joe Jackson-A&M*
16 STRAY CUT STRUT *Stray Cats-EMI America*	16 HEARTLIGHT *Neil Diamond-Columbia*	16 BUFFALO GALS *Malcolm McLaren–Charisma*	16 KILLER ON THE RAMPAGE *Eddy Grant-Ice*
17 PASS THE DUTCHIE *Musical Youth-MCA*	17 AMERICAN FOOL *John Cougar-Riva/Mercury*	17 TWISTING BY THE POOL *Dire Straits-Vertigo/Phonogram*	17 VISIONS *Various-K-tel*
18 ALLENTOWN *Billy Joel-Columbia*	18 SPRING SESSION M *Missing Persons-Capitol*	18 OH DIANE *Fleetwood Mac-Warner Bros.*	18 SKY FIVE LIVE *Sky-Ariola*
19 HAND TO HOLD ON TO *John Cougar-Riva*	19 RECORDS *Foreigner-Atlantic*	19 HOLD ME TIGHTER ... *Billy Griffin-CBS*	19 THRILLER *Michael Jackson-Epic*
20 YOU GOT LUCKY *Tom Petty-Backstreet*	20 FAMOUS LAST WORDS *Supertramp-A&M*	20 SAVE YOUR LOVE *Renée & Renato-Hollywood*	20 20 GREATEST HITS *The Beatles-Parlophone*

US SINGLES

1 **AFRICA**
Toto-Columbia
2 **DOWN UNDER**
Men at Work-Columbia
3 **SEXUAL HEALING**
Marvin Gaye-Columbia
4 **BABY, COME TO ME**
Patti Austin-Qwest
5 **SHAME ON THE MOON**
Bob Seger-Capitol
6 **MANEATER**
Daryl Hall & John Oates-RCA
7 **DIRTY LAUNDRY**
Don Henley-Asylum
8 **ROCK THE CASBAH**
The Clash-Epic
9 **YOU AND I**
Eddie Rabbitt/Crystal Gayle-Elektra
10 **YOU CAN'T HURRY LOVE**
Phil Collins-Atlantic
11 **THE OTHER GUY**
Little River Band-Capitol
12 **STRAY CAT STRUT**
Stray Cats-EMI America
13 **GOODY TWO SHOES**
Adam Ant-Epic
14 **PASS THE DUTCHIE**
Musical Youth-MCA
15 **HEART TO HEART**
Kenny Loggins-Columbia
16 **THE GIRL IS MINE**
Michael Jackson/Paul McCartney-Epic
17 **ALLENTOWN**
Billy Joel-Columbia
18 **YOUR LOVE IS DRIVING ME...**
Sammy Hagar-Geffen
19 **ALL RIGHT**
Christopher Cross-Warner Bros.
20 **YOU GOT LUCKY**
Tom Petty-Backstreet

US ALBUMS

1 **BUSINESS AS USUAL**
Men at Work-Columbia
2 **BUILT FOR SPEED**
Stray Cats-EMI America
3 **H$_2$O**
Daryl Hall & John Oates-RCA
4 **GET NERVOUS**
Pat Benatar-Chrysalis
5 **THRILLER**
Michael Jackson-Epic
6 **THE DISTANCE**
Bob Seger-Capitol
7 **COMBAT ROCK**
The Clash-Epic
8 **HELLO, I MUST BE GOING**
Phil Collins-Atlantic
9 **LONG AFTER DARK**
Tom Petty-Backstreet
10 **TOTO IV**
Toto-Columbia
11 **LIONEL RICHIE**
Lionel Richie-Motown
12 **THE NYLON CURTAIN**
Billy Joel-Columbia
13 **EMOTIONS IN MOTION**
Billy Squier-Capitol
14 **SPEAK OF THE DEVIL**
Ozzy Osbourne-Jet
15 **RECORDS**
Foreigner-Atlantic
16 **HEARTLIGHT**
Neil Diamond-Columbia
17 **AMERICAN FOOL**
John Cougar-Riva/Mercury
18 **SPRING SESSION M**
Missing Persons-Capitol
19 **TRANS**
Neil Young-Geffen
20 **CODA**
Led Zeppelin-Swansong

UK SINGLES

1 **DOWN UNDER**
Men at Work-Epic
2 **ELECTRIC AVENUE**
Eddy Grant-Ice
3 **YOU CAN'T HURRY LOVE**
Phil Collins-Virgin
4 **SIGN OF THE TIMES**
The Belle Stars-Stiff
5 **TOO SHY**
KajaGooGoo-EMI
6 **GLORIA**
Laura Branigan-Atlantic
7 **STORY OF THE BLUES**
Wah!-Eternal
8 **THE CUTTER**
Echo & The Bunnymen-Korova
9 **STEPPIN' OUT**
Joe Jackson-A&M
10 **NEW YEAR'S DAY**
U2-Island
11 **WHAM RAP!...**
Wham-Inner Vision
12 **UP WHERE WE BELONG**
Joe Cocker & Jennifer Warnes-Island
13 **HEARTACHE AVENUE**
The Maisonettes-Ready Steady Go!
14 **TWISTING BY THE POOL**
Dire Straits-Vertigo/Phonogram
15 **LAST NIGHT A D.J. ...**
Indeep-Sound of New York
16 **OH DIANE**
Fleetwood Mac-Warner Bros.
17 **HOLD ME TIGHTER...**
Billy Griffin-CBS
18 **ORVILLE'S SONG**
Keith Harris And Orville-BBC
19 **CHANGE**
Tears for Fears-Mercury/Phonogram
20 **BILLIE JEAN**
Michael Jackson-Epic

UK ALBUMS

1 **BUSINESS AS USUAL**
Men at Work-Epic
2 **RICHARD CLAYDERMAN**
Richard Clayderman-Delphine/Decca
3 **NIGHT AND DAY**
Joe Jackson-A&M
4 **RAIDERS OF POP CHARTS**
Various-Ronco
5 **HELLO, I MUST BE GOING!**
Phil Collins-Virgin
6 **HEARTBREAKER**
Dionne Warwick-Arista
7 **JOHN LENNON COLLECTION**
John Lennon-Parlophone
8 **KILLER ON THE RAMPAGE**
Eddy Grant-Ice
9 **FELINE**
The Stranglers-Epic
10 **CACHARPAYA**
Incantation-Beggars Banquet
11 **VISIONS**
Various-K-tel
12 **GREATEST HITS**
Olivia Newton-John-EMI
13 **THRILLER**
Michael Jackson-Epic
14 **ART OF FALLING APART**
Soft Cell-Some Bizzare/Phonogram
15 **RIO**
Duran Duran-EMI
16 **SKY FIVE LIVE**
Sky-Ariola
17 **FRIENDS**
Shalamar-Solar
18 **PEARLS II**
Elkie Brooks-A&M
19 **LIVE EVIL**
Black Sabbath-Vertigo/Phonogram
20 **20 GREATEST HITS**
The Beatles-Parlophone

US SINGLES

1 **DOWN UNDER**
Men at Work-Columbia
2 **BABY COME TO ME**
Patti Austin-Qwest
3 **SEXUAL HEALING**
Marvin Gaye-Columbia
4 **SHAME ON THE MOON**
Bob Seger-Capitol
5 **AFRICA**
Toto-Columbia
6 **MANEATER**
Daryl Hall & John Oates-RCA
7 **YOU AND I**
Eddie Rabbitt/Crystal Gayle-Elektra
8 **ROCK THE CASBAH**
The Clash-Epic
9 **STRAY CAT STRUT**
Stray Cats-EMI America
10 **YOU CAN'T HURRY LOVE**
Phil Collins-Atlantic
11 **THE OTHER GUY**
Little River Band-Capitol
12 **GOODY TWO SHOES**
Adam Ant-Epic
13 **PASS THE DUTCHIE**
Musical Youth-MCA
14 **YOU LOVE IS DRIVING ME...**
Sammy Hagar-Geffen
15 **HEART TO HEART**
Kenny Loggins-Columbia
16 **ALL RIGHT**
Christopher Cross-Warner Bros.
17 **ALLENTOWN**
Billy Joel-Columbia
18 **DO YOU REALLY WANT TO...**
Culture Club-Virgin/Epic
19 **HUNGRY LIKE THE WOLF**
Duran Duran-Harvest
20 **YOU GOT LUCKY**
Tom Petty-Backstreet

US ALBUMS

1 **BUSINESS AS USUAL**
Men at Work-Columbia
2 **BUILT FOR SPEED**
Stray Cats-EMI America
3 **H$_2$O**
Daryl Hall & John Oates-RCA
4 **GET NERVOUS**
Pat Benatar-Chrysalis
5 **THRILLER**
Michael Jackson-Epic
6 **THE DISTANCE**
Bob Seger-Capitol
7 **COMBAT ROCK**
The Clash-Epic
8 **HELLO, I MUST BE GOING**
Phil Collins-Atlantic
9 **TOTO IV**
Toto-Columbia
10 **RECORDS**
Foreigner-Atlantic
11 **LIONEL RICHIE**
Lionel Richie-Motown
12 **LONG AFTER DARK**
Tom Petty-Backstreet
13 **EMOTIONS IN MOTION**
Billy Squier-Capitol
14 **THE NYLON CURTAIN**
Billy Joel-Columbia
15 **RIO**
Duran Duran-Capitol
16 **HEARTLIGHT**
Niel Diamond-Columbia
17 **AMERICAN FOOL**
John Cougar-Riva/Mercury
18 **SPRING SESSION M**
Missing Persons-Capitol
19 **TRANS**
Neil Young-Geffen
20 **THREE LOCK BOX**
Sammy Hagar-Geffen

UK SINGLES

1 **DOWN UNDER**
Men at Work-Epic
2 **TOO SHY**
KajaGooGoo-EMI
3 **SIGN OF THE TIMES**
The Belle Stars-Stiff
4 **ELECTRIC AVENUE**
Eddy Grant-Ice
5 **CHANGE**
Tears for Fears-Mercury/Phonogram
6 **GLORIA**
Laura Branigan-Atlantic
7 **UP WHERE WE BELONG**
Joe Cocker & Jennifer Warnes-Island
8 **YOU CAN'T HURRY LOVE**
Phil Collins-Virgin
9 **WHAM RAP!...**
Wham-Inner Vision
10 **OH DIANE**
Fleetwood Mac-Warner Bros.
11 **THE CUTTER**
Echo & The Bunnymen-Korova
12 **STORY OF THE BLUES**
Wah!-Eternal
13 **NEW YEAR'S DAY**
U2-Island
14 **LAST NIGHT A D.J. ...**
Indeep-Sound of New York
15 **TWISTING BY THE POOL**
Dire Straits-Vertigo/Phonogram
16 **STEPPIN' OUT**
Joe Jackson-A&M
17 **BILLIE JEAN**
Michael Jackson-Epic
18 **CHRISTIAN**
China Crisis-Virgin
19 **AFRICA**
Toto
20 **HOLD ME TIGHTER...**
Billy Griffin-CBS

UK ALBUMS

1 **BUSINESS AS USUAL**
Men at Work-Epic
2 **PORCUPINE**
Echo & The Bunnymen-Korova
3 **JOHN LENNON COLLECTION**
John Lennon-Parlophone
4 **HELLO, I MUST BE GOING!**
Phil Collins-Virgin
5 **RICHARD CLAYDERMAN**
Richard Clayderman-Delphine/Decca
6 **NIGHT AND DAY**
Joe Jackson-A&M
7 **KILLER ON THE RAMPAGE**
Eddy Grant-Ice
8 **RAIDERS OF POP CHARTS**
Various-Ronco
9 **VISIONS**
Various-K-tel
10 **HEARTBREAKER**
Dionne Warwick-Arista
11 **THRILLER**
Michael Jackson-Epic
12 **CACHARPAYA**
Incantation-Beggars Banquet
13 **FELINE**
The Stranglers-Epic
14 **SKY FIVE LIVE**
Sky-Ariola
15 **ART OF FALLING APART**
Soft Cell-Some Bizzare/Phonogram
16 **20 GREATEST LOVE SONGS**
Nat King Cole-Capitol
17 **RIO**
Duran Duran-EMI
18 **PEARLS II**
Elkie Brooks-A&M
19 **20 GREATEST HITS**
The Beatles-Parlophone
20 **GREATEST HITS**
Olivia Newton-John-EMI

US SINGLES

#	Title / Artist
1	**BABY, COME TO ME** — *Patti Austin-Qwest*
2	**DOWN UNDER** — *Men at Work-Columbia*
3	**SHAME ON THE MOON** — *Bob Seger-Capitol*
4	**STRAY CAT STRUT** — *Stray Cats-EMI America*
5	**AFRICA** — *Toto-Columbia*
6	**BILLIE JEAN** — *Michael Jackson-Epic*
7	**YOU AND I** — *Eddie Rabbitt/Crystal Gayle-Elektra*
8	**DO YOU REALLY WANT TO...** — *Culture Club-Virgin/Epic*
9	**HUNGRY LIKE THE WOLF** — *Duran Duran-Capitol*
10	**YOU CAN'T HURRY LOVE** — *Phil Collins-Atlantic*
11	**THE OTHER GUY** — *Little River Band-Capitol*
12	**GOODY TWO SHOES** — *Adam Ant-Epic*
13	**PASS THE DUTCHIE** — *Musical Youth-MCA*
14	**YOUR LOVE IS DRIVING ME...** — *Sammy Hagar-Geffen*
15	**HEART TO HEART** — *Kenny Loggins-Columbia*
16	**ALL RIGHT** — *Christopher Cross-Warner Bros.*
17	**ALLENTOWN** — *Billy Joel-Columbia*
18	**YOU ARE** — *Lionel Richie-Motown*
19	**BACK ON THE CHAIN GANG** — *The Pretenders-Sire*
20	**TWILIGHT ZONE** — *Golden Earring-21 Records*

US ALBUMS

#	Title / Artist
1	**BUSINESS AS USUAL** — *Men at Work-Columbia*
2	**BUILT FOR SPEED** — *Stray Cats-EMI America*
3	**H₂O** — *Daryl Hall & John Oates-RCA*
4	**THRILLER** — *Michael Jackson-Epic*
5	**THE DISTANCE** — *Bob Seger-Capitol*
6	**GET NERVOUS** — *Pat Benatar-Chrysalis*
7	**COMBAT ROCK** — *The Clash-Epic*
8	**HELLO, I MUST BE GOING** — *Phil Collins-Atlantic*
9	**TOTO IV** — *Toto-Columbia*
10	**RECORDS** — *Foreigner-Atlantic*
11	**LIONEL RICHIE** — *Lionel Richie-Motown*
12	**RIO** — *Duran Duran-Capitol*
13	**EMOTIONS IN MOTION** — *Billy Squier-Capitol*
14	**LONG AFTER DARK** — *Tom Petty-Backstreet*
15	**THE NYLON CURTAIN** — *Billy Joel-Columbia*
16	**HEARTLIGHT** — *Neil Diamond-Columbia*
17	**AMERICAN FOOL** — *John Cougar-Riva/Mercury*
18	**SPRING SESSION M** — *Missing Persons-Capitol*
19	**TRANS** — *Neil Young-Geffen*
20	**THREE LOCK BOX** — *Sammy Hagar-Geffen*

UK SINGLES

#	Title / Artist
1	**TOO SHY** — *KajaGooGoo-EMI*
2	**DOWN UNDER** — *Men at Work-Epic*
3	**SIGN OF THE TIMES** — *The Belle Stars-Stiff*
4	**CHANGE** — *Tears for Fears-Mercury/Phonogram*
5	**BILLIE JEAN** — *Michael Jackson-Epic*
6	**AFRICA** — *Toto-CBS*
7	**UP WHERE WE BELONG** — *Joe Cocker & Jennifer Warnes-Island*
8	**WHAM RAP!...** — *Wham-Inner Vision*
9	**OH DIANE** — *Fleetwood Mac-Warner Bros.*
10	**ELECTRIC AVENUE** — *Eddy Grant-Ice*
11	**GLORIA** — *Laura Branigan-Atlantic*
12	**CHRISTIAN** — *China Crisis-Virgin*
13	**LAST NIGHT A D.J. ...** — *Indeep-Sound of New York*
14	**TUNNEL OF LOVE** — *The Fun Boy Three-Chrysalis*
15	**LOVE ON YOUR SIDE** — *Thompson Twins-Arista*
16	**NEVER GONNA GIVE YOU UP** — *Musical Youth-MCA*
17	**YOU CAN'T HURRY LOVE** — *Phil Collins-Virgin*
18	**THE CUTTER** — *Echo & The Bunnymen-Korova*
19	**TWISTING BY THE POOL** — *Dire Straits-Vertigo/Phonogram*
20	**STORY OF THE BLUES** — *Wah!-Eternal*

UK ALBUMS

#	Title / Artist
1	**BUSINESS AS USUAL** — *Men at Work-Epic*
2	**JOHN LENNON COLLECTION** — *John Lennon-Parlophone*
3	**PORCUPINE** — *Echo & The Bunnymen-Korova*
4	**ANOTHER PAGE** — *Christopher Cross-Warner Bros.*
5	**THRILLER** — *Michael Jackson-Epic*
6	**FRONTIERS** — *Journey-CBS*
7	**VISIONS** — *Various-K-tel*
8	**NIGHT AND DAY** — *Joe Jackson-A&M*
9	**HELLO, I MUST BE GOING!** — *Phil Collins-Virgin*
10	**RICHARD CLAYDERMAN** — *Richard Clayderman-Delphine/Decca*
11	**KILLER ON THE RAMPAGE** — *Eddy Grant-Ice*
12	**RIO** — *Duran Duran-EMI*
13	**MONEY AND CIGARETTES** — *Eric Clapton-Duck/Warner Bros.*
14	**RAIDERS OF POP CHARTS** — *Various-Ronco*
15	**THE BELLE STARS** — *The Belle Stars-Stiff*
16	**HEARTBREAKER** — *Dionne Warwick-Arista*
17	**CACHARPAYA** — *Incantation-Beggars Banquet*
18	**WAITING** — *The Fun Boy Three-Chrysalis*
19	**ALL THE BEST** — *Stiff Little Fingers-Chrysalis*
20	**PEARLS II** — *Elkie Brooks-A&M*

US SINGLES

#	Title / Artist
1	**BABY, COME TO ME** — *Patti Austen-Qwest*
2	**SHAME ON THE MOON** — *Bob Seger-Capitol*
3	**STRAY CAT STRUT** — *Stray Cats-EMI America*
4	**BILLIE JEAN** — *Michael Jackson-Epic*
5	**DO YOU REALLY WANT TO...** — *Culture Club-Virgin/Epic*
6	**HUNGRY LIKE THE WOLF** — *Duran Duran-Capitol*
7	**YOU AND I** — *Eddie Rabbitt/Crystal Gayle-Elektra*
8	**DOWN UNDER** — *Men at Work-Columbia*
9	**WE'VE GOT TONIGHT** — *Kenny Rogers & Sheena Easton-Liberty*
10	**PASS THE DUTCHIE** — *Musical Youth-MCA*
11	**BACK ON THE CHAIN GANG** — *The Pretenders-Sire*
12	**GOODY TWO SHOES** — *Adam Ant-Epic*
13	**YOUR LOVE IS DRIVING ME...** — *Sammy Hagar-Geffen*
14	**YOU ARE** — *Lionel Richie-Motown*
15	**HEART TO HEART** — *Kenny Loggins-Columbia*
16	**ALL RIGHT** — *Christopher Cross-Warner Bros.*
17	**ALLENTOWN** — *Billy Joel-Columbia*
18	**TWILIGHT ZONE** — *Golden Earring-21 Records*
19	**AFRICA** — *Toto-Columbia*
20	**SEPARATE WAYS** — *Journey-Columbia*

US ALBUMS

#	Title / Artist
1	**THRILLER** — *Michael Jackson-Epic*
2	**BUILT FOR SPEED** — *Stray Cats-EMI America*
3	**H₂O** — *Daryl Hall & John Oates-RCA*
4	**BUSINESS AS USUAL** — *Men at Work-Columbia*
5	**THE DISTANCE** — *Bob Seger-Capitol*
6	**FRONTIERS** — *Journey-Columbia*
7	**RIO** — *Duran Duran-Capitol*
8	**HELLO, I MUST BE GOING** — *Phil Collins-Atlantic*
9	**TOTO IV** — *Toto-Columbia*
10	**RECORDS** — *Foreigner-Atlantic*
11	**LIONEL RICHIE** — *Lionel Richie-Motown*
12	**GET NERVOUS** — *Pat Benatar-Chrysalis*
13	**EMOTIONS IN MOTION** — *Billy Squier-Capitol*
14	**LONG AFTER DARK** — *Tom Petty-Backstreet*
15	**COMBAT ROCK** — *The Clash-Epic*
16	**PYROMANIA** — *Def Leppard-Mercury*
17	**SPRING SESSION M** — *Missing Persons-Capitol*
18	**THREE LOCK BOX** — *Sammy Hagar-Geffen*
19	**TRANS** — *Neil Young-Geffen*
20	**THE NYLON CURTAIN** — *Billy Joel-Columbia*

UK SINGLES

#	Title / Artist
1	**TOO SHY** — *KajaGooGoo-EMI*
2	**BILLIE JEAN** — *Michael Jackson-Epic*
3	**AFRICA** — *Toto-CBS*
4	**CHANGE** — *Tears for Fears-Mercury/Phonogram*
5	**SIGN OF THE TIMES** — *The Belle Stars-Stiff*
6	**DOWN UNDER** — *Men at Work-Epic*
7	**UP WHERE WE BELONG** — *Joe Cocker & Jennifer Warnes-Island*
8	**NEVER GONNA GIVE YOU UP** — *Musical Youth-MCA*
9	**TOMORROW'S (JUST...)** — *Madness-Stiff*
10	**WHAM RAP!...** — *Wham-Inner Vision*
11	**TUNNEL OF LOVE** — *The Fun Boy Three-Chrysalis*
12	**LOVE ON YOUR SIDE** — *Thompson Twins-Arista*
13	**OH DIANE** — *Fleetwood Mac-Warner Bros.*
14	**TOTAL ECLIPSE...** — *Bonnie Tyler-CBS*
15	**CHRISTIAN** — *China Crisis-Virgin*
16	**SHINY SHINY** — *Haysi Fantayzee-Regard*
17	**HEY LITTLE GIRL** — *Icehouse-Chrysalis*
18	**LAST NIGHT A D.J. ...** — *Indeep-Sound of New York*
19	**BABY, COME TO ME** — *Patti Austin & James Ingram-Qwest*
20	**GLORIA** — *Laura Branigan-Atlantic*

UK ALBUMS

#	Title / Artist
1	**BUSINESS AS USUAL** — *Men at Work-Epic*
2	**THRILLER** — *Michael Jackson-Epic*
3	**JOHN LENNON COLLECTION** — *John Lennon-Parlophone*
4	**ANOTHER PAGE** — *Christopher Cross-Warner Bros.*
5	**VISIONS** — *Various-K-tel*
6	**PORCUPINE** — *Echo & The Bunnymen-Korova*
7	**RICHARD CLAYDERMAN** — *Richard Clayderman-Delphine/Decca*
8	**HEARTBREAKER** — *Dionne Warwick-Arista*
9	**WORKOUT** — *Jane Fonda-CBS*
10	**NIGHT AND DAY** — *Joe Jackson-A&M*
11	**RIO** — *Duran Duran-EMI*
12	**QUICK STEP & SIDE KICK** — *Thompson Twins-Arista*
13	**MONEY AND CIGARETTES** — *Eric Clapton-Duck/Warner Bros.*
14	**WAITING** — *The Fun Boy Three-Chrysalis*
15	**HELLO, I MUST BE GOING!** — *Phil Collins-Virgin*
16	**KILLER ON THE RAMPAGE** — *Eddy Grant-Ice*
17	**LIONEL RICHIE** — *Lionel Richie-Motown*
18	**RAIDERS OF POP CHARTS** — *Various-Ronco*
19	**FRONTIERS** — *Journey-CBS*
20	**THE BELLE STARS** — *The Belle Stars-Stiff*

WEEK ENDING MARCH 5 1983

US SINGLES

1. **BILLIE JEAN**
   Michael Jackson-Epic
2. **SHAME ON THE MOON**
   Bob Seger-Capitol
3. **STRAY CAT STRUT**
   Stray Cats-EMI America
4. **DO YOU REALLY WANT TO...**
   Culture Club-Virgin/Epic
5. **HUNGRY LIKE THE WOLF**
   Duran Duran-Capitol
6. **BABY, COME TO ME**
   Patti Austin-Qwest
7. **YOU AND I**
   Eddie Rabbitt/Crystal Gayle-Elektra
8. **WE'VE GOT TONIGHT**
   Kenny Rogers & Sheena Easton-Liberty
9. **BACK ON THE CHAIN GANG**
   The Pretenders-Sire
10. **PASS THE DUTCHIE**
    Musical Youth-MCA
11. **YOU ARE**
    Lionel Richie-Motown
12. **ALL RIGHT**
    Christopher Cross-Warner Bros.
13. **YOUR LOVE IS DRIVING ME...**
    Sammy Hagar-Geffen
14. **DOWN UNDER**
    Men at Work-Columbia
15. **SEPARATE WAYS**
    Journey-Columbia
16. **TWILIGHT ZONE**
    Golden Earring-21 Records
17. **ALLENTOWN**
    Billy Joel-Columbia
18. **ONE ON ONE**
    Daryl Hall & John Oates-RCA
19. **BREAKING US IN TWO**
    Joe Jackson-A&M
20. **MR. ROBOTO**
    Styx-A&M

US ALBUMS

1. **THRILLER**
   Michael Jackson-Epic
2. **BUILT FOR SPEED**
   Stray Cats-EMI America
3. **H₂O**
   Daryl Hall & John Oates-RCA
4. **FRONTIERS**
   Journey-Columbia
5. **THE DISTANCE**
   Bob Seger-Capitol
6. **BUSINESS AS USUAL**
   Men at Work-Columbia
7. **RIO**
   Duran Duran-Capitol
8. **HELLO, I MUST BE GOING**
   Phil Collins-Atlantic
9. **TOTO IV**
   Toto-Columbia
10. **RECORDS**
    Foreigner-Atlantic
11. **LIONEL RICHIE**
    Lionel Richie-Motown
12. **GET NERVOUS**
    Pat Benatar-Chrysalis
13. **ANOTHER PAGE**
    Christopher Cross-Warner Bros.
14. **LONG AFTER DARK**
    Tom Petty-Backstreet
15. **PYROMANIA**
    Def Leppard-Mercury
16. **FRIEND OR FOE**
    Adam Ant-Epic
17. **SPRING SESSION M**
    Missing Persons-Capitol
18. **THREE LOCK BOX**
    Sammy Hagar-Geffen
19. **TRANS**
    Neil Young-Geffen
20. **KISSING TO BE CLEVER**
    Culture Club-Virgin/Epic

UK SINGLES

1. **BILLIE JEAN**
   Michael Jackson-Epic
2. **TOTAL ECLIPSE...**
   Bonnie Tyler-CBS
3. **TOO SHY**
   KajaGooGoo-EMI
4. **AFRICA**
   Toto-CBS
5. **SWEET DREAMS...**
   Eurythmics-RCA
6. **NEVER GONNA GIVE YOU UP**
   Musical Youth-MCA
7. **CHANGE**
   Tears for Fears-Mercury/Phonogram
8. **TOMORROW'S (JUST...)**
   Madness-Stiff
9. **LOVE ON YOUR SIDE**
   Thompson Twins-Arista
10. **TUNNEL OF LOVE**
    The Fun Boy Three-Chrysalis
11. **UP WHERE WE BELONG**
    Joe Cocker & Jennifer Warnes-Island
12. **ROCK THE BOAT**
    Forrest-CBS
13. **GET THE BALANCE RIGHT!**
    Depeche Mode-Mute
14. **WHAM RAP!...**
    Wham-Inner Vision
15. **COMMUNICATION**
    Spandau Ballet-Reformation/Chrysalis
16. **SIGN OF THE TIMES**
    The Belle Stars-Stiff
17. **HEY LITTLE GIRL**
    Icehouse-Chrysalis
18. **BABY, COME TO ME**
    Patti Austin & James Ingram-Qwest
19. **SHE MEANS NOTHING TO ME**
    Phil Everly/Cliff Richard-Capitol
20. **SHINY SHINY**
    Haysi Fantayzee-Regard

UK ALBUMS

1. **THRILLER**
   Michael Jackson-Epic
2. **QUICK STEP & SIDE KICK**
   Thompson Twins-Arista
3. **BUSINESS AS USUAL**
   Men at Work-Epic
4. **TOTO IV**
   Toto-CBS
5. **VISIONS**
   Various-K-tel
6. **ANOTHER PAGE**
   Christopher Cross-Warner Bros.
7. **WORKOUT**
   Jane Fonda-CBS
8. **JOHN LENNON COLLECTION**
   John Lennon-Parlophone
9. **LIONEL RICHIE**
   Lionel Richie-Motown
10. **RICHARD CLAYDERMAN**
    Richard Clayderman-Delphine/Decca
11. **PORCUPINE**
    Echo & The Bunnymen-Korova
12. **HEARTBREAKER**
    Dionne Warwick-Arista
13. **RIO**
    Duran Duran-EMI
14. **WAITING**
    The Fun Boy Three-Chrysalis
15. **SWEET DREAMS...**
    Eurythmics-RCA
16. **NIGHT AND DAY**
    Joe Jackson-A&M
17. **HOTLINE**
    Various-K-tel
18. **THE BELLE STARS**
    The Belle Stars-Stiff
19. **FRONTIERS**
    Journey-CBS
20. **VERY BEST OF CILLA BLACK**
    Cilla Black-Parlophone

WEEK ENDING MARCH 12 1983

US SINGLES

1. **BILLIE JEAN**
   Michael Jackson-Epic
2. **SHAME ON THE MOON**
   Bob Seger-Capitol
3. **STRAY CAT STRUT**
   Stray Cats-EMI America
4. **DO YOU REALLY WANT TO...**
   Culture Club-Virgin/Epic
5. **HUNGRY LIKE THE WOLF**
   Duran Duran-Capitol
6. **BACK ON THE CHAIN GANG**
   The Pretenders-Sire
7. **YOU ARE**
   Lionel Richie-Motown
8. **WE'VE GOT TONIGHT**
   Kenny Rogers & Sheena Easton-Liberty
9. **BABY, COME TO ME**
   Patti Austin-Qwest
10. **SEPARATE WAYS**
    Journey-Columbia
11. **ONE ON ONE**
    Daryl Hall & John Oates-RCA
12. **ALL RIGHT**
    Christopher Cross-Warner Bros.
13. **MR. ROBOTO**
    Styx-A&M
14. **TWILIGHT ZONE**
    Golden Earring-21 Records
15. **DOWN UNDER**
    Men at Work-Columbia
16. **I KNOW THERE'S SOMETHING...**
    Frida-Atlantic
17. **ALLENTOWN**
    Billy Joel-Columbia
18. **FALL IN LOVE WITH ME**
    Earth, Wind & Fire-Columbia
19. **BREAKING US IN TWO**
    Joe Jackson-A&M
20. **COME ON EILEEN**
    Dexys Midnight Runners-Mercury

US ALBUMS

1. **THRILLER**
   Michael Jackson-Epic
2. **FRONTIERS**
   Journey-Columbia
3. **H₂O**
   Daryl Hall & John Oates-RCA
4. **BUSINESS AS USUAL**
   Men at Work-Columbia
5. **THE DISTANCE**
   Bob Seger-Capitol
6. **RIO**
   Duran Duran-Capitol
7. **LIONEL RICHIE**
   Lionel Richie-Motown
8. **TOTO IV**
   Toto-Columbia
9. **BUILT FOR SPEED**
   Stray Cats-EMI America
10. **PYROMANIA**
    Def Leppard-Mercury
11. **ANOTHER PAGE**
    Christopher Cross-Warner Bros.
12. **GET NERVOUS**
    Pat Benatar-Chrysalis
13. **HELLO, I MUST BE GOING**
    Phil Collins-Atlantic
14. **LONG AFTER DARK**
    Tom Petty-Backstreet
15. **KISSING TO BE CLEVER**
    Culture Club-Virgin/Epic
16. **FRIEND OR FOE**
    Adam Ant-Epic
17. **SPRING SESSION M**
    Missing Persons-Capitol
18. **THREE LOCK BOX**
    Sammy Hagar-Geffen
19. **TRANS**
    Neil Young-Geffen
20. **RECORDS**
    Foreigner-Atlantic

UK SINGLES

1. **TOTAL ECLIPSE...**
   Bonnie Tyler-CBS
2. **BILLIE JEAN**
   Michael Jackson-Epic
3. **SWEET DREAMS...**
   Eurythmics-RCA
4. **ROCK THE BOAT**
   Forrest-CBS
5. **AFRICA**
   Toto-CBS
6. **TOO SHY**
   KajaGooGoo-EMI
7. **NA NA HEY HEY KISS HIM...**
   Bananarama-London
8. **TOMORROW'S (JUST...)**
   Madness-Stiff
9. **LOVE ON YOUR SIDE**
   Thompson Twins-Arista
10. **NEVER GONNA GIVE YOU UP**
    Musical Youth-MCA
11. **BABY, COME TO ME**
    Patti Austin & James Ingram-Qwest
12. **COMMUNICATION**
    Spandau Ballet-Reformation/Chrysalis
13. **TUNNEL OF LOVE**
    The Fun Boy Three-Chrysalis
14. **SHE MEANS NOTHING TO ME**
    Phil Everly/Cliff Richard-Capitol
15. **GET THE BALANCE RIGHT!**
    Depeche Mode-Mute
16. **CHANGE**
    Tears for Fears-Mercury/Phonogram
17. **HEY LITTLE GIRL**
    Icehouse-Chrysalis
18. **HIGH LIFE**
    Modern Romance-WEA
19. **UP WHERE WE BELONG**
    Joe Cocker & Jennifer Warnes-Island
20. **GENETIC ENGINEERING**
    OMD-Telegraph/Virgin

UK ALBUMS

1. **WAR**
   U2-Island
2. **THRILLER**
   Michael Jackson-Epic
3. **HOTLINE**
   Various-K-tel
4. **THUNDER AND LIGHTNING**
   Thin Lizzy-Vertigo/Phonogram
5. **DAZZLE SHIPS**
   OMD-Telegraph/Virgin
6. **SWEET DREAMS...**
   Eurythmics-RCA
7. **TOTO IV**
   Toto-CBS
8. **QUICK STEP & SIDE KICK**
   Thompson Twins-Arista
9. **TRUE**
   Spandau Ballet-Reformation/Chrysalis
10. **VISIONS**
    Various-K-tel
11. **WORKOUT**
    Jane Fonda-CBS
12. **BUSINESS AS USUAL**
    Men at Work-Epic
13. **THE KEY**
    Joan Armatrading-A&M
14. **ANOTHER PAGE**
    Christopher Cross-Warner Bros.
15. **LIONEL RICHIE**
    Lionel Richie-Motown
16. **JOHN LENNON COLLECTION**
    John Lennon-Parlophone
17. **RICHARD CLAYDERMAN**
    Richard Clayderman-Delphine/Decca
18. **PYROMANIA**
    Def Leppard-Vertigo/Phonogram
19. **NIGHT AND DAY**
    Joe Jackson-A&M
20. **HEARTBREAKER**
    Dionne Warwick-Arista

WEEK ENDING MARCH 19 1983

US SINGLES	US ALBUMS	UK SINGLES	UK ALBUMS
1 **BILLIE JEAN** *Michael Jackson-Epic*	1 **THRILLER** *Michael Jackson-Epic*	1 **TOTAL ECLIPSE...** *Bonnie Tyler-CBS*	1 **THRILLER** *Michael Jackson-Epic*
2 **SHAME ON THE MOON** *Bob Seger-Capitol*	2 **FRONTIERS** *Journey-Columbia*	2 **SWEET DREAMS...** *Eurythmics-RCA*	2 **THE HURTING** *Tears for Fears-Mercury/Phonogram*
3 **DO YOU REALLY WANT TO...** *Culture Club-Virgin/Epic*	3 **H_2O** *Daryl Hall & John Oates-RCA*	3 **BILLIE JEAN** *Michael Jackson-Epic*	3 **HOTLINE** *Various-K-tel*
4 **HUNGRY LIKE THE WOLF** *Duran Duran-Capitol*	4 **BUSINESS AS USUAL** *Men at Work-Columbia*	4 **ROCK THE BOAT** *Forrest-CBS*	4 **WAR** *U2-Island*
5 **BACK ON THE CHAIN GANG** *The Pretenders-Sire*	5 **THE DISTANCE** *Bob Seger-Capitol*	5 **NA NA HEY HEY KISS HIM...** *Bananarama-London*	5 **SWEET DREAMS...** *Eurythmics-RCA*
6 **YOU ARE** *Lionel Richie-Motown*	6 **RIO** *Duran Duran-Capitol*	6 **SPEAK LIKE A CHILD** *The Style Council-Polydor*	6 **DAZZLE SHIPS** *OMD-Telegraph/Virgin*
7 **WE'VE GOT TONIGHT** *Kenny Rogers & Sheena Easton-Liberty*	7 **LIONEL RICHIE** *Lionel Richie-Motown*	7 **AFRICA** *Toto-CBS*	7 **TRUE** *Spandau Ballet-Reformation/Chrysalis*
8 **SEPARATE WAYS** *Journey-Columbia*	8 **TOTO IV** *Toto-Columbia*	8 **HIGH LIFE** *Modern Romance-WEA*	8 **THUNDER AND LIGHTNING** *Thin Lizzy-Vertigo/Phonogram*
9 **ONE ON ONE** *Daryl Hall & John Oates-RCA*	9 **PYROMANIA** *Def Leppard-Mercury*	9 **SHE MEANS NOTHING TO ME** *Phil Everly/Cliff Richard-Capitol*	9 **WORKOUT** *Jane Fonda-CBS*
10 **MR. ROBOTO** *Styx-A&M*	10 **KILROY WAS HERE** *Styx-A&M*	10 **RIP IT UP** *Orange Juice-Polydor*	10 **TOTO IV** *Toto-CBS*
11 **STRAY CAT STRUT** *Stray Cats-EMI America*	11 **ANOTHER PAGE** *Christopher Cross-Warner Bros.*	11 **BABY, COME TO ME** *Patti Austin & James Ingram-Qwest*	11 **RICHARD CLAYDERMAN** *Richard Clayderman-Delphine/Decca*
12 **ALL RIGHT** *Christopher Cross-Warner Bros.*	12 **BUILT FOR SPEED** *Stray Cats-EMI America*	12 **LOVE ON YOUR SIDE** *Thompson Twins-Arista*	12 **QUICK STEP & SIDE KICK** *Thompson Twins-Arista*
13 **TWILIGHT ZONE** *Golden Earring-21 Records*	13 **POWERLIGHT** *Earth, Wind & Fire-Columbia*	13 **COMMUNICATION** *Spandau Ballet-Reformation/Chrysalis*	13 **DEEP SEA SKIVING** *Bananarama-London*
14 **COME ON EILEEN** *Dexys Midnight Runners-Mercury*	14 **KISSING TO BE CLEVER** *Culture Club-Virgin/Epic*	14 **TOO SHY** *KajaGooGoo-EMI*	14 **VISIONS** *Various-K-tel*
15 **I KNOW THERE'S SOMETHING...** *Frida-Atlantic*	15 **GET NERVOUS** *Pat Benatar-Chrysalis*	15 **TOMORROW'S (JUST...)** *Madness-Stiff*	15 **THE KEY** *Joan Armatrading-A&M*
16 **JEOPARDY** *Greg Kihn Band-Beserkley*	16 **FRIEND OR FOE** *Adam Ant-Epic*	16 **YOU CAN'T HIDE...** *David Joseph-Island*	16 **LIONEL RICHIE** *Lionel Richie-Motown*
17 **FALL IN LOVE WITH ME** *Earth, Wind & Fire-Columbia*	17 **SPRING SESSION M** *Missing Persons-Capitol*	17 **NEVER GONNA GIVE YOU UP** *Musical Youth-MCA*	17 **HEARTBREAKER** *Dionne Warwick-Arista*
18 **BREAKING US IN TWO** *Joe Jackson-A&M*	18 **THREE LOCK BOX** *Sammy Hagar-Geffen*	18 **TUNNEL OF LOVE** *The Fun Boy Three-Chrysalis*	18 **BUSINESS AS USUAL** *Men at Work-Epic*
19 **I'VE GOT A ROCK 'N' ROLL...** *Eric Clapton-Warner Bros./Duck*	19 **MONEY AND CIGARETTES** *Eric Clapton-Warner Bros./Duck*	19 **WAVES** *Blancmange-London*	19 **JOHN LENNON COLLECTION** *John Lennon-Parlophone*
20 **DER KOMMISSAR** *After the Fire-Epic*	20 **JANE FONDA'S WORKOUT...** *Jane Fonda-Columbia*	20 **HEY LITTLE GIRL** *Icehouse-Chrysalis*	20 **NIGHT AND DAY** *Joe Jackson-A&M*

WEEK ENDING MARCH 26 1983

US SINGLES	US ALBUMS	UK SINGLES	UK ALBUMS
1 **BILLIE JEAN** *Michael Jackson-Epic*	1 **THRILLER** *Michael Jackson-Epic*	1 **IS THERE SOMETHING...** *Duran Duran-EMI*	1 **THE HURTING** *Tears for Fears-Mercury/Phonogram*
2 **DO YOU REALLY WANT TO...** *Culture Club-Virgin/Epic*	2 **FRONTIERS** *Journey-Columbia*	2 **TOTAL ECLIPSE...** *Bonnie Tyler-CBS*	2 **THRILLER** *Michael Jackson-Epic*
3 **HUNGRY LIKE THE WOLF** *Duran Duran-Capitol*	3 **H_2O** *Daryl Hall & John Oates-RCA*	3 **SWEET DREAMS...** *Eurythmics-RCA*	3 **SWEET DREAMS...** *Eurythmics-RCA*
4 **YOU ARE** *Lionel Richie-Motown*	4 **BUSINESS AS USUAL** *Men at Work-Columbia*	4 **SPEAK LIKE A CHILD** *The Style Council-Polydor*	4 **WAR** *U2-Island*
5 **BACK ON THE CHAIN GANG** *The Pretenders-Sire*	5 **THE DISTANCE** *Bob Seger-Capitol*	5 **LET'S DANCE** *David Bowie-EMI America*	5 **CHART RUNNERS** *Various-K-tel*
6 **WE'VE GOT TONIGHT** *Kenny Rogers & Sheena Easton-Liberty*	6 **RIO** *Duran Duran-Capitol*	6 **ROCK THE BOAT** *Forrest-CBS*	6 **HOTLINE** *Various-K-tel*
7 **MR ROBOTO** *Styx-A&M*	7 **LIONEL RICHIE** *Lionel Richie-Motown*	7 **NA NA HEY HEY KISS HIM...** *Bananarama-London*	7 **SCRIPT FOR A JESTER'S TEAR** *Marillion-EMI*
8 **SEPARATE WAYS** *Journey-Columbia*	8 **TOTO IV** *Toto-Columbia*	8 **BILLIE JEAN** *Michael Jackson-Epic*	8 **DEEP SEA SKIVING** *Bananarama-London*
9 **ONE ON ONE** *Daryl Hall & John Oates-RCA*	9 **PYROMANIA** *Def Leppard-Mercury*	9 **RIP IT UP** *Orange Juice-Polydor*	9 **TRUE** *Spandau Ballet-Reformation/Chrysalis*
10 **TWILIGHT ZONE** *Golden Earring-21 Records*	10 **KILROY WAS HERE** *Styx-A&M*	10 **HIGH LIFE** *Modern Romance-WEA*	10 **THE KEY** *Joan Armatrading-A&M*
11 **COME ON EILEEN** *Dexys Midnight Runners-Mercury*	11 **ANOTHER PAGE** *Christopher Cross-Warner Bros.*	11 **DROP THE PILOT** *Joan Armatrading-A&M*	11 **TOTO IV** *Toto-CBS*
12 **SHAME ON THE MOON** *Bob Seger-Capitol*	12 **POWERLIGHT** *Earth, Wind & Fire-Columbia*	12 **DON'T TALK TO ME...** *Altered Images-Epic*	12 **THUNDER AND LIGHTNING** *Thin Lizzy-Vertigo/Phonogram*
13 **I KNOW THERE'S SOMETHING...** *Frida-Atlantic*	13 **BUILT FOR SPEED** *Stray Cats-EMI America*	13 **YOU CAN'T HIDE...** *David Joseph-Island*	13 **DAZZLE SHIPS** *OMD-Telegraph/Virgin*
14 **JEOPARDY** *Greg Kihn Band-Beserkley*	14 **KISSING TO BE CLEVER** *Culture Club-Virgin/Epic*	14 **RUN FOR YOUR LIFE** *Bucks Fizz-RCA*	14 **QUICK STEP & SIDE KICK** *Thompson Twins-Arista*
15 **BEAT IT** *Michael Jackson-Epic*	15 **JANE FONDA'S WORKOUT...** *Jane Fonda-Columbia*	15 **VISIONS IN BLUE** *Ultravox-Chrysalis*	15 **POWER & THE GLORY** *Saxon-Carrere*
16 **DER KOMMISSAR** *After the Fire-Epic*	16 **MONEY AND CIGARETTES** *Eric Clapton-Warner Bros./Duck*	16 **SHE MEANS NOTHING...** *Phil Everly/Cliff Richard-Capitol*	16 **WORKOUT** *Jane Fonda-CBS*
17 **FALL IN LOVE WITH ME** *Earth, Wind & Fire-Columbia*	17 **SPRING SESSION M** *Missing Persons-Capitol*	17 **GARDEN PARTY** *Mezzoforte-Steinar*	17 **RICHARD CLAYDERMAN** *Richard Clayderman-Delphine/Decca*
18 **I'VE GOT A ROCK 'N' ROLL...** *Eric Clapton-Warner Bros./Duck*	18 **THREE LOCK BOX** *Sammy Hagar-Geffen*	18 **BABY, COME TO ME** *Patti Austin & James Ingram-Qwest*	18 **HAND CUT** *Bucks Fizz-RCA*
19 **ALL RIGHT** *Christopher Cross-Warner Bros.*	19 **HELLO, I MUST BE GOING** *Phil Collins-Atlantic*	19 **WAVES** *Blancmange-London*	19 **BUSINESS AS USUAL** *Men at Work-Epic*
20 **LITTLE TOO LATE** *Pat Benatar-Chrysalis*	20 **GET NERVOUS** *Pat Benatar-Chrysalis*	20 **COMMUNICATION** *Spandau Ballet-Reformation/Chrysalis*	20 **RIO** *Duran Duran-EMI*

US SINGLES

1. **BILLIE JEAN**
   Michael Jackson-Epic
2. **DO YOU REALLY WANT TO...**
   Culture Club-Virgin/Epic
3. **HUNGRY LIKE THE WOLF**
   Duran Duran-Capitol
4. **YOU ARE**
   Lionel Richie-Motown
5. **BACK ON THE CHAIN GANG**
   The Pretenders-Sire
6. **WE'VE GOT TONIGHT**
   Kenny Rogers & Sheena Easton-Liberty
7. **MR ROBOTO**
   Styx-A&M
8. **SEPARATE WAYS**
   Journey-Columbia
9. **ONE ON ONE**
   Daryl Hall & John Oates-RCA
10. **TWILIGHT ZONE**
    Golden Earring-21 Records
11. **COME ON EILEEN**
    Dexys Midnight Runners-Mercury
12. **JEOPARDY**
    Greg Kihn Band-Beserkley
13. **I KNOW THERE'S SOMETHING...**
    Frida-Atlantic
14. **BEAT IT**
    Michael Jackson-Epic
15. **DER KOMMISSAR**
    After the Fire-Epic
16. **SHAME ON THE MOON**
    Bob Seger-Capitol
17. **FALL IN LOVE WITH ME**
    Earth, Wind & Fire-Columbia
18. **I'VE GOT A ROCK 'N' ROLL...**
    Eric Clapton-Warner Bros./Duck
19. **ALL RIGHT**
    Christopher Cross-Warner Bros.
20. **LITTLE TOO LATE**
    Pat Benatar-Chrysalis

US ALBUMS

1. **THRILLER**
   Michael Jackson-Epic
2. **FRONTIERS**
   Journey-Columbia
3. **H$_2$0**
   Daryl Hall & John Oates
4. **BUSINESS AS USUAL**
   Men at Work-Columbia
5. **KILROY WAS HERE**
   Styx-A&M
6. **RIO**
   Duran Duran-Capitol
7. **LIONEL RICHIE**
   Lionel Richie-Motown
8. **TOTO IV**
   Toto-Columbia
9. **PYROMANIA**
   Def Leppard-Mercury
10. **THE DISTANCE**
    Bob Seger-Capitol
11. **ANOTHER PAGE**
    Christopher Cross-Warner Bros.
12. **POWERLIGHT**
    Earth, Wind & Fire-Columbia
13. **BUILT FOR SPEED**
    Stray Cats-EMI America
14. **KISSING TO BE CLEVER**
    Culture Club-Virgin/Epic
15. **JANE FONDA'S WORKOUT...**
    Jane Fonda-Columbia
16. **MONEY AND CIGARETTES**
    Eric Clapton-Warner Bros./Duck
17. **SPRING SESSION M**
    Missing Persons-Capitol
18. **THREE LOCK BOX**
    Sammy Hagar-Geffen
19. **HELLO, I MUST BE GOING**
    Phil Collins-Atlantic
20. **BLINDED BY SCIENCE**
    Thomas Dolby-Capitol

UK SINGLES

1. **IS THERE SOMETHING...**
   Duran Duran-EMI
2. **LET'S DANCE**
   David Bowie-EMI America
3. **TOTAL ECLIPSE...**
   Bonnie Tyler-CBS
4. **SPEAK LIKE A CHILD**
   The Style Council-Polydor
5. **SWEET DREAMS...**
   Eurythmics-RCA
6. **BOXERBEAT**
   JoBoxers-RCA
7. **DON'T TALK TO ME...**
   Altered Images-Epic
8. **RIP IT UP**
   Orange Juice-Polydor
9. **NA NA HEY HEY KISS HIM...**
   Bananarama-London
10. **ROCK THE BOAT**
    Forrest-CBS
11. **BILLIE JEAN**
    Michael Jackson-Epic
12. **DROP THE PILOT**
    Joan Armatrading-A&M
13. **FIELDS OF FIRE...**
    Big Country-Mercury/Phonogram
14. **YOU CAN'T HIDE...**
    David Joseph-Island
15. **WHISTLE DOWN THE WIND**
    Nick Heyward-Arista
16. **ORCHARD ROAD**
    Leo Sayer-Chrysalis
17. **BLUE MONDAY**
    New Order-Factory
18. **BREAKAWAY**
    Tracey Ullman-Stiff
19. **GARDEN PARTY**
    Mezzoforte-Steinar
20. **OOH TO BE AH**
    KajaGooGoo-EMI

UK ALBUMS

1. **THE FINAL CUT**
   Pink Floyd-Harvest
2. **THE HURTING**
   Tears for Fears-Mercury/Phonogram
3. **THRILLER**
   Michael Jackson-Epic
4. **CHART RUNNERS**
   Various-K-tel
5. **SWEET DREAMS...**
   Eurythmics-RCA
6. **WAR**
   U2-Island
7. **DEEP SEA SKIVING**
   Bananarama-London
8. **SCRIPT FOR A JESTER'S TEAR**
   Marillion-EMI
9. **HOTLINE**
   Various-K-tel
10. **THE KEY**
    Joan Armatrading-A&M
11. **RIO**
    Duran Duran-EMI
12. **TOTO IV**
    Toto-CBS
13. **TRUE**
    Spandau Ballet-Reformation/Chrysalis
14. **INARTICULATE SPEECH...**
    Van Morrison-Mercury/Phonogram
15. **THUNDER AND LIGHTNING**
    Thin Lizzy-Vertigo/Phonogram
16. **QUICK STEP & SIDE KICK**
    Thompson Twins-Arista
17. **POWER & THE GLORY**
    Saxon-Carrere
18. **BUSINESS AS USUAL**
    Men at Work-Epic
19. **DAZZLE SHIPS**
    OMD-Telegraph/Virgin
20. **HELLO, I MUST BE GOING!**
    Phil Collins-Virgin

US SINGLES

1. **BILLIE JEAN**
   Michael Jackson-Epic
2. **DO YOU REALLY WANT TO...**
   Culture Club-Virgin/Epic
3. **HUNGRY LIKE THE WOLF**
   Duran Duran-Capitol
4. **COME ON EILEEN**
   Dexys Midnight Runners-Mercury
5. **MR. ROBOTO**
   Styx-A&M
6. **WE'VE GOT TONIGHT**
   Kenny Rogers & Sheena Easton-Liberty
7. **ONE ON ONE**
   Daryl Hall & John Oates-RCA
8. **SEPARATE WAYS**
   Journey-Columbia
9. **JEOPARDY**
   Greg Kihn Band-Beserkley
10. **BEAT IT**
    Michael Jackson-Epic
11. **YOU ARE**
    Lionel Richie-Motown
12. **DER KOMMISSAR**
    After the Fire-Epic
13. **I KNOW THERE'S SOMETHING...**
    Frida-Atlantic
14. **BACK ON THE CHAIN GANG**
    The Pretenders-Sire
15. **TWILIGHT ZONE**
    Golden Earring-21 Records
16. **SHE BLINDED ME WITH...**
    Thomas Dolby-Capitol
17. **SHAME ON THE MOON**
    Bob Seger-Capitol
18. **I'VE GOT A ROCK 'N' ROLL...**
    Eric Clapton-Warner Bros./Duck
19. **LITTLE RED CORVETTE**
    Prince-Warner Bros.
20. **LITTLE TOO LATE**
    Pat Benatar-Chrysalis

US ALBUMS

1. **THRILLER**
   Michael Jackson-Epic
2. **FRONTIERS**
   Journey-Columbia
3. **H$_2$0**
   Daryl Hall & John Oates-RCA
4. **BUSINESS AS USUAL**
   Men at Work-Columbia
5. **KILROY WAS HERE**
   Styx-A&M
6. **RIO**
   Duran Duran-Capitol
7. **LIONEL RICHIE**
   Lionel Richie-Motown
8. **TOTO IV**
   Toto-Columbia
9. **PYROMANIA**
   Def Leppard-Mercury
10. **THE DISTANCE**
    Bob Seger-Capitol
11. **ANOTHER PAGE**
    Christopher Cross-Warner Bros.
12. **POWERLIGHT**
    Earth, Wind & Fire-Columbia
13. **BUILT FOR SPEED**
    Stray Cats-EMI America
14. **KISSING TO BE CLEVER**
    Culture Club-Virgin/Epic
15. **JANE FONDA'S WORKOUT...**
    Jane Fonda-Columbia
16. **MONEY AND CIGARETTES**
    Eric Clapton-Warner Bros./Duck
17. **THREE LOCK BOX**
    Sammy Hagar-Geffen
18. **THE CLOSER YOU GET**
    Alabama-RCA
19. **TOO-RYE-AY**
    Dexys Midnight Runners-Mercury
20. **BLINDED BY SCIENCE**
    Thomas Dolby-Capitol

UK SINGLES

1. **LET'S DANCE**
   David Bowie-EMI America
2. **IS THERE SOMETHING...**
   Duran Duran-EMI
3. **BOXERBEAT**
   JoBoxers-RCA
4. **SPEAK LIKE A CHILD**
   The Style Council-Polydor
5. **SWEET DREAMS...**
   Eurythmics-RCA
6. **BREAKAWAY**
   Tracey Ullman-Stiff
7. **OOH TO BE AH**
   KajaGooGoo-EMI
8. **TOTAL ECLIPSE...**
   Bonnie Tyler-CBS
9. **CHURCH OF POISON MIND**
   Culture Club-Virgin
10. **SNOT RAP**
    Kenny Everett-RCA
11. **DON'T TALK TO ME...**
    Altered Images-Epic
12. **RIP IT UP**
    Orange Juice-Polydor
13. **FIELDS OF FIRE...**
    Big Country-Mercury/Phonogram
14. **BLUE MONDAY**
    New Order-Factory
15. **WHISTLE DOWN THE WIND**
    Nick Heyward-Arista
16. **NA NA HEY HEY KISS HIM...**
    Bananarama-London
17. **ROCK THE BOAT**
    Forrest-CBS
18. **TWO HEARTS BEAT AS ONE**
    U2-Island
19. **ORCHARD ROAD**
    Leo Sayer-Chrysalis
20. **BILLIE JEAN**
    Michael Jackson-Epic

UK ALBUMS

1. **THE FINAL CUT**
   Pink Floyd-Harvest
2. **THRILLER**
   Michael Jackson-Epic
3. **THE HURTING**
   Tears for Fears-Mercury/Phonogram
4. **CHART RUNNERS**
   Various-Ronco
5. **SWEET DREAMS...**
   Eurythmics-RCA
6. **WAR**
   U2-Island
7. **RIO**
   Duran Duran-EMI
8. **DEEP SEA SKIVING**
   Bananarama-London
9. **HELLO, I MUST BE GOING!**
   Phil Collins-Virgin
10. **THE KEY**
    Joan Armatrading-A&M
11. **QUICK STEP & SIDE KICK**
    Thompson Twins-Arista
12. **TRUE**
    Spandau Ballet-Reformation/Chrysalis
13. **SCRIPT FOR A JESTER'S TEAR**
    Marillion-EMI
14. **TOTO IV**
    Toto-CBS
15. **HOTLINE**
    Various-K-tel
16. **DAZZLE SHIPS**
    OMD-Telegraph/Virgin
17. **HAND CUT**
    Bucks Fizz-RCA
18. **BUSINESS AS USUAL**
    Men at Work-Epic
19. **LIONEL RICHIE**
    Lionel Richie-Motown
20. **RICHARD CLAYDERMAN**
    Richard Clayderman-Delphine/Decca

US SINGLES

1. **BILLIE JEAN**
   Michael Jackson-Epic
2. **COME ON EILEEN**
   Dexys Midnight Runners-Mercury
3. **MR. ROBOTO**
   Styx-A&M
4. **JEOPARDY**
   Greg Kihn Band-Beserkley
5. **BEAT IT**
   Michael Jackson-Epic
6. **HUNGRY LIKE THE WOLF**
   Duran Duran-Capitol
7. **ONE ON ONE**
   Daryl Hall & John Oates-RCA
8. **SEPARATE WAYS**
   Journey-Columbia
9. **DER KOMMISSAR**
   After the Fire-Epic
10. **DO YOU REALLY WANT TO...**
    Culture Club-Virgin/Epic
11. **WE'VE GOT TONIGHT**
    Kenny Rogers & Sheena Easton-Liberty
12. **YOU ARE**
    Lionel Richie-Motown
13. **SHE BLINDED ME WITH...**
    Thomas Dolby-Capitol
14. **I KNOW THERE'S SOMETHING...**
    Frida-Atlantic
15. **LET'S DANCE**
    David Bowie-EMI America
16. **EVEN NOW**
    Bob Seger-Capitol
17. **LITTE RED CORVETTE**
    Prince-Warner Bros.
18. **BACK ON THE CHAIN GANG**
    The Pretenders-Sire
19. **OVERKILL**
    Men at Work-Columbia
20. **I WON'T HOLD YOU BACK**
    Toto-Columbia

US ALBUMS

1. **THRILLER**
   Michael Jackson-Epic
2. **FRONTIERS**
   Journey-Columbia
3. **H2O**
   Daryl Hall & John Oates-RCA
4. **BUSINESS AS USUAL**
   Men at Work-Columbia
5. **KILROY WAS HERE**
   Styx-A&M
6. **RIO**
   Duran Duran-Capitol
7. **LIONEL RICHIE**
   Lionel Richie-Motown
8. **TOTO IV**
   Toto-Columbia
9. **PYROMANIA**
   Def Leppard-Mercury
10. **THE DISTANCE**
    Bob Seger-Capitol
11. **THE FINAL CUT**
    Pink Floyd-Columbia
12. **POWERLIGHT**
    Earth, Wind & Fire-Columbia
13. **THE CLOSER YOU GET**
    Alabama-RCA
14. **KISSING TO BE CLEVER**
    Culture Club-Virgin/Epic
15. **JANE FONDA'S WORKOUT...**
    Jane Fonda-Columbia
16. **MONEY AND CIGARETTES**
    Eric Clapton-Warner Bros./Duck
17. **THREE LOCK BOX**
    Sammy Hagar-Geffen
18. **TOO-RYE-AY**
    Dexys Midnight Runners-Mercury
19. **WAR**
    U2-Island
20. **BLINDED BY SCIENCE**
    Thomas Dolby-Capitol

UK SINGLES

1. **LET'S DANCE**
   David Bowie-EMI America
2. **CHURCH OF POISON MIND**
   Culture Club-Virgin
3. **IS THERE SOMETHING...**
   Duran Duran-EMI
4. **BREAKAWAY**
   Tracey Ullman-Stiff
5. **BEAT IT**
   Michael Jackson-Epic
6. **BOXERBEAT**
   JoBoxers-RCA
7. **OOH TO BE AH**
   KajaGooGoo-EMI
8. **WORDS**
   F.R. David-Carrere
9. **SNOT RAP**
   Kenny Everett-RCA
10. **FIELDS OF FIRE...**
    Big Country-Mercury/Phonogram
11. **SPEAK LIKE A CHILD**
    The Style Council-Polydor
12. **HOUSE THAT JACK BUILT**
    Tracie-Respond
13. **WHISTLE DOWN THE WIND**
    Nick Heyward-Arista
14. **BLUE MONDAY**
    New Order-Factory
15. **SWEET DREAMS...**
    Eurythmics-RCA
16. **TOTAL ECLIPSE...**
    Bonnie Tyler-CBS
17. **DON'T TALK TO ME...**
    Altered Images-Epic
18. **RIP IT UP**
    Orange Juice-Polydor
19. **I AM (I'M ME)**
    Twisted Sister-Atlantic
20. **CELTIC SOUL BROTHERS**
    Kevin Rowland/Dexys-Mercury

UK ALBUMS

1. **FASTER THAN THE SPEED...**
   Bonnie Tyler-CBS
2. **THRILLER**
   Michael Jackson-Epic
3. **THE FINAL CUT**
   Pink Floyd-Harvest
4. **THE HURTING**
   Tears for Fears-Mercury/Phonogram
5. **SWEET DREAMS...**
   Eurythmics-RCA
6. **WAR**
   U2-Island
7. **CHART RUNNERS**
   Various-Ronco
8. **KIDS FROM FAME LIVE!**
   Kids From Fame-BBC
9. **RIO**
   Duran Duran-EMI
10. **TRUE**
    Spandau Ballet-Reformation/Chrysalis
11. **HELLO, I MUST BE GOING!**
    Phil Collins-Virgin
12. **TOTO IV**
    Toto-CBS
13. **THE KEY**
    Joan Armatrading-A&M
14. **DEEP SEA SKIVING**
    Bananarama-London
15. **QUICK STEP & SIDE KICK**
    Thompson Twins-Arista
16. **SCRIPT FOR A JESTER'S TEAR**
    Marillion-EMI
17. **DAZZLE SHIPS**
    OMD-Telegraph/Virgin
18. **POWER & THE GLORY**
    Saxon-Carrere
19. **JOURNEY THROUGH CLASSICS**
    Louis Clark/Royal Philharmonic-K-tel
20. **BUSINESS AS USUAL**
    Men at Work-Epic

US SINGLES

1. **COME ON EILEEN**
   Dexys Midnight Runners-Mercury
2. **BEAT IT**
   Michael Jackson-Epic
3. **MR. ROBOTO**
   Styx-A&M
4. **JEOPARDY**
   Greg Kihn Band-Berserkley
5. **BILLIE JEAN**
   Michael Jackson-Epic
6. **DER KOMMISSAR**
   After the Fire-Epic
7. **ONE ON ONE**
   Daryl Hall & John Oates-RCA
8. **SEPARATE WAYS**
   Journey-Columbia
9. **LET'S DANCE**
   David Bowie-EMI America
10. **SHE BLINDED ME WITH...**
    Thomas Dolby-Capitol
11. **HUNGRY LIKE THE WOLF**
    Duran Duran-Capitol
12. **LITTLE RED CORVETTE**
    Prince-Warner Bros.
13. **EVEN NOW**
    Bob Seger-Capitol
14. **DO YOU REALLY WANT TO...**
    Culture Club-Virgin/Epic
15. **OVERKILL**
    Men at Work-Columbia
16. **I WON'T HOLD YOU BACK**
    Toto-Columbia
17. **YOU ARE**
    Lionel Richie-Motown
18. **SOLITAIRE**
    Laura Branigan-Atlantic
19. **WE'VE GOT TONIGHT**
    Kenny Rogers & Sheena Easton-Liberty
20. **I KNOW THERE'S SOMETHING...**
    Frida-Atlantic

US ALBUMS

1. **THRILLER**
   Michael Jackson-Epic
2. **FRONTIERS**
   Journey-Columbia
3. **H2O**
   Daryl Hall & John Oates-RCA
4. **BUSINESS AS USUAL**
   Men at Work-Columbia
5. **KILROY WAS HERE**
   Styx-A&M
6. **RIO**
   Duran Duran-Capitol
7. **LIONEL RICHIE**
   Lionel Richie-Motown
8. **PYROMANIA**
   Def Leppard-Mercury
9. **THE FINAL CUT**
   Pink Floyd-Columbia
10. **TOTO IV**
    Toto-Columbia
11. **THE CLOSER YOU GET**
    Alabama-RCA
12. **THE DISTANCE**
    Bob Seger-Capitol
13. **POWERLIGHT**
    Earth, Wind & Fire-Columbia
14. **KISSING TO BE CLEVER**
    Culture Club-Virgin/Epic
15. **WAR**
    U2-Island
16. **TOO-RYE-AY**
    Dexys Midnight Runners-Mercury
17. **JANE FONDA'S WORKOUT...**
    Jane Fonda-Columbia
18. **KIHNSPIRACY**
    Greg Kihn Band-Berserkley
19. **THREE LOCK BOX**
    Sammy Hagar-Geffen
20. **BLINDED BY SCIENCE**
    Thomas Dolby-Capitol

UK SINGLES

1. **LET'S DANCE**
   David Bowie-EMI
2. **CHURCH OF POISON MIND**
   Culture Club-Virgin
3. **BEAT IT**
   Michael Jackson-Epic
4. **WORDS**
   F.R. David-Carrere
5. **BREAKAWAY**
   Tracey Ullman-Stiff
6. **LOVE IS A STRANGER**
   Eurythmics-RCA
7. **BOXERBEAT**
   JoBoxers-RCA
8. **OOH TO BE AH**
   KajaGooGoo-EMI
9. **HOUSE THAT JACK BUILT**
   Tracie-Respond
10. **TRUE**
    Spandau Ballet-Reformation/Chrysalis
11. **IS THERE SOMETHING...**
    Duran Duran-EMI
12. **BLUE MONDAY**
    New Order-Factory
13. **SNOT RAP**
    Kenny Everett-RCA
14. **TRUE LOVE WAYS**
    Cliff Richard/London Philharmonic-EMI
15. **FIELDS OF FIRE (400 MILES)**
    Big Country-Mercury/Phonogram
16. **(KEEP FEELING)...**
    Human League-Virgin
17. **WHISTLE DOWN THE WIND**
    Nick Heyward-Arista
18. **I AM (I'M ME)**
    Twisted Sister-Atlantic
19. **ROSANNA**
    Toto-CBS
20. **YOUNG, FREE AND SINGLE**
    Sunfire-Warner Bros.

UK ALBUMS

1. **LET'S DANCE**
   David Bowie-EMI America
2. **THRILLER**
   Michael Jackson-Epic
3. **FASTER THAN THE SPEED...**
   Bonnie Tyler-CBS
4. **THE FINAL CUT**
   Pink Floyd-Harvest
5. **SWEET DREAMS...**
   Eurythmics-RCA
6. **TRUE**
   Spandau Ballet-Reformation/Chrysalis
7. **THE HURTING**
   Tears for Fears-Mercury/Phonogram
8. **WAR**
   U2-Island
9. **CHART RUNNERS**
   Various-Ronco
10. **KIDS FROM FAME LIVE!**
    Kids From Fame-BBC
11. **TOTO IV**
    Toto-CBS
12. **RIO**
    Duran Duran-EMI
13. **QUICK STEP & SIDE KICK**
    Thompson Twins-Arista
14. **MUSIC FROM 'LOCAL HERO'**
    Mark Knopfler-Vertigo/Phonogram
15. **DEEP SEA SKIVING**
    Bananarama-London
16. **BUSINESS AS USUAL**
    Men at Work-Epic
17. **HELLO, I MUST BE GOING!**
    Phil Collins-Virgin
18. **THE KEY**
    Joan Armatrading-A&M
19. **JOURNEY THROUGH CLASSICS**
    Louis Clark/Royal Philharmonic-K-tel
20. **SCRIPT FOR A JESTER'S TEAR**
    Marillion-EMI

U S   S I N G L E S

1 **BEAT IT**
Michael Jackson-Epic
2 **COME ON EILEEN**
Dexys Midnight Runners-Mercury
3 **JEOPARDY**
Greg Kihn Band-Beserkley
4 **MR. ROBOTO**
Styx-A&M
5 **DER KOMMISSAR**
After the Fire-Epic
6 **LET'S DANCE**
David Bowie-EMI America
7 **BILLIE JEAN**
Michael Jackson-Epic
8 **SHE BLINDED ME WITH...**
Thomas Dolby-Capitol
9 **OVERKILL**
Men at Work-Columbia
10 **LITTLE RED CORVETTE**
Prince-Warner Bros.
11 **I WON'T HOLD YOU BACK**
Toto-Columbia
12 **SEPARATE WAYS**
Journey-Columbia
13 **EVEN NOW**
Bob Seger-Capitol
14 **SOLITAIRE**
Laura Branigan-Atlantic
15 **ONE ON ONE**
Daryl Hall & John Oates-RCA
16 **HUNGRY LIKE THE WOLF**
Duran Duran-Capitol
17 **RIO**
Duran Duran-Capitol
18 **DO YOU REALLY WANT TO...**
Culture Club-Virgin/Epic
19 **PHOTOGRAPH**
Def Leppard-Mercury
20 **YOU ARE**
Lionel Richie-Motown

U S   A L B U M S

1 **THRILLER**
Michael Jackson-Epic
2 **FRONTIERS**
Journey-Columbia
3 **KILROY WAS HERE**
Styx-A&M
4 **BUSINESS AS USUAL**
Men at Work-Columbia
5 **PYROMANIA**
Def Leppard-Mercury
6 **H₂O**
Daryl Hall & John Oates-RCA
7 **THE FINAL CUT**
Pink Floyd-Columbia
8 **LIONEL RICHIE**
Lionel Richie-Motown
9 **RIO**
Duran Duran-Capitol
10 **THE CLOSER YOU GET**
Alabama-RCA
11 **TOTO IV**
Toto-Columbia
12 **THE DISTANCE**
Bob Seger-Capitol
13 **WAR**
U2-Island
14 **TOO-RYE-AY**
Dexys Midnight Runners-Mercury
15 **KIHNSPIRACY**
Greg Kihn Band-Beserkley
16 **KISSING TO BE CLEVER**
Culture Club-Virgin/Epic
17 **POWERLIGHT**
Earth, Wind & Fire-Columbia
18 **WE'VE GOT TONIGHT**
Kenny Rogers-Liberty
19 **1999**
Prince-Warner Bros.
20 **CUTS LIKE A KNIFE**
Bryan Adams-A&M

U K   S I N G L E S

1 **TRUE**
Spandau Ballet-Reformation/Chrysalis
2 **WORDS**
F.R. David-Carrere
3 **BEAT IT**
Michael Jackson-Epic
4 **(KEEP FEELING)...**
Human League-Virgin
5 **CHURCH OF POISON MIND**
Culture Club-Virgin
6 **LET'S DANCE**
David Bowie-EMI America
7 **LOVE IS A STRANGER**
Eurythmics-RCA
8 **TRUE LOVE WAYS**
Cliff Richard-London Philharmonic-EMI
9 **WE ARE DETECTIVE**
Thompson Twins-Arista
10 **BREAKAWAY**
Tracey Ullman-Stiff
11 **FLIGHT OF ICARUS**
Iron Maiden-EMI
12 **ROSANNA**
Toto-CBS
13 **BLUE MONDAY**
New Order-Factory
14 **TEMPTATION**
Heaven 17-B.E.F./Virgin
15 **HOUSE THAT JACK BUILT**
Tracie-Respond
16 **OOH TO BE AH**
KajaGooGoo-EMI
17 **FRIDAY NIGHT (Live Version)**
Kids From Fame-RCA
18 **I AM (I'M ME)**
Twisted Sister-Atlantic
19 **BOXERBEAT**
JoBoxers-RCA
20 **DANCING TIGHT**
Galaxy with Phil Fearon-Ensign/Island

U K   A L B U M S

1 **LET'S DANCE**
David Bowie-EMI America
2 **THRILLER**
Michael Jackson-Epic
3 **TRUE**
Spandau Ballet-Reformation/Chrysalis
4 **FASTER THAN THE SPEED...**
Bonnie Tyler-CBS
5 **WHITE FEATHERS**
KajaGooGoo-EMI
6 **SWEET DREAMS...**
Eurythmics-RCA
7 **THE FINAL CUT**
Pink Floyd-Harvest
8 **CARGO**
Men at Work-Epic
9 **TOTO IV**
Toto-CBS
10 **THE HURTING**
Tears for Fears-Mercury/Phonogram
11 **QUICK STEP & SIDE KICK**
Thompson Twins-Arista
12 **KIDS FROM FAME LIVE!**
Kids From Fame-BBC
13 **WAR**
U2-Island
14 **RIO**
Duran Duran-EMI
15 **CHART RUNNERS**
Various-Ronco
16 **HIGHLY STRUNG**
Steve Hackett-Charisma/Phonogram
17 **BUSINESS AS USUAL**
Men at Work-Epic
18 **HELLO, I MUST BE GOING!**
Phil Collins-Virgin
19 **JOURNEY THROUGH CLASSICS**
Louis Clark/Royal Philharmonic-K-tel
20 **THE KEY**
Joan Armatrading-A&M

U S   S I N G L E S

1 **BEAT IT**
Michael Jackson-Epic
2 **JEOPARDY**
Greg Kihn Band-Beserkley
3 **LET'S DANCE**
David Bowie-EMI America
4 **COME ON EILEEN**
Dexys Midnight Runners-Mercury
5 **DER KOMMISSAR**
After the Fire-Epic
6 **OVERKILL**
Men at Work-Columbia
7 **SHE BLINDED ME WITH...**
Thomas Dolby-Capitol
8 **MR. ROBOTO**
Styx-A&M
9 **LITTLE RED CORVETTE**
Prince-Warner Bros.
10 **I WON'T HOLD YOU BACK**
Toto-Columbia
11 **SOLITAIRE**
Laura Branigan-Atlantic
12 **EVEN NOW**
Bob Seger-Capitol
13 **FLASHDANCE...WHAT A...**
Irene Cara-Casablanca
14 **BILLIE JEAN**
Michael Jackson-Epic
15 **PHOTOGRAPH**
Def Leppard-Mercury
16 **RIO**
Duran Duran-Capitol
17 **MY LOVE**
Lionel Richie-Motown
18 **STRAIGHT FROM THE...**
Bryan Adams-A&M
19 **TIME**
Culture Club-Virgin/Epic
20 **AFFAIR OF THE HEART**
Rick Springfield-RCA

U S   A L B U M S

1 **THRILLER**
Michael Jackson-Epic
2 **FRONTIERS**
Journey-Columbia
3 **KILROY WAS HERE**
Styx-A&M
4 **PYROMANIA**
Def Leppard-Mercury
5 **BUSINESS AS USUAL**
Men at Work-Columbia
6 **THE FINAL CUT**
Pink Floyd-Columbia
7 **LIONEL RICHIE**
Lionel Richie-Motown
8 **H₂O**
Daryl Hall & John Oates-RCA
9 **RIO**
Duran Duran-Capitol
10 **THE DISTANCE**
Bob Seger-Capitol
11 **CARGO**
Men at Work-Columbia
12 **WAR**
U2-Island
13 **THE CLOSER YOU GET**
Alabama-RCA
14 **TOO-RYE-AY**
Dexys Midnight Runners-Mercury
15 **KIHNSPIRACY**
Greg Kihn Band-Beserkley
16 **1999**
Prince-Warner Bros.
17 **CUTS LIKE A KNIFE**
Bryan Adams-A&M
18 **LET'S DANCE**
David Bowie-EMI America
19 **TOTO IV**
Toto-Columbia
20 **GOLDEN AGE OF WIRELESS**
Thomas Dolby-Capitol

U K   S I N G L E S

1 **TRUE**
Spandau Ballet-Reformation/Chrysalis
2 **WORDS**
F.R. David-Carrere
3 **(KEEP FEELING)...**
Human League-Virgin
4 **BEAT IT**
Michael Jackson-Epic
5 **PALE SHELTER**
Tears for Fears-Mercury/Phonogram
6 **DANCING TIGHT**
Galaxy with Phil Fearon-Ensign/Island
7 **WE ARE DETECTIVE**
Thompson Twins-Arista
8 **TEMPTATION**
Heaven 17-B.E.F./Virgin
9 **LET'S DANCE**
David Bowie-EMI America
10 **CHURCH OF POISON MIND**
Culture Club-Virgin
11 **TRUE LOVE WAYS**
Cliff Richard/London Philharmonic-EMI
12 **LOVE IS A STRANGER**
Eurythmics-RCA
13 **FRIDAY NIGHT (Live Version)**
Kids From Fame-RCA
14 **FLIGHT OF ICARUS**
Iron Maiden-EMI
15 **ROSANNA**
Toto-CBS
16 **OUR LIPS ARE SEALED**
The Fun Boy Three-Chrysalis
17 **BLUE MONDAY**
New Order-Factory
18 **BREAKAWAY**
Tracey Ullman-Stiff
19 **LAST FILM**
Kissing the Pink-Magnet
20 **I AM (I'M ME)**
Twisted Sister-Atlantic

U K   A L B U M S

1 **LET'S DANCE**
David Bowie-EMI America
2 **THRILLER**
Michael Jackson-Epic
3 **TRUE**
Spandau Ballet-Reformation/Chrysalis
4 **THE LUXURY GAP**
Heavey 17-Virgin
5 **SWEET DREAMS...**
Eurythmics-RCA
6 **FASTER THAN THE SPEED...**
Bonne Tyler-CBS
7 **MIDNIGHT AT THE LOST...**
Meat Loaf-Cleveland International/Epic
8 **THE HURTING**
Tears for Fears-Mercury/Phonogram
9 **WHITE FEATHERS**
KajaGooGoo-EMI
10 **CARGO**
Men at Work-Epic
11 **QUICK STEP & SIDE KICK**
Thompson Twins-Arista
12 **TOTO IV**
Toto-CBS
13 **THE FINAL CUT**
Pink Floyd-Harvest
14 **YOU CAN'T STOP ROCK...**
Twisted Sister-Atlantic
15 **KIDS FROM FAME LIVE!**
Kids From Fame-BBC
16 **LISTEN**
A Flock of Seagulls-Jive
17 **RIO**
Duran Duran-EMI
18 **LIONEL RICHIE**
Lionel Richie-Motown
19 **RICHARD CLAYDERMAN**
Richard Clayderman-Delphine/Decca
20 **CHART RUNNERS**
Various-Ronco

US SINGLES	US ALBUMS	UK SINGLES	UK ALBUMS
1 BEAT IT *Michael Jackson-Epic*	1 THRILLER *Michael Jackson-Epic*	1 TRUE *Spandau Ballet-Reformation/Chrysalis*	1 TRUE *Spandau Ballet-Reformation/Chrysalis*
2 LET'S DANCE *David Bowie-EMI America*	2 PYROMANIA *Def Leppard-Mercury*	2 (KEEP FEELING)... *Human League-Virgin*	2 THRILLER *Michael Jackson-Epic*
3 JEOPARDY *Greg Kihn Band-Berserkley*	3 FRONTIERS *Journey-Columbia*	3 TEMPTATION *Heaven 17-B.E.F./Virgin*	3 LET'S DANCE *David Bowie-EMI America*
4 OVERKILL *Men at Work-Columbia*	4 CARGO *Men at Work-Columbia*	4 WORDS *F.R. David-Carrere*	4 POWER CORRUPTION & LIES *New Order-Factory*
5 SHE BLINDED ME WITH... *Thomas Dolby-Capitol*	5 KILROY WAS HERE *Styx-A&M*	5 DANCING TIGHT *Galaxy with Phil Fearon-Ensign/Island*	5 THE LUXURY GAP *Heaven 17-Virgin*
6 COME ON EILEEN *Dexys Midnight Runners-Mercury*	6 THE FINAL CUT *Pink Floyd-Columbia*	6 PALE SHELTER *Tears for Fears-Mercury/Phonogram*	6 THE HURTING *Tears for Fears-Mercury/Phonogram*
7 FLASHDANCE....WHAT A... *Irene Cara-Casablanca*	7 BUSINESS AS USUAL *Men at Work-Columbia*	7 CANDY GIRL *New Edition-London*	7 FASTER THAN THE SPEED... *Bonnie Tyler-CBS*
8 LITTLE RED CORVETTE *Prince-Warner Bros.*	8 H₂O *Daryl Hall & John Oates-RCA*	8 WE ARE DETECTIVE *Thompson Twins-Arista*	8 SWEET DREAMS... *Eurythmics-RCA*
9 SOLITAIRE *Laura Branigan-Atlantic*	9 WAR *U2-Island*	9 OUR LIPS ARE SEALED *The Fun Boy Three-Chrysalis*	9 NIGHT DUBBING *Imagination-R&B*
10 DER KOMMISSAR *After the Fire-Epic*	10 LIONEL RICHIE *Lionel Richie-Motown*	10 CAN'T GET USED TO... *The Beat-Go Feet*	10 MIDNIGHT AT THE LOST... *Meat Loaf-Cleveland International/Epic*
11 I WON'T HOLD YOU BACK *Toto-Columbia*	11 RIO *Duran Duran-Capitol*	11 BEAT IT *Michael Jackson-Epic*	11 CARGO *Men at Work-Epic*
12 MY LOVE *Lionel Richie-Motown*	12 THE DISTANCE *Bob Seger-Capitol*	12 BLIND VISION *Blancmange-London*	12 THE FINAL CUT *Pink Floyd-Harvest*
13 PHOTOGRAPH *Def Leppard-Mercury*	13 FLASHDANCE *Soundtrack-Casablanca*	13 LET'S DANCE *David Bowie-EMI America*	13 TOTO IV *Toto-CBS*
14 RIO *Duran Duran-Capitol*	14 1999 *Prince-Warner Bros.*	14 TRUE LOVE WAYS *Cliff Richard/London Philharmonic-EMI*	14 KIDS FROM "FAME" SONGS *Kids From Fame-BBC*
15 STRAIGHT FROM THE... *Bryan Adams-A&M*	15 CUTS LIKE A KNIFE *Bryan Adams-A&M*	15 FRIDAY NIGHT (Live Version) *The Kids From Fame-RCA*	15 WHITE FEATHERS *KajaGooGoo-EMI*
16 MR. ROBOTO *Styx-A&M*	16 LET'S DANCE *David Bowie-EMI America*	16 CHURCH OF POISON MIND *Culture Club-Virgin*	16 QUICK STEP & SIDE KICK *Thompson Twins-Arista*
17 TIME *Culture Club-Virgin/Epic*	17 THE CLOSER YOU GET *Alabama-RCA*	17 LOVE IS A STRANGER *Eurythmics-RCA*	17 TWICE AS KOOL *Kool & The Gang-De-Lite/Phonogram*
18 EVEN NOW *Bob Seger-Capitol*	18 JARREAU *Jarreau-Warner Bros.*	18 BLUE MONDAY *New Order-Factory*	18 LISTEN *A Flock of Seagulls-Jive*
19 AFFAIR OF THE HEART *Rick Springfield-RCA*	19 TOTO IV *Toto-Columbia*	19 LAST FILM *Kissing the Pink-Magnet*	19 YOU CAN'T STOP ROCK... *Twisted Sister-Atlantic*
20 FAITHFULLY *Journey-Columbia*	20 GOLDEN AGE OF WIRELESS *Thomas Dolby-Capitol*	20 ROSANNA *Toto-CBS*	20 RIO *Duran Duran-EMI*

US SINGLES	US ALBUMS	UK SINGLES	UK ALBUMS
1 LET'S DANCE *David Bowie-EMI America*	1 THRILLER *Michael Jackson-Epic*	1 TRUE *Spandau Ballet-Reformation/Chrysalis*	1 THRILLER *Michael Jackson-Epic*
2 BEAT IT *Michael Jackson-Epic*	2 PYROMANIA *Def Leppard-Mercury*	2 TEMPTATION *Heaven 17-B.E.F. Virgin*	2 TRUE *Spandau Ballet-Reformation/Chrysalis*
3 FLASHDANCE...WHAT A... *Irene Cara-Casablanca*	3 CARGO *Men at Work-Columbia*	3 CANDY GIRL *New Edition-London*	3 LET'S DANCE *David Bowie-EMI America*
4 OVERKILL *Men at Work-Columbia*	4 FLASHDANCE *Soundtrack-Casablanca*	4 DANCING TIGHT *Galaxy with Phil Fearon-Ensign/Island*	4 THE LUXURY GAP *Heaven 17-Virgin*
5 SHE BLINDED ME WITH... *Thomas Dolby-Capitol*	5 LET'S DANCE *David Bowie-EMI America*	5 CAN'T GET USED TO... *The Beat-Go Feet*	5 POWER CORRUPTION & LIES *New Order-Factory*
6 LITTLE RED CORVETTE *Prince-Warner Bros.*	6 FRONTIERS *Journey-Columbia*	6 (KEEP FEELING)... *Human League-Virgin*	6 THE HURTING *Tears for Fears-Mercury/Phonogram*
7 SOLITAIRE *Laura Branigan-Atlantic*	7 KILROY WAS HERE *Styx-A&M*	7 OUR LIPS ARE SEALED *The Fun Boy Three-Chrysalis*	7 DRESSED FOR THE OCCASION *Cliff Richard/London Philharmonic-EMI*
8 JEOPARDY *Greg Kihn Band-Berserkley*	8 H₂O *Daryl Hall & John Oates-RCA*	8 PALE SHELTER *Tears for Fears-Mercury/Phonogram*	8 FASTER THAN THE SPEED... *Bonnie Tyler-CBS*
9 MY LOVE *Lionel Richie-Motown*	9 BUSINESS AS USUAL *Men at Work-Columbia*	9 WORDS *F.R. David-Carrere*	9 NIGHT DUBBING *Imagination-R&B*
10 TIME *Culture Club-Virgin/Epic*	10 THE FINAL CUT *Pink Floyd-Columbia*	10 BLIND VISION *Blancmange-London*	10 CARGO *Men at Work-Epic*
11 DER KOMMISSAR *After the Fire-Epic*	11 LIONEL RICHIE *Lionel Richie-Motown*	11 WE ARE DETECTIVE *Thompson Twins-Arista*	11 TWICE AS KOOL *Kool & The Gang-De-Lite/Phonogram*
12 PHOTOGRAPH *Def Leppard-Mercury*	12 RIO *Duran Duran-Capitol*	12 BAD BOYS *Wham-Inner Vision*	12 MIDNIGHT AT THE LOST... *Meat Loaf-Cleveland International/Epic*
13 STRAIGHT FROM THE... *Bryan Adams-A&M*	13 1999 *Prince-Warner Bros.*	13 WHAT KINDA BOY... *Hot Chocolate-RAK*	13 QUICK STEP & SIDE KICK *Thompson Twins-Arista*
14 RIO *Duran Duran-Capitol*	14 CUTS LIKE A KNIFE *Bryan Adams-A&M*	14 DON'T STOP THAT CRAZY... *Modern Romance-WEA*	14 SWEET DREAMS... *Eurythmics-RCA*
15 I WON'T HOLD YOU BACK *Toto-Columbia*	15 JARREAU *Jarreau-Warner Bros.*	15 FAMILY MAN *Daryl Hall & John Oates-RCA*	15 CHART ENCOUNTERS... *Various-Ronco*
16 AFFAIR OF THE HEART *Rick Springfield-RCA*	16 WAR *U2-Island*	16 BEAT IT *Michael Jackson-Epic*	16 TOTO IV *Toto-CBS*
17 COME ON EILEEN *Dexys Midnight Runners-Mercury*	17 THE DISTANCE *Bob Seger-Capitol*	17 BUFFALO SOLDIER *Bob Marley & The Wailers-Island*	17 THE FINAL CUT *Pink Floyd-Harvest*
18 ALWAYS SOMETHING... *Naked Eyes-EMI America*	18 GOLDEN AGE OF WIRELESS *Thomas Dolby-Capitol*	18 FRIDAY NIGHT (Live Version) *Kids From Fame-RCA*	18 KIDS FROM "FAME" SONGS *Kids From Fame-BBC*
19 FAITHFULLY *Journey-Columbia*	19 LIVING IN OZ *Rick Springfield-RCA*	19 LAST FILM *Kissing the Pink-Magnet*	19 LAUGHTER & TEARS... *Various-WEA*
20 DON'T LET IT END *Styx-A&M*	20 KISSING TO BE CLEVER *Culture Club-Virgin/Epic*	20 NOBODY'S DIARY *Yazoo-Mute*	20 WHITE FEATHERS *KajaGooGoo-EMI*

US SINGLES

1. FLASHDANCE...WHAT A...
   Irene Cara-Casablanca
2. LET'S DANCE
   David Bowie-EMI America
3. BEAT IT
   Michael Jackson-Epic
4. OVERKILL
   Men at Work-Columbia
5. SHE BLINDED ME WITH...
   Thomas Dolby-Capitol
6. LITTLE RED CORVETTE
   Prince-Warner Bros.
7. SOLITAIRE
   Laura Branigan-Atlantic
8. TIME
   Culture Club-Virgin/Epic
9. MY LOVE
   Lionel Richie-Motown
10. STRAIGHT FROM THE...
    Bryan Adams-A&M
11. AFFAIR OF THE HEART
    Rick Springfield-RCA
12. ALWAYS SOMETHING...
    Naked Eyes-EMI America
13. FAITHFULLY
    Journey-Columbia
14. DON'T LET IT END
    Styx-A&M
15. JEOPARDY
    Greg Kihn Band-Beserkley
16. PHOTOGRAPH
    Def Leppard-Mercury
17. FAMILY MAN
    Daryl Hall & John Oates-RCA
18. DER KOMMISSAR
    After the Fire-Epic
19. I WON'T HOLD YOU BACK
    Toto-Columbia
20. SHE'S A BEAUTY
    The Tubes-Capitol

US ALBUMS

1. THRILLER
   Michael Jackson-Epic
2. FLASHDANCE
   Soundtrack-Casablanca
3. CARGO
   Men at Work-Columbia
4. PYROMANIA
   Def Leppard-Mercury
5. LET'S DANCE
   David Bowie-EMI America
6. FRONTIERS
   Journey-Columbia
7. KILROY WAS HERE
   Styx-A&M
8. H2O
   Daryl Hall & John Oates-RCA
9. 1999
   Prince-Warner Bros.
10. LIONEL RICHIE
    Lionel Richie-Motown
11. THE FINAL CUT
    Pink Floyd-Columbia
12. CUTS LIKE A KNIFE
    Bryan Adams-A&M
13. JARREAU
    Jarreau-Warner Bros.
14. BUSINESS AS USUAL
    Men at Work-Columbia
15. GOLDEN AGE OF WIRELESS
    Thomas Dolby-Capitol
16. RIO
    Duran Duran-Capitol
17. LIVING IN OZ
    Rick Springfield-RCA
18. KISSING TO BE CLEVER
    Culture Club-Virgin/Epic
19. WAR
    U2-Island
20. ELIMINATOR
    Z.Z. Top-Warner Bros.

UK SINGLES

1. CANDY GIRL
   New Edition-London
2. TRUE
   Spandau Ballet-Reformation/Chrysalis
3. CAN'T GET USED TO...
   The Beat-Go Feet
4. TEMPTATION
   Heaven 17-B.E.F./Virgin
5. BAD BOYS
   Wham-Inner Vision
6. DANCING TIGHT
   Galaxy with Phil Fearon-Ensign/Island
7. EVERY BREATH YOU TAKE
   Police-A&M
8. NOBODY'S DIARY
   Yazoo-Mute
9. OUR LIPS ARE SEALED
   The Fun Boy Three-Chrysalis
10. WHAT KINDA BOY...
    Hot Chocolate-RAK
11. BUFFALO SOLDIER
    Bob Marley & The Wailers-Island
12. MONEY GO ROUND Part 1
    The Style Council-Polydor
13. GLORY, GLORY, MAN. UNITED
    Manchester United Football Team-EMI
14. BLIND VISION
    Blancmange-London
15. (KEEP FEELING)...
    Human League-Virgin
16. JUST GOT LUCKY
    JoBoxers-RCA
17. WORDS
    F.R. David-Carrere
18. PALE SHELTER
    Tears for Fears-Mercury/Phonogram
19. LOVE TOWN
    Booker Newberry 111-Polydor
20. FEEL THE NEED IN ME
    Forrest-CBS

UK ALBUMS

1. THRILLER
   Michael Jackson-Epic
2. TRUE
   Spandau Ballet-Reformation/Chrysalis
3. PIECE OF MIND
   Iron Maiden-EMI
4. LET'S DANCE
   David Bowie-EMI America
5. THE LUXURY GAP
   Heaven 17-Virgin
6. TWICE AS KOOL
   Kool & The Gang-De-Lite/Phonogram
7. CHART ENCOUNTERS...
   Various-Ronco
8. CONFRONTATION
   Bob Marley & The Wailers-Island
9. THE HURTING
   Tears for Fears-Mercury/Phonogram
10. DRESSED FOR THE OCCASION
    Cliff Richard/London Philharmonic-EMI
11. NIGHT DUBBING
    Imagination-R&B
12. QUICK STEP & SIDE KICK
    Thompson Twins-Arista
13. POWER CORRUPTION & LIES
    New Order-Factory
14. CARGO
    Men at Work-Epic
15. FASTER THAN THE SPEED...
    Bonnie Tyler-CBS
16. MIDNIGHT AT THE LOST...
    Meat Loaf-Cleveland International/Epic
17. FEAST
    The Creatures-Wonderland/Polydor
18. DIONNE WARWICK...
    Dionne Warwick-Arista/Dione
19. SWEET DREAMS...
    Eurythmics-RCA
20. KIDS FROM "FAME" SONGS
    Kids From Fame-BBC

US SINGLES

1. FLASHDANCE...WHAT A...
   Irene Cara-Casablanca
2. LET'S DANCE
   David Bowie-EMI America
3. OVERKILL
   Men at Work-Columbia
4. TIME
   Culture Club-Virgin/Epic
5. SHE BLINDED ME WITH...
   Thomas Dolby-Capitol
6. BEAT IT
   Michael Jackson-Epic
7. MY LOVE
   Lionel Richie-Motown
8. LITTLE RED CORVETTE
   Prince-Warner Bros.
9. SOLITAIRE
   Laura Branigan-Atlantic
10. STRAIGHT FROM THE...
    Bryan Adams-A&M
11. AFFAIR OF THE HEART
    Rick Springfield-RCA
12. ALWAYS SOMETHING...
    Naked Eyes-EMI America
13. FAITHFULLY
    Journey-Columbia
14. DON'T LET IT END
    Styx-A&M
15. FAMILY MAN
    Daryl Hall & John Oates-RCA
16. ELECTRIC AVENUE
    Eddy Grant-Portrait/Ice
17. PHOTOGRAPH
    Def Leppard-Mercury
18. NEVER GONNA LET YOU GO
    Sergio Mendes-A&M
19. SHE'S A BEAUTY
    The Tubes-Capitol
20. TOO SHY
    KajaGooGoo-EMI America

US ALBUMS

1. THRILLER
   Michael Jackson-Epic
2. FLASHDANCE
   Soundtrack-Casablanca
3. CARGO
   Men at Work-Columbia
4. PYROMANIA
   Def Leppard-Mercury
5. LET'S DANCE
   David Bowie-EMI America
6. FRONTIERS
   Journey-Columbia
7. KILROY WAS HERE
   Styx-A&M
8. H2O
   Daryl Hall & John Oates-RCA
9. 1999
   Prince-Warner Bros.
10. CUTS LIKE A KNIFE
    Bryan Adams-A&M
11. LIONEL RICHIE
    Lionel Richie-Motown
12. THE FINAL CUT
    Pink Floyd-Columbia
13. JARREAU
    Jarreau-Warner Bros.
14. GOLDEN AGE OF WIRELESS
    Thomas Dolby-Capitol
15. LIVING IN OZ
    Rick Springfield-RCA
16. KISSING TO BE CLEVER
    Culture Club-Virgin/Epic
17. BUSINESS AS USUAL
    Men at Work-Columbia
18. RIO
    Duran Duran-Capitol
19. ELIMINATOR
    Z.Z. Top-Warner Bros.
20. WAR
    U2-Island

UK SINGLES

1. EVERY BREATH YOU TAKE
   Police-A&M
2. BAD BOYS
   Wham-Inner Vision
3. CANDY GIRL
   New Edition-London
4. NOBODY'S DIARY
   Yazoo-Mute
5. CAN'T GET USED TO...
   The Beat-Go Feet
6. BUFFALO SOLDIER
   Bob Marley & The Wailers-Island
7. JUST GOT LUCKY
   JoBoxers-RCA
8. LOVE TOWN
   Booker Newberry III-Polydor/Montage
9. TEMPTATION
   Heaven 17-B.E.F./Virgin
10. TRUE
    Spandau Ballet-Reformation/Chrysalis
11. MONEY GO ROUND Part 1
    The Style Council-Polydor
12. WHAT KINDA BOY...
    Hot Chocolate-RAK
13. GLORY, GLORY, MAN. UNITED
    Manchester United Football Team-EMI
14. OUR LIPS ARE SEALED
    The Fun Boy Three-Chrysalis
15. LADY LOVE ME...
    George Benson-Warner Bros.
16. DANCING TIGHT
    Galaxy with Phil Fearon-Ensign/Island
17. FEEL THE NEED IN ME
    Forrest-CBS
18. IN A BIG COUNTRY
    Big Country-Mercury/Phonogram
19. STOP AND GO
    David Grant-Chrysalis
20. BLIND VISION
    Blancmange-London

UK ALBUMS

1. THRILLER
   Michael Jackson-Epic
2. TRUE
   Spandau Ballet-Reformation/Chrysalis
3. LET'S DANCE
   David Bowie-EMI America
4. TWICE AS KOOL
   Kool & The Gang-De-Lite/Phonogram
5. CONFRONTATION
   Bob Marley & The Wailers-Island
6. PIECE OF MIND
   Iron Maiden-EMI
7. THE LUXURY GAP
   Heaven 17-Virgin
8. CRISIS
   Mike Oldfield-Virgin
9. CHART ENCOUNTERS...
   Various-Ronco
10. THE HURTING
    Tears for Fears-Mercury/Phonogram
11. DRESSED FOR THE OCCASION
    Cliff Richard/London Philharmonic-EMI
12. POWER CORRUPTION & LIES
    New Order-Factory
13. NIGHT DUBBING
    Imagination-R&B
14. FASTER THAN THE SPEED...
    Bonnie Tyler-CBS
15. QUICK STEP & SIDE KICK
    Thompson Twins-Arista
16. CARGO
    Men at Work-Epic
17. DIONNE WARWICK ...
    Dionne Warwick-Arista/Dione
18. SWEET DREAMS...
    Eurythmics-RCA
19. FEAST
    The Creatures-Wonderland/Polydor
20. ANOTHER PERFECT DAY
    Motorhead-Bronze

WEEK ENDING JUNE 11 1983

US SINGLES	US ALBUMS	UK SINGLES	UK ALBUMS
1 FLASHDANCE...WHAT A... *Irene Cara-Casablanca*	1 THRILLER *Michael Jackson-Epic*	1 EVERY BREATH YOU TAKE *Police-A&M*	1 THRILLER *Michael Jackson-Epic*
2 LET'S DANCE *David Bowie-EMI America*	2 FLASHDANCE *Soundtrack-Casablanca*	2 BAD BOYS *Wham-Inner Vision*	2 LET'S DANCE *David Bowie-EMI America*
3 TIME *Culture Club-Virgin/Epic*	3 CARGO *Men at Work-Columbia*	3 NOBODY'S DIARY *Yazoo-Mute*	3 TRUE *Spandau Ballet-Reformation/Chrysalis*
4 OVERKILL *Men at Work-Columbia*	4 PYROMANIA *Def Leppard-Mercury*	4 BUFFALO SOLDIER *Bob Marley & The Wailers-Island*	4 TWICE AS KOOL *Kool & The Gang-De-Lite/Phonogram*
5 MY LOVE *Lionel Richie-Motown*	5 LET'S DANCE *David Bowie-EMI America*	5 CANDY GIRL *New Edition-London*	5 CHART ENCOUNTERS... *Various-Ronco*
6 BEAT IT *Michael Jackson-Epic*	6 FRONTIERS *Journey-Columbia*	6 LOVE TOWN *Booker Newberry III-Polydor/Montage*	6 CONFRONTATION *Bob Marley & The Wailers-Island*
7 SHE BLINDED ME WITH... *Thomas Dolby-Capitol*	7 KILROY WAS HERE *Styx-A&M*	7 JUST GOT LUCKY *JoBoxers-RCA*	7 THE LUXURY GAP *Heaven 17-Virgin*
8 ALWAYS SOMETHING... *Naked Eyes-EMI America*	8 H2O *Daryl Hall & John Oates-RCA*	8 CHINA GIRL *David Bowie-EMI America*	8 CRISES *Mike Oldfield-Virgin*
9 DON'T LET IT END *Styx-A&M*	9 CUTS LIKE A KNIFE *Bryan Adams-A&M*	9 FLASHDANCE...WHAT A... *Irene Cara-Casablanca/Phonogram*	9 TOO LOW FOR ZERO *Elton John-Rocket/Phonogram*
10 AFFAIR OF THE HEART *Rick Springfield-RCA*	10 1999 *Prince-Warner Bros.*	10 CAN'T GET USED TO... *The Beat-Go Feet*	10 PIECE OF MIND *Iron Maiden-EMI*
11 ELECTRIC AVENUE *Eddie Grant-Portrait/Ice*	11 LIONEL RICHIE *Lionel Richie-Motown*	11 LADY LOVE ME... *George Benson-Warner Bros.*	11 IN YOUR EYES *George Benson-Warner Bros.*
12 FAITHFULLY *Journey-Columbia*	12 THE FINAL CUT *Pink Floyd-Columbia*	12 WAITING FOR A TRAIN *Flash & The Pan-Easy Beat/Ensign*	12 THE HURTING *Tears for Fears-Mercury/Phonogram*
13 FAMILY MAN *Daryl Hall & John Oates-RCA*	13 LIVING IN OZ *Rick Springfield-RCA*	13 MONEY GO ROUND Part 1 *The Style Council-Polydor*	13 HOLY DIVER *Dio-Vertigo/Phonogram*
14 LITTLE RED CORVETTE *Prince-Warner Bros.*	14 GOLDEN AGE OF WIRELESS *Thomas Dolby-Capitol*	14 TEMPTATION *Heaven 17-B.E.F./Virgin*	14 WHITE FEATHERS *KajaGooGoo-EMI*
15 NEVER GONNA LET YOU GO *Sergio Mendes-A&M*	15 KISSING TO BE CLEVER *Culture Club-Virgin/Epic*	15 HANG ON NOW *KajaGooGoo-EMI*	15 WHAT IS BEAT?... *The Beat-Go Feet*
16 SHE'S A BEAUTY *The Tubes-Capitol*	16 JARREAU *Jarreau-Warner Bros.*	16 TRUE *Spandau Ballet-Reformation/Chrysalis*	16 FAST THAN THE SPEED... *Bonnie Tyler-CBS*
17 TOO SHY *KajaGooGoo-EMI America*	17 BUSINESS AS USUAL *Men at Work-Columbia*	17 IN A BIG COUNTRY *Big Country-Mercury/Phonogram*	17 NIGHT DUBBING *Imagination-R&B*
18 I'M STILL STANDING *Elton John-Geffen*	18 ELIMINATOR *Z.Z. Top-Warner Bros.*	18 I GUESS THAT'S WHY... *Elton John-Rocket/Phonogram*	18 SWEET DREAMS... *Eurythmics-RCA*
19 WANNA BE STARTIN'... *Michael Jackson-Epic*	19 WAR *U2-Island*	19 BABY JANE *Rod Stewart-Warner Bros.*	19 DIONNE WARWICK... *Dionne Warwick-Arista/Dione*
20 SOLITAIRE *Laura Branigan-Atlantic*	20 KILLER ON THE RAMPAGE *Eddy Grant-Portrait/Ice*	20 WHAT KINDA BOY... *Hot Chocolate-RAK*	20 QUICK STEP & SIDE KICK *Thompson Twins-Arista*

WEEK ENDING JUNE 18 1983

US SINGLES	US ALBUMS	UK SINGLES	UK ALBUMS
1 FLASHDANCE...WHAT A... *Irene Cara-Casablanca*	1 THRILLER *Michael Jackson-Epic*	1 EVERY BREATH YOU TAKE *Police-A&M*	1 THRILLER *Michael Jackson-Epic*
2 TIME *Culture Club-Virgin/Epic*	2 FLASHDANCE *Soundtrack-Casablanca*	2 CHINA GIRL *David Bowie-EMI America*	2 LET'S DANCE *David Bowie-EMI America*
3 LET'S DANCE *David Bowie-EMI America*	3 CARGO *Men at Work-Columbia*	3 BAD BOYS *Wham-Inner Vision*	3 IN YOUR EYES *George Benson-Warner Bros.*
4 ELECTRIC AVENUE *Eddy Grant-Portrait/Ice*	4 PYROMANIA *Def Leppard-Mercury*	4 FLASHDANCE...WHAT A... *Irene Cara-Casablanca/Phonogram*	4 TWICE AS KOOL *Kool & The Gang-De-Lite/Phonogram*
5 OVERKILL *Men at Work-Columbia*	5 LET'S DANCE *David Bowie-EMI America*	5 NOBODY'S DIARY *Yazoo-Mute*	5 OIL ON CANVAS *Japan-Virgin*
6 MY LOVE *Lionel Richie-Motown*	6 FRONTIERS *Journey-Columbia*	6 BABY JANE *Rod Stewart-Warner Bros.*	6 TRUE *Spandau Ballet-Reformation/Chrysalis*
7 DON'T LET IT END *Styx-A&M*	7 H2O *Daryl Hall & John Oates-RCA*	7 BUFFALO SOLDIER *Bob Marley & The Wailers-Island*	7 TOO LOW FOR ZERO *Elton John-Rocket/Phonogram*
8 ALWAYS SOMETHING... *Naked Eyes-EMI America*	8 KILROY WAS HERE *Styx-A&M*	8 LOVE TOWN *Booker Newberry III-Polydor/Montage*	8 PETER GABRIEL PLAYS LIVE *Peter Gabriel-Charisma/Phonogram*
9 AFFAIR OF THE HEART *Rick Springfield-RCA*	9 CUTS LIKE A KNIFE *Bryan Adams-A&M*	9 I GUESS THAT'S WHY... *Elton John-Rocket/Phonogram*	9 CRISES *Mike Oldfield-Virgin*
10 FAMILY MAN *Daryl Hall & John Oates-RCA*	10 1999 *Prince-Warner Bros.*	10 WAITING FOR A TRAIN *Flash & The Pan-Easy Beat/Ensign*	10 WHAT IS BEAT?... *The Beat-Go Feet*
11 BEAT IT *Michael Jackson-Epic*	11 LIONEL RICHIE *Lionel Richie-Motown*	11 LADY LOVE ME... *George Benson-Warner Bros.*	11 BODY WISHES *Rod Stewart-Warner Bros.*
12 FAITHFULLY *Journey-Columbia*	12 LIVING IN OZ *Rick Springfield-RCA*	12 JUST GOT LUCKY *JoBoxers-RCA*	12 CHART STARS *Various-K-tel*
13 NEVER GONNA LET YOU GO *Sergio Mendes-A&M*	13 GOLDEN AGE OF WIRELESS *Thomas Dolby-Capitol*	13 HANG ON NOW *KajaGooGoo-EMI*	13 CONFRONTATION *Bob Marley & The Wailers-Island*
14 EVERY BREATH YOU TAKE *The Police-A&M*	14 KISSING TO BE CLEVER *Culture Club-Virgin/Epic*	14 WANNA BE STARTIN'... *Michael Jackson-Epic*	14 THE HURTING *Tears for Fears-Mercury/Phonogram*
15 TOO SHY *KajaGooGoo-EMI America*	15 JARREAU *Jarreau-Warner Bros.*	15 DARK IS THE NIGHT *Shakatak-Polydor*	15 THE LUXURY GAP *Heaven 17-Virgin*
16 SHE'S A BEAUTY *The Tubes-Capitol*	16 KILLER ON THE RAMPAGE *Eddy Grant-Portrait/Ice*	16 PILLS AND SOAP *The Imposter-IMP/Demon*	16 FASTER THAN THE SPEED... *Bonnie Tyler-CBS*
17 WANNA BE STARTIN'... *Michael Jackson-Epic*	17 WAR *U2-Island*	17 CANDY GIRL *New Edition-London*	17 DIONNE WARWICK... *Dionne Warwick-Arista/Dione*
18 I'M STILL STANDING *Elton John-Geffen*	18 ELIMINATOR *Z.Z. Top-Warner Bros.*	18 WE CAME TO DANCE *Ultravox-Chrysalis*	18 WRAP YOUR ARMS... *Agnetha Faltskog-Epic*
19 COME DANCING *The Kinks-Arista*	19 OUTSIDE/INSIDE *The Tubes-Capitol*	19 DREAM TO SLEEP *H2O-RCA*	19 CHART ENCOUNTERS... *Various-Ronco*
20 SHE BLINDED ME WITH... *Thomas Dolby-Capitol*	20 BUSINESS AS USUAL *Men at Work-Columbia*	20 DEAD GIVEAWAY *Shalamar-Solar*	20 PIECE OF MIND *Iron Maiden-EMI*

196

WEEK ENDING JUNE 25 1983

	US SINGLES		US ALBUMS		UK SINGLES		UK ALBUMS
1	FLASHDANCE...WHAT A... *Irene Cara-Casablanca*	1	FLASHDANCE *Soundtrack-Casablanca*	1	EVERY BREATH YOU TAKE *Police-A&M*	1	SYNCHRONICITY *The Police-A&M*
2	TIME *Culture Club-Virgin/Epic*	2	THRILLER *Michael Jackson-Epic*	2	BABY JANE *Rod Stewart-Warner Bros.*	2	THRILLER *Michael Jackson-Epic*
3	ELECTRIC AVENUE *Eddy Grant-Portrait/Ice*	3	PYROMANIA *Def Leppard-Mercury*	3	CHINA GIRL *David Bowie-EMI America*	3	LET'S DANCE *David Bowie-EMI America*
4	EVERY BREATH YOU TAKE *The Police-A&M*	4	LET'S DANCE *David Bowie-EMI America*	4	FLASHDANCE...WHAT A... *Irene Cara-Casablanca/Phonogram*	4	IN YOUR EYES *George Benson-Warner Bros.*
5	LET'S DANCE *David Bowie-EMI America*	5	CARGO *Men at Work-Columbia*	5	BAD BOYS *Wham-Inner Vision*	5	BODY WISHES *Rod Stewart-Warner Bros.*
6	FAMILY MAN *Daryl Hall & John Oates-RCA*	6	FRONTIERS *Journey-Columbia*	6	I GUESS THAT'S WHY... *Elton John-Rocket/Phonogram*	6	TWICE AS KOOL *Kool & The Gang-De-Lite/Phonogram*
7	DON'T LET IT END *Styx-A&M*	7	H₂O *Daryl Hall & John Oates-RCA*	7	WAITING FOR A TRAIN *Flash & The Pan-Easy Beat/Ensign*	7	CHART STARS *Various-K-tel*
8	NEVER GONNA LET YOU GO *Sergio Mendes-A&M*	8	CUTS LIKE A KNIFE *Bryan Adams-A&M*	8	WANNA BE STARTIN'... *Michael Jackson-Epic*	8	OIL ON CANVAS *Japan-Virgin*
9	AFFAIR OF THE HEART *Rick Springfield-RCA*	9	KILROY WAS HERE *Styx-A&M*	9	NOBODY'S DIARY *Yazoo-Mute*	9	TRUE *Spandau Ballet-Reformation/Chrysalis*
10	TOO SHY *KajaGooGoo-EMI America*	10	1999 *Prince-Warner Bros.*	10	WHEN WE WERE YOUNG *Bucks Fizz-RCA*	10	TOO LOW FOR ZERO *Elton John-Rocket/Phonogram*
11	BEAT IT *Michael Jackson-Epic*	11	LIONEL RICHIE *Lionel Richie-Motown*	11	LADY LOVE ME... *George Benson-Warner Bros.*	11	DIONNE WARWICK... *Dionne Warwick-Arista/Dione*
12	FAITHFULLY *Journey-Columbia*	12	LIVING IN OZ *Rick Springfield-RCA*	12	DEAD GIVEAWAY *Shalamar-Solar*	12	CRISES *Mike Oldfield-Virgin*
13	ALWAYS SOMETHING... *Naked Eyes-EMI America*	13	GOLDEN AGE OF WIRELESS *Thomas Dolby-Capitol*	13	LOVE TOWN *Booker Newberry III-Polydor/Montage*	13	THE LUXURY GAP *Heaven 17-Virgin*
14	SHE'S A BEAUTY *The Tubes-Capitol*	14	KISSING TO BE CLEVER *Culture Club-Virgin/Epic*	14	BUFFALO SOLDIER *Bob Marley & The Wailers-Island*	14	WHAT IS BEAT?... *The Beat-Go-Feet*
15	WANNA BE STARTIN'... *Michael Jackson-Epic*	15	KILLER ON THE RAMPAGE *Eddy Grant-Portrait/Ice*	15	DARK IS THE NIGHT *Shakatak-Polydor*	15	PETER GABRIEL PLAYS LIVE *Peter Gabriel-Charisma/Phonogram*
16	I'M STILL STANDING *Elton John-Geffen*	16	ELIMINATOR *Z.Z. Top-Warner Bros.*	16	GARDEN PARTY *Marillion-EMI*	16	CONFRONTATION *Bob Marley & The Wailers-Island*
17	COME DANCING *The Kinks-Arista*	17	WAR *U2-Island*	17	DREAM TO SLEEP *H2O-RCA*	17	FASTER THAN THE SPEED... *Bonnie Tyler-CBS*
18	OVERKILL *Men at Work-Columbia*	18	JARREAU *Jarreau-Warner Bros.*	18	HANG ON NOW *KajaGooGoo-EMI*	18	BITE *Altered Images-Epic*
19	OUR HOUSE *Madness-Geffen*	19	OUTSIDE/INSIDE *The Tubes-Capitol*	19	MOONLIGHT SHADOW *Mike Oldfield-Virgin*	19	THE HURTING *Tears for Fears-Mercury/Phonogram*
20	MY LOVE *Lionel Richie-Motown*	20	BUSINESS AS USUAL *Men at Work-Columbia*	20	WE CAME TO DANCE *Ultravox-Chrysalis*	20	HOLY DIVER *Dio-Vertigo/Phonogram*

WEEK ENDING JULY 2 1983

	US ALBUMS		US SINGLES		UK SINGLES		UK ALBUMS
1	FLASHDANCE...WHAT... *Irene Cara-Casablanca*	1	FLASHDANCE *Soundtrack-Casablanca*	1	BABY JANE *Rod Stewart-Warner Bros.*	1	SYNCHRONICITY *The Police-A&M*
2	ELECTRIC AVENUE *Eddy Grant-Portrait/Ice*	2	THRILLER *Michael Jackson-Epic*	2	EVERY BREATH YOU TAKE *Police-A&M*	2	THRILLER *Michael Jackson-Epic*
3	EVERY BREATH YOU TAKE *The Police-A&M*	3	PYROMANIA *Def Leppard-Mercury*	3	FLASHDANCE...WHAT A... *Irene Cara-Casablanca/Phonogram*	3	LET'S DANCE *David Bowie-EMI America*
4	TIME *Culture Club-Virgin/Epic*	4	CARGO *Men at Work-Columbia*	4	MOONLIGHT SHADOW *Mike Oldfield-Virgin*	4	SECRET MESSAGES *ELO-Jet*
5	NEVER GONNA LET YOU GO *Sergio Mendes-A&M*	5	LET'S DANCE *David Bowie-EMI America*	5	I GUESS THAT'S WHY... *Elton John-Rocket/Phonogram*	5	BODY WISHES *Rod Stewart-Warner Bros.*
6	DON'T LET IT END *Styx-A&M*	6	FRONTIERS *Journey-Columbia*	6	CHINA GIRL *David Bowie-EMI America*	6	CRISES *Mike Oldfield-Virgin*
7	TOO SHY *KajaGooGoo-EMI America*	7	H₂O *Daryl Hall & John Oates-RCA*	7	I.O.U. *Freeez-Beggars Banquet*	7	IN YOUR EYES *George Benson-Warner Bros.*
8	FAMILY MAN *Daryl Hall & John Oates-RCA*	8	CUTS LIKE A KNIFE *Bryan Adams-A&M*	8	DEAD GIVEAWAY *Shalamar-Solar*	8	TWICE AS KOOL *Kool & The Gang-De-Lite/Phonogram*
9	WANNA BE STARTIN'... *Michael Jackson-Epic*	9	KILROY WAS HERE *Styx-A&M*	9	BAD BOYS *Wham-Inner Vision*	9	TRUE *Spandau Ballet-Reformation/Chrysalis*
10	SHE'S A BEAUTY *The Tubes-Capitol*	10	1999 *Prince-Warner Bros.*	10	WHEN WE WERE YOUNG *Bucks Fizz-RCA*	10	TOO LOW FOR ZERO *Elton John-Rocket/Phonogram*
11	COME DANCING *The Kinks-Arista*	11	KILLER ON THE RAMPAGE *Eddy Grant-Portrait/Ice*	11	WAITING FOR A TRAIN *Flash & The Pan-Easy Beat/Ensign*	11	THE LUXURY GAP *Heaven 17-Virgin*
12	AFFAIR OF THE HEART *Rick Springfield-RCA*	12	LIVING IN OZ *Rick Springfield-RCA*	12	WHEREVER I LAY MY HAT... *Paul Young-CBS*	12	CHART STARS *Various-K-tel*
13	OUR HOUSE *Madness-Geffen*	13	LIONEL RICHIE *Lionel Richie-Motown*	13	WANNA BE STARTIN'... *Michael Jackson-Epic*	13	OIL ON CANVAS *Japan-Virgin*
14	I'M STILL STANDING *Elton John-Geffen*	14	KISSING TO BE CLEVER *Culture Club-Virgin/Epic*	14	TAKE THAT SITUATION *Nick Heyward-Arista*	14	STREET SOUNDS—EDITION 4 *Various-Street Sounds*
15	LET'S DANCE *David Bowie-EMI America*	15	ELIMINATOR *Z.Z. Top-Warner Bros.*	15	ROCK'N'ROLL IS KING *ELO-Jet*	15	WHAT IS BEAT?... *The Beat-Go-Feet*
16	BEAT IT *Michael Jackson-Epic*	16	GOLDEN AGE OF WIRELESS *Thomas Dolby-Capitol*	16	COME LIVE WITH ME *Heaven 17-B.E.F./Virgin*	16	BITE *Altered Images-Epic*
17	IS THERE SOMETHING... *Duran Duran-Capitol*	17	SYNCHRONICITY *The Police-A&M*	17	WAR BABY *Tom Robinson-Panic*	17	DIONNE WARWICK... *Dionne Warwick-Arista/Dione*
18	ALL THIS LOVE *Debarge-Gordy*	18	OUTSIDE/INSIDE *The Tubes-Capitol*	18	DREAM TO SLEEP *H2O-RCA*	18	THE HURTING *Tears for Fears-Mercury/Phonogram*
19	STAND BACK *Stevie Nicks-Modern*	19	JARREAU *Jarreau-Warner Bros.*	19	LADY LOVE ME... *George Benson-Warner Bros.*	19	FASTER THAN THE SPEED... *Bonnie Tyler-CBS*
20	ALWAYS SOMETHING... *Naked Eyes-EMI America*	20	BETWEEN THE SHEETS *The Isley Brothers-T-Neck*	20	NOBODY'S DIARY *Yazoo-Mute*	20	LOVERS ONLY! *Various-Ronco*

US SINGLES	US ALBUMS	UK SINGLES	UK ALBUMS
1 EVERY BREATH YOU TAKE *The Police-A&M*	1 THRILLER *Michael Jackson-Epic*	1 BABY JANE *Rod Stewart-Warner Bros.*	1 FANTASTIC *Wham!-Inner Vision*
2 ELECTRIC AVENUE *Eddy Grant-Portrait/Ice*	2 FLASHDANCE *Soundtrack-Casablanca*	2 FLASHDANCE...WHAT A... *Irene Cara-Casablanca/Phonogram*	2 SYNCHRONICITY *The Police-A&M*
3 FLASHDANCE...WHAT A... *Irene Cara-Casablanca*	3 PYROMANIA *Def Leppard-Mercury*	3 WHEREVER I LAY MY HAT... *Paul Young-CBS*	3 THRILLER *Michael Jackson-Epic*
4 NEVER GONNA LET YOU GO *Sergio Mendes-A&M*	4 SYNCHRONICITY *The Police-A&M*	4 MOONLIGHT SHADOW *Mike Oldfield-Virgin*	4 LET'S DANCE *David Bowie-EMI America*
5 TOO SHY *KajaGooGoo-EMI America*	5 LET'S DANCE *David Bowie-EMI America*	5 I.O.U. *Freeez-Beggars Banquet*	5 BODY WISHES *Rod Stewart-Warner Bros.*
6 WANNA BE STARTIN'... *Michael Jackson-Epic*	6 CARGO *Men at Work-Columbia*	6 WAR BABY *Tom Robinson-Panic*	6 SECRET MESSAGES *ELO-Jet*
7 TIME *Culture Club-Virgin/Epic*	7 FRONTIERS *Journey-Columbia*	7 COME LIVE WITH ME *Heaven 17-B.E.F./Virgin*	7 CRISES *Mike Oldfield-Virgin*
8 COME DANCING *The Kinks-Arista*	8 CUTS LIKE A KNIFE *Bryan Adams-A&M*	8 DEAD GIVEAWAY *Shalamar-Solar*	8 JULIO *Julio Iglesias-CBS*
9 DON'T LET IT END *Styx-A&M*	9 1999 *Prince-Warner Bros.*	9 EVERY BREATH YOU TAKE *Police-A&M*	9 IN YOUR EYES *George Benson-Warner Bros.*
10 OUR HOUSE *Madness-Geffen*	10 H₂O *Daryl Hall & John Oates-RCA*	10 I GUESS THAT'S WHY... *Elton John-Rocket/Phonogram*	10 THE LUXURY GAP *Heaven 17-Virgin*
11 FAMILY MAN *Daryl Hall & John Oates-RCA*	11 KILLER ON THE RAMPAGE *Eddy Grant-Portrait/Ice*	11 TAKE THAT SITUATION *Nick Heyward-Arista*	11 FLASHDANCE SOUNDTRACK *Various-Casablanca/Phonogram*
12 I'M STILL STANDING *Elton John-Geffen*	12 THE WILD HEART *Stevie Nicks-Modern*	12 THE TROOPER *Iron Maiden-EMI*	12 LOVERS ONLY! *Various-Ronco*
13 IS THERE SOMETHING... *Duran Duran-Capitol*	13 KILROY WAS HERE *Styx-A&M*	13 WHEN WE WERE YOUNG *Bucks Fizz-RCA*	13 TOO LOW FOR ZERO *Elton John-Rocket/Phonogram*
14 STAND BACK *Stevie Nicks-Modern*	14 KISSING TO BE CLEVER *Culture Club-Virgin/Epic*	14 ROCK'N'ROLL IS KING *ELO-Jet*	14 TRUE *Spandau Ballet-Reformation/Chrysalis*
15 1999 *Prince-Warner Bros.*	15 ELIMINATOR *Z.Z. Top-Warner Bros.*	15 IT'S OVER *Funk Masters-Master-Funk Records*	15 TWICE AS KOOL *Kool & The Gang-De-Lite/Phonogram*
16 SHE'S A BEAUTY *The Tubes-Capitol*	16 LIONEL RICHIE *Lionel Richie-Motown*	16 BAD BOYS *Wham-Inner Vision*	16 CHART STARS *Various-K-tel*
17 ALL THIS LOVE *Debarge-Gordy*	17 LIVING IN OZ *Rick Springfield-RCA*	17 CHINA GIRL *David Bowie-EMI America*	17 STREET SOUNDS—EDITION 4 *Various-Street Sounds*
18 SHE WORKS HARD FOR... *Donna Summer-Mercury*	18 KEEP IT UP *Loverboy-Columbia*	18 WAITING FOR A TRAIN *Flash & The Pan-Easy Beat/Ensign*	18 DUCK ROCK *Malcolm McLaren-Charisma/Phonogram*
19 BABY JANE *Rod Stewart-Warner Bros.*	19 BETWEEN THE SHEETS *The Isley Brothers-T-Neck*	19 DOUBLE DUTCH *Malcolm McLaren-Charisma/Phonogram*	19 WAR *U2-Island*
20 SWEET DREAMS... *Eurythmics-RCA*	20 RETURN OF THE JEDI *Soundtrack-RSO*	20 FORBIDDEN COLOURS *David Sylvian/Riuichi Sakamoto-Virgin*	20 IN THE GROOVE... *Various-Telstar*

US SINGLES	US ALBUMS	UK SINGLES	UK ALBUMS
1 EVERY BREATH YOU TAKE *The Police-A&M*	1 THRILLER *Michael Jackson-Epic*	1 BABY JANE *Rod Stewart-Warner Bros.*	1 FANTASTIC *Wham!-Inner Vision*
2 ELECTRIC AVENUE *Eddy Grant-Portrait/Ice*	2 SYNCHRONICITY *The Police-A&M*	2 WHEREVER I LAY MY HAT... *Paul Young-CBS*	2 YOU AND ME BOTH *Yazoo-Mute*
3 FLASHDANCE...WHAT A... *Irene Cara-Casablanca*	3 FLASHDANCE *Soundtrack-Casablanca*	3 I.O.U. *Freeez-Beggars Banquet*	3 SYNCHRONICITY *The Police-A&M*
4 NEVER GONNA LET YOU GO *Sergio Mendes-A&M*	4 PYROMANIA *Def Leppard-Mercury*	4 MOONLIGHT SHADOW *Mike Oldfield-Virgin*	4 THRILLER *Michael Jackson-Epic*
5 WANNA BE STARTIN'... *Michael Jackson-Epic*	5 LET'S DANCE *David Bowie-EMI America*	5 FLASHDANCE...WHAT A... *Irene Cara-Casablanca/Phonogram*	5 JULIO *Julio Iglesias-CBS*
6 COME DANCING *The Kinks-Arista*	6 CARGO *Men at Work-Columbia*	6 COME LIVE WITH ME *Heaven 17-B.E.F./Virgin*	6 LET'S DANCE *David Bowie-EMI America*
7 TOO SHY *KajaGooGoo-EMI America*	7 THE WILD HEART *Stevie Nicks-Modern*	7 WAR BABY *Tom Robinson-Panic*	7 CRISES *Mike Oldfield-Virgin*
8 OUR HOUSE *Madness-Geffen*	8 KEEP IT UP *Loverboy-Columbia*	8 IT'S OVER *Funk Masters-Master-Funk Records*	8 BODY WISHES *Rod Stewart-Warner Bros.*
9 IS THERE SOMETHING... *Duran Duran-Capitol*	9 1999 *Prince-Warner Bros.*	9 WHO'S THAT GIRL? *Eurythmics-RCA*	9 FLASHDANCE SOUNDTRACK *Various-Casablanca/Phonogram*
10 OUR HOUSE *Culture Club-Virgin/Epic*	10 KILLER ON THE RAMPAGE *Eddy Grant-Portrait/Ice*	10 DOUBLE DUTCH *Malcolm McLaren-Charisma/Phonogram*	10 SECRET MESSAGES *ELO-Jet*
11 STAND BACK *Stevie Nicks-Modern*	11 FRONTIERS *Journey-Columbia*	11 DEAD GIVEAWAY *Shalamar-Solar*	11 IN YOUR EYES *George Benson-Warner Bros.*
12 I'M STILL STANDING *Elton John-Geffen*	12 CUTS LIKE A KNIFE *Bryan Adams-A&M*	12 THE TROOPER *Iron Maiden-EMI*	12 THE LUXURY GAP *Heaven 17-Virgin*
13 1999 *Prince-Warner Bros.*	13 H₂O *Daryl Hall & John Oates-RCA*	13 ROCK'N'ROLL IS KING *ELO-Jet*	13 TOO LOW FOR ZERO *Elton John-Rocket/Phonogram*
14 SHE WORKS HARD FOR... *Donna Summer-Mercury*	14 KILROY WAS HERE *Styx-A&M*	14 TAKE THAT SITUATION *Nick Heyward-Arista*	14 PIECE OF MIND *Iron Maiden-EMI*
15 SWEET DREAMS... *Eurythmics-RCA*	15 STATE OF CONFUSION *The Kinks-Arista*	15 I GUESS THAT'S WHY... *Elton John-Rocket/Phonogram*	15 TRUE *Spandau Ballet-Reformation/Chrysalis*
16 BABY JANE *Rod Stewart-Warner Bros.*	16 LISTEN *A Flock of Seagulls-Jive/Arista*	16 ALL NIGHT LONG *Mary Jane Girls-Gord-y*	16 LOVERS ONLY! *Various-Ronco*
17 ALL THIS LOVE *Debarge-Gordy*	17 PIECE OF MIND *Iron Maiden-Capitol*	17 THE WALK *The Cure-Fiction*	17 TWICE AS KOOL *Kool & The Gang-De-Lite/Phonogram*
18 DON'T LET IT END *Styx-A&M*	18 LIVING IN OZ *Rick Springfield-RCA*	18 FORBIDDEN COLOURS *David Sylvian/Riuichi Sakamoto-Virgin*	18 DUCK ROCK *Malcolm McLaren-Charisma/Phonogram*
19 MANIAC *Michael Sembello-Casablanca*	19 ELIMINATOR *Z.Z. Top-Warner Bros.*	19 TANTALISE (WO WO EE...) *Jimmy The Hoover-Inner Vision*	19 SWEET DREAMS... *Eurythmics-RCA*
20 CUTS LIKE A KNIFE *Bryan Adams-A&M*	20 RETURN OF THE JEDI *Soundtrack-RSO*	20 EVERY BREATH YOU TAKE *Police-A&M*	20 CARGO *Men at Work-Epic*

US SINGLES	US ALBUMS	UK SINGLES	UK ALBUMS
1 EVERY BREATH YOU TAKE *The Police-A&M*	1 SYNCHRONICITY *The Police-A&M*	1 WHEREVER I LAY MY HAT... *Paul Young-CBS*	1 YOU AND ME BOTH *Yazoo-Mute*
2 ELECTRIC AVENUE *Eddy Grant-Portrait/Ice*	2 FLASHDANCE *Soundtrack-Casablanca*	2 I.O.U. *Freeez-Beggars Banquet*	2 FANTASTIC *Wham!-Inner Vision*
3 FLASHDANCE...WHAT A... *Irene Cara-Casablanca*	3 THRILLER *Michael Jackson-Epic*	3 BABY JANE *Rod Stewart-Warner Bros.*	3 THRILLER *Michael Jackson-Epic*
4 NEVER GONNA LET YOU GO *Sergio Mendes-A&M*	4 PYROMANIA *Def Leppard-Mercury*	4 WHO'S THAT GIRL? *Eurythmics-RCA*	4 SYNCHRONICITY *The Police-A&M*
5 WANNA BE STARTIN'... *Michael Jackson-Epic*	5 THE WILD HEART *Stevie Nicks-Modern*	5 MOONLIGHT SHADOW *Mike Oldfield-Virgin*	5 JULIO *Julio Iglesias-CBS*
6 COME DANCING *The Kinks-Arista*	6 LET'S DANCE *David Bowie-EMI America*	6 COME LIVE WITH ME *Heaven 17-B.E.F./Virgin*	6 LET'S DANCE *David Bowie-EMI America*
7 OUR HOUSE *Madness-Geffen*	7 KEEP IT UP *Loverboy-Columbia*	7 DOUBLE DUTCH *Malcolm McLaren-Charisma/Phonogram*	7 THE LUXURY GAP *Heaven 17-Virgin*
8 IS THERE SOMETHING... *Duran Duran-Capitol*	8 CARGO *Men at Work-Columbia*	8 FLASHDANCE...WHAT A... *Irene Cara-Casablanca/Phonogram*	8 CRISES *Mike Oldfield-Virgin*
9 STAND BACK *Stevie Nicks-Modern*	9 1999 *Prince-Warner Bros.*	9 WAR BABY *Tom Robinson-Panic*	9 FLASHDANCE SOUNDTRACK *Various-Casablanca/Phonogram*
10 SHE WORKS HARD FOR... *Donna Summer-Mercury*	10 KILLER ON THE RAMPAGE *Eddy Grant-Portrait/Ice*	10 IT'S OVER *Funk Masters-Master-Funk Records*	10 PRINCIPLE OF MOMENTS *Robert Plant-WEA*
11 SWEET DREAMS... *Eurythmics-RCA*	11 FRONTIERS *Journey-Columbia*	11 CRUEL SUMMER *Bananarama-London*	11 BODY WISHES *Rod Stewart-Warner Bros.*
12 1999 *Prince-Warner Bros.*	12 H$_2$O *Daryl Hall & John Oates-RCA*	12 THE WALK *The Cure-Fiction*	12 IN YOUR EYES *George Benson-Warner Bros.*
13 TOO SHY *KajaGooGoo-EMI America*	13 STATE OF CONFUSION *The Kinks-Arista*	13 ALL NIGHT LONG *Mary Jane Girls-Gord-y*	13 BURNING FROM THE INSIDE *Bauhaus-Beggars Banquet*
14 MANIAC *Michael Sembello-Casablanca*	14 CUTS LIKE A KNIFE *Bryan Adams-A&M*	14 WRAPPED AROUND YOUR... *The Police-A&M*	14 SECRET MESSAGES *ELO-Jet*
15 BABY JANE *Rod Stewart-Warner Bros.*	15 PIECE OF MIND *Iron Maiden-Capitol*	15 NEVER STOP *Echo & The Bunnymen-Korova*	15 TOO LOW FOR ZERO *Elton John-Rocket/Phonogram*
16 CUTS LIKE A KNIFE *Bryan Adams-A&M*	16 LISTEN *A Flock of Seagulls-Jive/Arista*	16 FORBIDDEN COLOURS *David Sylvian/Riuichi Sakamoto-Virgin*	16 SWEET DREAMS... *Eurythmics-RCA*
17 ALL THIS LOVE *Debarge-Gordy*	17 KILROY WAS HERE *Styx-A&M*	17 ROCK'N'ROLL IS KING *ELO-Jet*	17 PIECE OF MIND *Iron Maiden-EMI*
18 (KEEP) FEELING... *The Human League-A&M*	18 KISSING TO BE CLEVER *Culture Club-Virgin/Epic*	18 TANTALISE (WO WO EE...) *Jimmy The Hoover-Inner Vision*	18 DUCK ROCK *Malcolm McLaren-Charisma/Phonogram*
19 HOT GIRLS IN LOVE *Loverboy-Columbia*	19 ELIMINATOR *Z.Z. Top-Warner Bros.*	19 THE TROOPER *Iron Maiden-EMI*	19 LOVERS ONLY! *Various-Ronco*
20 IT'S A MISTAKE *Men at Work-Columbia*	20 REACH THE BEACH *The Fixx-MCA*	20 DON'T TRY TO STOP IT *Roman Holliday-Jive*	20 TRUE *Spandau Ballet-Reformation/Chrysalis*

US SINGLES	US ALBUMS	UK SINGLES	UK ALBUMS
1 EVERY BREATH YOU TAKE *The Police-A&M*	1 SYNCHRONICITY *The Police-A&M*	1 WHEREVER I LAY MY HAT... *Paul Young-CBS*	1 YOU AND ME BOTH *Yazoo-Mute*
2 ELECTRIC AVENUE *Eddy Grant-Portrait/Ice*	2 THRILLER *Michael Jackson-Epic*	2 I.O.U. *Freeez-Beggars Banquet*	2 THRILLER *Michael Jackson-Epic*
3 FLASHDANCE...WHAT A... *Irene Cara-Casablanca*	3 FLASHDANCE *Soundtrack-Casablanca*	3 WHO'S THAT GIRL? *Eurythmics-RCA*	3 SYNCHRONICITY *The Police-A&M*
4 NEVER GONNA LET YOU GO *Sergio Mendes-A&M*	4 PYROMANIA *Def Leppard-Mercury*	4 DOUBLE DUTCH *Malcolm McLaren-Charisma/Phonogram*	4 FANTASTIC *Wham!-Inner Vision*
5 IS THERE SOMETHING... *Duran Duran-Capitol*	5 THE WILD HEART *Stevie Nicks-Modern*	5 COME LIVE WITH ME *Heaven 17-B.E.F./Virgin*	5 BEST OF THE BEACH BOYS *The Beach Boys-Capitol*
6 SWEET DREAMS... *Eurythmics-RCA*	6 LET'S DANCE *David Bowie-EMI America*	6 THE CROWN *Gary Byrd & G.B. Experience-Motown*	6 NO PARLEZ! *Paul Young-CBS*
7 WANNA BE STARTIN'... *Michael Jackson-Epic*	7 KEEP IT UP *Loverboy-Columbia*	7 MOONLIGHT SHADOW *Mike Oldfield-Virgin*	7 THE LOOK *Shalamar-Solar*
8 SHE WORKS HARD FOR... *Donna Summer-Mercury*	8 CARGO *Men at Work-Columbia*	8 WRAPPED AROUND YOUR... *The Police-A&M*	8 JULIO *Julio Iglesias-CBS*
9 STAND BACK *Stevie Nicks-Modern*	9 1999 *Prince-Warner Bros.*	9 BABY JANE *Rod Stewart-Warner Bros.*	9 THE LUXURY GAP *Heaven 17-Virgin*
10 OUR HOUSE *Madness-Geffen*	10 KILLER ON THE RAMPAGE *Eddy Grant-Portrait/Ice*	10 CRUEL SUMMER *Bananarama-London*	10 18 GREATEST HITS *Michael Jackson with Jackson 5-Telstar*
11 MANIAC *Michael Sembello-Casablanca*	11 FRONTIERS *Journey-Columbia*	11 DO IT AGAIN/BILLIE JEAN *Club House-Island*	11 CRISES *Mike Oldfield-Virgin*
12 1999 *Prince-Warner Bros.*	12 H$_2$O *Daryl Hall & John Oates-RCA*	12 IT'S LATE *Shakin' Stevens-Epic*	12 LET'S DANCE *David Bowie-EMI America*
13 COME DANCING *The Kinks-Arista*	13 STATE OF CONFUSION *The Kinks-Arista*	13 FLASHDANCE...WHAT A... *Irene Cara-Casablanca/Phonogram*	13 PRINCIPLE OF MOMENTS *Robert Plant-WEA*
14 BABY JANE *Rod Stewart-Warner Bros.*	14 CUTS LIKE A KNIFE *Bryan Adams-A&M*	14 IT'S OVER *Funk Masters-Master-Funk Records*	14 FLASHDANCE SOUNDTRACK *Various-Casablanca/Phonogram*
15 IT'S A MISTAKE *Men at Work-Columbia*	15 PIECE OF MIND *Iron Maiden-Capitol*	15 DON'T TRY TO STOP IT *Roman Holliday-Jive*	15 IN YOUR EYES *George Benson-Warner Bros.*
16 CUTS LIKE A KNIFE *Bryan Adams-A&M*	16 DURAN DURAN *Duran Duran-Capitol*	16 THE WALK *The Cure-Fiction*	16 BODY WISHES *Rod Stewart-Warner Bros.*
17 (KEEP FEELING)... *The Human League-A&M*	17 SPEAKING IN TONGUES *The Talking Heads-Sire*	17 NEVER STOP *Echo & The Bunnymen-Korova*	17 HITS ON FIRE *Various-Ronco*
18 HOT GIRLS IN LOVE *Loverboy-Columbia*	18 REACH THE BEACH *The Fixx-MCA*	18 WAR BABY *Tom Robinson-Panic*	18 SWEET DREAMS... *Eurythmics-RCA*
19 ROCK OF AGES *Def Leppard-Mercury*	19 SHE WORKS HARD FOR... *Donna Summer-Mercury*	19 GIVE IT UP *KC & The Sunshine Band-Epic*	19 BURNING FROM THE INSIDE *Bauhaus-Beggars Banquet*
20 CHINA GIRL *David Bowie-EMI America*	20 ELIMINATOR *Z.Z.Top-Warner Bros.*	20 FORBIDDEN COLOURS *David Sylvian/Riuichi Sakamoto-Virgin*	20 TOO LOW FOR ZERO *Elton John-Rocket/Phonogram*

QUOTES OF THE YEAR

❝WHEN MY DAUGHTER IS 16, I'LL BE 52. HER FRIENDS WILL COME ROUND AND I'LL HAVE TO LIFT UP THEIR FROCKS WITH MY STICK.❞
ROD STEWART

"There is hardly any logic to anything that goes on. You have to be flexible if you want to survive."
Marshall Crenshaw

"In London, you go out in the street and people point at you and you get approached for autographs every two minutes. You go into a shoe shop and the staff bring out a camera and start taking pictures of you."
Marc Almond, Soft Cell

"Sex is life and you have to do sex in order to get happy. I see myself as a nun."
Nina Hagen

"I think I'm a far better fucking actor than either David Bowie or Sting could ever be."
John Lydon, PiL

"I was striving for a lack of irony, but there's a limit to how little irony I can pull off at this point."
Donald Fagen

"We've written at least two classics and that's a fact."
Geoff Deane, Modern Romance

"I used to think one hit single and you get your Rolls Royce — but it takes about ten albums to be comfortably off."
Andy Fletcher, Depeche Mode

❝I'M LIKE EVERYONE ELSE — I GO HOME, KISS THE BABY, AND SIT ON THE SETTEE AND HAVE A CUDDLE WITH MY WIFE.❞
SUGGS, MADNESS

"I hate Bodymist, I think it stinks. I think Virgin Music stinks. I think the legal process stinks."
Sting, The Police

"There is not one utterance escapes our instruments that has not been programmed and shaped in advance by Don. Sometimes he'd draw a picture and say 'I want more of this' or he would crinkle up a piece of paper in your ear and say 'Sound like this.'"
Gary Lucas, Captain Beefheart & His Magic Band

"The thing about life, if you boil it down for me, is three things: keep a cool head, eat well and have free bowels — then you'll live as long as you want. You get there too fast, it will kill you."
Jimmy Cliff

"I suppose I see myself as a kind of Charles Darwin, a chap pottering about investigating strange species and occasionally coming up with something alien and totally new."
John Peel

❝I DON'T HAVE DREAMS ABOUT MEN ANYMORE, NOT IN THE SENSE OF THE WOMAN WAITING FOR THE KNIGHT ON THE WHITE HORSE.❞
YOKO ONO

"I LIKE BIG MEN BECAUSE I'M NOT A SMALL PERSON MYSELF. I LIKED OLIVER REED BEFORE HE GOT TOO FAT. BUT THE THING IS I DON'T MEET MANY MEN. BECAUSE MY SHOW IS RATHER CAMP, MOST OF THE MEN WHO COME TO SEE ME ARE GAY. THEY ARE EVER SO NICE, BUT THAT DOESN'T REALLY HELP."
MARI WILSON

"When I fuck, I play the dub version of 'Guilty' by Honey Bane, followed by the first Ramones album."
Kim Fowley

"I finally decided to fold the band after I heard the Blancmange album. I hated it. It's pinned to my wall as a reminder of how much I'm bored with the current music."
Julian Cope, The Teardrop Explodes

"Runaway kids still pour into LA looking for the golden vein — whatever that is. Quite often they end up on the street selling their butts to chicken hawkers."
Joe Nanini, Wall of Voodoo

"I'm not going with girls; I'm not going with anyone anymore. . . I don't want to get herpes."
Pete Wylie, Wah!

"ROCK'N'ROLL IS ALWAYS AT ITS BEST WHEN IT HAS IMPERFECTIONS AND ALWAYS AT ITS WORST WHEN THOSE IMPERFECTIONS ARE PADDED OUT BY THE CELEBRATED PRODUCERS THAT ARE AROUND TODAY. THE ORIGINAL SIN, THE BUM NOTE, HAS VANISHED. THE SPONTANEOUS VULGARITY HAS BEEN POLISHED OFF."
MALCOLM McLAREN

"I hate the idea of being on this planet. It's a terrible place and I always knew when I first arrived here."
Sun Ra

"I find it very hard to write a conventional love song — it would be like a virgin writing about sex. I just don't have those conventional feelings."
Toyah

"We want to give positive, responsible entertainment experiences. That's what art is. Not politics or violence or devil worship or sex or drugs or lunacy or stupidity."
Terry Bozzio, Missing Persons

"There's not that much money to be made in rock anymore. The people who've been in it for the money aren't going to be in it anymore — and that, to me, is healthy."
Paul Kantner, Jefferson Starship

"Watching *Top of the Pops* I'm embarrassed by half of what's selling and I laugh at the other half. I cannot understand how people can buy a Steve Strange record. What are they buying? The image is so wallysville and the music is non-existent. Maybe I'm getting too old and cynical."
John Lydon, PiL

"I've never explored anything to the point where it could be my life's work. I was never that kind of artist."
David Bowie

"Pop music is definitely going through a silly stage, but I think it's a short-lived one."
David Bowie

"MY MUSIC APPEALS TO ALL KINDS OF PEOPLE. HOUSEWIVES DOING THEIR IRONING FIND IT EASY TO LISTEN TO."
CHRISTOPHER CROSS

"I was introduced to Prince Charles last week and I said to him 'This is the proudest moment of my life.' I wouldn't let go of his hand."
Cheryl, Bucks Fizz

"There's a new blue movie out. It's got a pig in it."
Mike, Bucks Fizz

"PERSONALLY, I DON'T WANT TO BE KNOWN AS A NYMPHET OR A SEX SYMBOL. AS FAR AS I CAN SEE, A NYMPHET IS A GIRL WHO DOESN'T KNOW WHAT THE FUCK SHE'S TALKING ABOUT."
ANNABELLA, BOW WOW WOW

"I don't really like much of this new wave sound. Half the groups look like morons, completely without intelligence."
Christine McVie, Fleetwood Mac

"THE LOVE SONGS THAT I WRITE HAVE GOT DIFFERENT LYRICS; I USE WORDS LIKE TOBLERONE, NORWAY, TEA AND SCONES."
NICK HEYWARD, HAIRCUT 100

"People think you're always having a great time, with Rolls Royces, money and so on. If they knew the truth, they'd be disillusioned. It's a lot more hard work than fun. But that work can be fun...a lot more fun than working in a jam factory in Hereford."
Martin Chambers, The Pretenders

"Artists are a commodity. You have to stay aloof from it all. My friends are doctors, dentists, lawyers, accountants."
Harvey Goldsmith, promoter

"In this business, the ones who moan loudest are the ones who don't know what they're doing."
Harvey Goldsmith, promoter

"I got fed up with being piggy in the middle."
Malcolm McLaren

"I've always found musicians very coarse people, often quite uninspired and unintelligent."
Malcolm McLaren

"IT'S NOT THE ROAD AND IT'S NOT PERFORMING THAT I'VE GOT AN ARGUMENT WITH — IT'S THE FROZEN NATURE OF THE BAND. ROGER SAYS WE MUST STOP BEFORE THE WHO BECOMES A PARODY OF ITSELF...WELL, I THINK WE'VE BEEN PARODYING OURSELVES FOR A LONG, LONG TIME."
PETE TOWNSHEND, THE WHO

"You don't have to wear make-up in a limp-wristed way. If I adopt a particular expression on stage, I can scorch people's eyeballs in the back row."
Fish, Marillion

"For a long time, Australia had a chip on its shoulder about its art. We are now realising that what we have here is as good as anywhere else."
Colin Hay, Men at Work

"I'm smarter than your average rock pig. My IQ is 164."
Kim Fowley

"I'm competitive, egotistical, vain, arrogant — but underneath I try to be a nice human being. I don't like fucking people over in any respect."
Adam Ant

"MY ULTIMATE AIM IS TO RETIRE TO THE CHILTERNS AND WRITE MISERABLE BOOKS."
FISH, MARILLION

"Rotten was a marvellous poet. With me inspiring him, he was able to eloquently portray the feelings of a generation."
Malcolm McLaren

"It's clear to me that if you're hated in England, you've got to be doing something right, you've got to be changing something in this muddy old hole."
Malcolm McLaren

"I never vote. I never even filled in the census form. I simply refuse to do anything like that."
Malcolm McLaren

"Anybody creative in this country seems more interested in the idea than the selling. We're a land without very good salesmen. Same as we don't have good plumbers."
Malcolm McLaren

"I'm like a doctor — I can't really talk about my patients."
Trevor Horn, producer

"I am a dabbler, but that doesn't mean I'm not serious. It doesn't matter if you do several things well any more than if you devote a lifetime to interpreting one kind of pop music — like Frank Sinatra or Willie Nelson."
David Byrne, Talking Heads

"I signed into a motel once but I couldn't even remember my address — I'd gotten that wasted."
Jeffrey Lee Pierce, Gun Club

"Right now, everyone in America is walking around in a daydream — they're not interested in anything except videos and pot. They looked at the war between the English and the Argentines like it was some kind of TV show."
Jeffrey Lee Pierce, Gun Club

"I feel we have achieved all we can together as a group, both musically and commercially. I want us to finish with dignity."
Paul Weller, The Jam

"In a social situation, I'm absolutely at a loss. I loathe parties because I always feel so uptight. I never know what to say. I sort of hang about on the edge. My remedy used to be to get absolutely stoned."
David Bowie

"I used to have a very strong rivalry with Mick Jagger, but that's mellowed out over the past few years as we've realised, I guess, that we've established everything we thought we wanted."
David Bowie

"The game Monopoly has this card saying 'Get out of jail free.' Being in a group with a number one record is like having that card...we could use it to solve our problems with anyone who bothers us. But if I find out any of us is using it, I'd be very annoyed."
Michael Grant, Musical Youth

"Whenever I've been to record companies in the last six years they've just scratched their heads and said 'You must be joking — we're here to make money, not music, sonny.'"
Tymon Dogg

"I ALWAYS WANT TO KNOW WHAT MAKES GOOD PERFORMERS FALL TO PIECES. I JUST CAN'T BELIEVE IT'S THE SAME THINGS THAT GET THEM TIME AND TIME AGAIN."
MICHAEL JACKSON

"WHEN WE STARTED IN THIS BUSINESS, WE WERE THE ONES WHO SAID YOU CAN'T TRUST PEOPLE OVER THIRTY."
JONI MITCHELL, 39

"Along with the glamour and guilt of the theory heydays went the obverse side, which is a self-denial of the things beyond the rationale, which was succinct in terms of political theory we'd grown up with, which is basically a post-Marxist one."
Green, Scritti Politti

"I think rock'n'roll in its highest form is a death cult. The Gods of rock'n'roll are all dead...Sid Vicious, Janis Joplin, Jimi Hendrix, Jim Morrison. The best thing you can do in rock'n'roll is die."
Sting, The Police

"Rock'n'roll will last as long as people drink and fuck."
David Coverdale, Whitesnake

"Lately, I have been called Shithouse, Michael Wanker — all that kind of thing."
Michael Schenker

"I disliked everything at school apart from a little bit of Shakespeare. The rest I rejected."
Kirk Brandon, Spear of Destiny

"I feel as if the heavens opened and the gods said, 'We give you the gift of rock'n'roll...take it and do something with it.' "
Gene Simmons, Kiss

"I can't see why anybody would want to buy any of the singles in the Top Ten."
Robert Smith, The Cure

"There can't be anything nicer than getting married and having babies."
Clare Grogan, Altered Images

"An audience is like an animal; sometimes you have to tickle it under the chin but sometimes you have to slap it around the muzzle to get its attention."
Lemmy, Motorhead

"The other day I saw myself in the mirror and I realised I looked like a bank clerk."
Billy MacKenzie, The Associates

❝I THINK BOY GEORGE IS THE NEW ADAM ANT — AND I THINK HE REALISES THAT TOO. WE GET ON VERY WELL — WE'VE GOT TO OPEN FIVE HMV SHOPS TOGETHER OVER THE NEXT FEW WEEKS. ❞
STEVE STRANGE

"I promise a truly memorable performance."
Kevin Rowland, Dexy's Midnight Runners

"Music will always have a massive influence on the way people dress, where they go, what they do — but ultimately it'll have bugger all power come polling-day or come the revolution."
Chego, Hey Elastica

"I'd have to be in jail before somebody could organise me."
Billy Mackenzie, The Associates

"He never relied on drugs and he certainly never became addicted."
Jimmy Page's defence counsel

"I find it bloody irritating that people pay more attention to the 'sociological phenomenon' of Public Image than the music we play."
John Lydon, Public Image Ltd

❝1982 PROVIDED ME WITH ENOUGH MONEY TO BUY EVERY RECORD RAY CHARLES EVER MADE, PRODUCED OR TOUCHED, AND BE ABLE TO AFFORD A WILLIE TRANSPLANT IF I WANTED ONE. ❞
JOOLS HOLLAND

"I once said, 'Americans have no brains', just as a wind-up job, and it worked wonders. Our A&M contract was ripped up just like that."
Jean Jacques Burnel, The Stranglers

"I figure forty-five is a good age to go. Quick heart attack, something like that...or a nice clean decapitation in a car crash."
Lemmy, Motorhead

"To play support to the Feelgoods — that was the ultimate."
Alison Moyet, Yazoo

"When we first started to get a bit successful, some of the girls did start to treat me a bit different. They would buy me drinks 'cause they thought I was famous."
Kelvin, Musical Youth

"Exploiting yourself is much better than exploiting others."
Malcolm McLaren

"All the chicks I know are into shagging. They don't get uptight. Why is there such secrecy? Sex is a big motivation in my life, but if we admit that, we get called sexist."
Brian, Spider

"We don't do lots of drugs or drink because it tends to make life rather difficult . . . you can't go on stage feeling like a bag of old potatoes."
Simon LeBon, Duran Duran

"We had to fight the record company all the way to get it released. They said Simon Bates wouldn't play it — and we said we didn't write songs for Simon Bates."
Terry Hall, Fun Boy Three

❝ TO ME, SOMETHING LIKE STYX REPRESENTS EVERYTHING THAT'S WRONG WITH MUSIC. ❞
PAT BENATAR

❝ THE SORT OF CRITICISM WE RECEIVED FROM THE PRESS HERE WAS BASED ENTIRELY ON COLONIAL PATRONISATION... 'HERE'S ANOTHER BUNCH OF AUSTRALIAN BIMBOS' — THAT SORT OF THING. ❞
IVA DAVIES, ICE HOUSE

"I'm not interested in being a rebel for a weekend or a rebel on tour. Revolution ain't no tea party!"
Kirk Brandon, Spear of Destiny

"I hated Deep Purple's removed, moody, arrogant, asshole image and I refuse to make fat, lazy, boring records."
David Coverdale, Whitesnake

"I want to sink that ship they've just brought up, the *Mary Rose*. And I still want to fuck Maggie Thatcher."
Ozzy Osbourne

"I hate the press. I hate doing interviews. I don't even know why I did this one. I don't want to do any more."
Michael Schenker

"Religion is of no importance apart from the fact that it blinds the majority of the world."
Kirk Brandon, Spear of Destiny

❝ I'M NOT GOING TO DIE THE RICHEST MAN IN THE GRAVEYARD. I WANT TO DIE OWING LOTS OF MONEY. ❞
ROGER DALTREY, THE WHO

"The desire was to produce something special. There is no longer any point. The desire is no longer there."
Julian Cope, The Teardrop Explodes

"ABOUT THREE-QUARTERS OF THE PEOPLE I KNOW ARE UNEMPLOYED AND THEY ARE VERY HAPPY BECAUSE THEY'RE HAVING A GOOD TIME. YOU DON'T HAVE TO HAVE A FUCKING JOB TO ENJOY YOURSELF. "
PAUL CAPLIN, HAYSI FANTAYZEE

"You're supposed to eat when you're hungry, drink when you're dry, sleep when you're tired, and the rest of the time you should do what amuses you. It amuses me to work."
Frank Zappa

"We're not really into late nights and those groupies and parties and all that. I mean, that's all old hat...it's not modern anymore."
Limahl, KajaGooGoo

"Let's be honest, what's Britain got now? English people spend their lives paying for politicians' fuck ups. They should have a Maggie Thatcher Burning Night instead of Guy Fawkes. Politicians are scumbags; they're all fucked."
Ozzy Osbourne

"Just cos you're in a group, you can't forget about school."
Michael, Musical Youth

"I haven't slept with anyone for two years. I never sleep when I have sex. I usually try to stay awake."
Boy George, Culture Club

"The name remains our thirteen-year secret and it remains eternal."
Billy Gibbons, Z Z Top

"There's nothing worse than letting people backstage and they start eating all your food and drinking all your drink."
Steve Severin, Siouxsie & The Banshees

"I could never see myself doing this at David Bowie's age — even if I had his talent."
Gary Numan

"The problem with American record companies is they basically think that all musicians have got very short foreheads and walk with their knuckles on the ground."
Phil Oakey, Human League

"I think we've done more for the sales of double-breasted suits than anybody else."
Midge Ure, Ultravox

"Just because we don't sing about crucial issues doesn't mean we don't believe in them. I think fishing is wonderful, but I don't sing about it."
Baz, Farmer's Boys

"I think 99% of the British public are arseholes because they don't think for themselves, they accept their conditioning."
Ollie Wisdom, The Specimen

"Our records were like being punched in the teeth, but now they're like being punched in the teeth with an apology afterwards."
Phil Taylor, Motorhead

"WHEN YOU DANCE, YOU'RE SHAKING YOUR ARSE AROUND AT PEOPLE IN THE HOPE THAT THEY'LL WANT TO GET HOLD OF IT. "
KATE, HAYSI FANTAYZEE

"I think we have to do more chat shows — let people know we're not three little nigger boys from down the road who eat fish and chips and have snotty noses."
Leee, Imagination

"We're not dealing in violence or destructive self-abuse. We deal in fun."
Tom Bailey, The Thompson Twins

"In Liverpool, there really is nothing. Unless you're a footballer, a boxer, or in a band there's no way out."
Mike Head, Pale Fountains

"OBVIOUSLY, THE PEOPLE WHO I'D LIKE TO APPEAL TO MOST ARE THE SEVEN-YEAR-OLDS BECAUSE THEY AREN'T FULL OF SHIT LIKE OLDER PEOPLE. "
JEREMIAH, HAYSI FANTAYZEE

"The love story between Superman and Lois Lane reminds me of one of my own affairs. Oh, it was just one of those things, you know, things didn't work out. I can be very vulnerable."
Limahl, KajaGooGoo

"Quite honestly we're not qualified for anything except beachcombing and thieving."
Lemmy, Motorhead

"I really believe I should slag Blancmange off — because they have no redeeming features. They offend me no end."
Julian Cope

"I love stuff that isn't solely based in reality. There's like a twilight zone between reality and pure strangeness."
Julian Cope

"I wish people would at least back off a bit and realise that we're trying to do something a bit different — and there are few enough groups around now doing that."
Martyn Ware, Heaven 17

"We are aware that people would much rather know what Boy George thinks about his food than what Orchestral Manoeuvres in the Dark think about genetic engineering."
Andy McCluskey, OMD

"I've found I haven't got my naivety anymore...I still say the same things now, but with maturity."
Ian McCulloch, Echo & The Bunnymen

"I'm not a particularly sexual or sexy person — I just happen to have gorgeous red lips."
Ian McCulloch, Echo & The Bunnymen

" THERE'S A VULNERABILITY WITH PEOPLE LIKE DYLAN THAT MAKES YOU FEEL PROTECTIVE TOWARDS THEM — ALMOST AS IF YOU WANT TO PUT YOUR ARMS ROUND THEM. HE HAD SUCH A HARD TIME, BEING DEIFIED. HE KNEW WHAT HE WAS, AND IT WASN'T GOD. HE'S JUST A VERY SPIRITUAL, POETIC GENTLEMAN. "
MARK KNOPFLER, DIRE STRAITS

"I believe that a lot of young people have just gone off drugs and sex now. I think people are going back to morals."
Boy George, Culture Club

"I have a basic understanding of what interviewers want — so, of course, I told the guy from the *Sun* that we're all gay and fuck bears up the arse, and are members of the Ku-Klux-Klan."
Colin Hay, Men at Work

"I do refute the idea that we're just another electric duo. That's so facile. We think of ourselves as two people who organise sound. Neil and I can't write music — we tend to see it in blocks of colour."
Stephen Luscombe, Blancmange

"Do you really trust this megalomaniac (Margaret Thatcher) with your future? Are you prepared to see life destroyed by the insanity of her and her government?"
Penny Rimbaud, Crass

"I don't like this synthesiser stuff. I think it's very sterile. There's no guts, no soul, no heart. It's as crap as Styx. There's no difference."
Joey Ramone, The Ramones

"When Phil Spector was producing us, there was one chord in 'Rock'n'Roll High School' that he listened back to a thousand times. He wanted to make sure that the overtones and harmonies sounded right in the mix."
Joey Ramone, The Ramones

"The only thing that slightly worries me is if we move too fast for people. What I hope is that we don't go too far ahead to make our early stuff sound ridiculous."
Roland, Tears for Fears

"The trouble with this business is that it's full of peckerheads."
Greg Kihn

"Time for belt tightening. You can't live on a million a year anymore."
Randy Newman

"George is good for us, for our publicity. In fact, he's very normal really."
Michael Craig, Culture Club

"I wear my hair this way because it makes my face look longer, my hat because it makes me look taller, black clothes because they make me look thinner, and make-up because it makes me look prettier."
Boy George, Culture Club

"I always say everything boils down to sex in the end. I'm not trying to wind you up — sex is the driving force. . .and we ain't getting any tonight by the look of it."
Biff Byford, Saxon

"I've felt old all my life."
Pete Townshend

"There is humour in The Banshees — we laugh up our sleeves."
Budgie, Siouxsie & The Banshees

"Why do people come up to you on the street and want to feel your tie? I guess I'm still more attuned to appreciate music on the jazz level. You never ran after Rashied Ali and tried to cut off his coat tail."
Stan Ridgway, Wall of Voodoo

"Even without make-up people recognise me. I've got a big nose, a big mouth, a face people remember."
Boy George, Culture Club

"It would be wrong for me to say 'yes, we can change the world with a song' — but every time I try writing, that's where I'm at. I'm not stupid. I'm aware of the futility of rock'n'roll music, but I'm also aware of its power."
Bono, U2

"Sometimes Ultravox seems to us like a big monster sitting in this sea of fashionable music that keeps waffling past."
Midge Ure, Ultravox

"All round the country the reaction's been bloody brilliant. At one gig someone threw a dead hedgehog at me while I was drumming."
Sean McClusky, JoBoxers

"Well, if I sing the lead, then what's *he* going to do?"
Keith Richards, Rolling Stones

"All the talk about me retiring to become a housewife in Swansea was rubbish. I spent the time looking for songs that would establish me as a rock singer."
Bonnie Tyler

" IT'S NOT JUST A CLOUD CUCKOO LAND THAT I LIVE IN, YOU KNOW. I'M DEBONAIR AND I'M DANGEROUS, I LOVE AND I SUFFER "
MARTIN FRY, ABC

❝I WAS TAUGHT BY JESUITS — THEY ARE RESPONSIBLE FOR MY VENOMOUS NATURE.❞
STING, THE POLICE

"I believe that through working hard, being sensitive, and wanting to be an artist, I got good at what I was doing. My music got good, got unique."
Ric Ocasek, The Cars

"When we started, I was listening to people like John Coltrane more than anything else."
Mark Hollis, Talk Talk

"I got fed up of singing. It was like having Pete Townshend singing with The Who instead of Roger Daltrey."
Steve Jones, The Professionals

"I'd probably find more in a Haircut 100 single than Haircut 100 put into it."
Green, Scritti Politti

"There was a time that I thought we were aspiring to make well-produced melodic records, but we're not — because I bloody well can't sing."
Edwyn Collins, Orange Juice

"Anybody who's naive enough to think they're going into the army to learn a trade deserves to get his head blown off."
Fad Gadget

"We've only just started having to shave every day."
Andy Fletcher, Depeche Mode

"I'd like to have Bo Derek's body with someone else's brain — maybe David Bowie's."
Toyah

"I remember the Clash at the 100 Club saying 'If we ever make money, we are going to be doing things for you people — the kids.' They've never done nothing for anyone."
Rat Scabies, The Damned

"When the Rolling Stones first went to Muscle Shoals, they arrived in the biggest plane that had ever landed at the airport there — and only five people got off it! The people at the Holiday Inn literally had no idea who the Stones were. The last day we were there, we were eating breakfast before flying out again, and one of the waitresses said to Bill Wyman, 'You in a group?' and he said 'Yes, we're Martha & the Vandellas.' "
Jim Dickinson, session man

"I don't like happy songs because that's never been my experience of love affairs."
Marc Almond, Soft Cell

"I feel there are some great pop records with really shitty lyrics."
Peter Gabriel

"I know I'm a tosser. There's nothing wrong with being a tosser — it's a way of life."
Captain Sensible, The Damned

"The cabaret circuit was good enough as training, but you can't really get any satisfaction from playing to people eating chicken in a basket."
Paul Gendler, Modern Romance

"It's not a matter of playing any musical form for the sake of keeping it alive. When I play, I want the air to move."
Ry Cooder

"We are a club band, even though we don't play clubs anymore."
Malcolm Young, AC/DC

"I was stoned for every bit of music I've ever played. Every record, every performance — I was stoned halfway out of my gourd."
David Crosby, Crosby, Stills & Nash

"I don't get out as much as I used to."
Arthur Lee

"I've got a few sexual vices, baby lotion and the like, but I don't feel the need to sing about them."
Abbo, UK Decay

"At school, the teachers were convinced I was a drug addict. The headmaster once summoned me to his office and asked me if I'd tripped lately."
Marc Almond, Soft Cell

"I am a man now too. I think even Freddie Mercury is falling in love with me because I am a man."
Nina Hagen

"I don't mind when critics put down our music by saying it sounds like Styx or Journey or Boston or Aerosmith . . . those are my favourite bands, so I'm flattered."
Craig Chaquico, Jefferson Starship

"I read things about, say, ABC and think 'what are they doing that Hot Chocolate hasn't been doing for years?' These days, every band likes to be thought of as dance-oriented — so I guess they've caught up with us."
Errol Brown, Hot Chocolate

❝YOU'VE GOT TO TRY AND KEEP YOUR HEAD ABOVE WATER AND THE ONLY WAY WE CAN DO THAT IS BY TRYING TO KEEP OUR FACES IN THE CHARTS. IT'S ALL VERY WELL BEING AN UNDERGROUND GROUP, BUT 'UNDERGROUND' IS JUST A WORD FOR UNPOPULAR.❞
RODDY FRAME, AZTEC CAMERA

"FASHION HAS CHANGED. NO LONGER IS IT UNHIP TO ACHIEVE COMMERCIAL RECOGNITION. INDEED, WHERE COMMERCIALITY ONCE WAS SCORNED, IT IS NOW EMBRACED."
ALISON MOYET, YAZOO

"It's difficult to make a commercial album that doesn't mention sex. Writing about sex is pretty easy. I get extremely bored doing these sexual numbers anyway."
Marvin Gaye

"It's important that people understand that I'm not a mercenary, a commercialist or just a singer. It takes a lot of balls to do the things I have done in life. One has to be strong willed in his art and truly believe that he's an artist."
Marvin Gaye

"When he took all our money I said 'Malcolm (McLaren), you took all our money' and he said 'But I taught you all about wine!' and I said 'Fair enough!' I love the geezer! That's his trick — he gets you to love him, then he rips you off blind. He's a dodgy bastard!"
Dave Barbe, Bow Wow Wow

"If we stay in small clubs we'll develop small minds, and then we'll start making small music."
Bono, U2

"I just don't fit into the predominant image of rock'n'roll. I saw what drugs were doing to people and, in most cases, I had to suffer the consequences of their substandard work."
Steve Winwood

"I tried to charm the pants off Bob Dylan but everyone will be disappointed to learn that I was unsuccessful. I got close...a couple of fast feels in the front seat of his Cadillac."
Bette Midler

"I bought Lou Reed's *Sally Can't Dance* and listened to both sides six hundred times. When you bought a record then, it was a big fucking deal."
Johnny Cougar

"I think we've shown that you can be hugely successful, which we are, and still remain decent, caring and honest. I think we're the first group ever to do that."
Paul Weller, The Jam

"There's chaos in this country right now; this is not going to be a peaceful decade."
Paul Kantner, Jefferson Starship

"How can you be a rebel when rebellion is the norm? Rock'n'roll has lost its power as a revolutionary force, it really has, and there's no way it can actually get that back."
Sting, The Police

"My mother isn't particularly impressed by my music, although I think she's relieved that I didn't overdose on drugs or become a fully-fledged petty criminal."
Richard Hell

"Rock'n'roll is trying to convince girls to pay money to be near you."
Richard Hell

"I wanted to go bald once, because of Howard Devoto."
Garry Daly, China Crisis

"Our ideas are emotional and each one is a seed. The degree to which we're successful is the degree to which we plant a fertile seed in somebody's mind."
Chuck, Black Flag

"IF I REALLY WANTED JUST TO FURTHER MY CAREER I'D DO ALL THOSE AWFUL PROGRAMMES LIKE *PUNCHLINES*. I DID *BLANKETY BLANK* ONCE AND HATED IT. I WON'T DO THINGS LIKE THAT AGAIN."
TRACEY ULLMAN

"The British music scene is absolute crap. There are still all these guitar-based bands churning out the same stuff, and it's meaningless. It doesn't do anything, it doesn't achieve anything, and it's just boring."
Paul Weller, Style Council

"I have become more spiritual in the last two weeks. I know God wants me to be a singer."
Rod Stewart

"Pain is my girlfriend, that's how I see it. I feel pain every day of my life. When you see me perform, it's that pain you're seeing, coming out. I put all my emotions, all my feelings, and my body on the line. People hurt me, I hurt myself — mentally, physically."
Henry Rollins, Black Flag

"I wanted to be a pimp, but I thought 'wait a minute, how can I have money and drugs and women and not be running from the FBI?...music!'"
Charles Alexander, Prince Charles & The City Beat Band

"I have emotion in my music. I like writing songs like 'Big chested girls'. I might write a song about big asses next."
Charles Alexander, Prince Charles & The City Beat Band

"If everyone takes ABC seriously then perhaps there is no hope."
Tracey Thorn

ROCK REFERENCE

RECORD COMPANIES/UK

A&M Records
(01) 736 3311
136/140 New Kings Road,
London SW6.

Abstract Records Ltd.
(01) 969 4018
35 Kempe Road,
London NW6 6SP.

Ace Records
(01) 267 5192
132/134 Grafton Road,
Kentish Town,
London NW5.
Labels: Big Beat, Kent, Damned, Thrust,
Ear to Ear, Cascade, Nitelife.

Albion Records Ltd.
(01) 243 0011/221 3113
119/121 Freston Road,
London W11 4BD.

Arista/Ariola
(01) 580 5566
3 Cavendish Square,
London W1.

Aura Records and Music Ltd.
(01) 486 5288
1 Kendall Place,
London W1H 3AG.

Backs Recording Company Ltd.
(0603) 26221
St. Mary's Works,
St. Mary's Plain,
Norwich NR3 3AF.

BBC Records and Tapes
(01) 580 4468
The Langham,
Portland Place,
London W1A 1AA.

Beggar's Banquet
(01) 870 9912
17/19 Alma Road,
London SW18.

Big Bear Records
(021) 454 7020
190 Monument Road,
Birmingham B16 8UU.
Labels: Grandstand, Truckers Delight.

Bridge House Records Ltd.
(01) 476 9947
15 Tinto Road,
London E16 4BB.

Bright Records
(01) 408 0288
34/36 Maddox Street,
London W1R 9PD.

Bronze Records
(01) 267 4499
100 Chalk Farm Road,
London NW1 8EH.

Burning Rome Records
(01) 240 7443
25 Denmark Street,
London WC2.

Carrere Records UK
(01) 493 7406
22 Queen Street,
Mayfair,
London W1X 7PJ.

CBS
(01) 734 8181
17/19 Soho Square,
London W1.
Labels: Epic, Portrait, Full Moon,
Monument, Philadelphia International,
Kirshner, Tabu, Caribou, Unlimited Gold,
Boardwalk, Prelude, Blue Sky, Alfa,
Geffen, Scotti Bros, Inner Vision.

Charisma
(01) 434 1351
90 Wardour Street,
London W1.

Charly Records Ltd.
(01) 639 8603/4/5/6
156/177 Ilderton Road,
London SE15 1NT.

Cherry Red Records
(01) 229 8854/5
53 Kensington Gardens Square,
London W2 4BA.
Labels: Pipe, Kathedral, City, Zebra,
Anagram.

Chiswick Records
(01) 267 5192
132 Grafton Road,
Kentish Town,
London NW5.

Chrysalis
(01) 408 2355
12 Stratford Place,
London W1N 9AF.
Labels: Two Tone, Reformation.

Clay
(0782) 273324
26 Hope Street,
Stoke-on-Trent,
Staffordshire.

Cocteau Records
(01) 398 6413
PO Box 134A,
Thames Ditton,
Surrey.

Crass Records
(01) 888 8949
PO Box 279,
London Road,
London N22.

Creole Records Ltd.
(01) 965 9223
91/93 High Street,
Harlesden,
London NW10.
Labels: Polo, Dynamic, Ecstasy, Replay,
Ocean, Cactus, Blast From the Past.

Decca International Ltd.
(01) 743 9111
1 Rockley Road,
London W14.
Labels: Ace of Clubs, Ace of Diamonds,
Argo, Eclipse, L'Oiseau, Lyre, Threshold,
Viva.

Demon Records Ltd.
(01) 847 2481
28 The Butts,
Brentford,
Middlesex TW8 8BL.
Label: Edsel.

Dep International
(021) 643 1321
92 Fazeley Street,
Digbeth,
Birmingham B5 5RD.

DJM Records
(01) 242 6886
James House,
5/11 Theobalds Road,
London WC1X 8SE.
Label: Champagne.

Don't Fall Off the Mountain
(01) 870 9912
17/19 Alma Road,
Wandsworth,
London SW5.

EG Records
(01) 730 2162
63a Kings Road,
London SW3 4NT.
Label: Editions EG.

EMI Records (UK)
(01) 486 4488
20 Manchester Square,
London W1A 1ES.
Labels: Harvest, Parlophone, Columbia,
Zonophone, Starline, Capitol, Liberty,
HMV, EMI America, MFP, LFP, CFP,
World Records, Sunset, Rolling Stones.

Ensign Records Ltd.
(01) 727 0527
3 Monmouth Place,
Off Monmouth Road,
London W2 5SH.

F-Beat Records
(01) 847 2481
28 The Butts,
Brentford,
Middx TW8 8BL.

Factory Records
(061) 434 3876
86 Palatine Road,
Manchester 20.

Fiction Records
(01) 723 9269
46a Montagu Square,
London W1.

Flicknife
(01) 743 9412
82 Adelaide Grove,
London W12.

Glass Records
(01) 289 3108
79 Wellesley Court,
Maida Vale,
London W9.

Go! Discs (Universal)
(01) 995 6131
Go! Mansions,
1 Gleve Street,
Chiswick,
London W5.

Graduate Records Ltd.
(0384) 59048/211159
196 Wolverhampton Street,
Dudley,
West Midlands.
Labels: Ready Steady Go!, Fifth Column,
CMS Records Jamaica.

Greensleeves Records Ltd.
(01) 749 3277/8
44 Uxbridge Road,
Shepherd's Bush,
London W12.

Hannibal Records
(01) 381 5119
Unit 1,
21/27 Seagrave Road,
London SW6.

Heartbeat Productions
(0272) 730458
14c Lansdown Place,
Clifton,
Bristol BS8 3AF.
Labels: Riot City Records, Disorder
Records, Riot State Records.

Ice Record Company
(01) 607 6183
85 Richmond Avenue,
Islington,
London N1.

Illuminated Records
452 Fulham Road,
London SW6.

Imperial Records
(01) 969 9414
Imperial Records,
Kensaltown Works,
Kensal Road,
London W10.

Independent Record Labels Ltd.
(01) 727 0734
194 Kensington Park Road,
London W11 2ES.
Labels: IRS, Illegal, Step-Forward, Total
Noise, WXYZ, Deptford Fun City.

Island Records
(01) 741 1511
22 St Peters Square,
London W6L 9NW.
Labels: Springtime, Taxi, Shelter, Ze,
Genetic, Crepuscule.

Jamming Records
(01) 602 0048
69 Hammersmith Road,
London W14.

Jet Records
(01) 637 2111
35 Portland Place,
London W1N 3AG.

K-Tel International (UK) Ltd.
(01) 992 8055
620 Western Avenue,
London W3.
Labels: Lotus, Era.

Lamborghini Records
(01) 286 1283
Flat 14,
Vale Court,
Maida Vale,
London W9.

Lightning Records
(01) 969 5255
841 Harrow Road,
London NW10 5NH.

London Records
(01) 491 4600
13-14 George Street,
London W1R 9DE.
Labels: Compact, Deram, Qualiton, Rex,
Vocalion.

Magnet Records
(01) 486 8151
Magnet House,
22 York Street,
London W1H 1FD.

MCA Records Ltd.
(01) 439 9951
1 Great Pulteney Street,
London W1.

Motown
(01) 636 8311
1 Bedford Avenue,
London WC1.

Music for Pleasure
(01) 561 3125
1/3 Uxbridge Road,
Hayes,
Middx UB4 0SY.

Mute Records
(01) 221 4840
49/53 Kensington Gardens Square,
London W2.

Neat Records
(0632) 624999
71 High Street,
East Wallsend,
Tyne and Wear NE28 7RJ.
Labels: Wudwink, Rigid, Completely,
Different.

No Future Records
(06845) 65319/68036
3 Adelaide House,
21 Wells Road,
Malvern,
Worcestershire W14 4RH.

Oily Records
(0224) 632749
6 Cedar Place,
Aberdeen,
Scotland AB2 3SZ.

Old Gold Records Ltd.
(01) 969 0155
350 Kilburn Lane,
London W9 3EF.

Oval Records
(01) 622 0111
11 Liston Road,
London SW4.

People Unite Musicians Co-Op
(01) 574 0888/541 0653
45 Lea Road,
Southall,
Middx.

Phonogram Ltd.
(01) 491 4600
50 New Bond Street,
London W1Y 9HA.
Labels: Mercury, Vertigo, Philips,
Fontana, De-Lite, Casablanca, Some
Bizzare, Rocket, Charisma, Neutron,
20th Century.

Pickwick International Inc. (GB) Ltd.
(01) 200 7000
The Hyde Industrial Estate,
The Hyde,
London NW9 6JU.
Labels: Hallmark, Contour, Marble Arch,
Camden, Contour Classics, Spot, Ditto.

Polydor Ltd.
(01) 499 8686
13/14 George Street,
London W1R 9DE.
Labels: RSO, MGM, Verve, Obscure,
Fiction, Energy, Dreamland, CTI, Kudu,
Spring, Capricorn, Privilege, Helidor,
Twenty One, Wonderland, Archive,
Editions EG.

Pop Aural
(031) 661 5811/2
3/4 East Norton Place,
Abbeyhill,
Edinburgh.
Labels: Fast Product, Accessory.

President Records Ltd.
(01) 839 4672/5
Broadmead House,
21 Panton Street,
London SW1Y 4DR.
Labels: Aquarius, Barak, Bulldog,
Crystal, Dart, Energy, Enterprise, Gemini,
Jayboy, Joy, Max's Kansas City, New
World, Rhapsody, Seville, Spiral,
Thunderbird, Torpedo.

Probe
(051) 227 5646
8-12 Rainford Gardens,
Liverpool 2.

PRT Records
(01) 262 8040
ACC House,
17 Great Cumberland Place,
London W1A 1AG.

Radialchoice Records
(01) 853 5899
17 Nelson Road,
Greenwich,
London SE10.

RAK Records Ltd.
(01) 586 2112
42 Charlbert Street,
London NW8.

RCA
(01) 636 8311
1 Bedford Avenue,
London WC1.
Labels: Motown, Carrere, Ice, Regard,
Salsoul, KR Records, Red Seal.

Recreational Records
(0272) 299105
1 Berkeley Crescent,
The Triangle,
Clifton,
Bristol BS8 1HA.

Red Flame Ltd.
(01) 743 0006
The Metrostore,
231 The Vale,
Acton,
London W3 7QS.

Red Rhino
(0904) 36499
9 Gillygate,
York.

Revolver Records
(0272) 211115/299105
1 Berkeley Crescent,
The Triangle,
Bristol BS8 1HA.
Labels: Riot City, Recreational, Round
Ear, Dakka Da Dak, Take A Hammer,
Freedom City, Insane, Resurrection,
Fried Egg.

Riva Records Ltd.
(01) 731 4131
2 New Kings Road,
London SW8.
Label: GM.

The Rocket Record Company Ltd.
(01) 938 1741
125 Kensington High Street,
London W8 5SN.

Ronco Teleproducts Ltd.
(01) 274 7761
Ellerslie Park,
11 Lyham Road,
London SW2.

Rough Trade Records
(01) 229 2146/727 6085
137 Blenheim Crescent,
London W11.
Label: DATC.

Safari Records
(01) 723 8464
44 Seymour Place,
London W1.
Label: Singing Dog Records.

Saga Records Ltd.
(01) 969 6651
Labels: Trojan, B&C, Mooncrest.

Satril Records
(01) 435 8063
Satri House,
444 Finchley Road,
London NW2.

Secret Records (London) Ltd.
(01) 870 8522
362 York Road,
London SW18 1SP.

Shout Records
(01) 381 1393
452 Fulham Road,
London SW6.

Situation 2
(01) 870 9912
17/19 Alma Road,
London SW18.

Small Wonder Records Ltd.
(01) 520 5036
162 Hoe Street,
London E17.

Sonet Records
(01) 229 7267
121 Ledbury Road,
London W11.

Statik Records
(01) 381 0116/385 0567
1a Normand Gardens,
Greyhound Road,
London W14.

Stiff Records
(01) 485 5622
115/123 Bayham Street,
Camden Town,
London NW1 0A1.
Label: Ranting Records.

Superville Records
(0904) 55584
9/10 Bridge Street,
York YO1 1DD.
Labels: Supermusic, Exploited.

Towerbell Records
(01) 794 6702
32/34 Gondar Gardens,
London NW6.
Labels: Rockney, Shelf, Cockerel.

Trojan Recordings Ltd.
(01) 969 6651
326 Kensal Road,
London W10 5BL.
Label: Mooncrest.

Upright
(01) 229 8856
49/53 Kensington Gardens Square,
London W2 4BA.
Label: Alternative Tentacles.

Virgin Records Ltd.
(01) 727 8070
2/4 Vernon Yard,
119 Portobello Road,
London W11 2DX.
Labels: Caroline, Frontline,
WMOT.

WEA Records Ltd
(01) 434 3232
20 Broadwick Street,
London W1V 2BH.
Labels: Asylum, Atlantic, Cotillion, Dark
Horse, Elektra, Korova, Radar, Reprise,
Warner Brothers, Sire, Swansong.

Wonderful World of...
(051) 708 0193
16 Benson Street,
Liverpool 1.

Y Records
(01) 743 2318/2336
70a Uxbridge Road,
London W12.

Zomba Productions Ltd.
(01) 451 3044
Zomba House,
165/167 Willesden High Road,
London NW10 2SG.
Label: Jive.

RECORD COMPANIES/US

Alternative Tentacles
PO Box 11458
San Francisco, CA 94101

A&M Records
(213) 469 2411
1416 North La Brea,
Hollywood, CA 90028.
New York office:
(212) 826 0477
595 Madison Avenue,
New York, NY 10022.
Affiliated labels: I.R.S., Horizon.

Arista Records
(212) 489 7400
6 West 57 Street,
New York, NY 10019.
Affiliated labels: Jive, Buddah, GRP,
Ariola, Savoy, Genetic.

Atlantic Recording Corp.
(212) 484 6000
75 Rockefeller Plaza,
New York, NY 10019.
L.A. office:
(213) 278 9230
9229 Sunset Boulevard,
Los Angeles, CA 90069.
Affiliated labels: Atco, Cotillion, Emerald
City, Finnadar, Mirage, Modern, Pacific,
RFC, Radio, Rolling Stones, Swansong,
Duke, Island.

Bearsville Records
(914) 679 7303
PO Box 135,
Bearsville, NY 12409.

The Boardwalk Entertainment Co.
(213) 656 2840
8255 Sunset Boulevard,
Los Angeles, CA 90046.
New York office:
(212) 765 5103
888 Seventh Avenue,
New York, NY 10019.

Bomp Records
(213) 227 4141
2702 San Fernando Road,
Los Angeles, CA 90065.
Labels: Quark, Voxx, Invasion.

Buddah Records Inc.
(212) 582 6900
1790 Broadway,
New York, NY 10019.
Affiliated label: Kama Sutra.

Cachalot Records
(212) 254 1979
611 Broadway,
New York, NY 10012.

Capitol Records
(213) 462 6252
1750 North Vine Street,
Hollywood, CA 90028.
New York office:
(212) 757 7470
1370 Avenue of the Americas,
New York, NY 10019.
Affiliated labels: Angel, Blue Note, EMI
America, Gold Coast, Harvest, Seraphim,
Sunbird.

CBS Records
(212) 975 4321
51 West 52 Street,
New York, NY 10019.
L.A. office:
(213) 556 4700
1801 Century Park West,
Los Angeles, CA 90067.
CBS labels: Epic, Columbia, Portrait,
CBS Masterworks, Odyssey, CBS.
CBS associated labels: BID, Bang, Blue
Sky, Caribou, Coast to Coast, Chrysalis,
Curb, Johnston, Kirshner, Lynx,
Nemperor, Pasha, Pavillion,
Philadelphia Int'l, Precision,
Rock'n'Roll, Scotti Brothers, T-Neck,
TSOP, Uncle Jam, Unlimited Gold,
John Hammond.

Chrysalis Records
(212) 758 3555
645 Madison Avenue,
New York, NY 10022.
Affiliated labels: Animal, 2 Tone,
Radialchoice, Bronze, Air.

Columbia Records
Same as CBS Records.
Associated labels: ARC, Stiff-Columbia,
415.

Compendium Inc.
(404) 525 1679
432 Moreland Avenue,
Atlanta, GA 30307.
Labels: DB, Press.

Cream Records
(213) 655 0944
8025 Melrose Avenue,
Los Angeles, CA 90046.
Affiliated label: Hi.

Dischord Records
(703) 243 2454
3819 Beecher Street NW,
Washington, DC 20007.

ECM Records
(212) 888 1122
509 Madison Avenue,
New York, NY 10022.

Elektra/Asylum/Nonesuch Records
(212) 355 7610
665 Fifth Avenue,
New York, NY 10022.
L.A. office:
(213) 655 8280
962 North LaCienega,
Los Angeles, CA 90069.
Affiliated labels: Beserkley, Curb, Solar,
Musician, Ze.

EMI America/Liberty Records
(213) 462 6252
1750 North Vine Street,
Hollywood, CA 90028.
New York office:
(212) 757 7470
1370 Avenue of the Americas,
New York, NY 10019.
Affiliated labels: United Artists,
Blue Note.

Enigma Records
(213) 533 8075
PO Box 2896,
20445 Gramercy Place,
Torrance, CA 90509.

Epic/Portrait/Associated Labels
Same as CBS.
Associated labels: City Lights, Cleveland
Int'l, Full Moon, Park Lane, Lorimar,
Stiff-Epic, Virgin, Carrere.

Fantasy/Prestige/Milestone/Stax
(415) 549 2500
10th and Parker Streets,
Berkeley, CA 94710.
Affiliated labels: Galaxy, Riverside.

Folkways Records and Service Corp.
(212) 586 7260
43 West 61 Street,
New York, NY 10023.
Labels: Asch, Broadsides, RBF.

415 Records
(415) 552 1379
PO Box 14563,
San Francisco, CA 94114.

Frontier Records
(213) 765 4850
Box 22,
Sun Valley, CA 91352.

Geffen Records
(213) 278 9010
9126 Sunset Boulevard,
Los Angeles, CA 90069.
New York office:
(212) 484 8000
75 Rockefeller Plaza,
New York, NY 10019.

Handshake Records
(212) 245 3600
730 Fifth Avenue,
New York, NY 10022.
L.A. office:
(213) 655 8635
8304 Beverly Boulevard,
Los Angeles, CA 90048.

Hannibal Records
(212) 420 1780
611 Broadway,
New York, NY 10012.

International Record Syndicate (I.R.S.)
(213) 489 2411
1416 North LaBrea,
Hollywood, CA 90028.
New York office:
(212) 826 0477
595 Madison Avenue,
New York, NY 10022.
Affiliated labels: Faulty Products,
Illegal Records.

Island Records
(212) 355 6550
444 Madison Avenue,
New York, NY 10022.
Affiliated labels: Mango, Antilles.

Jem Records Inc.
(201) 753 6100
3619 Kennedy Road,
South Plainfield, NJ 07080.
West Coast office:
(213) 996 6754
18629 Topham Street,
Reseda, CA 91335.
Associated labels: Passport, PVC, Visa,
Editions EG.

Landslide Records Inc.
(404) 873 3918
450 14 Street NW,
Atlanta, GA 30318.

Lovely Music Ltd.
(212) 243 6153
325 Spring Street,
New York, NY 10013.
Affiliated label: Antarctica.

MCA Records Inc.
(213) 985 4321
70 Universal City Plaza,
Universal City, CA 91608.
New York office:
(212) 888 9700
10 East 53 Street,
New York, NY 10022.
Affiliated labels: Backstreet, Coral, Dot,
Duke, Dunhill, Impulse, Paramount,
Sweet City.

Mobile Fidelity Sound Lab.
(213) 709 8440
21040 Nordhoff Street,
Chatsworth, CA 91311.

Modern Method
(617) 247 7590
268 Newbury Street,
Boston, MA 02116.

Motown Record Corp.
(213) 468 3500
6255 Sunset Boulevard,
Los Angeles, CA 90028.
Labels: Gordy, Natural Resources,
Prodigal, Rare Earth, Soul, Tamla.

99 Records
(212) 777 4610
99 MacDougal Street,
New York, NY 10012.

PolyGram Records Inc.
(212) 399 7100
810 Seventh Avenue,
New York, NY 10019.
L.A. office:
(213) 277 1412
1930 Century Park West,
Los Angeles, CA 90067.
Affiliated labels: Casablanca, Mercury,
London, MGM, Verve, Chocolate City, De-
Lite, MVP, RSO, Riva, Spring, Polydor,
Twin Tone.

Posh Boy Records and Tapes
(213) 466 7755
PO Box 38861,
Los Angeles, CA 90038.

Propellor Records
Box 658,
Allston Station,
Boston, MA 02134.

Ralph Records
(415) 543 4085
109 Minna Street,
San Francisco, CA 94105.

RCA Records
(212) 930 4000
1133 Avenue of the Americas,
New York, NY 10036.
L.A. office:
(213) 468 4000
6363 Sunset Boulevard,
Hollywood, CA 90028.
Affiliated labels: Grunt, Millenium,
Gold Seal, Pure Gold, Bluebird, Salsoul,
Pablo.

Reachout International Records (ROIR)
(212) 477 0563
611 Broadway,
New York, NY 10012.

Rhino Records
(213) 450 6323
1201 Olympic Boulevard,
Santa Monica, CA 90404.

Rollin' Rock Records
(213) 781 4805
6918 Peach Avenue,
Van Nuys, CA 91406.
Labels: American Rhythm Music,
Boppin' Belle, California Rockabilly, Ray
Campi, Ollie, Ragin' Rockabilly,
Rockabilly Rebellion, Rockin' Ronny,
Rockin' Weiser.

Rough Trade Inc.
(415) 621 4186
326 Sixth Street,
San Francisco, CA 94103.
Associated label: Factory.

Rounder Records
(617) 354 0700
1 Camp Street,
Cambridge, MA 02140.

Salsoul Record Corp.
(212) 889 7340
401 Fifth Avenue,
New York, NY 10016.
Labels: Bethlehem, Dream, Gold Mind.

Shanachie Records Corp.
(201) 445 5561
Dalebrook Park,
HoHoKus, NJ 07423.

Slash Records
(213) 937 4660
7381 Beverly Boulevard,
Los Angeles, CA 90036.
Label: Ruby.

Sounds Interesting Records
PO Box 54,
Stone Harbor, NJ 08247.

SST Records
(213) 376 5887
Box 1,
Lawndale, CA 90260.

Subterranean Records
(415) 841 3488
577 Valencia,
San Francisco, CA 94110.

Sugar Hill Records Inc.
(201) 569 5170
96 West Street,
Englewood, NJ 07631.

Tommy Boy Records
(212) 348 4700
210 East 90 Street,
New York, NY 10028.

Twin Tone Records
(612) 377 9541
445 Oliver Avenue South,
Minneapolis, MN 55405.

Vanguard Recording Society, Inc.
(212) 255 7732
71 West 23 Street,
New York, NY 10010.
Labels: O, Flip.

Warner Bros Records Inc.
(213) 846 9090
3300 Warner Boulevard,
Burbank, CA 91510.
New York office:
(212) 702 0318
3 East 54 Street,
New York, NY 10022.
Affiliated labels: Sire, Bearsville, Slash,
ECM, Geffen, Reprise, Dark Horse.

Wasp Records
(703) 522 6497
821 North Taylor Street,
Arlington, VA 22203.

ZE Records and Tapes
(212) 245 7233
154 West 57 Street,
New York, NY 10019.

MUSIC PUBLISHERS/UK

Albion Music Ltd.
(01) 243 0011
119/121 Freston Road,
London W11 4BD.

Ambassador Music Ltd.
(01) 836 5996
22 Denmark Street,
London WC2.

April Music Ltd.
(01) 439 1845
37 Soho Square,
London W1V 5DG.

Arnakata Music Ltd.
(01) 723 8424
10L Oxford & Cambridge Mansions,
Transcept Street,
London NW1.

Arretta Music Ltd.
(66) 27099/25741
Electron House,
Cray Avenue,
St. Mary Cray,
Orpington,
Kent BR5 8QJ.

Ash Music Publishers
(0623) 752448
Cropwell House,
Salmon Lane,
Kirkby-in-Ashfield,
Notts.

ASL Publishing
(0633) 856327
5 Ogmore Crescent,
Bettws,
Newport,
Gwent NPT 6SP.

Asterisk Music
(01) 397 9857
PO Box 18F,
Chessington,
Surrey KT9 1UZ.

ATV Music Ltd.
(01) 409 2211
19 Upper Brook Street,
London W1Y 1PD.

Automatic Music
5 Avery Row,
London W1X 9HA.

Balgier Ltd.
(021) 643 7727
Room 32,
Princes Chambers,
6 Coronation Street,
Birmingham B2 4RN.

Banks Music Publications
(0904) 21818
139 Holgate Road,
York YO2 4DF.

Barn Publishing Ltd.
(01) 637 2111
35 Portland Place,
London W1.

Beadle Music Ltd.
(0444) 457454
The Old Cottage,
Lunces Common,
Haywards Heath,
Sussex.

Belsize Music Ltd.
(01) 491 3175
38 North Row,
London W1R 1DH.

Big Ben Music Ltd.
(01) 723 4499
18 Lancaster Mews,
London W2 3QE.

Big Secret Music
(0735) 213623
Havoc House,
Beenham,
Berkshire.

Black Sheep Music Ltd.
(395) 2109/2143
Fulmer Gardens House,
Fulmer,
Bucks.

Bocu Music Ltd.
(01) 402 7433/4/5
1 Wyndham Yard,
Wyndham Place,
London W1H 1AR.

Bourne Music Ltd.
(01) 493 6412
34/36 Maddox Street,
London W1R 9PD.

Bread Lion Music
Lion Studios,
Aire Street Workshops,
31 Aire Street,
Leeds LS1 4HT.

Bridge House Music Ltd.
(01) 476 9947
15 Tinto Road,
Canning Town,
London EJ6 4BB.

Sydney Bron Music Co. Ltd.
(01) 267 4499
100 Chalk Farm Road,
London NW1 8EH.

Brothers Music Ltd.
(01) 794 9177
5 Hollycroft Avenue,
London NW3 7QG.

BTW (Music) Ltd.
(01) 888 6655
125 Myddleton Road,
Wood Green,
London N22 4NG.

Bullseye Music Ltd.
(0388) 814632
AIR House,
Spennymoor,
Co. Durham DL16 7SE.

Burlington Music Co. Ltd.
(01) 499 0067
40 South Audley Street,
London W1.

Cambar Music Ltd.
(01) 434 2525
17 Newburgh Street,
London W1V 1LE.

Carlin Music Corporation
(01) 734 3251
14 New Burlington Street,
London W1X 2LR.

Centridge Ltd.
(01) 272 7501
PO Box 137,
London N7 0EF.

Chappell Music Ltd.
(01) 629 7600
129 Park Street,
London W1Y 3FA.

Charly Publishing Ltd.
(01) 732 5647
46/47 Pall Mall,
London SW1 5JG.

Cherry Music
(01) 437 7418/9
49 Greek Street,
London W1.

Chevron Music Publishing Ltd.
(0532) 38283
The Television Centre,
Leeds LS3 1JS.

Christabel Music Ltd.
(0532) 677480
73 The Avenue,
Alwoodley,
Leeds 17.

Chrysalis Music Ltd.
(01) 408 2355
12 Stratford Place,
London W1N 9AF.

Barry Cole Music Ltd.
(02273) 67241
65/69 Mortimer Street,
Herne Bay,
Kent CT6 5PR.

Collins Music Company
(01) 258 3891
38 Kendal Street,
London W2.

Barry Collings Music Ltd.
(0702) 43464
15 Claremont Road,
Westcliff-on-Sea,
Essex.

Creole Music Ltd.
(01) 965 9223
91/93 High Street,
Harlesden,
London NW10.

Eaton Music Ltd.
(01) 235 9046
8 West Eaton Place,
London SW1X 8LS.

Ebony Music
(0482) 25850
18 Mayfield Street,
Spring Bank,
Hull HU3 1NS.

John Edward Music Ltd.
(01) 806 1121/2
38/40 Upper Clapton Road,
London E5 8BQ.

Edwardson Music Ltd.
(01) 935 7615
106 Bickenhall Mansions,
London W1H 3LB.

EG Music Ltd.
(01) 730 2162
63a King's Road,
London SW3 4NT.

EMI Music Publishing
(01) 836 6699
138/140 Charing Cross Road,
London WC2H 0LD.

E & S Music Ltd.
(01) 409 3122
46 South Molton Street,
Mayfair,
London W1Y 1HE.

TRO Essex Music Ltd.
(01) 637 7665
85 Gower Street,
London WC1.

Faber Music Ltd.
(01) 278 6881
3 Queen Square,
London WC1N 3AU.

Fast Western Ltd.
(01) 723 9559/402 4024
2 York House,
Upper Montagu Street,
London W1.

Fentone Music Ltd.
(05366) 60981
Fleming Road,
Earlstrees,
Corby,
Northants.

Noel Gay Music Co. Ltd.
(01) 836 3941
24 Denmark Street,
London WC2H 8NJ.

Graduate Music Ltd.
(0384) 59048/211159
Chaddesley House,
196 Wolverhampton Street,
Dudley,
W. Midlands.

Halcyon Music Ltd.
(01) 586 0288
11 Howitt Road,
London NW3.

Handle Music Ltd.
(01) 493 9637
1 Derby Street,
London W1.

Hansa Productions
(01) 402 2191
26 Castlereagh Street,
London W1.

Happy Face Music
(0905) 820659
The Old Smithy,
Post Office Lane,
Kempsey,
Worcs.

Heath Levy Music Co. Ltd.
(01) 439 7731
184/186 Regent Street,
London W1R 5DF.

Hedley Music
(0246) 79976
71 Rutland Road,
Chesterfield,
Derbys S40 1ND.

Heisenberg Ltd.
(01) 703 7677
18 Crofton Road,
London SE5 8NB.

Hensley Music Publishing Co. Ltd.
(01) 727 5118
29 Clarendon Road,
London W11 4JB.

Hollywood Music
(01) 806 0071
38/40 Upper Clapton Road,
London E5.

Hub Music
(01) 891 3146
4/10 Queens Road,
Twickenham TW1 4ES.

Hush Music Ltd.
(01) 589 6293
117c Fulham Road,
London SW3.

Intersong Music Ltd.
(01) 499 0067
40 South Audley Street,
London W1Y 5DH.

Island Music Ltd.
(01) 741 1511
22 St. Peter's Square,
Hammersmith,
London W6 9NW.

Ivory Coast Music Ltd.
(01) 381 1393
452 Fulham Road,
London SW6.

Kamela Music Ltd.
(061) 652 2491
225 Ripponden Road,
Oldham,
Lancs OL1 4HR.

Edward Kassner Music Co. Ltd.
(01) 839 4672
21 Panton Street,
London SW1.

Kenmar Music Company
(01) 437 3711/2
11 Great Marlborough Street,
London W1A 4QD.

Kennick Music
(01) 589 7711/8861
Flat 3,
50 Cadogan Square,
London SW1X 0JW.

Lantern Music Publishing Co. Ltd.
(01) 828 4595
66 Roebuck House,
Palace Street,
London SW1.

Logorhythm Music Ltd.
(01) 734 7443
6/10 Lexington Street,
London W1.

Louvigny Music Co. Ltd.
(01) 493 5961
38 Hertford Street,
London W1Y 8BA.

Magnet Music Ltd.
(01) 486 8151
22 York Street,
London W1H 1FD.

MAM (Music Publishing) Ltd.
(01) 629 9255
24/25 New Bond Street,
London W1Y 9HD.

Sue Manning Music Publishing Ltd.
(01) 831 8796
161 Drury Lane,
London WC2.

Martin-Coulter Music Ltd.
(01) 582 7622
11th Floor,
Alembic House,
93 Albert Embankment,
London SE1 7TY.

MCA Music Ltd.
(01) 629 7211
139 Piccadilly,
London W1V 9FH.

Midnight Music Ltd.
(01) 845 1518
58 Islip Manor Road,
Northolt,
Middx.

Morrison Leahy Music Ltd.
(01) 402 9238
Flat 3,
1 Hyde Park Place,
London W2 2LH.

MPL Communications Ltd.
(01) 439 6621
1 Soho Square,
London W1V 6BQ.

The Music Production Co. Ltd.
(01) 567 7039
2 Springbridge Mews,
London W5.

Neptune Music Ltd.
(01) 437 2066/7
31 Old Burlington Street,
London W1X 1LB.

No Future Music
(068 45) 68036
3 Adelaide House,
21 Wells Road,
Malvern,
Worcs WR14 4RH.

Orange Publishing Ltd.
(01) 351 3340/2008
15 Old Church Street,
Chelsea,
London SW3 5DL.

Oval Music
(01) 622 0111
11 Liston Road,
London SW4.

Page One Music Ltd.
(01) 221 7179/7381
29 Ruston Mews,
London W11 1RB.

Palace Music Co. Ltd.
(01) 499 0067
40 South Audley Street,
London W1.

Paper Music Ltd.
(01) 580 1544/5
Walmar House,
1st Floor, Suite 106,
296 Regent Street,
London W1.

Paragon Music Co. Ltd.
(01) 681 6663
Park House,
22 Park Street,
Croydon,
Surrey.

Pattern Music Ltd.
(01) 836 5996
22 Denmark Street,
London WC2.

Peers Music
(01) 836 6699
6 Denmark Place,
London WC2.

Pink Floyd Music Publishers Ltd.
(01) 734 6892
27 Noel Street,
London W1V 3RD.

Plangent Visions Music Ltd.
(01) 734 6892
27 Noel Street,
London W1V 3RD.

Point Music Ltd.
(01) 730 9777/4201
The Point,
9 Eccleston Street,
Victoria,
London SW1W 9LX.

RAK Publishing Ltd.
(01) 586 2012
42/48 Charlbert Street,
London NW8 7BU.

The Really Useful Company Ltd.
(01) 734 2114
20 Greek Street,
London W1V 5LF.

Red Bus Music (International) Ltd.
(01) 258 0324/5/6/7/8
Red Bus House,
48 Broadley Terrace,
London NW1.

RCA Music Ltd.
(01) 437 2468
155/157 Oxford Street,
London W1.

Riva Music Ltd.
(01) 731 4131
2 New King's Road,
London SW6.

Rock Music Co. Ltd.
(01) 734 6892
27 Noel Street,
London W1V 3RD.

Rock City Music Ltd.
(09328) 66531
Shepperton Studio Centre,
Shepperton,
Middlesex.

Rocket Music and Big Pig Music Ltd.
(01) 938 1741
125 Kensington High Street,
London W8 5SN.

Rondor Music (London) Ltd.
(01) 731 4161/5
Rondor House,
10a Parsons Green,
London SW6 4TW.

Sarm Songs Ltd.
(01) 247 1311
Osborn House,
9/13 Osborn Street,
London E1 6TD.

Satril Music Ltd.
(01) 435 8063/4/5
444 Finchley Road,
London NW2 2HT.

Scorpio Music
(01) 455 4556
9 Ravenscroft Avenue,
London NW11 0SA.

Shapiro Bernstein and Co. Ltd.
(01) 439 7731
186 Regent Street,
London W1R 5DF.

Sonet Records & Publishing Ltd.
(01) 229 7267
121 Ledbury Road,
London W11 2AQ.

Sound Diagrams Ltd.
21 Atholl Crescent,
Edinburgh,
Scotland EH3 8HQ.

Southern Music Publishing Co. Ltd.
(01) 836 4524
8 Denmark Street,
London WC2H 8LT.

St. Annes Music Ltd.
(061) 941 5151
Kennedy House,
31 Stamford Street,
Altrincham,
Cheshire WA14 1ES.

Storm Music
(0253) 27357
133 Park Road,
Blackpool FY1 4ET.

Street Music Ltd.
(01) 451 3044
Zomba House,
165/167 Willesden High Road,
London NW10.

Summit Music Ltd.
(01) 491 3175
38 North Row,
London W1R 1DH.

Sunbury Music Ltd.
(01) 437 2468
155/157 Oxford Street,
London W1R 1TB.

Tabitha Music Ltd.
(0392) 79914
39 Cordery Road,
St Thomas,
Exeter,
Devon EX2 9DJ.

Tembo Music Ltd.
(01) 586 5591
50 Regents Park Road,
London NW1 7SX.

Thames Music Ltd.
(01) 741 2406
117 Church Road,
Barnes,
London SW13 9HL.

Tristan Music Ltd.
(01) 836 5996
22 Denmark Street,
London WC2.

United Music Publishers Ltd.
(01) 729 4700
42 Rivington Street,
London EC2A 3BN.

Valentine Music Group
(01) 240 1628
7 Garrick Street,
London WC2E 9AR.

Valley Music Ltd.
(01) 629 7211
138 Piccadilly,
London W1V 9FH.

Virgin Music (Publishers) Ltd.
(01) 229 1282
95/99 Ladbroke Grove,
London W11 1PG.

Warner Brothers Music Ltd.
(01) 637 3771
17 Berners Street,
London W1P 3DD.

Bruce Welch Music Ltd.
(01) 434 1839
64 Stirling Court,
Marshall Street,
London W1V 1LG.

Westminster Music Ltd.
(01) 734 8121
19/20 Poland Street,
London W1V 3DD.

Zebra Publishing (Songs) Ltd.
(01) 408 1611
243 Regent Street,
London W1R 8PN.

MUSIC PUBLISHERS/US

ATV Music Corp.
(213) 462 6933
6255 Sunset Boulevard,
Hollywood, CA 90028.

Abkco Music Inc.
(212) 399 0300
1700 Broadway,
New York, NY 10019.

Acuff-Rose Publications Inc.
(615) 385 3031
2510 Franklin Road,
Nashville, TN 37204.

Alfa Music Group
(213) 654 1100
1015 Fairfax Avenue,
Los Angeles, CA 90046.

Allied Artists Music Co. Inc.
(212) 541 9200
15 Columbus Circle,
New York, NY 10023.

April/Blackwood Music Inc.
(212) 975 4886
1350 Avenue of the Americas,
New York, NY 10019.

Arista Music Publishing Group
(213) 852 0771
8304 Beverly Boulevard,
Los Angeles, CA 90048.

Augsburg Publishing House
(612) 330 3300
426 South Fifth Street,
Minneapolis, MN 55415.

Baruth Music
(213) 650 0060
8033 Sunset Boulevard,
Hollywood, CA 90046.

Beechwood Music Corp.
(213) 469 8371
6255 Sunset Boulevard,
Hollywood, CA 90028.

M. Bernstein Music Publishing Company
(303) 755 0093
2122D South Victor Street,
Aurora, CO 80014.

Beserkley
(415) 848 6701
2054 University Avenue,
Berkeley, CA 94704.

Big Music
(203) 269 4465
10 George Street,
Wallingford, CT 06492.

Big Seven Music Corp.
(212) 582 4267
1790 Broadway,
New York, NY 10019.

Blendingwell Music Inc.
(212) 752 3033
488 Madison Avenue,
New York, NY 10022.

Buddah Music Inc.
(212) 582 6900
1790 Broadway,
New York, NY 10019.

Bug Music
(213) 466 4352
6777 Hollywood Boulevard,
Hollywood, CA 90028.

Cameron Organisation Inc.
(312) 246 8222
822 Hillgrove Avenue,
Western Springs, IL 60558.

Carrere Music
(212) 772 2475
300 East 75 Street,
New York, NY 10021.

Cascade Mountain Music
(213) 537 5476
18039 South Crenshaw Boulevard,
Torrance, CA 90504.

Chappell Music Co.
(212) 399 7373
810 Seventh Avenue,
New York, NY 10019.

**Cherry Lane Music Publishing
Company Inc.**
(914) 937 8601
110 Midland Avenue,
Port Chester, NY 10573.

Chrysalis Music Group
(212) 758 3555
645 Madison Avenue,
New York, NY 10022.

Cotillion Music Inc.
(212) 484 8208
75 Rockefeller Plaza,
New York, NY 10019.

Crazy Cajun Music
(713) 926 4431
5626 Brock,
Houston, TX 77023.

Cream Publishing Group
(213) 655 0944
8025 Melrose Avenue,
Los Angeles, CA 90046.

Doppler Effect Music
(216) 372 2510
1798 Maplewood NE,
Warren, OH 44483.

Duane Music Inc.
(408) 739 6133
382 Clarence Avenue,
Sunnyvale, CA 94086.

Elm Publishing Co.
(714) 898 7317
14621 Allen Street,
Westminster, CA 92683.

Elvis Music Inc.
(212) 489 8170
1619 Broadway,
New York, NY 10019.

Entertainment Company Music Group
(212) 265 2600
40 West 57 Street,
New York, NY 10019.

Evansongs Ltd.
(212) 765 8450
1790 Broadway,
New York, NY 10019.

Famous Music Corp.
(212) 333 3433
1 Gulf + Western Plaza,
New York, NY 10023.

Carl Fischer Inc.
(212) 777 0900
62 Cooper Square,
New York, NY 10003.

Flying Fish Music
(312) 528 5455
1304 West Schubert,
Chicago, IL 60614.

Fort Knox Music Co.
(212) 489 8170
1619 Broadway,
New York, NY 10019.

Al Gallico Music Corp.
(212) 355 5980
120 East 56 Street,
New York, NY 10022.

Garrett Music Enterprises
(213) 467 2181
6255 Sunset Boulevard,
Hollywood, CA 90028.

Al Green
(901) 794 6220
3208 Winchester Road,
Memphis, TN 38118.

Hallnote Music Co.
(615) 373 5221
PO Box 40209,
Nashville, TN 37204.

Hilaria Music Inc.
(608) 251 2644
315 West Gorham Street,
Madison, WI 53703.

Home Grown Music Inc.
(213) 985 3800
4852 Laurel Canyon Boulevard,
North Hollywood, CA 91607.

House of Cash Inc.
(615) 824 5110
700 Johnny Cash Parkway,
Hendersonville, TN 37115.

Illegal Songs
(212) 489 6336
1697 Broadway,
New York, NY 10019.

Intersong Music Inc.
(213) 469 5141
6255 Sunset Boulevard,
Hollywood, CA 90028.

Island Music
(213) 469 1285
6525 Sunset Boulevard,
Hollywood, CA 90028.

Jobete Music Co. Inc.
(213) 468 3400
6255 Sunset Boulevard,
Hollywood, CA 90028.

Kirshner/CBS Music Publishing
(212) 974 8870
101 West 55 Street,
New York, NY 10019.

Laurie Publishing Group
(914) 425 7000
20-F Robert Pitt Drive,
Monsey, NY 10952.

Lady Jane Music
(916) 583 1322
PO Box 614,
Tahoe City, CA 95730.

Largo Music Inc.
(212) 371 9400
425 Park Avenue,
New York, NY 10022.

Hal Leonard Publishing Corp.
(414) 774 3630
8112 West Bluemound Road,
Milwaukee, WI 53213.

MCA Music
(213) 508 4550
70 Universal City Plaza,
Universal City, CA 91608.

MPL Communications Inc.
39 West 54 Street,
New York, NY 10019.

Marielle Music Publishing Group
(212) 580 9723
PO Box 842,
Radio City Station,
New York, NY 10019.

Marsaint Music Inc.
(504) 949 8386
3809 Clematis Avenue,
New Orleans, LA 70122.

Ivan Mogull Music Corp.
(212) 355 5636
625 Madison Avenue,
New York, NY 10022.

Neil Music Inc.
(213) 656 2614
8400 Sunset Boulevard,
Los Angeles, CA 90069.

Open End Music Inc.
(213) 851 9115
7720 Sunset Boulevard,
Los Angeles, CA 90046.

Pale Pachyderm Publishing
(415) 543 4085
109 Minna Street,
San Francisco, CA 94105.

Phonetones
(617) 744 7678
400 Essex Street,
Salem, MA 01970.

Rough Trade Inc.
(415) 621 4186
326 Sixth Street,
San Francisco, CA 94103.

Salsoul Music Publishing Corp.
(212) 889 7340
401 Fifth Avenue,
New York, NY 10016.

Screen Gems-EMI Music Inc.
(213) 469 8371
6255 Sunset Boulevard,
Hollywood, CA 90028.

Paul Simon
(212) 541 7571
1619 Broadway,
New York, NY 10019.

Skyhill Publishing Co. Inc.
(213) 469 1285
6525 Sunset Boulevard,
Hollywood, CA 90028.

Special Rider Music
(212) 473 5900
PO Box 860,
Cooper Station,
New York, NY 10276.

The Richmond Organisation (TRO)
(212) 765 9889
10 Columbus Circle,
New York, NY 10019.

Thirty Four Music
(213) 766 6411
4329 Colfax Avenue,
Studio City, CA 91604.

20th Century Fox Music Corp.
(213) 203 1487
8544 Sunset Boulevard,
Los Angeles, CA 90069.

United Artists Music
(213) 469 3600
PO Box 572,
6753 Hollywood Boulevard,
Los Angeles, CA 90028.

Var Music Publishing
PO Box 2392,
Woburn, MA 01888.

WPN Music Co. Inc.
(516) 796 3698
10 Swirl Lane,
Levittown, NY 11756.

Warner Bros Music
(213) 273 3323
9200 Sunset Boulevard,
Los Angeles, CA 90069.

Word Music
(817) 772 7650
4800 Waco Drive,
Waco, TX 76796.

Yuggoth Music Co.
(213) 550 1010
9465 Wilshire Boulevard,
Beverly Hills, CA 90212.

INDEPENDENT RECORD DISTRIBUTORS/UK

Back Records Ltd.
(0603) 26221
St. Mary's Works,
St. Mary's Plain,
Norwich NR3 3AF.

Terry Blood
(0782) 620321/6, 620621/721
18/20 Rosevale Road,
Parkhouse Industrial Estate,
Chesterton,
Newcastle-under-Lyme,
Staffs.

Cadillac Music
(01) 836 3646/340 3933
180 Shaftesbury Avenue,
London WC2H 8SJ.

Caroline Exports
(01) 961 2919
56 Standard Road London NW10.

The Cartel
See Backs Records, Fast Product,
Probe Records, Red Rhino, Revolver
Records, Rough Trade.

Daddy Kool Records
(01) 437 3535/734 5920
94 Dean Street, London W1.

Discovery Records
(067 285) 406
Broad Street,
Beechingstoke,
Pewsey,
Wilts.

**ESSP
(Electronic Synthesiser Sound Projects)**
(01) 979 9997
The Sound House,
PO Box 37b,
East Molesey,
Surrey KT8 9JB.

Fast Product
(031) 661 5811/2
3/4 East Norton Place,
Edinburgh.

Graduate Records Ltd.
(0384) 59048/21159
196 Wolverhampton Street,
Dudley,
West Midlands.

Greensleeves Records Ltd.
(01) 749 3277/8
44 Uxbridge Road,
Shepherd's Bush,
London W12.

Independent Distribution Services Ltd.
(01) 476 1476
7 Deanstone Wharf,
Bradfield Road,
London E16 2BJ.

Independent Record Labels Association
(01) 935 2303
56-60 Wigmore Street,
London W1.

Jazz Horizon (Importers/Distributors)
(0279) 725863/724572
103 London Road,
Sawbridgeworth,
Herts.

Jet Star Phonographics Ltd.
(01) 961 5818
78 Craven Park Road,
London NW10.

JSU Distribution Ltd.
(0422) 64773
21 Bull Green,
Halifax,
W. Yorkshire HX1 2RZ.

Jungle Records (Bravour Ltd.)
(01) 359 8444/9161
24 Gaskin Street,
Islington,
London N1 2RY.

Lightning Records & Video Ltd.
(01) 969 5255
841 Harrow Road,
London NW10 5NH.

Lugton and Company Ltd. (Distributors)
PO Box 182,
Cross Lane,
Hornsey,
London N8 7SB.

Lotus Records
(0782) 628916
23 High Street,
Newcastle-under-Lyme,
Staffs ST5 1QZ.

Making Waves Ltd.
(01) 481 9917
6/8 Alie Street,
London E1.

Multiple Sound Distributors Ltd.
(01) 961 5646
3 Standard Road,
London NW10 6EX.

Neon Records Ltd.
(093 63) 5029
PO Box 459,
Lawton Road,
Alsager,
Stoke-on-Trent.

Pinnacle Records
(66) 27000
Pinnacle House,
1 Oasthouse Way,
Orpington,
Kent.

Pizza Express Music Distribution
(01) 734 6112
29 Romilly Street,
London W1.

Probe Records
(051) 236 6591
Enterprise House,
8-12 Rainford Gardens,
Liverpool 2.

Projection Records Distribution
(0702) 72281/714025
74 High Street,
Old Town,
Leigh-on-Sea,
Essex.

PRT Distribution
(01) 648 7000
132 Western Road,
Mitcham,
Surrey CR4 3UT.

Recommended Records
(01) 622 8834
583 Wandsworth Road,
London SW8.

**Red Lightnin' Records,
Blues and R&B Specialists**
(0379) 88693
The White House,
N. Lopham,
Diss,
Norfolk.

Red Rhino Distribution Ltd.
(0904) 641415
The Coach House,
Fetter Lane,
York YO1 1EM.

Red Rhino (Midlands)
(0926) 26376
Lower Avenue,
Leamington Spa,
Warwickshire.

Relay Records (Distribution)
(01) 579 2400
9 Cherrington Road,
Hanwell,
London W7.

Revolver Records
(0272) 211115/299105
1 Berkeley Crescent,
The Triangle,
Bristol BS8 1HA.

Rough Trade Distribution
(01) 727 1098
137 Blenheim Crescent,
London W11.

Scotia Distribution
(021) 557 0029
37 Jeffrey Street,
Edinburgh.

Small Wonder Records Ltd.
(01) 520 5036
162 Hoe Street,
London E17.

Spartan Records
(01) 903 4753
London Road,
Wembley,
Middlesex.

Stage One (Records) Ltd.
(0428) 4001
Parshire House,
2 Kings Road,
Haslemere,
Surrey.

Swift Record Distributors,
3 Wilton Road,
Bexhill-on-Sea,
East Sussex TN40 1HY.

**TOL —
The Other Labels Distribution Ltd.**
(01) 624 1843/328 9455
39/41 Lonsdale Road,
London NW6 6RA.

Wynd-Up
(061) 872 0170 (enquiries);
(01) 872 5020 (telephone sales)
Turntable House,
Unit 11,
Guinness Road Trading Estate,
Trafford Park,
Manchester 17 1SD.

Wynd-Up (Scottish office)
(041) 429 5155
7 Kilbirnie Place,
Tradeston Industrial Estate,
Glasgow G5 8QR.

RECORD DISTRIBUTORS/IMPORTERS/US

Dutch East India Trading
(516) 432 3500
45 Alabama Avenue,
Island Park, NY 11558.

Greenworld Distribution
(213) 533 8075
PO Box 2896
Torrance, CA 90509.

Important Records
(212) 995 9200
149-03 New York Boulevard,
Jamaica, NY 11434.

Jem Records
(201) 753 6100
3619 Kennedy Road,
South Plainfield, NJ 07080.
West Coast office:
(213) 996 6754
18629 Topham,
Reseda, CA 91335.

Rough Trade
(415) 621 4307
326 Sixth Street,
San Francisco, CA 93103.

Rounder Records
(612) 354 0700
186 Willow Avenue,
Somerville, MA 02144.

Sounds Good Import Co.
(213) 452 5949
1201 Olympic Boulevard,
Santa Monica, CA 90404.

Square Deal Records
(805) 543 3636
169 Prado Road,
San Luis Obispo, CA 93406.

Systematic Record Distributors
(415) 845 3352
729 Heinz Avenue,
Berkeley, CA 94710.

RECORDING STUDIOS/UK

Abbey Road Studios
(01) 286 1161
3 Abbey Road,
London NW8 9AY.

Alaska Rehearsal and Recording Studios
(01) 928 7440
127/129 Alaska Street,
London SE1.

Alvic Sound Studio
(01) 385 8244/0700
17 Barons Court Road,
London W14 9DP.

Amazon Recording Studios
(051) 546 6444
I.S.D. Stopgate Lane,
Simonswood,
Liverpool 33.

Angel Recording Studios Ltd.
(01) 354 2525
311 Upper Street,
London N1.

The Barge
(01) 289 6204
Opposite No. 63 Blomfield Road,
Little Venice,
London W9.

Berwick Street Recording Studios
(01) 734 5750
8 Berwick Street,
Soho,
London W1V 3RG.

Britannia Row Recording Studios Ltd.
(01) 226 3377/354 3390
35 Britannia Row,
Islington,
London N1 8QH.

Ca Va Sound Workshops
(041) 334 5099/6330
49 Derby Street,
Kelvingrove,
Glasgow G3 7TU.

Cargo Studios
(0706) 524420
Kenion Street,
Rochdale,
Lancashire.

Castle Recording Studio
(0942) 58777
The Castle,
Castle Hill Road,
Hindley,
Wigan,
Lancashire.

CBS Recording Studios
(01) 636 3434
31/37 Whitfield Street,
London W1P 5RE.

Chipping Norton Recording Studios Ltd.
(0608) 36367
28/30 New Street,
Chipping Norton,
Oxfordshire OX7 5JL.

Craighall Studio
(031) 552 3685
68 Craighall Road,
Edinburgh EH6 4RL.

De Wolfe Ltd.
(01) 437 4933/439 8481
80/88 Wardour Street,
London W1V 3LF.

Decibel Studios
(01) 802 7868
19 Stamford Hill,
London N16 5TU.

Denmark Street Studios
(01) 836 6061
9 Denmark Street,
London WC2.

DJM Recording Studios
(01) 242 6886
5/11 Theobalds Road,
London WC1.

Duffy's Studio
(01) 737 0817/703 9608
1/2 The Parade,
Dog Kennel Hill,
East Dulwich,
London SE22.

Easy Street Studios
(01) 739 1451/8887
45 Blythe Street,
London E2.

Eden Studios Ltd.
(01) 995 5432
20/24 Beaumont Road,
London W4.

Eel Pie Studios
(01) 892 3642
The Boathouse,
Ranelagh Drive,
Twickenham TW1 1QZ.

The Elephant Recording Studio
(01) 481 8615
Basement N,
Metropolitan Wharf,
Wapping Wall,
London E1.

The Factory, Sound (Woldingham) Ltd.
(01) 905 2386
Toftrees Church Road,
Woldingham,
Surrey.

Fairworld Recording Studio
(0385) 887811
West Lane,
Chester Le Street,
Co. Durham.

Fallout Shelter
(01) 741 1511
47 British Grove,
London W4 2NL.

Farmyard Recording Studios
(02404) 2912
Bendrose House East,
White Lion Road,
Little Chalfont,
Buckinghamshire.

Focus Studios
(01) 403 0007/0020
Vineyard off Sanctuary Lane,
London SE1.

Foel Recording Studio Ltd.
(0938) 810758
Llanfair Caereinion,
Powys,
Mid Wales.

Good Earth Productions Ltd.
(01) 734 0864/434 1490
59 Dean Street,
London W1.

Gooseberry Gerrard Street Studios
(01) 437 6255
19 Gerrard Street,
London W1.

Gooseberry Hillside Road Studios
(01) 674 0548
2 Hillside Road,
Tulse Hill,
London SW2.

Grosvenor Recording Studios
(021) 356 9636
16 Grosvenor Road,
Handsworth Wood,
Birmingham B30 3NP.

Herne Place Studios
(0990) 26639
Herne Place,
London Road,
Sunningdale,
Ascot,
Berkshire.

Hollywood Studios
(01) 806 1121/2
38/40 Upper Clapton Road,
London E5 8BQ.

Horizon Recording Studios
(0203) 21000
Horizon House,
Warwick Road,
Coventry.

Jacobs Studio
(0252) 723518
Ridgway House,
Runwick,
Nr. Farnham,
Surrey.

Jam Recording Ltd.
(01) 272 2906
106 Tollington Park,
London N4.

Jamm Studios
(0204) 286040/493126
Flash Mill,
Great Moor Street,
Bolton.

R G Jones Recording Studio
(01) 540 9881
Beulah Road,
London SW10 3SB.

Kaleidophon Electronic Music Recording Studio
(01) 485 6464
283 Camden High Street,
London NW1.

Kirkland Park Studios
(0236) 821081
Letham Road,
Strathaven M40 6EE.

Konk "Kinks" Productions Ltd.
(01) 340 7873/4757
84/86 Tottenham Lane,
London N8 7EE.

Lansdowne Recording Studios Ltd.
(01) 727 0041
Lansdowne House,
Lansdowne Road,
London W11 3LP.

Livingston Studios Ltd.
(01) 889 6558
Brook Road,
Wood Green,
London N22.

Lysander Studios
(0225) 705514
Unit 4,
Lysander Road,
Bowerhill,
Melksham,
Wiltshire.

The Manor Studios
(08675) 77551
Shipton-on-Cherwell,
Nr Kidlington,
Oxfordshire.

Marcus Music UK
(01) 229 9599
49/53 Kensington Gardens Square,
London W2.

Marquee Studios
(01) 437 6731
10 Richmond Mews,
Dean Street,
London W1.

Mayfair Recording Studios
(01) 586 7746
11a Sharpleshall Street, London NW1.

Misty Recording Studio
(0202) 295961
24 Norwich Road,
Bournemouth.

Mushroom Studios
(0272) 735994/735867
18 West Mall,
Clifton,
Bristol BS8 4BQ.

Music Works
(01) 609 0808
23 Benwell Road,
London N7.

The Nova Suite
(01) 493 7403
21/27 Bryanston Street,
Marble Arch,
London W1H 7AB.

Odyssey Recording Studios
(01) 402 2191
26-27 Castlereagh Street,
London W1.

Old Barn Recorders
(01) 657 7113
39 Croham Road,
South Croydon CR2 7HD.

One Two Three Music Studios
(0222) 373135
123 Butte Street,
Cardiff.

Outlet Recording Studios
(0232) 22826
48 Smithfield Square,
Belfast,
Northern Ireland.

Pathway
(01) 359 0970
2a Grosvenor Avenue,
London N5.

Pennine Studios
(061) 655 2278
225 Ripponden Road,
Littlemoore,
Oldham OL1 4HR.

Pineapple Recording Studios
(01) 571 4591
Abbottsbury House,
Priory Way,
Southall,
Middlesex.

Pluto Recording Studios
(061) 228 2022
36 Granby Row,
Manchester 1.

PolyGram Studio
(01) 402 6121
Garden Entrance,
Stanhope House,
Stanhope Place,
London W2 2HH.

Portland Recording Studios Ltd.
(01) 637 2111
35 Portland Place,
London W1N 3AG.

Producers Workshop Ltd.
(01) 589 8341
117c Fulham Road,
London SW3.

PRT Studios
(01) 402 8114
40 Bryanstone Street,
London W1.

Q Studios
(0533) 608813
1487 Melton Road,
Queniborough Industrial Estate,
Queniborough,
Leicester.

RAK Studios
(01) 586 2012
42/48 Charlbert Street,
London NW8 7BU.

Ramport Studios
(01) 720 5066
115 Thessaly Road,
London SW8.

Redan Recorders Ltd.
(01) 229 9054
23 Redan Place,
Queensway,
London W2.

Regal Sound Recorders
(0462) 54332
50 Bancroft,
Hitchin,
Herts.

Regents Park Studios
(01) 586 7576
27a Queens Terrace,
St. John's Wood,
London NW8 6DY.

REL Studios
(031) 229 9651
7a Atholl Place,
Edinburgh EH3 8HP.

Ridge Farm Studios
(0306) 711202
Ridge Farm,
Capel,
Surrey RH5 5HG.

Riverside Recordings Ltd.
(01) 994 3142
78 Church Path,
London W4 5BJ.

Rockfield Studios
(0600) 2449/3625
Amberley Court,
Rockfield Road,
Monmouth,
Gwent.

Roundhouse Recording Studios
(01) 485 0131
100 Chalk Farm Road,
London NW1 8EH.

Sain (Recordiau) Cyf
(0286) 831111
Llandwrog,
Caernarfon,
Gwynedd,
Cymru,
Wales.

Sarm Recording Studios (East)
(01) 24/ 1311
Osborn House,
9/13 Osborn Street,
London E1 6TD.

Sarm Recording Studios (West)
(01) 229 1229
8/10 Basing Street,
London W11 1ET.

Satril Studio
(01) 435 8063
444 Finchley Road,
London NW2.

SAV Studios Ltd.
(01) 278 7893
26 Harrison Street,
London WC1H 8JG.

Scorpio Sound
(01) 388 0263/4
19/20 Euston Centre,
London NW1 3JH.

September Sound Studios
(0484) 643211
38 Knowl Road,
Golcar,
Huddersfield DH7 4AN.

Sin City Studios
(0602) 784714/708622
22a Forest Road West,
Nottingham NG7 4EQ.

Sirocco Recording Studio
(0563) 36377
1 Glencairn Square,
Kilmarnock,
Ayrshire,
Scotland.

Sound Suite Recording Studios
(01) 485 4881
92 Camden Mews,
London NW1.

Southern Studios
(01) 888 8949
10 Myddleton Road,
London N22 4NS.

Spaceward Recording Studios
(035) 389 600/776
The Old School,
High Street,
Stretham,
Cambridge CB6 3LD.

Surrey Sound Studio Ltd.
(0372) 379444
70 Kingston Road,
Leatherhead,
Surrey.

Tapestry Studio
(01) 878 3353
67 First Avenue,
Mortlake,
London SW14 8SP.

Town House Studios
(01) 743 9313
150 Goldhawk Road,
London W12.

Trident Studios
(01) 734 9901
17 St. Anne's Court,
Wardour Street,
London W1.

Utopia Studios
(01) 586 3434
Utopia Village,
7 Chalcot Road,
London NW1 8LH.

Wessex Studios
(01) 359 0051
106 Highbury New Park,
London N5 2DW.

Woodlands Recording Studio
(0924) 896293
6 Garden Street,
Normanton,
W. Yorks.

The Workhouse
(01) 237 1736/7/8
488 Old Kent Road,
London SE1.

RECORDING STUDIOS/US

Alpha Audio
(804) 358 3852
2049 West Broad Street,
Richmond, VA 23220.

A&M Recording Studios
(213) 469 2411
1416 North LaBrea,
Hollywood, CA 90028.

A&R Recording
(212) 397 0300
322 West 48 Street,
New York, NY 10036.

Audio Innovators
(412) 471 6220
216 Boulevard of the Allies,
Pittsburgh, PA 15222.

Bee Jay Recording Studios
(305) 293 1781
5000 Eggleston Avenue,
Orlando, FL 32810.

Bullet Recording
(615) 327 4621
49 Music Square West,
Nashville, TN 37203.

Capitol Studios
(213) 462 6252
1750 North Vine Street,
Hollywood, CA 90028.

CBS Studios
(212) 975 5901
49 East 52 Street,
New York, NY 10022.

Cherokee Recording Studios
(213) 653 3412
751 North Fairfax,
Hollywood, CA 90046.

Clover Recorders
(213) 463 2371
6232 Santa Monica Boulevard,
Hollywood, CA 90038.

Criteria Recording Studios
(305) 947 5611
1755 NE 149 Street,
Miami, FL 33181.

Different Fur Recording
(415) 864 1967
3470 19 Street,
San Francisco, CA 94110.

Electric Lady Studios
(212) 677 4700
52 West 8 Street,
New York, NY 10011.

Fantasy Studios
(415) 549 2500
10th and Parker,
Berkeley, CA 94710.

Hit Factory
(212) 664 1000
237 West 54 Street,
New York, NY 10019.

House of Music
(201) 736 3062
1400 Pleasant Valley Way,
West Orange, NJ 07052.

Kendun Recorders
(213) 843 8096
619 South Glenwood Place,
Burbank, CA 91506.

Larrabee Sound
(213) 657 6750
8811 Santa Monica Boulevard,
Los Angeles, CA 90069.

MCA/Whitney Recording Studios
(213) 241 4228
1516 West Glen Oaks Boulevard,
Glendale, CA 91201.

Media Sound
(212) 765 4700
311 West 57 Street,
New York, NY 10019.

Mitch's Drive-In Studio
(919) 724 3772
124 Shady Boulevard,
Winston-Salem, NC 27101.

Motown/Hitsville USA
(213) 850 1510
7317 Romaine Street,
Los Angeles, CA 90046.

Muscle Shoals Sound Studios
(205) 381 2060
1000 Alabama Avenue,
Muscle Shoals, AL 35660.

National Recording Studios
(212) 279 2000
460 West 42 Street,
New York, NY 10036.

Ocean Way Recording
(213) 467 9375
6050 West Sunset Boulevard,
Los Angeles, CA 90028.

Pierce Arrow Recorders
(312) 328 8950
1911 Ridge Avenue,
Evanston, IL 60202.

Power Station
(212) 246 2900
441 West 53 Street,
New York, NY 10019.

RCA Studios
(212) 930 4062
110 West 44 Street,
New York, NY 10036.

Record Plant
(213) 653 0240
8456 West 3 Street,
Los Angeles, CA 90098.

Record Plant
(212) 582 6505
321 West 44 Street,
New York, NY 10036.

Sheffield Recording
(301) 628 7260
13816 Sunnybrook Road,
Phoenix, MD 21131.

Sigma Sound Studios
(215) 561 3660
212 North 12 Street,
Philadelphia, PA 19107.

Sigma Sound Studios
(212) 582 5055
1697 Broadway,
New York, NY 10019.

Sound City
(213) 873 2842
15456 Cabrito Road,
Van Nuys, CA 91406.

Sound Emporium
(615) 383 1982
3102 Belmont Boulevard,
Nashville, TN 37212.

Sound 80
(612) 339 9313
2709 East 25 Street,
Minneapolis, MN 55406.

Sound Labs
(213) 466 3463
1800 North Argyle Street,
Los Angeles, CA 90028.

Suma Recording Studio
(216) 951 3955
5706 Vrooman Road,
Cleveland, OH 44077.

Syncro Sound
(617) 424 1062
331 Newbury Street,
Boston, MA 02115.

Technisonic Studios
(314) 727 1055
1201 South Brentwood Boulevard,
St. Louis, MO 63117.

Universal Recording
(312) 642 6465
46 East Walton,
Chicago, IL 60611.

Village Recorder
(213) 478 8227
1616 Butler Avenue,
West Los Angeles, CA 90025.

Wally Heider Recording
(213) 466 5474
1604 North Cahuenga Boulevard,
Hollywood, CA 90028.

Warner Bros Recording Studios
(213) 980 5605
1114 Cumpston Avenue,
North Hollywood, CA 91601.

Westlake Studios
(213) 654 2155
8447 Beverly Boulevard,
Los Angeles, CA 90048.

Allen Zentz Recording
(213) 851 8300
1020 North Sycamore Avenue,
Hollywood, CA 90038.

ROCK PUBLICATIONS/UK

COMPILED BY *GIOVANNI DADOMO*

Black Echoes
(01) 405 0461
113 High Holborn,
London WC1.
Large-format weekly at 40p covering all aspects of black music. Reviews and interviews tend to be in the MOR tradition of the mainstream weeklies and the photo quality leaves something

to be desired, but the chart and gig/club sections are invaluable to the serious·soul/funk/reggae enthusiast.

BM and Jazz Review
(01) 402 5051
153 Praed Street,
London W2.
Once an extremely valuable magazine,

but less so lately. And it's not just the paper quality that's coarsened; the general approach and design too are now closer to a monthly version of the above, plus colour pix. 70p. The "BM" is, of course, short for *Black Music*.

BLITZ

1 Lower James Street,
London W1.
Monthly at 75p and no more or less than the latest of many attempts to jump on the *Face* bandwagon. Design and writing are better than most, but other than that the only real differences are that this one's about half an inch bigger all round and several pages shorter. Likely to go the way of *Noise*, *Kicks* etc., etc. Who'll weep?

Blues Unlimited

36 Belmont Park,
London SE13.
75p, bi-monthly, and a thorough and readable commentary on vintage blues and r'n'b written by experts for experts.

Comstock Lode

(01) 747 0916
51 Bollo Lane,
London W4.
Handsome fanzine with its roots in sixties' West Coast pop and branches in related areas throughout the succeeding decades. Quarterly at 75p and best enjoyed sitting on a large mushroom with the "cans" turned way up on Uncle Jerry.

Country Music People

17 Broomwood Road,
St. Paul's Clay,
Orpington,
Kent BR5 2JH.
Glossy magazine concentrating on the more well-pressed, popular aspects of cowboy music. Interviews, reviews, colour snaps etc., but a little too respectable for genu-ine shitkickers. 80p, monthly.

Disco International and Club News

(01) 278 3591
41 St. John Street,
London EC1.
The title says most of it: reports on the current scene from active participants (DJs, broadcasters), plus ads, pix, charts. Rather humdrum unless you're a fully paid up member, but Biblically essential for freaks. 90p, monthly.

Electronic and Music Maker

(0702) 338878
282 London Road,
Westcliff-on-Sea,
Essex SS0 7JG.
Technical manual for keyboard addicts — product reviews, tests, analyses, filled out by the odd name interview, with the emphasis on equipment and technique. A keyboard persons' *Which?* and more than useful if you want to go shopping and need some expert advice first. 90p, monthly.

Elvis Costello Information Service

c/o Ian Cheetham,
14 Woodgrange Close,
Kenton,
Harrow,
Middlesex HA3 0XH.
Costello isn't just the best songwriter this country has produced in a good decade, he's also the most collected artist, something manager Jake Riviera's policy of specialising in collectible rarities (see early Stiff stunts) helps no end. This is a pocket-size xerox job with reviews of gigs, discs (legal and illegal) and — until recently — the odd snippet of "rare" interview. Essential reading matter for the EC completist. £4.80 for six issues (one approximately every eight weeks) from the above for UK fans. US and Euros send $9.00 (or D.Fl. 19.00) to: Richard Groothuizen, Primulastraat 46, 1441 HC Purmerend, Holland.

The Face

(01) 580 6756
5/11 Mortimer Street,
London W1.
Style and visuals are king, which is about the only negative thing you could say about Nick Logan's masterly monthly: it always looks great, but what's it really saying? Great, great images and a brief that takes in threads, print, movies — even the occasional bit of music. Pop culture's answer to *Life*; loud, proud, bursting with energy and inspiration. 75p every month and always worth the wait.

Fan Library Monthly

(01) 836 1522
40 Long Acre,
London WC2.
Something the staff of *Sounds* and *Record Mirror* cobble together in their spare time — glossy magazines concentrating on one artist in (shortish) words and plenty (biggish) pictures. The latter are above average, the former somewhere around the middle of the brow. The same team also produce *Guitar Heroes*: snaps of long-haired chaps leaning over backwards in colour with brief life histories attached. Both monthly, both 90p.

Flexipop

(01) 402 8586
80 Bell Street,
London NW1.
Long-running competitor to *Smash Hits* utilising almost exactly the same approach in every respect (design, choice of acts, style of interviews etc.); the main difference is this one's a lot more sexist — in a really infantile, pee-po-belly-bum-wee-who's-buying-the-next-round way — plus it pays more attention to the ongoing punk band-bus. Rumours say the writing is on the wall.

I-D

c/o Better Badges,
286 Portobello Road,
London W10.
Innovative pop-fashion catwalk that lets the little guys and gals have their say. Sometimes brilliant; at other times élitist manure, but you gotta give it a flip if you wanna stay hip. Fashion note: be the first on your block to wear an old lorry tire for a belt, sez our source at the ice-cool I-D office!

International Musician and Recording World

Grosvenor House,
141/143 Drury Lane,
London WC2.
Heavyweight glossy monthly — i.e., it's got a lot of pages, many of them ads — with the emphasis on equipment reviews and FX-related interviews. Used to be somewhat dated in its choice of acts but it's recently made a big effort to get hep. This, along with a breezier design, have turned it into a pretty reasonable quid's-worth if you're interested in chords, humbucking pick-ups and the like.

Jamming

45/53 Sinclair Road,
London W11.
Haven't been able to trace *In the City* for months, so this is presumably now the longest-surviving punk era fanzine. Still the same friendly, misspelt, sweaty dressing-room-after-the-gig approach but pluses such as colour covers, broader approach to music, thoughtful reviews etc. 40p every couple of months.

Kerrang!

(01) 836 1522
40 Long Acre,
London WC2.
Glossy spawn of the HM revival and still going strong. Actually, this *Sounds* spin-off is becoming an interesting mag in its own right, having expanded to include such, ahem, cultural side-links as splatter movies etc. No doubt it'll be quick to get in on the wrestling/horror sub-genre currently sweeping the US when it hits the UK. Fortnightly, 65p. Less literate HM fans will be best served by the *Metal Fury* rip-off cooked up by the *Flexipop* enterprise: that one has very few words and turns into a giant wall poster at a flick of the wrist. All together now: Uuurrghh!

Melody Maker

(01) 379 3581
Berkshire House,
168/173 High Holborn,
London WC1.
A year ago I'd have said *MM* was on its last legs and few would have disagreed. But things change, and while its rivals have got soggier, it's probably the best-looking (don't count photos and cartoons though, that's still where *NME* tops all comers) and most enjoyably readable of the Big Three taken week for week. 40p.

MUSIC

MLP Ltd.,
Payne House,
23/24 Smithfield Street,
London EC1.
Laughingly sub-titled "The Alternative Music Paper", this is the latest in a long line of doomed attempts to crash the big three (*NME*, *MM*, *Sounds*) monopoly: it looks and reads like a bad pastiche of all three and is, to be blunt, a crock of shit in a colour cover. The last one I saw resembled a golden age (circa 1966-7) *Record Mirror* in places, but I'm sure this was accidental.

New Kommotion

3 Bowrons Avenue,
Wembley,
Middlesex.
Collector's quarterly with its heart in the fifties: lists, discographies, catalogue numbers, histories of obscure acts and labels. Vital if you're of the opinion that the sun never set on Sun.

NME

(01) 439 8761
5/7 Carnaby Street,
London W1.
The cartoons of Serge Clerc, Benyon and Lowry, the photography of Pennie Smith and Anton Corbijn, the brilliant cassette compilations; these are currently the best (only?) reasons for stopping off at this station. The last batch of "name" writers are all TV personalities and no one seems to have arrived with sufficient character, spirit, and plain old style to wear the crown. 40p.

Not Fade Away

(051) 426 9100
16 Conston Avenue,
Prescott,
Merseyside L34 2SW.
Oldies quarterly with the usual thoroughness enhanced by better than usual visual presentation and bouncy, idiosyncratic writing. 75p.

No. 1!

(01) 251 6958
Room 2614,
King's Reach Tower,
Stamford Street,
SE1 9LS.
Out-and-out *Smash Hits* replica. What'll probably keep it going longer than most of the competition is the big (IPC) money that's meant a staff recruited from the best(ish) talent on the weeklies — editor Phil McNeill, ex-*NME*, was a glossy-pops pioneer, heading up the Rollers-era *Rainbow Giant* poster mag — plus nation-wide ads, distribution etc. Pity that all that cash and talent couldn't have been put to slightly more imaginative use.

Outlet

c/o Trev,
33 Aintree Crescent,
Barkingside,
Ilford,
Essex.
Well-written specialist fanzine specialising on contemporary obscurities and weirdies with The Residents high in its pantheon. Sporadic, but worth checking. £1.20 including post and packing.

Pickin' the Blues
57 East Main Street,
East Calder,
West Lothian EH53 0ES.
Handsome blues fanatics' guidebook, impeccable on facts and figures, engagingly fleshed out by biographical and review material. 30p, bi-monthly.

Record Collector
45 St. Mary's Road,
London W5 RQ.
What it says: features, lists galore, re-issues noted and reviewed and, first and foremost, miles and miles of want and sell lists. Just enlarged its format to A4-size, so it looks a lot better as well as being the best way to stay clued on to what the market-place is charging for that old gold.

Record Mirror
(01) 836 1522
40 Long Acre,
London WC2.
Belatedly noting that most of its teen/chart market had been filched by the far bouncier *Smash Hits*, *RM*'s supremos have turned it into yet another *SH* imitator. Unfortunately the paper's of a low, coarser quality — and what's printed on it isn't too hot either.

Smash Hits
(01) 439 8801
Lisa House,
52/55 Carnaby Street,
London W1.
Reflecting (and no doubt partly responsible for) the glitzy but ultimately gutless silicon pop that dominates the current day, *Smash Hits* is, above all, the most light, digestible fun a fortnightly 40p can buy. The number of imitations alone testify to its popular success. The trouble, if any, is: how long can its principles singlehandedly seem to dominate the pop media — they all do radio and TV as well — without stopping for a breather/running out of ideas/having collective nervous breakdowns? At the moment their kingship seems unassailable.

Sounds
(01) 836 1522
40 Long Acre,
London WC2.
Youngest of the pop weeklies and still the most daring/least conscientious. The *Sun* approach to pop — write down, exploit any bandwagon as soon as possible... if necessary, invent one (*vide* the HM "New Wave" launched by now ed Geoff Barton) and if things get

tough, throw in a pair of tits. As the weeklies waver uneasily in the presence of *Smash Hits* and *The Face*, *Sounds* is in danger of getting its several identities confused (particularly after sacrificing its long-supporting HM audience to offspring *Kerrang!*). But it still has the great cartoonist Savage Pencil, plenty of unknown act coverage and a good chart section to see it through its thinner issues. 40p.

Stick It In Your Ear
c/o Geoff Wall,
9 Gladstone Road,
Sholing,
Southampton 2.
Cassette magazine in the style of the much-lamented *SFX*. This one's an altogether more home-made affair, but done with zest and care and specialising in the more *outré* sounds of the day. Any reviewer who can actually play you some of the music he's talking about has to be miles ahead of the poor bastards who only have newsprint. 60p, irregular but improving.

Swing 51
(01) 641 1308
41 Bushey Road,
Sutton,
Surrey SM1 1QR.
Folk, bluegrass and beyond.

ZG
(01) 671 3772
Hallery House Press,
23 Mantrell Road,
London SW2.
Inventive, visually brilliant, verbally highly articulate culture parade with pop just one of its concerns. A sort of UK answer to *Wet*. And, in other words, probably one of the main sources of inspiration for the way your "proper" pop papers will be looking in six months/a year.

Zig Zag
(01) 229 5115
118 Talbot Road,
London W11.
Monthly, 60p. The real problem with Britain's oldest fanzine is that its big plans are usually grounded by its miniscule budgets. What happened to the *Zigzag* club? Writer's School? Floundering somewhat since the loss of madman editor Kris Needs, but shouldn't be counted out quite yet.

ROCK PUBLICATIONS/US

BAM
(415) 652 3810
5951 Canning Street,
Oakland, CA 94609.

(213) 467 7878
1800 North Highland,
Hollywood, CA 90028.
Bi-weekly, the two editions of BAM cover northern and southern California's scenes with class and quality.

Billboard
(212) 764 7300
1515 Broadway,
New York, NY 10036.

(213) 273 7040
9000 Sunset Boulevard,
Los Angeles, CA 90069.
The leading record trade magazine, *Billboard*'s weekly charts are still the ones to watch. A recent emphasis on video should guarantee the magazine's pre-eminence for some time.

The Bob
508 Whitby Drive,
Wilmington, DE 19803.
A neat tabloid fanzine, published monthly, covering the Philadelphia scene.

Boston Rock
(617) 266 8787
268 Newbury Street,
Boston, MA 02116.
Monthly tabloid that blends local Boston doings with national and international coverage.

Cash Box
(212) 586 2640
1775 Broadway,
New York, NY 10019.
Billboard's only competition, this trade weekly has been suffering due to the troubles of the record business, but continues to hang in there.

Circus
(212) 685 5050
419 Park Avenue South,
New York, NY 10016.
The magazine for metal and arena-rockers; each monthly issue features glossy pix of sweating superstars and undemanding prose.

Creem
(313) 642 8833
210 South Woodward,
Birmingham, MI 48011.
Published monthly, with special-edition one-shots also appearing regularly. Although the editorial direction continues to shift, the sniggering photo captions remain the magazine's one steady component.

Down Beat
(312) 346 7811
222 West Adams Street,
Chicago, IL 60606.
Thanks to last year's graphic redesign, and a broader editorial reach, the venerable jazz monthly has been looking hipper lately.

Flipside
PO Box 363,
Whittier, CA 90608.
Irregular but exciting, this hardcore fanzine is indispensable for punks.

Goldmine
(715) 445 2214
700 East State Street,
Iola, WI 54990.
This is the leading magazine for record collectors who want to buy or sell fifties' and sixties' rarities.

Guitar Player
(408) 446 1105
20605 Lazaneo,
Cupertino, CA 95014.
The first and still the best magazine for guitarists, rock and otherwise.

High Fidelity
(212) 887 8337
825 Seventh Avenue,
New York, NY 10019.
Mainstream audio monthly with some material of interest to rockers.

Illinois Entertainer
(312) 298 9333
PO Box 356,
Mt. Prospect, IL 60056.
Published monthly. Editorial coverage of local and national acts with cover story concentrating on Illinoians. Includes personality profiles and regular features.

International Musician and Recording World
(212) 947 6740
12 West 32 Street,
New York, NY 10001.
Monthly, combining equipment reviews with articles and interviews with musicians.

Jazz Times
(301) 588 4114
8055 13 Street,
Silver Springs, MD 20910.
Monthly tabloid for jazz fans.

Keyboard
(408) 446 1105
20605 Lazaneo,
Cupertino, CA 95014.
Monthly for ivory-ticklers, covering a wide range of musics that employ keyboards.

LA Reader
(213) 930 1214
5225 Wilshire Boulevard,
Los Angeles, CA 90036.
Weekly giveaway; not strictly a music
paper, but often influential in the
local rock scene.

Living Blues
(312) 281 3385
2615 North Wilton Avenue,
Chicago, IL 60614.
Published quarterly by and for fans of
classic blues.

Matter
(312) 491 9112
624 Davis Street,
Evanston, IL 60201.
Excellent free bi-monthly fanzine
covering local and world-wide new wave
doings with uncommon skill and style.

Maximum Rock'n'Roll
PO Box 288,
Berkeley, CA 94701.
Controversial hardcore fanzine with
national impact.

Modern Recording and Music
(516) 883 5705
14 Vanderventer Avenue,
Port Washington, NY 11050.
Monthly that approaches rock from the
studio angle.

Music and Sound Output
(516) 334 7880
220 Westbury Avenue,
Carle Place, NY 11514.
Recently converted to a monthly
schedule, this eclectic glossy covers art
and technique in rock and other fields.

Musician
(617) 281 3110
31 Commercial Street,
Gloucester, MA 01930.

(212) 764 7400
1515 Broadway,
New York, NY 10036.
Slick, successful monthly with the most
impressive interviews in the business.
The editorial blend mixes credible rock
and established superstars with jazz and
avant-garde performers.

OP
(206) 352 9735
PO Box 2391,
Olympia, WA 98507.
Now in magazine format, this bi-
monthly is the most comprehensive
source of information on underground/
obscure/independent records.

Progressive Media
(516) 248 9600
185 Willis Avenue,
Mineola, NY 11501.
Aimed mainly at college radio, this
hybrid trade/consumer monthly is still
developing an editorial focus.

Radio and Records
(213) 553 4330
193 Century Park West,
Los Angeles, CA 90067.
Highly regarded trade publication for
radio and record people.

The Record
(212) 350 1235
745 Fifth Avenue,
New York, NY 10151.
Rolling Stone's monthly music

publication, currently undergoing a
transition from tabloid to magazine
format.

Record Review
(213) 886 4432
PO Box 91878,
Los Angeles, CA 90009.
Like the title says — mostly record
reviews of various genres.

Recordings of Experimental Music
104 Fern Avenue,
Collingswood, NJ 08108.
Bi-monthly review journal of esoterica
and extremism.

Relix
(212) 645 0818
PO Box 94,
Brooklyn, NY 11229.
Monthly general-interest rock magazine.

RockBill
(212) 977 7745
850 Seventh Avenue,
New York, NY 10019.
Pocket-sized and colourful, with brief
articles on current rock bands and lots
of big-name advertisers. Monthly.

Rockpool Newsletter
(212) 686 7410
50 West 29 Street,
New York, NY 10001.
Bi-weekly batch of charts and reports
on new music that are influential in
"new music" circles.

Rock & Roll Confidential
Box 2060,
Teaneck, NJ 07666.
Dave Marsh's monthly newsletter —
intelligent and articulate.

Rock Wire Service Report
PO Box 56,
Rego Park, NY 11374.
Lou O'Neill Jr.'s bi-weekly news/gossip
newsletter. Great for those who need to
be the first to know about goings-on in
the world of rock'n'roll.

Rolling Stone
(212) 758 3800
745 Fifth Avenue,
New York, NY 10151.
The biggest youth-culture magazine in
America; the rock coverage continues to
be solid, with up-to-date record reviews
now the norm.

Smash Hits
(203) 735 3381
Charlton Building,
Derby, CT 06418.
Hit Parader's sister publication, this
song-lyrics magazine is unrelated to the
British magazine of the same name.

Stereo Review
(212) 725 3500
1 Park Avenue,
New York, NY 10016.
The leading audiophile magazine; some
rock coverage amidst the classical.

Suburban Relapse
PO Box 610906,
North Miami, FL 33261.
Entertaining, gutsy fanzine, covering
mostly Florida, but national acts as well.

Trouser Press
(212) 889 7145
212 Fifth Avenue,
New York, NY 10010.
America's leading "new music"
monthly; coverage includes local scenes
as well as chart-toppers. Subscription
copies include a flexi-disc every issue.

MUSIC RELATED ASSOCIATIONS

US

Academy of Country Music
(213) 462 2351
6255 Sunset Boulevard,
Hollywood, CA 90028.

American Federation of Musicians
(212) 869 1330
1500 Broadway, New York, NY 10036.

American Musicians Union
(201) 384 5378
8 Tobin Court, Dumont, NJ 07628.

ASCAP
(212) 595 3050
1 Lincoln Plaza,
New York, NY 10023.

**Association of Independent Music
Publishers**
(213) 466 3834
6253 Hollywood Boulevard,
Hollywood, CA 90028.

Black Music Association
(215) 545 8600
1500 Locust Street,
Philadelphia, PA 19102.

BMI
(212) 586 2000
320 West 57 Street,
New York, NY 10019.

Country Music Association
(615) 244 2840
7 Music Circle North,
Nashville, TN 37203.

Jazz Composers' Orchestra Association
(212) 925 2121
500 Broadway,
New York, NY 10022.

**National Academy of Recording Arts
and Sciences**
(213) 843 8233
4444 Riverside Drive,
Burbank, CA 91505.

**National Association of Independent
Record Distributors**
c/o Richman Brothers Records
(att. Jerry Richman),
6935 Airport Highway Lane,
Pennsauken, NJ 08109.

National Association of Music Merchants
(312) 527 3200
500 North Michigan Avenue,
Chicago, IL 60611.

**National Association of Record
Merchandisers**
(609) 795 5555
1008F Astoria Boulevard,
Cherry Hill, NJ 08034.

**Recording Industry Association
of America**
(212) 765 4330
888 Seventh Avenue,
New York, NY 10106.

SESAC Inc.
(212) 586 3450
10 Columbus Circle,
New York, NY 10019.

UK

**American Society of Composers,
Authors and Publishers**
(01) 930 1121
Suite 9,
4th Floor,
52 Haymarket,
London SW1Y 4RP.

**Association of Professional
Recording Studios**
(0923) 772907
23 Chestnut Avenue,
Chorleywood,
Herts WD3 4HA.

**British Academy of Songwriters,
Composers and Authors**
(01) 240 2823
148 Charing Cross Road,
London WC2.

**The British Library
(National Sound Archive)**
(01) 589 6603
29 Exhibition Road,
London SW7.

British Music Information Centre
(01) 499 8567
10 Stratford Place,
London W1N 9AE.

British Phonographic Industry Ltd.
(01) 629 8642
4th Floor,
Roxburghe House,

273/287 Regent Street,
London W1R 8BN.

British Tape Industry Association
(01) 688 4422
7/18 Lansdowne Road,
Croydon CR9 2PL.

Community Radio Association
(01) 263 6692
92 Huddleston Road,
London N7.

Composers Guild of Great Britain
(01) 499 4795
10 Stratford Place,
London W1N 9AE.

Country Music Association Inc.
(01) 930 2445
Suite 3,
52 Haymarket,
London SW1Y 4RP.

English Folk Dance and Song
(01) 485 2206
2 Regents Park Road,
London NW1.

Independent Records Labels Association
(01) 935 2303
56/60 Wigmore Street,
London W1.

Jazz Centre Society
(01) 580 8532
35 Great Russell Street,
London WC1.

London Musicians Collective
(01) 722 0456

42 Gloucester Avenue,
London NW1.

Mechanical-Copyright Protection Society
(01) 769 4400
Elgar House,
41 Streatham High Road,
London SW16 1ER.

Music Publishers Association
(01) 831 7591
7th Floor,
Kingsway House,
103 Kingsway,
London WC2B 6QX.

Musicians Union
(01) 582 5566
60/62 Clapham Road,
London SW9 0JJ.

Performing Rights Society Ltd.
(01) 580 5544
29/33 Berners Street,
London W1P 4AA.

**Royal Society of Musicians
of Great Britain**
(01) 629 6137
10 Stratford Place, London W1.

Society for the Promotion of New Music
(01) 491 8111
10 Stratford Place,
London W1N 9AE.

Variety Club of Great Britain
(01) 491 4521
Avon House,
360 Oxford Street, London W1.